Prof... Mr. Gregg Falls...

This book was definitely a great help to you as you can see that it is all worn out!

Let me hear ? ? ? ? ? ? ? ?
? ? cause ? ? ? ? ? !

January 20, 1953.
("Ike" is
the President)

PUBLIC SPEAKING:
PRINCIPLES AND PRACTICE.

THE UNITED NATIONS AND THE SPOKEN WORD

Through their representatives, the peoples of fifty-eight member nations make themselves heard before the international forum. Public speaking assumes an important role in international affairs. (Photo, Black Star and United Nations.)

PUBLIC SPEAKING:
PRINCIPLES AND PRACTICE

Giles Wilkeson Gray
and Waldo W. Braden
LOUISIANA STATE UNIVERSITY

HARPER & BROTHERS
PUBLISHERS · NEW YORK

PUBLIC SPEAKING: Principles and Practice

*Copyright, 1951, by Harper & Brothers
Printed in the United States of America*

*All rights in this book are reserved.
No part of the book may be used or reproduced in any manner whatsoever without written permission except in the case of brief quotations embodied in critical articles and reviews. For information address Harper & Brothers
49 East 33rd Street, New York 16, N. Y.*

C-A

FURTHERMORE, mark you, the man who wishes to persuade people will not be negligent as to the matter of character; no, on the contrary, he will apply himself above all to establish a most honourable name among his fellow-citizens; for who does not know that words carry greater conviction when spoken by men of good repute than when spoken by men who live under a cloud, and that the argument which is made by a man's life is of more weight than that which is furnished by words? Therefore, the stronger a man's desire to persuade his hearers, the more zealously will he strive to be honourable and to have the esteem of his fellow-citizens.

ANTIDOSIS

Contents

	Preface	xi
I.	The Attitude of the Speaker	1
II.	Some First Principles	25
III.	Motivation	52
IV.	Attention and Interest	78
V.	Occasion and Audience	109
VI.	Speech Goals	138
VII.	Subjects, Sources, and Materials	154
VIII.	The Informative Speech	183
IX.	Analysis and Organization of Argumentative Speeches	208
X.	The Occasional Speech	243
XI.	Forms of Support	280
XII.	Visual Supports	316
XIII.	The Introduction	333
XIV.	The Discussion	355
XV.	The Conclusion	372
XVI.	Using Language for Clarity	391
XVII.	Using Language for Vividness	415
XVIII.	Using Language for Impressiveness	438
XIX.	Memory	460

CONTENTS

XX.	General Principles of Delivery	475
XXI.	Vocal Aspects of Delivery	493
XXII.	Bodily Aspects of Delivery	539
	Index of Authors and Speakers Cited	567
	Index of Subjects	570

Illustrations

The United Nations and the Spoken Word	FRONTISPIECE
	Faces page
The American Way	16
The Ability to Speak in Public Is a Necessity in Nearly Every Vocation and Profession	17
Democracy at Work: The New England Town Meeting	48
The New England Town Meeting at Work	49
Good Speaking Requires a Realization of Social Responsibility	56
A Great Assembly of Freedom	57
The Security Council of the United Nations in Action	72
Free Government Places Great Responsibilities on Its Leaders	73
The Time and the Place Greatly Influence the Audience, the Speaker, and the Speech	80
The Times and Places Men Speak Are Legion	81
Types of Audiences	112
Types of Audiences: Inactive Audience	113
Types of Audiences: Selected Audience	120
Types of Audiences: Concerted Group	121
Franklin D. Roosevelt	136

ix

ILLUSTRATIONS

Eric Johnston	137
The General Goal of Speaking Is Response	144
A Speaker Must Judge His Success in Terms of Response	145
In a Free Society the Sermon Is a Prevalent Type of Public Speech	176
The Speaker's Attitude Will Be Reflected in His Audience	177
The Informative Speech Is Delivered in Many Different Places	184
The Critique Is a Common Type of the Informative Speech	185
Wendell Willkie	200
Winston Churchill	201
A Speech of Welcome for Mrs. Eleanor Roosevelt	272
Dr. Ralph Bunche Delivers an Occasional Speech	273
Supporting Materials	304
Supporting Materials	305
Blackboard Sketches	312
Presentation	313
Visual Aids	328
Practical Devices: Models and Actual Objects	329
Projected Pictures May Make Your Talk More Effective	336
Pictorial Aids	337
A Great General Is a Great Speaker	368
The Speaker Reveals Much by the Visual Aspects of His Delivery	369
President Franklin D. Roosevelt Speaks to 30,000	496
The Speaker Must Adjust His Voice to the Speaking Situation	497
Good Delivery Is Animated	528
Facial Expression Gives Many Clues to a Speaker's Personality	529
A Gesture May Be Worth a Dozen Words	536
Gestures Must Be Adapted to the Speaking Situation	537
Types of Gestures	552
Types of Gestures	553

Preface

In presenting still another textbook in public speaking, the authors are under no illusions of having written with a high degree of originality in either subject matter or organization. Even the casual reader will discern throughout the pages of this book ample evidence of borrowings from sources that go back as far as the origins of speech education itself. Easily recognized, too, in the very sequence of chapters are the classical canons of rhetoric, which the authors confess themselves unable to improve upon. Much of what is said here under those five canons has been said before in the numerous good texts that have been published within the past half century, to say nothing of those which were written hundreds of years ago.

If there be anything of the unique to be found in the present work, it may perhaps be found in the emphasis placed upon the ethical point of view—and yet, as will be observed, even in that connection reference is made to Quintilian's *Institutes,* and the principle was far from original with him. The authors have felt that it was high time to call attention again sharply to the fact, sometimes overlooked, that speech is a terrific force in human relations for either good or ill; that because of its potentialities, the acquisition of ability in speaking carries with it a deep responsibility for its ethical use; that in scarcely any period in our history has the need existed as it exists today for a type of honest thinking and speaking that is motivated by a genuine and consistent concern for the well-being of humanity.

For more than a century and a half we have been committed to a democratic principle of self-government, in which speech has always played a vital role. Government by talk, instead of being a target for slurs, has in fact been one of our most valuable contributions to civilization. So vital to democracy is the function of speech that it can be used even to destroy the societal forms which make it possible! It is the belief of the authors that a course in public speaking should, therefore, offer more than an understanding of the psychological and rhetorical techniques used in public utterance; it should offer an opportunity to examine the function of speech in the development and maintenance of those social and individual values which have derived from our public and private institutions. It should further make an effort to orient the student in a wholesome point of view toward that function. Freedom of speech, with all its social, psychological, and educational implications, can exist only in a form of society essentially democratic in its philosophy; conversely, such a form of society is the only one that can exist where freedom of speech, with all its accompaniments, prevails. The study of public speaking, therefore, becomes in large part a study of public relations at their highest level and of the place of speech in the rational solution of the manifold problems that arise in those relations.

A textbook written from such a point of view will inevitably consist of something more than a manual of instruction, although the techniques of effective speaking are treated. Such a book seeks to go back of the rhetorical and the psychological and to inquire into some of the principles that enable human beings to live and work together for their mutual good. It must perforce be prescriptive at times; but an effort is constantly made to base the prescription on the social and the ethical as well as on the rhetorical and the psychological. It goes further than immediate utility; it looks to the lifelong effectiveness of the speaker on the basis of a personal integrity, the importance of which was recognized a hundred or more years before Aristotle.

The point of view thus incorporated into the text will be found in the very first chapter and through the succeeding chapters. It will be noted in the discussion of goals, in the treatment of language, and even in the chapters on delivery. The attitude consistently held is that no treatment of rhetorical theory can be complete or adequate unless it takes into consideration the relation of that body of theory to human society and the impact of both theory and practice on human welfare and human aspirations. It holds that no principles of public speaking can be sound, *even on a purely theoretical basis*, which ignore a solid foundation of fact—and truth, so far as it can be identified with facts, is on the side of ethics. Unethical speaking, therefore, is untruthful speaking, which cannot be sound on any basis.

This, then, is the credo to which the authors are committed in the presentation of *Public Speaking: Principles and Practice*.

It is quite evident that full acknowledgment of our indebtedness to all who have influenced the content of the present text and its writing is quite impossible. The material has been drawn from too many sources the identity of which has been completely lost. Whenever material has been drawn from specific sources, references have been made to those sources in the footnotes; we believe that our indebtedness will be more obvious in that way than if all such acknowledgments were gathered together in some place apart from the material itself. We should, however, like to express our deep gratitude for permissions to use many of the excerpts from speeches and from writings. Full recognition is given in each case in direct connection with its appearance.

We cannot forego this opportunity of recognizing our deep obligation to Dr. C. M. Wise, who gave so generously of his time and editorial experience in going over the manuscript in minute detail. To Miss Edith Dabney also we hereby express our grati-

PREFACE

tude for the drawings which accompany the discussion of Visual Supports. To Miss Jeannette Hodson, Editor of the *L.S.U. Alumni News,* we are deeply indebted for aid and counsel. We also wish to express our appreciation of the coöperation of the Esso Standard Oil, Baton Rouge Refinery, and of the Ethyl Corporation, Baton Rouge Plant, in providing us with a not inconsiderable amount of illustrative material. There are undoubtedly dozens of others to whom some acknowledgment is due—our students, who have listened with at least the appearance of patience while we expounded some of the principles set down here; our colleagues, who have encouraged the writing and have kindly refrained from making excessive demands on our time and energies.

G. W. G.
W. W. B.

Baton Rouge, Louisiana
January, 1951

PUBLIC SPEAKING:
PRINCIPLES AND PRACTICE

CHAPTER I

The Attitude of the Speaker

THE study of public speaking, which you are now entering, is by no means new to the educational program. It is, in fact, almost as old as civilization itself. Even before the building of the Great Pyramid of Khufu, about 2900 B.C., the Egyptians had mentioned speech in their writings, and some two centuries later Ptah Hotep, the old vizier to the reigning Pharaoh Isesi, called his children about him and gave them instruction in "fair speaking." There is also some evidence that before the Trojan War a school of speech was set up in Greece by Theseus (he who, according to legend, slew the Minotaur); and in Homer's *Iliad* and *Odyssey* are many fine speeches by the warriors who took part in the long siege of Troy.

The present development of the principles and practices of public speaking may be traced in an unbroken line back to the middle of the fifth century B.C., when Corax, a Sicilian, formulated some of the ideas which you will be studying in this course. Other ideas were provided a hundred years later by Aristotle and still later by Cicero, the great Roman orator and writer of the first century B.C.; by Quintilian, who in the first century A.D. was appointed by the Emperor to the first state-supported professorship of speech. Further ideas were added by still other writers in later periods.

It is not the purpose of this discussion to give a detailed history of public speaking or of its teaching. Let it suffice to say, first, that there has been no time during the past twenty-five centuries when speech and speaking have not been taught; and second, that from the experiences of two and a half millennia have emerged a number of principles that are found to be just as valid today as they were in the time of Aristotle. One of the most important of these has to do with your personal attitude toward public speaking and toward the study of the subject. Much of your influence as a speaker will depend on your developing certain points of view with respect to your study of the principles and practices, as well as with respect to your recognition of the function, of public utterance.

PUBLIC SPEAKING IS AN ASSET

In the minds of many the ability to speak is of importance only to those whose vocations depend primarily on speaking, such as the ministry, the law, lawmaking, teaching, and perhaps a few others. Such an idea is erroneous. In nearly every vocation the ability to speak is not only an asset, it is a positive necessity. The dean of an engineering college recently asked a number of practicing engineers what courses in school he should give his students to fit them better for their profession. Near the top of the list they had placed public speaking. "Teach them how to express themselves!" they said. Dr. M. P. Martin, President of the State Association of Health Physicians of Louisiana, insists that a good public-health officer must be more than a good doctor; he must be a good administrator, a diplomat, an expert in public relations, and a good public speaker.[1]

Not only will you find it necessary to speak occasionally to general groups outside your own vocation; you will even more frequently be called on to speak within your group: at the meetings of your clubs, professional associations, trade unions, scientific societies, and similar organizations. A successful physician recently enrolled in an evening class to learn how to speak in public so that he would be able to read his professional papers more effectively. Extension and evening classes all over the country are filled with adult men and women from all walks of life who feel that the ability to speak well is an absolute necessity for advancement in their work. Without it, they feel, they are limited in their capacities for growth.

It is not only professionally that the ability to speak is important. You will all enter into the life of your community, your state, your country, in greater or lesser degrees of activity. Our whole society is based on the principle of freedom of exchange of ideas, opinions, experiences. Freedom of utterance is one of our most jealously guarded rights. But it is more than a right; it is also a responsibility. The effectiveness of a democratic order is determined by the effectiveness with which the individual members participate in its activities. The greatest threat to those institutions is not so much from definitely subversive elements as from indifferent or ineffective participation, or total lack of participation, on the part of the members themselves.

Your privilege or right of exercising your freedom of speech is of little practical value to you, however, unless you possess also the *ability* to exercise it. The effectiveness of your own function as a citizen is essentially a matter of your individual participation in the affairs of your community, large or small. That participation, in turn, is largely dependent on two things: having ideas

[1] Richard Thruelson, "Public Health Doctor," *Saturday Evening Post,* May 13, 1950, pp. 36, 170 ff.

that will contribute to the welfare of the group, and your ability to present those ideas clearly, forcibly, and convincingly. As Thomas Mann says in his *Joseph in Egypt*, "Who knows how to set his words well and hath a gift of expression, upon him gods and men nod with applause, and he findeth inclined ears."[2]

GOOD SPEAKING CAN BE LEARNED

There is an old Latin saying, *"Orator fit, non nascitur,"* meaning, "The orator is made, not born." It is not expected that everyone will become a Demosthenes, a Cicero, a Bryan, a Roosevelt, or a Churchill. There are natural aptitudes in speech as in every other activity. Only a relatively small number of athletes each season become superlatively skillful in golf, in football, in baseball, in track. Not everyone, regardless of the time and effort expended, can become a Jascha Heifetz, a Lily Pons, or a Katherine Hepburn. Individual differences account for the Einsteins, the Whiteheads, the Hemingways, and the Websters.

But even though you may not win any major golf tournaments, any of you can, under competent instruction and diligent, directed practice, lower your score appreciably. Although you may not become accomplished musicians, most of you can learn to carry a tune and participate in group singing. Similarly, although few if any of you will reach the heights of oratorical greatness, all of you can, by judicious study and practice, learn to speak more effectively than you can now. It is probable that few of you will find yourselves in situations calling for the type of exalted speaking that goes by the name of oratory; but none of you will escape entirely the opportunity, even the responsibility, of saying simply, clearly, and with some force, the things that will need to be said if you are to participate actively in the affairs of the various groups in which you are to live.

It is toward this type of speaking that the present course is directed. Later, if you want to pursue your study and practice

[2] Reprinted from *Joseph in Egypt* by Thomas Mann, by permission of Alfred A. Knopf, Inc. Copyright 1938 by Alfred A. Knopf, Inc.

further, you may go as far as your ambitions, your individual ability, and your persistence can take you. You will not become an orator or even a good speaker overnight. But for the present it should be remembered that any one of you who is willing to expend a reasonable amount of time and effort on the work will make a significant improvement in his ability to speak before a group of listeners. Some of the specific directions which that improvement is to take will appear in the succeeding chapters of this text. The old saying that "Practice makes perfect" is not altogether true; it only fixes habits and tends to make them permanent. But intelligent practice, based on an understanding of what you are trying to do and why you are doing it, and on a conscious (and conscientious) effort to apply the principles of good speaking, will bring about an improvement. How much is a matter for you alone to determine.

GOOD SPEAKING DEMANDS CERTAIN MINIMUM ESSENTIALS

If you are desirous of learning how to speak well in public, you will need to consider a few minimum essentials in the study and practice of speaking. You will, of course, learn how to do some things that are necessary to make a good speech; but you will also need to examine some of the basic attitudes which effective speaking of today requires. In other words, you should give some thought to the question of *why* public speaking is so vital in such a society as ours, as well as to the matter of your own place in that society, once you have acquired something of an ability to influence the behavior of others. The following five points will suggest to you a few of the attitudes which all good speakers, consciously or unconsciously, have acquired in their period of preparation.

Study Is an Essential

There have been "natural" speakers, perhaps, who could hold and sway audiences without knowing how they did it or without knowing anything about the principles of public speaking; but they have been extremely rare. It is highly probable, even, that many of them, who later learned something about these principles, were like the industrial foreman who for some weeks attended an extension course in public speaking. After class one evening he stopped to speak to the instructor. "These techniques you have been giving us," he said, "I have been using for several years; but this is the first time I ever understood why."

It has been the experience of most people that effective speaking requires much study. In his first attempt to address the Athenian public, Demosthenes was a total failure and was laughed out of the assembly; but after long study with his teacher, Isaeus, and after much practice, he became one of the world's greatest orators. Some of you have read Cicero's orations. Cicero spent many years, first in Rome and later in Athens and on the island of Rhodes, in so perfecting his abilities that he too became a great orator. St. Augustine not only studied the principles of speaking, but for eleven years before his conversion to Christianity, he was a teacher of rhetoric, which at that time was equivalent to speech. Others of the Church Fathers—the Gregorys, Basil, Jerome, Chrysostom—all were profound students of speaking, some of them traveling as far as Antioch in Asia Minor to study under the great teacher Libanius.

So it has been through the centuries. When men have aspired to success in any vocation in which speaking played an important part—and it is difficult to find one which does not involve some speech—they have spent much time and effort in learning the principles of good speech and in practicing their application. When Walter Reuther, President of the United Automobile Workers, was a youth, his father, who had studied public speaking by correspondence, used to take him and his three brothers into an upstairs room on Sunday afternoons and require them to debate some current topic. Reuther's ability to engage in the rough-and-tumble of union controversy was the result of those exercises. Cardinal Spellman was a college debater, as were Senators Humphrey of Minnesota and Russell Long of Louisiana. Senators Morse of Oregon and Mundt of South Dakota were not only profound students of public speaking; they also taught it for some years. Former Senator Lee of Oklahoma and Governor Maw of Utah were likewise teachers of speech. Woodrow Wilson, an enthusiastic sponsor of debating clubs at Princeton and Wesleyan, never lost his interest in improving the effectiveness of his speaking.[3]

William Jennings Bryan, who in 1896 at the age of thirty-six won the Democratic nomination for the Presidency with his "Cross of Gold" speech, had studied speech at a small college in Illinois; Wendell Phillips was a student at Harvard, Henry Ward Beecher at Amherst, Chauncey M. Depew at Yale, and Henry W. Grady at the University of Georgia. Matthew Arnold, the great English essayist and historian, took lessons in elocution (a term in much higher repute then than now) from a certain Reverend J. W. Churchill; when Macaulay was planning to come to America in the middle of the last century, he took lessons in speech to ensure that his lectures would be more certain of success; and Paul Lawrence Dunbar, the Negro poet, studied speech so that he could become a successful public reader, especially of his own poems. Many women who became highly influential because of their speaking ability also made a careful study of public speaking. Among these may be mentioned Ida M. Tarbell, Ruth Bryan Owen, Eleanor Roosevelt, and Dorothy Thompson.

It would be possible to extend this list almost indefinitely. Perhaps enough examples have been given to illustrate the point that for many centuries men—and women—have found it necessary, whenever their work demanded some proficiency in speaking, to make a careful study of the principles and practices of speech.

In speech it is unsafe to depend wholly on your own native ability, just as it is in any activity which is based on understand-

---

[3] Robert T. Oliver, "Wilson's *Rapport* with his Audience," *The Quarterly Journal of Speech*. February, 1941, pp. 79-90.

ing and skill. You may become a fairly fast runner, but if you want to break records, you have to train. There is such a thing, even in running, as form. The individual who "never had a lesson" may be a nuisance when he sits down at the piano. Successful writers spend seemingly fruitless hours writing pages that will never be published in order to learn how to write. Effective public speech is an art based on a solid body of theory that has developed over a period of two and a half thousand years. As such it is not to be picked up in "ten easy lessons" or by no lessons at all.

For one more reason study and practice are essential. The old story is told of the man who would not write or speak until he had developed his ideas fully, all ready to be broadcast to the world. When he finally felt that he was ready, he learned to his dismay that he had lost even the capacity to have ideas. *Study and practice in the expression of ideas is the best possible means of developing the capacity to have ideas.*

Good Speaking Requires Broad Knowledge

In the early days of the study of public speaking, in ancient Athens, it was expected that the individual master the whole world of knowledge. With the present accumulation of the world's store of information, however, such an achievement would obviously be impossible. At the same time, it is essential in the development of your own maximum effectiveness in speech to secure as broad an understanding as possible. The person who knows only one field, even though he may know that one thoroughly, is certain to be limited in his ability to speak to general audiences even on that field. The dean of a medical school, when asked recently what sort of premedical education his prospective students should be given, replied, "Give them anything but medical subjects; give them an education!"

Your chosen field of specialization, whatever it may be, will not stand alone. It will be closely related to and interdependent with many other subjects. To be thoroughly grounded in your own field of knowledge you should be able to orient it with those other subjects; you should be able to appreciate those interdependencies. Literary history, for example, is unintelligible without social history; physics cannot be understood without a knowledge of mathematics. Many orthodontists, in addition to performing necessary oral operations, are increasingly interested in the effect of those operations on the formation of the sounds of speech. An engineer who builds a bridge across the Mississippi River may see that structure not only as an engineering achievement but as a means to further social facilitation. The road builder may understand his technical job, but he may also appreciate the effect of highways on the breaking down of social and economic isolation. The speaker who addresses an audience of farmers may wish to show them how they can increase their crops; he should also have some understanding of rural economics and rural sociology and of what increased crops will mean to his listeners in terms of certain economic and social advantages.

Your illustrative material can be drawn from a wide variety of sources. Webster opened his "Reply to Hayne" with a reference to the practice of mariners after a storm. Literary and Biblical allusions are often effective; but to be able to use them you must know your literature, both secular and sacred. The recounting of a course of events leading up to some final outcome may require a knowledge of history. Instances are known in which a lawyer's knowledge of chemistry was a vital factor in the case; and it is said that Lincoln once "broke" a trial by showing that, on the night in question, an alleged identification by moonlight would have been impossible because on that night, according to the almanac, the moon had not yet risen.

Preparation for speaking is of two sorts. The first involves the acquisition of broad knowledge and experience. Everything you read, every new place you visit, every different thing you do, may provide, sometimes unexpectedly, valuable material for your speeches. This sort of *general preparation* you are constantly making because you are constantly acquiring new experiences, new information, new ideas. This is not the preparation that goes into any single speech; it is the preparation that you will be making all your lives for speaking in general. When Webster was asked how long it had taken him to prepare the speech mentioned above, he replied, "I have been preparing for that speech all my life." Great speakers have always been great readers.

It is in the acquisition of broad understanding that your general preparation for speaking—not for planning *a* speech—is made. The broader and more deeply the foundation of that understanding is laid, the more solid will be the preparation you will be able to make for your specific speeches. "Besides the art of words," said a sixteenth-century educator,[4] "he [the student] must be stuffed with a store of matter."

For still another reason a broad education is essential for the good speaker. Someone has recently said, "Ignorant eloquence is as subversive as heresy." It should not need to be said that the speaker should be sincere in his utterances. But important as sincerity is, it is not enough alone: <u>enlightened sincerity</u> is essential. Twenty-four centuries ago the great philosopher Plato wrote, "A solid art of speaking without a grip on truth, there is not nor will be hereafter, ever." "Freedom of speech," says Walter Generazzo, President of the American Watch Workers' Union, "carries with it an obligation to tell the truth."[5] It is only the broadly educated person who is truly educated, for only he may come most close to gaining the "grip on truth" of which Plato wrote. But Plato also said, "Mere knowledge of the truth will not give you the art of persuasion."[6] "A merely well informed man," says

---

[4] Laurence Humphrey, *The Nobles; or, of Nobilitye: the original nature, dutyes, right and Christian institution thereof three bookes. . . .*, T. Marshe, 1563. Quoted in Foster Watson, *The English Grammar Schools to 1660*, Cambridge University Press, 1908, p. 87.

[5] Walter Generazzo, "How to Lick Class Struggle," *Reader's Digest*, September, 1949, pp. 81-85.

[6] Both quotations from the *Phaedrus*.

Whitehead, "is the most useless bore on earth."[7] And wisdom without eloquence, according to Cicero, is of no benefit to the state, whereas eloquence without wisdom is a great danger.[8]

The other sort of preparation takes place when you get ready for a specific speech to a specific audience on a specific occasion. It is then that you make your *special preparation*; it is then that you will assemble all the pertinent material available, selecting that which will contribute most to the accomplishment of your purpose. You will organize it and work out in some detail exactly what you plan to say. In this specific preparation you will draw on the experiences and information and knowledge you have gained through your years of general preparation, taking an item from this field, another from a second field, still another from a third, and so on.

Good Speaking Requires the Urge to Communicate

It may be said with some justification that in any speaking situation there are two basic factors: what is being said and the people to whom it is being said. The immediate purpose of the speaker is to get across to his audience a specific idea. The broad effects of successfully joining these two elements constitute what have been called the *general ends* of speech. As an immediate result of getting the speaker's idea, the listeners may (1) acquire new information, new experiences; (2) they may have their already accepted beliefs and attitudes strengthened and revitalized; (3) they may have those beliefs and attitudes changed, even reversed; (4) they may decide upon a new and altered course of action, different from that which they have hitherto been following or even directly opposed to it; (5) they may derive amusement, entertainment, diversion as a result of an idea which has been aroused or stimulated by the speaker.

[7] Quoted by George D. Stoddard, in a panel discussion, "Are We Educating for the Needs of the Modern Man?" *Representative American Speeches, 1948-1949*, A. Craig Baird (ed.), The H. W. Wilson Company, 1949, p. 188.

[8] Adapted from *De Inventione*.

The communicative situation arises whenever one individual with an idea and the urge to share it finds one or more persons who are willing or can be persuaded to listen to him. The types of occasion giving rise to such situations are obviously many and varied, no two being exactly alike. The speaker himself is essentially the medium through which idea and listener are brought together.

As has already been pointed out, the acquisition of the means by which this objective is reached necessitates considerable thought. Essentially, the study of public speaking involves three aspects:

1. It involves an examination into the attitudes and motives of the speaker himself in an attempt to find justification for his own desire to join these two basic factors of idea and listener.
2. It involves an examination into the emotional and logical and ethical aspects of human nature through which the listener may be reached.
3. It involves a study and application of the methods by which the speaker achieves his purpose, that is, by which he seeks to bring his idea to his audience.

There are various reasons for speaking. As a young speaker, eager to gain further experiences in addressing groups, you may justifiably seize upon every reasonable opportunity to speak in public. If you are really interested in improving your own abilities, you should never refuse such opportunities, so long as you have a worth-while contribution to make to the discussion and so long as you stop well short of making a nuisance of yourself. You may feel the need of adding an item of information in the discussion of some subject of interest or importance; you may advocate the acceptance or rejection of some proposal which has come before your group for decision. If none of these opportunities presents itself, you can follow the example of the former Senator Ashurst of Arizona, who, it is said, used to declaim to the mountains and to his cattle as he rode the range in his own state. As you gain in experience and knowledge, in confidence and poise, you will find plenty of occasions for speaking.

In all these situations the speaker, to be most effective, must feel the urge to communicate. He must, in other words, feel that the idea which is in his mind is one that should be in the possession of his hearers and that he is the medium by which this audience and this idea are to be brought together. *There is no effective speaking that does not arise from the urge to communicate.*

Good Speaking Demands Honest Thinking

Broad knowledge is of great importance to the speaker, but in order for it to be of greatest value, it must be interpreted through honest thinking. The true scientist understands what is meant by intellectual honesty, and his studies, at least in his own field, are characterized by that type of thinking. He examines the facts as they come to him through his investigations, interprets those facts in the light of what is already known, and arrives at his conclusions on the basis of those interpretations. *He sees what is there rather than what he is looking for.* Sometimes what he sees is quite different from what he anticipated; but unless he is willing to accept those interpretations and to base his conclusions on the facts as he discovers them, he is no true scientist. For generations after Magellan's little fleet completed its voyage around the world, people refused to discard the idea that the phrase, "the four corners of the earth," was to be taken literally. The members of the French Academy persisted in their rejection of the findings of Pasteur until the sheer weight of evidence forced them to recognize the validity of his findings.

In your thinking, then, you should follow those procedures which contribute to intellectual honesty and avoid those which violate the principles of sound thinking. In arriving at your judgments you will encounter favorable as well as unfavorable facts, that is, details which agree or disagree with your present beliefs and attitudes. Do not permit your emotional biases to outweigh your reason in evaluating these apparently contradictory data. Do not ignore the unfavorable in arriving at your final judgments.

In other words, do not allow your prejudices to govern your selection of facts or your evaluation of those facts. ". . . absolute correspondence between certain beliefs and fact is very difficult to establish. We should therefore always be on the alert for possible changes in our accepted beliefs which serve as basic assumptions, for the conclusions that depend on them may change markedly when we accept a change in the foundation framework."[9]

If your judgments are formed only after you have accumulated sufficient knowledge of the problem, they will then be the more easily defended because they have a sounder basis in fact; even then, you must be ready to accept new information as it comes to you and to modify your judgments accordingly. The process of rationalization, generally to be avoided, consists in first making up your mind and then trying to find reasons for taking the attitude you do, or in determining a course of action and then seeking to justify that course. William Jennings Bryan once said, "It is a poor head that cannot find a reason for doing what the heart wants to do."

In your speaking make it your aim to clarify rather than to confuse the thinking of your listeners. Half-truths are to be avoided; it should be remembered that in being only half truth, they are likely to be also half falsehood. Falsification through omission is no less misleading than through commission. Misrepresentation, distortion, and concealment of facts for your own purposes are to be condemned. As will be pointed out in a succeeding chapter, you will inevitably appeal to motives, which are closely related to the emotions. But when you do, put those appeals on a rational basis. Back up your emotional appeal by sound reasoning.

PROPAGANDA. Propaganda is not always pernicious, although the term has acquired a somewhat unsavory connotation. It is often distrusted because it makes extensive use of the techniques of confusion and deception. Despite Hitler's insistence that

---

[9] Lee Emerson Boyer, *Mathematics, A Historical Development*, Henry Holt and Company, Inc., 1945, p. 387. Quoted by special permission.

people will believe any lie if it is repeated often enough and loudly enough, it is still true, as Lincoln said, "You can't fool all the people all the time." "To deceive through words is no less reprehensible than to cheat through more overt and demonstrable ways."[10]

One of the techniques of deception and confusion used in propaganda consists of what is known as *name calling*. This is, in brief, the process by which emotional attitudes are directed toward something, a person or a proposal, by applying to it a term which has a particularly favorable or unfavorable association or connotation. So long as these terms are actually applicable and there is a sound factual justification for the attitudes aroused, the propaganda itself may be considered salutary. It is when the terms are entirely inappropriate and the attitudes quite unjustified that the propaganda becomes pernicious.

In this technique we seek approval of a proposed measure by associating it with the "American way of life" or by connecting it in some way, which is never clarified, with Thomas Jefferson or Abraham Lincoln. To many people, applying the label *socialistic* to a given proposal is enough to condemn it utterly. This is not an argument for or against socialism; it merely utilizes the fact that many people dislike what they have vaguely associated with the term, so that whenever it is applied they automatically dislike whatever it is made to refer to. When the late President Roosevelt coined the term "economic royalists," he was seeking to generate unfavorable emotional attitudes through the technique of name calling.

Another of the devices of confusion and deception used in much propaganda consists of what is known as the *red-herring* technique. This process involves the introduction of some argument not connected with the point at issue and raising a great furor over that irrelevant matter in order to draw the attention of the reader or listener away from the real issues at stake. It

[10] Lester Thonssen and A. Craig Baird, *Speech Criticism*, The Ronald Press Company, 1948, p. 470.

is usually resorted to when one's own position is insecure and when it would be unsafe, for one's own purposes, to allow the basic issues to be brought to light. If the issue is doubtful, it is more honest to face it fairly and to dispose of the opposition by sound argument if possible. If it cannot be so disposed of, the probabilities are that the opposition has a sound-enough basis to warrant at least careful consideration by all concerned. "If I can carry you with me by sound convictions," said Beecher to a hostile audience at Liverpool, "I shall be immensely glad; but if I cannot carry you with me by facts and sound arguments, I do not wish you to go with me at all; and all that I ask is simply *fair play*."[11]

In a later chapter it will be pointed out that one's clearness and honesty of thinking are revealed to a great extent by the degree of definiteness in the meanings which he attaches to the words he uses. Good speaking demands that the speaker be honest in his thinking and that he carry this integrity into his public utterances as well as his private conversations.

Good Speaking Requires Realization of Social Responsibility

From what has been said, it seems obvious that in such a form of social organization as our own the ability to speak effectively is highly important. Yet that ability in itself is not enough. If we are to preserve our present social structure or to make those changes which seem advisable from time to time, it is vital that the members of the social organization be able to express their ideas and opinions clearly and forcibly; it is equally important that they know when to use that ability and to what social ends it is to be employed. Consider, for example, the medical profession. Students in medical colleges not only learn the arts of disease pre-

---

[11] Henry Ward Beecher, "Liverpool Address," October 16, 1863, *Classified Speech Models*, William Norwood Brigance (ed.), F. S. Crofts & Co., 1928, pp. 40-65.

THE AMERICAN WAY. *(Photo, Black Star.)*

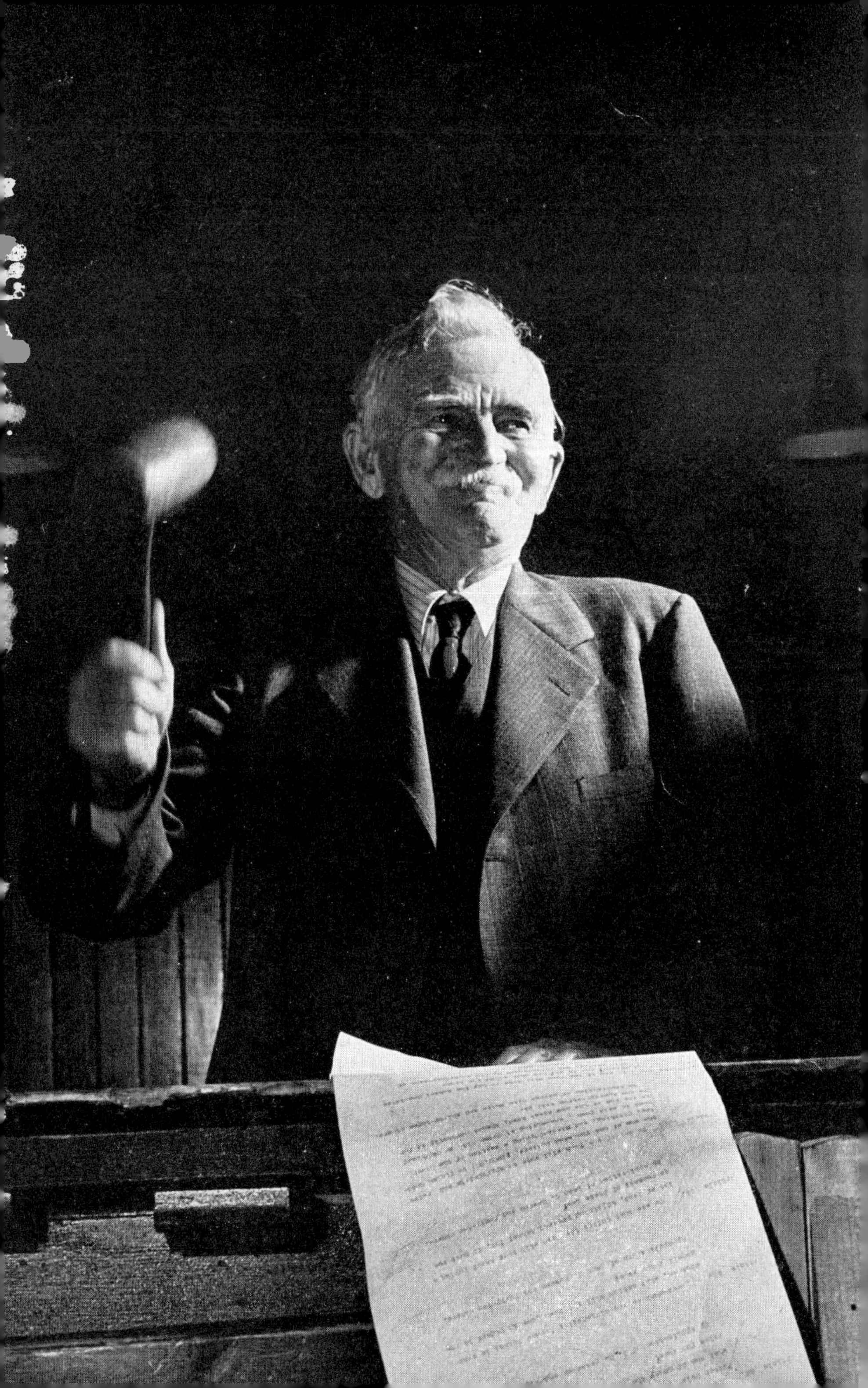

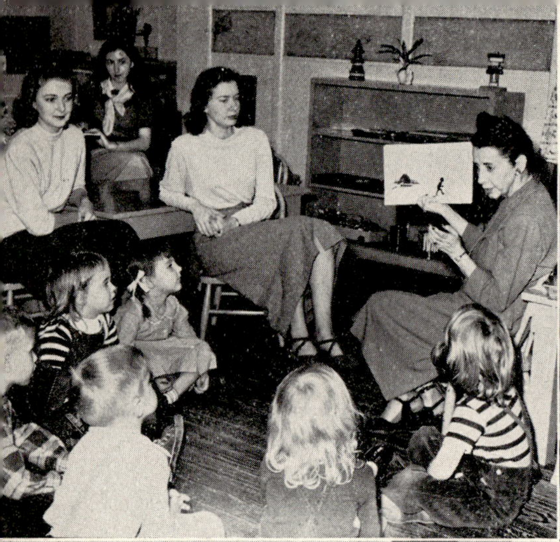

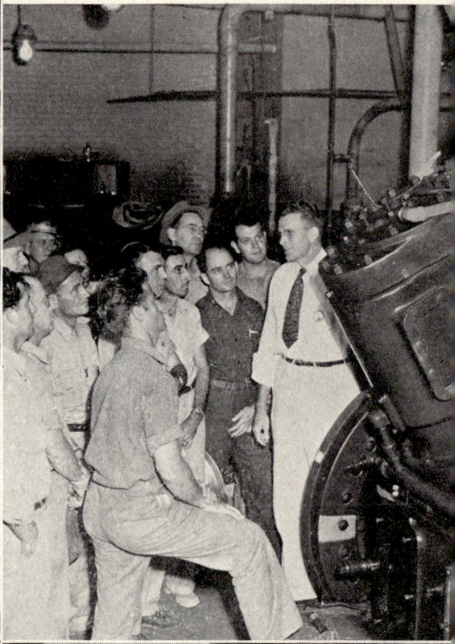

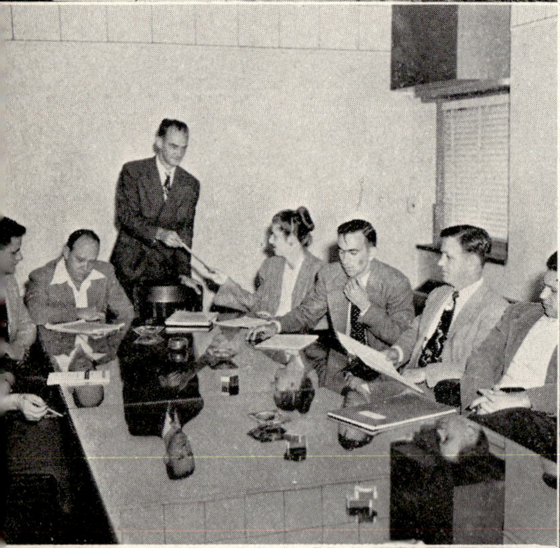

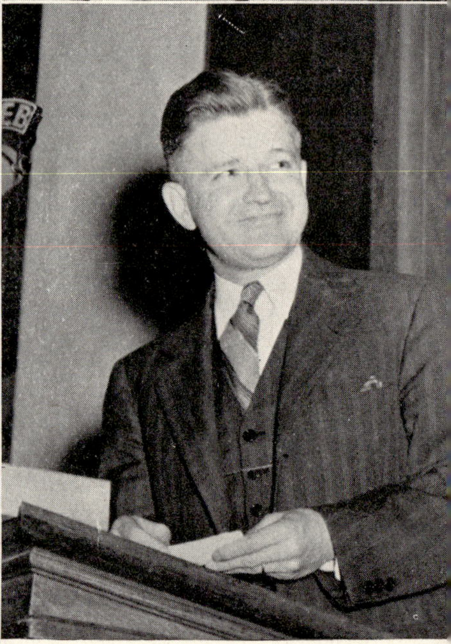

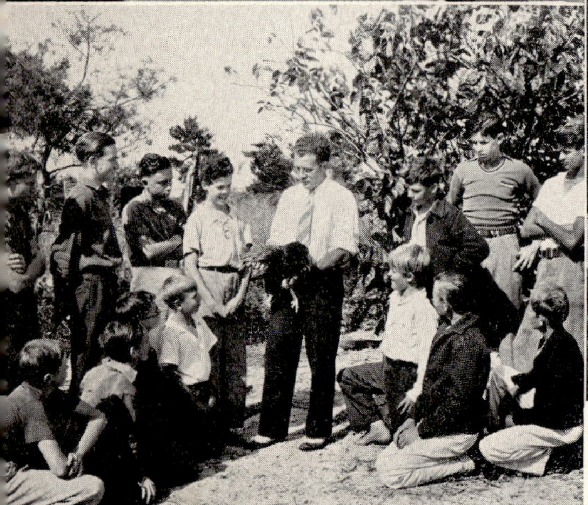

THE ATTITUDE OF THE SPEAKER

vention and healing; they also learn the rigid code of ethics which governs the practice of medicine. The "Oath of Hippocrates" is for the physician a statement of the principles by which he determines his professional conduct. The oath reads in part as follows:

> I will follow that method of treatment which, according to my ability and judgment, I consider for the benefit of my patients, and abstain from whatever is deleterious and mischievous. I will give no deadly medicine to anyone if asked, nor suggest any such counsel; . . . With purity and holiness I will pass my life and practice my art. . . . Into whatever houses I enter I will go into them for the benefit of the sick and will abstain from every voluntary act of mischief and corruption. . . .

The very first section of the modern version of the code of medical ethics, as adopted by the American Medical Association, states:

> A profession has for its prime object the service it can render to humanity; reward or financial gain should be a subordinate consideration. The practice of medicine is a profession. In choosing this profession an individual assumes an obligation to conduct himself in accord with its ideals.[12]

The speaker, like the physician, also has a social responsibility. In his acquired ability to affect the thinking, the feelings, the actions of those who come under his influence, he has the oppor-

---

[12] Leo F. Simpson, M.D., "The Doctor and Public Health," *Vital Speeches,* August 14, 1948, pp. 654-657.

THE ABILITY TO SPEAK IN PUBLIC IS A NECESSITY IN NEARLY EVERY VOCATION AND PROFESSION

The effectiveness of the teacher, the foreman, the supervisor, the doctor, the lawyer, and the college president depends upon the ability to express ideas clearly and forcefully. (Photos, Ethyl Corporation, Baton Rouge Plant; Esso Standard Oil, Baton Rouge Refinery; L.S.U. Alumni News; U.S.D.A. Extension Service; L.S.U. Bureau of Public Service.)

tunity of contributing to either the welfare or the detriment of the social order and of the individual members of that order. This is not to imply that one should never advocate change at all; but it does suggest that whatever changes in the social order are urged should be such as are calculated to be for the benefit of the maximum number of persons concerned and not for any single individual or group of individuals at the expense of the others.

As students of speech, therefore, your concern should be not only with the improvement of your capabilities for public utterance but also with the question of the uses to which you intend to put that ability.

As a people we are committed to the maintenance of what is called the democratic way of life. The term has meant many things to many people. Essentially, it refers to the willingness to grant to others the same privileges we ask for ourselves; the insistence on as much freedom in our own action as will not interfere with the like freedom of others; the insistence upon determining without coercion our own course of conduct and granting to our neighbor the same right; the right to discuss freely and openly the problems that arise from time to time and to exchange as freely and openly our ideas, information, opinion, experiences with our associates; the arrival at decisions on group action only after full, open, and free discussion participated in by all concerned and the acceptance of the expressed decision of the majority; the unrestricted selection of those who are to lead us in our group activities and the removal of such leaders as do not perform the group will.

We are committed to the preservation of this type of organization because we believe that any such association exists primarily for the benefit of the individual members and that only through a democratic form of society can the individual reach his highest development. This is, in fact, the fundamental purpose of a democracy: to permit, even to encourage, the realization of the highest capacities of the several members of that society, intellect-

THE ATTITUDE OF THE SPEAKER 19

ually, socially, economically, spiritually. Speaking which does not contribute to those objectives, or which obstructs their attainment, or which deliberately leads others away from their progress toward those goals, falls short of its opportunities; the speaker is failing to meet his social obligation. If our form of social organization is worth preserving at all, and we all believe that it is in its essential features, then it is worth while to develop the means by which it is fostered and perpetuated. In such a society it should be obvious that speech, both private and public, plays a vital role not only in the processes of social interaction but in the very process of thought itself. "*Effective speech*," says Taeusch, "is a *necessary instrument* in *social thinking*."[13]

How one uses his ability in speaking, whether for the good or ill of society, is essentially a matter of the speaker's own sense of ethical and moral values, of his own motives in speaking, of the honesty of his own thinking, and of the genuineness of his concern for human welfare. There is not, nor has there ever been, any great speaking which was directed toward the abasement of humanity, toward the enslavement of people, or the destruction of human freedoms. There has never been a truly great speaker whose efforts were directed toward such end results. As Emerson once said, "There is no true eloquence, unless there is a man behind the speech."

In recent years we have heard much about the potentialities of atomic energy. Its terrific destructive force has been demonstrated; we are assured that it has equally great possibilities for constructive work. What may not be so clearly realized is that tremendous as that energy is, it is still relatively insignificant in its possibilities for good or ill as compared with the power of the spoken word. The atom bomb at Hiroshima snuffed out the lives of some sixty thousand victims in a single, searing, blinding, instant; the hydrogen bomb may make that one look like a Fourth

---

[13] Carl F. Taeusch, "Effective Speaking as an Index of Thought," *The Quarterly Journal of Speech*, April, 1941, pp. 195-197. Italics are in the original.

of July firecracker. But it was the fiery harangues of Hitler and Mussolini that brought on World War II which cost the lives of millions and the destruction of untold billions in material values—and the end is not yet in sight! Hitler's threat, "If I fall, I'll take the whole world with me," has not been made innocuous, even as this is written.

Even more tragically, through the passionate speech of the dictators, the minds of whole nations of people, adults and children, were warped almost beyond recovery. Hitler himself testified that to accomplish his ends he had relied almost entirely on the power of speech. And so strong is that power that in the postwar world the minds of yet further millions are still being warped through its destructive force. Skill in the techniques of speech is one of the chief weapons for those charged with the responsibility for the spread of ideologies subversive to democratic thought. The techniques of group manipulation, of parliamentary procedure, are also used for purposes of deception and confusion. The workers have received intensive training and know all the tricks. The one thing they cannot and will not survive is the full, free, open discussion of the issues at stake under conditions in which everyone who wishes may enter into the discussion with no fear of punishment for the views he may hold. "Tyranny cannot flourish," say Thonssen and Baird, "where responsible men have the right to say responsible things."[14] If the fundamental purposes of a democracy are to be achieved, and tyranny prevented or overthrown, this right becomes an obligation.

The most effective way of combatting these enemies of such a system of free participation is to know the techniques of democracy just a little more thoroughly than they, to develop an even greater skill in their application, and above all, to bring to the controversy an openness and honesty of thought and purpose, a meticulous regard for facts, a tolerance for the opinions of others, and a genuine interest in human welfare.

[14] Thonssen and Baird, *op. cit.*, p. 468.

THE ATTITUDE OF THE SPEAKER

In opposition to the destructive speaking of Hitler and Mussolini, it was Roosevelt who, through his speaking, quieted the fears of America during the dark days of the depression which began in 1929. It was Churchill who by his speech welded the British people into a solid wall of resistance to the onslaughts of the Nazis, even though he had nothing to offer but "blood, sweat, and tears." The growth of religion has taken place primarily through speech. In all the most important steps forward in the development of civilization, speech has played a significant role. It has had its constructive as well as its destructive aspects.

Because of the power of effective speech to influence others to think, to feel, and to act very much as the speaker wants them to, it is not difficult to understand why the speaker himself, as his speech becomes more and more effective, assumes so grave a responsibility. He needs, then, to examine closely his own ethical standards, his motives in speaking, and the effect of his utterances on his listeners and on the welfare of those affected. Here again a comparison might be made between the speaking of Hitler on the one hand, and of Churchill on the other. Both were, for their respective audiences, immediately and outstandingly effective speakers. But Hitler was motivated by a craving for power for himself, for absolute power of life and death over all other peoples, for the rise of a new Germany, with himself as the dictator, at the expense of all the world. Churchill was motivated by a desire to preserve not only for himself, but for that world, the advantages which had been won through centuries of striving toward the individual freedom of mankind. Of the two it is Churchill who will be remembered as a good, even a great, speaker.

As has been truly said, "Skillful utterance can be totally destructive unless it is motivated by honest thinking, a feeling for justice, and a genuine concern for the well-being of humanity."[15] Nineteen centuries ago Quintilian wrote in his *Institutes of Oratory*,

---

[15] Joseph F. Smith, quoted in Giles Wilkeson Gray and Claude Merton Wise, *The Bases of Speech*, Harper & Brothers, rev. ed., 1946, p. 374.

When Nature, that indulgent Mother, endowed Man with Speech, to distinguish him from other Creatures, she would have acted the Part not of a Parent, but a Tyrant, had she intended that Eloquence should herd with Wickedness, oppose Innocence and destroy Truth. It had been more kind in her, to have ordered Man to be born mute, nay, devoid of all reason, rather than that he should employ the Gifts of Providence to the Destruction of his Neighbour.

. . . should a wicked man be eloquent, then Eloquence herself becomes Wickedness; because she furnishes that Man with the Means of being more wicked; and a bad Man will be sure to use them.[16]

About the time these lines were being written in Rome, another man in the East, who also claimed Roman citizenship but with a basic philosophy quite different from Quintilian's enlightened paganism, was writing to his friends in Corinth a parallel sentiment which is equally valid today. "Though I speak with the tongues of men and of angels, and have not love, I am become as sounding brass, or a tinkling cymbal."[17]

EXERCISES

1. In a two- to four-minute speech introduce yourself to your classmates. Give your name, your home town, your major field of interest, and some interesting facts in your own experiences. Attempt to establish with your fellows the impression that you are a person of some intelligence, good will, character, and personal worth.
2. During the present course your speech class will be your audience. Although it will consist of the same personnel from day to day, it will in effect be constantly changing because of varying relations with the things you will be talking about. During the speeches of introduction, study each individual as he speaks; attempt to determine what types of speeches he will probably like to hear and his possible fixed attitudes and his personality. Prepare and hand in a *written analysis* of your class as an audience in relation to your probable subjects.

[16] William Guthrie's translation, T. Waller, 1756, vol. 2, Book XII, chap. 1, pp. 495, 503.

[17] I Corinthians xiii: 1.

THE ATTITUDE OF THE SPEAKER

3. Write a speech biography in which you analyze your own assets and liabilities as a speaker. Consider such questions as the following, in so far as they may apply:
   a. Why I enrolled in a public-speaking course (If it is required, state the probable reasons why it is required.)
   b. What I hope to accomplish as a result of taking the course
   c. The kind of speaker I should like to be
   d. The social uses to which I might put my ability in speaking
   e. Any pleasant or unpleasant experiences I may have had as a speaker
   f. My present recognized faults in speaking

   Attempt to look at yourself as objectively as possible. If you are timid, say so frankly, and attempt to determine why. If you have difficulty in expressing yourself, look for the cause of the problem.

4. *Discussion Questions for Class Symposiums.* Your instructor may decide that the symposium method is a more effective way of presenting the subject matter of some of the chapters in this text than question and answer sessions or lecturing. In such cases he will select a panel of four or five members and a chairman, who will be responsible for discussing before the class the questions given below, as well as others which may be raised. You may consider one or more of these questions, which are not directly answered in the text. You will need to draw on additional information for your discussion.
   a. Why is training in public speaking essential in a democratic society?
   b. What is the function of speech in what is called the "American way of life"?
   c. What are the relations between speech and "personality?"
   d. Is there a correlation between proficiency in speech and success in the rest of your school work?
   e. Why, in case of an armed invasion, are the communication centers (the telephone exchanges, the radio stations, etc.) among the first points to be attacked and captured?

5. Read one of the speeches in *Vital Speeches,* and try to determine what different fields of knowledge contributed to the speaker's information. Discuss the results of your inquiry before the class.

6. Give a talk in which you show how, in order to discuss some topic you want to speak about, you must draw on a number of different areas of knowledge.

SUPPLEMENTARY READINGS

1. Baird, A. Craig, and Knower, Franklin H., *General Speech: An Introduction*, McGraw-Hill Book Company, Inc., 1949, chap. 11, "The Speaker's Personality," pp. 159-182.
2. Bryant, Donald C., and Wallace, Karl R., *Fundamentals of Public Speaking*, Appleton-Century-Crofts, Inc., 1947, pp. 374-377.
3. Campbell, George, *The Philosophy of Rhetoric*, Harper & Brothers, 1946, chap. IX, "Of the Consideration Which the Speaker Ought to Have of Himself"; chap. X, Sec. I, "The Different Kinds of Public Speaking."
4. Gray, Giles Wilkeson, and Wise, Claude Merton, *The Bases of Speech*, Harper & Brothers, rev. ed., 1946, pp. 372-374; chap. IX, "The Semantic Basis of Speech," pp. 505-546.
5. Oliver, Robert T., *Training for Effective Speech*, The Cordon Company, Inc., 1939, chap. 3, "The Ethics of Speech," pp. 63-77.
6. Overstreet, H. A., *Influencing Human Behavior*, W. W. Norton & Company, 1925, chap. IX, "The Building of Habits: Associative Techniques," pp. 159-168; chap. X, "Unconscious Fabrication Habits," pp. 169-183; chap. XI, "The Problem of Straight Thinking," pp. 184-200.
7. Quintilian, *Institutes of Oratory*, Book X, chap. I, "Concerning the Benefit of Reading." (In chap. II Quintilian discusses the authors whom he thinks the orators of his day should read.)
8. Sarett, Lew, and Foster, William Trufant, *Basic Principles of Speech*, Houghton Mifflin Company, rev. ed., 1946, pp. 25-30.
9. Thonssen, Lester, and Baird, A. Craig, *Speech Criticism*, The Ronald Press Company, 1948, chap. 13, "The Character of the Speaker," pp. 383-391; chap. 18, "Toward a Philosophy of Rhetoric," pp. 465-472.
10. Winans, James A., *Speech-Making*, Appleton-Century-Crofts, Inc., 1938, chap. XIX, "The Speaker Himself," pp. 378-403.
11. Yeager, Willard Hayes, *Effective Speaking for Every Occasion*, Prentice-Hall, Inc., 1940, chap. I, "Beginning Principles of Effective Speaking," pp. 1-35.

CHAPTER II

Some First Principles

IN PLANNING assignments for your class in public speaking, your teacher faces a dilemma: which should come first—principles or practice? If you are required to give talks before you have had an opportunity to study the text, you may develop undesirable habits and waste much time and effort in searching for methods. On the other hand, if you wait to present your first talk until after you have thoroughly studied the text, you will undoubtedly be denied many opportunities to practice and to perfect your skills. But like many a dilemma, this one does not run true to form: it is not really a dilemma, for it permits more than two possibilities. There is a third alternative: during our early preview of certain of the basic principles of public speaking we shall be able to mingle principles and practice and have you talking to the group from the beginning of the course. The objective of this chapter is to give you some of the first principles needed.

When you later study the various principles in more detail, you will become increasingly aware of their complexities, and you will consequently be in a better position to refine your techniques. For the present these refinements can be delayed. In keeping with the foregoing explanation, the assignments throughout this course are planned with two purposes in mind: first, to provide for you as many and as varied speaking assignments as possible, and second, to stress one principle at a time until you have built up a substantial body of information about speaking in public.

YOUR APPROACH TO EARLY SPEECHES

In the preceding chapter you learned that your development as a speaker will depend much on your attitudes toward public speaking. The preparation and delivery of your early speeches in class will bring into the open and crystallize many of your attitudes. Some of you will notice little difference between your opening assignments and numerous other speaking activities in which you have engaged for many years—at Scout meetings, at Sunday School, before your clubs, and of course in your numerous school activities. As a result, you will look upon these assignments as experiences similar to those of the past; and you probably will not waste your energy in worrying about yourself or your progress. But although these assignments are so much like your previous experiences in speaking, do not make the mistake of thinking that they can be carried out successfully without preparation. You will learn quite as much about public speaking from the planning as you will from the presentation.

Others of you may react quite differently. Some of you will magnify some aspect of your past experience in speaking, or of the present situation, beyond its proper importance and as a result may indulge in unnecessary anxiety and needless worry. Alarm may arise because of your inexperience, fear of your classmates, a feeling of inadequacy, an awareness that you are to be graded, a dislike of personal criticism, a belief that the speech class will approximate some past unhappy experience, or a failure to understand the nature of what is called stage fright.

You certainly are not alone in such attitudes. Many of these negative reactions are typical responses to a new speaking situation and, if not allowed to persist, are not serious. Many of them should disappear after a few speeches to the class. However, you must work consciously to eliminate these negative or fear reactions and attempt to substitute positive or favorable ones in their stead.

Study carefully the two lists of student reactions given below. Notice that those on the left resist and defy improvement, while those in the other column look toward the future and toward improvement. If you find that you react negatively to speechmaking, begin at once to substitute attitudes similar to those on the right.

Negative Reactions	Positive Reactions
1. "I know that I shall make a fool of myself when I get up to speak."	1. "I am eager to learn to speak effectively in public."
2. "Public speaking will be of no value to me in my future profession."	2. "Public speaking will be an asset to me in the future."
3. "I have nothing interesting or worth while to talk about."	3. "Each time I speak I shall attempt to improve."
4. "My personality (or my voice) is a great handicap to me."	4. "I hope that my teacher will give constructive criticism in order that I may improve my performance."
5. "I am not capable of delivering a speech in public."	5. "I am going to observe carefully the performances of my classmates in order that I may avoid their mistakes."
6. "I am unfortunate because my classmates are all superior to me."	6. "I like to talk to my classmates."
7. "I know that I am going to flunk this course."	7. "I shall strive to get as much out of this class as possible."

Sound advice to the beginning speaker is, "Stop feeling sorry for yourself. Think about your subject; develop an eagerness to talk about it to other people." Try to realize that

1. You are probably very much like most of the other members of the class.
2. Your problems are probably in no way different from those of other beginners.
3. Your teacher does not expect you to be a polished speaker.
4. The goals of the course are to overcome your fears, to give you understanding, and to improve your skills.
5. Your speech class provides you with a real opportunity to experiment in the art of public speaking, in influencing others, in expressing your ideas, and in learning to master the techniques of social control in so far as speech is involved.

SELECTING A SUBJECT

In considering a subject for an early speech, first, select one that will enable you to draw heavily on your private stock of personal experiences and personal convictions. As a starting point, ask yourself this question, "What do I know most about?" Each of you has his own specialties, hobbies, preferences, and individual experiences. Speakers are, as a rule, most fluent, most dynamic, and most persuasive about those subjects with which they are thoroughly familiar and in which they intensely believe. Even the untrained speaker, when forced to defend what he regards as sacred or precious, often forgets himself, speaks with vigor and force, and utters forceful and compelling oratory which in its abandon approaches eloquence. You will probably be most effective on those subjects which you are eager to share with your listeners.

Second, select a subject in which your listeners are interested or in which you can interest them. The members of the speech class are your audience. Already you have had some opportunity to get acquainted with them as they introduced themselves. Their opening speeches should have yielded much valuable information about their experience, training, interests, and wants. You may be sure that those pursuits and activities which make their lives easier, which promise them security, which increase their incomes, or which promote the welfare of their loved ones are usually the most important and interesting to them. Furthermore, they dislike the commonplace and the routine; consequently, if you are wise, you will attempt to use a fresh approach without seeming to be peculiar.

3. Third, select a topic that is specific in nature, limited in scope, and well within the listeners' experiences. Avoid the philosophical, the subjective, and the theoretical. For your first appearances talk about familiar objects that can be seen or activities that can be personally performed by the listener. The two lists given below illustrate the difference between concrete and abstract subjects:

Abstract Subjects	Specific Subjects
The struggle for freedom	How to operate a voting machine
The meaning of democracy	How to cast an absentee-voter's ballot
The hope for peace	
The value of patriotism	The operation of the electoral college
My philosophy of life	
The improvement of personality	The duties of the county recorder
The importance of agriculture	
Engineering as a profession	The two-cycle gasoline motor
	Building a chicken house
	Life in a bee hive
	The refining of sugar

Many abstract subjects can be transformed into good speech topics if they are narrowed and limited in phase well within the interest and experience of the hearers. What can be done with an abstraction is illustrated in the example given below. Notice how the idea of democracy is successively narrowed in scope until at the end we have a good subject for a speech.

Democracy
Democratic government
Democratic government in the United States
Democratic government in New England
Democratic government in Massachusetts

The town meeting in Concord
The rules of procedure in the Concord town meeting

Even some subjects that at first glance may seem to be good speech topics may be improved if you will narrow them so that they may be adequately developed within the time allotted.

Fourth, choose for your first talks informative subjects. Such speeches make relatively simple demands on both you and your listeners; consequently, they are much easier to present than some other types. Here are some examples of suitable subjects for informative talks:

Making a simple pinhole camera	Building a boat
Chair construction	Building a duck blind
Hunting 'coons	Growing dahlias
Artificial respiration	Mining copper
Making gumbo	Telling time by the stars
Trapping rabbits	Using a map
Life on the Burma front	Training a rabbit dog
Improving your golf game	Cattle brands
Constructing a sundial	Locating oil deposits
The Geiger counter	Duties of a forester

As you see, these subjects call for simple sequences of information. After you have gained confidence and experience, you will be ready to give talks intended to stimulate or to persuade.

Fifth, for your beginning talks select topics the presentation of which requires some physical activity: the operation of a gadget, writing or drawing on the blackboard, the use of a map or chart, or movement about the room. If you do experience stage fright, physical activity will give you a release for your nervous tension and enable you to throw off feelings of timidity.

PLANNING THE SPEECH

Frame a Central Thought

If possible, expand your speech topic into a simple declarative sentence which expresses the idea which you wish to convey to your listeners. This sentence should be short and to the point.

Draft the Main Points

Select two or three points which will develop the central thought into a speech. If possible, word these points also in simple declarative sentences. Arrange the points in what seems to be a strong order. You should now have an outline like one of the following:

Central Thought: Bees have a complicated social organization.
    I. The queen lays the eggs.
   II. The females are the workers.
  III. The males are the drones.

Central Thought: The mighty Mississippi is a real antagonist.
    I. Its floods are constant threats to life and property.
   II. Its channels are constantly shifting.
  III. Its currents carry away millions of tons of rich soil.

Central Thought: The muskrat lives an interesting life.
    I. He is an ardent homemaker.
   II. He is blessed with many children.
  III. He is a ward of the state.

Gather Your Supporting Material

An outline is not a speech; it is only a beginning, a series of related thoughts, a skeleton which probably will have little, if any, effect on your listeners. If you intend to hold interest and accomplish your goal, you must put meat on those bones, clothe them in an attractive outfit, and generally glamorize the result.

One of the best ways to make a speech impelling is to pack into it many examples and extended illustrations. Audiences like specific instances, and they like stories. Here you can learn a lesson from Abraham Lincoln. When an important premise was involved or when the atmosphere was tense, Lincoln in his simple subtle way made his point by telling a story. In so doing, he was using a form of proof that ordinarily is effective for most speakers. You need not go far afield to find this type of supporting material, for your own experience should offer an unlimited supply. But if you are not satisfied with what you find at home, look to your daily reading, to the biographies of famous men, to history, and to literature.

If you feel the need of additional support, there are many other types as the following list will suggest:

1. Statistics
2. Competent statement from authority
3. Comparisons and contrasts
4. Reasoning
5. Explanation
6. Descriptions

In a later chapter each of these will be discussed at length.

Plan an Interest-getting Introduction

Your opening sentences make a first impression for you and your speech. Since they may determine the success of your entire effort, they must be carefully planned. Strive to accomplish two objectives in the opening remarks: (1) gain attention, and (2) clarify the subject.

The attention of the audience may be attracted by one of the following methods:

1. Arousing their curiosity
2. Making a startling statement
3. Relating an exciting incident
4. Telling an amusing story

Clarifying the topic means announcing the subject and explaining any confusing terms. Occasionally you may wish to trace the development of the subject or to show that the subject itself is timely. Speakers ordinarily find that a *preview* of the main points of the speech helps in achieving unity and clarity. If you feel that your effectiveness may be hampered somewhat by feelings of nervousness, you can avoid inarticulateness in the opening moments by writing out and memorizing the first few sentences.

Plan a Short Conclusion

The conclusion should be as carefully planned as the introduction. Ordinarily your objective will be twofold: to summarize and to appeal for acceptance.

The beginning speaker may well employ a summarization which restates the central thought of the speech and then repeats the main points in one-two-three order. For your parting words, do not say, "That is all I have to say," "I guess I'll conclude now," "I hope you see what I mean," "I hope that's all right," or "Why not do thus and so?" Too many times these apologies serve only to emphasize your timidity or nervousness; they certainly add nothing to what you have to say. As for the trite "Why not," your listeners will be able to find plenty of reasons why not, once you have suggested that they look for those reasons. Simply close your summary with a carefully worded telling statement, and sit down.

Formula for Putting a Speech Together

The foregoing paragraphs may be epitomized in outline form:

1. Attract attention and interest.
2. Preview what you intend to say by listing the main points.
3. Develop each point around the following pattern:
   a. State the point.
   b. Give the evidence.
   c. Restate the point.
4. Summarize: repeat the main points.

COMPLETE SPEECH OUTLINE

Muskrats

INTRODUCTION

Let me tell you about an important inhabitant of our state.
I. The muskrat provides employment for 100,000 persons.
II. Eight to ten million are trapped each year.
III. The muskrat brings an income of $10,000,000 a year.

Central Thought: The muskrat lives an interesting life.

Discussion

I. He is an ardent home builder.
   A. He selects a swamp or bayou for his site.
   B. He builds a dome-shaped mound.
      1. His materials are mud, grass, and reeds.
      2. Sometimes he locates his home in water not over two feet deep.
      3. His living room is in the top of the mound above the water level.
II. He is blessed with many children.
   A. There are from four to twelve in a litter.
   B. There may be as many as five litters in a year.
   C. The mother takes care of the "kits."
III. He is a ward of the state.
   A. He is protected from nine to ten months of the year.
   B. Trapping is carefully regulated.
   C. There are severe penalties for mistreating him.

Conclusion

I hope that now you will have a greater understanding of Mr. Muskrat and the life he leads.
I. He is an ardent homemaker.
II. He is blessed with many children.
III. He is a ward of the state.

PRACTICING YOUR SPEECH

Oral Practice

Earlier it was suggested that you might prefer to write out and memorize your opening sentences. But you should not attempt to commit the entire speech to memory. For the beginner especially, memorizing a speech has two hazards: first, during delivery the student is haunted by the fear of forgetting. Sometimes the failure to recall a single word may completely upset the whole presentation. Second, the student may sound artificial and mechanical in his delivery; he may lose that spontaneity which accompanies the presentation of a thought for the first time. Memorization often if not usually, results in concentration upon remembering rather than on the communication of ideas.

In rehearsing your speech, use what is called the *extemporaneous* method. After you have prepared your outline and collected your supporting material, practice your speech by "talking" it out, that is, by discussing aloud the ideas you wish to present until you can crystallize your thinking and your language.

As a first step, memorize your central thought and your two or three main points. It is desirable to keep the wording of these the same throughout the speech in order to aid the listeners in following your development. You will probably repeat the main points at least three times during the speech: when you *preview* the points in your introduction, when you *present* each point individually, and when you *summarize* the speech. As the old colored preacher said in describing his method of building a sermon, "Fust I tells 'em what I'se gwine to tell 'em; then I tells 'em; and finally, I tells 'em what I'se done tole 'em!"

Although unnecessary in many cases, the writing out of the speech may be your second step. Setting down your thoughts early in the preparation may help you to arrange your supporting material in an orderly fashion and to determine the most effective sequence of presentation. Reading and rereading what you have written will serve to test the organization and to set the pattern in your mind.

But you should stop short of complete memorization, put aside your manuscript, and continue by extemporizing on the topic. In successive practices do not endeavor to duplicate the language of a previous trial, but think the thought, and select words which express the idea at the moment. If you find yourself merely uttering phrases without thinking the thoughts, you are wasting time. Concentrate not on how you sound but on *what you are saying as you are saying it*.

Do not be discouraged if your first oral attempts are hesitant and awkward. With continuing practice your fluency and confidence will increase; but you must work for them. Two or three short periods of rehearsal well spaced are superior to a single extended period.

Use of Notes

In your first speeches you may find that the use of a few notes will relieve you of anxiety about forgetting, keep you from rambling, and serve to remind you of the main points. Your notes should be brief enough to be placed on a small card (a three-by-five-inch index card should be large enough) which can be easily held, will not attract attention, and can be disposed of at any time. Above all, do not try to conceal your notes; you will succeed only in making them more conspicuous.

The following outline suggests what you might include in your notes:

Muskrats

Important to Louisiana
    I. One hundred thousand persons employed
    II. Eight to ten million trapped
    III. Ten-millon-dollar income
The muskrat lives an interesting life
    I. Homemaking
        A. Swamp or bayou
        B. Dome-shaped mound
    II. Many children
        A. Four to twelve in litter
        B. Five litters a year
    III. Ward of state
        A. Protected nine or ten months
        B. Trapping regulated
        C. Penalties for mistreatment
Summary

Mental Preparation

The word *worry* comes from the Anglo-Saxon *wyrgan*, meaning "to strangle"! Truly, worry about a speech can strangle a speaker and render him inarticulate. In the interim between the time of preparing your speech and delivering it, constant anxiety about your success, abnormal dissatisfaction with yourself, the belittling of your ability, and the anticipation of dire consequences will serve only to increase your tenseness and your inarticulateness. These are the very things you want to avoid. Do not let worry be your master. Do not let yourself be strangled.

By mental discipline it is possible to avoid thinking about unpleasant aspects of the speaking situation. As suggested earlier in the chapter, the easiest way to accomplish this is to substitute wholesome attitudes for the negative ones. Think about how to make your presentation more compelling; develop an eagerness to speak on your subject, an "urge to communicate."

DELIVERY OF THE SPEECH

Your Approach

When your turn comes to speak, walk to the front of the room with quiet dignity, and stop at about the center of the platform or stage. If you are speaking from a platform, do not stand on the edge; if in a classroom, do not crowd the front row of chairs. In an effort to appear informal, students will occasionally half sit on the edge of the table, lean on the lectern or reading stand, or even put one foot on the rung or seat of a front-row chair. Learn to stand on your own two feet without support from the furniture. Even in an informal situation, informality can be overdone. Take your position, and pause two or three seconds before speaking in order to give your listeners an opportunity to prepare themselves to listen. Do not start your speech while you are still walking.

Posture and Bodily Activity

As a general rule, and for the time being, if your physical activity does not call attention to itself, it is probably satisfactory.

The excellent speaker shows his alertness by his posture; he stands up straight but not stiff, with his feet not too far apart, his hands at his sides, his head erect. He does not hide behind or lean on a lectern or table.

If you are nervous and ill at ease, you may want to put a hand in your pocket or behind you. So long as such devices do not interfere with your ability to communicate, they are not to be condemned.

Face your listeners, and make them feel that you are speaking to them, that you expect them to listen, and that you have something important and interesting to say. Borden suggests the following:

> Look at your listeners.
> Look at your listeners all the time.
> Look at all your listeners.
> Actually see your listeners.[1]

Albert J. Beveridge's description of the delivery of Robert G. Ingersoll provides us with an excellent example of effective platform technique.

> In the first place he was perfectly attired, freshly shaved, well groomed, neatly turned out in every particular. He came to the front of the platform in the most natural manner and, looking us in the eye in a friendly fashion, began to talk to us as if he were conversing with each of us personally.
>
> He stood still, made no gestures for a long time, and when they came at last, they were, seemingly, so spontaneous and unstudied that we scarcely noticed them, so much a part of his spoken word did they appear to be. His gestures added to the force of his remarks. Only once did he show emotion, and then it was so appropriate, so obviously sincere, gestures so well expressing the physical reaction of his sentiments, that even this outburst was engaging.[2]

Voice

Longfellow once said, "The soul of man is audible, not visible." There can be no doubt that your auditors will base many of their impressions of you on how you sound. If you have a voice like William Jennings Bryan, you will be able to thrill people by the

---

[1] Richard C. Borden, *Public Speaking as Listeners Like It*, Harper & Brothers, 1935, pp. 93-96.

[2] Albert J. Beveridge, *The Art of Public Speaking*, Houghton Mifflin Company, 1924, pp. 11-12. Quoted by special permission.

richness of your tones. But few people are so gifted. No matter how good or how bad your vocal equipment may be, there are certain minimum essentials which probably are entirely within your capacity.

First, you can be heard if you are willing to put forth sufficient effort. You can also be understood if you will give careful attention to your articulation. At all times strive for distinctness and for audibility. There are very few inviolable rules in public speaking; two of them are quite simple: you *must* be heard, and you *must* be understood!

Second, you can be conversational in your tone and manner. You need not preach or "orate," thereby making yourself ridiculous and giving the impression of insincerity. You must, of course, amplify your conversational style sufficiently to put over your meaning. But at the same time, strive to give the impression that you are sincerely conversing with each member of the audience.

Third, you can attempt to make your voice fit the occasion and the subject. The humorous talk may demand gaiety and joviality, while the sales talk demands a businesslike approach. You need not drone along in a monotone.

Fourth, you can talk at a rate commensurate with distinctness and with your listeners' rate of easy comprehension. If you speak too slowly, you put them to sleep; if you speak too rapidly, you wear them out with trying to keep up with you.

Fifth, you can avoid unpleasant and distracting "and-a," "uh," and other meaningless vocalizations. Normally these are simple matters of habit which can be eliminated if you try.

The five requirements named here are minimum essentials. If you cannot meet these elementary standards, you probably need the special guidance of a speech clinic. On the other hand, if you can meet them at the beginning of your course of study, you can hope confidently to make steady improvement in the use of your voice.

Mannerisms

You will reveal your nervousness and other interfering attitudes by your individual mannerisms. Work to eliminate those which prevent your freest and easiest communication with your audience or which may even make you seem peculiar and ridiculous. Here are some common annoying habits:

1. Wringing hands
2. Folding and unfolding notes
3. Jingling money or keys
4. Buttoning and unbuttoning coat
5. Pulling ear or nose
6. Fumbling with pencil
7. Putting thumbs under belt
8. Standing with arms akimbo (hands on hips)
9. Scratching
10. Fussing with ring, watch, or beads
11. Fixing tie or pin
12. Clutching or straightening skirt
13. Cracking knuckles
14. Constantly looking at ceiling or out the window
15. Shifting eyes from place to place without letting them come to rest definitely
16. Looking constantly at the floor
17. Folding arms
18. Giving nervous or silly laugh
19. Standing with feet wide apart or too close together
20. Rocking backward and forward from heels to toes and back again
21. Standing cross legged
22. Pacing excessively
23. Shifting sidewise from one foot to the other
24. Placing foot on chair or table
25. Leaning heavily on lectern or reading stand
26. Wetting lips too frequently
27. Repeatedly smoothing hair or replacing stray wisps

YOUR ATTITUDE TOWARD CRITICISM

One of the essential phases of a public-speaking course is criticism. Admittedly you can learn much by studying speech principles and by striving to put them into practice, but your progress will be greatly facilitated if you have someone to evaluate your performance, to ascertain your weaknesses, and to suggest ways in which you can improve. Points in which you are already strong will also be noted, so that you will know where to put the emphasis in the matter of improvement.

Making such evaluations and giving criticism is one of the chief responsibilities of the instructor. At the mere thought of having a speech criticized many students assume that the criticism will be adverse and hence unpleasant. But criticism is not necessarily destructive. Good criticism is an evaluation in which the critic observes favorable as well as unfavorable characteristics of your performance. Its objectives are (1) to strengthen good points, (2) to correct weak points, and (3) to eliminate errors.

No matter how observing, how tactful, and how skillful your instructor may be in explaining how you can go about improving your speech, you will derive no benefit whatever if you turn a deaf ear to his comments, reject his evaluation, or refuse to follow his suggestions. To get the greatest value from the discussion of your presentations, follow these suggestions:

First, it is important that you understand the criticism itself. Criticism must be definite and intelligible, so that you can understand it. Your instructor has the responsibility of making it clear, and if he does not, that is likely to be his fault. But you too have a duty. If you do not understand his comments, seek additional information; if you do not, that is *your* fault. If you feel embarrassed about asking questions in class, make an appointment for a personal conference.

Second, you need to develop, if you do not already have it, a wholesome attitude toward criticism. Instead of fearing or dreading or even resenting what your teacher may say about your speaking, you should look forward eagerly to his suggestions. Insist that he tell you how you can improve.

Third, avoid emotionalized self-defense and rationalization when a fault is pointed out. Many students fail to improve because they are continually excusing themselves for their failures. They rationalize with such excuses as these:

1. I didn't have time to prepare.
2. The teacher picks on me.
3. The teacher (or the class) dislikes me.
4. I can't be expected to do as well as the others in the class.
5. If I really wanted to, I could improve.
6. I am much better than some of those the teacher compliments.
7. The teacher does not know a good speech when he hears one.
8. It isn't worth the effort anyway.

You must view yourself as objectively as possible, which means that you must see yourself as others see you. The instructor is really interested in your improvement; that is his purpose in being in the class. Remember that criticism is given you to make you more effective in your speaking.

Fourth, avoid developing a feeling of hopelessness or futility. Many students feel, they apparently believe, that after attending classes for two or three weeks, they will have learned all there is to know about speaking; and when they discover that they are not yet fluent and polished in their performances, they give it up as hopeless. They do not appreciate the fact that the preparing, the practicing, and the presentation of speeches is not something they can learn immediately or, as has been suggested, in "ten easy lessons." When they discover, therefore, that learning to speak in public requires effort, they become discouraged. Each time the instructor offers another suggestion, they become even more disheartened and finally drop out altogether.

Development in public speaking is usually slow; years of study go into the making of a truly great orator. Your improvement in the present course will depend on several factors, among which are your native ability, your eagerness to improve, your willingness to work, and your receptivity to criticism. The individual who cannot make some improvement probably should not be in college at all.

YOUR ATTITUDE AS A LISTENER

In Chapter I it was pointed out that the audience, or the people to whom an idea is presented, is one of the two basic factors in the speaking situation. You will not always be the speaker on such occasions; more often you will be a member of the audience, one of the listeners. As a listener you will not be a mere passive recipient of stimuli from the speaker; you will be an integral part of the entire situation, and as such you will have certain responsibilities, one to the speaker and one to yourself. In your study of public speaking you will listen to many more speeches than you will give; your fellow students will be working to improve their speech, just as you are to improve yours. Whether you know it or not, you may have much to contribute to their individual success. You and your classmates are the speaker's audience. What can you do to help him?

First, you can give the speaker your undivided and complete attention. Class speaking is difficult enough under the most favorable conditions. As a listener you need to remember that the Golden Rule is applicable here as well as in other situations: give to each speaker the same courteous hearing that you like to have when you are speaking. This means that you should push aside distracting thoughts and refrain from engaging in diverting activities. Put away your newspaper; close your economics text; postpone that problem in mathematics. Look at the speaker; be alert and responsive to what he is saying.

Second, you can be sympathetic and encouraging in your attitude. You have undoubtedly discovered how pleasant it is to have someone express and demonstrate an interest in your welfare, in the progress of your work, in the attainment of your ambitions. The beginning speaker will have an easier time if he realizes that as a part of his audience you are sympathetic and responsive. Do not be afraid to respond overtly to his speech; register your reaction by facial expression and bodily attitude. Your responsiveness should of course be genuine and sincere.

Flattery may act as a hindrance rather than a help. If a fellow classmate experiences difficulty in speaking, you can attempt to focus on what is effective about his presentation. Avoid expressions of censure and superiority, lack of interest or boredom.

Third, if you are called on to give criticisms yourself, *attempt to be encouraging in what you say, even when you are pointing out errors.* Tell the student how in your opinion he can improve. Remember that your criticism must be (1) definite, (2) intelligible, and (3) constructive. Confine your remarks to the particular phase of speech theory under consideration.

Earlier it was said that as a listener you have a responsibility to yourself. By carefully observing the speaking of your classmates and listening to the criticisms of their speeches, you can learn much that will be applicable to your own speaking. Evaluate each performance, and check your observations against those of others. If you find that your standards of effectiveness or your criteria of judgment are significantly different from those of your instructor, perhaps you need to arrange a conference with him.

EXERCISES

1. *Speaking Assignment.* Give a talk of two to four minutes (from three hundred to six hundred words) on a subject with which you have had direct personal experience. You may wish to speak on a subject similar to one of the following:
    a. The author or poet of the year
    b. How to select a good movie
    c. How to spend your leisure time
    d. A "pet peeve"
    e. An embarrassing moment
    f. Finding and holding a job
    g. How to be the "life of the party"
    h. A vacation I shall never forget
    i. A business experience
    j. My experiences on the farm (in the shop, behind the counter, as a door-to-door salesman, etc.)
    k. Any topic of a similar nature.

2. *Speaking Assignment.* Deliver a five-minute informative talk in which you develop three or four points. Follow this procedure: after a brief introduction, give a preview of your points. As you present each point, write it on the blackboard. In your conclusion, review the points developed by pointing to them as you repeat them orally.
3. *Written Assignment.* Prepare a written analysis of the most effective speaker you know. Prepare a list of his speaking qualities. What are his unusual characteristics?
4. *Discussion Questions for Class Symposiums:*
   a. How can a negative or unfavorable attitude reduce your proficiency in a field of endeavor?
   b. Why are positive or favorable attitudes especially important in public speaking?
   c. What are the characteristics (symptoms) of stage fright?
   d. What personal experiences have you had with stage fright?
   e. Is stage fright related to a negative attitude?
   f. What qualities characterize the following (from your own point of view; do not repeat or paraphrase what the book says): (1) a good introduction; (2) interesting material; (3) an appropriate conclusion; (4) a pleasant voice; (5) effective delivery.
   g. What qualities do you like in your listeners?
   h. What is constructive criticism? When is criticism unfair?
5. *Research Assignment.* Observe the platform manner of some local speaker. Tabulate the following information:
   1. Number of times he looks away from the audience
   2. His posture
   3. Number of times he gestures with his right hand
   4. Number of times he gestures with his left hand
   5. Number of times he changes his position
   6. His strong and his weak points
6. *Speech Analysis.* The speech given below can be delivered in less than a minute and a half, and yet it demonstrates many of the principles that have been discussed in this chapter. What principles does it illustrate? What are its strong points? How could the speech be improved?

The Camel That Broke the Man's Back

Remember the old story about the merchant and the camel? It was a cold night, and the camel begged to warm his nose—only his nose—in the tent. Then what happened? Little by little, the camel inched in his shoulders, his front legs—until he took over the whole tent. And the merchant was out in the cold.

That's how government agencies are inching their way into the electric business. First, public funds were set aside to build dams—*for flood control and navigation.* Then it was argued that the water behind the dams could be used to make electricity.

That led to the building of power lines, and then to more dams, more lines, and so on. Now these same agencies want more millions of dollars to build fuel-burning power plants—*which have nothing to do with floods or navigation at all.*

Yes, the camel of State Socialism is creeping farther and farther into the tent of the electric business. What it is doing here it can do in other industries. For when a government can enter *one* business in unfair competition with its own citizens, it is but a short step to entering *all* businesses—and eventually taking over *all business.*

Like the camel and the tent. What business are *you* in? This can affect you, too. Write your Congressman about it.[3]

7. Study carefully the following speech by William G. Carleton. Notice how the speaker has carefully organized his material and how he has drawn supporting material from his own experience. Do you think the speech was appropriate for an audience of college and high-school students? What was the speaker's purpose in delivering this speech? If you had talked to such an audience would have approached the subject in a different manner?

Let Us Keep Debating in Our Schools[4]

Periodically, the place of high school and college debating in our educational schemes comes up for re-examination. At such times it is appropriate for those of us who see lasting values in school debating to review those values. There are, it seems to me, four distinct educational opportunities to be derived from a program of high school and college debating. I welcome this opportunity to discuss these opportunities in general terms and,

---

[3] From a full-page advertisement of the Electric Light and Power Companies, which appeared in *Time Magazine*, May 23, 1949, p. 103. Used by special permission of N. W. Ayer and Son, Inc.

[4] By William G. Carleton, Professor of Political Science, University of Florida, Gainesville, Florida. Delivered before a Banquet of High School and College Debaters of South Florida, Miami, Florida, June 16, 1949. Quoted by permission.

if I may be allowed, in terms of my own personal experience. And what are these opportunities?

First, effective speech is largely a matter of practice, and the earlier one takes part in public address the surer and readier a speaker he is likely to be in maturity. Like the learning of a language, practice in public speaking cannot begin too early. Learning to think on one's feet, spontaneous and ready speech, comes with *doing*, and doing *early*.

A long period of time is required to develop the indispensable elements of distinguished speech—self-assurance, poise, urbanity; a nice sense of rhythm; the ability to make meaningful shifts in volume, pitch, intensity, and pace; a balanced combination of form and content; and intelligent blending of language and thought; freedom on occasion to let one's self go and in a kind of disciplined spontaneity pour out one's deepest convictions in sincere and passionate earnestness. The "born" speaker is usually one who starts public speaking while still an adolescent.

Second, high school and college debating is likely to direct students to serious study of public questions at an early age. Debate questions usually involve important issues of high conflict, and youthful minds are attracted to them by the lively and controversial way in which they are put. Most average students, even if they are majoring in one of the social sciences, will not delve deeply into such questions as labor relations, foreign policy, the control of business cycles, the tariff, public finance, and so forth, unless they are challenged by active participation in debate. In my own case, I recall, while only a sophomore in high school, going rather deeply into the intricate question of the graduated income tax for the purpose of contesting in a state-wide debate—a debate, incidentally, which I won, and nothing has ever made me as proud as the victory won in sophomore days. Thus at a relatively tender age I was personally introduced to the complexities of economics by way of school debate. A thorough knowledge of a subject is the surest way of winning a debate—for rebuttals cannot be won without finger-tip knowledge that comes out spontaneously, and most debates are won on rebuttals.

Third, debating forces a student to consider all sides of a particular question. It is a mistaken notion that debating requires a student to think in distinct terms of black and white. Usually, the student learns to take all sides of a question, and often the question is phrased in a variety of ways in order to exploit it from different points of view. This training in seeing all around a question, its many sides, its various facets, is invaluable. It affords significant training in flexibility and breadth of view. However, further to assure the student an opportunity to develop a subject in his own personal way, it is well to schedule a few discussions as well as debates, discussions in which the student is freed from any fixed statement of the problem and may state the problem and develop it in any way he sees fit.

Fourth, and most important, public speech allows valuable training in clear and precise thinking. Indeed, clear expression, both written and oral, is inseparable from clear thinking. The debater thinks through a proposition over and over again, phrases it any number of ways, and publicly experiments with it on numerous occasions before he finally achieves the crystal clarity he is seeking. This passion for clear expression develops into a passion for clear thinking, for the young debater soon learns that without clear thinking there can be no clear expression. The late Senator Albert J. Beveridge, himself an able orator, observes in his monumental biography of Abraham Lincoln that Lincoln's speeches at the end of any given political campaign were always better than they were at its beginning—by a process of selective repetition Lincoln distilled in clearer and clearer fashion his political arguments and ideas.

Personally, I have been appreciably helped in my profession of college teaching by my high school and college debating experience. In the very earliest days of my college teaching I never experienced the self-consciousness and even stage fright so often betrayed by the beginning teacher. Moreover, in my very first year of teaching I was called upon to lecture to hundreds of freshmen in large lecture sections but, because of previous practice in public address, I looked upon these lectures, even at the beginning, as a challenge that could be successfully met rather than as a frightful hurdle somehow to be overcome.

The most important lesson learned in school debating, however, is respect for that rigorous winnowing process whereby the rele-

DEMOCRACY AT WORK: THE NEW ENGLAND TOWN MEETING
In the upper picture the chairman recognizes a speaker. In the lower picture a member presents a detailed report to the meeting. (Photos, Black Star.)

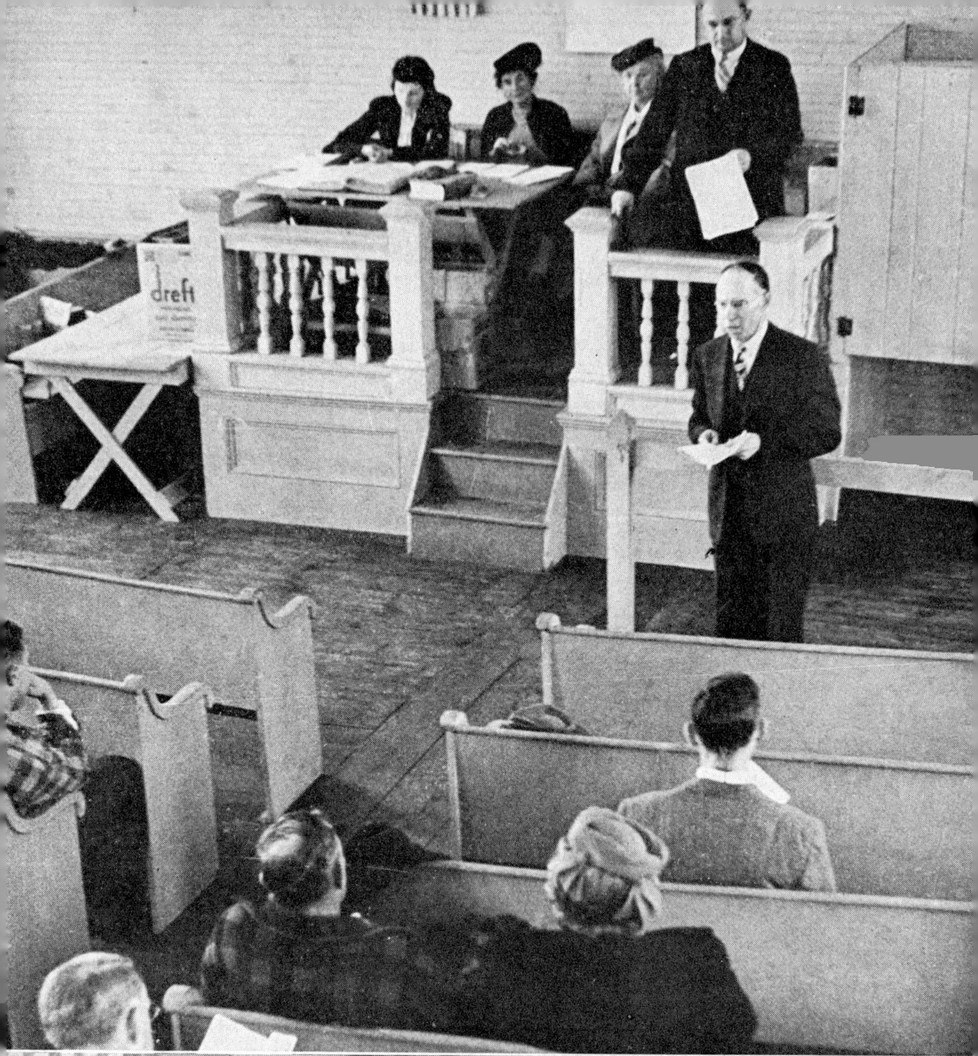
dreft

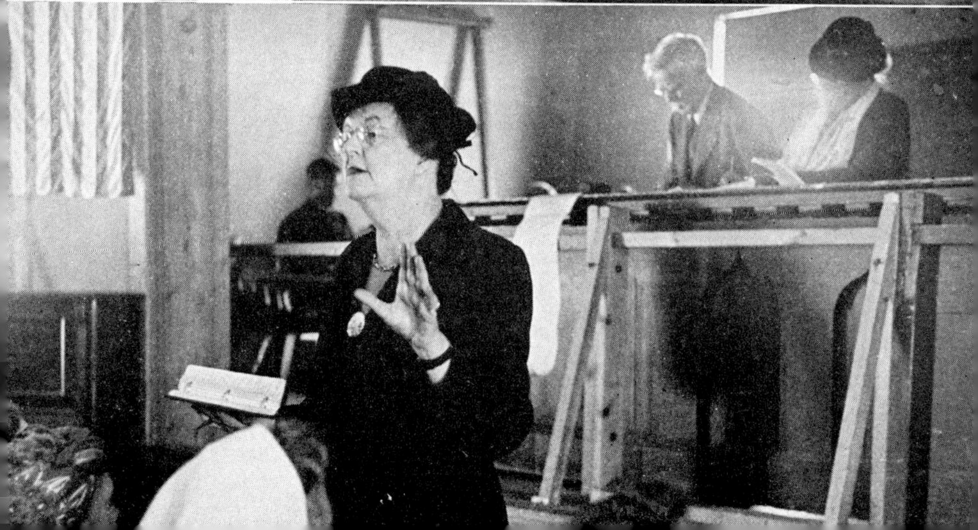

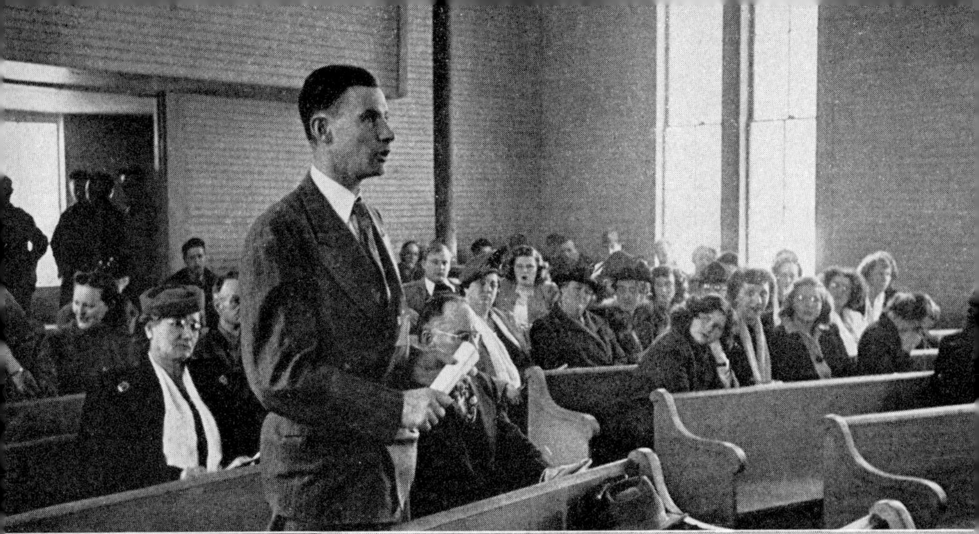
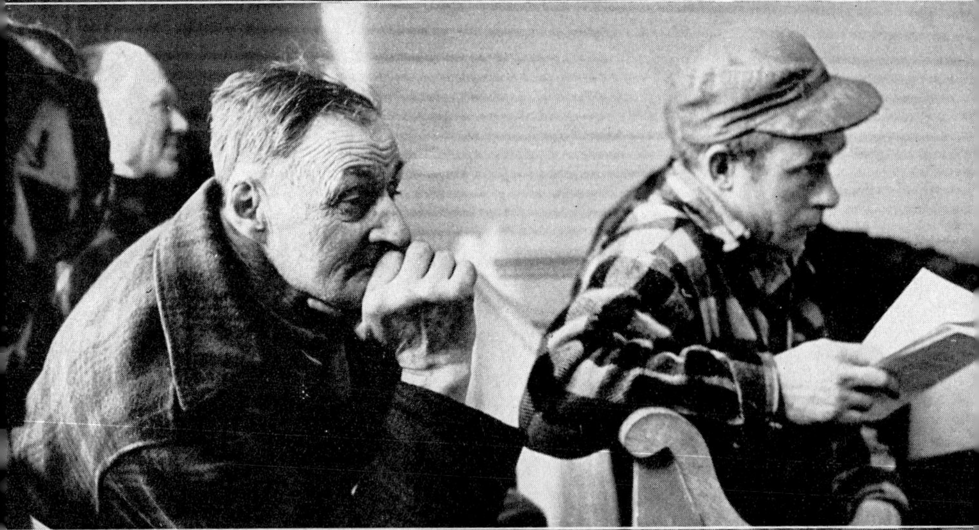
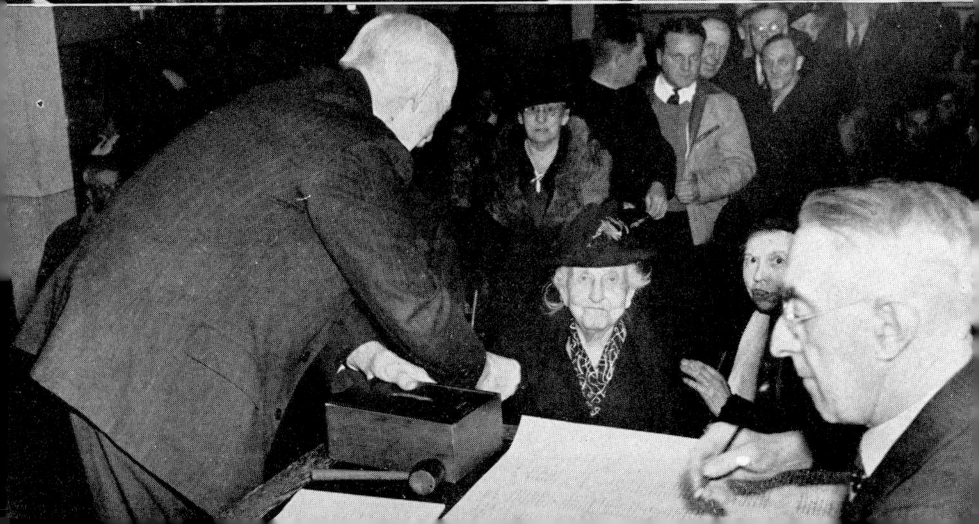

vant factors are called from the irrelevant and presented in the simplest and clearest way—respect for classic clarity of thought and expression.

SUPPLEMENTARY READINGS

1. Baird, A. Craig, and Knower, Franklin H., *General Speech: An Introduction*, McGraw-Hill Book Company, Inc., 1949, chap. 3.
2. Barnes, Harry G., *Speech Handbook*, Prentice-Hall, Inc., 1945, pp. 26-80.
3. Beveridge, Albert J., *The Art of Public Speaking*, Houghton Mifflin Company, 1924.
4. Borden, Richard C., *Public Speaking as Listeners Like It*, Harper & Brothers, 1935.
5. Lee, Josh, *How to Hold an Audience Without a Rope*, Ziff-Davis Publishing Company, 1947, chaps. 1, 3, 6.
6. Murray, Elwood, *The Speech Personality*, J. B. Lippincott Company, rev. ed., 1944, chap. 6.
7. Monroe, Alan H., *Principles and Types of Speech*, Scott, Foresman & Company, 3d ed., 1949, chap. 1.
8. Thonssen, Lester, and Gilkinson, Howard, *Basic Training in Speech*, D. C. Heath and Company, 1947, chaps. 3, 4.

SEMESTER PROJECTS

Early in the term you should begin to consider what you want to do for your semester project. An early start will enable you to complete your work more efficiently and with greater ease. Below are some suggested projects that you may want to consider.

1. *A Drill Project.* Students who use substandard pronunciation or who have voice problems should undertake a systematic drill program. It will be necessary for your instructor to diagnose your individual problems and to provide drill materials for you. (See Grant Fairbanks, *Voice and Articulation Drillbook*, Harper & Brothers, 1940;

THE NEW ENGLAND TOWN MEETING AT WORK

Top, a member of the audience replies. Center, members of the meeting weigh the arguments. Bottom, the ballot box is used to determine the final outcome. (Photos, Black Star.)

Borchers and Wise, *Modern Speech*, Harcourt, Brace & Company, Inc., 1947.)

You should agree on a definite time and place for your work. If possible, it should be under the direction of a trained speech clinician. It is obvious that not all students will need this type of work.

2. *Join the Speakers' Bureau.* Some members of the class may wish to gain additional speaking experiences outside the class. The Speakers' Bureau is organized to accommodate outside groups that want programs. Four types of activities are in demand: discussions, speeches, debates, and readings. If you have something in mind that would make a suitable fifteen-minute program for a service club or adult group, talk to your instructor about it. It will be necessary for you to prepare carefully and to try out in order to determine whether your offering is worthy of a listing with the Speakers' Bureau.

3. *Participate in Extracurricular Debate or Discussion.* You may adopt as your project participation in extracurricular debate or discussion. If you want to follow such a program, you must try out for and attend most of the scheduled meetings of the extracurricular debate or discussions group.

4. *A Research Project.* a. Write a speech biography of one of your fellow students in your public-speaking class. Base your biography on day-to-day observations of how he carries out the various assignments and on the progress that he makes. You may want to interview him to procure information concerning his speech background. At the close of the semester prepare a detailed report of your observations, and determine his strong and weak points. You may want to recommend a future program for him in your biography.

b. Write reports of from fifty to one hundred words on each of the following: (*a*) three sermons; (*b*) three radio addresses; (*c*) two of the following: after-dinner speech, debate, discussion, campaign speech, presentation speech, or speech of farewell.

c. Investigate the speaking career of some prominent speaker. If possible, select a person whom you can hear personally or over the radio. Consider such items as the following: (1) speech training, (2) general study habits, (3) methods of speech preparation, (4) types of speaking, (5) organization, (6) forms of support, (7) delivery, (8) general effectiveness.

For additional guidance see Thonssen and Baird, *Speech Criticism*, The Ronald Press Company, 1948.

5. *Scrapbook on Important Speeches of the Semester.* Follow care-

fully the newspapers and magazines for reports of important speeches. Include reports and pictures in your scrapbook.

6. *A Project of Your Own Choice.* If none of the suggestions above appeals to you, you may want to devise a project more to your own liking. Work out in writing what you propose to do, and submit it to your instructor for approval. This should be done before the end of the first six weeks.

Speech-Criticism Blank
(For Beginners)

	Poor	Below average	Average	Excellent	Superior
1. Did the speaker choose an interesting subject?	1	2	3	4	5
2. Did the speaker supply the audience with any new information?					
3. Did the material presented seem to be from the speaker's own experience?					
4. Did the speaker look at his audience?					
5. Did the speaker talk to his audience?					
6. Did the speaker show his enthusiasm and interest in the subject?					
7. Did the speaker assume a pleasing posture?					
8. Did the speaker manifest a sufficient amount of physical activity?					
9. Did the speaker reflect a wholesome attitude toward the speaking situation?					
10. Did the speaker seem to notice and respond to the reactions of the audience?					

Additional remarks:

Grade........

CHAPTER III

Motivation

UNDERSTANDING MOTIVES

ALL your speaking will be an effort on your part to secure from your auditors some kind of response. This response may be one of simple enjoyment, understanding of a hitherto unknown set of facts, the intensification of already held beliefs and attitudes, the acceptance of new beliefs, or the adoption of a new course of action. All these are types of reactions which may be made by the members of your audience. In order to make your efforts successful, therefore, you should know something of the background for human behavior, the reasons why people do the things they do, the impulsions behind the choices of action they make from time to time. Without some understanding of these bases, you will be likely to flounder aimlessly or to select an appeal to which your listeners will not respond at all.[1]

Why did you come to college? If you enrolled voluntarily for this course, what was back of your reasons for taking public speaking? Why did you choose the particular vocation for which you are studying, or, for that matter, why are you studying at all? Why do we surround ourselves with objects of beauty—music, pictures, flowers, literature, well-kept lawns? Why do we contribute to the Red Cross, the Community Chest, or to other worthy charities, or to the church? Why do we take measures to protect our health, to ensure reasonably long life? Why do we seek the approval of others or avoid their disapproval? Why do we work to improve our economic status; or run for office on the campus, in the community, or in the state or nation? Why do we reject the philosophy of communism and adhere to those principles of democracy which we have taken the trouble to understand? In short, why do we do the things we do?

These questions cannot be referred to cold reason. We do not have to discover logical reasons for seeking social approval; we just seek it. It takes no argument to convince us that we want to live to a ripe old age; most people cling to life rather tenaciously. No one has to tell us that we should prefer pleasant to squalid surroundings or that we should choose the freedom of a democratic society to the restrictions on our activities imposed by totalitarian regimes. These are things we want or need; and their acquisition or preservation constitutes a strong impelling force in our lives. In the last analysis, these impulsions provide the only basis upon which must rest any appeal that the speaker can make.

---

[1] The term *appeal*, which will be used frequently, does not refer necessarily to perfervid exhortations or supplications but rather to any procedures which may bring about some response, whether it be to impel the listeners to think, to feel, or to act. The "appeal" is usually directed toward some factor in the human constitution which contributes to the tendency to respond in certain ways.

Motives Basic to Behavior

Psychologists have long recognized that within each organism are strong internal forces which direct the individual toward certain goals[2] and without which there would be no directed activity; there would be only a random, futile sort of behavior for its own sake. When properly stimulated, these forces may set off a chain reaction of behavior which does not entirely subside until the goal is achieved. Such goals are usually referred to as *motives*. Much of our existence is spent in satisfying these motives. Thus, we go to great lengths to *conserve our health* and *prolong our lives*. We join certain organizations partly to gain a measure of *social approval* and partly in quest of *congenial companionship*. We keep our houses painted to add to their *appearance* and to *keep longer what we have*. We contribute to the Community Chest, the Red Cross, the church, in order to satisfy the normal human desire *to be helpful* where help is needed. We react vigorously against flagrant attempts to place rigid restrictions on our *freedom of action*; we resent coercion.

As we said earlier, these desires are not basically matters of reason, although once having determined certain goals, we can and should resort to reason to discover how these end results can best be achieved. Motives have been called the "mainsprings of action." They are what give us the drive; they are the impelling forces which form the basis for all our behavior. They are among the most important aspects of human existence. So far as it is related to speaking, *motivation* is the process by which the speaker arouses or stimulates these motives or internal compulsions to such a degree that the listeners are more favorably inclined to respond as he intends they should.

CLASSIFICATION OF MOTIVES

Many attempts have been made by psychologists as well as by teachers of public speaking to classify motives, to reduce their

[2] Floyd L. Ruch, *Psychology and Life*, Scott, Foresman and Company, new ed., 1941, pp. 65 ff.

apparently large numbers, and in many cases to attribute all of them to a very small group of fundamental biological needs. Many of them, however, are far more social than biological: social approval, for instance, is considered by many authorities to be the strongest of all the impelling motives. It would be difficult to find two lists of motives that agree entirely. ". . . motives are as numerous," says Dewey, "as are original impulsive activities multiplied by the diversified consequences they produce as they operate under diverse conditions."[3] "Any classification of human motives would be merely for convenience in talking about them," says Ruch.[4]

"Lower" and "Higher" Motives

For purposes of convenience, then, let us roughly classify these impelling motives first into two general types, which, for some reason, have been called the "lower" and the "higher" motives. The former direct our actions toward those goals which bring satisfactions more or less directly to ourselves, either individually or in groups. They have also been called the "selfish" motives. The latter are concerned with those forms of behavior which are engaged in primarily because of the benefits or advantages which may be brought to others. They may also be thought of as "altruistic." It should be pointed out that there is in this distinction, or in the labels which have been attached to the two general types, no implication that the "lower" or "selfish" goals are in themselves always reprehensible or that the "higher" or "altruistic" motives are necessarily always justifiable. There certainly is nothing blameworthy in maintaining one's own good health; on the other hand, one may request favors for other people who do not deserve them at all.

Motives Rarely Single

These various motives rarely stand alone; it is seldom that a given act arises from a single motive. Usually a number of them

---

[3] John Dewey, *Human Nature and Conduct,* Henry Holt and Company, Inc., 1932, p. 122. Quoted by special permission.
[4] Ruch, *op. cit.,* p. 86.

are active simultaneously. Often, too, the "lower" and the "higher" motives may be found side by side, so to speak, both giving impulsion to the same activity. The player who hits a "grand-slam" home run undoubtedly gets a keen satisfaction over the power he has exhibited as well as over a few other elements of superiority; but he may also have driven in three runs besides his own for the team—of which he is a member. The man who puts up an extensive low-cost housing development to relieve the slum conditions in his city may at the same time reasonably hope for some financial return on his investment. The most potent argument for aiding European recovery is that it will benefit not only the peoples of Europe—a humanitarian objective—but ourselves as well. It is becoming increasingly recognized that the prosperity of any one part of the country, or of the world, depends on the welfare of every other part. These are all examples of what has been called *enlightened self-interest.*

Motives Vary in Strength

The same motives do not seem to be equally strong among all people, nor are all motives equally strong in the same person. Furthermore, any motive may be for a time dormant, that is, in any one person a motive may vary in strength from time to time. Too, the various motives may on occasion come into conflict. When these conflicts arise, decisions have to be made on the basis of which particular motive is strongest at the time. Thus, a factory owner may, in time of financial disturbance, relinquish his profits in order to ensure that his workers will not be laid off and lose their own living. Parents give up things they have long wanted in order to send their children to college.

GOOD SPEAKING REQUIRES A REALIZATION OF SOCIAL RESPONSIBILITY

At the top is Ernest Bevin of England, speaking to a labor conference in 1944. At the bottom is Trygve Lie of the United Nations, holding a press conference in Paris. (Photos, Black Star.)

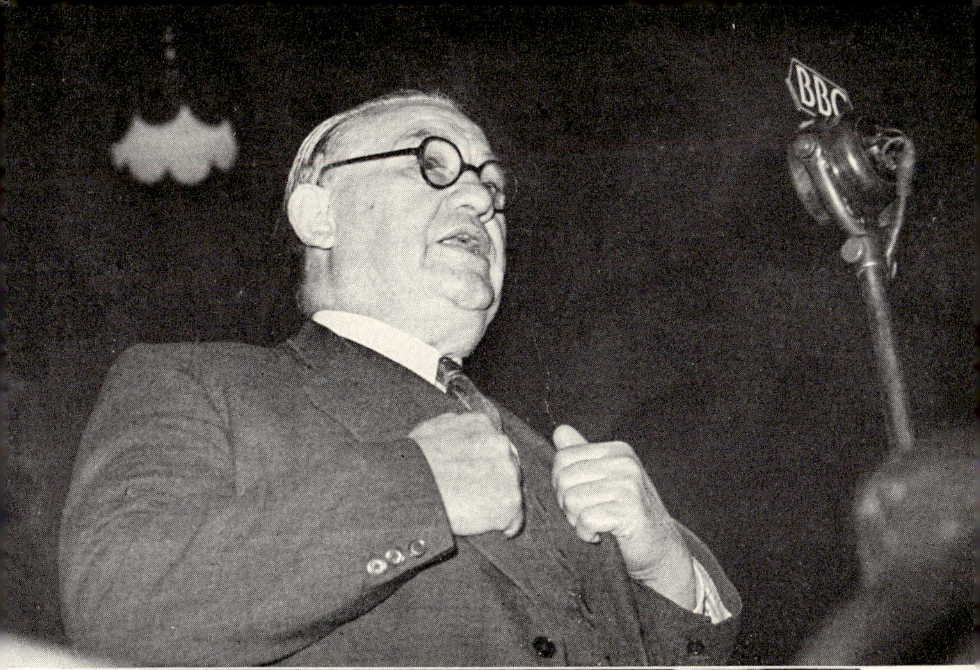
BBC

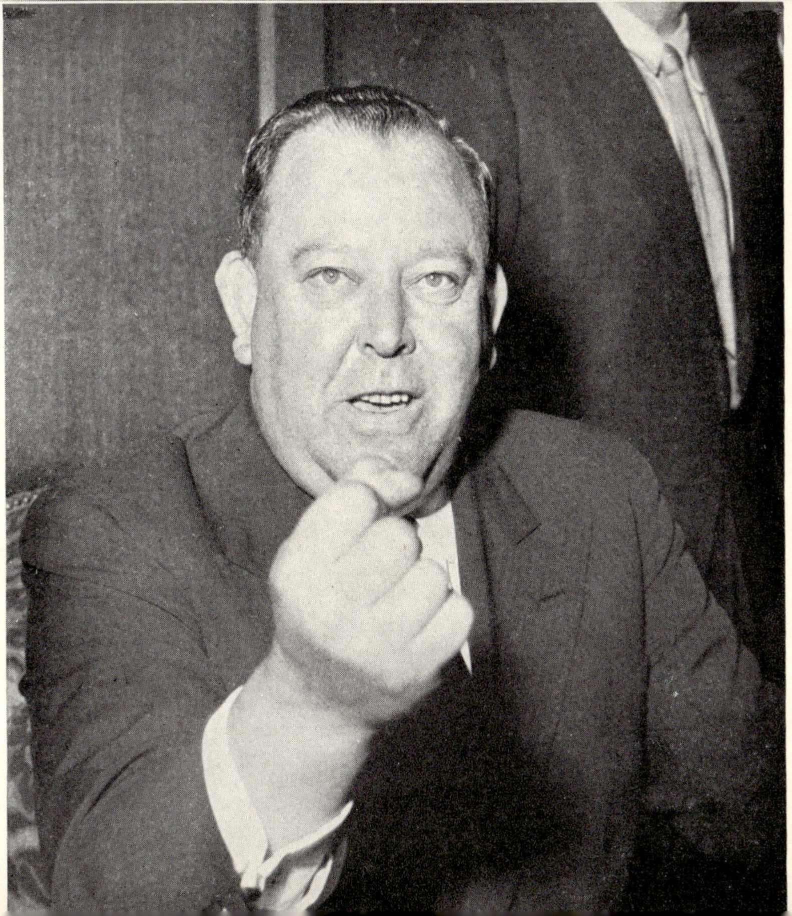

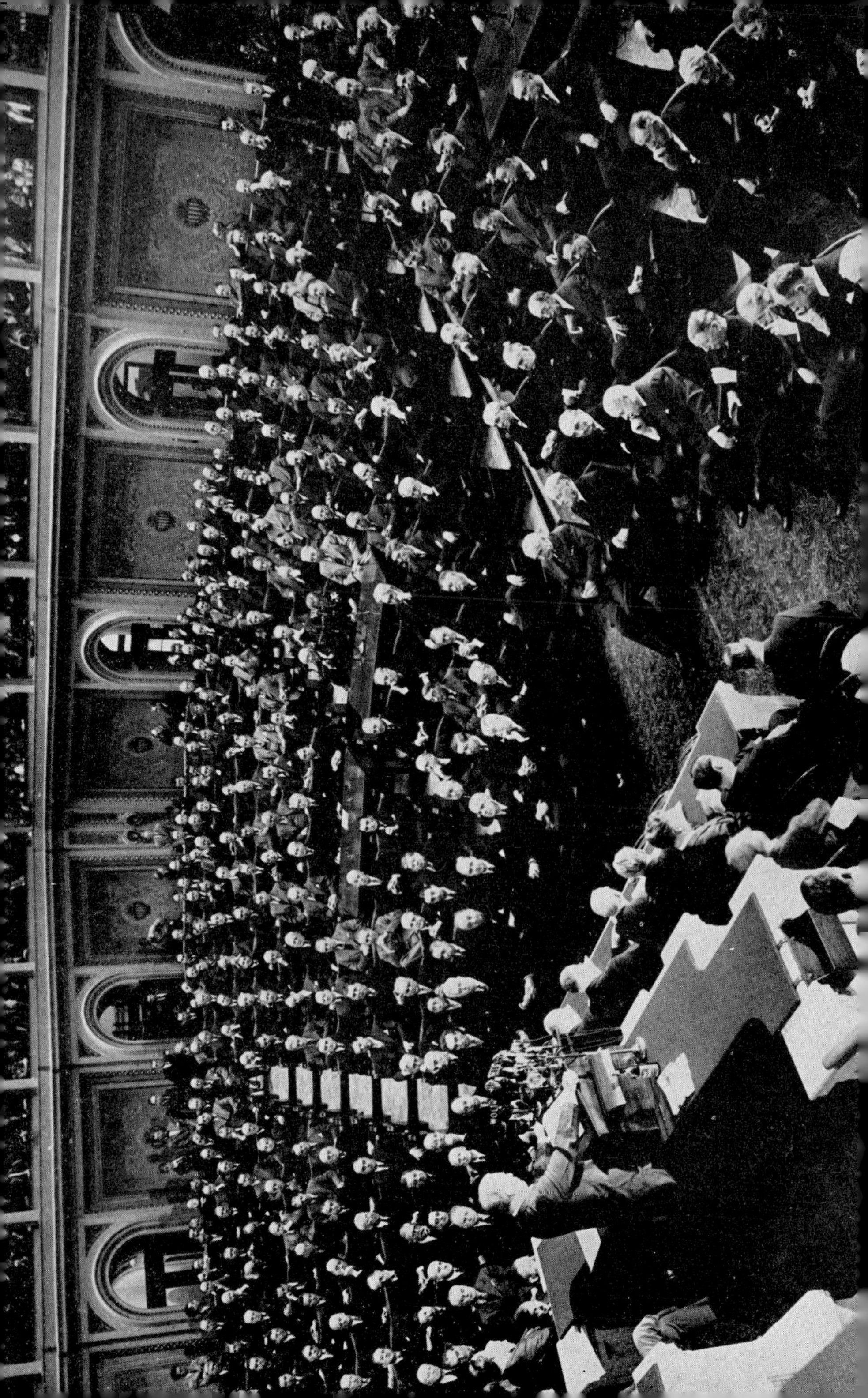

Choosing the Motive Appeals

In attempting to win the responses you want from your audience, then, you must in your speaking stimulate, arouse, or strengthen these motives which are present in some degree in nearly everyone. The selection of the particular motive to which you will appeal will usually depend on (1) the present situation, (2) the events of the immediate past, and (3) the habitual attitudes and modes of thought of the people to whom you are talking. Often, however, you may find it more to your purpose to awaken dormant motives, that is, to stimulate those which for one reason or another have been allowed to lapse into quiescence. The need for adequate national defense before World War II was not admitted by many high in authority until world events made the necessity obvious to everyone. The people of an entire nation may find their freedom of action greatly limited if they permit their resentment of undue restrictions to become dulled. The inhabitants of one choice residential street may be indifferent to the deplorable slums in the next block unless the dormant desire on the part of all decent people to relieve distress is awakened or unless they are made to realize that their own welfare is in jeopardy. Minority groups are permitted to live in social and economic squalor unless the members of majority groups are stimulated to provide better living and working conditions.

TYPES OF MOTIVE APPEAL

In the discussion up to the present, a number of the various types of motive appeal have been mentioned. Let us examine

A GREAT ASSEMBLY OF FREEDOM

President Roosevelt delivers his annual report on the state of the Union before a joint session of Congress, January 7, 1943. Free men reach their decisions by parliamentary means even in times of war. (Photo, Wide World.)

some of these more closely. It is not intended to present a complete list here; all that is being attempted is to suggest some of those which you as a speaker will find most readily adaptable to your purposes.

Security

The desire for security is strong in most of us. It may be directed into many channels: avoidance of physical danger, provision for financial support in old age, investment in safe securities, assurance of happiness in the afterworld, guarding against contaminated foods which endanger health, and so on. In making your appeal to such a motive, you might, for example, open with a warning, describing the present situation and its tendencies and pointing out the inevitable disastrous consequences if the course of action now being followed is not changed. Typical "central ideas" which you can present to an audience are these:

1. Protect your health by insisting on pasteurized milk.
2. Take out an annuity now so that when you retire you will not have to live on charity.
3. Deposit your savings in the First National Bank; they are protected by the Federal Deposit Insurance Corporation.
4. Use Delite deodorant and feel safe.
5. See that the Underwriters' Laboratories label is stamped on your electric wiring to be sure that it is safe to use.
6. Put a set of Autoseal inner tubes on your car and stop worrying about punctures or blowouts.
7. "An ounce of prevention is worth a pound of cure."
8. The teacher-tenure law is a good one for teachers because it removes the profession from the vagaries of politics.
9. We should strengthen the levees to protect the people living along the river from disastrous floods.
10. Your best protection against unemployment is thorough preparation for your job.
11. Government bonds are your safest investment.
12. Don't take a chance on being swindled; know your dealer.
13. "Slow down! School! Speed Limit 10 Miles per Hour!"
14. Drive carefully; the life you save may be your own.

15. Support the United Nations Organization and make our democratic way of life more secure.
16. Strengthening our democracy strengthens democracy everywhere.
17. Be safe; have your brakes tested periodically.
18. Have your dog vaccinated against rabies and protect the children of your community.

If you can find the things that threaten the security of your listeners in these or other ways, you have a powerful appeal upon which to base your proposals. But you must, if your speech is to be permanently effective, show *how* the desire for added security, whether it be economic, social, physical, or whatnot, will be satisfied by following your suggestions. Merely to insist over and over that such a desire will be satisfied is not enough for the good speaker, even though you can, as Lincoln said, fool all the people some of the time, and some of the people all of the time. In order to establish and maintain your own reputation for integrity, as well as give a sound basis for your appeal, you must go further than mere reiteration. Through the use of facts, figures, statistics, examples, and other factual means of support, you must lead your audience toward an intelligent acceptance that will not be repudiated the first time an opposing idea is presented to them.

It will readily be seen that an appeal for security may as easily stimulate the altruistic as the selfish motives. We are as often keenly interested in the security of others as we are of our own security. Drives against disease are carried on for the most part by people who do not expect to benefit personally from the researches being conducted or from new and better methods of treatment being developed. The Damon Runyon Cancer Fund was not started by people hoping to find a cure for themselves, nor were the discoverers of insulin sufferers from diabetes. The Friendship Trains which collected enormous amounts of goods as well as of good will to be shipped to the people of Europe originated partly as a gesture of encouragement to those people in their struggle against the threat of communism; they also originated in the belief that whatever strengthened the position of democracy in western Europe would make our own that much more secure. Of the two motives involved here, the unselfish and the selfish, who can say that the former was not the stronger?

Social Approval

According to some psychologists, the strongest of all motives is the desire for the good opinion of others, for social acceptance, for the feeling of "belonging" in some social group. This motive may be operative not only in individuals but among groups themselves. On the campus fraternities and sororities and other social groups vie for honors, for cups to display in the trophy cabinet; they enter their members in various activities, campaign for the election of their members to office. Schools themselves engage in more or less friendly rivalry in sports, although not so much in academic pursuits, outside of debating and other types of speaking competition. Communities institute clean-up campaigns, build up their industries, improve their parks, boast of their schools and churches, partly because these things are in themselves worth while and partly also because the residents may gain the good opinion of the people of their own and of other communities. Nations maintain representatives in other civilized countries in part to establish and further good opinion among the nationals of those countries. Business firms plan extensive advertising campaigns to build up public good will toward themselves as well as for the specific purpose of selling their goods.

Students themselves gain the favorable opinion of their fellow students by engaging in various campus activities, such as going out for athletic teams; in only rare instances, it is feared, by setting up high standards of scholarship; by joining societies; by always being well groomed. And their professors likewise gain public approval by giving interesting lectures in their courses, by making fair examinations, by publishing books and articles, by conducting and engaging in research, by participating in their professional organizations, and by engaging in community enterprises.

The negative aspect of the desire for social approval must also be recognized: we are almost as assiduous in avoiding unfavorable opinions of others as we are in cultivating the favorable. The fear of being put into jail, with its attendant stigma, is undoubtedly a powerful deterrent to doing many of the things we sometimes would like to do. Mrs. Grundy has always been a powerful influence in the shaping of human conduct.

Typical of the "central ideas" through which you may appeal to the desire for social approval are these:

1. It is better to be a servant in the house of the Lord than to dwell in the tents of iniquity.
2. This is the brand used "by men of distinction."
3. Try ——— soap to have "the skin you love to touch."
4. "Cremol" will give your hair that well-groomed look.
5. If we could break through the Iron Curtain, we could tell Eastern Europe the truth about America.
6. Some things just aren't done by careful people.
7. The correct use of the mother tongue is one of the marks of an educated person. Don't use slovenly speech.
8. Prevent halitosis so you won't be a wallflower.
9. We can't have our town looking like a junk heap.
10. Excessive slang, an indication of sloppy thinking, should be avoided.
11. The world dislikes a poor loser—or a poor winner.
12. We must maintain the academic prestige of the university.
13. Advertising is a powerful medium for building good will for your product.
14. Keep up with the Joneses—but pick the right Jones.
15. If we want to hold our heads up, we must have a football team that will win its share of games.
16. This town is the laughing stock of the whole state; let's clean it up.
17. This university will establish an enviable reputation among other schools by providing for the publication of significant research.
18. Who steals my purse steals trash; 'tis something, nothing;
    'Twas mine, 'tis his, and has been slave to thousands;
    But he that filches from me my good name
    Robs me of that which not enriches him
    And makes me poor indeed.

Ownership, or Possession

In a little one-act play, "Joint Owners in Spain,"[5] one of the characters, an old woman living in the poorhouse, is made to say, "I don't want much, but I want it mine." People take great satisfaction in acquiring and saving, that is, in becoming owners and in preserving what they have. Many prefer to own their own homes, although there has been some debate as to whether ownership is more economical in the long run than renting. People collect many different, strange things, not for their intrinsic value but to satisfy a desire for ownership.

Closely allied to this desire for possession is what has been called the "profit motive." The businessman hopes to make a profit from his business and will be greatly influenced by anyone who can convince him that by adopting a new merchandising policy he can increase his profits. He may be more easily convinced if he can be assured that he will at the same time maintain his business integrity and give his customers more for their money. The laborer will listen eagerly to the labor leader who will promise to get higher wages, shorter hours, and larger pensions. Stores advertise bargain days to attract buyers who are hopeful of purchasing more economically. We are advised that, in the matter of house paints, "if we save the surface, we save all." A certain make of automobile, we are assured, will give thousands of miles of economical service. We work hard to improve our vocational proficiency, hoping that our superiors will reward us by a substantial raise in salary.

Profits, increased income, savings on expenditures, all enable us to acquire more of the things we want or need. These in turn satisfy the desire for ownership and at the same time enable us to live more comfortably, to move in more desirable social circles, to provide adequate medical care for ourselves and those dependent on us, to enjoy vacations, to have more beautiful things around us, and so on.

[5] Alice Brown, *Joint Owners in Spain*, Walter H. Baker Company, 1925.

The following are illustrative of the appeals you may make to the desire for ownership or possession:

1. Install Automatic Business Machines and save on costs, time, and labor.
2. Use steel in your product to increase your profits, and give the customer more for his money.
3. Travel the economical way: go by bus.
4. Have your car greased regularly and avoid costly repair bills.
5. Our new gasoline gives you more miles per gallon.
6. Many of our salesmen have earned more than six hundred dollars a month; you can do as well.
7. Wearproof hosiery will give you added wear.
8. Would you like to increase your income by fifty percent? Then investigate our proposition.
9. Put your savings to work for you; invest in guaranteed bonds.
10. You get more for your dollar by trading at the Emporium Department Store.
11. Here is a home you will be proud to own.
12. This company gives its employees excellent opportunities for advancement.
13. This car is priced very low; it is also economical to operate.
14. Earn while you learn.
15. For a fascinating hobby, try collecting old books (or stamps, or old glassware, autographs, match folders, etc.).
16. Now the inside facts about the situation are these. . . .
17. Let us set you up in your own business.
18. Our taxes could be greatly reduced if the government would eliminate waste in its operations.

Learn your listeners' particular type of acquisitiveness, and you have a powerful leverage to persuasion. Whenever possible, however, tie the "selfish" motive of possession to some "unselfish" motive such as social welfare, the advancement of individual opportunity, giving the customers their money's worth, or the like.

Exploration

As soon as the infant learns to crawl, he begins to explore. About the house are dozens of fascinating places to examine, things to handle, steps to climb, cabinets to open. He wants to go places he hasn't been, to see things he hasn't seen, to do things he hasn't done. His small world is full of interesting things; and as his world expands, the number of these interesting things also increases, so that he never quite loses his desire to explore. In boyhood, the streams, woods, caves, even new roads or strange parts of the city, beckon him to adventure. Later, if he is free to travel, he may go for adventures in strange, faraway places, studying exotic peoples, unfamiliar customs, long-forgotten ruins of ancient cultures. If travel is denied him, he may find his interest satisfied in investigating new fields of thought in science, literature, history, art, or philosophy.

Exploration may thus take various forms. There are adventures to be found, curiosities to be satisfied in science or history, for example, no less than in mountain climbing or in big-game hunting. For most of us the impulse to delve into the unknown remains strong throughout the greater part of our lives. An appeal to this motive, therefore, can be a powerful stimulant to audience response. One lecture by a noted astronomer on "The Expanding Universe" drew a packed audience of people drawn by the opportunity to explore vicariously into the well-nigh infinite distances of interstellar space. Another large audience gathered to hear of some of the adventures of the Byrd South Polar Expedition, as related by one of the members; and still another sat for nearly two hours while an official of the Bell System explained and demonstrated some of the wonders of modern methods of communication. Any exploring expedition being organized will have more applicants for membership than can possibly be accepted. A member of one of the groups attempting to scale Mt. Everest was once asked why he wanted to make the climb. "Because it is there," was the entirely understandable reply.

Arouse the exploratory tendencies of the audience, stimulate their curiosity, and then proceed to give the information that will satisfy that curiosity. A speaker introduced an otherwise probably very dull talk on spelling by the statement that, according to an authority on the subject, there were more than forty thousand different ways of spelling the word *circus*: when a child had one chance in forty thousand, he could not always be expected to know which of these was generally accepted as *the* correct one.

Effective stimulation of this motive may be accomplished by such topic sentences as these:

1. Join the Navy and see the world.
2. The truth is not generally known, but the inside facts are. . . .
3. What is inside the atom?
4. Join the students' European tour this summer and visit the Land of the Midnight Sun.
5. The Palomar telescope will enable man to see worlds not even suspected before.
6. Visit America first: go by bus and stop wherever you please.
7. To know the literature of a people you must know its language: learn at least one foreign language.
8. Wide reading introduces you to the great minds of the world's history.
9. The plot of this story, which you will have to unravel yourselves, has to do with the loss of a supposedly costly diamond necklace.
10. "Listen to history in the making."
11. What is the truth about communism?
12. The frontiers of thought are every bit as intriguing as are those of geography.

The curiosity of the audience can be aroused by proposing to give them information they do not already have. You can often do this by opening with some statement that on casual hearing is well-nigh incredible. "Do you know, . . ." is frequently an attention-getting beginning. One speaker began a talk on coddling criminals with the startling statement, phrased in the form of a rhetorical question, "Do you know that there are more murderers at large today than there are members of all the police forces of this country?"

Freedom from Restraint

When personal freedoms are threatened, people are likely to swing into vigorous action. Groups resent the attempt on the part of outside forces to control their authority to determine their own course of conduct. It was no accident that almost a hundred and seventy-five years ago liberty was proclaimed as one of man's inalienable rights. Among our own people, as among the peoples of many other nations, freedom of action has been one of the goals toward which the processes of social evolution have been directed. Wars have been waged, internecine struggles have been fought, in an effort to secure to the people the right to govern themselves, to be free from external restraint. You can make powerful appeals if you can show how this freedom can be made more secure or how it can be enlarged still further. Similarly, if you can show your listeners how they are threatened, you have a strong leverage with which to move them.

It should be obvious that freedom is only relative because of the very nature of society itself. Complete and absolute liberty of action is as impossible of achievement as perpetual motion; it could result only in anarchy, in chaos, for conflicts arise inevitably among individuals even as among nations. By and large, that freedom is most effective when it permits the individual members of a society to follow their own inclinations so long as they do not interfere with comparable inclinations of others. The advocate of freedom must, therefore, be cautioned against attempting to stimulate the sort of activity which would result in interference with the activities of others who may have the same or equal rights to liberty. The day of the railway magnate who proclaimed, "The public be damned," is past. The industrialist who squeezed the last bit of energy from his laborers in order to increase his own profits is gone. Child labor is a practice of yesterday. The liberty of a few has often had to be restricted in order that a larger liberty for everyone may be achieved. These are factors which must be considered by the speaker who is making an appeal to the widespread desire for freedom from external restraint.

The deep-lying demand for such freedom readily comes into conflict with some of the other motives which direct human conduct. Perhaps the one with which it has come into most vigorous opposition within the past two decades is that having security as its end result. This is not the place to enter into an argument as to whether freedom from external restraint or security is in the long run the more desirable. It might be apropos, however, to point out that in any instance of such a conflict as this, into which the whole political, social, and economic system is drawn, you must recognize that there are limits to which it is possible to advance the one without encroaching seriously on the other. You cannot, for example, honestly pretend to your listeners that it is possible for them to obtain the maximum of guaranteed "unearned" security from whatever source and still retain the maximum of freedom from the control of those in charge of that source. You cannot offer to a group of farmers the maintenance of their tradition of "independence" and at the same time advocate a system of price supports and crop control. In your appeals to conflicting motives, then, you must make the choice: you may either base your appeal on what you estimate to be the strongest of the opposing factors, or you may as a matter of honest judgment seek to stimulate that particular motive which in your opinion will bring about the greatest benefit to all concerned. Do not hold out to your listeners the hope of attaining goals which are mutually incompatible or deliberately conceal from them the implications in their choice of goals.

The problem of freedom from restrictions involves not only limitations imposed by other people; it may relate to those limitations imposed by physical factors, personal inabilities, even by geographical features. Fifty years ago one's neighborhood was bounded by the space one could cover in an hour or so with a horse and buggy. The telegraph, the telephone, the radio, television, have all contributed immeasurably to the removal of former limitations on one's communication. Fast trains, the airplane, the automobile, speedy ocean liners, have likewise extended beyond the dream of our grandfathers the possibility of expanding human intercourse. These all have to do with the breaking down of many of the old limitations on freedom of action and of communication.

There are many approaches that you can make in appealing to this powerful motive of freedom from external restraint. Following are some examples of topic sentences that might be utilized:

1. Know the truth, and the truth will make you free.
2. Fly to Europe, and give yourself more time to visit the historical spots of the Old World.
3. The rural areas of this state should be provided with all-weather roads.
4. Communism is a direct threat to the liberties we have always prized so highly.
5. In union there is strength.
6. Develop your ability to speak, and thus make freedom of speech a reality.
7. "Is life so dear, or peace so sweet, as to be purchased at the price of chains and slavery?"
8. Live in a trailer, and have a home on wheels.
9. Government by bureau is our greatest present domestic threat to individual liberty.
10. The laborer's right to work is seriously jeopardized by irresponsible labor leaders.
11. Don't be a wallflower; learn the modern dances.
12. The college curriculum should permit a wide choice of electives.
13. Let us resist this aggression, which would deprive us of our liberties.
14. The first article in the Bill of Rights has given inestimable benefits to the American people.
15. "There are no free wills in police states."[6]

Relief of Distress

As has been said, not all behavior is based on anticipated benefits to the individual himself. Much of what we do is done because of the benefits it will bring to others. While it is un-

[6] Arthur H. Vandenberg, "European Recovery Program," *Representative American Speeches, 1947-1948*, A. Craig Baird (ed.), The H. W. Wilson Company, 1948, pp. 24-47.

doubtedly true that we may derive much personal satisfaction from generous acts, it is also true that our own feelings of self-gratification are usually in the background and are probably not the determining factor. Examples of the working of this type of motivation may be found in the many instances of immediate and generous aid in times of disaster, even though the tragedy may occur thousands of miles from us to people with whom we have no acquaintance. When San Francisco and Tokyo were struck by devastating earthquakes, when the lower Mississippi Valley was visited by a ruinous flood, when the Eastern seacoast was hit by a terrific hurricane that wrought destruction as far north as New England, supplies, food, clothing, medicines, money, personnel, were rushed from all parts of the country, not because the givers were taking to themselves credit for giving but simply because in these places people were in need of help. For several weeks a large signboard beside the street leading from a college campus into the city carried nothing more than this appeal:

Children in Europe Are Hungry. Send a CARE Package.

It is also true that by benefiting others we often benefit ourselves. We recognize that by assisting the peoples of Europe we are furthering our own welfare.[7] By working for improvements in our own community we are giving ourselves a better place in which to live. But it is often the case that our efforts are directed in such a way that we ourselves derive benefit from our acts only indirectly if at all. Not everyone asks, with reference to some proposal, "What is there in it for me?" In fact, many people would be deeply offended by the implication that what they were doing was being done with even half an eye to their own advantage.

At the same time, it often makes a more effective appeal if it can be shown how some good can be done to others and at the same time some benefit brought to the benefactor. Our efforts

---

[7] See Vandenberg, *op. cit.*, for an excellent development of this argument.

to strengthen the democracies of Europe and throughout the world are a case in point in which the "higher" and "lower" motives are working together to accomplish some highly desirable end result. The purchase of war bonds during both World Wars provided our armed forces with the needed supplies; it also gave the purchaser a return on his investment. But many blood donors had no sons or other close relatives in the services.

The speaker is confronted with many opportunities to appeal to these higher motives of his listeners. In fact, when attempts to persuade the audience to some action that will bring to them certain benefits, he may himself be acting on the basis of a higher motive, in that their action can bring to him no appreciable advantage. Some illustrative topic sentences that may be used in appealing to this motive are these:

1. Drive carefully, and protect the children.
2. Contribute to the Community Chest (Red Cross, etc.).
3. The teaching profession (or the ministry, or medicine) will give you a great opportunity for service to humanity.
4. Your dimes will help some child to recover from poliomyelitis.
5. Send your contribution to the Damon Runyon Cancer Fund.
6. Let's clear up these slums, and provide decent places for the people to live.
7. Farm prices should be supported, even though the cost of living will be raised thereby.
8. Send your used books to help build up the destroyed libraries of European universities.
9. Save your old clothes to give to the Red Cross.
10. A federal system of scholarships would enable many a young man and woman to go to college who could not otherwise afford it.
11. If you want to render a much-needed service to humanity, become a country doctor (or the editor of a country newspaper).

People will often rise to meet a need or to give some service to their community, to the state, or to the country, if they are shown that the need exists and that the opportunity is theirs. Sometimes they can be persuaded to action because of benefits already received: we owe, for example, certain duties to the country because of the opportunities it has afforded us—educational, economic, political, social.

It would be possible to enumerate many more of the motives that underlie human behavior, but those discussed above will be sufficient to illustrate the principle that, if you want to influence your listeners, you must stimulate those internal drives and impulsions which lead human beings to do the things they do.

Need for Studying the Situation

Motives vary in strength, as has been said, among different persons and in the same individuals at different times. Among the factors which tend to bring them to the fore may be recent events, climatic conditions, geographical features, social habit, religious fervor, and so on. Those motives which would be very strong in the people of one area might have little or no effect in another. A settled, cultured community might entertain an appeal to beautify its environs; while a frontier town, in which the inhabitants are primarily interested in wresting a living from reluctant Nature, would hardly respond as enthusiastically to such an appeal. In time of war, donations of blood are likely to come far easier than in times of peace.

People generally are not easy to interest actively in winter sports when the temperature is reaching for the hundred-degree mark or in summer activities when the ground is covered with snow and ice. But a highway accident resulting in the deaths of two well-known students was followed by several strong class talks on traffic safety. A forest fire in which a number of smoke chasers lost their lives was the incentive for a number of effective appeals for extreme care in the use of fire. The introduction into Congress of a bill proposing restrictions on labor will usually arouse stirring speeches having to do with freedom of action, "slave-labor laws," and similar general topics.

Know your audience. Study their interests, their habitual attitudes and modes of thinking, the particular motives which seem uppermost in their minds at the time, and if possible base your appeal on those characteristics. Frequently your proposal will touch no motive that is especially active at the moment. In such a case you may find it necessary to arouse some dormant motive, often by connecting it with one which is already active.

GENERAL PRINCIPLES GOVERNING MOTIVE APPEALS

In your use of the motive appeals, there are a few general principles[8] which you should follow:

1. The motive itself must be "worthy of the deed."[9] Most people do not like to admit that they are selfish, inconsiderate, uninterested in human welfare; they can often be aroused by an appeal to a motive that is socially acceptable, even when they tend to decry any particular altruism on their own part. In fact, those whose actions are most often directed toward some social benefit are often the very ones to be modest with regard to their "public spirit." As an investment, a slum-clearance project might not appeal; if to the expectation of a modest return on one's investment is added a reference to the social value of decent living quarters for low-income groups, the motive appeal would thereby be elevated to the point where it becomes "worthy of the deed," as Winans expresses the idea.

2. You must also show that the end result itself is worth the effort put into its attainment. If it can be shown to a group of

[8] The first four of these are adapted from Giles Wilkeson Gray and Claude Merton Wise, *The Bases of Speech*, Harper & Brothers, rev. ed., 1946, pp. 366-388.
[9] James A. Winans, *Speech-Making*, Appleton-Century-Crofts, Inc., 1938, p. 313.

THE SECURITY COUNCIL OF THE UNITED NATIONS IN ACTION

A significant question before the nations of the world today is, Can world government be made to work? Is it possible to substitute talk and discussion for aggression, intrigue, and war? (Photo, Black Star.)

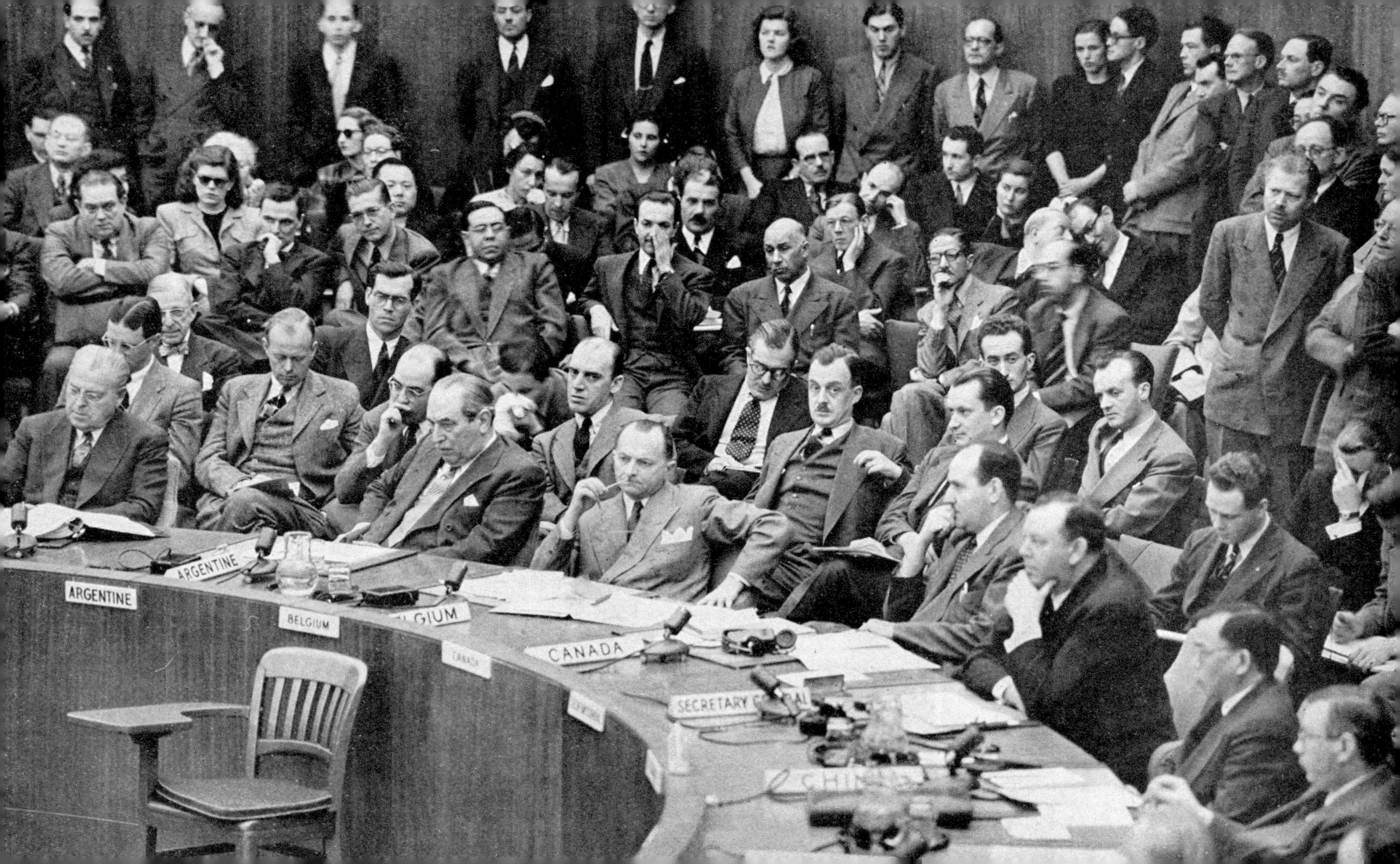
ARGENTINE
ARGENTINE
BELGIUM
CANADA
BELGIUM
CANADA

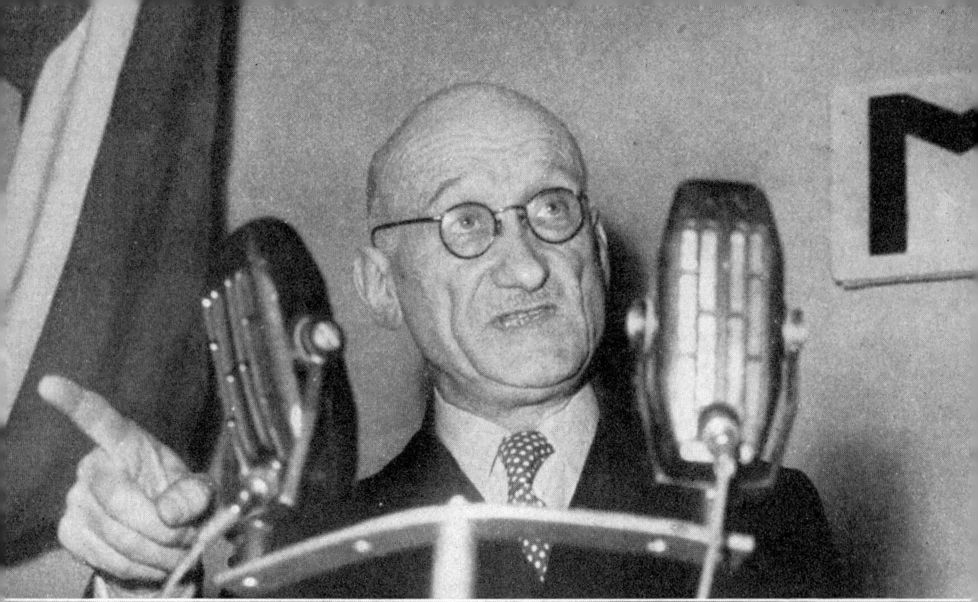

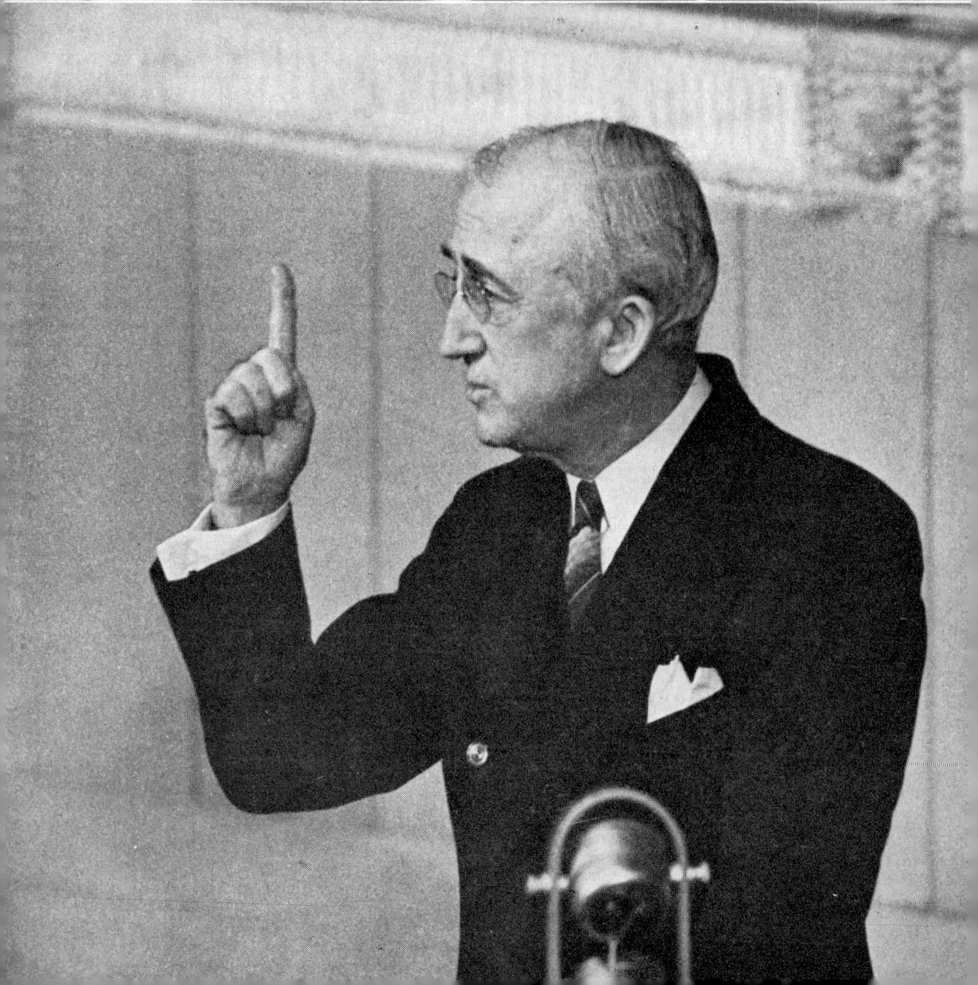

college or high-school students that the study of public speaking will repay them handsomely, they are more likely to work just a little harder on the course. You yourself have come to college because you believe that your education will enable you to secure for yourself many things you would not otherwise be able to have and that it will afford the preparation you need for a life of greater social usefulness. You believe that these objectives are worth the four to seven years it will take you to complete your courses.

Is the gain achieved by a long-drawn-out strike worth the lost income due to the resulting unemployment? Is the security of America and of the entire western world worth the expenditures it is costing the American people? Is our freedom of action of such value as to warrant a defense of that freedom at all hazards? Or is a security under the protection of a paternalistic government worth what it costs in terms of freedom from external restraints? Do the activities made possible by our contributions to the Community Chest justify our giving as generously as our finances permit?

3. You must be able to show further that by following the course of action prompted by the aroused motives, there is a strong likelihood that the desired end result will be achieved. If you did not feel that your education would actually enable you to obtain the results you want, you might be very reluctant to spend these years in college. If America had not felt that sending billions of dollars in goods and credits to western Europe would bring at least some degree of peace and security to a part of the world, the entire program would have been no more than a futile gesture.

FREE GOVERNMENT PLACES GREAT RESPONSIBILITIES ON ITS LEADERS

At the top Mr. Robert Schuman speaks in behalf of France. At the bottom James Byrnes speaks on atomic energy before United Nations Assembly. (Photos, Black Star.)

Sometimes an individual or a group can be persuaded to undertake some enterprise in which there is no reasonable expectation of success, simply because the element of "rightness" is a predominant factor. While their own efforts may not prevail at the time, there is the hope that they may pave the way for someone's later success. Suffrage for women was not adopted into the Constitution until generations after it was first proposed. A candidate may be persuaded to run for public office as a protest against a corrupt opposition, primarily in an attempt to arouse the voters to a sense of civic and political betterment. His own candidacy is no more than one step in the broader campaign ultimately to dislodge the predatory interests. Once the citizenry is aroused, the end result of such continued struggling will, it is hoped, be all that can be desired.

4. Make your appeal to the highest motives to which your listeners are likely to respond.[10] If an appeal to motives of self-interest is necessary, attempt, if possible, to associate them with motives having to do with the welfare of others. Thus, an automobile driver may respond to a safety campaign for the sake of his own life; but it can also be shown that his life is of some value to others and that reckless driving endangers others as well as himself. One might not be drawn into the teaching profession solely by the promise of monetary rewards; but he might be if he were convinced that he might live in reasonable comfort and at the same time perform a much-needed service to the youth of the community. The merchant may be induced to improve his store in order to draw more customers and increase his profits; as a result of better facilities and more economical methods of handling his merchandise, he may also give those customers more for their money.

5. Make your appeal, as a rule, to more than one motive, on the theory that if one will not have the desired effect perhaps another will! Actually, a number of good reasons or motives can

---

[10] George Pierce Baker and Henry Barrett Huntington, *The Principles of Argument,* Ginn & Company, revised and augmented, 1905, p. 321.

usually be found for most actions, and if more than one of these is presented, there is more likelihood of your getting the desired response.

6. Often it is best not to mention motives at all; the desirability of the end result may be so obvious or may be so effectively presented that nothing more is needed. People do not like to be appealed to on the basis of the purely selfish and are sometimes embarrassed by appeals to altruism, especially when made too obvious; they may even refuse to admit any influence of the "higher" motives at all.

7. Do not dictate motives. You cannot tell people what they ought to feel. You cannot insist that they should be under the impulsion of certain motives. The best you can do is to discover those motives which are already operative, or which can be aroused indirectly, and make use of them.

8. Do not overwork any motive. Most people, for example, are willing to do their "duty" but will resent the persistent repetition of the appeal. They would much rather determine for themselves where their duty lies. Generosity can usually be appealed to successfully, but it can easily be overworked. Vary your appeals; you will probably find that you will not have occasion to use the same appeal very often, anyway.

EXERCISES

1. Analyze your own motives in (a) seeking an education, (b) choosing your particular vocation. Exactly what part does the acquiring of ability in public speaking contribute to the satisfaction of these motives?
2. Present an account of an instance in your own experience of a conflict of motives. What were the deciding factors in the final resolution of the conflict?
3. Bring to class a half dozen or more full-page advertisements from magazines, posters, and the like, and make a talk with these as visual aids, showing how advertisers in attempting to sell their merchandise appeal to certain motives.

4. Read a persuasive speech, and analyze the motives to which the speaker is appealing. What does he offer in his speech by way of satisfaction of those motives?
5. Give a talk in which you make a definite link between one of the "selfish" and one of the "unselfish" motives. Make use of the idea of "enlightened self-interest." In your preparation, analyze your own motives in urging the course of action you propose for your listeners to follow. What is your particular interest in the matter?
6. Present a talk in which you appeal primarily to one of the motives discussed in the chapter. Observe carefully the general principles, and *show* that the end result is worthy, attainable. Do not specifically mention the particular motive to which you are appealing.
7. Select some individual who has recently been before the public eye largely through his speaking. On the basis of his public utterances correlated with his public actions, what would you say of his probable motives in (a) requesting support at the polls, (b) urging the adoption of certain policies, (c) urging support of another candidate for office?

SUPPLEMENTARY READINGS

1. Baird, A. Craig, *Argumentation, Discussion, and Debate*, McGraw-Hill Book Company, Inc., 1950, chap. 18, "Persuasion: Techniques of Motivation," pp. 214-234.
2. Baird, A. Craig, and Knower, Franklin H., *General Speech: An Introduction*, McGraw-Hill Book Company, Inc., 1949, pp. 389-392.
3. Brigance, William Norwood, *Speech Composition*, F. S. Crofts & Co., 1937, pp. 181-190.
4. Gray, Giles Wilkeson, and Wise, Claude Merton, *The Bases of Speech*, Harper & Brothers, rev. ed., 1946, pp. 340-374.
5. Monroe, Alan H., *Principles and Types of Speech*, Scott, Foresman & Company, 3rd ed., 1949, pp. 192-207.
6. Oliver, Robert T., *The Psychology of Persuasive Speech*, Longmans, Green & Co., 1945, chap. VI, "Reaching the Sources of Motivation," pp. 163-196.
7. Oliver, Robert T., *Training for Effective Speech*, The Cordon Company, Inc., 1939, chap. 12, "Motivating the Audience," pp. 307-348.
8. Overstreet, H. A., *Influencing Human Behavior*, W. W. Norton & Company, 1925, pp. 28-49.

9. Phillips, Arthur Edward, *Effective Speaking*, The Newton Company, 1908, pp. 48-62.
10. Weaver, Andrew Thomas, *Speech: Forms and Principles*, Longmans Green & Co., 1942, pp. 349-352.
11. Winans, James A., *Speech-Making*, Appleton-Century-Crofts, Inc., 1938, chap. XV, "Motives," pp. 304-322.
12. Woolbert, Charles Henry, and Smith, Joseph F., *The Fundamentals of Speech*, Harper & Brothers, 1934, pp. 367-374.
13. Young, Paul Thomas, *The Motivation of Behavior*, John W. Wiley Sons, Inc., 1936.

CHAPTER IV

Attention and Interest

IT SHOULD be obvious that unless you can get your audience to listen to you there is no point in speaking at all; you actually have no audience. One of your primary problems, therefore, is to secure and hold the attention and interest of your listeners. This is true regardless of the type of speaking situation, whether it be conversation, a classroom lecture or demonstration, the reading aloud of a piece of literature, the presentation of a play, or the delivery of a speech.

ATTENTION DEFINED

Attention may be defined from two points of view. In the first place, it may be thought of as a bodily "set," in which the responsive apparatus is made more sensitive to certain stimuli impinging upon it while it is less sensitive to other stimuli momentarily less significant. Thus, in a crowd we may often pick out the face of someone we know, while all others fade, so to speak, into the background. From the highly complex sounds emanating from an orchestra we can often isolate a single violin or other instrument. From a babel of conversation we can often select a single voice. One whose sense of taste has been highly developed can pick out of the complexity of a salad dressing a single ingredient. These selections are made through a process of sharpening our acuteness for some particular stimulus which may have special significance at the moment. It is a sensory-neuro-muscular act. It may be thought of as a physiological phenomenon.

Attention may also be considered as a process by which our awareness of a given stimulus is heightened, the stimulus thereby entering more directly into what the psychologist James called the "focus of consciousness," while all other stimuli are relegated to the "fringe" or margin. From this point of view attention is a psychological phenomenon, that is to say, an element of consciousness.

It should be borne in mind that no distinction can actually be made between the physiological and the psychological descriptions of attention; any differentiation is essentially a matter of how one may look at the phenomenon. Both aspects are present in every act involving attention.

Your problem as a speaker, then, is to bring your subject into the "focus of consciousness" of your listeners, while other matters are permitted to fade or are perhaps even forced into the background or "fringe." If you can maintain the attention and interest of your audience on the problem at hand, without their being diverted to other subjects or to conflicting ideas, your success is more nearly assured. Woodrow Wilson once said that the first job of any book is to get itself read. Similarly, the first job of any speech is to get itself heard. Your hearers may not accept your ideas, but at least they have listened. Sometimes that will be as much as you can expect.

Adaptation

No one can attend strictly to any stimulus for more than a few seconds at a time. We soon become so accustomed to many of the sounds, sights, and other sensations about us that we are hardly aware of them at all. We rarely listen to a car passing along the street, even though it may come within a few yards of us. As this is being written, the sounds of the night—the crickets, the katydids, the occasional distant toot of an automobile horn, the clank of steel against steel on an oil derrick being erected not far away—all these require a conscious act of listening, or attending, in order for them to be brought into the consciousness at all. The contact of clothing on the skin, the odor of freshly cut grass—all the myriads of stimuli of various kinds impinging on our sense organs have by their very constancy lost their attention-getting value. We have become *adapted* to them to such an extent that whatever response they may arouse remains itself far in the margin of consciousness.

Once you have lost the attention of your audience, it is extremely difficult to regain it with any degree of effectiveness. For one thing, the continuity of your thought has been broken, and it will not be easy for your listeners to pick up in the middle of an explanation or an argument. Again, they will already have formed their judgment of you, a judgment which you may have trouble in dislodging or reversing.

THE TIME AND THE PLACE GREATLY INFLUENCE THE AUDIENCE,
THE SPEAKER, AND THE SPEECH

Compare the three pictures and note how the physical environment sets the mood. In the first picture the supporters of Harry Truman are attempting to disrupt a demonstration for Senator Richard Russell of Georgia at the Democratic National Convention in 1948. (Photo, Wide World.)

Why did Charles De Gaulle choose to speak from a high platform bearing a symbol of Free France? (Photo, Black Star.)

What limitations does a church place upon a speaker? (Photo, Black Star.)

HAWAII
PUERTO RICO
VIRGIN ISLANDS
ALASKA
ILLINOIS
HE IS HUMAN
Our
HARRY

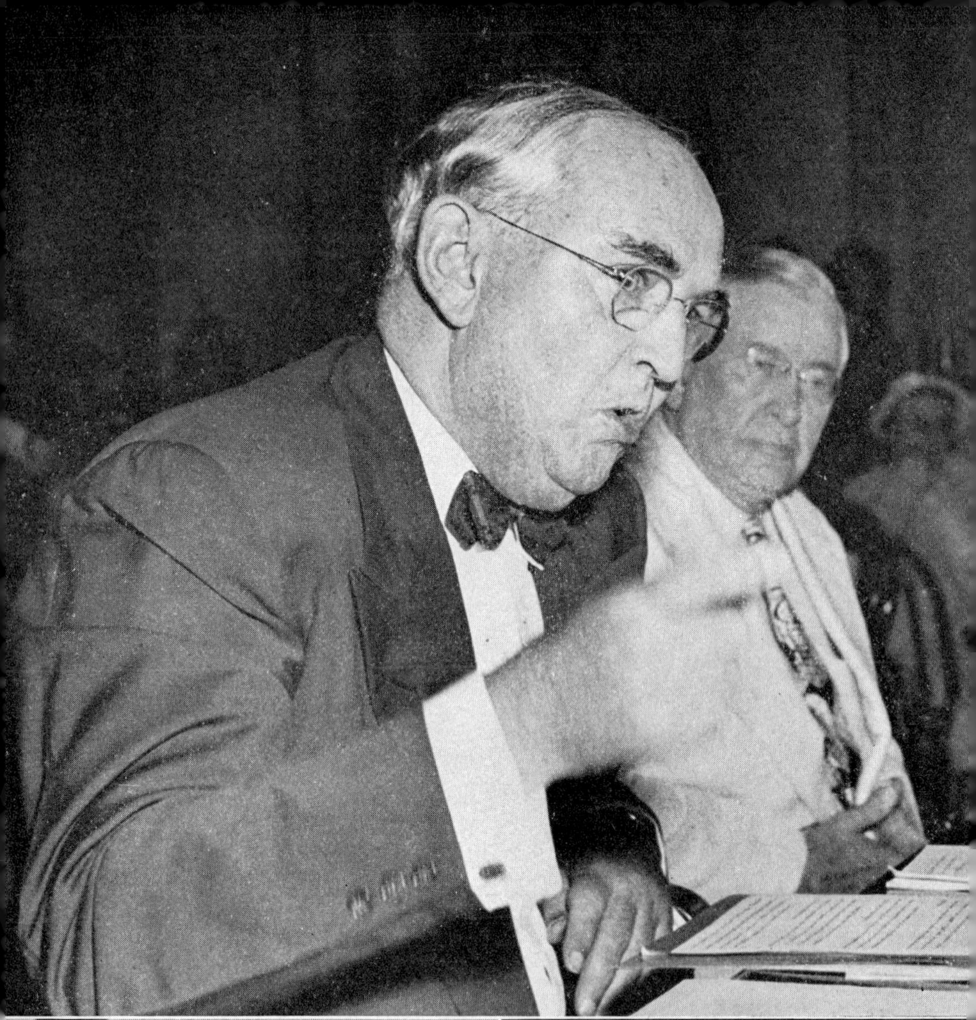

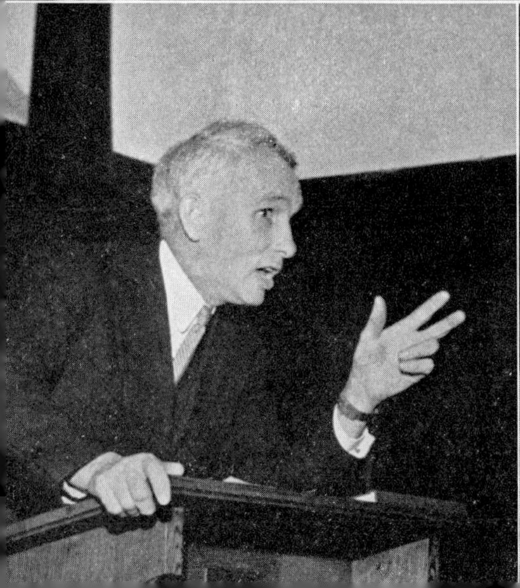

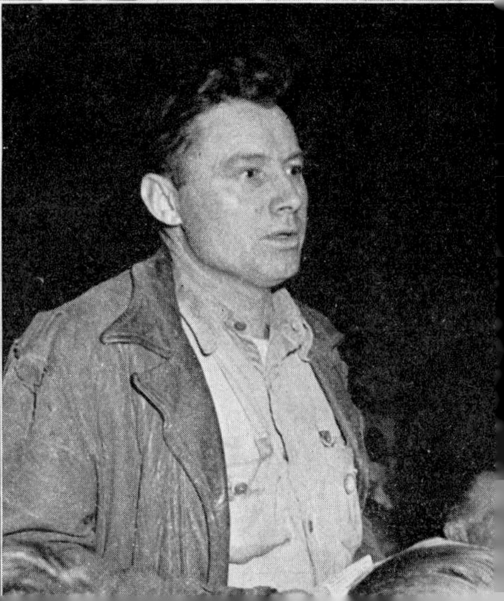

Attention and Interest

Attention and interest are usually thought of together and are often identified with one another. However, it is probably best to think of them as more or less distinct, though correlated, phenomena. Attention is a definite act, though not always voluntary, by which, as has been said, stimuli are brought into sharper focus. Interest is likely to be of longer duration and arises as a rule out of the motives through the force of which we obtain our satisfactions. Each act of attending is a separate act; but one's interest in a given subject may persist through any number of such acts. One may be continuously interested in civic improvement, even though he may be giving his attention during business hours to his own commercial enterprises. The fact that a statesman may for relaxation enjoy mystery stories, and while reading them give his undivided attention to them, does not argue that he is no longer interested, even for the time being, in the national welfare. His interest is simply temporarily quiescent.

We attend more readily to those things in which we are interested, but just as our active interest fluctuates from time to time, so also does our attention. We may be interested in many things, and this interest is often maintained over a period of years. As various occasions arise, we give attention now to one, now to another of these interests. From the point of view of the speaker, the problem, then, is one of selecting those interests which may have the greatest present attention value.

FACTORS OF ATTENTION

Attention may be drawn by any one or a combination of a number of aspects of the situation. For instance, any *sudden*

THE TIMES AND PLACES MEN SPEAK ARE LEGION

The pictures on the facing page show Senator Arthur Vandenberg (photo, Wide World), a minister, and a laborer (photos, Black Star).

change in the stimulus pattern is likely to draw that changed element into the focus of consciousness. A loud or sudden noise or a flash of light, a sudden touch, an unaccustomed odor, a peculiar taste in our food, will cause an immediate awareness of that new element. A sudden movement in otherwise quiet surroundings will attract attention, as any hunter will testify who does not see the squirrel up in the tree until it flicks its tail. A fisherman may drowse on the banks of his favorite spot until a vigorous tug on his line arouses him to instant action.

This factor of sudden change is operative both in the relatively simpler and in the more complex behavior situations. We easily fall into a more or less fixed pattern of living, adapting ourselves to the regularity of our existence; but if something occurs to upset the routine, we are at once conscious, often uncomfortably so, of the difference. We may even recoil at the very thought of such a change and resist innovations with considerable energy. Changes in our social, economic, and political structure are rarely made without widespread attention being given to them; whereas too many people rarely give a thought to the normal everyday processes by which the social order is maintained or social evolution proceeds. Petty crime too often is tolerated until some major offense is committed, whereupon our attention is immediately fixed on the "crime wave" which has apparently suddenly descended upon us. Any sudden change in the stimulus pattern to which we have become even partially adapted is likely to arouse attention, whether that pattern be of a simple or a complex nature.

The speaker can make use of the attention value of sudden change either by the use of ideas that represent sudden and great deviations from the normal pattern or by the use of techniques of delivery which break into the regular, accustomed manner of presentation. Typical of the former is the injection of the "startling statement"—an idea that is almost incredible because it represents a sudden deviation from the usual modes of thinking. We know, for instance, that traffic accidents cause a great many fatalities every year, and we are likely to go on taking the fact for granted. But when we are told that, since Armistice Day, 1918, seven times as many Americans have been killed in traffic accidents as were killed in both World Wars, we are likely to give the matter some attention.

Similarly, the speaker can often draw attention by means of a sudden strong emphasis, a complete stop, a forceful gesture, because these are abrupt changes in the general overall stimulus pattern. One must be careful that these methods are not so startling as to draw attention to themselves; they should be so used as to direct attention to what is being said.

Magnitude

We are also drawn by the magnitude of the stimulus as well as by its suddenness. Every tourist is impressed by the magnificence of the Grand Canyon, even though he may have come upon it gradually. It takes no startling suddenness to become keenly aware of the giant sequoias of California, the exquisite beauty of the Berkshire Hills, or the tranquillity of the Maine woods. Byron was quite familiar with the sea when he penned his moving "Apostrophe to the Ocean." We might not be attracted by a shooting star; but a meteor which lights up the whole sky could not fail to draw our attention. When the "Airflow" automobile was built several years ago, it was such a radical departure from the type of body then in vogue as to attract a great deal of attention, much of it unfavorable. Today, when most cars are using lines somewhat similar, no one pays much attention to the differences in appearance among the various makes of 1951 automobile or to the changes in model from one year to the next.

The principle of magnitude of change is operative again in the social, political, and economic world. It is here that the speaker can make his applications. Proposals which fifty years ago were considered "radical" because they represented a change of great magnitude in our social processes have since been adopted with scarcely a ripple; today they do not represent so wide a departure.

Repetition

Up to a certain point, repetition of a stimulus adds to the attention value. We do not mind if someone strikes a single note on the piano; we should certainly notice it if that same note were to be repeated over and over for any length of time. We usually give the other ring on our telephone party line no more than a passing notice further than to observe that it is not our own. But let that telephone ring almost incessantly for two entire days, and it becomes more noticeable. Like many repeated stimuli, it may become even irritating. A repeated stimulus may, on the other hand, like the refrain in much poetry as well as in public speech, become highly impressive. Lincoln's Cooper Union Address is illustrative of the effect of repetition in public speaking. In this speech Lincoln used just enough repetition to gain attention and to make his ideas impressive but not enough to create monotony.

Reference to Experience

We attend, as a rule, to those stimuli which may be related to our own experiences perhaps as much as to those which may be entirely new. One who sees the mountains for the first time is highly conscious of them; they are impressive largely because of their contrast with the things with which one is familiar. On the other hand, we are also attracted by those things which are similar to what we have known. If the new can be associated, either by contrast or similarity, with the old, then its attention value may be greatly enhanced. Totally novel ideas presented along with the familiar have a much better chance of gaining the attention of the listener. That is what makes the Parables so impressive: "A certain man had two sons";[1] "Behold, there went out a sower to sow";[2] "There was a certain rich man, which had a steward";[3] "A certain man went down from Jerusalem to

[1] Luke xv: 11.
[2] Mark iv: 3.
[3] Luke xvi: 1.

Jericho, and fell among thieves."[4] In each narrative a new idea is presented through a comparison with a situation with which all the hearers were familiar.

Effect of Interest

Generally speaking, people give attention to those aspects of a situation in which they are interested. A couple is downtown window-shopping. The wife will want to stop and look at the new hats and dresses; her husband will see the sporting goods a little farther down the street. If a botanist and a zoologist are walking together through the fields, one will "see" (that is, he will attend to) the plants and the flowers, while the other will see the birds and the insects.

These different interests which lead us to attend to different aspects of the total situation also lead to varying interpretations of the same phenomena. Thus, a new bridge across the Mississippi may be viewed by one man as an engineering triumph, by another as a means for improved and accelerated social intercourse, for the breaking down of isolation. The network of hard-surface highways represents to one a tremendous material achievement; to another it represents a great step forward in social facilitation. What you "see" in any given phenomenon depends largely on what your interests are.

Interest, in this connection, is closely related to those motives which impel the individual "to pay attention to a certain thing or class of things."[5] In other words, we are prone to pay attention to those things which give promise of providing the end results toward which our motives impel us. The businessman will listen with interest to proposals which will enable him to increase his profits and give better service. The physician will pay attention to new and more effective methods of treating diseases. The farmer will listen to a discussion of ways that will enable him to increase his yield per acre.

[4] Luke x: 30.
[5] John Frederick Dashiell, *Fundamentals of General Psychology*, Houghton, Mifflin Company, 1937, p. 102n.

TYPES OF ATTENTION

Psychologists recognize that attention may take one of three general forms, which may be thought of also as stages of development. The first of these has been called the *involuntary* or sometimes the *primary* type of attention. This is the type which results when certain factors in either the stimulus or in the organism itself cause our attention to be drawn without effort on our part. In the stimulus such factors as suddenness or magnitude of change and repetition of stimulus have attention value. Just as effective as increase in intensity is a decrease: people may be awakened by the stopping of the clock. A speaker who by his continual loudness has put his audience to sleep may arouse them by suddenly dropping his voice so that it is barely audible. The speaker may occasionally resort to this type of attention by making use of either sudden increases or decreases in stimulus intensity; but it is a method that can easily be overworked.

Within the organism there are also certain factors that contribute to the attention value of a given stimulus. Among these are one's own habits of attention and inattention, one's emotional state, and the interest of the moment.[6] The orchestra conductor has developed habits of attention to such a degree that he can detect slight deviations from the musical score when only a single instrument of the whole ensemble makes the error. As Woodworth points out, if you are angry with someone you are more sensitive to his faults than otherwise. If you are in the market for a new car, the latest models have an irresistible attraction for you. As has been pointed out, you see what you are interested in.

While the speaker may be limited in his use of the physical aspects of the stimulus pattern which attract attention, his use of those factors which reside within the organism, that is, within his listeners, is well-nigh unlimited. The attentive habits of his

[6] Robert S. Woodworth, *Psychology*, Henry Holt and Company, Inc., 4th ed., 1940, pp. 43-51.

hearers, their present emotional states, and their interests of the moment all provide avenues for immediate appeals to the attention. Through these avenues he can direct the attention of his audience to the subject under discussion.

The second type of attention has been called *voluntary*, or *secondary*, attention. It occurs when the individual forces his attention upon some object or activity, usually with some sense of effort and strain. You settle down for an evening of study and attack a subject which has not as yet aroused your keen interest. Recognizing that the work must be done, however, if you want to pass the course, you force yourself to get to work and give your attention to the text. So long as the attention is given by direct act of will, it remains voluntary, and the sense of effort will persist. It tires you to have to attend to such tasks for any length of time because attention itself involves muscle strain. You attend a lecture not because you are interested but because you feel you should, and you force yourself to listen carefully to everything that is said. At the end of the lecture you are worn out.

Some speakers make it extremely difficult to listen to them without such strain. They speak indistinctly or in such a low voice that they are neither easily audible nor readily intelligible. Their discussion itself is dull, dry, unrelieved by any sort of liveliness. Their language is obscure, their ideas abstract. They wear us out trying to listen to them and understand them. Many people simply will not expend the effort necessary to follow such a speaker who depends entirely on the voluntary or forced attention of his audience. It is to be suspected that some college and university professors never get beyond this kind of attention in their lectures.

The third type of attention has been called the *derived primary*. Sometimes, after you have directed your attention by sheer effort to a given activity or phenomenon, you may find after a time that your interests are awakened, and your attention is held thenceforth without further effort on your part. This type of attention partakes somewhat of the nature of the primary or involuntary in that it requires no conscious effort; since it arises or is derived from the voluntary type, it is designated as the derived primary.

You may start to read a book which you feel you ought to read and at first find it necessary to direct your attention forcibly to it; as you go further into the subject, however, you find that it is in fact highly interesting, and you read on, unconscious of the passage of time. Attention, which began by being consciously directed, is no longer a strain; it requires no effort, and the feeling of weariness from the expended energy does not ensue.

You have all entered into the study of subjects for no other reason than that they were required in your course. For the first few weeks considerable effort was undoubtedly needed to apply yourselves to getting the assignments. As time progressed, however, you found yourselves becoming more and more interested, until it required no heroic act of will at all to continue your study; attention had passed into the third stage where it was almost entirely effortless.

APPLICATION TO THE SPEAKER'S PROBLEM

It is not safe for a speaker to depend entirely on the involuntary form of attention from his audience. Occasional wide departures from the usual pattern may be permitted; but if they are indulged in too often the audience will become adapted to them, and they will lose their attention value. They may even take on the nature of an exhibition to be enjoyed by the audience for their own sake but diverting the attention of the listeners away from the subject the speaker is trying to present. Avoid making extensive use of the physical aspects of the stimulus pattern for the primary purpose of gaining attention. So long as they are a part of the act of communication, however, and contribute to the meanings you are trying to arouse, they may be used freely.

You *may* have to arouse involuntary attention at the outset by the use of heightened stimulation; you may have to ask your listeners to give you their voluntary attention for a time. But the sooner you can pass from the stage of either involuntary or voluntary to the derived primary, or *interested* attention, the easier your task will be. And the longer you can maintain your hearers' interest, the longer you can hold their attention. In those relatively rare instances in which you cannot assume that your audience is already interested either in you or in what you are going to say, your problem is one of striking immediately at their interests and of maintaining throughout your speech a high level of that interest.

It should be emphasized that as a rule subjects in themselves are neither interesting nor uninteresting. Almost any audience can be interested in almost any subject if approached by relating the subject to those things in which they are already interested. When Woodrow Wilson was a professor at Princeton, he told his class one day that Gladstone could make even a four-hour speech on the budget interesting. "Young men," he said, "it is not the subject that is dry; it is you that are dry!"[7]

AUDIENCES NOT PASSIVE

Audiences are not passive. They may be relaxed, inactive so far as may be observed. But because they have assembled for some fairly definite purpose, even though they may reveal no intense eagerness externally, they have assumed a certain mental or bodily "set" which has the effect of directing their attention to the speaker as soon as he appears. If through his own ineptness he loses that attention, it is likely to be his own fault.

As a rule, therefore, it is unnecessary for the speaker to stimulate either the voluntary or the involuntary attention. Outside classrooms and penal institutions, people rarely go to hear a speaker through coercion: they are already interested either in the speaker or in what he has to say or in the occasion itself.

[7] James A. Winans, *Speech-Making*, Appleton-Century-Crofts, Inc., 1938, p. 224.

They are present for the reason that he is to speak; or they have come together, for example, because some problem which touches their interests is to come under discussion, and they will listen attentively to anyone who offers a reasonable solution: that is why they are there. If they were not interested to begin with, they would stay away. The speaker usually has at the outset, therefore, the attentiveness that arises from interest. His problem is not so much one of gaining that attention as of holding and directing it.

APPEALS TO ATTENTION AND INTEREST

How can you apply the principles of attention and interest in the construction and delivery of your speeches? You can make the application by using certain specific appeals which are calculated to stimulate the interests of your listeners. Somewhat as in the case of motives, no final and rigid classification of these appeals is possible; there are about as many lists as there are people making them out. In any such classification the various categories are not mutually exclusive; you may make use of two or three appeals at the same time. For purposes of convenience the following list is suggested:

1. Vital
2. New and old
3. Concrete
4. Activity
5. Suspense
6. Struggle
7. Humor

Vital

As was pointed out earlier in this chapter, those things which give promise of satisfying human motives are likely to arouse keen attention and interest. Whatever affects life, freedom of action, comfort, property, security—the satisfaction of basic motives—is of immediate concern to everyone; such things are vital to human existence, to physical and mental welfare, or the welfare of those for whom our sympathy or pity has been aroused. Because they are of such importance in the business of living, discussions of topics related to them are listened to attentively. Find out, therefore, what the active motives are at the time, and relate your subject to them.

Occasionally you will want to talk on some subject on which your audience has no particular feelings at the time and which at the outset has no relation to their present active motives. In such a case you may find it necessary to stimulate dormant motives. In the Town Meeting of the Air on July 3, 1947, Mr. Denny stimulated interest in the question, "Has Twentieth Century Civilization Improved Mankind," by relating it to other questions of vital interest: "How can we assure ourselves that these products of research of twentieth century civilization will not be used to destroy twentieth century civilization itself?" . . . "Why do we fear so deeply the possibility of the use of the radio as a means of enslaving millions of people through lies and propaganda?" These and other questions were deliberately raised in order to arouse a dormant interest in the specific problem under discussion.[8]

Special devices may sometimes be used to direct what may be thought of as involuntary attention to a subject generally considered of little interest. When a speaker said to a class, "I don't know which one it is going to be, but one of you will spend some time as a patient in a mental hospital," he got immediate attention. From that opening he led his listeners through a statement of the surprising prevalence of mental disorders and thence to a consideration of the treatment given to mental patients in many state institutions. Another began, "The house you intended building this year burned down last summer," and thereby stimulated interest in the prevention of forest fires. Still another created interest in a rather humorous description of the

[8] *Representative American Speeches, 1947-1948*, A. Craig Baird (ed.), The H. W. Wilson Company, 1948, pp. 188-205.

divergent timepieces on the campus by beginning, "You were late to class this morning because the clock in the tower lied to you; in fact, it told four lies, because no two of the four faces on that clock were together, and no one of them was correct."

New and Old

People are interested in familiar scenes, familiar faces, accustomed activities; they are also interested in new scenes, making new acquaintances, and doing different things. Similarly, they like to hear old ideas, but they also want a new one now and then. Entirely new ideas which have no relation to what is known, however, have little appeal. Neither the new nor the old by itself is interesting.[9] The principle generally accepted in educational theory to proceed from the known to the unknown is equally applicable in speaking. You will want to present new ideas; but they will be more readily listened to if they are associated with already understood ideas. On the other hand, you will on occasion reiterate old, familiar thoughts. In such cases they will create more interest if you can give them a novel slant, a different approach, a new emphasis. You cannot take the attitude of the rustic who was asked by a bewildered traveler how to get to a distant city. The native pondered for some time. Finally, "Stranger," he replied, "if I wanted to go to that place, I wouldn't start from here." You must start from where your listeners are, whether in knowledge, understanding, or in their attitudes.

Huxley, the great English scientist, introduced a discussion of the chemistry of chalk to an audience composed of workingmen in southeast England thus: "If a well were to be sunk at our very feet in the midst of the city of Norwich, the diggers would very soon find themselves at work in that white substance almost too soft to be called rock, with which we are all familiar as chalk."

[9] William James, *Talks to Teachers on Psychology, and to Students on Some of Life's Ideals*, Henry Holt and Company, Inc., 1907, p. 108.

In attempting to impress an audience of businessmen with a few basic principles of advertising, Bruce Barton took as his theme the well-known passage from the Bible, "And Joseph died, and there arose a new King in Egypt which knew not Joseph." Mark Antony, in his funeral oration in *Julius Caesar*, raises a question in his listeners' minds regarding Caesar's supposed ambition by reminding them,

> You all did see that on the Lupercal
> I thrice presented him a kingly crown,
> Which he did thrice refuse! Was this ambition?

In presenting material that is familiar to your listeners, do not present it as something new; they are likely to resent your seeming attempt to palm off "old stuff" about which they already know. Similarly, new ideas should not be given as if they were old; you may leave your audience bogged down in a mass of unfamiliar material, and they will soon lose interest.

If your listeners already know something of your subject, start from there, with perhaps a brief summary of what is known to serve as a background for the new. Draw upon the experiences of your hearers, but go on from those experiences in describing new ones. Observe how Henry W. Grady reminded his audience, members of the staid old New England Society meeting in New York, of the fact that "the Cavalier as well as the Puritan was on the continent in its early days, and that he was 'up and able to be about,'" and that "while Miles Standish was cutting off men's ears for courting a girl without her parents' consent, and forbade men to kiss their wives on Sunday, the Cavalier was courting everything in sight, and that the Almighty had vouchsafed great increase to the Cavalier colonies, the huts in the wilderness being as full as the nests in the woods." Then he advanced further the newer idea that the characteristics of both Puritan and Cavalier had been merged into the one common strain, the American citizen.

It is for the reason that new material based on the old has

attention value, that illustrative material drawn from instances nearby in both time and space is likely to be especially effective. The report of a traffic accident occurring today, or yesterday, in your own locality, bringing injury or death to a friend or acquaintance, will have a far greater effect than a report of one a year ago, in some distant part of the country, and involving no one your listeners ever heard of. A student in Louisiana talking about forest fires to an audience of that state will do well at least to mention the fact that such fires do occur in Louisiana, not merely in the Pacific Northwest, and that they actually have broken out recently. A speaker discussing soil conservation should present information on what is happening or has happened recently in the area in which he is talking. A student speaker on juvenile delinquency, although treating the topic as a widespread problem, made her speech effective by gathering much of her material from the social welfare and police agencies in the city in which the university was located.

That is not to say that the more remote incidents and localities are of no interest at all. The point is that distant events and scenes are clarified and made more impressive by comparison with those near at hand. A discussion in the North of the race question in the South, for example, might very well, by way of comparison or contrast, make mention of somewhat similar problems in the large cities of the North, in some sections of the Southwest with large Mexican populations, or in the West, of the problem of Asiatics on the Pacific Coast prior to World War II.

On the other hand, the remote may often serve to illustrate and to clarify a discussion of a present problem. If we know the causes for the downfall of the Roman Republic or of the Greek democracy, perhaps we can preserve our own more effectively. If we can show that those speakers in the past who have not been motivated by "a genuine concern for the well-being of humanity" have passed under partial if not total eclipse, we may have more concern for our own ethics in speaking.

Concrete

Concrete terms generally hold greater interest than abstract terms because they come closer to actual experience and arouse more specific imagery. *Dwelling* is more specific than *building*: if you want to make the concept still more definite you might use *cottage, mansion, palace, bungalow, cabin, shanty, hovel,* and so on. Similarly, there are scores of words having to do with one's moving from one place to another under one's own power: *walk, dash, stroll, stagger, stalk, totter, plod, stride, march, run, gallop, trot,* to say nothing of the more picturesque and colloquial *hightail, highball,* and *hotfoot.* These specific terms come nearer to our actual experience than the more inclusive and general *dwelling* or *go,* and call up a more concrete imagery.

It is unavoidable that some abstract terms will be used. We speak of *democracy, laissez faire, integration* in education, *Americanism,* or "the American way of life," and so on, as if everyone understands exactly what we mean when we use the terms. Every field of thought which departs from the objectivity of material science has such expressions. So long as they are used in a sense that will be understood by everyone working in that field, no damage is done. There is no objection to your talking about such topics, even if you are not a thorough student of the subject in which they have definite meanings; but somewhere along the line it would be helpful if you were to present in concrete terms a brief statement of just what you do mean when you use the terms. We excoriate communism and all other forms of totalitarianism; but the terms are very abstract, requiring considerable explanation. If you will exercise great care to put your understanding in terms of direct experience, of concrete reality, and specific imagery, you will be in a better position to form intelligent attitudes yourself toward the things represented by the words; you will also be able to arouse intelligent attitudes toward these things on the part of your listeners.

Activity

The stationary soon loses its interest for us. People are interested in events, in things happening. The narrative therefore is often more effective in presenting a statement of principle than any amount of explanation. Lincoln's stories made his point far better than lengthy argument could have. Bruce Barton, in impressing his listeners with the importance of continuous advertising, even though the merchant and his goods were well known, told the simple story of the church which had been on the same spot for years and which everyone knew was there; yet the bell was rung every Sunday morning.

Your examples and illustrations can be presented as *factual, fictional,* or *hypothetical.* Factual examples are specific instances of actual occurrences, of conditions as they actually exist or have existed, procedures which have actually taken place or are taking place, descriptions of scenes which can actually be visited. In these instances you should use every means of making your descriptions or narratives alive. Introduce people and make them move; let them be doing something. Use fictitious names if necessary, but avoid such designations as "Mr. X," or as frequently seen in the Victorian novel, "Mr. S——." You can sometimes mention as the central character "A friend of mine. . . ."

The short anecdote is an example of the *fictitious instance*; the fable, the parable, the allegory are others. While John Bunyan could write a book-length allegory in *Pilgrim's Progress,* it is much better to limit yourself to a short narrative in which you come quickly to a point, make it, and then move on. It is doubtful if the fictitious description is as effectual as the factual.

The *hypothetical* example is usually introduced by some such expression as "Suppose," "It is as if," "Imagine this instance," or the like. It consists of a suppositious instance, either narrative or descriptive. The story told *might* have happened but, so far as you know, actually never did; the things described might have existed but really never did outside the imagination. Such an instance can be used effectively for clarification, perhaps more effectively in many cases than a factual example, in that you can fill in the details to fit the necessities of the situation. At the same time, your hypothetical account must be plausible; the instance could have taken place just as you described it, *unless* for some specific effect you deliberately exaggerate, in which case you should so inform your audience.

Activity and Delivery

The element of activity may also be applied in the speaker's own behavior before the audience. People get tired of listening to the same tones of voice for any length of time. Develop, therefore, vocal flexibility, partly for the sake of the variety itself and partly because the flexible voice can say more than the monotonous voice and say it more precisely.

Your behavior on the platform should be active, alert, animated. Show that you yourself are alive. Move about freely, but move purposefully. Don't just "go" without going somewhere for some purpose. Use your head, arms, hands to contribute to the communication. Keep your listeners' interest awake by exhibiting your own interest in the subject and in the discussion itself. Your "urge to communicate," if genuine and sincere, will in itself give you a foundation upon which to build an effective manner of speaking. It is highly probable that no lackadaisical speaker ever aroused a high interest either in himself or in what he was saying.

Your ideas should progress in such a way that your audience will be able to follow you. Keep moving in your development, and carry your hearers along with you. Once a point is taken up, finish with it before going on to the next; then you will not have to retrace. But avoid remaining on any one point so long that it becomes overworked and loses interest. Make the point, and move on to the next, and be sure that you let your hearers know that you are moving. The progression should be orderly. Aimless, disorganized shifting from one idea to another and back again will give only the effect of incoherent rambling.

Suspense

The popularity of the mystery story, the crime novel, is due in large part to the high degree of suspense that the author succeeds in creating. Uncertainty as to the outcome of some event is almost certain to arouse great interest; witness, for example, the manner in which the "soap operas" hold their listeners for week after week or in which Li'l Abner or Andy Gump keep their readers on edge while the hero struggles to extricate himself from some predicament.

Mark Antony made effective use of the element of suspense in his funeral oration by presenting the subject of the will, then withholding from the mob its provisions until he had aroused them almost to a frenzy.

Suspense in a speech may be aroused in various ways. In the first place, you may present no more than a broad, initial outline of the points you intend to bring out. These points should be of sufficient significance to stimulate a desire on the part of the audience to hear them discussed and a willingness to wait until they are developed. Second, you can in your discussion mention in passing, so to speak, a point which you expect to bring out in detail later on. The relevance of this point must be shown, however, when you finally develop it. Third, you can trace a chain of events, withholding the inciting incident until the chain has been firmly forged and then presenting the beginning, or cause; or, conversely, withholding the final outcome until your audience has been mentally and emotionally prepared for the denouement.

Causal relations can be treated to create high suspense in either a cause-to-effect or an effect-to-cause development. Suspense can also be created by leading your audience through a chain of steps in such a way that, although they can follow your argument easily, they are unable to see exactly where you are leading them until the final step. Such a technique is the so-called "yes-response" method, in which the speaker, starting with an idea that is generally and readily accepted, leads his listeners through a series of ideas, each following from the preceding one, until, by getting them to agree to each successive point, he reaches a final step with which, in order to be consistent, they must also agree.

It should be pointed out, however, that this technique lends itself quite readily to persuasive trickery. It is the familiar procedure of the unscrupulous door-to-door encyclopedia salesman who opens his sales campaign with an expression of deep solicitude over the educational welfare of your children, or the salesman who begins by apparently wanting to give you something for nothing. Like many other argumentative techniques, in the hands of a charlatan or a trickster it can be devastating in its potency. One's best defense is often a direct question which demands a direct answer, "Just what is your specific proposition?" The suspense in such situations may be intriguing; but if one is not careful, it may be quite expensive.

Struggle

Most people enjoy games either as participants or as spectators. Usually, the closer the game, the harder the struggle, and the more uncertain the outcome, the greater is the enjoyment. Struggle is often closely associated with suspense, although not all suspense involves struggle. Most people enjoy an argument because it represents an opposition of ideas and opinions. A public discussion will be much more interesting if there is a clash of opinion. Speeches on controversial issues are almost certain to draw interest. Attacks on entrenched political figures, on waste in government, on negligence of public officials, on economic, juridical, or social injustice, provide good opportunity for making the maximum use of the appeal to public interest in conflict, in competition.

Humor

It is not true that every speech must have some humor injected into it. However, some element of humor is often very helpful in disarming an oppositious audience and in illustrating a point, even to a favorable audience. Grady, for example, in his after-dinner speech on "The New South," succeeded in creating a favorable attitude on the part of his listeners partly by injecting frequent bits of humor into an otherwise serious speech. David E. Lilienthal tells of his eggman who quit work at Oak Ridge during the war because he felt that, whatever it was the government was making there, it would be cheaper to go out and buy it.

To have the best effect humor should have certain characteristics:

1. *Humor should be appropriate to the occasion.* There are some situations in which any humor at all would be out of place. You must be able to sense the prevailing mood of your listeners before indulging in what may prove to be misplaced humor. A group of townspeople assembled to consider what steps may be taken to combat a sudden wave of juvenile delinquency are probably in no frame of mind to entertain any genial humor; the situation is serious, and no nonsense is to be tolerated.

Broad, obvious types of humor may be suitable to an audience not accustomed to making fine distinctions; with groups whose habitual modes of thought and behavior are on a high level of discrimination, a more delicate type may be suitable. This may in such instances take the form of peculiar twists of language, an unexpected turn of a phrase, a short, pungent characterization.

2. *Humor should contribute to the point that is being made.* It is a mistaken notion that one should always begin a speech with a funny story, to create a feeling of good will on the part of the audience. Stories, anecdotes, humorous incidents, or any other forms of humor should be introduced only when they serve to clarify a point, to make it vivid, or to make it impressive.

In the purely entertaining speech, on the other hand, humor may be introduced at almost any point, particularly when there is no significant developmental sequence of ideas that should not be broken. An entertaining speech may at times consist of no more than a series of more or less unrelated stories, anecdotes, or incidents related entirely for their entertainment value.

3. *Humor should be genial.* All the world laughed with Will Rogers when he poked fun at dignity; but although there was underneath his witticisms a solid basis of truth, no one, not even those at whom his barbs were aimed, could resent his genial humor. It should be pointed out that he rarely used the names of the victims of his wit.

Biting humor, especially when directed at individuals, often arouses resentment and antagonism even among those not the victim. In a public speech, giving personal offense is even more to be avoided, especially when those attacked have no opportunity for defense. Taking such undue advantage is not consistent with what we like to believe is our sense of fair play. Furthermore, although it is a minor point, the humor may be turned against the speaker and become a boomerang, to his extreme discomfiture. In order to be able to use genial humor, you must be able to laugh at yourself. Former President Taft often referred in his speeches to his four years in the White House, but never without his famous infectious chuckle. Mark Twain is said once to have remarked that no one could make a humorous speech if he lacked self-confidence, "or if he was afraid of the occasion or the audience."[10]

Although humor should generally be genial, especially where individuals are involved, it can be scathing or grim when directed at social, economic, or political abuses.

4. *Humorous passages should be brief.* If you use a funny story, make it short. Don't drag it out interminably. Come to the point, and then go on. Humorous or witty remarks injected into the body of the speech should be brief and unexpected. They should be like a rapier thrust, quick and sharp. The element of surprise is an important aspect of humor: many of O. Henry's

---

[10] Loren D. Reid, "Private John Allen: A Humorist in Politics," *The Quarterly Journal of Speech*, December, 1942, pp. 414-421.

stories are so charmingly humorous because of their unexpected endings.

5. *Humor should always be in good taste, whether it is genial or grim.* Different occasions call for different types of humor, but in any situation, a violation of good taste can easily mar the pleasant atmosphere; it can also reflect seriously on the judgment and good sense of the speaker himself. On some occasions a broad, obvious type of humor may be effectively used, whereas on another a delicate, subtle type will be demanded. In any event, the humor must not violate the standards which are set up for the general cultural level of the audience.

As an instance of such a violation, it would certainly be in extremely poor taste to single out the physical infirmities of some individual and play them up by exaggeration, by emphasizing the incongruous, or by any other technique of humor. The extremely rare references to Franklin D. Roosevelt's physical disability made by irascible, irresponsible speakers were promptly and properly condemned by everyone, even by his political opponents. It would be equally bad taste to select some genuinely venerable person, someone highly regarded for his intrinsic merit, and hold him up to ridicule. Humorous stories and anecdotes are often permissible; but they should never in a public-speaking situation be tinged with the off-color, the risqué, the bawdy, introduced for their own sake.

Humor has for its purposes, first, relaxation, enjoyment, relief from the long-continued serious; second, to make a point that will stick because it is told in a unique manner. It denotes a delicate perception. Violations of good taste are in themselves incongruous in that they denote exactly the opposite, namely, a lack of social perception. The jarring impressions so created will be deep and long lasting.

6. *Humor should be spontaneous.* If you plan to introduce a humorous anecdote, make it seem to fall into place easily and spontaneously, never dragged in forcibly. Have it so perfectly in mind that in the telling you will not have to grope and

stumble. *Never attempt to tell a story if there is the slightest chance that you will be unable to come to the point.* Unless you are adept at dialect, it is probably better to avoid trying it. Your humorous phrases and turns of language should seem to come naturally, fitting easily into the train of thought. Notice how President Stoddard, speaking on "Education and Civilization," moves into his point: "To be linked with a distinguished physicist under the general umbrella of 'Science and Civilization' produced in me a slight 'startle' reaction. I know that I am not nearly as civilized as Professor Bacher is scientific."[11] To illustrate the difficulty that Becquerel had in isolating the factor in uranium that made photographic plates turn black, the same speaker told of the "statistician who, having consumed rye and soda, bourbon and soda, and scotch and soda, only to feel bad each time, swore a solemn oath to stay away from the obvious common element, soda!"

7. *The effective use of humor requires in the speaker a delicate perception of the incongruous, even in himself.*[12] No one, however, enjoys prolonged association with the individual who sees something funny in everything. There are times, there are situations, there are moods, in which the audience response to the speaker's misguided humor is extremely disadvantageous to him. The required sensitivity of perception for its use includes the sensing of the situation before making any attempts at being humorous.

8. One more caution with respect to the use of humor in public speaking: *Do not allow yourself to get such a reputation as a humorist that no one will take you seriously.* Tom Corwin, "King of the Stump,"[13] whose wit was famous during the middle of the nineteenth century, always regretted that he would be remem-

---

[11] Baird, *op. cit.*, p. 170. The reference is to Professor Robert F. Bacher, at the time a member of the United States Atomic Energy Commission.

[12] Humor has in fact been defined as "the juxtaposition of incongruous concepts."

[13] J. Jeffery Auer, "Tom Corwin: 'King of the Stump,'" *The Quarterly Journal of Speech*, February, 1944, pp. 47-55.

bered as a joker[14] and repeatedly warned his friends, "for God's sake, never cultivate the reputation of being a wit."

Senator John Proctor Knott gave such a humorous and satirical speech[15] in the Senate on a proposed grant for a railroad into Duluth, Minnesota, that, although he won the argument, he ruined himself politically, for no one would ever again take him seriously.

Humor in its place is effective; it can serve also to lighten up an otherwise deadly serious situation. Shakespeare introduced humorous scenes into some of his deepest tragedies to provide relief for pent-up emotions. Unless it is your deliberate intention to establish yourself as a humorist, it will be better to employ it sparingly. Then when you do use it the effect will be all the more powerful.

The stimulation of attention and interest is as a rule the means to an end rather than the end in itself. It is very seldom that the speaker stops when he has secured the attention of his audience or even when he has aroused their interest. The basic purpose of these devices and methods is to get the audience to listen to him in order that he may more effectively accomplish his real purpose, which is to elicit the desired response. The one exception is perhaps the purely entertaining speech in which the sole objective is to maintain audience interest. In all other types of public address, attention and interest are aroused for objectives over and above themselves.

EXERCISES

1. Cite an instance in which two or more persons, though in the same situation, "saw" different things because of their differences in interests.
2. Present a speech in which you make an appeal to two or more of the factors listed on page 90. You do not need to indicate these

[14] J. Jeffery Auer, "Tom Corwin: Men Will Remember Me as a Joker," *The Quarterly Journal of Speech*, February, 1947, pp. 9-14.
[15] "The Glories of Duluth," *Classified Models of Speech Composition*, James Milton O'Neill (ed.), The Century Co., 1921, pp. 317-327.

factors by name; your appeal may be more effective if you do not. They should be readily identifiable, however.
3. Give a speech on some subject in which your listeners are not particularly interested; in fact, one they have not even been thinking about, so far as you know. Show how it is related to one or more of the factors listed on page 90, and attempt through those avenues to arouse interest. You must in your presentation give ample evidence of your own interest.
4. Give a talk on a generally serious subject, enlivening the discussion by the injection of occasional bits of humor. Be sure that your humor meets the requirements discussed in the text.
5. Bring to class six full-page magazine advertisements which have appealed to you. Discuss why you looked at them a second time, what particular factors of interest are used, and with what success.
6. Analyze the factors of interest in one of the speeches in a recent issue of *Vital Speeches*.
7. Give a five-minute speech in which you concentrate on making specific application of two or three of the factors of attention and interest. At the close of your speech your classmates will be asked to identify the factors you have used and to evaluate your effectiveness in using them.
8. Give a five- to ten-minute speech in which you stimulate interest at the opening by exhibiting a picture or an object of unusual nature. Be sure that your display has a direct bearing on the subject; show how it is of significance to your listeners.
9. Present an oral analysis of some interesting speech you have recently heard. Point out those aspects of the content of the speech which first drew your attention and then held your interest. Differentiate, if possible, between the factors of attention and those of interest. Note, second, what aspects of the speaker's presentation attracted your attention and interest. To what extent, would you estimate, did the manner of presentation add to or detract from your interest? Would the speech be as interesting if you were to read it to yourself as it was when you heard it? Try to analyze the reasons for your answer.
10. Study the speech, "Live Magnanimously," by President Charles Seymour (pp. 308-315). In consideration of the occasion on which this address was given, the audience, the speaker himself, determine the method or methods by which the speaker gets the attention of his audience or directs it to the subject which he is

to discuss. To what degree is it necessary that he use attention-getting devices? Second, determine the methods by which the speaker maintains the attention of his listeners. Third, determine the specific interests of his audience to which he appeals. How are these interests related to his use of attention-getting techniques?

11. Discussion questions for class symposiums:
   a. How does magazine advertising utilize the factors of attention and interest? Does it use techniques not available to the speaker? Have you observed instances of the use of these techniques in ways that may have been misleading or otherwise unethical?
   b. How does the speaker utilize techniques of gaining attention and interest not available to the magazine advertiser?
   c. Are there significant differences in the speaker's and the radio advertiser's use of attention- and interest-gaining techniques when appearing directly before the audience?
   d. Discuss in symposium the methods of stimulating interest in a subject which is ordinarily thought to be dull and uninteresting.
   e. What part can the listeners play in arousing interest in a speech?

12. The lyceum and chautauqua lectures of several years ago revealed great skill on the part of the speakers in gaining and holding the interest of their listeners. A speaker might present the same address to from fifty to a hundred audiences. Study one of the following named speeches (or a similar talk) and make a written analysis of the factors of attention and interest used. Remember that these talks were prepared for audiences of several years ago, but many of them contain ideas that are still worth consideration:
   a. William Jennings Bryan, "The Prince of Peace," *Modern Eloquence*, Ashley Thorndike (ed.), Modern Eloquence Corp., 1923, vol. VIII, pp. 68-88. (You may have a different edition of *Modern Eloquence* in your library; check the volume on "Famous Lectures.")
   b. Robert Jones Burdette, "The Rise and Fall of the Moustache," *Modern Eloquence*, vol. VIII, pp. 102-130.
   c. Mark Twain, "The Sandwich Islands," *Modern Eloquence*, vol. VIII, pp. 131-168.
   d. Russell H. Conwell, "Acres of Diamonds," *Modern Eloquence*, vol. VIII, pp. 138-168. This speech is found in many other collections.

ATTENTION AND INTEREST

    e. Thomas H. Huxley, "On a Piece of Chalk," *Modern Eloquence*, vol. VIII, pp. 215-236.
    f. Wendell Phillips, "The Lost Arts," *Modern Eloquence*, vol. VIII, pp. 276-290. This address is found in many other collections.
    g. Roe Fulkerson, "Inheritance Tax," *Classified Speech Models*, William Norwood Brigance (ed.), Appleton-Century-Crofts, Inc., 1928, pp. 407-413.
    h. Thomas DeWitt Talmage, "Big Blunders," *Classified Models of Speech Composition*, James Milton O'Neill (ed.), The Century Co., 1921, pp. 828-844.

13. Attention and interest can be evaluated only in terms of the audience. Any appeals to interest, any attempts to stimulate attention, must consider the listeners in relation to the total situation. Study the situations as they are described in connection with the speeches listed in some current collection, such as Baird's *Representative American Speeches* or *Vital Speeches of the Day*. Determine the basic interests of the listeners on those occasions and the extent to which the speaker made use of those interests. Were dormant interests stimulated, or were the appeals to already active interests? What specific techniques were employed by the speaker in stimulating attention and arousing interest or in maintaining it?

SUPPLEMENTARY READINGS

1. Brigance, William Norwood, *Speech Composition*, F. S. Crofts & Co., 1937, pp. 123-133.
2. Bryant, Donald C., and Wallace, Karl R., *Fundamentals of Public Speaking*, Appleton-Century-Crofts, Inc., 1947, pp. 94-118.
3. Gray, Giles Wilkeson, and Wise, Claude Merton, *The Bases of Speech*, Harper & Brothers, rev. ed., 1946, pp. 374-380.
4. Monroe, Alan H., *Principles and Types of Speech*, Scott, Foresman & Company, 3rd ed., 1949, chap. 13, "Choosing Material that Will Hold Attention," pp. 249-260.
5. Oliver, Robert T., *The Psychology of Persuasive Speech*, Longmans, Green & Co., Inc., 1945, chap. VII, "Attention," pp. 199-226.
6. Oliver, Robert T., Cortright, Rupert L., and Hager, Cyril D., *The New Training for Effective Speech*, The Dryden Press, Inc., 1946, chap. 13, "Interesting the Audience," pp. 282-306.
7. Overstreet, H. A., *Influencing Human Behavior*, W. W. Norton & Company, 1925, chap. I, "The Key Problem, Capturing the At-

tention," pp. 9-27; chap. VI, "Crossing the Interest Deadline," pp. 110-124.
8. Parrish, Wayland Maxfield, *Speaking in Public*, Charles Scribner's Sons, 1947, pp. 346-373.
9. Phillips, Arthur Edward, *Effective Speaking*, The Newton Company, 1908, chap. VI, "Entertainment and the Factors of Interestingness," pp. 63-78.
10. Williamson, Arleigh B., Fritz, Charles A., and Ross, Harold Raymond, *Speaking in Public*, Prentice-Hall, Inc., 2nd ed., 1948, pp. 20-46.
11. Winans, James A., *Speech-Making*, Appleton-Century-Crofts, Inc., 1938, chap. VII, "Interest," pp. 131-154; chap. VIII, "Methods of Interesting," pp. 155-179.
12. Yeager, Willard Hayes, *Effective Speaking for Every Occasion*, Prentice-Hall, Inc., 1940, chap. 2, "Audience Interest and Speech Composition," pp. 36-77.

CHAPTER V

Occasion and Audience

YOUR success in public speaking will rest many times upon your ability to understand the speech situation and upon your shrewdness in adapting your materials to its peculiar requirements. An effective speech is timely and appropriate for the occasion. In addition, it appeals to the listeners and promises satisfaction for their desires, their moods, their biases, and their preferences.

Study of the occasion and the audience is therefore a necessary early step in planning a speech. In most instances it is the first step. On the basis of what you learn about your audience and the occasion you will determine your goals, frame the thesis or central thought, select the pattern of development, weigh the supporting material, and choose the language.

OCCASION

The times and places men speak are legion. They make talks on the slightest provocation. Inaugurations, farewells, political rallies, meetings of service clubs, banquets, community forums, barbecues, funerals, prayer meetings, and worship services are all occasions for speeches. Each event requires a different approach, different subject matter, and a different delivery. In choosing your strategy, weigh the following elements of the occasion: the time of the meeting, the assembly place, the prevailing customs of the locality, and the purpose of the gathering.

The exact hour of your appearance may make considerable difference in your success. What immediately precedes and follows your speech should also be weighed thoughtfully. But your analysis may not stop here; it may consider the broad historical trends which have given rise to the assembly. For this reason it is immediately apparent why a knowledge of history may be of great advantage to you. Some of our greatest speakers have been thorough students of history, sometimes spending months, even years, in acquiring insight into the background of an occasion. When he delivered his address at Plymouth, Massachusetts, December 22, 1820, Webster, for example, was well aware of the significance of commemorating the landing of the Pilgrims. With carefully selected evidence, a magnificent manner, and elevated language, he inspired his fellow citizens also to take pride in that two-hundredth anniversary.

Speaking at Cooper Union in New York, February 27, 1860, Abraham Lincoln was conscious of the historical forces at work, particularly in the North. He recognized that the opportunity for a Western lawyer to address influential New Yorkers did not come often. Contrary to his practice in some of his earlier speeches, he now marshalled many facts with which to persuade his educated Eastern listeners. His speech was successful because he adapted it to that occasion.

In studying the time, consider such questions as these:

1. What are the broad historical antecedents of the speech?
   a. Political?
   b. Economic?
   c. Religious?
2. What immediate past events give rise to the meeting?
   a. Are these known to the audience?
   b. Has the program committee or chairman been aware of these in calling the meeting?
3. How does the time of the meeting affect the speaker and the audience?
   a. Is it a convenient time?
   b. How does the time affect the speaker?
   c. How does it affect the auditors?
      (1) Alert?
      (2) Sleepy?
      (3) Tired?
      (4) Bored?
      (5) Neutral or passive?

The importance of giving careful thought to the place in which you are to speak cannot be overstressed. The physical surroundings may be an asset or a liability. One place may require restraint and awe, while a second may call for frivolity and gaiety. The church, a historical landmark, a cemetery, or a lodge room often inspires contemplative silence. On the other hand, the stadium, the opera house, the gymnasium-auditorium may stimulate incessant chatter and laughter. Poor ventilation may contribute to drowsiness and inattentiveness. The size of the place, its acoustical properties, and the comfort of the audience must be carefully studied by the speaker.

Consider for a moment how the physical surroundings affected Lincoln when he spoke at Gettysburg, Pennsylvania, November 19, 1863.

On the credit side of the ledger, Lincoln, of course, talked to an audience who deeply revered the setting. On that site Confederate and Union armies had engaged in a fierce battle and had buried there thousands of their finest young men. Those present had come to dedicate a national cemetery. During the four minutes he spoke, Lincoln made three references to the place, referring to it as "a great battlefield of that war," "a portion of that field," and "this ground." He closely associated his remarks with "this ground" in order to heighten the emotional effect of his speech.

But what difficulties did the surroundings provide? Lincoln spoke outdoors to a crowd of fifteen to thirty thousand, most of whom were standing and many of whom could not push close enough to the speakers' stand to hear or even to see the President. The nature of the gathering and the surroundings meant that persons could wander away from the area without embarrassment. In addition to these difficulties, already many were no doubt weary of listening to Edward Everett, who, preceding Lincoln, had talked for over two hours. It goes without saying that these were challenging circumstances, some of which, incidentally, Lincoln could not overcome.

As a speaker, you must decide what the place of the meeting requires of you. In a small room, you must exercise restraint and finesse, keeping your voice conversational and quiet, your gestures few in number, and your movements subdued. Since there are probably fewer distracting influences in a small room than elsewhere, you can present your material more concisely. To be effective in a larger room or in an outdoor situation, you must be more vigorous and energetic, especially if no public-address system is available. You must use more movement, broader gestures, and an amplified conversational tone. Your rate of speaking should necessarily be slower. The more difficult

---

TYPES OF AUDIENCES

Top, a casual gathering: passersby stop momentarily to listen to the speaker. Center, a conversational group: workmen talk about the political situation. Bottom, a discussional group: directors of Chamber of Commerce examine and discuss plans for new swimming pool. (Photos, Black Star.)

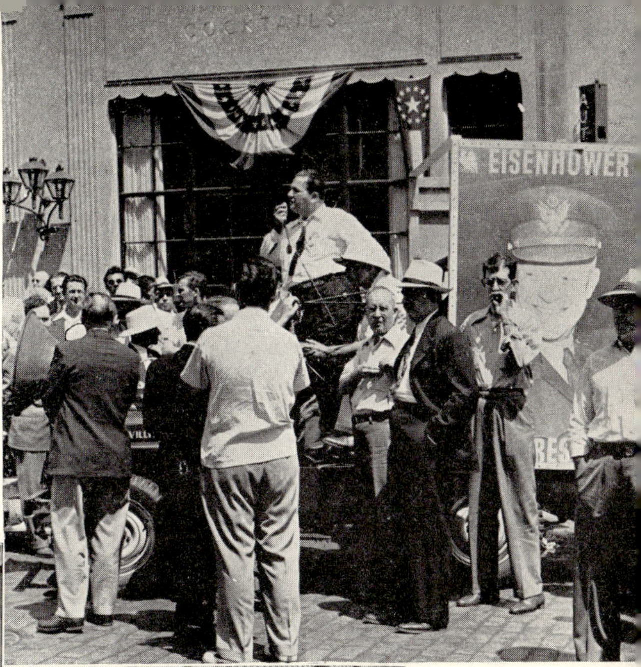
COCKTAILS
EISENHOWER

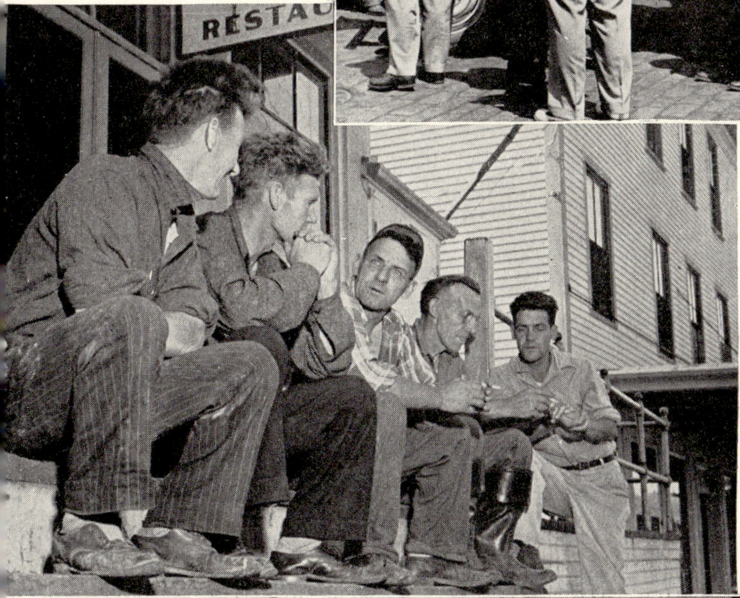
RESTAU

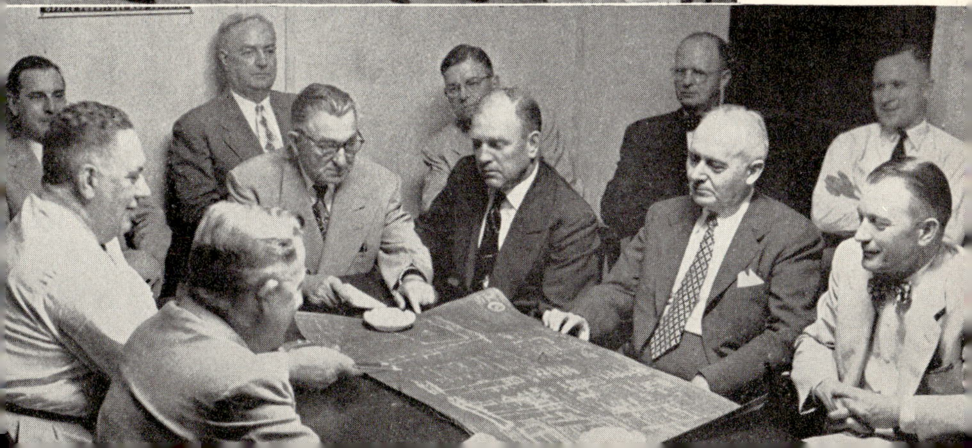

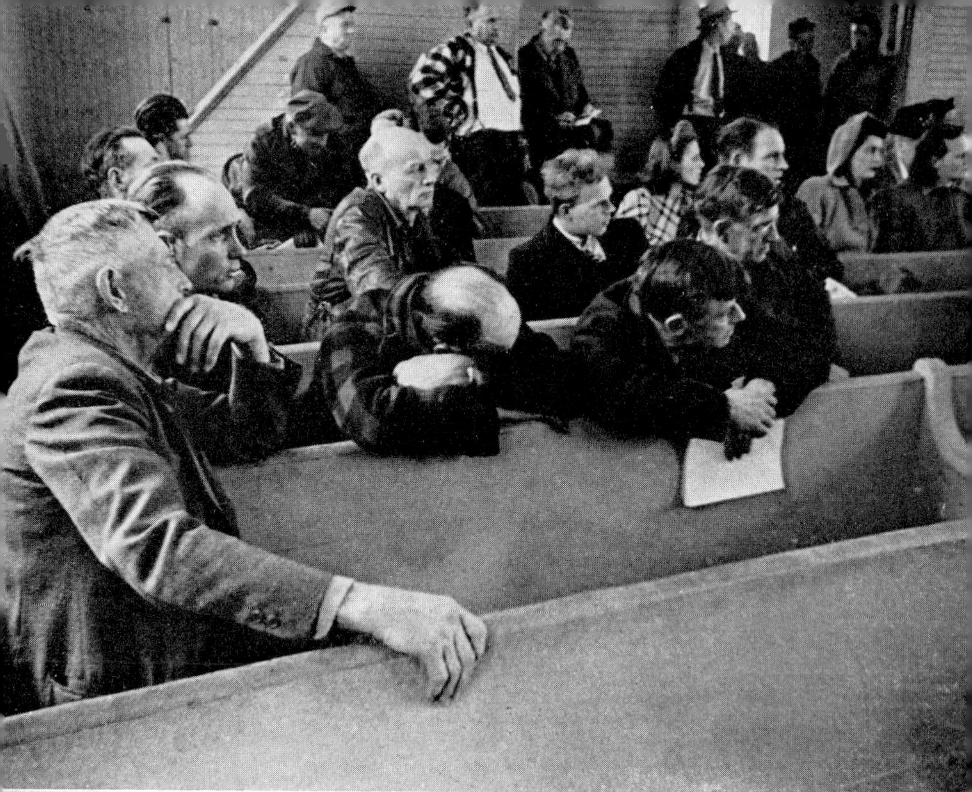

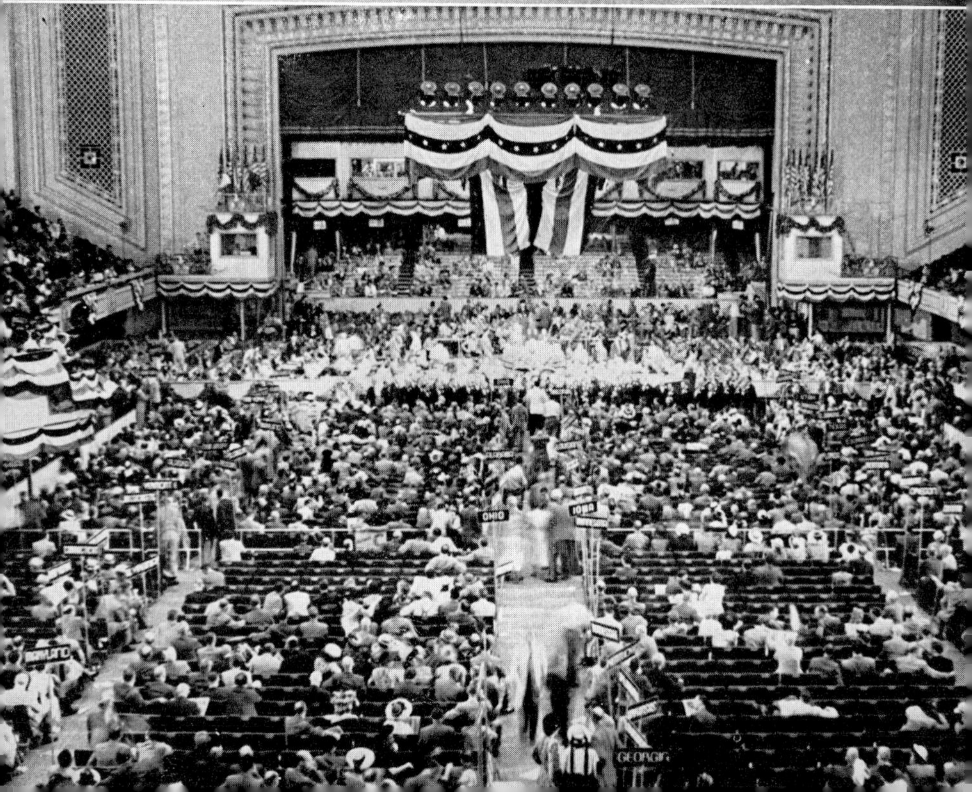
OHIO
IOWA
GEORGIA

OCCASION AND AUDIENCE

speaking situations will require more thought breaks. They may require greater use of humor, and more illustrations and examples.

Study carefully *where* your speech is to be delivered. Take an inventory of the items suggested below:

1. Where is the speech to be delivered?
   a. Is the speech to be delivered indoors or outdoors?
   b. Is the meeting place famous (or infamous)?
      (1) Have important events occurred there?
      (2) What important speakers have spoken there?
      (3) How familiar is the audience with this place?
   c. In what kind of community is the meeting place located?
      (1) Rural or urban?
      (2) Industrial or residential?
         (a) Cottages or mansions?
      (3) Business district or suburb?
   d. What are the taboos of the place?
   e. Is it a "hired" hall, a permanent meeting place, or a community center?
2. What will be the comfort of the auditors?
   a. Will they sit, stand, or both?
   b. Will they be crowded or scattered?
   c. Will they be confined to a small area?
   d. Will there be adequate ventilation?
      (1) Air conditioning?
      (2) Fans?
   e. How will the surroundings influence the auditors?
      (1) Are there distractions with which to compete?
      (2) Are the surroundings pleasant or unpleasant?
      (3) Will all auditors see the speaker with ease?
3. What are the lighting facilities?
   a. Will the speaker be able to see facial reactions of the listeners?

TYPES OF AUDIENCES: INACTIVE AUDIENCE

The upper picture shows members of an audience who are willing to listen but have no intention to act. At the moment the lower picture was taken, members of the Republican National Convention were inactive. Notice scattered auditors and apparent lack of interest. (Photos, Black Star.)

  b. Will the room be darkened?
  c. Will natural or artificial lighting be used?
  d. Will footlights or a spotlight be used on the speaker?
 4. What are the acoustical problems facing the speaker?
  a. Will a public-address system be available?
  b. Will the speech be broadcast or recorded as it is being presented?
  c. Is the place acoustically treated?
  d. Will there be disturbing reverberations?
 5. What are the comforts of the speaker?
  a. Is there to be a lectern?
  b. Is the speaker to be above or below the auditors?
  c. Are the listeners directly in front or on all sides of the speaker?

  The prevailing customs you should note are those which dictate what you may or may not do as a public speaker. Think for a moment about the wide difference in the conduct of the various religious groups. In some church buildings the men wear hats; in others the practice is very much out of place. Clergymen of one faith prefer to be called Father, others insist on Reverend, while the Quakers ask that their leaders be addressed simply as Mister. Some congregations would be shocked if their pastor did not speak from the pulpit in a subdued, mystical manner; others expect much pounding and shouting. Equally wide differences can be found in the practices of secular groups. These habit patterns may be dictated by the community as a whole, by the nature of the occasion, or by the place of assembly. Good advice is "When in Rome, do as the Romans do."

  Of value in discovering "what the Romans do" are the following questions:

1. What is considered appropriate public-speaking practice?
 a. With reference to dress?
 b. With reference to delivery?
 c. With reference to language and diction?
2. What is the audience etiquette?
3. What is the custom with reference to admissions and honorarium?
 a. Is an admission to be charged?
 b. Will the speaker receive an honorarium?
  (1) Is this the usual or a greater amount?

4. Is the group regulated by parliamentary laws?
    a. Robert's Rules of Order?
    b. Individual bylaws?
    c. Informal rules?
    d. No rules?
    e. Mob rule?

The purpose for which the meeting is called may place additional restrictions upon you as a speaker. If you speak to a businessmen's luncheon club, you will probably find that fellowship, fun, and good food prevail. The members of a trade union may assemble in an angry mood to discuss a violation of contract, strike strategy, or grievances against a foreman.

Contrast the difference in purpose of a Sunday-morning worship service and a social meeting of a church brotherhood. In the former, speaker and the audience are required to follow a ritual. In the latter, the same auditors may meet in the same building (in a different room), but they feel none of the restraints of the former meeting.

In your analysis of the purpose of the meeting, consider the questions given below. Many of these will overlap with queries given later under audience analysis:

1. Is it a regular or called meeting?
    a. Is the purpose of the meeting well known to the auditors?
    b. Is there general agreement on the advisability of the goal?
2. Who formulated the goal of the meeting?
    a. Did the group participate in its formulation?
    b. Did a select group decide on the goal?
    c. Did some outside source determine the goal?
    d. Did you participate in its formulation?
3. Is instruction or training a goal of the meeting?
    a. Is instruction to be administered to all or some?
    b. Has instruction been a previous goal?
    c. Is the speaker to help in giving instruction?
4. Is entertainment of the auditors a goal?
    a. Is it to be the broad, slapstick type?
    b. Do they expect restraint and dignity?
5. Does the meeting commemorate or celebrate an important event?

a. Is the event related to the history of the group?
   (1) To other similar groups?
   (2) Only to this group?
b. Did the auditors participate in the revered event?
c. What are their sources of information about the event?
6. Is the purpose of the meeting associated with persuasion?
   a. What kind of change is expected?
      (1) Covert?
      (2) Overt?
   b. Does the audience expect to profit from the meeting?
   c. How is the purpose related to your betterment?

AUDIENCE

What to say and how to say it are related to "where," "when," and "to whom." In their famous debates in 1858 for the Illinois senatorship, Lincoln and Douglas were adroit in altering their arguments as they moved from antislave northern to proslave southern Illinois and back again. The state of Louisiana offers a real challenge to the stump speaker because northern Louisiana differs markedly from the southern French parishes. Furthermore, to employ the same arguments and techniques in the hill country beyond the Red River and in cosmopolitan New Orleans would be to invite failure. "The first simple rule in all good speaking, in any situation," advises Overstreet, "is: think of your audience."[1]

Although Dr. Russell Conwell presented his "Acres of Diamonds" over sixty-one hundred times over a period of fifty years, he never lost sight in all that time of the importance of studying his immediate listeners and then attempting to adapt his presentation to the peculiar requirements of the situation. Said Conwell,

This lecture has been delivered under these circumstances: I visit a town or city, and try to arrive there early enough to see the postmaster, the barber, the keeper of the hotel, the principal of the schools, and the ministers of some of the churches, and then go into

[1] H. A. Overstreet, *Influencing Human Behavior*, W. W. Norton & Company, 1925, pp. 72-73.

some of the factories and stores, and talk with the people, and get into sympathy with the local conditions of that town or city and see what has been their history, what opportunities they had, and what they had failed to do—and every town fails to do something—and then go to those people about the subjects which applied to their locality.[2]

Never before our time has the speaker had available so much information, so many techniques, or so much help. The social psychologist, the sociologist, and the geographer, with their extensive studies of group conduct, population trends, attitudes, and prejudices, make valuable allies. The public-opinion poll and consumer's research yield much information that you can often utilize.

Although you may not have the resources or the time to conduct elaborate studies or to hire the services of the professional pollster, you can learn much from them. The public-opinion polls published in the newspapers and magazines give many hints concerning trends in popular thinking on a wide variety of subjects.[3]

For a political unit as small as the township or ward, the state and federal census reports give detailed population statistics relative to age, sex, education, occupation, racial background, religious affiliation, school attendance, illiteracy, and many other related topics. Many times when political issues are analyzed, election returns serve as another valuable source. In addition, the *Statistical Abstract,* the *World Almanac,* and *Information Please Almanac* may be helpful.

In some cases the local newspapers or magazines give information valuable in audience analysis. Before you formulate opinions you of course should ascertain the political bias of the editor as well as the unique features of the publication, and you should remember that newspapers mold as well as reflect local attitudes. The editorial page will contain many clues concerning the nature

[2] Russell H. Conwell, *Acres of Diamonds*, Harper & Brothers, 1915, p. 2.
[3] Each week Gallup has four releases to one hundred twenty-six newspapers. *Time,* May 3, 1948, p. 21.

and policy of a paper. One newspaper should be checked against other papers and against additional sources and observers.

In every community there are key persons whose judgment regarding the community mores and local attitudes is astute and trustworthy. On many occasions such persons will be your principal source of information about what is expected of you and about what is appropriate. Ordinarily, the program chairman, the outstanding citizen, a speaker who has previously addressed the group, the committee in charge, or the officers will make valuable informants. The more individuals you consult, the more likely you are to make an accurate judgment about your audience.

The discussion above no doubt gives the impression that audience analysis is an endless and tedious task. Indeed, your conclusion is correct. Naturally, for the five-minute class performance or an appearance before a luncheon club, a detailed study is probably unwarranted. Some speaking situations will necessitate consulting many sources, while others may be handled successfully if you talk with a few persons in the community. *But the resourceful speaker is constantly alert to signs indicating shifts in opinion. Flexibility* and *adaptability* are important qualities of the effective speaker.

AUDIENCE ANALYSIS

The case of effective speaking may be put into a single sentence: "You must speak in terms of people's wants." The principle enunciated is not new; indeed, it dates back almost to the beginning of what we sometimes call *human relations*. Persons will listen, will consider, and will act if a proposal promises satisfaction of their wants. Audience analysis resolves, therefore, into an attempt to determine the motivation of the group and what of these aspects can be ultilized in a given speech:

1. What is the nature of the audience?
2. What is the basis for assembling?
3. In what ways are the auditors homogeneous?
4. What are the fixed attitudes of the group?

5. What does the audience know about you?
6. What does the audience know about your subject?
7. Does a division of opinion exist on your subject?

What Is the Nature of the Audience?

Speaking of the audience in this sense we are referring to those persons who constitute your listeners. In the face-to-face situation you have a visible audience, those within the natural or amplified range of your voice. For classroom performance your auditors will be your fellow students. On other occasions you may have for a visible audience a Rotary Club, a jury, a community forum, the Ladies Aid, or a trade-union council.

The printing press, the motion picture, the radio, and television have made possible what may be called a *greater audience* or an absent audience, consisting of those persons who hear the speech by radio or read it. Describing this group, Hollingworth points out, "There is of course usually no aggregation or congregation of people involved, and hence the group phenomena which an assembled audience may display will be missing."[4] On many occasions today this greater audience dwarfs the importance and size of the immediate audience. On the evening of May 27, 1941, President Franklin Roosevelt spoke to an immediate, select audience of three hundred persons assembled at the White House. Before him were Western Hemisphere diplomats and their families, but out on the airways an estimated sixty-five million tuned in to listen. Later the same speech was broadcast by short wave in fourteen languages to additional millions abroad.[5]

Former Prime Minister Winston Churchill journeyed thousands of miles to present an address at small Westminster College at Fulton, Missouri. His visible audience was a handful

[4] H. L. Hollingworth, *The Psychology of the Audience*, American Book Company, 1935, p. 26.
[5] Franklin Delano Roosevelt, "A State of Emergency Exists," *Representative American Speeches: 1940-1941*, A. Craig Baird (ed.), The H. W. Wilson Company, 1941, pp. 57-74.

of Middle Westerners, but his greater audience extended around the world. His English colleagues were definitely interested in what he said. He no doubt had a small but select audience in the Russian Kremlin. Other diplomats and thousands of John Does the world over studied that speech, for it predicted the future attitude of Russia and indicated what he thought would be the best strategy of the non-Communist world, particularly the English-speaking world.[6]

The radio audience may be augmented by millions who gain their impressions by what they read on the printed page. Unfortunately, many of these readers never see a full text of the speaker's remarks; consequently, in some cases they read only garbled half statements or whatever the censors permit to slip through. Quotation marks frequently are omitted; a reporter or an editor may do a thorough "rewrite."[7] Nevertheless, this reading audience is of great significance to many speakers.

Some speakers actually project their audiences into the future by addressing their remarks to posterity. What the historians will say becomes important to many, particularly if they imagine that "the halo of greatness" is descending upon them. For this reason our congressmen many times take particular care to revise what appears in the *Congressional Record*.[8] A senator or representative may frankly admit in opening that he intends his remarks "for the record," meaning that he wants a printed state-

---

[6] Winston Churchill, "The Sinews of Peace," delivered March 5, 1946, found in *Representative American Speeches: 1945-1946*, pp. 20-32.

[7] See Walter Lippmann, *Public Opinion*, Harcourt, Brace and Company, Inc., 1922, chap. 5.

[8] Zon Robinson, "The Accuracy With Which Speeches Are Reported in the Congressional Record," *Eastern Public Speaking Conference 1940*, Harold F. Harding (ed.), The H. W. Wilson Company, 1940, pp. 290-300.

TYPES OF AUDIENCES: SELECTED AUDIENCE

The first picture shows a ministerial group listening to a report by one of its members. The second picture shows internes listening to a professor of surgery. (Photos, Black Star and L.S.U. Alumni News.)

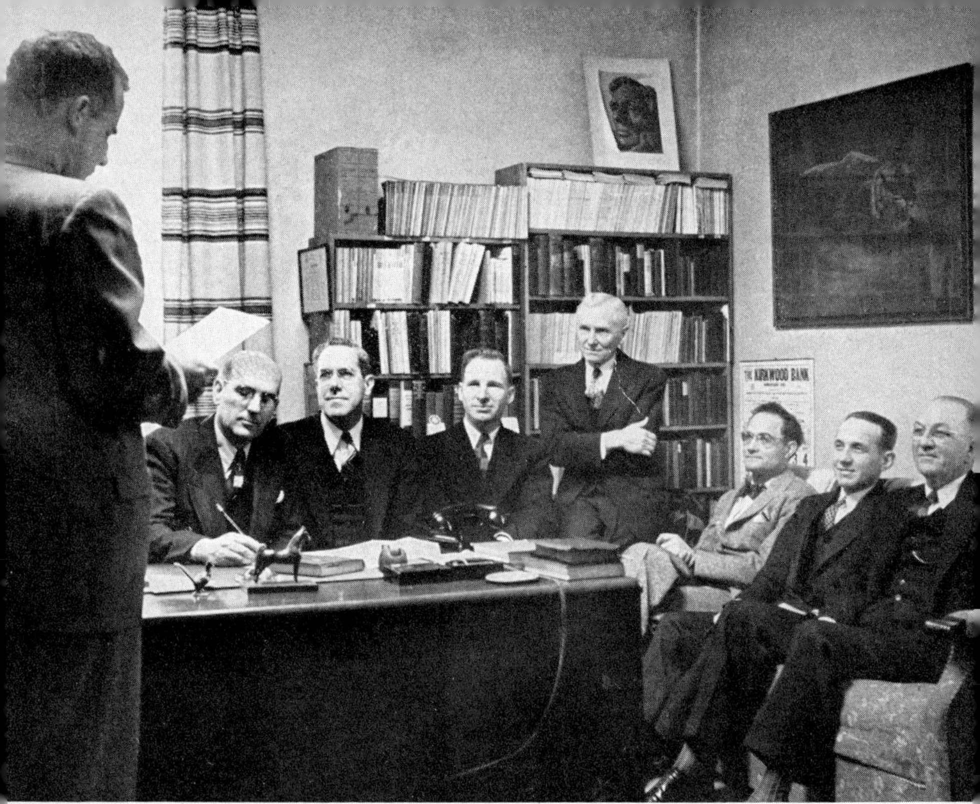
THE KIRKWOOD BANK

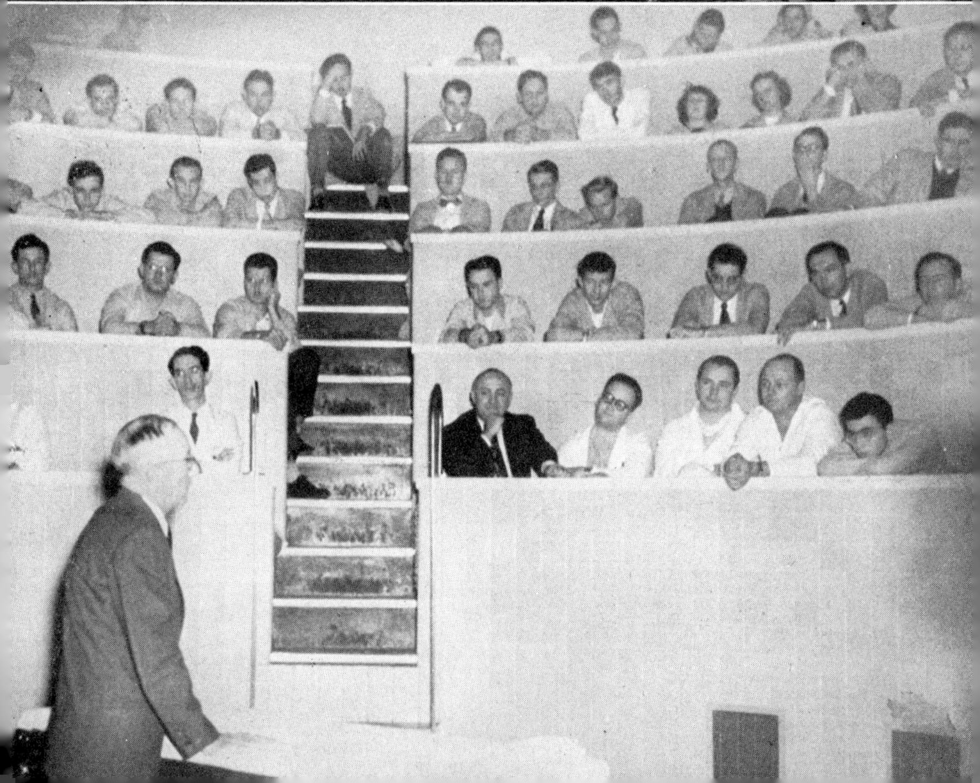

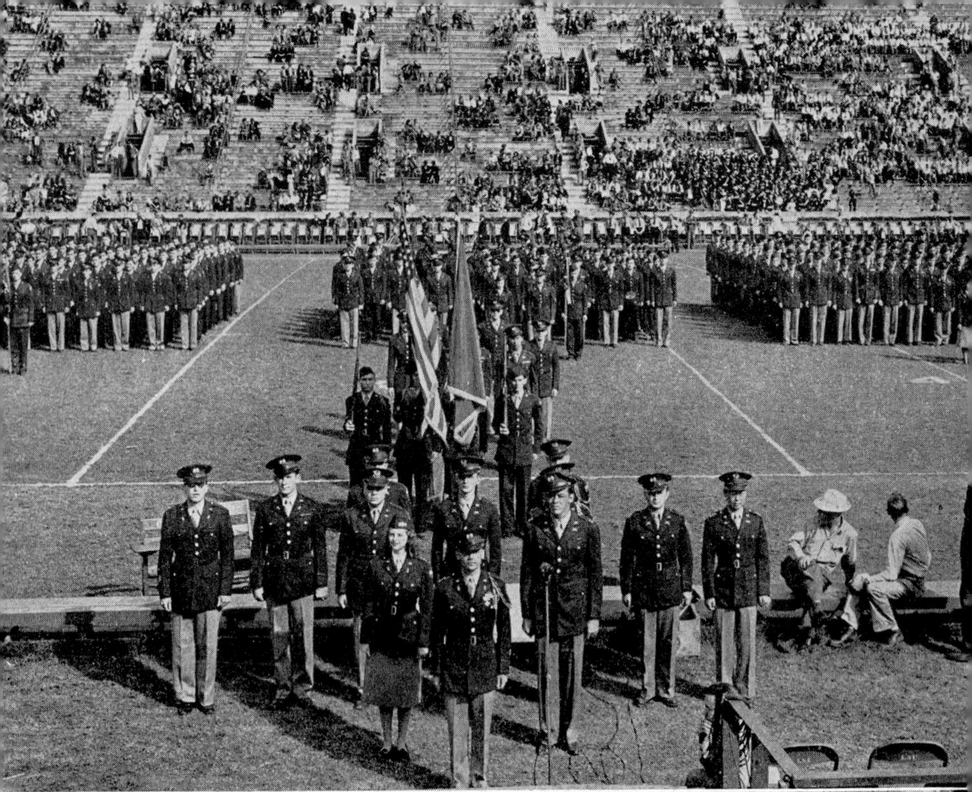

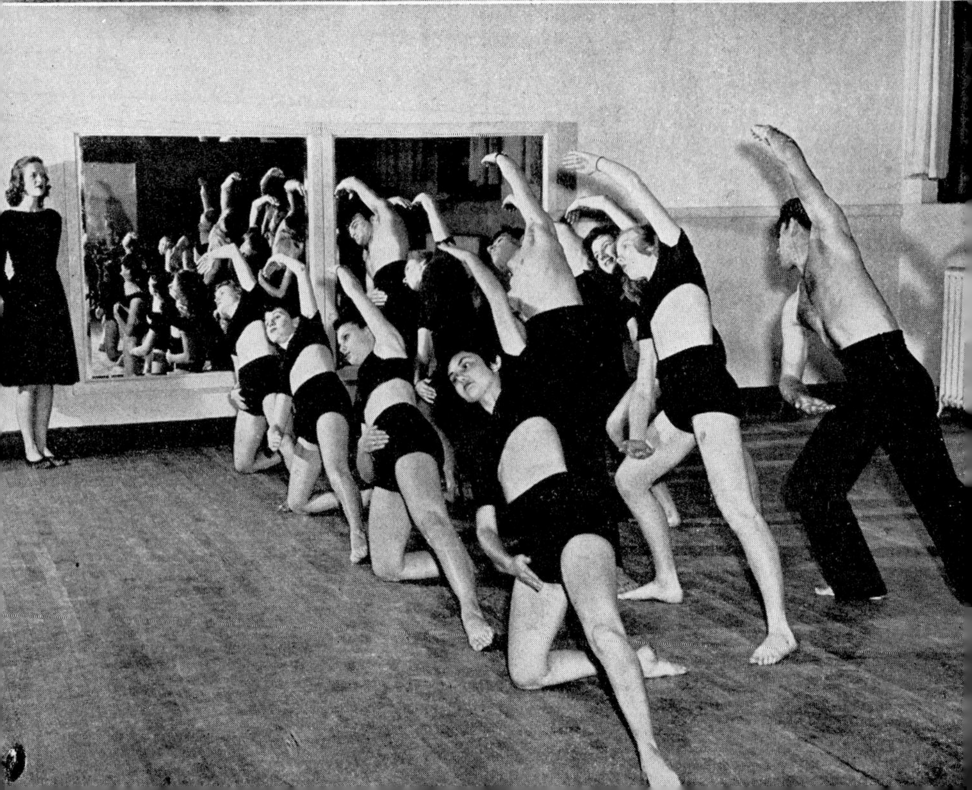

ment upon which to be judged at a later date—perhaps at the next election or even by generations unborn.

To summarize, your audience may include those persons in the immediate assembly and those reached through the press, radio, or television. Just as it cannot be limited in place, neither can the audience be limited in time; the speaker may even address his remarks to the reader of the future.

What Is the Basis for Assembling?

A group of persons does not congregate or remain assembled as a rule by mere chance or accident. Some motivating force in the speaking situation pulls them together and unites them into what we commonly refer to by the collective noun *audience*.

Persons may attend a lecture for the purpose of satisfying their curiosity about the speaker. For this reason, public figures often command large lecture fees, not because they can speak effectively but because at the moment they bask in public attention. On other occasions auditors may assemble because they are loyal or obligated to an organization such as Rotary, Lions, and Kiwanis. Another group, a student body, for example, may meet because it is commanded to be present.

To be successful, the speaker must consider carefully these cohesive forces, the degree of organization that has taken place, and the group anticipations. As a speaker, you must decide why the auditors have come to the meeting and why they remain.

The casual or spontaneous group possesses the lowest degree of integration and organization, for the individual members possess few common grounds of understanding or sympathy. The membership is determined almost entirely by chance. The street-

---

TYPES OF AUDIENCES: CONCERTED GROUP

Top, the military unit responds immediately to a command given by officer in charge. Bottom, modern dance class executes movements when instructor gives command. (Photos, L.S.U. Alumni News.)

corner gathering, observers of an unusual window display, commuters waiting in a subway station, or people huddled together in the same bomb shelter are casual or spontaneous groups. To transform a group of this kind into an audience presents a great challenge to the speaker, for he has no outside aids to mold them into an integrated unit. He must gain a hearing, enlist attention, and develop interest in the subject before he can hope to present his main thoughts.

The discussional or conversational group cannot be considered an audience in the usual sense of the word, for each member looks upon himself as a participant or speaker with an equal right to speak at any moment he wishes to break into the discussion. When he is not speaking, he is, of course, an auditor; but he is hesitant to let anyone monopolize the time.

Any attempt to take the floor is regarded as a breach of etiquette. To transform a discussion group into an audience, the speaker must gain the consent of the other members.

The inactive audience, unlike the first two groups, is bound together by the willingness of its members to recognize and give attention to something—whether it be a speaker, a singer, a juggling act, or a play. Members regard themselves as onlookers and listeners, not speakers nor participants.

Ordinarily they come with the purpose of remaining passive, of being spectators, of remaining inactive and sometimes even inert. The lyceum, the dinner club, the theater crowd, and some classes are inactive groups. After the auditors come and pay whatever admission there is, they expect to be entertained.

With an inactive group, the speaker is assured of an initial hearing; consequently, holding attention and directing interest are less of a problem than with the casual group. If the speaker expects more, he must work for it. Something about the speaker, the occasion, or the subject has attracted the auditors to the meeting place and makes them ready to listen. Discovery of this something is the key to reaching this group. Either this anticipation must be satisfied, or something more urgent must be substituted.

The selected audience possesses greater unity and organization than the previous type because there is a common basis for membership in the group. The P.T.A., a lodge, a patriotic society, or an alumni group are typical examples. Selectivity and membership requirements result in more homogeneity, thus simplifying somewhat the speaker's problem. Group objectives further unite the group and offer the speaker a common ground upon which to reach the members. If you ally yourself and your cause with these ideals, symbols, and taboos, you are assured of interest and attention, and you are probably ready to present your analysis or course of action.

The concerted audience is usually characterized by previous training, complete orientation, and rigid discipline. The athletic team, the military unit, and the airplane crew have been regimented. An order from the leader is sufficient to secure action without question or hesitation. Since freedom of choice is not a possibility, this type ordinarily falls beyond the realm of persuasion.

The basis of assembling will frequently determine your approach and the materials that are necessary. Weigh carefully the following questions:

1. Did the auditors assemble to hear you as a speaker?
    a. Are they interested in you because of your reputation?
    b. Do they want to hear you discuss your subject?
    c. Do they want to hear other auditors question you?
        (1) Are they interested in additional information?
        (2) Do they want to see you "put on the spot"?
2. Did they assemble because of the occasion?
    a. Do they come to celebrate a holiday or an event?
    b. Do they come to pay homage to a hero?
    c. Do they come to show respect to the group?
3. Is attendance of the group a matter of habit?
    a. Is it a regularly scheduled meeting?
    b. Is it a called meeting?

4. Is attendance compulsory?
   a. Who required attendance?
   b. What are the penalties for nonattendance?
5. Is attendance motivated by some other factor?
   a. Do the people come to hear another speaker?
   b. Are they present to see a famous (or infamous) person?
   c. Are they present to participate in group activities?
      (1) Discussion?
      (2) Singing?
      (3) Refreshments?
      (4) Good fellowship?

In What Ways Are Your Auditors Homogeneous?

Many persons speak of audience adjustment as if the speaker's task were simply to adapt his materials to the group as a whole. But as Hollingworth puts it, ". . . the audience is an unreal abstraction."[9] Certainly a number of persons meeting together do not lose their identity and fuse into a single entity with an oversoul or superpersonality. They may keep their individuality, or most likely they may group themselves around certain conditioners of opinion. Adjustment to each individual is highly desirable but impossible if the gathering is of large size. You must adapt your materials and appeal to certain groupings or segments of those present. Accomplishment of this task depends upon learning in what respect your listeners are homogeneous. Polling agencies provide us with a convenient list of topics around which they believe people group themselves. They insist that the important conditioners of opinion are occupational groups, sex, age, place of residence, education, income level, race, religion, and political preference.[10]

You therefore will do well to find the answers to the following questions:

1. What are the predominant characteristics of the majority of the prospective audience?
   a. Is the audience to be composed of men, women, or both?

[9] Hollingworth, *op. cit.*, p. 27.
[10] George Gallup, *A Guide to Public Opinion Polls,* Princeton University Press, 1948, pp. 31-33.

b. What are the age characteristics?
    (1) Juvenile?
    (2) Young adult?
    (3) Middle age?
    (4) Old age?
    (5) Mixed?
c. Where do the majority of the members of the audience live?
    (1) Large city?
    (2) Suburban area?
    (3) Village?
    (4) Rural area?
    (5) Mixed?
d. What is the average income of the listeners?
    (1) Wealthy?
    (2) Average?
    (3) Poor?
    (4) On relief?
    (5) Mixed?
e. What are the racial characteristics?
    (1) Foreign born or first-generation Americans?
    (2) Colored?
    (3) White?
    (4) Minority group?
    (5) Mixed?
f. What are the religious characteristics?
    (1) Protestant?
        (a) Fundamentalists?
        (b) Modernists?
    (2) Catholic?
    (3) Non-Christian?
g. What are the political affiliations?
    (1) Democrats?
        (a) Northern?
        (b) Southern?
    (2) Republicans?
    (3) Third-party groups?
    (4) Independents?
    (5) Mixed?
2. What other characteristics might be significant in influencing opinions?
    a. Secret societies?
    b. Fraternal affiliations?

What Are the Fixed Attitudes Toward Your Subject?

We all possess our wishes, our preferences, our moods, our biases, our desires, our quirks, and our inclinations. Because of our previous environment, we have developed certain fixed attitudes toward most issues, most institutions, and most people. The speaker cannot afford to ignore these sets of attitudes. In fact, on the basis of how we feel about certain political, social, economic, or religious questions, we are labeled as radicals, moderates, or conservatives. Our attitudes on national defense are illustrative of fixed attitudes. If you live on the West Coast, you no doubt are much interested in Pearl Harbor as a bastion of defense. If you reside on the Atlantic seaboard, you may think of England in this regard. But if you live in the great Corn Belt, you regard the great expanses of water as ample protection from attack from either Asia or Europe. Of course, if you have studied the possibilities of air power and the great-circle route, you may think all these points of view are obsolete. Each case, however, has its set of fixed attitudes with reference to defense.

The speaker must weigh carefully what the fixed attitudes are with reference to his subject. Your success will depend upon how well you align your objectives with these predispositions. When he spoke at the opening of the Cotton State and Industrial Exposition at Atlanta in 1895, Booker T. Washington, famous Negro educator, showed great sagacity in adapting his materials to the fixed attitudes on race which existed in Georgia at that time. His plea was not for "social equality" but for recognition of the Negro's worth to the South. He avoided the controversial issue and made his plea for something on which each group could agree. He aligned his argument with the fixed attitudes of his audience.

When you prepare a speech, give careful thought to how you make use of fixed attitudes in achieving your goal.

What Does the Audience Know About You?

If you are to be effective, you must also attempt to ascertain what your reputation is with your hearers and how the audience has arrived at its conclusions. On the basis of what you learn, you must determine the kind, the amount, and the type of personal appeal (ethical proof) essential for the success of your speech.

When he arose to deliver his Bunker Hill oration,[11] Daniel Webster found little need to establish himself with his listeners, for he knew that those present held him in high esteem. On that occasion extensive personal appeals would have been most inappropriate. In direct contrast with Webster, William L. Yancey, ardent states' righter and secessionist, found it necessary to pack much personal appeal into his speeches before northern audiences during the presidential campaign of 1860. His political foe, Stephen A. Douglas, the senator from Illinois, came to a similar conclusion when he spoke to Southerners. Both Yancey and Douglas, experienced speakers, strove to disarm their listeners before attempting serious presentations of their ideas.

In evaluating the attitudes of the audience toward yourself, be as objective as possible. If possible, determine what the real attitudes are, no matter how much some of them may irritate or disturb you.

Put the following questions to yourself:

1. What are the attitudes of the majority of the audience toward me as a speaker?
    a. How familiar are they with my background and reputation?
        (1) What are their sources of information?
            (a) Are these sources reliable?
            (b) Are they biased?
        (2) Is ethical proof necessary?
2. What are the similarities and differences in my background and that of the majority of the auditors?

[11] Delivered June 17, 1825, at the laying of the cornerstone of the Bunker Hill Monument at Charlestown, Massachusetts.

a. Are these known to the audience?
   b. Do they constitute a basis upon which to establish a "common ground"?
3. What does the majority of the auditors expect from me?
   a. Did they come to hear me?
   b. Do they have selfish motives in coming?

What Does the Audience Know About Your Subject?

To cover ground familiar to the audience and not be aware that it is familiar is to waste valuable time and to risk putting your auditors to sleep. But to assume that they know more than they actually do is equally disastrous. The purposeful speaker starts with the audience where they are and moves them toward his desired goal. What your audience knows then becomes an important consideration.

Frequently in these days of rapid communication and extensive news coverage, it is not unusual for an audience to have a résumé or even a complete copy of a talk before it is delivered. In this event, the speaker must take special pains to adapt carefully his presentation to the local situation.

The speech that is delivered more than once may actually acquire a reputation. Such was the case with many of William Jennings Bryan's lectures. Year after year Chautauqua crowds looked forward to hearing the Great Commoner give "The Prince of Peace" and "The Price of a Soul." The same was true of Russell Conwell's "Acres of Diamonds," Wendell Phillips' "The Lost Arts," and Thomas DeWitt Talmage's "Big Blunders."

What the audience knows about your subject will be an important determinant in your strategy. You will do well, therefore, to investigate the following questions:

1. What is the attitude of the majority of the auditors toward the speech?
   a. Has the title aroused curiosity?
      (1) Is it misleading?
      (2) Does it need clarification?
   b. What advance publicity has the speech received?
      (1) Amount?
      (2) Type?

(3) By whom?
(4) Purpose?
  c. How much does the majority know about the subject?
    (1) Source of information?
      (a) Careful study?
      (b) Hearsay?
      (c) Habitual association?
    (2) Has the audience had the opportunity to read the speech or a résumé?
2. Will the text be available afterward?

Does a Division of Opinion Exist on Your Subject?

Of course a division of opinion does not exist on all subjects, particularly those of an informative nature. But on most argumentative issues, the auditors may be divided into three arbitrary groups: partisans, neutrals, and opponents or for, undecided, and against. But no "hard-and-fast" dividing lines exist between these categories, for ordinarily on most issues there are all shades of opinion extending from that of the fanatical devotee to that of the fanatical antagonist. The following diagram shows shades of opinion graphically:

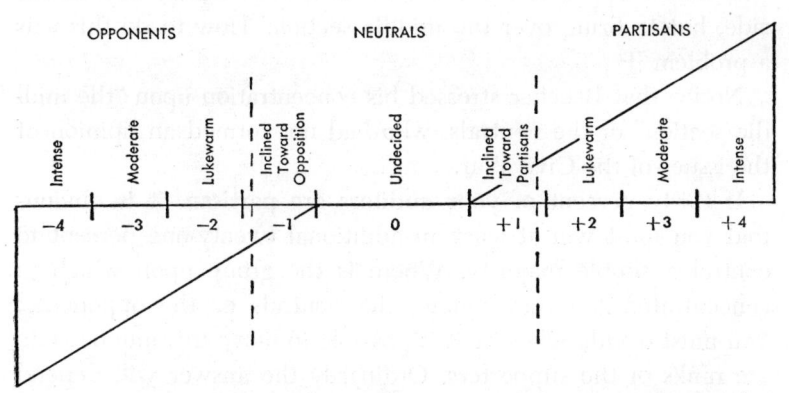

The horizontal line represents the extent of the group. Notice that the group has been arbitrarily divided into thirds for illustrative purposes. The vertical plane represents the intensity of the attitude. Furthermore, the numbers give another index of intensity with 4 representing the extremes.

In making realistic preparation, you must ascertain how many persons must be won to achieve your objective. Under standard parliamentary procedure, most decisions require only a simple majority, of fifty-one percent of those present, but more serious proposals take greater percentages. The rules of the Senate of the United States, for example, require a two-thirds majority (of ninety-six members) to ratify a treaty. To obtain a conviction in American Courts, unanimity is necessary, that is, twelve jurors must be persuaded that the accused is guilty.

But in audience analysis you must proceed beyond learning what constitutes parliamentary control; you must determine what segment holds "the balance of power."

Henry Ward Beecher faced this problem when he spoke to a hostile English audience in Manchester in 1863. At that time thousands of Englishmen who worked in cotton mills had been made idle by the Northern blockade of the Confederacy. Beecher explains his audience analysis as follows: "I took the measure of the audience and said to myself, 'About one fourth of this audience are opposed to me, and about one fourth will be rather in sympathy, and my business now is not to appeal to that portion that is opposed to me nor to those that are already on my side, but to bring over the middle section.' How to do this was a problem."[12]

Notice that Beecher stressed his concentration upon "the middle section" or the neutrals, who had not formed an opinion of the issues of the Civil War.

If thirty percent of your auditors are partisan, it is obvious that you must win at least an additional twenty-one percent to control a simple majority. Where is the group upon which to concentrate? Are they among the neutrals or the opponents? You must decide whether it is possible to move this number into the ranks of the supporters. Ordinarily the answer will depend upon the size of the in-between group. If there are enough neutrals to supply the desired number, you must choose one set

---

[12] Lyman Abbott, *Henry Ward Beecher: A Sketch of His Career*, American Publishing Company, 1887, pp. 171-172.

OCCASION AND AUDIENCE

of goals, but if the opposition controls the remaining group, you modify your goals considerably.

Determine the part of the audience that controls the group.

EXERCISES

1. *Speaking Assignments.* Deliver a five-minute talk on the analysis of the audience and the occasion. Analyze for your classmates how a speaker that you have heard personally succeeded or failed because of good or poor adjustment. You may wish to speak on a topic similar to the following:
    a. How a poor audience analysis caused a speaker to fail
    b. How on-the-spot adjustment to the speaking situation saved the day
    c. How an unforeseen incident wrecked a speech
    d. How an inappropriate subject embarrassed a speaker
    e. How a speaker's appearance or platform deportment contributed to ineffectiveness
    f. How a speaker made a difficult subject meaningful
    g. A difficult subject that caused a speaker trouble
    h. How courage scattered a mob
    i. How a famous speaker coped with a difficult speaking situation
    j. My "pet peeves" about speakers
2. *Research Assignment.* Prepare a written analysis of the prevailing customs concerning speaking that exist in your home community. Make your study as complete as you can.
3. *Research Assignment.* Prepare a written analysis of a typical visible audience in your home community.
4. *Research Assignment.* Prepare a written analysis of a typical radio audience which listens to a radio station in your home town or one nearby.
5. *Discussion Questions for Class Symposium.*
    a. Should a speaker tell his listeners what they would like to hear or what they should hear?
    b. Do political speakers lead or follow public opinion?
    c. What dominant attitudes in your home community are so strong that opposition to them means failure?
    d. Is it possible for a radio speaker to analyze his possible audience?
    e. Is interschool debating conducted in your school for the audience or for some other reason?

PUBLIC SPEAKING

6. *Research Assignment.* Investigate how some famous speaker made adjustment to some aspect of the speaking situation. Consider one of the following or some other speaker of note:
   a. Lincoln in the Lincoln-Douglas Debates, 1858. (Albert J. Beveridge, *Abraham Lincoln*, Houghton Mifflin Company, 1928, vol. II, pp. 641-694.)
   b. Lincoln at Gettysburg, November 19, 1863. (Carl Sandburg, *Abraham Lincoln, The War Years*, Harcourt, Brace and Company, 1939, vol. 2, chap. 44.)
   c. William Jennings Bryan at Democratic National Convention, Chicago, Illinois, July 6, 1896. (Wayne C. Williams, *William Jennings Bryan*, G. P. Putnam's Sons, 1936, chap. 8.)
   d. Booker T. Washington at Atlanta, Georgia, September 18, 1895. (Basil Mathews, *Booker T. Washington*, Harvard University Press, 1948, chap. 6.)
   e. Henry Ward Beecher speaking in England in 1863. (Lyman Abbott, *Henry Ward Beecher*, American Publishing Company, 1887, pp. 161-185.)
   f. Robert Emmet before the Court, September 19, 1803. (See Helen Landreth, *The Pursuit of Robert Emmet*, McGraw-Hill Book Co., Inc., 1948.)
7. Analyze Mark Antony's audience adaptation in his speech to the Roman mob. Remember that he was speaking to a hostile audience.

Speech of Mark Antony from Julius Caesar *by William Shakespeare*

ANT. Friends, Romans, countrymen, lend me your ears!
I come to bury Caesar, not to praise him.
The evil that men do lives after them,
The good is oft interred with their bones;
So let it be with Caesar. The noble Brutus
Hath told you Caesar was ambitious;
If it were so, it was a grievous fault,
And grievously hath Caesar answer'd it.
Here, under leave of Brutus and the rest—
For Brutus is an honorable man;
So are they all, all honorable men—
Come I to speak in Caesar's funeral.
He was my friend, faithful and just to me;
But Brutus says he was ambitious,
And Brutus is an honorable man.
He hath brought many captives home to Rome,
Whose ransoms did the general coffers fill;

Did this in Caesar seem ambitious?
When that the poor have cried, Caesar hath wept;
Ambition should be made of sterner stuff:
Yet Brutus says he was ambitious,
And Brutus is an honorable man.
You all did see that on the Lupercal
I thrice presented him a kingly crown,
Which he did thrice refuse. Was this ambition?
Yet Brutus says he was ambitious,
And, sure, he is an honorable man.
I speak not to disprove what Brutus spoke,
But here I am to speak what I do know.
You all did love him once, not without cause;
What cause withholds you then to mourn for him?
O judgment! thou art fled to brutish beasts,
And men have lost their reason. Bear with me;
My heart is in the coffin there with Caesar,
And I must pause till it come back to me.

1. PLEB. Methinks there is much reason in his sayings.
2. PLEB. If thou consider rightly of the matter,
Caesar has had great wrong.
3. PLEB.   Has he, masters?
I fear there will a worse come in his place.
4. PLEB. Mark'd ye his words? He would not take the crown;
Therefore 'tis certain he was not ambitious.
1. PLEB. If it be found so, some will dear abide it.
2. PLEB. Poor soul! his eyes are red as fire with weeping.
3. PLEB. There's not a nobler man in Rome than Antony.
4. PLEB. Now mark him, he begins again to speak.
ANT. But yesterday the word of Caesar might
Have stood against the world; now lies he there,
And none so poor to do him reverence.
O masters, if I were dispos'd to stir
Your hearts and minds to mutiny and rage,
I should do Brutus wrong, and Cassius wrong,
Who, you all know, are honorable men.
I will not do them wrong; I rather choose
To wrong the dead, to wrong myself and you,
Than I will wrong such honorable men.
But here's a parchment with the seal of Caesar;
I found it in his closet; 'tis his will.
Let but the commons hear this testament—

	Which, pardon me, I do not mean to read—
	And they would go and kiss dead Caesar's wounds
	And dip their napkins in his sacred blood,
	Yea, beg a hair of him for memory,
	And, dying, mention it within their wills,
	Bequeathing it as a rich legacy
	Unto their issue.
4. Pleb.	We'll hear the will. Read it, Mark Antony.
All.	The will, the will! we will hear Caesar's will.
Ant.	Have patience, gentle friends, I must not read it;
	It is not meet you know how Caesar lov'd you.
	You are not wood, you are not stones, but men:
	And, being men, hearing the will of Caesar,
	It will inflame you, it will make you mad.
	'Tis good you know not that you are his heirs;
	For, if you should, O, what would come of it!
4. Pleb.	Read the will; we'll hear it, Antony.
	You shall read us the will, Caesar's will.
Ant.	Will you be patient? Will you stay a while?
	I have o'ershot myself to tell you of it.
	I fear I wrong the honorable men
	Whose daggers have stabb'd Caesar; I do fear it.
4. Pleb.	They were traitors; honorable men!
All.	The will! the testament!
2. Pleb.	They were villains, murderers. The will!
	Read the will.
Ant.	You will compel me, then, to read the will?
	Then make a ring about the corpse of Caesar,
	And let me show you him that made the will.
	Shall I descend? and will you give me leave?
All.	Come down.
2. Pleb.	Descend.
3. Pleb.	You shall have leave.
	[*Antony comes down from the pulpit.*]
4. Pleb.	A ring; stand round.
1. Pleb.	Stand from the hearse, stand from the body.
2. Pleb.	Room for Antony, most noble Antony.
Ant.	Nay, press not so upon me; stand far off.
All.	Stand back; room; bear back!
Ant.	If you have tears, prepare to shed them now.
	You all do know this mantle; I remember
	The first time ever Caesar put it on.

'Twas on a summer's evening, in his tent,
That day he overcame the Nervii.
Look, in this place ran Cassius' dagger through;
See what a rent the envious Casca made;
Through this the well-beloved Brutus stabb'd,
And as he pluck'd his cursed steel away,
Mark how the blood of Caesar followed it,
As rushing out of doors, to be resolv'd
If Brutus so unkindly knock'd, or no;
For Brutus, as you know, was Caesar's angel.
Judge, O you gods, how dearly Caesar lov'd him!
This was the most unkindest cut of all;
For when the noble Caesar saw him stab,
Ingratitude, more strong than traitors' arms,
Quite vanquish'd him. Then burst his mighty heart;
And, in his mantle muffling up his face,
Even at the base of Pompey's statue,
Which all the while ran blood, great Caesar fell.
O, what a fall was there, my countrymen!
Then I, and you, and all of us fell down,
Whilst bloody treason flourish'd over us.
O, now you weep, and I perceive you feel
The dint of pity. These are gracious drops.
Kind souls, what, weep you when you but behold
Our Caesar's vesture wounded? Look you here:
  [*Lifting Caesar's mantle.*]
Here is himself, marr'd, as you see, with traitors.

1. PLEB. O piteous spectacle!
2. PLEB. O noble Caesar!
3. PLEB. O woeful day!
4. PLEB. O traitors, villains!
1. PLEB. O most bloody sight!
2. PLEB. We will be reveng'd!
(ALL.) Revenge! About!
Seek! Burn! Fire! Kill! Slay!
Let not a traitor live!
ANT. Stay, countrymen.
1. PLEB. Peace there! hear the noble Antony.
2. PLEB. We'll hear him, we'll follow him, we'll die with him.
ANT. Good friends, sweet friends, let me not stir you up
To such a sudden flood of mutiny.

They that have done this deed are honorable.
What private griefs they have, alas, I know not,
That made them do it; they are wise and honorable,
And will, no doubt, with reasons answer you.
I come not, friends, to steal away your hearts.
I am no orator, as Brutus is;
But, as you know me all, a plain blunt man
That love my friend; and that they know full well
That gave me public leave to speak of him;
For I have neither wit, nor words, nor worth,
Action, nor utterance, nor the power of speech
To stir men's blood; I only speak right on.
I tell you that which you yourselves do know;
Show you sweet Caesar's wounds, poor poor, dumb mouths,
And bid them speak for me. But were I Brutus,
And Brutus Antony, there were an Antony
Would ruffle up your spirits, and put a tongue
In every wound of Caesar, that should move
The stones of Rome to rise and mutiny.

ALL. We'll mutiny.
1. PLEB. We'll burn the house of Brutus.
3. PLEB. Away, then! come, seek the conspirators.
ANT. Yet hear me, countrymen; yet hear me speak.
ALL. Peace, ho! hear Antony, most noble Antony!
ANT. Why, friends, you go to do you know not what.
Wherein hath Caesar thus deserv'd your loves?
Alas, you know not; I must tell you, then.
You have forgot the will I told you of.
ALL. Most true. The will! Let's stay and hear the will.
ANT. Here is the will, and under Caesar's seal.
To every Roman citizen he gives,
To every several man, seventy-five drachmas.
2. PLEB. Most noble Caesar! We'll revenge his death.
3. PLEB. O royal Caesar!
ANT. Hear me with patience.
ALL. Peace, ho!

FRANKLIN D. ROOSEVELT

President Roosevelt at the dedication of the T.V.A. Chickamauga Dam, Chattanooga, Tennessee, 1940. (Photo, Wide World.)

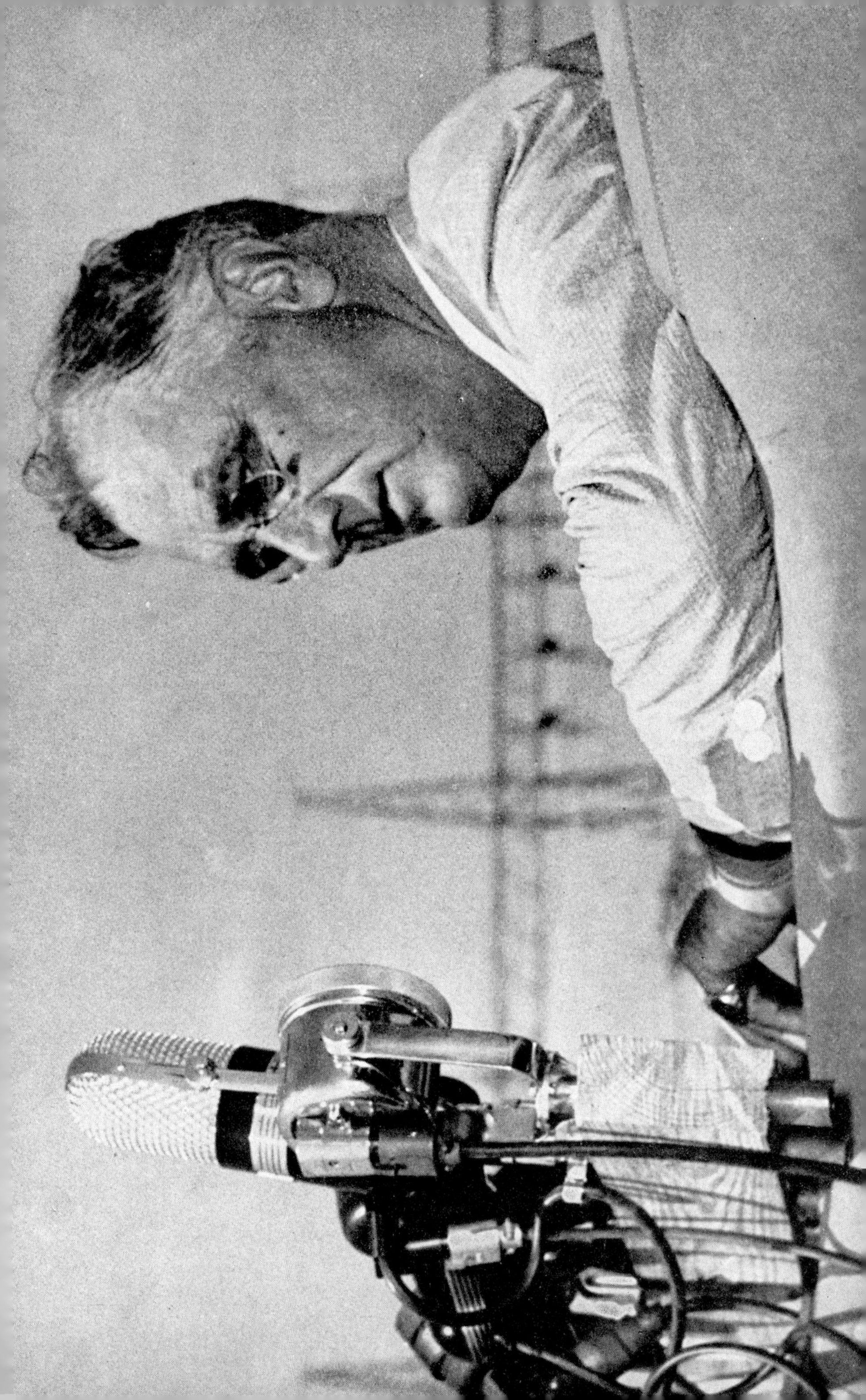

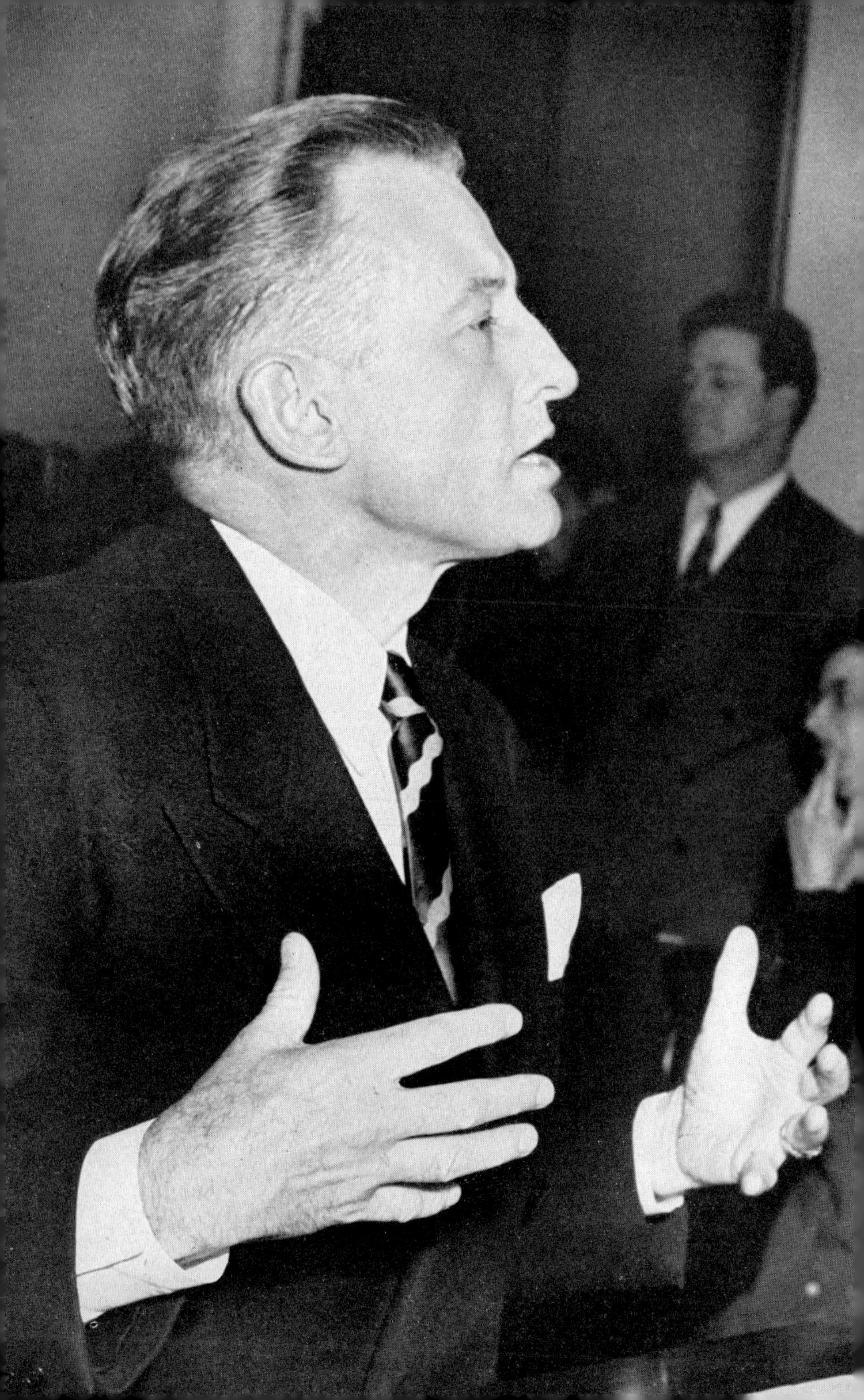

Ant.	Moreover, he hath left you all his walks,
	His private arbours and new-planted orchards,
	On this side Tiber; he hath left them you,
	And to your heirs forever, common pleasures,
	To walk abroad, and recreate yourselves.
	Here was a Caesar! When comes such another?
1. Pleb.	Never, never! Come, away, away!
	We'll burn his body in the holy place,
	And with the brands fire the traitors' houses.
	Take up the body.
2. Pleb.	Go fetch fire.
3. Pleb.	Pluck down benches.
4. Pleb.	Pluck down forms, windows, anything.
	Exeunt Plebeians [with the body].
Ant.	Now let it work. Mischief, thou art afoot,
	Take thou what course thou wilt!

SUPPLEMENTARY READINGS

1. Bryant, Donald C., and Wallace, Karl R., *The Fundamentals of Public Speaking*, Appleton-Century-Crofts, Inc., 1947, chap. 18.
2. Hollingworth, H. L., *The Psychology of the Audience*, American Book Company, 1935, chaps. 1-5.
3. Monroe, Alan H., *Principles and Types of Speech*, Scott, Foresman & Company, 3rd ed., 1949, chap. 9.
4. Oliver, Robert, *The Psychology of Persuasive Speech*, Longmans, Green & Co., Inc., 1942, chaps. 4, 10.
5. Overstreet, H. A., *Influencing Human Behavior*, W. W. Norton & Company, 1925, chaps. 1, 4, 12.
6. Thonssen, Lester, and Baird, A. Craig, *Speech Criticism*, The Ronald Press Company, 1948, chap. 10.
7. Whan, Forest L., "Stephen A. Douglas," *History and Criticism of American Public Address*, McGraw-Hill Book Company, Inc., 1943, vol. II, pp. 777-795.

ERIC JOHNSTON

The alert speaker is animated and direct. Mr. Johnston, president of the Motion Picture Association, is speaking to the House Un-American Activities Committee. Notice how his whole body emphasizes what he is saying. (Photo, Wide World.)

CHAPTER VI

Speech Goals

IN THE light of your studies of the audience and the occasion, you need to determine and carefully consider your speech purpose. To ensure purposeful activity, you must know what response you want in order to select materials and to make plans that enable you to achieve it. Keep your speech moving toward your objective.

The general goal of all speaking is response or, if you prefer more technical language, a neuromuscular or neuroglandular activity of one kind or another. When at dinner you say in a quiet voice, "Please pass the sugar," you hope that your neighbor will satisfy your request. If your car mires in the mud, you call anxiously for help, hoping for a response—a push or a pull. Before you drive the golf ball down the fairway, you shout a healthy "fore" with the intention of clearing the line of flight. In each case your objective is a *response*.

Likewise in a public speech you have a similar goal—some kind of response. Your goal must meet at least two requisites: First, you must have a definite idea of what you want. Second, you must select a response which you have a reasonable expectation of eliciting. In other words, the goal must be one which you can achieve by your speech. It must be neither theoretical nor ideal. Its selection must be based upon careful study of the attitudes, biases, preferences, and beliefs of your listeners and upon a thorough analysis of the occasion. *There is nothing haphazard or accidental about an effective speech; it is the result of careful thought and thorough planning.*

AUDIENCE RESPONSE

If you are to let the advice above be your guiding philosophy, early in your preparation you must answer four questions:

1. What kind of a response do I want?
2. When do I want my listeners to respond?
3. How long do I want them to respond?
4. Do I want my listeners to respond as individuals or as a group?

Let us consider each of these queries briefly.

What Kind of Response Do I Want?

Is the response to be *covert*, entirely within the auditor? Or is it to be *overt*, openly manifested? In the first, you may ask the listener to do no more than to think, to recall, to evaluate, to associate, to be amused, or to feel excited. When you unfold a new procedure to your colleagues, you work for understanding. The droll story usually has as its objective quiet unobservable delight. Many patriotic speeches attempt to do no more than stimulate additional pride in country. In each case the goal is a covert response.

On the other hand, you may work for a response that you can

see, an overt response, that is, demonstrate a skill, applaud loudly, shed tears, buy a vacuum cleaner, or cheer the home team.

The preceding discussion is not meant to imply that *overt* and *covert* responses are opposites; more correctly, they should be viewed as parts of the same process, differing only in degree. Indeed, it is difficult to say where one stops and the other begins.

When Do I Want My Listeners to Respond?

Is the reaction to be immediate or delayed? When you explain a simple gadget, you expect almost immediate understanding, but if you are discussing a complicated machine, you may give considerable explanation before you can hope for understanding from your auditor. In this latter case you are working for a delayed reaction. If you ask for a show of hands, a contribution, or a signature on a petition, the reaction is to be immediate, that is, it occurs during or immediately after the speech. If, however, the goal involves getting the auditors to write to their congressmen, read the newspapers, or boycott a merchant, the reaction is delayed. You must generate enough urgency to motivate your listeners to act sometime after the speech has been concluded.

How Long Do I Want the Audience to Respond?

Is the response to be momentary or sustained? How long is it to continue? Understanding a fact may be momentary, but retention of that fact is a sustained response. To cheer the coach for an inspirational pep talk may be momentary, but to play sixty minutes of "heads-up" football requires continued effort. A show of hands or a signature is momentary. If at the right instant you can bring sufficient pressure to bear, you succeed. In "converting" a "sinner," the minister hopes to do far more than to get the person to signify his intention to join the congregation; he wants the man to change his way of life. The insurance salesman has a particularly difficult task in this regard, for the signature on the original application is immediate and momentary; but payment of the premium should be continued fifteen or twenty years or even a lifetime. It is evident that momentary response is much more simple to arouse than a reaction which is to be sustained.

Do I Want Individual or Group Response?

If an individual response is your goal, you attempt to inform, to stimulate, or to influence members of the audience individually. No set number of conversions is required for success. The teacher, of course, works on the basis of individual response, for learning is an individual response. Another excellent example of this phenomenon is the revival meeting in which the minister asks that his converts come forward when they "feel the call."

In the case of group response, you seek a favorable vote of the group, a show of hands, or some other indication that the gathering affirms your stand and will follow your directions. You seek to commit the group to your program. As indicated in the previous chapter, if many ties bind the listeners together, the task of securing a group response is easier. In fact, with the regimented audience such as an airplane crew or a military unit, the social integration has been sufficient to ensure that a mere command will result in action. In less indoctrinated groups the significant question is, What percentage of the auditors can obligate or compel the whole group to act?

METHODS OF OBTAINING GOALS

In addition to knowing where you want to go with your speech, you should know what *route* you wish to travel in order to reach your destination. In general, five routes are available: entertaining, informing, stimulating, convincing, and actuating. Of course, two or more of these may be brought into play in the development of a single subject. In an informative talk you may include entertaining material for interest purposes. Of course, in an attempt to persuade, you may resort to humor, to information, and to stimulating material.

Entertaining

The term speech to entertain is self-defining. Since its nature is obvious, let us direct our attention to its purposes or goals. In seeking to amuse your listeners, you may seek either a *covert* or an *overt* response, that is, you may be satisfied if your auditors quietly attend to your speech, or you may strive to elicit from them perceptible evidences of amusement ranging from faint smiles to boisterous laughter. Ordinarily, the reaction desired is immediate and momentary. Of course, if the development is subtle or the listeners are slow to see the point of the humor, you may have to be content with silence or delayed laughter, not fully gratifying to the speaker. Little more than attention and interest, however, are required for the success of this type of speech.

Perhaps it will be helpful to view the entertaining speech from the auditor's point of view. To the auditor, this type of speech is solely a means of passing the time, of forgetting cares and troubles, and of relaxation. Once the speech is completed, he feels free to go his own way with no further responsibilities or obligations.

Informing

The informative speech may involve description, narration, definition, interpretation, analysis, synthesis, explanation, demonstration, or criticism. It demands in addition to attention and interest that the audience understand, retain, and often recall what is said. Sometimes the sign of success is performance or demonstration by the auditor. The reaction may be immediate or delayed, sustained, covert or overt.

What does the auditor expect from the informative speech? Since a premium is placed upon understanding and retention, the auditor demands above all else that the speech be clear and specific. Ordinarily he prefers many illustrations and demonstrations; he resists attempts to present material too rapidly; and he is pleased with thought breaks, shorter sentences, and the inclusion of entertaining materials. In many cases he fears being questioned and hopes to depart without being tested.

Stimulating

The stimulating speech strives to strengthen attitudes, opinions, or beliefs already present but ineffective or inactive in the listener. You hope to rekindle or heighten the appreciation for a principle, a person, a group of persons, or an institution. In this type of speech you seek mainly *covert* response; you may want either an immediate or delayed response, but probably you desire a sustained reaction. Classical rhetoricans referred to this type as a ceremonial speech or one of "praise or blame." Eulogies, pep talks, some sermons, reunion addresses, speeches of courtesy, patriotic orations, and dedicatory talks are stimulating talks.

Since it is based upon revitalizing latent wants, the auditors often find little in the stimulating speech to resist. The covert response is in no way embarrassing. If the talk is based upon the pleasant emotions (pride, reverence, patriotism), the auditor finds the presentation pleasant. On the other hand, if the motivation utilizes unpleasant or negative emotions (fear, horror, shame), the auditor may decide that the speech is unpleasant.

Convincing

Argumentative speeches seek to change attitudes and beliefs and in some cases strive to move the auditor to action. Herein they differ from stimulating speeches which seek to strengthen and revitalize attitudes present but dormant. A basic requirement of the argumentative speech then is that you as a speaker hold a position *which differs from that held by a significant number of your auditors.*

Argumentative speeches may be divided into two types: those which convince and those which actuate.

In the convincing speech you may seek either an immediate or a delayed reaction. It may be momentary, but more frequently it is a sustained reaction. The distinguishing characteristic here, however, is that the goal is a *covert* response. For example, you may speak on such propositions as the following: the chain store is detrimental to our community; the church is worthy of your support; oleomargarine has the same food value as butter. In any of these cases you ask for no more than mental agreement. Your speech may be preparatory to another in which you urge action, but so far as the present occasion is concerned, you are satisfied with mental acceptance.

Actuating

The so-called actuating speech goes a step further than the convincing talk in that it urges the auditor to pursue a course of action or, in other words, to give an *overt* response. The propositions cited earlier may be adapted to this type by changing the wording to read as follows: Mississippi should tax the chain stores; you should give ten percent of your income to the church; or the Iowa tax on oleomargarine should be discontinued.

The two types of argumentative speeches are, of course, complementary. The first may ordinarily be transformed into the second by adding a section proposing a solution to the problem and by including additional and more powerful motive appeals.

THE GENERAL GOAL OF SPEAKING IS RESPONSE

In the first picture a pollster is conducting an interview. The desired responses are correct answers to the questions. In the second picture the clinician is attempting to show youngster correct position of the teeth and tongue in making a sound. The response desired is correct pronunciation. (Photos, Black Star and L.S.U. Alumni News.)

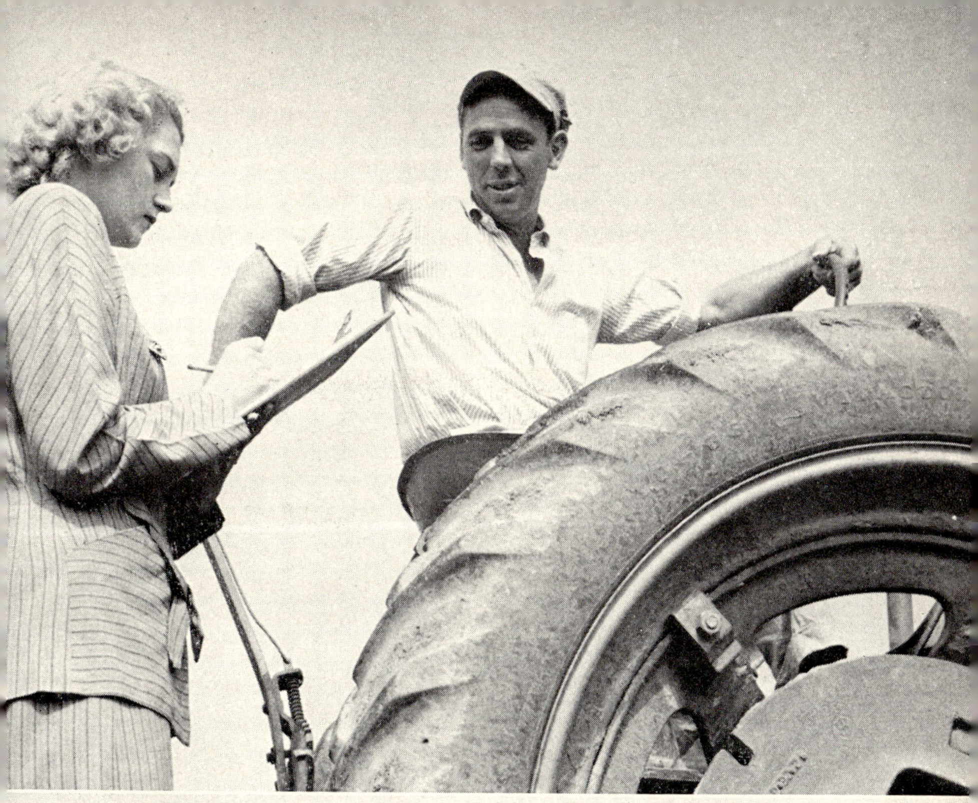

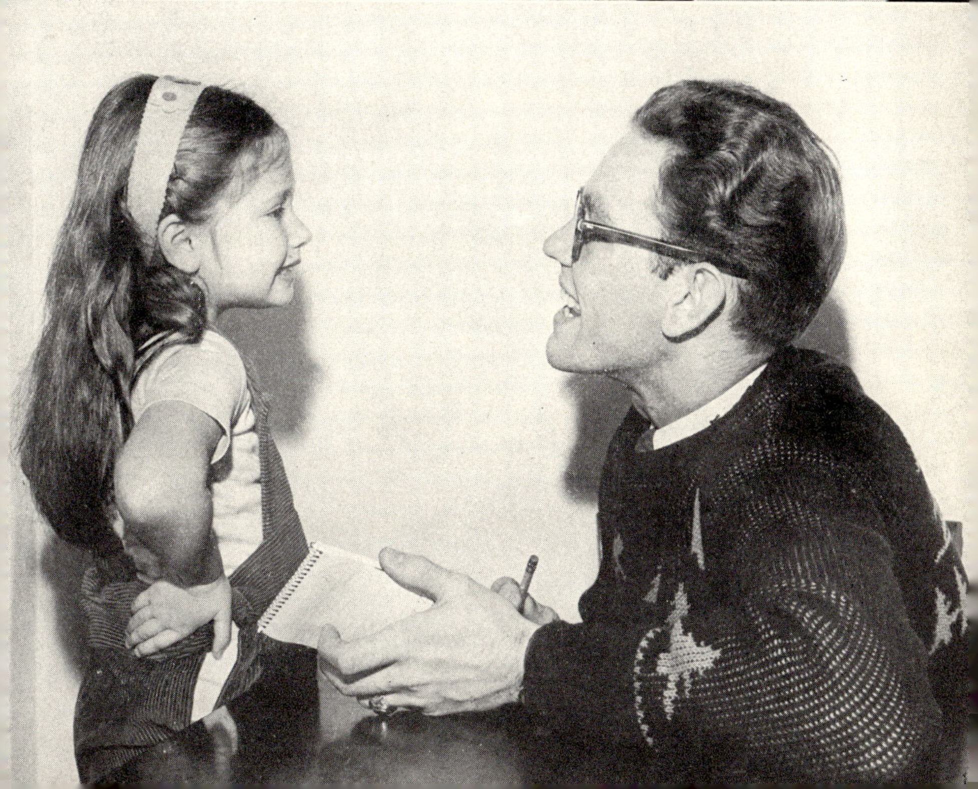

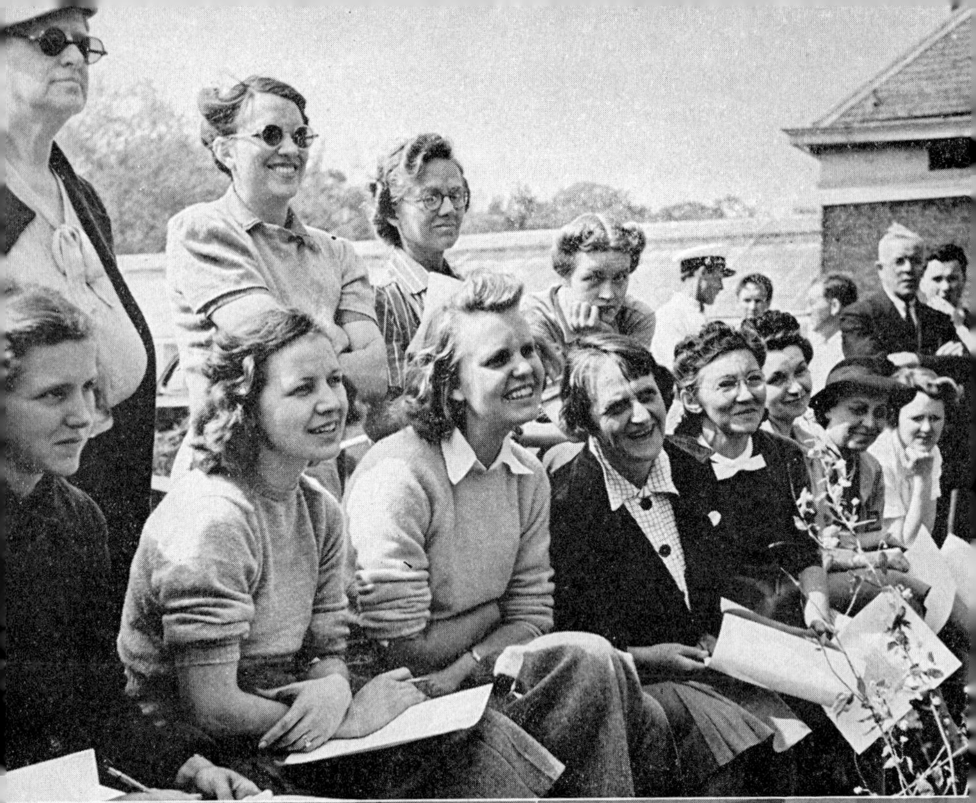

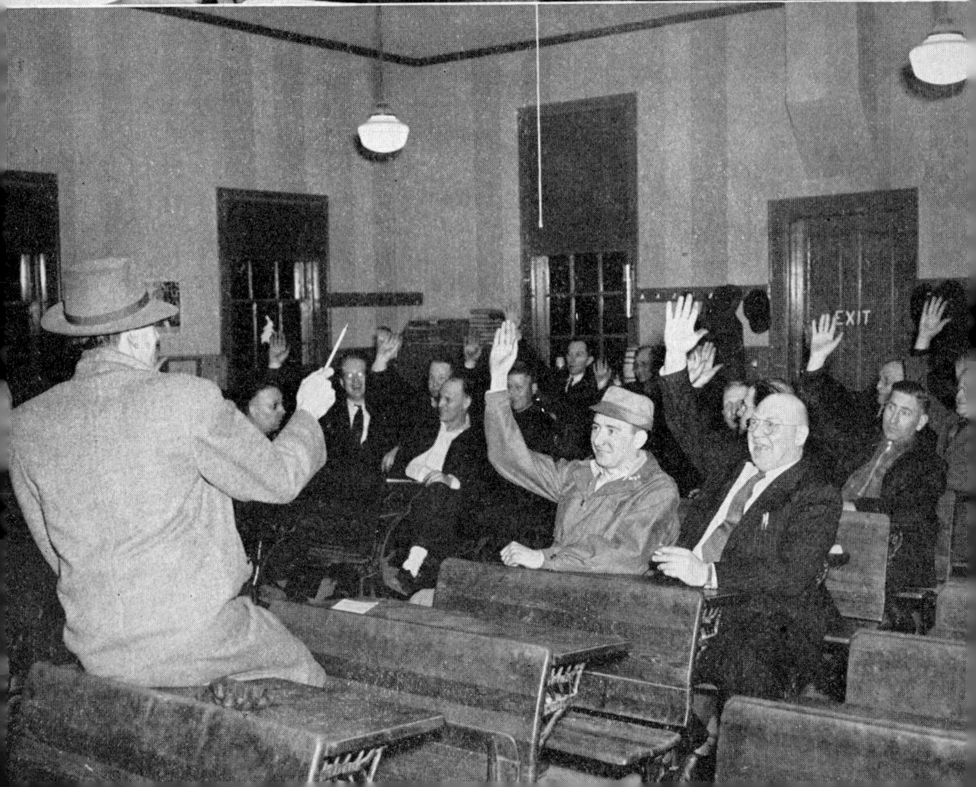
EXIT

It is evident that demand for overt response requires greater effort than the demand for a covert response. Of the various types, the argumentative talks are the most difficult, for they aim at changes of attitudes and beliefs. Departures from the *status quo* may seem frustrating to the listener in that he senses a threat to his security, dislikes the thought of deserting tested modes of behavior, and objects to having his past thinking challenged. He may feel that to accede to your demands constitutes a blow to his prestige.

Summary Chart

Methods of obtaining goals	General ends	Kind of response?	When?	How long?
Entertaining	Enjoyment Diversion	Covert or overt	Immediate	Momentary
Informing	Understanding	Covert or overt	Immediate or delayed	Sustained
Stimulating	Appreciation	Covert or overt	Immediate or delayed	Sustained
Convincing	Mental agreement	Covert	Immediate or delayed	Sustained
Actuating	Action	Overt	Immediate or delayed	Momentary or sustained

A SPEAKER MUST JUDGE HIS SUCCESS IN TERMS OF RESPONSE

The observant speaker looks for overt signs which indicate that his auditors agree or disagree with him. (Photos, Black Star.)

KINDS OF GOALS

Immediate and Remote Goals

The previous section has discussed what we have called methods of obtaining goals and the general end to which each leads, namely, diversion, information, appreciation, mental agreement, or action. But for a given speech, these general ends must be phrased in terms of specific immediate goals or responses which you intend to elicit. In the determination of the goal of a speech, you should realistically ask yourself, What is the most that I can hope to achieve with this audience? The wise solicitor seeks a donation well within his patron's capacity to pay. The effective teacher weighs carefully the intellectual capacity of a class before making an assignment.

But objectives selected in light of prevailing attitudes and intellectual capacities may fall far short of what you really hope to accomplish; consequently, for a given speech you may also select an *ultimate or remote* goal, a distant objective. When you achieve this remote objective will be determined by the number and size of the obstacles to be overcome and the skill with which you move your listeners step by step toward overcoming them. Perhaps it may require a dozen speeches, supplemented by other techniques such as advertising, group pressure, or dramatization. A college president who speaks on the "school spirit" may have in mind the day when he intends to ask you to contribute to the college endowment. Strong loyalties now may mean donations later when you have a substantial income. The politician gives to charity now with an eye on the future; admiration today means votes tomorrow, he hopes.

It becomes evident that the purposeful speaker must have clearly in mind his remote goal as well as his immediate one.

Announced and Concealed Goals

Ordinarily, the immediate goal, whether stated or implied, becomes evident to the audience by the close of the speech.

Often remote goals must be obscured or concealed, because the speaker realizes that for the moment his auditors are not ready for the final plunge. Premature revealing of future objectives may make the listeners more difficult to manage.

Is it ethical to have a goal which you cannot announce? Are you not deceiving your listeners? The answers to these questions depend upon whether your goals are consistent with the best interests of the group. If they are, you need feel no chagrin at not announcing your ultimate objectives. But if your ends are selfish and injurious to the welfare of the group, you should indeed be censured. (See Chapter I, "The Attitude of the Speaker," for further discussion of ethics.)

SELECTING A GOAL

Normally we assume that the speaker is a free agent in selecting the goal which he wishes to achieve. But seldom is this entirely true. Actually, the goal many times grows out of the demands of the listeners or requirements of the occasion. Much depends upon why the group assembles.

If the meeting has been called for the specific purpose of giving you an opportunity to speak, then you may determine what your method and objective will be. But if the audience assembles because of some aspect of the occasion—a patriotic celebration, a presentation ceremony, or a dedication service—then you must be guided by the requirements of the occasion. The humorous talk is frequently associated with the after-dinner occasion. The persuasive talk is often associated with churches, in some of which the preacher is expected to give a persuasive talk, concluding in an invitation for converts. The informative talk is often associated with the classroom. You must, therefore, always ask yourself, Does my proposed goal fit the requirements of the occasion?

Sometimes the audience invites you through a program chairman to speak on a certain subject. The representative may say,

"We should like to hear an entertaining talk on your recent trip to Hawaii." Or you may be asked to tell the local service club "How to make a successful speech," or "How to solicit funds," or "What is democracy?" You must honor such a request, else you may disappoint or even offend the group. In such cases, what is important is *that you align your own purposes with those of the audience.*

It is important in the matter of determining goals to consider how the audience is divided upon your topic. Ordinarily a group can be divided into three large categories: opposition, neutrals, and partisans. These terms are sometimes used to refer to argumentative speeches, but they may also be adapted to the other types of speeches, as the following chart shows:

Attitudes the Auditors May Hold with Reference to Your Subject

Type of Speech	Opposition	Neutral	Partisan
Speech to entertain	Bored	Passive	Attentive
Speech to inform	Uninformed (Ignorant)	Indifferent	Informed
Speech to stimulate	Lethargic	Uninterested	Enthusiastic
Argumentative a. To convince	Antagonistic	Undecided	Mental agreement
b. To actuate	Antagonistic	Undecided	Ready to act

Your goal must be aimed at the dominant segment of the audience or the group or combination which seems most important to you. If the majority is unfavorably disposed toward the subject, the speaker must choose an immediate goal less ambitious than he would for an audience in which there were many partisans. For illustration, consider the informative speech. If an instructor finds a majority of his class totally uninformed on the subject, he must present his material at a slower rate than for a group with some previous training. If seventy-five percent of his listeners have already mastered the subject, he must plan how to inform the other twenty-five percent without boring the majority. Furthermore, to the uninformed group, the speaker probably cannot hope by means of one speech to impart complete mastery of his material. Perhaps an opening speech can achieve no more than to focus attention upon the subject.

If the audience is largely partisan, at least to the extent that a majority is present, your task ordinarily will be to stir up great fervor. You may urge the group to finish a project in a shorter time than first planned, to be more overt in their responses, or to advance beyond the predetermined objective. The means to attain such a goal is the stimulating speech.

If the neutrals or a combination of neutrals and partisans hold the balance of power, they must receive major consideration.

Naturally, powerful motivation and concrete supporting material are necessary if the in-between group is to be moved toward or into the ranks of the partisans. A definite course of action well within the ability of the assembly may be proposed.

But what if the opposition controls more than fifty-one percent of the votes? What can you reasonably expect to accomplish with those who oppose you fundamentally and completely? To answer this question you must first consider the sources and the intensity of prevailing attitudes. Did the people reach their present beliefs after thoughtful meditation? Or did they form their attitudes in a more or less accidental or casual manner? If the issues are simple and not emotionalized, you may succeed in moving some lukewarm opponents into the ranks of supporters. Attitudes toward the types of clothing we wear or the custom of tipping the hat or where we park our cars are usually unemotionalized. But if the problem involves deep-seated prejudice, antagonism, antipathy, or extensive conditioning, your goals must be considerably modified. Race problems, segregation, party affiliation, and religious preference are subjects which have been intensely emotionalized. Many politicians take great pains to avoid declaring themselves on certain issues of this type. Congress on one occasion pushed aside a bill for federal aid to education because a religious controversy was suddenly stirred up. In 1948 the Dixiecrats won votes by raising the issues of "states rights," "poll tax," and "white supremacy"; many others won favor by declaring just as vehemently their opposition to such doctrines. Each of these themes had been emotionalized on both sides by generations of conditioning.

In many such cases a persuasive speech, particularly a speech to actuate, may accomplish little more than to crystallize opposition and promote great reluctance to change. In dealing with prejudiced opponents, perhaps you should strive to do no more in a single speech than to attempt to move them in the direction of uncertainty. To convert such opponents, a series of persuasive efforts is necessary. The election of 1928 offers an excellent example of this point. In that campaign the several states of the traditionally Democratic South were stirred up to oppose Alfred E. Smith, the Democratic standard bearer. The Republicans aligned their attacks with the widespread southern attitudes concerning Catholicism and prohibition. Then by numerous rallies, articles, radio broadcasts, and even a whispering campaign, they kept hammering away to intensify the attitudes on these two issues. On election day thousands of Southerners were willing to cast their votes for Herbert Hoover, a Republican!

When you are faced by strong opposition, all you can hope to do in a given speech is to "soften up" your listeners. With extreme opponents, a speech to inform, rather than to convince, may be advisable. If your ultimate goal is equal pay for Negro teachers, in some communities you will do well on a given occasion to do no more than to call attention to the problem and to show what is being done elsewhere. In other cases, a stimulating talk designed to gain a recognition of the problem or to

SPEECH GOALS

conciliate the listeners may be all that should be attempted. If the opposition is in the "lukewarm" stage, a convincing speech may be in order.

You should select a goal which you can reasonably expect to reach.

WORDING THE SPECIFIC PURPOSE

The wording of the specific purpose must relate the speaker's goal to the audience and the occasion. The importance of the specific purpose becomes more apparent when it is realized that the remainder of the analysis must stem from it. For an entertaining speech, a speaker might word his specific purpose as follows:

> To amuse my fraternity by ridiculing our rival fraternity
> To entertain the members of the speech class by discussing Santa Claus
> To entertain the Kiwanis Club by relating the events of my recent trip to Mexico

The specific purpose of an informative speech may read:

> To tell the speech class about my survey in sociology
> To relate to the members of the debate squad the history of Pi Kappa Delta
> To demonstrate to the first-aid class how to apply a tourniquet
> To discuss before the community forum the city-manager plan

If it is to be a stimulating talk, you may word the specific purpose in this manner:

> To praise in the presence of the Down Town Kiwanis Club the OHS football team
> To stir up the hatred of my social club for the Communists
> To stimulate the student body to appreciate Coach Smith
> To heighten the appreciation of the Ramblers for Shakespearean plays

The convincing speech may involve such specific purposes as follow:

> To convince the members of the society that communism is a threat to our way of life
> To move the members of the Ladies Aid Society to feel that Lloyd Douglas is a great novelist
> To convince the speech class that weight lifting is a good reducer
> To convince the Y.M.C.A. that Hawaii is ready for statehood

The specific purpose of an actuating speech may be worded as follows:

> To solicit gifts from the American Legion for the local orphanages
> To "sell" the bankers on the need for advertising
> To persuade the Cub Scouts that they should study the Manual
> To persuade Professor Jones that my grade should be raised

Notice that each of these specific purposes mentions the following elements: (1) the method (to tell, to stimulate, to convince, to persuade), (2) the audience, and (3) the specific subject.

EXERCISES

1. *Speaking Assignment.* Explain the correct as opposed to the incorrect way of doing something such as (a) a golf stroke, (b) playing tennis, (c) washing dishes, (d) diving, (e) a dance step, (f) casting, (g) playing a musical instrument.
2. *Speaking Assignment.* Deliver an oral analysis of the goals of three advertisers as shown in full-page newspaper or magazine advertisements.
    a. Determine what were the immediate, the remote, the concealed goals.
    b. Explain fully how you reached your conclusions.
    c. Determine whether you think the advertiser is ethical in his objectives.
    d. Carefully organize and rehearse your speech before you come to class.
3. *Discussion Questions for Class Symposiums*
    a. Is it possible for a speech to have two goals? More than two?
    b. Is it always necessary to determine the specific goal of a speech?
    c. What were the speech goals of the various candidates in the last presidential election? How did these goals affect their speaking?

d. As a listener, how can you determine a speaker's goals? Why is it important for you to ascertain his goal as soon as possible?

e. If you discover that a speaker has an undesirable goal, what should be your course of action?

SUPPLEMENTARY READINGS

1. Brigance, William Norwood, *Speech Composition*, F. S. Crofts & Co., 1937, chap. III.
2. Gray, Giles W., and Wise, Claude M., *The Bases of Speech*, Harper & Brothers, rev. ed., 1946, pp. 50-63.
3. Monroe, Alan H., *Principles and Types of Speech*, Scott, Foresman & Company, 1949, 3rd ed., pp. 163-177.
4. Oliver, Robert T., Cortright, Rupert L., and Hager, Cyril F., *The New Training for Effective Speech*, The Dryden Press, Inc., 1946, chap. 12.
5. O'Neill, James Milton, and Weaver, Andrew Thomas, *The Elements of Speech*, Longmans, Green & Co., Inc., 1935, chap. XXI.
6. Phillips, Arthur Edward, *Effective Speaking*, The Newton Company, 1908, pp. 17-27.
7. Sandford, William Phillips, and Yeager, Willard Hayes, *Principles of Effective Speaking*, The Ronald Press Company, 1942, chap. 10.

CHAPTER VII

Subjects, Sources, and Materials

"THE grass is always greener on the other side of the fence." Far-off places, the events of long ago, and the lives of strange tribes always seem to possess more charm and enchantment than life close to home. His own experience ordinarily seems commonplace to the beginning speaker. Frequent complaints are "Nothing exciting has ever happened to me"; "My home town is just like other small towns"; "I have not lived long enough to have had any exciting experiences." So it goes. As a result, the beginner may choose from a magazine digest a subject such as "Life in the Arctic," "Giant Ants of the Amazon," or "Tribal Customs of the Senegalese."

When these topics fail to turn into successful speeches, the beginner feels frustrated and discouraged. Was the topic not unusual? Was it not exciting? Did he not read a whole magazine article in gathering his material? Did he not almost memorize what the author had written? Why, after all this preparation, did he not sound convincing?

We must admit that this student did partially fulfill the requirements of *specific preparation*. But he was reporting the experience of another; consequently, he was limited by the number of details that the author had presented. Unfortunately, there was nothing in his own experience or background to enrich his presentation. As a result, what he said did not ring true, it was not convincing, it was not a part of him. He probably failed to put over his ideas because he was concentrating upon the *remembering* of ideas instead of the *presentation* of ideas.

Speaking technique cannot cover up shallow thinking, trite commonplaces, and ill-digested facts. Nor can it give a speaker the assurance, poise, and the persuasiveness that come with rich experience, with being generally well read, and with being specifically well informed upon a given subject.

The point here is well illustrated by a story around which Russell Conwell built his lecture, "Acres of Diamonds." Al Hafed became obsessed with a desire to find diamonds and to become immensely rich. He sold his farm and set out to wander in far-distant lands in quest of his dream. Another man chanced along and found diamonds in the very garden that Al Hafed had sold. The same is true with the speaker who overlooks his personal experience as a source. To have a rich storehouse of pertinent material, you need not be a world traveler, a thrill hunter, or even a Ph.D. But you must possess at least one quality—you must be alert and aware of what captures and holds human interest. Look into your specialties, your hobbies, your business experience, your preferences, and your fields of special endeavors. Here you will find rich reserves which await investigation and selection.

In summary, therefore, it appears that the wise speaker is one who selects a subject which will enable him to draw extensively upon his general background.

GENERAL BACKGROUND

Already we have emphasized in Chapter I, "The Attitude of the Speaker," that a broad background is an essential for effective speaking.

Through direct experience, conversation with your friends, listening to the radio, seeing movies, and reading current magazines and newspapers as well as serious books, you can increase your reservoirs and your effectiveness as a speaker.

Students of public address have long recognized that serious reflection, systematic thought, and extensive reading are primary requisites of excellence in public speaking. In this sense Cicero was an extremist when he observed, ". . . no man could ever excel and reach eminence in eloquence, without learning, not only the art of oratory, but every branch of useful knowledge." By eloquence Cicero refers to the ideal toward which most speakers strive.

A study of great speakers substantiates the importance of having an extensive background. Edmund Burke, remembered as a writer and political philosopher as well as a parliamentary orator, committed large portions of Vergil, Horace, and Lucretius to memory. Bacon, Milton, and Shakespeare were among his favorites. Among his companions in conversation were the leading intellectuals of his day.

Trained as a lawyer, Daniel Webster included Pope, Addison, Shakespeare, and Milton among his favorite English writers. He mastered Latin literature and frequently quoted it in his speeches. He kept Caesar, Vergil, and Livy on his desk. In addition, he was a careful student of history and law.

Calhoun, Webster's great rival, was equally at home with the classics of England and of the ancient world. Theodore Parker accumulated a library of twenty thousand volumes in thirty languages and in such diverse fields as history, literature, theology, philosophy, logic, mathematics, zoology, chemistry, physics, law, and biography. The evidence is that he used most of these.

Abraham Lincoln, reared on the American frontier where printed materials were luxuries, developed an insatiable hunger for knowledge. When new volumes were not available, young Abe reread what was at hand. When a copy of Blackstone accidentally fell into his hands, he studied it at length. Nothing escaped his attention. His debates, his pleadings before the courts, and his presidential utterances reflect his broad background and his astuteness in marshalling facts.

Theodore Roosevelt wrote an imposing historical series, *Winning of the West*. Long before he attracted public attention, Woodrow Wilson was a recognized authority on congressional government and had written an impressive list of books and articles. Ordinarily thought of as a lawyer and congressional debater, William E. Borah read and reread the writings of Shakespeare and Milton, memorized masterpieces of American and British oratory, and knew his Bible thoroughly. Much of his leisure reading was devoted to a study of history and the rise of constitutional government. Among his acquaintances he won the reputation of being "a great bookworm" and "an omnivorous reader," not a bad reputation to have but one not too common among senators.

Expansion of the list above seems unnecessary, for the implication is clear. Many orators of the past were more than masters of technique, they were profound students and thinkers. Because of the richness of their backgrounds, they brought to the platform a persuasiveness which transcended the glibness of many of their contemporaries. Men were attentive to these speakers because they had something significant to say, messages too important not to be heard.

Broad cultural background cannot be acquired in a day, a semester, or even a year. If the would-be speaker has a narrow outlook, if his attitudes are warped, or if his perceptive powers are dull, he probably will have difficulty in achieving eloquence. His intellectual sterility will be a factor in his ineffectiveness.

What are the signs of intellectual sterility? The student who is constantly complaining that he has nothing worth while to say is troubled with this complaint. He probably does not know how to utilize his previous experience. He ought to do some serious thinking about the needs of his community and the needs of his auditors. What does he have personally to say that is important? His difficulty may, of course, be that he is unaware of or not sensitive to the cultural, political, social, and economic problems that exist all around him; or perhaps the sphere in which he lives is so limited that he possesses insufficient confidence to express himself outside his little circle. Again, overspecialization may have made him a hermit.

The person who suspects that he needs to broaden his outlook should set for himself a definite program of reading. At the top of his list he should place "the great books,"[1] the Harvard Classics, or some other set of distinguished volumes. He needs to do what Emerson referred to as "creative reading," or reading with inquiring alertness and constant questioning. "One must be an inventor to read well," said Emerson. "As the proverb says, 'He that would bring home the wealth of the Indies, must carry out the wealth of the Indies.' There is then creative reading as well as creative writing. When the mind is braced by labor and invention, the page of whatever book we read becomes luminous with manifold allusion. Every sentence is doubly significant, and the sense of our author is as broad as the world."[2] Certainly the speaker needs to be "as broad as the world," forgetting his provincialism.

But the student faced with the prospect of meeting a speech class two or three times weekly demands to know what he can do immediately to get additional ideas for his speeches. Some excellent sources of speech material are your own experience, the radio, current newspapers and magazines. The adoption of the following program is a step in the right direction:

[1] For an excellent list, see Mortimer J. Adler, *How to Read a Book*, Simon and Schuster, Inc., 1940, pp. 377-389.

[2] Ralph Waldo Emerson, "The American Scholar," oration delivered before the Phi Beta Kappa Society, Cambridge, August 31, 1837.

SUBJECTS, SOURCES, MATERIALS

1. Read at least one newspaper daily (don't limit your reading to the comics; don't overlook the editorials).
2. Listen to at least thirty minutes of radio news daily.
3. Read weekly a news magazine such as *Newsweek, Time, Pathfinder, United States News,* or *The New Republic*.
4. Read each month a literary magazine: *Harpers', Atlantic Monthly,* or *Yale Review*.
5. Read at least one nonfiction book for every novel read.
6. When a good speech topic occurs to you, write it down for future reference.

THE SPEAKER'S NOTEBOOK

To digest and to remember all that is significant in your reading is, of course, an impossible task. At most to remember the general theme, a pertinent thought, or perhaps a quotation is about all that you can expect to do. Therefore the necessity of jotting down pregnant ideas and interesting information is quite evident. Ralph Waldo Emerson daily recorded his meditations in his *Journal*, which he called his "savings bank." This storehouse served him well when he prepared a lecture or an essay.

William E. Borah filed pertinent material away in large manila envelopes properly labeled. Into these repositories went clippings, letters, petitions, pamphlets, magazine articles, personal reflections, and outlines. Choice sentences were underlined, and marginal comments were made. He directed his stenographer to copy quotations that he particularly liked. For a given subject this collecting process might continue for several months or even years. But when the occasion to speak arose, Borah had an extensive accumulation from which to draw.[3]

You too will probably find it profitable to keep a speaker's notebook in which to accumulate speech materials.

1. One section should be devoted to speech topics. When a likely subject is suggested by reading, by meditation, or by a speech, record it immediately. In this manner you can soon collect a long list of excellent topics.

[3] Waldo W. Braden, "The Bases of William E. Borah's Speech Preparation," *The Quarterly Journal of Speech*, February, 1947, pp. 28-30.

2. Another section should be devoted to quotations, anecdotes, jokes, and unique illustrations. Clippings may be pasted in for future reference.

3. It will probably be profitable for you to retain written speech criticisms, speech outlines, and other material which your teacher may ask you to save.

IMMEDIATE PREPARATION

Frequently students inquire, "How much time should I devote to preparing a speech?" Some answer that little immediate preparation is necessary; the clever student, they argue, can make a good five-minute speech by just "shooting the breeze"—meaning, of course, that the clever student needs to give little actual thought to a speech before facing his colleagues. Preparing a speech for any audience is often an arduous task which should be spread out over a considerable period. As in other learning situations, work at spaced intervals will probably yield greater results than continuous concentration for a long period.

Considerable speculation has taken place concerning how much time Abraham Lincoln devoted to the preparation of the Gettysburg Address, which he delivered in less than five minutes. Modern Lincoln scholars now assure us that this gem of American eloquence was far more than an overnight production; it represented the thought of a man who had devoted his lifetime to the study of government and politics, of a man whose sympathies had been mellowed by three years of awful war, of a man keenly aware of the import of the occasion. The manuscript that Lincoln carried to Gettysburg was the product of much reflection. The night before the ceremony the Illinoian felt compelled to rewrite his speech once more. The version we revere thus went through additional revision before it reached its present form.[4]

Daniel Webster, student of the constitution and government, frequently spent from two weeks to two months preparing his

[4] For an interesting discussion, see James G. Randall, *Lincoln, the President*, Dodd, Mead & Company, Inc., 1945, vol. II, pp. 303-320.

SUBJECTS, SOURCES, MATERIALS

speeches.[5] After diligent research to collect material, Theodore Roosevelt sometimes revised his speeches five or six times.[6]

There is no simple answer to the question of how much time it takes to prepare a good speech. These matters cannot and must not be judged in terms of time. The amount of time spent depends upon how eager you are to succeed, how much you already know about the subject, the availability of materials, the enthusiasm with which you work, and the type of standards which you impose upon yourself.

The research for a speech may be divided into eight steps:

1. Finding a subject
2. Taking an inventory of what you already know about the subject
3. Acquiring additional general background on the subject
4. Crystallizing, rewording, and narrowing the subject
5. Formulating an appropriate thesis
6. Locating additional material; preparing a bibliography
7. Selecting material to be covered
8. Reading, synthesis, and note taking

FINDING A SUBJECT

The selecting of a speech topic is, indeed, an individual matter depending upon many variable factors. Therefore it does seem futile to list a large number of specific subjects which might catch the fancy of the student. A complete list, of course, would be as broad as life itself, for speeches are made about all phases of human conduct.

Taking a suggestion from the ancient rhetoricians, we list the following areas or realms of activity to stimulate your thinking. The topics are by no means mutually exclusive; there is much overlapping. Hundreds or thousands of subjects may be developed from each area. What the student makes out of the following suggestions will depend largely upon his creative inventiveness.

[5] Glen Mills, "Misconceptions Concerning Daniel Webster," *The Quarterly Journal of Speech*, December, 1943, pp. 423-428.

[6] William A. Behl, "Theodore Roosevelt's Principles of Speech Preparation and Delivery," *Speech Monographs*, 1945, pp. 112-122.

Sources of Speech Subjects

Speeches to Inform	Speeches to Entertain	Speeches to Stimulate	Speeches to Convince and to Actuate

1. Criticism
   a. Movies
   b. Plays
   c. Speeches
   d. Literature
2. Current events
3. Definitions
4. Descriptions
5. Explanations and demonstrations
   a. Apparatus
   b. Machines
   c. Tools
   d. Processes
   e. Procedures
6. Reviews
   a. Books
   b. Plays
   c. Movies
7. Interpretations
   a. Social customs and mores
   b. Religion
   c. Political affairs
   d. Government
   e. History
8. Travelogues
	1. True stories
	   a. About yourself
	   b. About others
	2. Travel accounts
	3. Character studies
	4. Fantastic or unbelievable tales
	5. Reports
	   a. Books
	   b. Plays
	   c. Movies
	6. Humorous situations
	7. The trivial but spectacular mishap
	8. Exaggeration
	9. Paradox
	10. Parody-travesty
	11. Satire
		1. Acts of courage and bravery
		2. Heroes and great characters
		3. Memorable and revered events
		4. Significant institutions and organizations
		5. Patriotic themes
		6. Religious themes
			1. Political problems
			   a. International
			   b. Regional
			   c. National
			   d. Sectional
			   e. State
			   f. County
			   g. Local
			   h. Personal
			2. Agricultural problems
			3. Industrial problems
			4. Business problems
			5. Labor problems
			6. Educational problems
			7. Family problems
			8. Religious problems
			9. Philosophical and ethical problems
			10. Social problems
			11. Scientific problems
			12. Personal affairs

The resourceful speaker should be constantly on the alert for good subjects. Creative thinking may be stimulated by creative reading of challenging editorials, magazine articles, and thought-provoking books and by listening to news commentators and to significant speakers. In this respect the beginning speaker may find help in listening to a daily news broadcast, the Chicago Round Table, Town Meeting of the Air, and similar programs or in reading *Vital Speeches,* the *Congressional Digest,* and the weekly news magazines. Excellent collections of speeches are Chauncey Goodrich's *Select British Eloquence* (Harper & Brothers, 1854), *Modern Eloquence* (D. F. Colliers, 1936), and Baird's annual *Representative American Speeches* (The H. W. Wilson Company).

The inspiration for the speech topic should grow out of the speech situation, that is, the speaker, the audience, or the occasion. Some important considerations are the following:

1. What "leads" has the program chairman or committee-in-charge given?
2. What do your motives in delivering the speech suggest?
3. What subjects are you most capable of presenting under the given conditions?
4. What is considered appropriate and inappropriate for the occasion?
5. What would the audience like to hear discussed?
6. What topics are in the public eye?

TESTING THE SUBJECT

In the chapter on Some First Principles we made several suggestions to the beginner concerning the choosing of a topic. Our emphasis in each case was upon simplifying the beginner's task. Now let us broaden our treatment to consider criteria that can be used in testing the suitability of any speech topic. Necessarily, some of these tests will be only a further development of what was said earlier.

Test 1: Do I Have a Reserve of Information About the Subject?

Or phrase the question another way, Am I qualified to discuss it? Have I had personal, direct experience with the subject? This test is an outgrowth of a suggestion made in Chapter II and needs little elaboration beyond what was said earlier. Conservation of time demands that you concentrate on those areas about which you know the most. To go far afield in search for a speech topic is to invite certain failure.

Test 2: Am I Enthusiastic About the Subject?

Do I have an urge to communicate this subject to an audience? Do I look forward to delivering a speech on this topic? This test is further development of a point discussed in Chapter II. The old adage that "Enthusiasm is contagious" explains the importance of this test. Your eagerness and enthusiasm are reflected in your preparation, in your manner, and in your voice. In turn, sensing your interest the listeners are swept along toward the goal which you hope to achieve.

After a lifetime of speaking and of observing and studying other great speakers, Albert J. Beveridge wrote, ". . . speak only when you have something to say. Be sure that you have a message to deliver. . . . This means, of course, utter sincerity. Never under any circumstances or for any reward tell an audience what you, yourself, do not believe or are even indifferent about."[7]

Test 3: Are Other Sources of Information Readily Available?

Can additional materials be found in the local library? Are there local persons who through interviews may give you information?

Personal experience, invaluable as it is, seldom is sufficient for the complete development of a speech. Embarrassing gaps ordinarily exist in your information. If you are to study the sub-

---

[7] Albert J. Beveridge, *The Art of Public Speaking*, Houghton Mifflin Company, 1924, pp. 19-20.

ject from many angles, you must have close at hand abundant reserves.

Test 4: Can the Subject Be Made to Interest the Audience?

What aspects of the subject will be interesting to the listeners? Can the subject be adapted to fit their wants? Russell Conwell, famous American lecturer, presented his talk "Acres of Diamonds" over sixty-one hundred times in a period of fifty years. And yet Conwell's speech seemed never to grow old to his generation; he built it around an appeal which peculiarly touched Americans of that time. Keenly aware of the social, political, and economic forces at work, he emphasized that opportunity and riches were actually close at hand for the man who would but look for them. His appeal to the fundamental wants of security and well-being was one that few Americans could resist.[8]

Since subjects related to the auditor's wants are likely to stimulate greater responsiveness, they require less effort for successful presentation. It is a wise speaker who keeps this fact in mind in selecting a subject.

Test 5: Is the Subject as Stated Well Within the Listeners' Understanding?

It is not difficult to see that the general level of intellectual ability of an audience becomes another important determinant in choosing a speech topic. Some groups might have some difficulty comprehending certain aspects of the fourth dimension, general semantics, relativity, atomic research, radar, and calculus. But any of these topics, if sufficiently limited and clearly presented, might fall within their comprehension. If you have a topic which appears to be above the intellectual capacity of a group, either limit it to a phase well within their intellectual attainment or select another subject.

---

[8] Mary Louise Gehring, "The Invention of Russell H. Conwell in His Lecture, 'Acres of Diamonds,'" unpublished M.A. thesis, Louisiana State University, 1949.

Test 6: Is Oral Presentation of the Topic Possible Under the Circumstances?

The physical surroundings and the available equipment must also be considered in deciding on a subject. Motion-picture projectors, film strip projectors, charts, chart racks, and blackboards may make considerable difference in the final outcome of your speech.

If, for an expository talk, you choose to discuss "the operation of a B-36," you need certain equipment. Since it is hardly possible to bring a B-36 to class or to take the class to the airport, you should have charts, pictures, and models available or at least a blackboard. If none of these is available, your talk is probably doomed to failure.

Test 7: Is the Subject Timely? Is It an Opportune Time to Discuss the Topic?

Has the subject received favorable attention recently? Although the subject of dueling was timely during the first half of the nineteenth century, it is no longer of general interest. For the same reason, trial by jury, popular election of senators, a six-year term for the President, and military occupation of Haiti hold less interest for us today than they once did.

Carefully weigh what advantages will accrue from a presentation of the subject at a given moment. Those subjects which have received attention in the press and over the radio will already be familiar to your auditors. Your success on many occasions may depend upon how skillfully you read the signs of the times and take advantage of current interest.

Test 8: Is the Subject Appropriate for the Occasion?

Will a discussion of it be considered in harmony with the spirit of the assembly? It is important that you do not give the impression of being inconsiderate and thoughtless about community customs. To violate the spirit of an occasion reflects upon your good judgment and good character.

SUBJECTS, SOURCES, MATERIALS

Such thoughtlessness could have had a serious consequence when Lincoln spoke at Gettysburg. When the news was released that he had accepted an invitation to appear, the story was circulated that Lincoln would deliver a political stump speech. Recognizing that such a choice was inappropriate for the dedication of a national cemetery, he naturally chose to do otherwise. After reading the advance copy of Edward Everett's two-and-a-half-hour address, he planned a short, five-minute inspirational talk, which proved to be most "fitting and proper" for that occasion. You too should always make sure that your subject will be "fitting and proper" for the meeting.

Test 9: Is the Subject Sufficiently Limited in Scope for Adequate Development Within the Time Limit?

As a general rule, a topic should be as specific as possible. As we have said earlier, broad philosophical and theoretical questions are difficult to treat, especially within a short period. Limit your subject sufficiently to ensure complete development. Instead of attempting to speak upon the general subject of world government in a ten-minute speech, you will probably be more successful if you discuss a limited phase such as "United Nations efforts to institute atomic control," "how the individual citizen can contribute to the United Nations," or "what the United Nations accomplished in Indonesia." The student who decides to speak upon the topic of "industrialization of the South" in a five-minute speech has failed to consider this test. His talk will be improved if he narrows his subject to the industrialization of one city or one county. If he does not narrow it, his treatment will be superficial and hurried, his assertions sweeping, and his evidence scant.

In light of the extensive discussion of this test in the chapter on some first principles, further discussion hardly seems necessary.

SURVEYING THE SUBJECT

Your inventory of what you already know about the tentative subject should reveal the areas in which you are weak. A more rigid definition of terms may be necessary before you can go further. In fact the exploratory phase of your research should institute a continual attempt to redefine the topic in light of new evidence.

In order to see the implications of the topic, to test its appropriateness, and to uncover new approaches, some reading in standard reference works may prove advisable. Upon the basis of such reading, you may decide whether to abandon the topic, recast it, or do further research upon it.

Some of the better known reference works which may prove helpful are given below:

> *The Encyclopedia Americana, The Encyclopaedia Britannica, Nelson's Perpetual Loose-Leaf Encyclopedia, The International Encyclopedia*
>
> *Who's Who, Who's Who in America, The Dictionary of American Biography, National Cyclopedia of American Biography, Dictionary of National Biography, Webster's Biographical Dictionary, Twentieth Century Authors, Current Biography*
>
> *Monroe's Cyclopedia of Education*
>
> *Cambridge Ancient History, Cambridge Medieval History, Cambridge Modern History, The New Larned History for Ready Reference, Pageant of America*
>
> *Cambridge History of American Literature, Cambridge History of English Literature, Library of Southern Literature*
>
> *Cyclopedia of American Government*
>
> *Encyclopedia of Religion and Ethics*
>
> *Encyclopedia of the Social Sciences*

PREPARING A BIBLIOGRAPHY

In order to have a comprehensive view of the pertinent material, for many speeches it is advisable to prepare a bibliography: a list of books, articles, and materials on the subject. Entries may be classified under the following headings: (1) books, (2) magazine articles, (3) government documents, (4) newspapers, (5) miscellaneous. Other categories may be added to meet the needs of a specific topic. To aid in later classification and alphabetizing, it is wise to record each reference on a separate small index card (three by five inches) or slip of paper. For books, include name of author with surname first, title, publisher, and date of publication as indicated in the illustration below:

> Gray, Giles Wilkeson, and Wise, Claude Merton, *The Bases of Speech*, Harper & Brothers, rev. ed., 1946.

If available also include on the card the library call number for future use. For magazines include items given in the *Periodical Guide to Literature*. Note the two examples given:

> *Newsweek* 33:36, January 3, 1949.
> *Sch & Soc* 69:14-15, January 1, 1949.

Bibliography

The assembling of a bibliography is a challenge to your resourcefulness. Many general reference works such as the *Dictionary of American Biography* give valuable bibliographical suggestions following each article. Ordinarily it is possible to locate prepared bibliographies on your subject or on a similar subject. *The Bibliographical Index* (The H. W. Wilson Company), published since 1937, provides an extensive list of bibliographies. In the first volume, 1937 to 1942, over fifty thousand are indexed. Better books on the subject may include a selected list of references. The card catalogue should furnish additional ideas.

Books

If exhaustive research is the goal, horizons should not be limited to the holdings of the local library. The most complete source of information concerning American books is the *Cumulative Book Index* (The H. W. Wilson Company), which includes a listing in alphabetical order by author, title, and subject all books published in this country. *The Book Review Digest*, which includes condensed reviews of current books, offers a convenient source for locating current publications.

Periodicals

For the periodical field, numerous indexes are published. The most widely used of these is the *Readers' Guide to Periodical Literature*, which has appeared since 1900. It indexes articles from a selected list of the more popular periodicals of the United States and Canada (see front of any volume) by author, title, and subject matter. Earlier American periodicals are indexed in *Poole's Index*, which extended from 1802 to 1907. *The International Index to Periodicals* aids in locating references in more scholarly journals of the humanities and sciences. More specialized are *Education Index, Agricultural Index, Catholic Periodical Index, Index to Legal Periodicals, Biography Index, Engineering Index, Industrial Arts Index, Art Index, Dramatic Index,* and *Occupational Index*.

Worthy of special note is the *Public Affairs Information Service*, which is a subject index in the fields of sociology, economics and political science. It indexes books, pamphlets, and government documents, as well as current periodicals.

Government Publications

For government publications published through 1940, consult the *Document Catalogue*. This index is kept up to date by the *Monthly Catalogue*. The indexes to the various volumes of the *Congressional Record* provide insight into subjects discussed in Congress, but many times much effort is required to ferret out the grain of wheat in the bushel of chaff.

Newspapers

Unfortunately most newspapers are not indexed, and no guides to them have been published. The one notable exception is the *New York Times Index*, which has appeared since 1913. Each entry gives exact reference to date, page, and column. It is valuable in locating materials in other papers, for once the date of publication of a story is determined, similar dates may be checked in other papers.

Special Fields

In the special fields, numerous helps are available for the student who will search them out. Lester Thonssen and Elizabeth Fatherson's *Bibliography of Speech Education* (The H. W. Wilson Company, 1939) provides a bibliography in the area of speech. Particularly valuable to the student of American history is *Writing on American History, 1906-1940,* which indexes numerous materials in the historical field. Recent doctoral studies may be located in the series entitled *Doctoral Dissertations Accepted by American Universities* (The H. W. Wilson Company), edited by Arnold H. Trotier. Each year *Speech Monographs* publishes a list of the graduate studies completed in leading departments of speech in the United States. Similar lists are prepared in other fields.

SPECIAL SOURCES OF MATERIAL

The beginning speaker should familiarize himself with certain well-known almanacs, handbooks, and compilations. The three most frequently used books of this kind are *The World Almanac* (World-Telegram), *The Statesman's Yearbook* (The Macmillan Company), and *Information Please Almanac* (The Macmillan Company). Contained in each of these books are facts and statistics on a great variety of subjects. Brief descriptions of the nations of the world, lists of educational institutions, population figures, postal regulations, leading events of the previous year, world's records in sports, industrial earnings as well as sundry other information are among the offerings of these yearly publications. The major encyclopedias issue annual supplements to keep abreast of the times.

Rich in factual material are two government publications, *The Statistical Abstract of the United States,* an annual summary of statistical information from the various agencies of the Federal government, and *The United States Census Reports,* a collection of data on population, employment, agriculture, manufacturing, and business for a ten-year period. These reports have been issued each decade since 1790.

The Reference Shelf series, published by The H. W. Wilson Company, is sometimes extremely helpful in giving an overall view of a subject. In each volume devoted to a particularly controversial topic are included articles, both pro and con, an excellent bibliography, and frequently a complete brief on each side of the proposition. Of a similar nature is the *Debate Handbook* series, published annually under the auspices of the National University Extension Association. The *Annals of the American Academy of Political and Social Science,* a periodical, devotes each issue to a current problem, with articles by leading authorities. *The Congressional Digest,* not to be confused with the *Congressional Record,* gives the pros and cons on leading controversial topics of the day.

Periodicals provide an almost inexhaustible source, as is indicated by Ulrick's *Periodical Directory* (R. R. Bowker Company, 1947), which lists over seventy-five hundred entries. Familiarity with each of the selected lists given below will aid you considerably in locating speech materials:

General Magazines

American Magazine
American Mercury
Atlantic Monthly
Catholic World
Commonweal
Christian Century
Collier's
Coronet
Current History
Fortune
Forum
Harpers Magazine

National Geographic
Nation
Newsweek
New Republic
Pathfinder
Reader's Digest
Survey
Saturday Evening Post
Time
United States News
Yale Review

Special Magazines

American City
American Home
American Photography
Better Homes and Gardens
Business Week
Congressional Digest
Foreign Affairs
Holiday
House Beautiful
Hygeia
Musical America

Nature
Nation's Business
Natural History
Parents' Magazine
Popular Mechanics Magazine
Popular Science
Saturday Review of Literature
School and Society
Scientific American
Science

Scholarly Journals

American Economic Review
American Historical Review
American Journal of International Law
American Journal of Psychology
American Journal of Sociology
American Literature
American Journal of Physics
Annals of American Academy of Political and Social Science
Canadian History Review
Classical Quarterly
Classical Review
English Journal
Journal of Home Economics

Journal of Negro History
Journal of Politics
Journal of Political Economy
Journal of Social Psychology
Journal of Religion
Journal of Southern History
Library Journal
Monthly Labor Review
Mississippi Valley Historical Review
Political Science Quarterly
Quarterly Journal of Economics
Social Research
Social Forces

Speech Magazines

Central States Speech Journal
Educational Theatre Journal
Forensic
Gavel
Journal of Speech and Hearing Disorders
The Quarterly Journal of Speech

Southern Speech Journal
Speaker
Speech Activities
Speech Monographs
Theatre Arts Monthly
Vital Speeches
Western Speech

Ordinarily, the numerous associations representing pressure groups are eager to forward pamphlets and materials on request. Such material, written from a particular bias, is valuable if the reader is discerning. *The World Almanac* for 1950 provides a list of over one thousand of these groups.[9] Some of the more prominent are the following:

American Bar Association, 140 North Dearborn St., Chicago, Ill.

American Farm Bureau Federation, 109 North Wabash Ave., Chicago 2, Ill.

American Federation of Labor, AF of L Bldg., 9th St. and Mass. Ave., N. W., Washington, D. C.

American Friends Service Committee, 20 South 12th St., Philadelphia 7, Pa.

American Medical Association, 535 North Dearborn St., Chicago 10, Ill.

American National Red Cross, 17th and E St., N. W., Washington, 13, D. C.

Chamber of Commerce of the United States of America, 1615 H St., N. W., Washington 6, D. C.

Congress of Industrial Organizations, 718 Jackson Place, N. W., Washington 6, D. C.

Federal Council of Churches of Christ in America, 297 Fourth Ave., New York 10, N. Y.

League of Women Voters of the United States, 726 Jackson Place, Washington, D. C.

National Association of Manufacturers, 14 West 49th St., New York 20, N. Y.

National Council for Prevention of War, 1013 18th St., N. W., Washington 6, D. C.

National Grange, Patrons of Husbandry, 744 Jackson Place, N. W., Washington 6, D. C.

COLLECTING EVIDENCE

Once the bibliography is completed, the speaker is ready to collect additional arguments and evidence. As early as possible

[9] See pp. 575-594.

the subject should be narrowed to fit the time limit, and a thesis should be formulated. (The subject of framing the proposition is dealt with at length in the next chapter.) Of course, as the speaker pursues his study, he may recast his main thought several times. The argument and type of evidence he selects to substantiate his position depend upon his own familiarity with the subject, the length of the speech, and the time available for study. In light of these, the speaker can choose references listed in his bibliography and read until he feels adequately prepared.

As he reads, he should keep before him such queries as the following:

1. Is the material primary or secondary?
2. What are the reputation and professional standing of the author and publisher?
3. Does the date of publication affect the validity of the material?
4. What was the author's purpose in presenting the material?
5. Are the materials and conclusions based upon careful and thorough research?
6. Is the author consistent?
7. Has the author explained his method of research sufficiently that his findings can be checked?
8. Are his conclusions verified by other authorities in the field?

RECORDING NOTES

The most frequently recommended method of note taking involves recording materials on index cards or small slips of paper easily filed. If slips of paper are used, they should probably conform to standard sizes of filing boxes—3 by 5 and 4 by 6 inches.

Some uniform system of labeling should be adopted. As soon as possible a standard set of topics should be drafted under which to file information. The subject should be placed in the upper left corner with the source immediately following the quotation or evidence.

> Requisites of good speaking
>
> "The art of speaking depends on great labor, constant study, varied exercise, repeated trials, the deepest sagacity, and the readiest judgment."
>
> Quintilian, <u>Institutes of Oratory</u>, John S. Watson, translator, Henry G. Bohn, 1856, vol. 1, pp. 136-137.

Care should be taken that the bibliographic reference is complete, that is, the same information recorded in a bibliography. The following suggestions should be observed:

1. Label clearly and uniformly.
2. Write clearly, and do not crowd material.
3. Place one subject on a card.
4. Do not distort meaning by lifting material out of context.
5. If you copy verbatim, enclose in quotation marks. For a quotation within a quotation, use single quotes.
6. Delete unnecessary portions and indicate by using three dots (...) for deletion within a sentence and four dots (....) for deletions at end of sentence.

IN A FREE SOCIETY THE SERMON IS A PREVALENT TYPE OF PUBLIC SPEECH

Each Sunday millions assemble in church to hear their pastors preach according to the dictates of their own consciences. In a democratic society Protestants, Jews, and Catholics worship without fear, whether it be in a country chapel, a tabernacle, or a great cathedral. These are rights which free men fight to preserve.

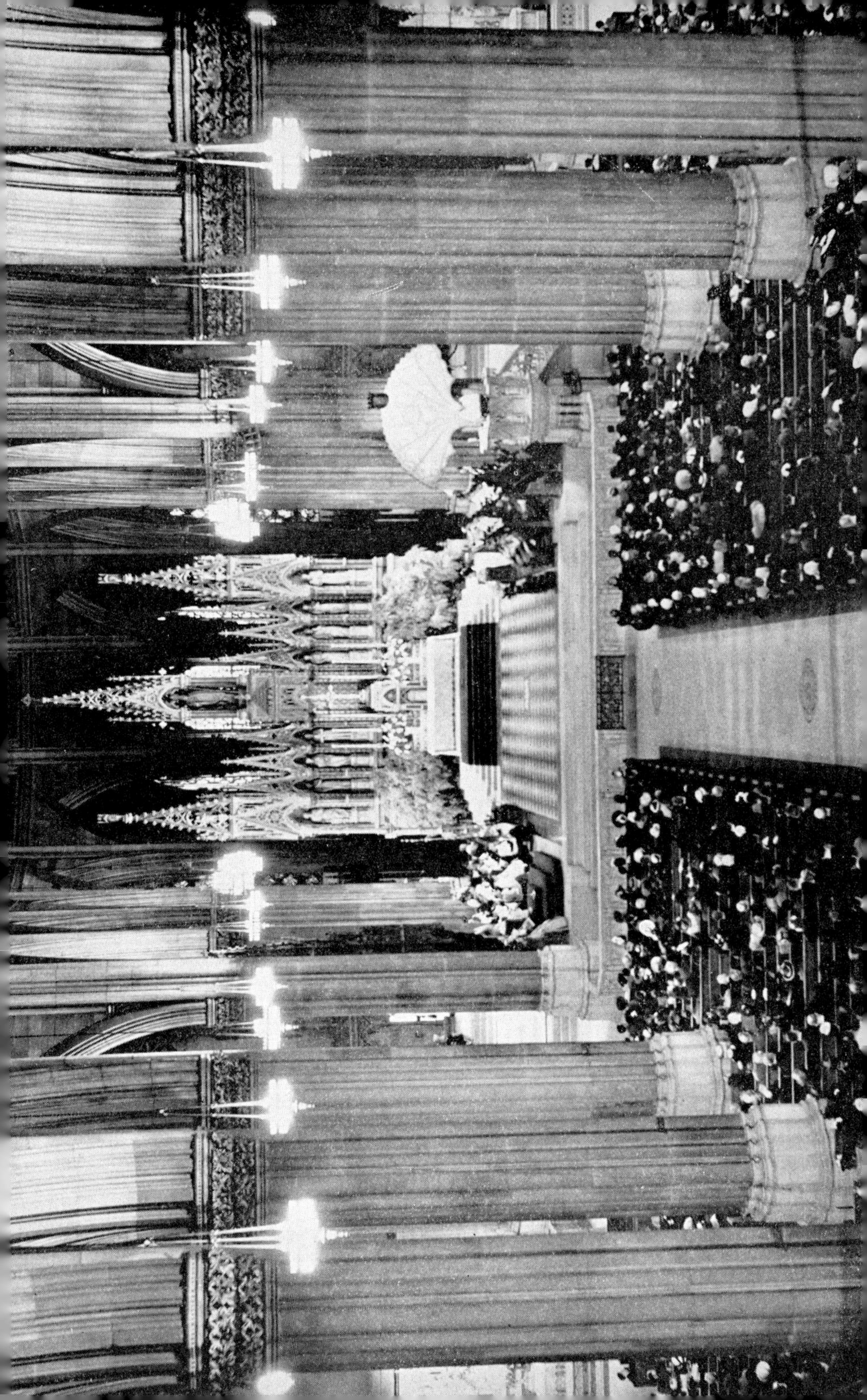

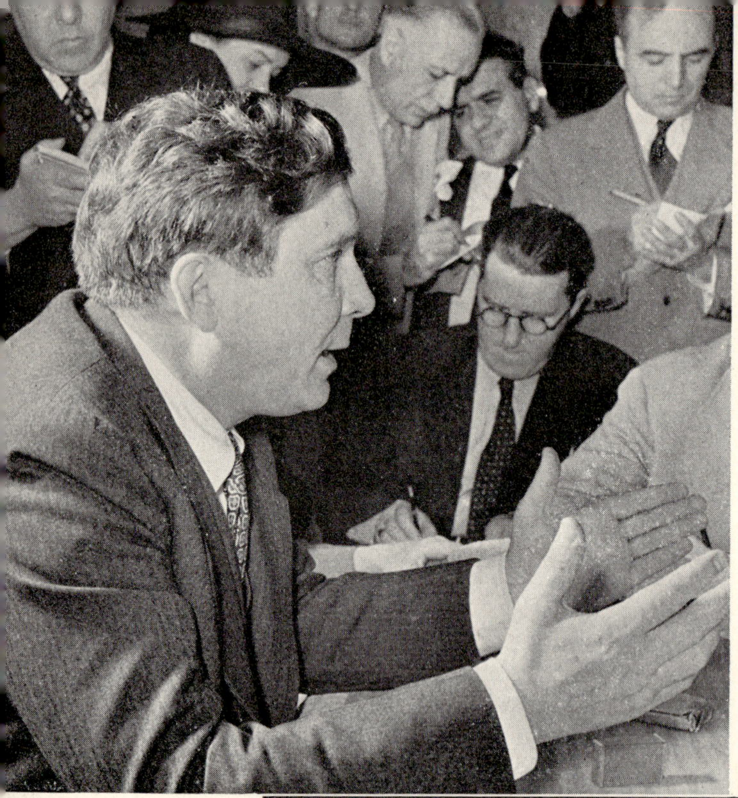

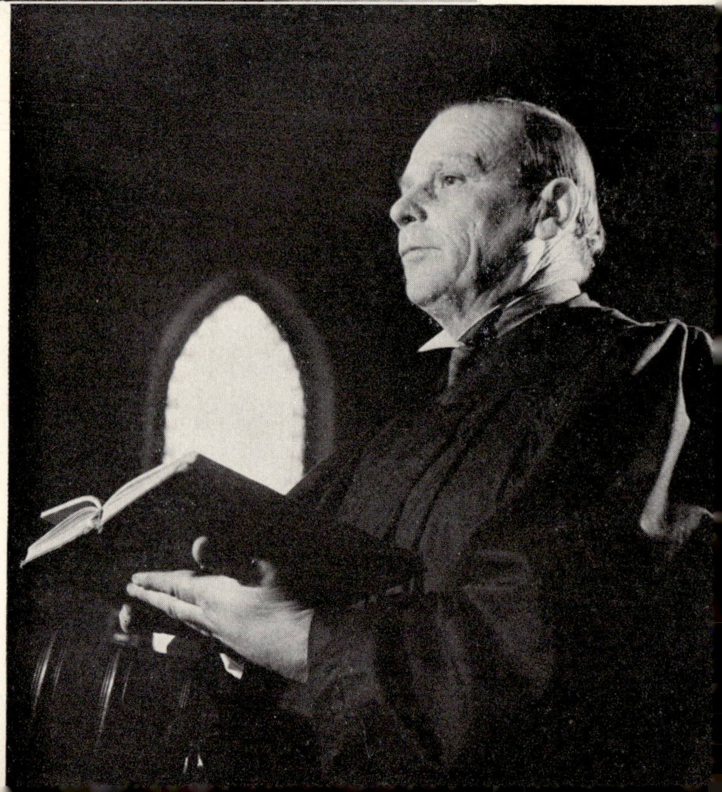

SUBJECTS, SOURCES, MATERIALS

7. Quote exactly. If the material seems in error, if words are omitted, or if words are misspelled, place [sic] immediately following the discrepancy to indicate that the mistake or deletion has been noted.
8. To indicate interpolation within a quotation, place remark within brackets, not parentheses.
9. Indicate italicized words by underlining.
10. After copying material, check it against original before proceeding.

Supplementary Bibliography of Useful References for a Speaker

Atlases

Hammond's *New World Atlas*, Garden City Publishing Company, Inc., 1947.

Books About Words

Barnhart, Clarence (ed.), *The American College Dictionary*, text ed., Harper & Brothers, 1948.

Crabb, George, *English Synonyms*, Grosset & Dunlap, Inc., 1945.

Fernald, James C., *Synonyms, Antonyms, and Prepositions*, Funk & Wagnalls Company, 1947.

Funk and Wagnalls' *New Standard Dictionary*, Funk & Wagnalls Company, 1946.

Kenyon, John Samuel, and Knot, Thomas Albert, *A Pronouncing Dictionary of American English*, G. & C. Merriam Company, 1944.

Roget, Peter M., *Thesaurus of English Words and Phrases*, Grosset & Dunlap, Inc., 1945.

Webster's *New Collegiate Dictionary*, G. & C. Merriam Company, 1949.

Webster's *New International Dictionary*, G. & C. Merriam Company, 1945.

THE SPEAKER'S ATTITUDE WILL BE REFLECTED IN HIS AUDIENCE

The seriousness and businesslike manner of Wendell Willkie resulted in a similar attitude among the newspaper correspondents who were attending his press conference.

In the second photograph the solemnity and garb of the minister helped to stimulate an attitude of reverence among his listeners. (Photos, Black Star.)

Dictionaries—Specialized

Adams, James Truslow, *Dictionary of American History*, Charles Scribner's Sons, 1940, 6 vols.
The Oxford Classical Dictionary, Oxford University Press, 1949.
Webster's *Biographical Dictionary*, G. & C. Merriam Company, 1943.
Webster's *Geographical Dictionary*, G. & C. Merriam Company, 1949.

Guides to Literature

Hart, John (ed.), *The Oxford Companion to American Literature*, Oxford University Press, 1948.
Harvey, Paul (ed.), *The Oxford Companion to English Literature*, Oxford University Press, 1946.
Harvey, Paul (ed.), *The Oxford Companion to Classical Literature*, Oxford University Press, 1937.
Spiller, Robert E., et al., *Literary History of the United States*, The Macmillan Company, 1948, 3 vols.

Familiar Quotations

Bartlett, John, *Familiar Quotations*, Little, Brown & Company, 1948.
Mencken, H. L. (ed.), *A New Dictionary of Quotations*, Alfred A. Knopf, Inc., 1942.
The Oxford Dictionary of Quotations, Oxford University Press, 1941.
Stevenson, Burton (ed.), *Home Book of Quotations*, Dodd, Mead & Company, Inc., 1947.

Style—Correct Usage

A Manual of Style, University of Chicago Press, 1949.

Parliamentary Law

Roberts, Henry M., *Rules of Order Revised for Deliberative Assemblies*, Scott, Foresman & Company, 1943.

Collections of Speeches

Baird, A. Craig (ed.), *Representative American Speeches*, The H. W. Wilson Company, published annually.
Brewers, David J. (ed.), *The World's Best Orators*, F. P. Kaiser, 1901.
Brigance, William Norwood, *Classified Speech Models*, F. S. Crofts & Co., 1928.
Bryan, William Jennings, *The World's Famous Orations*, Funk & Wagnalls Company, 1906, 10 vols.

SUBJECTS, SOURCES, MATERIALS

Goodrich, Chauncey A., *Select British Eloquence*, Harper & Brothers, 1854.
Harding, Samuel Bannister, *Select Orations*, The Macmillan Company, 1924.
Hicks, Frederic, *Famous American Jury Speeches*, West Publishing Company, 1925.
Lee, Guy Carleton, *The World's Orators*, G. P. Putnam's Sons, 1900, 10 vols.
Lindgren, Homer D., *Modern Speeches*, F. S. Crofts & Co., 1926.
O'Neill, James M., *Modern Short Speeches*, The Century Co., 1925.
O'Neill, James M., *Classified Models of Speech Composition*, The Century Co., 1921.
O'Neill, James Milton, and Riley, Floyd K., *Contemporary Speeches*, The Century Co., 1930.
Sandford, William Phillips, and Yeager, Willard Hayes, *Business Speeches by Business Men*, McGraw-Hill Book Company, Inc., 1930.
Sarett, Lew, and Foster, William Trufant, *Modern Speeches on Basic Issues*, Houghton Mifflin Company, 1939.
Thorndike, Ashley (ed.), *Modern Eloquence*, P. F. Collier and Son, 1936, 15 vols.

EXERCISES

1. *Speaking Assignment.* Deliver a three- to five-minute speech in which you explain the operation of some apparatus. If possible, actually bring the apparatus to class for demonstration. Divide your explanation into three or four steps or points.
2. *Speaking Assignment.* Report orally to the class on the steps you followed in finding the answer to one of the problems given below. Tell why you know that your answer is correct. (Review section on Collecting Evidence.) If you are unable to find what you consider a satisfactory answer, discuss with the class the steps you followed, and analyze why you failed. The answers *are not* as simple as they may appear.
   Questions for research:
   a. What was the speaking rate of Franklin D. Roosevelt?
   b. How many speeches did Harry Truman deliver in the campaign of 1948?

c. Did Napoleon sell Louisiana because he needed the money?
   d. Who won the Lincoln-Douglas debates?
   e. What was the physical appearance of Lincoln in March, 1860?
   f. Did George Washington write his Farewell Address?
   g. Who wrote Shakespeare's plays?
   h. How many official versions are there of the Gettysburg Address?
   i. Can you verify the handwriting of Franklin D. Roosevelt?
   j. In 1860 how many persons in Alabama owned more than three hundred slaves each?
   k. How many horses were there in Knox County, Tennessee, in 1860?
   l. Who won the World Series in 1924?
   m. What color clothes did the Pilgrims wear?
   n. Did the Pilgrims land on Plymouth Rock?
   o. Did Patrick Henry utter the phrase "Give me liberty or give me death"?
3. *Speaking Assignment.* Read carefully one of the following speeches or a similar one from another source. Prepare a four-minute oral summary or criticism of the speech as a whole or of some pertinent idea found in the speech. Notice also the sources indicated by your speaker.

   William G. Carleton, "Take Your College in Stride," *Vital Speeches*, February 1, 1947, p. 320. Also found in *Representative American Speeches: 1946-47*, pp. 222-225.

   Lionel Crocker, "On Seas of Ink," *Vital Speeches*, February 1, 1947, pp. 249-252.

   George V. Denny, et al., "Is the American Press Really Free?," *Representative American Speeches: 1946-47*, pp. 159-176.

   Monroe E. Deutsch, "A Life Without Books," *Vital Speeches*, January 15, 1944, pp. 220-223.

   Eberhard P. Deutsch, "Advertising and a Free Press," *Vital Speeches*, December 15, 1946, pp. 158-160.

   Grove Patterson, "Social Responsibilities of American Newspapers," *Vital Speeches*, May 1, 1948, pp. 435-438.

   Charles Seymour, "To Listen and To Inquire," *Vital Speeches*, August 1, 1948, pp. 623-625.

   Dorothy Thompson, "Stopping Propaganda," *Representative American Speeches: 1938-39*, pp. 87-93.
4. *Discussion Questions for Class Symposiums.*
   a. What is the "truth"? What is a fact? What is an opinion? What is a bias?

SUBJECTS, SOURCES, MATERIALS

    b. What is a primary source? How does a primary source differ from a secondary one?
    c. How can you ascertain the correctness of facts? That you read in a newspaper? Hear over the radio? See with your own eyes?
    d. What is the political bias of a local newspaper? Does this bias affect the reporting and selection of the news?
    e. What are the biases of a prominent radio newscaster? How does this affect his reporting of the news?
    f. Should we have censorship of the news, comic books, novels, movies, and the radio?
    g. Do you think that all libraries should publicly burn *Mein Kampf*? Advantages? Disadvantages?
    h. As a listener, how can you check a speaker's facts?
5. *Research Assignment.* Select a tentative speech topic for investigation, and prepare a list of the following bibliographical materials:
    a. Five private organizations with their addresses to which you might write for information
    b. Five national authorities with their addresses to whom you might write
    c. Five magazines that you might read for pertinent material
    d. Five local persons whom you might interview; justify your choice
6. *Written Assignment.* In light of what you already know about your classmates, prepare a list of fifty topics which would be appropriate for five-minute speeches. Make your topics as specific as possible. List them under these headings: speeches to stimulate, speeches to entertain, speeches to inform, and speeches to persuade.
7. *Research and Speaking Assignment.* Investigate how some famous speaker prepared his speeches. On the basis of your findings, deliver a five-minute oral report to your classmates.

    For interesting material on the speech preparation of famous speakers, see the following:

    William A. Behl, "Theodore Roosevelt's Principles of Speech Preparation and Delivery," *Speech Monographs*, (1945), pp. 112-122.

    Waldo W. Braden, "The Bases of William E. Borah's Speech Preparation," *The Quarterly Journal of Speech*, February, 1947, pp. 29-30.

    Earnest Brandenburg, "The Preparation of Franklin D. Roosevelt's Speeches," *The Quarterly Journal of Speech*, April, 1949, pp. 214-221.

William Norwood Brigance (ed.), *A History and Criticism of American Public Address*, McGraw-Hill Book Company, Inc., 1943, 2 vols.

Dayton D. McKean, "Notes on Woodrow Wilson's Speeches," *The Quarterly Journal of Speech*, April, 1930, pp. 176-184.

Glen Mills, "Misconceptions Concerning Daniel Webster," *The Quarterly Journal of Speech*, December, 1943, pp. 423-428.

Loren Reid, "Did Charles Fox Prepare His Speeches?" *The Quarterly Journal of Speech*, February, 1938, pp. 17-26.

Charles Ross, "How Truman Did It," *Collier's*, December 25, 1948, pp. 13, 87-88.

SUPPLEMENTARY READINGS

1. Adler, Mortimer J., *How to Read a Book*, Simon and Schuster, Inc., 1940.
2. Aldrich, Ella V., *Using Books and Libraries*, Prentice-Hall, Inc., 1946.
3. Baird, A. Craig, and Knower, Franklin H., *General Speech: An Introduction*, McGraw-Hill Book Company, Inc., 1949, chaps. 4, 5.
4. Bryant, Donald, and Wallace, Karl R., *Fundamentals of Public Speaking*, Appleton-Century-Crofts, Inc., 1947, chaps. 7, 8.
5. Oliver, Robert T., Cortright, Rupert L., and Hager, Cyril F., *The New Training for Effective Speech*, The Dryden Press, Inc., 1946, chap. 7.
6. Parrish, Wayland Maxfield, *Speaking in Public*, Charles Scribner's Sons, 1947, chap. 4.
7. Williamson, Arleigh B., Fritz, Charles A., and Ross, Harold Raymond, *Speaking in Public*, Prentice-Hall, Inc., 2nd ed., 1948, chap. 5.
8. Winans, James A., *Speech-Making*, Appleton-Century-Crofts, Inc., 1938, chap. 4.

CHAPTER VIII

The Informative Speech

IN OUR society the informative talk is probably delivered more frequently than any other type of speech. It prevails wherever instruction is in order—in the classroom, the laboratory, machine shop, the trade school, the factory, boys' and girls' camps, the lodge conclave, the study club, the Farm Bureau meeting, and the Sunday School. The informative speaker may be known by any of a number of names: instructor, leader, coach, teacher, critic, guide, tutor, counselor, director, or lecturer.

Since it is delivered under so many diverse conditions, the informative talk exists in many forms as the following outline will suggest:

1. Simple instructions (giving directions)
2. Informative description
3. Informative narrative

a. Simple narrative
  b. Autobiography
  c. Biographical sketch
  d. Historical account
  e. Travelogue
4. Exposition
5. Appraisal or criticism
  a. Simple criticism
  b. Rhetorical criticism
  c. Dramatic criticism
  d. Literary criticism (book review)

NATURE OF THE INFORMATIVE TALK

Regardless of its form, the informative talk is always directed toward the accomplishment of a twofold objective: to elicit understanding and retention. The development of understanding may involve the correcting of misinformation, the increasing of insight, the presenting of new facts, or the sharpening of critical powers of observation and discrimination. However, giving understanding may be broadened to include what we refer to as training—breaking old habits, developing new skills, or teaching how to manipulate a machine or even a gadget.

Retention is the power to remember or to hold mentally for a period of time what the speaker has said. It hardly seems worth while to make something understandable if immediately thereafter the auditor or student forgets what has been said. The informative speaker, therefore, must not only make his subject clear and meaningful, he must also make it vivid and impressive.

In contrast to the argumentative speech, the informative talk is not concerned with changing attitudes or beliefs or with producing action. The use the listener makes of the knowledge or skill which you impart is not your concern; that choice remains

THE INFORMATIVE SPEECH IS DELIVERED IN MANY DIFFERENT PLACES

Top and bottom photos, L.S.U. Alumni News; left, Esso Standard Oil, Baton Rouge Refinery; right, Black Star.

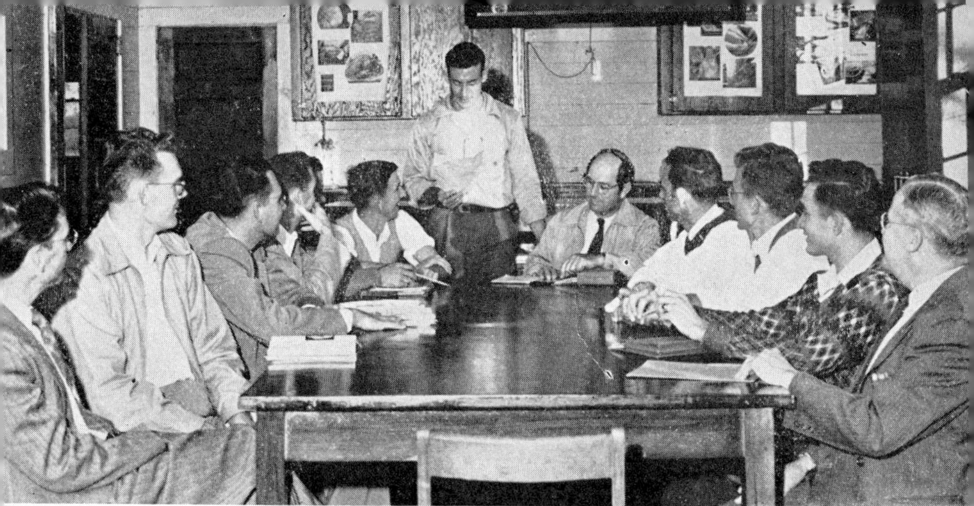
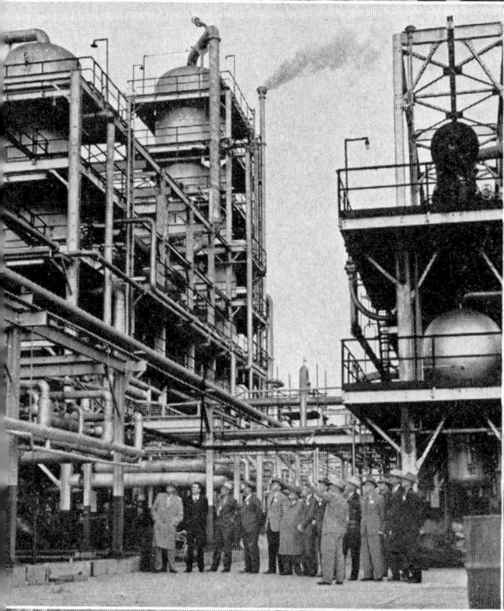
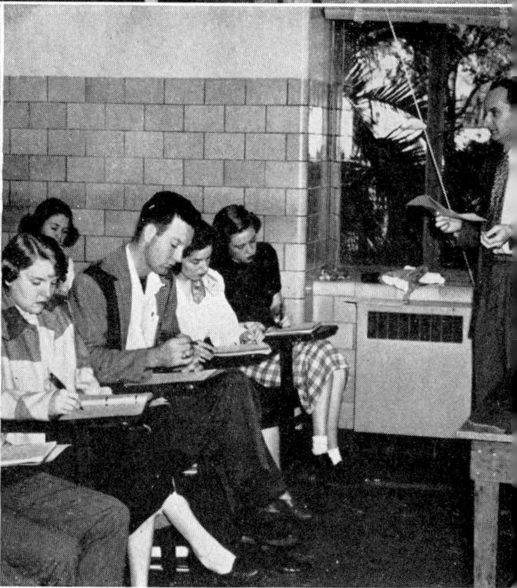
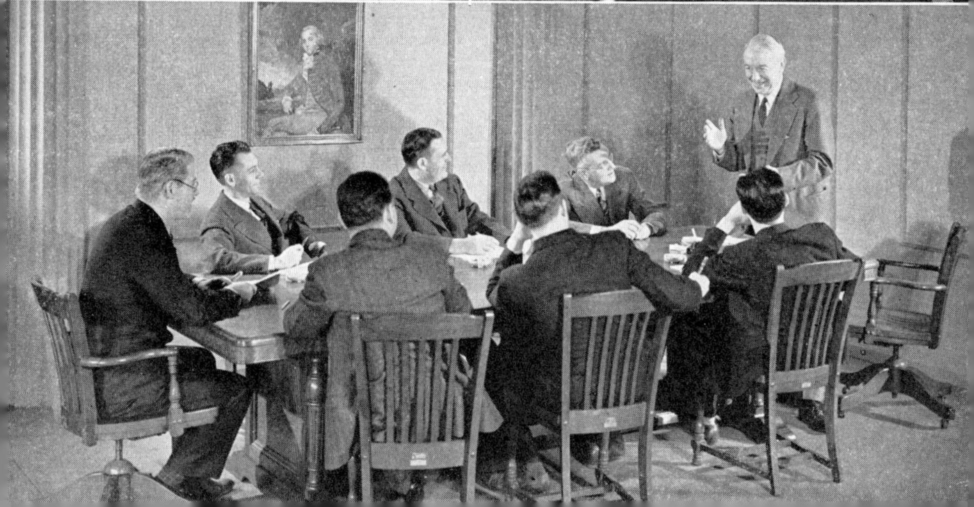

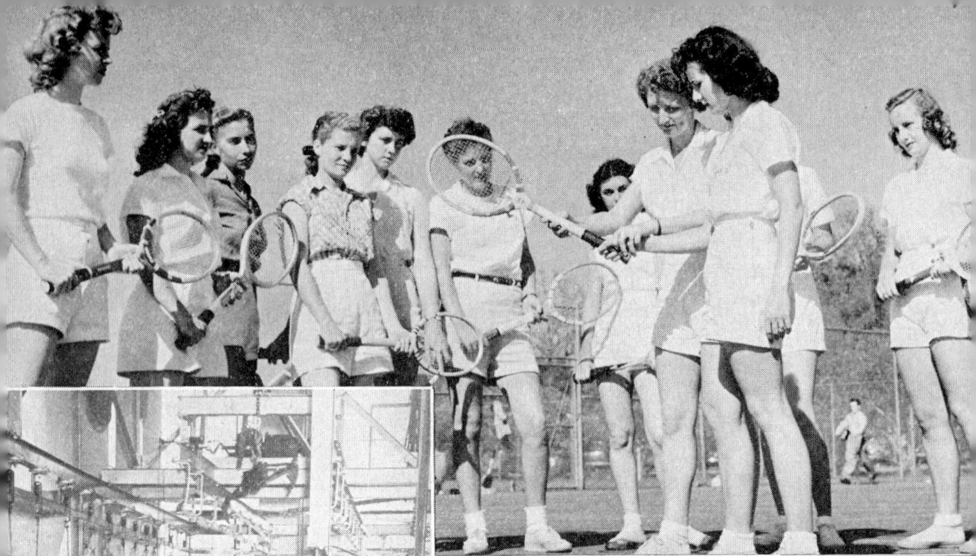
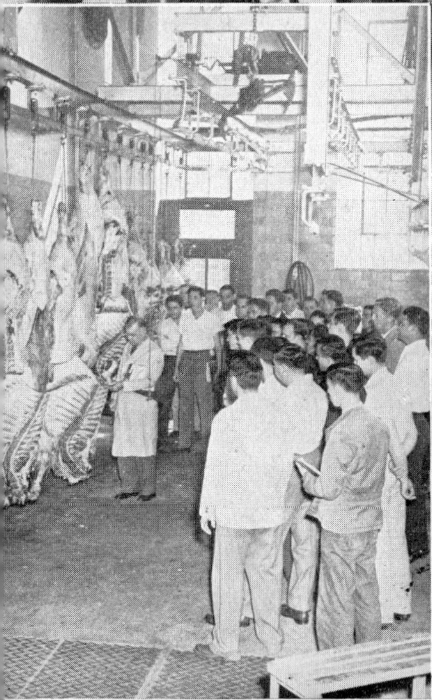
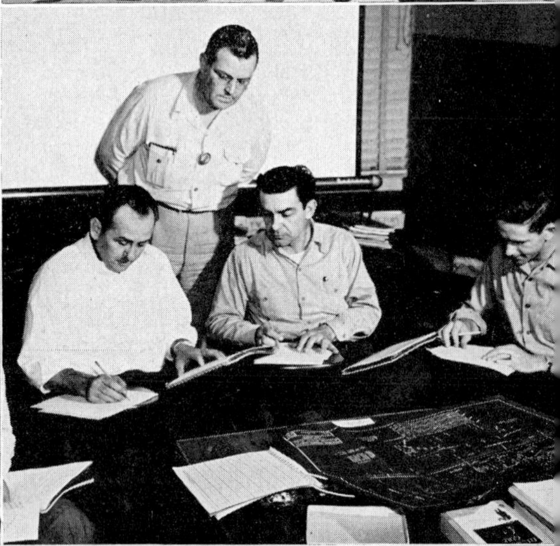
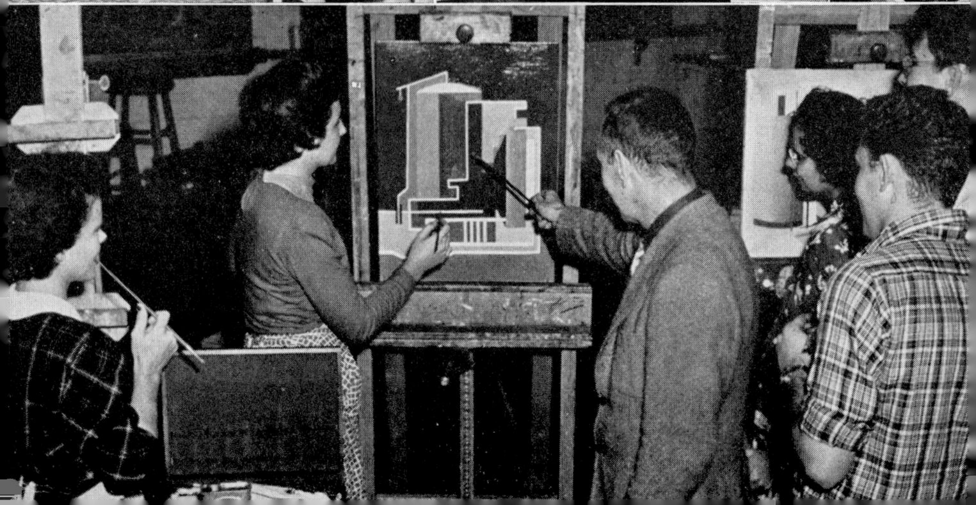

THE INFORMATIVE SPEECH

with the listener. Once the auditor understands and remembers the information presented, your task as a speaker is accomplished.

Later you will learn that comprehension and retention depend upon three qualities: clarity, vividness, and impressiveness. The achievement of these involves all the elements of speechmaking: analysis of the subject matter, organization, choice of language, and delivery. The primary concern of the present chapter is to discuss the analysis and organization of the different types of informative talks for maximum effectiveness.

The analysis and organization of an informative talk may be divided into six steps:

1. Studying and comprehending the materials
2. Selecting the materials for presentation
3. Phrasing a central thought
4. Determining the type of informative speech best suited to presentation of materials
5. Partitioning the subject
6. Developing an outline for presentation

STUDYING AND SELECTING MATERIALS FOR THE INFORMATIVE TALK

If you are to make ideas clear to an audience, you must first understand those ideas. Failure to comprehend your subject is sure to result in an unconvincing, uninspiring performance. To deliver an informative talk effectively, you must meet the following five requirements:

1. You should be objective.
2. You should be thorough.
3. You should be accurate.
4. You should be selective.
5. You should be adaptable.

First, the informative speaker must be objective about the materials he intends to present. In your study and analysis, you

---

THE CRITIQUE IS A COMMON TYPE OF THE INFORMATIVE SPEECH
Top and bottom photos, L.S.U. Alumni News; left, L.S.U. Alumni News; right, Esso Standard Oil, Baton Rouge Refinery.

must attempt to see details and relationships as they really are. Your point of view must be detached and impersonal. If you have preferences and biases, you must by-pass them in an effort to make the listener actually understand the facts.

Second, the informative speaker must be thorough in gathering material for his speech. Your goal in studying your subject should be to accumulate ample reserves upon which to draw. Then you will have no difficulty with the unexpected question, and your reserves will give you additional confidence in your delivery.

Third, the informative speaker must be accurate in recording and reporting details. This requirement should need little elaboration. If you accept the responsibility of presenting information to an audience, you must report the facts—the embarrassing ones as well as those that seem to favor or to be consistent with your "pet" theory.

Fourth, the informative speaker must exercise careful judgment in selecting details for presentation. In this regard you must select your details with reference to the intellectual capacity of your listeners and the amount of time available. Representative details must be selected to give a faithful picture. Enough details must be presented to ensure understanding.

Fifth, the informative speaker must, above all, be able to adapt his materials to the changing elements of the speaking situation. In addition to the ability to extemporize, the speaker must have made extensive preparation which will give him insight into what may or may not be confusing to the learner. You must be prepared to understand and answer the poorly phrased question, the confused question, and the searching question. When queries come, you must be able to give your answer within the framework of your development. Some questions must be ignored, some delayed, and some answered.

FRAMING A CENTRAL THOUGHT

As a starting point in the preparation of the informative talk, you will want first to frame, in a single sentence, a central thought around which to build your talk. But you have great latitude in phrasing this sentence. The only requirement is that you make clear to the listener your particular approach to the subject. The sentence may take any one of the following forms:

1. It may be stated as a question to be answered by the speech.
2. It may consist of a brief definition of the subject.
3. It may evaluate the subject.
4. It may state your intentions in giving the speech.
5. It may partition the subject.

The central thought in question form is frequently used in the lecture. You pose a question to the listeners and then proceed to answer it in your development. The query may ask how, when, why, what, or where. For example, the following questions might be developed into informative speeches: What are the qualities of an effective speech? How can you improve your personality? How can the meaning of the atomic age be made clear to the public?

When the central thought constitutes a brief definition of the subject, it answers the question, "What is it?" The remainder of the speech is devoted to expansion of the definition by the use of facts, illustrations, diagrams, comparisons, or whatever is necessary to make the audience understand. Frequently the speech concerning a process, a procedure, or an operation employs this type of central thought. Below are several examples of this type:

Speech is an overlaid function.
Rhetorical criticism contains a process, a method, and a declaration of judgment.
Poi is a simple Hawaiian food.
The life of a football player is not "the life of Riley."

The central thought may evaluate the subject. Ordinarily, it answers the question, "What is its value?" In the presentation of oral criticism, this type of central thought is used. For example, you may build a talk around the following sentence: "Lloyd Douglas' *Magnificent Obsession* is a thought-provoking novel."

The development of your speech will show in one-two-three order why you hold this opinion concerning the book. Listen to your instructor give an evaluation of the performance of your colleagues. In each instance he may present an informative talk built around a central thought, such as "your indirectness is a serious handicap to your effectiveness" or "your organization was confused."

Other examples of the central thought which evaluates are the following:

Carelessness causes many forest fires.
Group insurance operates on sound business principles.
Adequate nutrition is essential to happy living.
The Frasch process of extracting sulfur is a simple one.

Sometimes the central thought may simply reveal the plan or parts of the speech. In other words, you may say that there are two, three, or four steps in the procedure or process. You actually tell the listeners what to expect. In your speech class you hear a lecture developed around central thoughts like these:

Three major speech dialects exist in the United States.
The effective speech possesses nine essentials.
The refining of sugar is a four-step process.

The speech may be built around a central thought that reveals what the speaker intends to do in the speech. In such a declaration you say, "I wish to describe the latest Paris fashions," or "Permit me to relate to you events of my recent trip to Denver," or "I want to make clear to you how sulfur is mined in Sicily." Such purpose sentences are frequently the central thoughts of the informative description and the informative narration.

SIMPLE INSTRUCTIONS

The simplest and probably the most frequently used type of informative talk is the one in which you give instructions or directions to an auditor. For example, if a passer-by asks the way to the nearest town, you may point in the right direction and say, "Go five miles north, turn left at the schoolhouse, and follow the blacktop for two miles." Some may feel that this does not constitute a "talk" in the formal sense, but in an expanded form it represents a typical informative situation.

Keep in mind three suggestions:

1. Emphasize brevity and simplicity.
2. Carefully enumerate the steps to be followed.
3. Give the listener ample opportunity to ask questions concerning what is not clear.

INFORMATIVE DESCRIPTION

Another common type of the informative speech is the description. Engineers, teachers, foremen, sales managers, supervisors, or department heads may be called on to describe to their protégés a new model, a layout, a display, a new building, a geological formation, an attitude, or even a quality. You too will discover that you will be asked often to give oral informative descriptions.

Description is the portrayal of a scene, person, object, quality, or emotion by means of language. This definition contains three parts worthy of further comment. First, the word "portrayal" implies more than mere enumeration or cataloging of details. It implies that discussion of the object, as a whole and in its parts, will produce a unified and consistent picture to the listener. Through the use of vivid, specific, and concrete words you bring imagery into play and thus move your auditor to envision or to sense the object under consideration. For example, if you use the phrase "bright-red hat" it should give your listener a vivid realization of what you have said. If your language is clear, specific, and well chosen, your words will be translated into shape, color, light, sound, odor, taste, and movement.

Second, note that description deals with an individual object, not a class. Genung explains, "The aim of description . . . is to give the qualities wherein one object is individualized, unlike other objects; and has nothing to do with the class except in so far as referring it to a class may serve to localize it."[1]

The third implication of the definition is that you may describe qualities, attitudes, mental states, or characteristics as well as material objects such as automobiles, salt domes, or diamond rings. When the doctor asks, "How do you feel?" he wants you to describe one of these intangibles. Often in the courtroom, a lawyer describes an intense emotion which somehow helps to explain an act of the accused. At a patriotic gathering it is not unusual to hear talks on "loyalty," "patriotism," "courage," or "fortitude." The play director may stop a rehearsal in order to describe how he thinks Shylock must have felt about the Christian. In each of these cases, the speaker gives an informative description of what may be referred to as an immaterial thing.

Analysis of the Informative Description

The preparation of an informative description involves the following:

1. Analysis of the whole and its parts
2. Selection of details
3. Arrangement of the details for presentation

ANALYSIS OF THE WHOLE AND ITS PARTS. As a starting point in preparation, study the structure or make-up of the object to be described. For the concrete object, consider its class, its shape, its size, its position, its location, and its dominant sensory appeals. Furthermore, investigate how it is put together and how it may be utilized in presenting the details to the listener.

For the immaterial thing you will be interested in predominant qualities, characteristics, and traits. The description of a man's character, for example, will necessitate an attempt to assess the traits which he possesses. The portrayal of a fear will involve its characteristics.

[1] John F. Genung, *The Practical Elements of Rhetoric*, Ginn & Company, 1899, p. 327.

SELECTION OF DETAILS. After you are thoroughly familiar with the object and its parts or divisions, you are ready for the second step. Put to yourself two questions: Which particulars shall I choose? How many will I need to make the subject clear? If you are to succeed in your description, you must select those particulars which give a fair representation of the whole and will result in accurate insight and lasting retention. Presentation of exceptional details, of course, will result in distortion and misunderstanding.

The particulars must be sufficient in number to give a clear picture of the whole but sufficiently limited for presentation within the time limit. The story of the blind men's description of an elephant exemplifies the points made above: asked to describe an elephant, they described what they could feel. Hence the one that touched the animal's side reported that the elephant was like a wall. His colleague that grasped the tail disagreed, for he thought that it was like a rope. Each blind man failed in his description because he knew only an isolated characteristic which was not representative or of sufficient magnitude to give an adequate picture of the whole elephant.

Once you have selected the details for presentation you probably have already reached some conclusion about arrangement, the third step.

ARRANGEMENT OF DETAILS FOR PRESENTATION. In ordering your points, you must obey two voices: that of the subject and that of the audience. The subject may suggest an arrangement, but this arrangement must be planned also to facilitate understanding and retention.

If you are describing a tangible object, you probably will discover that *contiguity*, or what lies next in space, serves as a basis for arranging your points. The description of a drainage project may follow the flow of the stream. If you are describing the Empire State Building, you may choose to move from bottom to top, or vice versa. The play director, in describing a stage setting to his cast, may move from left to right or from upstage to downstage. Below are some possible orders that you may pursue:

1. From far to near or near to far
2. From top to bottom or bottom to top
3. From front to rear or rear to front
4. From right to left or left to right
5. From corner to corner
6. From outside to inside or inside to outside

For the description of an immaterial thing you probably need to arrange the details according to a natural sequence, such as similarity and contrast, cause and effect, or some other system. Since such qualities are abstract and subjective in meaning, it is necessary for you to compare or contrast them with qualities or feelings which have meaning in common for you and your listener. You may describe, for instance, the insecurity that the speaker feels (stage fright) by comparing it with "buck fever" or the parachute jumper's fear.

Below are listed a few hints for making the presentation of the informative description more effective:

1. Orient the listener in order that he will understand his physical position with reference to the object. In other words, is he supposed to assume that he is looking at the side, the top, or the bottom of the object?
2. Make clear your starting point. Where does the sequence of details start? At the northwest corner? At the extreme right? At the bottom? At downstage left?
3. At the beginning announce the order you intend to follow. In what direction are you moving in presenting your descriptive details?
4. Frequently reorient your listener as to his position, your position, the direction you are traveling, and how far you have progressed.

INFORMATIVE NARRATIVE

From the beginning of time, storytelling has been a favorite pastime in all circles and thus has been associated with entertainment. But the relating of a true story may likewise constitute a way to enlighten and to inform. The informative narrative places primary concern upon accurate reporting of the actual sequence of events with little effort to develop characterization or suspense. The participants, complicating forces, and setting are presented as impersonally and objectively as possible. You must make every effort to avoid emotional coloring and loaded words which may distort the meaning. These may be used in storytelling for entertainment but not here. The final test is "Does the listener know what happened?"

The recounting of a process or procedure is usually in narrative form. It follows the natural sequence of events as they occur. Of course, each phase, step, or period in the development may actually involve a minute description. Because of its dependence upon description, some writers place it in that category. Ordinarily, informative description falls under one of two headings:

1. An operational pattern
2. A developmental pattern

Other types of the informative narrative are (1) simple narrative, (2) autobiography, (3) biographical sketch, (4) travelogue, and (5) historical account.

The simple narrative relates the events of a short incident. Examples are on-the-spot reporting of a search or rescue, a radio broadcast of a fire, or events leading up to an accident. At times many radio, sports-, and newscasters and news analysts give little more than simple narrative in broadcasting news. For example, Boake Carter told his numerous listeners on March 11, 1938, how Hitler took over Austria. In his dramatic way he reported the events as he saw them.[2]

Autobiography and *biography* consist of information about human beings. The employer frequently asks the prospective employee to give an autobiographical sketch. The displaced person tells of his past life in his homeland. Judge M. A. Mus-

[2] Boake Carter, "Germany Takes Austria," *Representative American Speeches, 1937-1938*, A Craig Baird (ed.), The H. W. Wilson Company, 1938, pp. 97-100.

manno told a radio audience about his experience of spending three days in the Penitentiary of Western Pennsylvania. The good judge gave an autobiographical account of his reaction to the prisoners and prison life.[3] Or the speaker may choose to recount the stirring events in the life of another—George Washington, Babe Ruth, or Buffalo Bill.

A *travelogue* is an account of a trip, expedition, or exploration. During World War II American flyers gave this type of talk upon returning from each mission over Germany or Japan. They reported the raid as accurately and completely as possible to intelligence officers. Upon his return from Antarctica, Dr. Thomas Poulter, who served with Admiral Byrd (at Little America), gave a travelogue to his fellow townsmen. Actually he simply retold the stirring events of his trip to the South Pole.

A *historical account* is concerned with more general events of the past: the fall of the Bastille, the capture of Cornwallis, the defeat of Rommel, the development of Standard Oil. Incorporated in such accounts may be autobiographical or biographical sketches and travelogues. The lecture on history in the classroom is often an excellent example of this type. It is evident that these types of narrative overlap. Frequently one type is subordinated to another, or two or more are combined to make a more complete presentation.

You will do well to make your speech follow the chronological sequence of the events. In other words, if your subject is the refining of oil, you may well trace the product from the crude-oil stage to the refined product of gasoline or of the various by-products. If you wish to trace the growth of your home town you will follow the little town from its founding to the present.

In presenting an informative narrative, you can improve your effectiveness by following these suggestions:

1. Divide the process of procedure into two to five steps.
2. Give your listeners a preview of the steps early in the speech.

[3] M. A. Musmanno, "A Judge in Jail," *Vital Speeches*, October 15, 1936, p. 221.

3. Tell your listeners frequently how far you have progressed in your development.
4. Use visual supports such as diagrams, flow charts, slides, etc.

EXPOSITION

The third general informative type is exposition or explanation. The word *explain* comes from the Latin *explanare* which means *to spread out*. In other words, explanation implies the spreading out of an object, process, or procedure in order that it may be understood; it defines or relates how and why something operates or evaluates something. Exposition comes from the Latin *exponere, to place*. Exposition, then, is a working equivalent of explanation. Genung says, ". . . By exposition people generally understand setting forth the meaning of things; and this we may regard as its fundamental office. It is not concerned primarily with establishing the truth or falsity of a thing; it seeks rather what the thing is—what is its real nature, its scope, its relation."[4]

Exposition or explanation involves two phases: (1) definition and (2) logical analysis or partition.

Definition in Exposition

An expository talk ordinarily has at its nucleus a definition. This statement may attempt to establish the limits or nature of the subject by classification, gradation, comparison, or contrast. Or it may attempt to make the subject meaningful by one of the other types of definition. For example, the speaker may spend considerable time attempting to place the topic in its proper context, to give examples of it, or to tell what it is not (negation). He may explain the subject by giving numerous synonyms or even by tracing the etymology of the word. In light of the treatment of the subject of definition in the chapter on using language for clarity (Chapter XVI), further development here hardly seems necessary.

[4] Genung, *op. cit.*, p. 383.

If the talk is short, the exposition may be no more than an enlarged definition. In this case, you will be wise to combine several of the methods of definition.

Partitioning of an Exposition

The second step of exposition involves logical analysis or dividing the whole into its parts.

The definition may suggest a plan, the parts of the definition becoming the principal points in the speech. In such a case, then, the definition becomes the thesis sentence of the talk.

Ordinarily, exposition may fall into at least four patterns.[5] First, it may involve the analysis of the component parts of a thing.[6] This approach is concerned with composition and structure. The following questions are pertinent:

1. What are the parts?
2. What are their relationships?
3. How do the parts fit together into the whole?

The outline of an expository talk on the human body might approach the subject from the point of view of the principal parts: head, trunk, and limbs.

A second approach to exposition involves an attempt to discover the connection between one "thing" and another. Circumstances and conditions become the main concern in this type. The explainer seeks to make clear how a particular detail is related to and dependent upon its environment. In contrast to the first type, which discussed the internal parts, this approach is devoted to information outside the object concerning its environment. Important questions are the following:

1. What is necessary for the existence of the thing?
2. How is it related to other objects?
3. Is its existence more dependent on certain elements than on others?

[5] These were suggested by H. E. Manders, *Logic for Millions,* Philosophical Library, Inc., 1947.

[6] For the word "thing" any of the following might be substituted: mechanism, machine, apparatus, institution, production, construction, formation, process, procedure, performance, problem, organization, etc.

If the human body were again the subject, with this approach the speaker would seek to explain how the body must have food, sunshine, air, and protection.

A third approach seeks to view "things" in terms of causes. The previous approach explains relations of things that exist at the same time, while the present one involves the sequence of events in time. The speaker seeks answers to such queries as follow:

1. What event or events explain the given event?
2. Is the alleged cause sufficient in scope to explain the "thing"?
3. Are other causes operating?

Returning to the subject of the human body, the speaker might now seek to explain how climatic conditions affect skin coloring, body structure, and emotional make-up.

A fourth approach to exposition involves the analysis of the influence of a "thing" upon its neighbors and its surroundings. The two previous approaches have emphasized the conditions and the causes which account for the existence of the "thing." This last approach seeks to explain how an object influences its environment and shapes the destiny of its neighbors.

Returning to the subject of the human body, such an approach might explain how the human being influences his fellows and his habitat.

In summary, these four approaches to exposition may be clearly differentiated if applied to the same subject, such as "The Place of the Social Fraternity in Campus Life."

First approach (component parts): The membership of a social fraternity may be divided into three classes—(1) pledges, (2) actives, (3) alumni.

Second approach (circumstances and conditions): The social fraternity requires (1) the cooperation of the alumni, (2) the recognition of the national organization, and (3) the support of the faculty.

Third approach (causes): Social fraternities developed because of a need (1) for congenial companions, (2) for wholesome fellowship, (3) for group guidance.

Fourth approach (effects): The social fraternity (1) makes a man of the timid freshman, (2) stimulates cooperative effort, and (3) results in lifelong friendships.

In many expositions, complete development necessitates the combination of all four approaches. The auditor may need to have a knowledge of (1) the component parts, (2) the circumstances and conditions necessary for a survival, (3) the causes and (4) influences of the organization under consideration.

APPRAISAL AND CRITICISM

A fourth general type of informative speech is the type which appraises or evaluates. It ordinarily is referred to as *criticism*. As used here, the word criticism denotes the process of interpretation and evaluation of an activity, performance, or achievement. It is not used in the limited sense of referring solely to the formation of statements concerning appreciation of artistic achievement. Some, of course, regard appraisal as the prerogative solely of the written word; but reflection brings to mind many situations in which it is applied orally. In such a form it sometimes evaluates the efforts of a gun crew, a football team, or a cast of actors, a play, movie, or novel, a building, a landscape, or flower arrangement.

Criticism is the very essence of teaching. The good instructor, whether he is a factory foreman, an automobile demonstrator, a county agent, or an army sergeant, gives critiques after observing the performance of his charges. He attempts to point out wherein his pupils have succeeded or failed in order that they may improve subsequent performances. Any person who served in World War II was constantly subjected to "critiques."

Criticism as applied in public speaking may be subdivided into many types. The four most frequently used are (1) the simple critique, (2) rhetorical criticism, (3) dramatic criticism, and (4) literary criticism.

THE INFORMATIVE SPEECH

Analysis

Each type of criticism has its own distinct approach. However, seemingly there are three or four steps common to all types:

1. The formulation of standards by which to judge the activity.
2. The examination of the activity in light of these standards.
3. A summary of the weaknesses and strong points revealed in analysis.

The critic might approach his evaluation by posing such questions as follow:

1. How did the performer come to do it?
2. What has the performer done?
3. What method did the performer employ in accomplishing the task?
4. What are the effects of what the performer has done?[7]

Biography of an Informative Speech

Steps in Preparation	Application of Steps
1. Locate a subject	1. Sugar
2. Narrow the subject	2. Refining of raw sugar
3. Study the occasion and audience	3. To be delivered before Speech 51 class composed of fifteen Arts and Science majors
4. Select a desired response	4. To gain understanding and retention
5. Word the specific purpose	5. To inform Speech 51 class about the refining of raw sugar
6. Phrase central thought	6. The refining of raw sugar involves four steps

[7] Thomas E. Rankin, *The Methods and Practice of Exposition*, The Macmillan Company, 1917, pp. 192-195.

7. Determine type of informative speech
7. Informative narrative

8. Choose pattern of partition
8. Chronological order: operational pattern

9. Partition subject
9. The refining of raw sugar involves four "C's," namely
   1. Crushing
   2. Clarification
   3. Concentration
   4. Crystallization

10. Develop sentence outline

11. Collect and fit evidence into development
(See Chapters XI and XIV.)

OUTLINING THE INFORMATIVE TALK

Study of the biography above should suggest that, if you have followed step by step the development recommended in this book, you should have accomplished for a given speech the following:

1. You have a subject.
2. You have studied the occasion and audience.
3. You know where and what your goal is.
4. You have worded a specific purpose and central thought.
5. You have selected a basis of division and carried it as far as wording your points.
6. You have subdivided your main points.

It goes without saying that, if you have accomplished the six

~~~~~~

WENDELL WILLKIE

The effective speaker shows his alertness by his posture. In the presidential campaign of 1940, Wendell Willkie, Republican nominee, won the admiration of millions of Americans by his directness and enthusiasm. (Photo, Black Star.)

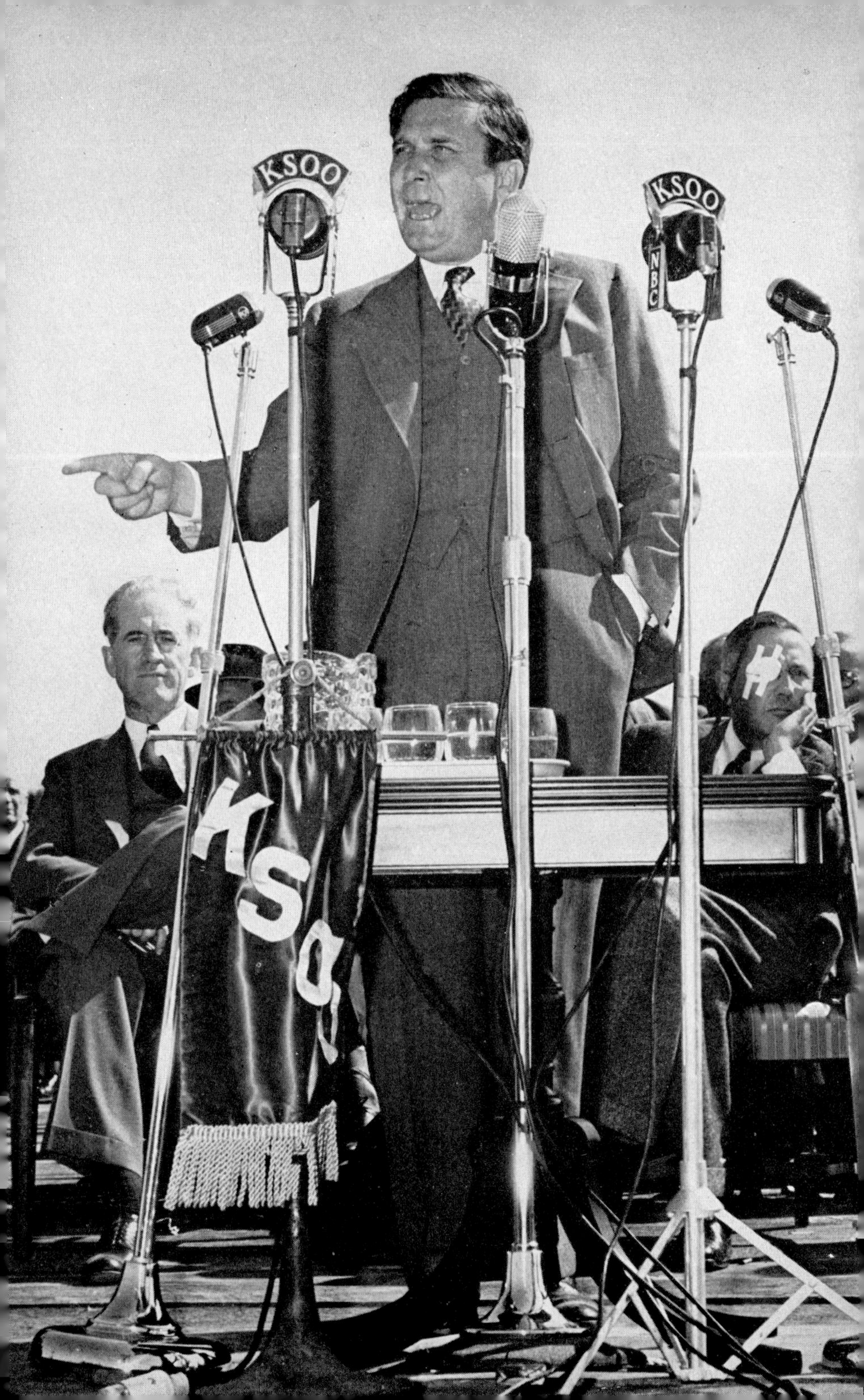
KSOO
KSOO
NBC
KSO

CHURCHILL HERE TO-DAY
STEWART
LABOUR'S CHOICE EAST FULHAM
ASTOR
DANCE
HELP HIM

things suggested above, you already have a superstructure. You may feel, however, that you need additional help in Steps 10 and 11 in the Biography. Therefore, let us consider more in detail the question of outlining.

First, let us anticipate a typical student's reaction to outlining. The student may ask, why not prepare the speech and then prepare the outline, or for that matter, why prepare an outline at all? This attitude probably indicates that you do not understand the principles of analysis and partitioning. Actually, outlining should make speech preparation easier and provide a method whereby you can systematically break a subject into its parts, arrange the parts, and then check for yourself the speech structure.

Why outline? *To ensure precise, orderly thinking.*

A speech outline will make it easier for those persons who are to listen to you also, for the outline will make your presentation more systematic and more orderly. It will help you to see your subject as a whole and to make clear to your listeners how you propose to develop it. Furthermore, during your speech you will be able to make it clear where you are in the development and when you have reached your destination.

Why outline? *To ensure precise, orderly presentation of your ideas.*

Kinds of Outlines

Ordinarily there are two kinds of speech outlines which may be used in the preparation of the informative talk: the topical outline and the sentence outline.

WINSTON CHURCHILL

Many persons regard Winston Churchill as England's greatest living orator. On this occasion, July 3, 1945, Churchill made a short speech to his London constituents. Even a prime minister must answer to the people in a democracy. You will find throughout this book several examples taken from the oratory of this great Englishman. (Photo, Black Star.)

The type of outline you select for a given speech will depend upon two factors: first, the nature and scope of the subject, and second, the use to which you wish to put the outline.

The topical outline is often cryptic and therefore meaningful only to the person who prepares it. The following is a specimen topical outline.

Refining of Raw Sugar

I. Remember the C. C. C.
II. Refining involves four C's
    A. Crushing
    B. Clarification
    C. Concentration
    D. Crystallization
III. Summary

This abbreviated type of outline requires the same thoughtful analysis and partitioning that the sentence outline involves. For short talks and simple subjects the topical outline may be all that is necessary. It is quite adequate for a speaker's notes or a speaker's outline.

Ordinarily we recommend, however, that you prepare a sentence outline for your class assignments and for more serious efforts. Putting your thoughts into sentences will give you a greater opportunity to crystallize the key ideas of your speech and to make sure that you have ordered your materials wisely. You will want to follow a form similar to that given below:

Model Skeleton Outline

Title

Specific Purpose:

Introduction

I. . . . .
II. . . . .

Central Thought:

Discussion

I. . . . .
    A. . . . .

THE INFORMATIVE SPEECH

      1. . . . .
         a. . . . .
           (1) . . . .
           (2) . . . .
         b. . . . .
      2. . . . .
   B. . . . .
      1. . . . .
      2. . . . .
II. . . . .
   A. . . . .
   B. . . . .
III. . . . .

Conclusion

I. . . . .
II. . . . .

Following are two specimen outlines conforming to the skeleton outline on pages 202-203.

Operational Pattern

Title: The Four "C's" of Sugar Refining
Specific Purpose: To tell the speech class about the refining of raw sugar

INTRODUCTION

I. During the last depression, we all heard about C.C.C. or the three "C's."
II. Today I want to discuss the four "C's" of sugar refining.

Central Idea: The refining of raw sugar involves four "C's."

DISCUSSION

I. The first "C" stands for crushing.
   A. The cane is placed on a conveyor belt.
   B. It is carried through two sets of knives.
   C. The finely chopped cane is passed through crushers.
   D. The juice is carried into next step.
   E. The bagasse is sent to furnace room or to storage area.
II. The second "C" stands for clarification.
   A. The juice contains many impurities such as mud and particles of fiber

    B. Lime is added to accomplish the following:
       1. To neutralize the natural acidity
       2. To remove suspended impurities
       3. To precipitate dissolved nonsugar
       4. To decolorize the juice
    C. Lime is permitted to settle.
III. The third "C" represents concentration.
    A. Juice is sent through a series of multiple-effect evaporators.
    B. Excess water is evaporated.
IV. The fourth "C" stands for crystallization.
    A. Concentrated juice is passed through vacuum pans which facilitate the formation of crystals.
    B. By a centrifugal action crystals are separated from molten liquor.

Conclusion

Remember the four "C's" of sugar refining
   I. Crushing
  II. Clarification
 III. Concentration
 IV. Crystallization

Operational Pattern

Title: The Frasch process of extracting sulfur

Introduction

I. Until recently the United States imported large quantities of sulfur from Sicily, where it is mined from open pits.
II. Louisiana and Texas have large deposits of sulfur, but they are too far underground for mining from open pits.
III. The Frasch process made possible the mining of this sulfur.

Central Thought: The Frasch process of extracting sulfur is a simple one.

Discussion

I. A hole large enough to accommodate a ten-inch pipe is drilled to the sulfur deposit.
II. Four concentric pipes are sunk into borehole to the sulfur level.
    A. The pipe diameters are 10, 6, 3, and 1 inches.
III. The sulfur is forced to the surface by the following method:
    A. Superheated steam is forced down the three-inch pipe to melt the sulfur.

THE INFORMATIVE SPEECH

B. Compressed air is pumped down the center pipe to apply pressure on mixture of water and molten sulfur.
C. Liquid molten sulfur is forced to surface through outside pipes.

IV. Sulfur is run into settling tanks where water is allowed to evaporate.

Conclusion

I. The Frasch process has made the people of Louisiana thousands of dollars.

RÉSUMÉ OF OUTLINING

A significant part of your speech preparation is outlining. It is not an easy or simple task, but it is one that requires concentration and effort. If it is carefully done, it provides you with another opportunity to test your materials and the ordering of your points and to check the unity and coherence of your thinking. It will increase your mastery of the subject.

Study carefully the model outlines given above. Notice the following points:

1. The outlines contain six parts: title, specific purpose, introduction, central thought, discussion, and conclusion.
2. Standard outlining symbols are used:
   I.
     A.
       1.
         a.
           (1)
             (a)
3. Subpoints are indented to indicate an inferior position.
4. Only complete sentences are used.
5. Points are worded in the language which the speaker intends to utter in his speech.
6. Subpoints explain main points. If you wish, they may be related by such connectives as *namely, as the following, as follows, or in cases such as the following.*

EXERCISES

1. *Speaking Assignment.* Deliver a five-minute informative talk in which you tell the class how to construct a map locating your home.

Ask members of the class to draw the map as you give instructions. When you have finished your speech, collect the maps, and determine how effective you were in giving simple instructions. Write a brief estimate of your effectiveness.

2. *Speaking Assignment.* Deliver a five-minute informative talk in which you use one of the following types:
    a. An informative description of a building in your home town
    b. An informative narrative of a trip you have taken
    c. A historical narrative
3. *Speaking Assignment.* Deliver a five-minute explanation in which you explain a plan of organization, a procedure, or an operation.
4. *Speaking Assignment.* Deliver a five-minute talk in which you attempt to make the audience appreciate (a) a great distance, (b) a great value, or (c) a great size.
5. *Speaking Assignment.* Deliver a five-minute informative talk in which you attempt to stimulate questions from the floor. (See Alan H. Monroe, *Principles and Types of Speech*, 3rd ed., chap. 23.) You will be graded partially on the questions you stimulate and the manner in which you answer them.
6. *Discussion Questions for Class Symposiums.*
    a. What were the teaching methods of your most effective high-school teacher? Can any of these methods be applied to the delivery of an informative talk?
    b. What were the teaching methods of your most ineffective high-school teacher? Can you profit by his or her mistakes?
    c. How much do listeners remember of what you say in an informative speech?
    d. How can you as an informative speaker improve retention?
    e. How can a speaker stimulate a listener to ask questions?
    f. Should the speaker ever refuse to answer questions? When? How?
    g. To what group should the informative speaker adapt his material in the informative speech? the slowest group? the average? the most intelligent?
7. *Research Assignment.* Which of the following would be suitable as the central thought for an informative speech of between five and ten minutes? Determine how the ones which you discard could be reworded into effective central thoughts.
    a. The open-stock law protects livestock on the highway.
    b. Haste makes waste.
    c. Advertising is an essential part of our lives.

d. Germany was the aggressor in World War I.
e. A large college offers a student many advantages.
f. Woman is the stronger of the sexes.
g. An ideal vacation.
h. What to do about hot weather.
i. Woodrow Wilson was a great president.
j. A large part of a college day is spent in walking.
k. Everyone should take swimming.
l. Swimming builds muscles.
m. To get anywhere in the world you must have a clear head on your shoulders—not an empty one.
n. The Boston Red Sox and the New York Giants are good ball teams.
o. Football is a game of skill.
p. Motorcycling is an exciting sport.
q. We do not want communism.
r. The advantages of playing tennis.
s. A university is a marriage bureau.
t. Exercise colors your attitudes.
u. The ant has great intelligence.
v. Life in Boone County.
w. Why I wanted to be a fireman.
x. The nature of the earth.
y. Keeping books.

SUPPLEMENTARY READINGS

1. Baird, A. Craig, and Knower, Franklin H., *General Speech: An Introduction*, McGraw-Hill Book Company, Inc., 1949, chap. 18.
2. Genung, John F., *The Practical Elements of Rhetoric*, Ginn & Company, 1899, pp. 217-405.
3. Hayworth, Donald, *An Introduction to Public Speaking*, The Ronald Press Company, rev. ed., 1941, pp. 297-311.
4. Oliver, Robert T., Dickey, Dallas C., and Zelko, Harold P., *Essentials of Communicative Speech*, The Dryden Press, Inc., 1949, chap. 8.
5. Soper, Paul L., *Basic Public Speaking*, Oxford University Press, 1949, chap. 10.
6. Williamson, Arleigh B., Fritz, Charles A., and Ross, Harold Raymond, *Speaking in Public*, Prentice-Hall, Inc., 2nd ed., 1948, chaps. 13, 17.

CHAPTER IX

Analysis and Organization of Argumentative Speeches

IN THE present chapter we wish to discuss the framing of argumentative propositions, the dividing or partitioning of these statements into their logical parts, and the preparing of argumentative speech outlines.

The principles of analysis and organization discussed in the preceding chapter on the informative speech are not necessarily applicable to the argumentative talk. Since the goal of the argumentative speech is different, naturally the method of planning must also be different. The outline for the argumentative talk seeks to give reasons for belief or for action, while that for the informative talk ordinarily explains or makes clear with the hope of gaining understanding and retention.

Let us for a moment compare the planning of the argumentative and the stimulating talk. Although the purposes of the stimulating and argumentative speeches are different, the planning of the two is similar. The stimulating speech many times strives *to give reasons* for rekindling or heightening your appreciation, but this process does not involve any principles of analysis, partitioning, and outlining which would be inappropriate to the argumentative type. Therefore, we see little need for a separate chapter on the planning of the stimulating talk.

For the argumentative speech, John Dewey's formula for reflective thought serves as a useful guide.[1] Many times your preparation will progress through the five steps listed by Dewey:

Step 1. Recognition of a felt difficulty or discrepancy
Step 2. Definition and location of the difficulty
Step 3. Discovery of the possible solutions (supposition, conjecture, guess, hypothesis, or theory) to the problem
Step 4. Examination of the various solutions
Step 5. The testing of the most feasible solution, or in the words of Dewey, "further observation and experiment leading to acceptance or rejection; that is, the conclusion of belief or disbelief"

Careful scrutiny of the five steps named above reveals that the process described actually starts when the speaker feels the urge to deliver a speech or senses a difficulty faced by his group. This recognition constitutes Step 1. In the process of studying the audience and occasion, selecting a goal, and formulating a proposition, the speaker moves into Step 2. However, this step is not completed until the speaker has decided the extent and nature of the difficulty. In the remaining three steps, the speaker seeks a way to solve the problem and accomplish his goal.

[1] John Dewey, *How We Think,* D. C. Heath and Company, 1910, pp. 68-78.

THE PROPOSITION
Definition

A pertinent question to ask of the augumentative speaker is, What are you trying to prove? Throughout his speech the speaker must make the answer to this question apparent to the largest possible percentage of his auditors. If at any moment the speaker loses sight of his proposition, that is, what he is trying to prove, he is wasting your time. Of course, in his presentation he may choose to withhold an exact statement of his central point until he considers that it will receive a favorable reception, but whatever he says and does should be directed toward making his listeners think, feel, believe, or do what he says.

This key or central idea around which the speech is built is called the proposition. It is the epitome or very heart of what the speaker says. Or, to describe it in another way, if the speaker suddenly finds that his extended remarks are to be limited to a single sentence, he will doubtlessly deliver his *proposition*, for its acceptance means the accomplishment of his goal. It is not difficult to see that, if a unified impression is made, the proposition must be worded in a single meaningful sentence. If your listeners fail to hear or to understand the proposition, they are sure to be confused. If they try to decide what they "think you are driving at," they may develop a dozen different interpretations of your line of thought or the course of action you propose. Under such conditions of uncertainty, unity of thought, feeling, or action is impossible.

Kinds of Propositions

In the stimulating or argumentative speech, propositions fall under two headings: those of fact (value) and those of policy.[2]

[2] Although some writers include a third type, those of value, in our treatment this type is discussed under propositions of fact. "Propositions of value are those which assess the worth of a subject in dispute. They assert that something is or is not beneficial; they call for approval or disapproval of a belief or an idea." (Russell H. Wagner, *Handbook of Argumentation*, Thomas Nelson & Sons, 1936, p. 16.)

ARGUMENTATIVE SPEECHES 211

The proposition of fact (value) affirms or denies the existence of a fact, a truth, a condition, an influence, a quality, or a relationship. It demands of the listener no more than a covert response, mental agreement. Naturally stated or implied in this type of statement is some form of the verb "to be." Note the following propositions: (1) There is a communistic influence in our state. To develop a speech around this statement, the speaker must prove that a communistic influence does exist, but recognition of the threat is all that is sought. (2) Our church needs (is in need of) a new organ. As stated, the speaker again asks no more than recognition of the need or of a condition. You might deliver a stimulating talk on "Hitler was an evil man." Although in such a talk the speaker's goal might be to stir up anger, disgust, or horror, notice that the subject is primarily a proposition of fact.

Other examples of propositions of fact are as follow:

1. Baton Rouge provides many business opportunities.
2. Democracy is superior to communism.
3. All men are not created equal.
4. Washington was a greater military strategist than Cornwallis.
5. The pen is mightier than the sword.
6. The Interstate Commerce Commission discriminates against the South.
7. The South is America's new frontier.
8. Labor unions are undemocratic.
9. Labor has a right to use the sit-down strike.
10. The meek shall inherit the earth.
11. Passive resistance is the best policy.
12. Latin America is a great potential market for consumer goods.
13. There is no Santa Claus.
14. Our taxes are too high.
15. Eugene O'Neill is America's greatest playwright.
16. Bacon is the author of Shakespeare's plays.
17. My grade in history was too low.
18. The objective test is unfair.
19. A fur coat increases a girl's self-esteem.
20. The home is losing its influence.
21. Our schools are understaffed.

22. We need more money for our department.
23. John Smith is guilty of first-degree murder.
24. William Jennings Bryan was a great orator.
25. Public-school teachers are overpaid.

The proposition of policy goes one step further than that of fact. In addition to telling what the listener is to believe, it proposes to him what he should do, thus demanding an *overt* response. In other words, it advocates the expediency or advisability of following a certain course of action. Perhaps it rightly should be called a "should" or "ought" proposition, for one of these words, either stated or implied, is usually combined with a transitive verb such as build, demand, join, buy, sell, support, give, adopt, or vote.

The following are examples of this type:

1. You should vote for Home Rule.
2. You should support the Community Chest.
3. You should establish a business in Baton Rouge.
4. Traffic laws should be enforced.
5. You should contribute to the March of Dimes.
6. You should buy U.S. Savings Bonds.
7. You should give five dollars to the Red Cross.
8. You should make a contribution to relief for Greece.
9. Go West, young man.
10. You should buy me a new coat.
11. You should tithe for your church.
12. Our teachers should receive higher pay.
13. The football team should have more support.
14. We must enlarge our stadium.
15. The United States should return to the gold standard.
16. You should buy a health-insurance policy.
17. You should buy a Mayfield washer today.
18. John Smith should be sentenced to life imprisonment.
19. Teachers should not grade by the "curve."
20. You should demand your rights as a veteran.
21. Let us sell our quota of bonds.
22. The states should not pay bonuses to veterans.

23. You should not eat starchy foods.
24. Louisiana should conserve its wild life.
25. Iowa farmers should cooperate in soil conservation.

Framing the Proposition

Framing the proposition is the crystallization of a speech topic into a single meaningful thought. This process may sometimes be a slow one. It may be much easier to express the key idea of the speech in two or three sentences or in a paragraph than in a fully developed speech. Consequently, the temptation is to say, "Oh, well, I am sure that they get the general idea anyway." But this rationalization should be countered with the question, How can a speaker communicate an idea so nebulous that he cannot phrase it concisely?

There are at least two ways to arrive at a wording of a proposition. The first is to wait until the inspiration strikes, but the objection to this is that inspiration seldom comes when it is most needed.

The second method of finding a proposition is to work deliberately and systematically. The method of exploration must be an individual matter, each person following the system best adapted to himself. We cannot hope to give a complete explanation to this process because it involves the whole question of how to think, which indeed is beyond the scope of this book. The following suggestions may prove helpful to some in framing a proposition:

1. Prepare a list of speech topics that seem appropriate for the speaking situation. At this stage expand the list as much as possible.
2. Study the list carefully. Strike out duplicates, combine those which overlap, and eliminate doubtful choices.
3. From the remaining list select the topic that seems most appropriate.
4. Expand the topic into a written paragraph or two which summarize your view of the subject. It may help to "talk the subject out," that is, present it orally as you would to an audience. In writing down an idea, do it as rapidly as possible without regard to style, word choice, or sentence structure.

5. Give the paragraph the *rest* treatment by laying it aside until you have had time to relax and forget it. Then check to see if it expresses the general idea. If it does not, improve the paragraph or discard it and start over.
6. By careful scrutiny of your paragraph you may find a sentence which with some rewording and alteration can be made into a proposition. If you see several possibilities, write them all down for further study. Take plenty of time to weigh the various possibilities.
7. Select one thought and reword it into a meaningful, simple, declarative sentence.

In many cases it may not prove necessary to use all seven steps. Naturally you should make the process as short and efficient as possible. As a rule, some orderly process designed to crystallize your thoughts will prove superior to waiting passively for an inspiration.

Wording the Proposition

Future analysis and later acceptance of the speech will depend upon how well the proposition is worded. The following principles should be remembered as guides in the wording process:

The proposition should be worded in a complete declarative sentence. A topic or a phrase may announce a title but does not express a point of view. A question is also neutral. A declarative sentence by its very nature is a complete thought; it cannot be neutral. If a speaker announces that he is going to speak upon "intercollegiate football," he has revealed nothing concerning his point of view. The speech may be one to entertain, to stimulate, or to persuade. He may be for or against football. But if he puts the topic into a sentence, "Intercollegiate football is detrimental to college life" or "Football at Tabor should be resumed next year," he has taken a stand. A declarative sentence gives the audience a clear understanding of what the speaker is trying to prove.

The proposition should be a simple sentence—limited to one thought. Compound, complex, or compound-complex sentences should be avoided because they express two or more thoughts. If the proposition is a single thought, the unity of the speech will be easier to maintain. Furthermore, the fewer words the proposition contains, the simpler it will be for the listener to remember. Although no iron-clad rule can be formulated, the chances of retention are much higher if the proposition is short.

The proposition should be stated in language instantly intelligible. The language should require as little definition as possible. Ambiguous or unfamiliar terms result in a multiplicity of impressions. For the same reason, figures of speech should be used sparingly. The proposition, "Democracy needs us to take up for it" is vague because of the phrase, "to take up for it." An improved wording might be "You should defend the American form of government," or "The army needs you to fight in Korea," or "We should teach more history in our schools." Each represents an attempt to put the phrase "to take up for it" into concrete, meaningful language, instantly intelligible.

The proposition should be worded in the language of the auditors. Each listener must be made to feel that the speaker is talking directly to him. A common fault is that a proposition is impersonal. In the statement, "The United States should adopt socialized medicine," the individual listener is completely ignored. This proposition, worded in terms of the audience, might read, "You should urge your senator to vote for socialized medicine." The use of collective words—people, persons, citizens, voters, the American public, men, ladies, everyone, as well as the third person pronouns, he, she, they—also contributes to indirectness. The proposition "every home should own a pressure cooker" can be made more impelling when reworded "you should buy a pressure cooker." Let there be no doubt as to whom the speaker is directing his remarks.

The verb in the proposition should be in the active voice. The passive voice is indirect. An example of this weakness can be observed in the following proposition, "A new suit should be bought by you." Such a statement may be made more direct by this wording: "You should buy a new suit."

The proposition should attract attention and be easy to remember. Since it embraces the very essence of the speech, the proposition must stand out. In this respect the problem of wording is much the same as that of the slogan maker; the wording and the title must be unique.

The proposition must be adapted to the audience and the occasion. Care must be taken not to alienate the listener. For example, for many groups south of the Mason-Dixon line, the proposition "segregation should be eliminated" would not be given a hearing, because once the word "segregation" is mentioned, they would become emotional and refuse to listen. The mere mention of segregation is a stimulus sufficient to arouse an unfavorable response.

A dignified formal occasion demands a formally stated proposition elevated in general implications. For this reason, a speaker finds a marked advantage with church groups in giving a quotation from Scripture as a thesis. On the other hand, "Beat 'Bama for Bernie" would be appropriate and extremely effective at pep meetings.

The proposition should be sufficiently short to fit the time limit and to ensure adequate development. The person who insists upon exceeding his time limit is extremely discourteous to his audience, to other speakers on the program, and to the chairman. His thoughtless enthusiasm or his inability to come to the point may be a source of ineffectiveness. His audience may become tired and restless, or his treatment may be hurried and superficial.

The proposition must be narrowed to the extent that the speaker can maintain maximum interest and attention and can develop the subject sufficiently to obtain his desired goal.

In summary, therefore, a proposition should be a complete,

declarative, simple sentence, stated in language instantly intelligible, and worded in terms of the audience. It should be stated in the active voice, and it should be easy to remember, appropriate to the speaking situation, and sufficiently limited for development within the time limit.

PARTITION OF A PROPOSITION OF POLICY

The question here is, How can such a proposition be divided logically into its parts? Of course, by its very nature the proposition of policy contains two elements: a problem (a felt difficulty) and a recommended solution. These two are discernible in the sentence "You should contribute five dollars to the Community Chest." The problem probably is that in the community there are many worthy charities and philanthropic causes, such as Y.M.C.A., Boy Scouts, Salvation Army, and Red Cross, that need financial support. The solution is "You should contribute five dollars." The word "should" implies that you "ought" to do it because it is highly desirable or expedient for you to do your part.

Immediately it becomes apparent that certain key questions can be devised which may be utilized in the study of most propositions of policy. The stock or key questions may be worded as follows:

1. What is the problem or what conditions make a change necessary?
   a. What are the causes of the problem?
   b. Does the problem arise from a structural or inherent weakness of the system?
   c. Do the weaknesses seriously impair the operation of the system?
2. Is the proposal or solution desirable?
   a. How is it an improvement over the *status quo*?
   b. How will it benefit the parties involved?
   c. Is it legally and morally justifiable?
   d. Will the proposal correct the difficulties without introducing new difficulties?
3. Is the proposal feasible?
   a. When would it be put into operation?

b. Who would administer it?
c. What would be the cost of such a plan?
d. How will the change from old to new be made?

The list of questions above must be altered and adapted to fit a given proposition. The subquestions are not mutually exclusive and are not intended to be, nor can all the questions be applied to every problem. They are suggestive of queries that may be raised. The amount of time devoted to each will be determined by the speaker's interests, the occasion, and the audience.

PARTITION OF A PROPOSITION OF FACT OR VALUE

Many propositions of fact are in reality a part of some larger proposition of policy. This relationship is evident in the following outline:

Proposition: You should join the Hospital Insurance Plan, for
 I. Hospital bills are difficult to pay.
 II. Hospital insurance provides a cooperative way of sharing costs.
 III. Payments are easily made in monthly installments.

The proposition is clearly one of policy because it advocates the advisability of "you" following a course of action. However, notice that the subpoints have the characteristics of propositions of fact. They seek to prove three premises involving what is: "bills are. . . ," "insurance provides. . . ," and "payments are. . . ." Taken alone, each premise demands only mental agreement, but each one is designed to move the listener a step nearer complete acceptance of the main proposition.

The same is true of the following outline:

Proposition: The state of Louisiana should launch an extensive program of advertising, for
 I. Persons outside the state are unaware of the potentialities within the state.
 II. Such a program would result in many benefits to the state.

The course of action proposed is "an extensive program of

advertising," but the subpoints supporting the proposition possess the characteristics of the proposition of fact.

Therefore, it seems logical that in the analysis of the proposition of fact, two steps are necessary.

First, determine if the statement is a part of a larger proposition of policy. In other words, it seems futile to consider the statement "a communistic threat exists in the United States" without thinking in terms of the ultimate goal. If the speaker is purposeful, he has in mind a larger thesis which might be worded as follows: "the United States should outlaw the Communist Party," or "the United States should declare war on any foreign power responsible for fostering subversive activities in this country."

Second, divide the proposition into subpoints. Obviously, this type does not lend itself to the use of the key questions applied to propositions of policy. Each statement of this type must be approached on the basis of its individual merit. In this respect the following *patterns of partition* may prove useful:

According to chronological development: past, present and future or the reverse order. In a speech the first point might be worded in terms of what has happened; the second point in terms of what is happening; and the third point from the point of view of the future.

According to the parties involved: that is, students, faculty, and alumni; Democrats, Republicans, and Progressives; Protestants, Catholics, and Atheists; or French, Germans, and Italians. In this type a point is directed at each party.

According to spatial arrangement or the physical layout: This basis of division ordinarily is most commonly associated with description, but a speech can be planned on the basis of geographical location. Such an approach might involve the South, the West, and the North or the state, the nation, and the world.

According to a causal pattern: Normally such a development involves two points: cause and result. The order is not important.

According to the order used by the opposition: The refutative order is used when a speaker is answering points advanced by an opponent.

According to fields of endeavor: This basis is probably employed more frequently than any of the others. Fields might be political, social, and economic; the home, the school, and the church, etc.

To illustrate these methods of partition, let us apply several to the proposition: *Tabor is a great institution.*

Chrono-logical	Parties Involved	Spatial	Fields of Endeavor	Causal
1. Tabor has an illustrious past.	Tabor makes a great contribution to high-school students.	Tabor has meant much to Milford.	Tabor has made significant findings in science.	Tabor's Christian ideals explain its greatness.
2. Tabor is doing an excellent job today.	Tabor makes a great contribution to the undergraduate.	Tabor has meant much to Georgia.	Tabor has made significant contributions to social science.	Tabor's students reflect its ideals.
3. Tabor has a bright future.	Tabor makes a great contribution to the graduate student.	Tabor has meant much to the nation.	Tabor has made significant contributions to the humanities.	

From the discussion above, it becomes evident that in a proposition of policy both schemes of analysis will be utilized. To determine the large main points, the speaker will use the stock issues, but to subdivide the resulting contentions, he will probably employ one of the methods of partition described above.

OUTLINING THE ARGUMENTATIVE TALK

The topical and sentence outlines are both applicable to the argumentative as well as the informative talk. Much of what has been said earlier may serve as a guide in drafting outlines[3] for the stimulating, convincing, or actuating talks. There is one important distinction. *The outline for the informative talk is expository*: subpoints explain main points; while that for the *argumentative speech is logical* in nature: the subpoints normally give reasons for acceptance of the main points; consequently they

[3] See chap. VIII, The Informative Speech.

ARGUMENTATIVE SPEECHES

may be related to main points by means of such words as "for" or "because." Observe how the points are related to the proposition in the example given below:

Nationalist China is worth saving, for
I. It exercises a desirable influence in the United Nations.
II. It is a great potential customer of the United States.
III. It controls the continent of Asia.
IV. It will serve as a buffer state against Russia.
V. Its political program has a democratic objective.

For review purposes study the following biography of an argumentative speech. Compare it with the one given for the informative talk.

Biography of an Argumentative Speech

Steps in Preparation	Application of Steps
1. Locate a subject.	1. China.
2. Narrow the subject.	2. U.S. support of nationalist China.
3. Study the occasion and audience.	3. To be delivered before Speech 51, a class composed of fifteen men: eleven from College of Agriculture and four from Engineering.
4. Select a desired response.	4. To gain (a) immediate (b) mental agreement (c) which continues to dominate thinking.
5. Word specific purpose.	5. To convince (1) class (2) that nationalist China should have (3) our support.
6. Phrase proposition.	6. Nationalist China is worth saving.

7. Determine type of proposition: policy or fact.

7. Answer: fact (value) proposition.

8. Choose pattern of partition: (a) chronological, (b) spatial, (c) causal, (d) parties involved, (e) fields of endeavor, (f) another order.

8. Answer: fields of endeavor
   a. Military
   b. Economic
   c. Political

9. Word main points in sentence form.

9. Nationalist China is worth saving, for
   a. It is a valuable political ally in United Nations.
   b. It is a good customer.
   c. It will serve as a buffer against Communist Russia.

10. Check logical structure of speech outline.

11. Arrange points in most effective order.

(See Chapter XIV.)

12. Develop each point; fit evidence into proper place.

Study of the speech biography will show that argumentative analysis should provide you with the following:

I. A clearly worded proposition
   A. Proposition of policy
   B. Proposition of fact
II. A pattern of partitioning
   A. Chronological
   B. Spatial
   C. According to parties involved
   D. According to field of endeavor
   E. Causal

If you have a proposition and pattern of partitioning, you are ready to draft an outline. For the short speech a topical outline such as the following may be adequate:

ARGUMENTATIVE SPEECHES

Nationalist China
  I. Desperate need of help
 II. It is worth saving
    A. Military standpoint
    B. Business standpoint
    C. Political standpoint
III. Will we give—we must

Note that the foregoing outline contains only phrases or topics. However, for most class assignments, it is advisable to prepare as complete a sentence outline as possible. In this way logical relationships may be checked much more easily. The following principles should be observed:

1. Outline in simple sentences; avoid complex and, especially, compound sentences.
2. Relate subpoints to main points by using "for."
3. When partitioning a point, divide it into at least two subpoints. Too often, if only one point appears, it constitutes only a rewording and not an actual division.
4. It is not essential that introductions and conclusions follow strict outline form. You may find it helpful actually to write out in full the opening and closing sentences.
5. For preparation purposes, place thesis sentence between introduction and discussion. This procedure enables you to make sure of the logical sequence of the points. In oral presentation, however, the thesis may be stated at any place in the speech.
6. Evidence may be put in outline if you wish.
7. Word points in the language which you intend to use in the speech.

Study carefully the specimen sentence outlines given below. In what ways have they failed to meet the requirements just cited?

Specimen Outlines

Let Them Rest in Peace

Specific Purpose: To persuade the speech class that the war dead should not be disturbed in their graves overseas

Introduction

I. We shall soon witness in this country the strangest and most melancholy immigration in our history.
II. Congress has authorized the War Department to bring home the remains of our military dead.
III. American soldiers and sailors of World War II lie in cemeteries around the world.

Proposition: We should not bring our war dead home, for

Discussion

I. They would not want to be brought back, for
  A. Their comrades in arms made their final resting places beautiful.
  B. They would choose to remain with their buddies who died with them.
  C. They would not want to open old wounds of their dear ones.
II. Their return would be most difficult, for
  A. Many remain unidentified.
  B. Many rest in unmarked graves.
  C. Exhumation is difficult in many cases.
III. We can give them nothing by bringing them back, for
  A. They have won far greater honor than we can bestow.
  B. Monuments can be erected in their honor.

Conclusion

I. Let those honored heroes rest in peace.
II. Let us the living make sure that they did not die in vain.

A Profitable Business

Specific Purpose: To persuade my hearers that rabbit breeding is an excellent opportunity to earn money.

Introduction

I. Last night at 7:15 the annual meeting of the Baton Rouge Rabbit Breeders Association was held in the Parish Court House.
  A. Clarence Williams, the president of the association, and John Jones, Agricultural Economist, reported on the Rabbit Conference held at Texarkana last month.
II. The meeting was attended by twenty-five local citizens interested in this new business.

ARGUMENTATIVE SPEECHES

III. For many years now the rabbit industry has been growing and prospering in California and in other western states.

Proposition: Rabbit breeding is an excellent opportunity to earn money in your spare time.

Discussion

I. You need little capital to become a rabbit breeder, for
   A. The initial investment is small, for
      1. You can start with only one buck and one doe.
      2. You can grow into the business by keeping all females and selling only the males as fryers.
   B. You receive a quick return on your investment, for
      1. Each doe produces and raises to fryer size (four pounds) about twenty-eight rabbits per year.
      2. Fryers sell for seventy-six cents per pound dressed weight or twenty-seven cents per pound live weight.
         a. Net profit per fryer is about forty cents.
         b. Net profit for twenty-eight fryers is about eleven dollars.
         c. Therefore, each doe should net eleven dollars per year.
      3. The size of your income depends on the number of breeding does you keep, for
         a. Ten does will make about one hundred dollars per year.
         b. One hundred does will make about one thousand dollars per year.
         c. One thousand does will make about ten thousand dollars per year.

II. Rabbit breeding does not require much special knowledge or training, for
   A. Information on housing, feeding, breeding, sanitation, can be obtained from the local Rabbit Breeders Association.
   B. The use of automatic waterers and feeders is a tremendous timesaver.
      1. About one hour per day is required to look after five hundred does and fifty bucks.
   C. Rabbits are not susceptible to many diseases.
   D. The rabbits actually raise themselves, for
      1. A good doe will nurse her young for eight weeks, at which time they are sold for fryers.
      2. The only work involved is once every three months in mating the does to the bucks.

III. There is a ready market here for all the fryers you can produce.
    A. The Rabbit Breeders Association has its own slaughter house and freezing locker and have numerous outlets to dispose of the fryers.
    B. Marketing is no problem.
    C. Eventually when enough persons here raise rabbits the Association will send a truck twice a week to collect the fryers that are ready for market.

Conclusion

I. I think by now you realize that if you are interested there is easy money for you in the rabbit industry.
    A. There is a good profit in selling only fryers.
    B. By selling breeding stock you also can clear ten thousand dollars a year.
II. If you are interested, you can telephone or write the Rabbit Breeders Association or contact Mr. John Jones in Agricultural Extension, or see me after class.

Join Now

Specific Purpose: To actuate my fellow teachers to join a union.

Introduction

I. You teachers have an important place in our society.
II. In many communities you draw smaller salaries than janitors and garbage collectors.
III. Unless you organize you are helpless.

Proposition: You should join a teachers' union, for

Discussion

I. You do not have adequate economic security, for
    A. Your salaries are not sufficient to meet the rising cost of living, for
        1. From 1940 to 1947 the average elementary and high-school teacher's salary increased only forty-five percent while the general price level increased eighty-six percent.
    B. You do not have an adequate pension system to protect you in your old age, for
        1. A teacher in Indiana may retire after forty years of service with a maximum of seven hundred dollars paid quarterly.
    C. You do not have adequate tenure protection.

II. Many unqualified teachers are permitted to teach, for
   A. The untrained are permitted to teach on temporary certificates, for
      1. One of eight teachers is now teaching on temporary certificates.
   B. Laws of certification are unsatisfactory.
   C. Standards in teacher training institutions are low, for
      1. Many are understaffed.
      2. Entrance requirements are low.
      3. Many provide little opportunity for demonstration of instructional methods.
III. You are not provided decent working conditions, for
   A. Classroom enrollment is too great.
   B. School buildings and equipment are outmoded.
   C. The teaching load is too heavy.
IV. A teachers' union offers you many advantages, for
   A. A union gives you an affiliation with a national organization.
   B. It would unify your efforts with those of others.
   C. Minimum standards could be demanded.
   D. Constructive programs could be encouraged.
V. The teachers' union would not be expensive, for
   A. Only one percent of your salary would go to the union.
   B. State and local association dues exceed the amount due the union.

Conclusion

I. Your profession deserves your best.
II. A union will enable you to give your best.

THE BRIEF

For more extensive preparation, however, the speaker may need to draft a more detailed and more analytical outline. In such an event, he should consider the making of a brief.

The process of setting down in logical written form a concise statement of the analysis with evidence to support the subpoints may be referred to as *briefing*. This logical condensation involves, therefore, the breaking of the proposition into its parts (arguments), relating these parts to each other, determining the order in which they are to be arranged, and the grouping of them under the appropriate headings. *Theoretically, the brief should include all the possible arguments in support of the speaker's position.* Says A. Craig Baird, "The brief is a storehouse of information, including a complete analysis of a given proposition and all the representative arguments and evidence on a given side of the resolution."[4]

The outline of a speech designed for audience presentation should not be confused with the brief. The speech outline may be based upon a psychological approach to gain acceptance; the brief is arranged in a deductive, logical order, constructed for the speaker's benefit. It is put in a succinct form in order that logic can be more readily checked. It is too compact and impersonal for the listener. In other words, the brief is only a logical skeleton. From the brief the speech outline is made.

Parts of a Speech Brief

A brief is composed of three parts: (1) an introduction, (2) a discussion, and (3) a conclusion.

The introduction includes explanatory background material such as (a) the cause for discussion, (b) history of the question, (c) definition of terms, and (d) other necessary background material. The introduction of a brief is not the same as the introduction of the speech. The first is to aid in more clearly seeing the question in its proper context. The second serves the purpose of getting attention and interest and stating the proposition.

The introduction utilizes expository development, that is, subpoints *explain* but do not *prove*. Points are related by such connectives as "namely," "as follows," "for example." Two examples of expository briefing are given below:

Senate Bill No. 472 provides for the distribution of federal funds to equalize educational opportunity in the following manner:

[4] A. Craig Baird, *Public Discussion and Debate*, Ginn & Company, 1937, p. 89.

I. The federal government is to exercise no control in determining how funds are to be spent.
II. The federal government is to spend three hundred million dollars per year.
III. Funds will be granted on the following basis:
 A. Each state will receive five dollars per educable between the ages of five and seventeen;
 B. In cases of need, a state can receive up to forty-five dollars per child.

The history of the tidelands problem is as follows:
I. The present controversy originated when oil was discovered in the tidelands off the coasts of Texas, Louisiana, and California.
II. Federal officers first challenged the claims of the states in 1937.
III. In 1946 Congress passed a bill giving clear title to the states, but the bill was vetoed by President Truman.
IV. On June 23, 1947, the Supreme Court made a ruling in the case the United States versus California as follows:
 A. California does not own lands.
 B. United States has "paramount rights and dominion."
 C. Ownership was not clearly defined.
V. In December, 1948, United States Attorney General Tom Clark filed suit against Louisiana and Texas for jurisdiction.
VI. In 1950 the Supreme Court decided against the states of Louisiana and Texas.

The brief proper, called the discussion or the proof, contains the arguments that support or prove the proposition. Unlike the introduction, the discussion employs argumentative briefing in its development, that is, the subpoints give the reasons for acceptance of main premises. Subpoints are related to main points by the connective *for*. Below is an illustration of argumentative briefing:

You should buy a new car, for
 I. Your old one is no longer safe to drive;
 II. Your old one makes a poor impression;
 III. Your old one is expensive to operate.

In briefing a proposition of policy, the stock issues transformed into declarative sentences become the main headings. Subheadings follow the principles discussed above under analysis of the propositions of fact.

Below is a portion of a brief prepared by a student[5] advocating that atomic energy be placed under international control.

    I. International control of atomic energy is necessary, for
       A. The use of atomic energy as a weapon of war would result in great destruction, for

Cord Meyer, Jr., *Peace or Anarchy*, Little, Brown & Company, 1947, p. 15.

          1. The first bombs dropped at Hiroshima wrought great destruction, for

Bernard Brodie (ed.), *The Absolute Weapon*, Harcourt, Brace and Company, Inc., 1946, pp. 24-27.

            a. The area of total destruction was four square miles and the area of substantial damage was 27 square miles.
            b. The casualties were 77,000 dead; 13,000 missing; 300,000 injured.
          2. Even more destructive bombs are being developed, for

Cord Meyer, Jr., *Peace or Anarchy*, p. 19.

            a. It is predicted that within the next ten years, bombs of the power equivalent of one hundred thousand to two hundred and fifty thousand tons of TNT can be made, with some over ten times more powerful than the original bomb.
            b. ". . . . Professor Edward Teller, who played a prominent role in the development of the first bomb has declared, 'One consequence of such bigger bombs would be that instead of three or four square miles three or

---

[5] Prepared as a class project by James Woodland at Louisiana State University, January, 1950.

four hundred square miles might be devastated at a single blow.'"

United States News & World Report, January 13, 1950, p. 21.

c. "A major decision now is being faced by United States on whether to try to build a new type atom bomb. The new bomb, if successful, would be at least 1,000 times as powerful as the existing bomb. Its power could be multiplied far beyond that."

B. There is no adequate defense against the atomic bomb, for
  1. Dispersion is not feasible, for
    a. The cost would be prohibitive, for
      (1) According to estimates given in Senate hearings, the dispersion of U.S. industries would cost $300,000,000,000.

Atlantic Monthly 181 (April, 1948), pp. 51-53. "Russia, The U.S., and the Atom," by a foreign observer.

   b. The American people would never accept the degree of coercion involved.
   c. Dispersion would disrupt the economy.
   d. America's freedom would be jeopardized.
  2. Adequate countermeasures do not exist, for
    a. Existing radar system cannot differentiate friendly from enemy aircraft or missiles.

L. N. Redenour, "There is No Defense" found in *One World or None*, McGraw-Hill Book Company, Inc., pp. 33-38.

   b. A radar detection is not feasible, for
      (1) A radar detection net would represent a tremendous national

investment and a continual drain on manpower.
c. It would be impossible to prevent all bombs from exploding, for
(1) Initial effectiveness of our defenses in a surprise attack will be small.
(2) Maximum efficiency that can be expected is 90 percent which is too low to provide adequate protection.
(3) Specific countermeasures that will explode such a bomb while it is still a great distance from its target are unknown.
C. American monopoly of the bomb is not possible, for
1. Russia has the bomb, for
a. "We have evidence that within recent weeks an atomic explosion occurred in the U.S.S.R."
b. "The Russians have exploded one atom bomb. It may be their only bomb. But the plant which was used to make it can turn out others. Within a very short time, one year, perhaps, the Russians will have bombs in significant quantity—significant at least from the point of view of Western Europe."
2. Other nations can develop atomic bombs, for
a. "There is no reason to think

President Truman, *New York Times*, September 24, 1949.

Leo Szilard, "America, Russia, and the Bomb," *New Republic*, October 31, 1949, pp. 11-13.

Ellen D. Ellis, "The

Atomic Bomb—The Key to International Sanction," *Current History*, October, 1945, pp. 293-298.

New York Times, September 25, 1949.

United States News and World Report, October 31, 1947, pp. 13-14.

Summary found in Ernest K. Lindley and William A. Higgenbotham, *Atomic Challenge, Headline Series* (Foreign Policy Association), No. 63, May-June, 1947, p. 34.

that the secret of releasing atomic energy cannot sooner or later be available to any state desiring it."
b. Other countries that have atomic-energy programs include France, Holland, Denmark, Norway, Sweden, Switzerland, and Italy.
D. An armament race in atomic bombs might lead to war, for
1. An atomic armament race would breed insecurity.
2. Nations might fight to gain or maintain superiority, for
a. Already there is talk of waging a preventive war against the U.S.S.R.
b. There is warning of the effect of an atomic armament race on international relations.
II. The proposed plan for international control of atomic energy is feasible, for
A. It is technically feasible, for
1. Mining can be controlled, for
a. Only two natural elements need to be controlled, for
(1) "The only scientific evidence worthy of regard makes it clear that . . . uranium is indispensable in the production of fissionable materials on a scale large enough to make explosives for power."
(2) Uranium is the only relatively abundant element that can maintain a chain reaction.

  (3) Thorium with uranium can be used to make atomic explosions.
 b. These two elements are mined only for their use in the atomic field.
 c. There are relatively few rich deposits of these two elements.
2. Production can be controlled, for
 a. Supply of raw materials can be controlled.
 b. Inspectors with unlimited inspecting powers could detect illegal production.
3. Qualified scientists could be secured to serve in the International Atomic Authority, for
 a. There would be the greatest opportunity for creative research, for
  (1) They would be the only scientists unlimited in the field of atomic research.
  (2) They would have access to all the latest developments in the field.
 b. There would be great opportunity for service to mankind.

B. The proposed plan is politically feasible, for
1. No nation would seize the plants within its boundaries, for
 a. Such an act would proclaim to the world its aggressive intentions.
 b. The plants could be so placed that no nation would

Bernard Brodie, *The Absolute Weapon*, p. 184.

J. Robert Oppenheimer, *Bulletin of Atomic Scientists*, June, 1946, pp. 1-5, quoted in *Reference Shelf*, Vol. 19, No. 2, pp. 173-187. Walter Lippmann, "International Control of Atomic Energy," found in *One World or None*, pp. 66-75.

have more than a minority of plants within its quick grasp.
2. The international field is well suited for such a plan of inspection and control, for
 a. There has been sufficient experience in international regulation to prove that it is possible, for
  (1) International attempts to regulate the narcotics traffic demonstrate the feasibility.
 b. The field of international regulation is new enough to be free of hampering traditions.
3. Personal liability is the only practicable method of punishing violations, for
 a. It is not possible to punish a state.
 b. Existing international law provides for punishment of individual.
4. Universal acceptance of this plan is possible, for
 a. Many nations have already indicated their approval of a plan, for
  (1) United States proposed a similar plan to the U.S. Atomic Energy Commission.
  (2) United Nations Atomic Energy Commission approved a similar plan.
 b. It is to the interests of other nations to accept such a plan.

The *Conclusion* of a speech brief serves to summarize the main arguments developed in the discussion. The following form may be used:

I. Since . . . . . .
II. Since . . . . . .
III. Since . . . . . .
Therefore the proposition is acceptable.

RÉSUMÉ OF THE RULES OF BRIEFING

For the brief above, the conclusion would read,

I. Since there is a need for international control of atomic energy;
II. Since such control is desirable;
III. And since control is feasible;
Therefore atomic energy should be placed under international control.
1. The introduction involves an expository or explanatory development.
2. The discussion follows a logical development with relationships indicated by the word *for*.
3. Standard outline symbols should be used.
4. Sources of evidence should be indicated either immediately after the evidence is given or in the margin.
5. Loaded words, figurative language, and ambiguities should be avoided.

CHECKING THE LOGICAL STRUCTURE OF A SPEECH OUTLINE OR BRIEF

The logical structure of a speech outline may be checked by asking a series of questions.

Is the outline divided on the basis of one principle only? This test can best be explained by an analogy. To sort apples by using the divisions of large, small, and red would be foolish because some red apples are large and others are small. In other words, the division was based upon two principles—size and color. Similarly, in planning a speech you must be consistent, using only one basis of division.

Summary Chart

Brief	Rhetorical Sentence Outline	Topical Outline
1. Preparatory step	1. Second step in development	1. Third step
2. For longer and more serious subjects	2. Drafted from brief	2. Drafted from sentence outline
3. Storehouse for speaker	3. Planned for audience	3. Planned for speaker
4. Logical arrangement	4. Psychological in arrangement	4. Same as sentence outline
5. Exhaustive in development	5. Selective in development	5. Suggestive in development
6. In complete sentences	6. In complete sentences	6. In phrases
7. Impersonal in language	7. Worded in language of auditor (first and second person)	7. Key phrases

Is there overlapping in the outline? Each point should be mutually exclusive, that is, no two points should cover the same materials. The principle is violated if a student attempts to treat his speech from the point of view of fraternity men, independents, and members of the Y.M.C.A. The first two are mutually exclusive, but the third is not. A member of the Y.M.C.A. might be either a fraternity member or an independent.

Are parallel points of equal value? A fault of this nature occurs when a speaker makes a major point and a subpoint of equal value. Such is the case in the following partition:

Milford should build a larger stadium, for
  A. The present bowl cannot accommodate the crowds.
  B. The showers are inadequate for the visiting teams.

Probably B is a subpoint of a larger unstated premise which is of more equal value to A.

Are any subpoints equal to main points? Partition, of course, implies dividing a proposition into its parts. If a subpoint equals a main point, no partition has taken place. This fault ordinarily occurs when the student merely restates a point, believing that he has divided it. The fault is apparent in the following:

The Utah legislature should appropriate money to build a new stadium, for
  A. The old stadium is inadequate.
  B. A new stadium should be built.

This second point is not a reason for building the new stadium but a restatement of the main statement.

SUMMARY

The steps in analysis and synthesis are as follows:

1. Recognition of a difficulty, need, or desire.
2. Framing proposition concerning difficulty.
3. Determinating the type of proposition stated.
4. Division of proposition into arguments.
   a. For proposition of policy, use stock issues.
   b. For proposition of fact, select basis of division.
5. Preparation of an outline or brief or both.
   a. Brief subject.
   b. Prepare sentence outline.
   c. Prepare speaker's outline.
6. Check division by use of following principles.
   a. Was one principle of division used?
   b. Is there overlapping?
   c. Are the parallel points of equal value?
   d. Do any subpoints equal main points?
7. Selection of arguments to be used in a speech.

EXERCISES

1. *Speaking Assignment.* Deliver a five-minute convincing speech on some local problem. Be sure to impress upon your audience your proposition. Ask the class to write down your proposition. If there is disagreement as to what your thesis is, you have failed.
2. *Speaking Assignment.* Deliver an actuating speech with an immediate goal which you can actually achieve in class. You may urge a small donation to a local charity, the buying of Christmas seals, the purchase of some article, or some similar subject.
3. *Speaking Assignment.* Deliver a five-minute actuating speech in which you strive for delayed response.
4. *Speaking Assignment.* Deliver a five-minute sales talk in which you attempt to sell an object which you can demonstrate. Be sure to put your plea in terms of your auditors' wants.
5. *Speaking Assignment.* Deliver a five-minute sales talk in which you attempt to sell some intangible.
6. *Speaking Assignment.* Deliver a ten-minute convincing or actuating talk on some important national issue.
7. *Written Assignment.* Prepare five propositions on each of the following topics:
   Conservation
   Ownership of the Mississippi barge lines
   High- and low-cost housing
   Our local schools
   Our local church
   Improving participation in government
8. *Written Assignment.* Determine what patterns of partitions you would use and how you would word your main points for the following propositions:
   a. Mercy killing should be legalized.
   b. Professional football is more exciting than intercollegiate football.
   c. A dog is man's best friend.
   d. A college education is essential to success.
   e. Franklin Roosevelt was our greatest President.
9. *Written Assignment.* Write a detailed evaluation of the following student outline.
   a. Consider its strong and its weak points.
   b. Revise the outline into one that you consider logical and effective.

Socialized Medicine, Yes or No?

Specific Purpose: To persuade my listeners that socialized medicine should not be adopted.

Introduction: One of the features of President Truman's so-called "Fair Deal" is the socialization of the medical profession. This he believes will help give the American people freedom from want. This is an extremely important issue and has met with a great deal of opposition, mainly from the medical profession. It is therefore important that the American people express themselves on this issue.

Proposition: Socialized medicine should not be adopted in the U.S.

I. Socialized medicine would impair the quality of medical service.
   A. The best men would not enter the medical profession.
      1. Doctors should be a select group.
      2. The best men enter fields where there is the best opportunity for personal remuneration and advancement.
      3. Socialized medicine would not be such a field.
   B. The "spoils system" would enter into the medical profession.
      1. The "spoils system" infiltrated the postal system.
      2. The "spoils system" infiltrated the Veterans Administration.
      3. The "spoils system" infiltrated the W.P.A.
      4. The "spoils system" infiltrated the P.W.A.
      5. It is reasonably certain that it will infiltrate all governmental institutions.
      6. Socialized medicine would be such an institution.

II. Socialized medicine would be harmful to the medical profession.
   A. It would discriminate against the medical profession.
      1. Doctors are entitled to the rights of American citizenship.
      2. Manufacturers are entitled to the rights of American citizenship.
      3. Free enterprise is a right of American citizenship.
      4. Socialized medicine would deprive doctors but not manufacturers of free enterprise.

III. Socialized medicine would be harmful to the country as a whole.
   A. It would lead to further socialization of our economic system.
      1. It would establish a precedent.
      2. The medical profession is similar to other professions and services.

Conclusion: You should write your congressman and demand that he vote against this harmful legislation.

ARGUMENTATIVE SPEECHES 241

10. *Written Assignment.* Prepare a detailed brief of a speech that you have read in *Vital Speeches, Representative American Speeches, Modern Eloquence,* or some other collection.
11. *Research Assignment.* Prepare a brief of some famous speech such as one of the following:
    Burke's Speech on Conciliation With America, delivered March 22, 1775.
    Webster's Reply to Hayne, January 22, 1830.
    Webster's Reply to Calhoun, February 16, 1833.
    Lincoln's The Cooper Union Address, February 27, 1860.

SUPPLEMENTARY READINGS

1. Baird, A. Craig, *Argumentation, Discussion and Debate,* McGraw-Hill Book Company, Inc., 1950, chaps. 6-7.
2. Baird, A. Craig, and Knower, Franklin H., *General Speech: An Introduction,* McGraw-Hill Book Company, Inc., 1949, chap. 19.
3. Foster, William Trufant, *Argumentation and Debating,* Houghton Mifflin Company, rev. ed., 1936, chaps. 2-3.
4. Nichols, Alan, *Discussion and Debate,* Harcourt, Brace and Company, Inc., 1941, pp. 113-126.
5. Williamson, Arleigh B., Fritz, Charles A., and Ross, Harold Raymond, *Speaking in Public,* Prentice-Hall, Inc., 2nd ed., 1948, chap. 18.
6. Winans, James A., *Speech-Making,* Appleton-Century-Crofts, Inc., 1938, chaps. 5-6.

Evaluation Sheet

Name_____Section_____

	Inferior 11 Poor 22 Fair 33 Average 44 Above average 55 Excellent 66 Superior 77	Inferior	Poor	Fair	Average	Above average	Excellent	Superior
		1	2	3	4	5	6	7
Choice of subject								
Organization								
Development: Introduction								
Development: Discussion								
Development: Conclusion								
Bodily control: Facial Expression, Gestures, Posture, Movement								
Putting over ideas: Communicativeness, persuasiveness								
Language: Clarity, Vividness, Impressiveness								
Voice and pronunciation								
Attitudes: Toward Speaking Situation								
Overall effectiveness								

Score _____

CHAPTER X

The Occasional Speech

NOT long ago a prominent surgeon made a hurried call upon a speech teacher friend with an urgent request for some assistance. As head surgeon at a local Catholic Hospital he had been asked by a group of his colleagues to present a gift to the Mother Superior. Although he had the knowledge, the skill, and control to perform several delicate and difficult operations daily, even before a number of internes, he was terrified at the thought of standing before a group of listeners and making a five-minute talk. "How do you make a speech of presentation," he asked. To tell him just to utter "what was in his heart" was not enough. He wanted to know exactly what was appropriate for such an occasion and how to go about preparing a suitable speech, and he had come to find out what to do.

Another well known physician would not even go that far. He

had been asked to make a short talk to a class of graduating nurses, but would not trust himself to speak at all without a carefully prepared manuscript—and he had someone else to write the speech for him!

Actually, the occasional speech is simple; it does not require great oratory, although the situation which calls for an occasional speech may at times bring forth speaking of the highest degree of eloquence. Like any other speech, however, it may present a few difficulties for those who are not familiar with it. This chapter is dedicated to those physicians and surgeons who allowed a simple speech to worry them, and to the many other people who like them find that they have been selected to represent special groups on special occasions, or who are thrust into situations calling for the simple expression of a genuine sentiment.

You too will need now and then to know what is appropriate for speeches like the ones the physician and the surgeon were asked to give. You will have the opportunity to present talks which find their *cause for being in some aspect of the occasion*: a situation arises which demands a speech of a special type, in other words, an occasional speech.

The extent of this type of speaking is suggested by the following outline, which is by no means exhaustive:

1. Speeches of Courtesy
    a. Introductions
    b. Welcomes
    c. Responses
    d. Presentations
    e. Acceptances
    f. Farewells
2. Speeches of Inspiration
    a. Eulogies
    b. Commendations
    c. Commemorations
3. Speeches of Good Will
4. Speeches of Entertainment
    a. After dinner speeches
    b. Story telling
    c. Book reviews

SPEECHES OF COURTESY

Ceremonial occasions usually call for speeches of courtesy. You may be asked to introduce a speaker or guest, to extend a welcome to newcomers, or to present a gift or an award to someone. On the other hand, if you are the recipient of an award or honor, you will want to reply to similar acts of courtesy: a speech of welcome usually calls for a response, and the receipt of an honor or a gift may necessitate in turn a speech of acceptance. If you are leaving the group, you may be moved by a desire to express your regrets in a speech of farewell. On some of these occasions you may act as a spokesman for a group, or you may act for yourself. When you represent a group you will utter those sentiments which express the common feelings of the members of the organization. When you speak for yourself you will express the feelings and emotions which are most deeply felt at the time.

In general, speeches of courtesy have in common five characteristics:

1. They are usually short. Verboseness is looked upon as a sign of insincerity and vain display. Seldom should these speeches take more than five minutes to deliver.

2. They are streamlined in organization and do not fall into traditional patterns of organization. Attention and interest are rarely a problem because, since the speaker is already held in high esteem, little need exists for a formal introduction. In the development, subpoints are blended together and may be difficult to identify. Furthermore, the summary-appeal conclusion is unnecessary and inappropriate. Every effort is made to fuse the speech into a unified whole, expressive of some deep and fitting sentiment.

3. These speeches usually have one of three goals: to entertain, to inform, and to stimulate. They rarely if ever attempt to convince or to actuate.

4. They are sincere and genuine in tone. The language and delivery should give the impression of modesty and genuineness. High-flown language and a grand manner which attract attention

to themselves and distract attention from the occasion are in these, as in all other types of public address, highly inappropriate.

5. They are normally pleasant in mood. They need not be sober or solemn; in fact, well chosen humor is often considered quite refreshing and fitting, especially if it creates an atmosphere of good cheer and good fellowship.

The Speech of Introduction

Of all the speeches of courtesy the speech of introduction is probably the most common, and is also, probably, the one that is most poorly done. One authority epitomizes the perfect introduction in a single clause: ". . . one that puts the audience in an expectant state of mind."[1] This writer means that the introduction must make the audience expectant with reference to the speaker being introduced, and to his speech. By his few remarks the introducer should make the audience receptive, establish why the speaker is qualified to speak on the subject, focus attention on the subject, and impress the audience with the importance of paying close attention. He seeks, in other words, to secure for the speaker a favorable hearing.

In preparing the introductory speech, remember four simple rules:

1. *Subordinate your own speech to the main speech.* Like the best man or the maid of honor at a wedding, you must help to make the occasion a success. In no way should you compete with the speaker. The chairman, or whoever does the introducing, should be seen, and should be heard no more than is absolutely necessary.

2. *Prepare your introduction carefully.* Before you start your preparation you will want to gather such information as the following: the nature of the meeting, the duties expected of you, and as much significant data on the speaker as possible. Your remarks should be thought out carefully and rehearsed. However, if at

---

[1] G. Lynn Sumner, *We Have With Us Tonight,* Harper & Brothers, 1941, p. 56.

all possible, speak extemporaneously, without notes. The memorized introduction usually sounds stilted and mechanical.

3. *Be brief.* Most authorities agree that one minute, or a hundred to a hundred fifty words, is enough for any speech of introduction. One of the most famous of all speeches of introduction is that in which Dean Shailer Mathews, of the University of Chicago Divinity School, introduced Woodrow Wilson:

> LADIES AND GENTLEMEN: THE PRESIDENT.[2]

When you exceed such limits you are on precarious ground, in that it is easily possible to ramble on indefinitely.

4. *Order your introduction as follows:*

a. Greet your audience.

b. Give biographical data necessary to identify the speaker and to make him interesting as a person. These data may include his place of residence, educational and professional background, present business or profession, and his connection with the present group.

c. Hold any mention of the speaker's name or subject until the end in order that you may present it as a climax.

If the audience is already familiar with many of these data, there is no need to use up the time of the speaker in reviewing them. In the speech just cited, nothing that Dean Mathews could have said would have added to the audience's knowledge of President Wilson.

Below are some introductions which exemplify the principles which have just been stated. The first is one in which Sam Rayburn, Speaker of the House of Representatives, introduced Cordell Hull, Secretary of State, to a joint session of the Senate and the House. Speaker Rayburn said:

> Members of the Senate and the House of Representatives, it gives me great pleasure to welcome back to this Chamber one of its most distinguished ex-members. It was here he began a career that has led to world wide fame. By his great work at Moscow, in my humble

---

[2] In *Classified Models of Speech Composition,* James Milton O'Neill (ed.), The Century Co., 1921, p. 671.

opinion, he has interpreted the inarticulate longings of millions here and of millions over there who, through fear today, cannot speak for themselves. It is my privilege, and my great privilege to present to you the Secretary of State, Mr. Cordell Hull.[3]

Notice that in this speech Mr. Rayburn used less than one hundred words, and that his language was simple and free of "honey dripping" superlatives. On the other hand, his words were quite appropriate and fitting for a man of the stature of Cordell Hull.

Lieutenant Colonel Elizabeth Smith, Commandant of WAC training Center, Camp Lee, Virginia, presented the Honorable Edith Nourse Rogers, Congresswoman from Massachusetts, to WAC officer candidates at their graduation on April 11, 1949, with this introduction:

The exigencies of total war presented demands upon the resources of our country far beyond any which we had ever known. The utilization of the skills and the patriotism of American women presented itself as a national potentiality to many of our country's leaders. From one of these came a positive, strong, courageous advocacy of this utilization in its most practical form as a part of the Army of the United States.

Edith Nourse Rogers, who was that advocate, is our distinguished guest this afternoon. Her record as dean of our congress-women speaks for itself in constructive legislation. Her faith and confidence in the abilities of American women is also a matter of historical record.

Her championship of the WAC as a permanent part of our plan of national security made an inestimable contribution to our present legal status as part of the Regular Army.

It is my privilege to present to this audience the woman who introduced, sponsored, and championed the original legislation which brought into existence the WAC—the Honorable Edith Nourse Rogers.[4]

In this introduction the speaker has also maintained the dignity of the occasion with her well chosen words. She devoted most of

[3] Delivered November 18, 1943, during the First Session of the 78th Congress. In *Congressional Record*, Vol. 89, Part 7, p. 9677.
[4] *Congressional Record*, Vol. 95, Part 13, Appendix, p. A 1988.

her 175 words to building up the reputation of the speaker in relation to the interests of the listeners. The formality of the speech was extremely appropriate for the occasion; a less formal occasion would demand more informality.

The third example is a slightly different type of introduction. On this occasion Bruce Barton, author and advertising executive, was introduced at an annual dinner of the Advertising Federation of America, to a group who knew him well. He was one of several speakers on the program.

> The next speaker is difficult to classify. He is so versatile in his talents—so much more than an advertising agent. He makes me feel like the young lady up in Maine last summer who met a young man and she couldn't figure him out. Finally she asked him, "What is your vocation?" And he answered, "It's the first week in August, I'm on it now!"
>
> I first knew Bruce Barton when he was Editor of *Every Week*—that brilliant weekly that was one of the early casualties of the first World War. And I have followed him at a respectful distance ever since, through the years when we have all seen him become famous the world over as the author of best-selling books, and when products to which he has applied the magic of his copy have become best-selling merchandise.
>
> There is a secret back of Bruce Barton's pen. He knows people— knows how to touch their hearts—knows those simple fundamentals of life that make the world go round. And he is going to talk to us now on the subject he knows so well—"Better Understanding of Human Nature." I present—Bruce Barton.[5]

In using humor to introduce Mr. Barton the speaker was reflecting the spirit of the occasion. Since there were to be several speakers, this tone of levity was no doubt a welcome relief and may be considered to be in good taste. Furthermore, it no doubt helped the speaker because it put his listeners into a cheerful, even jovial mood.

The chairman or person who introduces a speaker may find that he has other duties and responsibilities. Whenever you are called on to serve in such a capacity, you will do well to check

[5] Sumner, *op. cit.*, pp. 97-98.

with the program chairman to make sure that you understand fully what is expected of you. In your capacity as host you may have the responsibility of recognizing distinguished guests, checking the public address system, if any, of quieting hilarious and possibly impolite members, of keeping the program moving on schedule, of making the speaker aware of his time limits, and of conducting the question period if one is to follow the main speech.

In summary, then, here are several important final hints that should be observed in making speeches of introduction:

1. An introduction should be carefully prepared; don't try to do it impromptu.
2. An introduction should be spontaneous and natural; don't read an introduction.
3. When presenting an introduction, look at the audience; don't talk to the person being introduced.
4. Just mention the speaker's subject; don't discuss it.
5. Play a supporting role; don't try to steal the show or embarrass the speaker with profuse compliments.
6. Avoid insincere flattery, and rarely if ever use glamour words or superlatives such as "greatest," "famous," "darling," "unique," "wonderful," and the like.
7. Avoid hackneyed sentences such as "Our speaker needs no introduction . . ."
8. Avoid anything that might give offense, or which might otherwise be considered to be in poor taste.

Speeches of Welcome and Response

When newcomers are in our midst, we often feel a desire and obligation to extend to them a few well chosen words of welcome. Mayors and secretaries of Chambers of Commerce, as representatives of their organizations, make frequent speeches of welcome to distinguished guests, to conventions, and to other visiting groups. The speech of welcome is also used to greet a new member of a club, or to extend a welcome to visitors. In speeches of this type, the speaker attempts to make the newcomer feel at home, to utter appropriate pleasantries, and to express appreciation of the opportunity to enjoy the presence of the visitors.

In the preparation of one of these speeches you should ask yourself these questions, in so far as they apply to the specific occasion:

1. Who is the person to whom you are extending the welcome?
2. What is the nature of the organization you are greeting? What is its purpose, its history, its program?
3. Why has the person or the organization come to your community?
4. What common bonds exist between you and the newcomer or newcomers?
5. What can the newcomer be expected to contribute to your organization or to your community?
6. What can your organization or your community offer to the newcomer?

Like the speech of introduction, the speech of welcome should be kept genuine, direct, and short. Good humor and graciousness must prevail.

The welcome which George Ainslie, Mayor of Richmond, Virginia, extended to the Sixteenth Conference for Education in the South, April 16, 1913, is typical of this type of speech. The mayor said:

Mr. Chairman, Ladies and Gentlemen: Richmond has been the meeting place of many large, distinguished and important conventions and conferences, but it has had none so large, more distinguished or more important than this one. It has had none so pregnant with great benefits to the people of the States here represented; it has had none with so large an attendance of many specialists as the distinguished men and women who are here to confer upon questions of such moment to the people of the entire South. Therefore the city of Richmond is deeply appreciative of the high honor that has been paid to it by its selection as the meeting place of this Conference, and in its behalf I have the pleasure to extend to you a cordial greeting and welcome. It is an additional pleasure to welcome to the city our distinguished fellow-citizen soon to represent the United States as its Ambassador at the Court of Great Britain. As rich as we are in pleasant and honored memories and traditions, we truly feel that the holding of this Conference here will largely add to our treasures of that character.[6]

In this speech Mr. Ainslie included four elements of a good speech of welcome: (1) He complimented the conference on its size and significance; (2) he took cognizance of what the conference had to offer the participants and the South; (3) he expressed the gratitude of the city of Richmond in being selected as the convention city; and (4) he specifically extended a greeting and welcome.

Ordinarily upon receiving a welcome some representative of the group, or the person himself who is so honored, gives an impromptu reply which is referred to as a *speech of response*. The materials for this type must come directly out of the immediate speaking situation, particularly from the remarks made in the welcome. The theme of all such responses is, "We are glad to be here. Thank you for your hospitality."

Speeches of Presentation and Acceptance

The presentation of a gift or the awarding of a prize often calls for some representative of the donors to make a speech of presentation. For example, a club may wish to present a gift to a retiring officer; a philanthropist may give a building to a college; a coach may wish to present letters to members of the football squad.

This type of speech attempts to put into words the feeling of the group for the recipient. In other words, the speaker must transmit (1) the admiration, the respect, and even the affection of a group to (2) the person being honored. Therefore the speech ordinarily attempts to include the following:

1. It must tell why the presentation is being made.
2. It must summarize the sentiments of the group.
3. It must make the recipient aware of the esteem in which he is held.

[6] For other excellent models, see *Modern Short Speeches*, James M. O'Neill (ed.), The Century Co., 1925, pp. 13-24.

In accomplishing these objectives the speaker must keep in mind two important "don'ts." First, he must avoid over-praise which will seem insincere or which will embarrass the recipient. Second, he must not overstress the gift or its value. Emphasis should be placed upon *why* the presentation is being made, and not upon the gift itself.

Thomas R. Marshall, Vice President from 1913 to 1921, was extremely popular as a presiding officer of the Senate. His fairness won him many friends on both sides of the Chamber. Upon his retirement in 1921, the Senators presented him with a silver vase in appreciation of his service. Henry Cabot Lodge spoke in behalf of the Republicans as follows:

Mr. President, the Sixty-sixth Congress is drawing to its close. For eight years, sir, you have presided over the deliberations of the Senate. By the passage of time and the process of election you will leave on the 4th of March.

It is the desire of the Senate to manifest in something more than a formal resolution the personal regret which all of us feel at the fact that we are about to separate. Separation in the brief life allotted to us here always has an element of sadness. But I desire—and I am sure I am speaking in behalf of all Senators—to express to you the affection that we feel for you, our sense of your unvarying kindness to each one of us, the thoroughly human way in which you have always dealt with us individually, and we wish that you should take with you a symbol of our feelings. We know that you are not going to forget us, any more than we shall forget you and all our many pleasant relations over a period of great strain and great events; but we have felt that some gift, an inanimate object, might serve from time to time, when your eye rested upon it, to remind you of the feeling that we all have and the regret that we all feel personally that the hour of parting is so close at hand.

On behalf of the Senate—and I know that the leader on the other side will express the same feeling—we all desire to give you every good wish in the future, and that you should know that you take with you our affection, our hopes for your happiness and prosperity, and although I need not express a hope on this that you will not forget the many days we have spent together in the service of our common and beloved country.[7]

Mr. Lodge made his speech genuine and sincere. The spirit expressed can be more fully appreciated when it is remembered that in the year prior to the date of this speech, the Senate had been deadlocked in bitter debate over the question of whether the United States should participate in the League of Nations, and whether the Senate should ratify the treaty of peace. The speaker accomplished three objectives: (1) he mentioned the occasion for the presentation; (2) he expressed the affection that the members of the Senate felt for the retiring Vice President Marshall; and (3) he wished for the Vice President a pleasant future. Noteworthy are his choice of simple words and the suppressed emotion reflected by the speech.

The *speech of acceptance* is much like the speech of response. Of course normally it is impromptu and grows out of the occasion, and its subject matter is suggested by the preceding speech of presentation. If it is prepared it must be made to seem spontaneous and heartfelt. The recipient must remain modest, and above all he must make his listeners feel his gratitude for the gift or award as well as for the sentiment behind it. This type of speech should normally be extremely short.

Mr. James V. Forrestal, upon his retirement as Secretary of Defense, was presented a remembrance by the Committee on Armed Services of the House of Representatives. In reply to Mr. Overton Brooks's speech of presentation, Mr. Forrestal said:

Mr. Chairman, I am too much overcome by what I consider to be a very gracious and a very moving testimonial of your friendship and of those deeper feelings that come from the heart.

I should like to say for the record, however, without venturing to contradict the rhetoric of the chairman, that that tribute which he gave should properly be directed to himself and to the members of this committee because it was the unfailing zeal, the high intelligence, and the continuing zest for work which really built the American

---

[7] Delivered before the Senate February 28, 1921. *Congressional Record*, Vol. 60, Part 4, p. 4021.

Navy and which under the chairmanship of Mr. Vinson will also build the defense forces under the unification which I know will be ably guided by Colonel Johnson, my successor.

I am much too moved to go into a longer appreciation of this most generous and exceptional act. I thank you deeply.[8]

Each paragraph of this speech accomplishes a purpose: the first expresses the appreciation for the gift, the second pays tribute to the committee making the presentation, and the third concludes the speech by thanking the group. Wisely the speaker devotes more than half of his time to talking about the committee.

Speeches of Farewell

Like other occasional addresses the speech of farewell is primarily a stimulating speech. When a person leaves an organization, accepts a position in another firm, or moves to another city, he may feel an urge to express his regret over breaking up a pleasant association. Such speeches may express the following points:

1. Regrets over leaving
2. Appreciation for the group
3. Reminiscence of happy times and memories
4. Indebtedness or obligations to the group
5. Closing words of farewell

Perhaps the best known speech of farewell, which embodies in a few lines all the essential characteristics of such a speech, is Lincoln's, delivered on the occasion of his leaving his home in Springfield, Illinois, for the White House in Washington:

My friends, No one not in my situation can appreciate my feeling of sadness at this parting. To this place, and the kindness of these people, I owe everything. Here I have lived a quarter of a century, and have passed from a young to an old man. Here my children have been born, and one is buried. I now leave, not knowing when or whether ever I may return, with a task before me greater than that which rested upon Washington. Without the assistance of that Divine Being who ever attended him, I cannot succeed. With that assistance,

[8] Delivered March 29, 1949. *Congressional Record*, Vol. 95, Part 3, Appendix pp. A1878-1879.

I cannot fail. Trusting in Him who can go with me, and remain with you, and be everywhere for good, let us confidently hope that all will yet be well. To his care commending you, as I hope in your prayers you will commend me, I bid you an affectionate farewell.[9]

SPEECHES OF INSPIRATION

In an earlier chapter[10] you read that the general goal of all speaking is the response of the listeners. As a rule the goal of the inspirational speech is to strengthen or intensify attitudes, opinions, or beliefs already held by the auditors. The stimulating talk is designed to create a greater appreciation of some person, an institution, or an event. In preparation it is much like the argumentative speech; consequently many of the principles of partition discussed in Chapter IX are applicable here. Like the argumentative speech, the inspirational talk is also built around a single key sentence or proposition. Below are some propositions which might be developed into excellent talks of this kind.

1. George Washington deserves to be called "the Father of his Country."
2. Theodore Roosevelt was a rugged individualist in the highest sense.
3. Al Smith was justly called "the happy warrior."
4. The landing of the Pilgrims was a significant event in world history.
5. Woodrow Wilson merits emulation as a great American.
6. We must rededicate our lives to the achievement of our objectives.
7. The erection of this monument is a fitting tribute to our war dead.
8. The history class is deeply indebted to Professor Jones.
9. My father stood for high ideals.
10. The spirit of the pioneer must be preserved.

A study of these topic sentences will reveal that under nearly every circumstance the speaker and the auditors would be at the outset in general agreement on these and kindred subjects. Such

[9] Delivered in Springfield, February 11, 1861. *Classified Models of Speech Composition*, p. 690.
[10] Chapter VI.

differences as might exist would be only a matter of the degree of enthusiasm. Since there is no disagreement, no argument is possible. Sometimes the speaker finds his listeners lethargic or passive, or only mildly interested, in which case he seeks to stir greater fervor and enthusiasm, which may, of course, lead to overt action.

Howell and Hudson in their discussion of Daniel Webster and his great ceremonial speeches give us an excellent analysis of the nature of inspirational or epideictic speaking. They say,

> The persuasive end of such oratory, according to Aristotle, is to establish honor or shame; that is, the epideictic speaker persuades an audience that some man or action or institution is to be praised or to be reviled. Yet such an orator, as a rule, has no heavy task of changing people's minds. Most American listeners already believe that the American Revolutionists deserve honor. The orator's task is rather to objectify those deserts and that honor (just as the deliberative orator objectifies the expediency of a proposed action), making them have palpable reality and weight. He is working for the most part with intangibles, and his success depends upon the truth and force of his imagination. He will draw word pictures; he will dramatize; he will elevate, enlarge, and dignify. Above all he will stir and create emotions, knowing that imaginations are released by emotional disturbance and then act to heighten the very emotion that has set them free.[11]

Remember that inspirational speaking attempts to intensify, to revivify, to elevate, to enlarge, and to dignify.

The Eulogy

The eulogy is a speech commending the character and actions of a deceased person. Sometimes the term connotes the praise of a hero or some famous person of another age or another country, but here the term is used in a more general sense. Depending on the occasion, it may be long or short. The funeral oration many times falls under this classification.

---

[11] Wilbur Samuel Howell and Hoyt Hopewell Hudson, "Daniel Webster." In *A History and Criticism of American Public Address*, William Norwood Brigance, (ed.), McGraw-Hill Book Company, 1943, Vol. II, pp. 665-733.

Aristotle says, "The eulogist draws his materials from the noble deeds, actual or reputed, of the man he is praising."[12] The speaker must show that his subject by his character and actions demonstrated that he possessed the virtues esteemed by the society of which the audience is a part. Evidence is drawn from such sources as (1) traits of character, (2) aspirations and goals, (3) outstanding accomplishments, (4) influences on men and the times. Naturally, episodes, comparisons, and analogies are the most effective types of supporting material. Ordinarily appreciation may be aroused by showing the accomplishment of the subject as compared favorably with those of other great men. Wendell Phillips elevated, enlarged, and dignified the character of Toussaint L'Ouverture, the Negro general of Santo Domingo, by comparing him with Cromwell, Napoleon, and Washington. The following paragraph is typical of his treatment:

You remember Macaulay says, comparing Cromwell with Napoleon, that Cromwell showed the greater military genius, if we consider that he never saw an army till he was forty; while Napoleon at the age of twenty-seven was placed at the head of the best troops Europe ever saw. They were both successful; but, says Macaulay, with such disadvantages, the Englishman showed the greater genius. Whether you allow the inference or not, you will at least grant that it is a fair mode of measurement. Apply it to Toussaint. Cromwell never saw an army till he was forty; this man never saw a soldier till he was fifty. Cromwell manufactured his own army—out of what? Englishmen—the best blood in Europe. Out of the middle class of Englishmen,—the best blood of the island. And with it he conquered what? Englishmen,—their equals. This man manufactured his army out of what? Out of what you call the despicable race of negroes, debased, demoralized by two hundred years of slavery, one hundred thousand of them imported into the island within four years, unable to speak a dialect intelligible even to each other. Yet out of this mixed, and, as you say, despicable mass, he forged a thunderbolt and hurled it at what? At the proudest blood in Europe, the Spaniard, and sent him home conquered [cheers]; at the most warlike blood in Europe, the French, and put them under his feet; at the pluckiest blood in Europe,

---

[12] Lane Cooper, *The Rhetoric of Aristotle*, Appleton-Century-Crofts Inc., 1932, p. 156.

the English, and they skulked home to Jamaica. [Applause] Now if Cromwell was a general, at least this man was a soldier. I know it was a small territory; it was not as large as that Attica, which, with Athens for a capital, has filled the earth with its fame for two thousand years. We measure genius by quality, not by quantity.[13]

The speech of praise must be more than a biographical summary or an enumeration of dates, events, and places. Indeed a prolonged recitation of dates, number of children, years of schooling, and membership in professional societies is likely to put almost any audience to sleep. The eulogist strives to make his subject unique in character and stature.

The inexperienced speaker may find the following suggestions helpful in preparing a eulogy. Ordinarily since the speaker wishes to praise his subject, he will use a central thought similar to either of the following: "_____ is worthy of praise," or "_____ is a great man worthy of emulation." Of course these topic sentences may be expressed in countless different ways and in more polished language, but essentially they express the theme of most eulogies.

The subpoints used to develop such a central theme will be statements about the traits, virtues, or accomplishments. They may be worded somewhat as follows:

1. He is brave.
2. He is kind.
3. He is sincere.
4. He is generous.

Or if the speaker wishes to use comparisons to develop his central thought, the subpoints may read:

1. He is more intelligent than _____.
2. He is more generous than _____.
3. He is more daring than _____.

For supporting material the speaker will search his subject's life for episodes that illustrate the subpoints. In other words, the

[13] Wendell Phillips, *Speeches, Lectures and Letters,* Lee and Shepard, 1863, pp. 468-494.

eulogy will be composed of a central theme or thought, statements concerning the man's traits, and illustrations to support each statement. Below is a skeleton outline of a eulogy:

Theodore Roosevelt was a great man, for
A. He was a brave soldier.
B. He was an excellent scholar.
C. He was a great statesman.

Do not attempt a eulogy which consists entirely of a chronological account of a man's life, for such an account is in fact no eulogy at all. Too often such a speech is no more than a factual report, and falls far short of being a speech of praise.

The Commendation

The commendation is a speech which strives to show the affection, the admiration, or the respect of a group for a living person. Such speeches grow out of situations like these: a worker achieves a new production record; a business man is recognized for his work in civic improvement; a local citizen demonstrates great valor; the high school football coach has a winning team. Ordinarily a spokesman reviews in some detail the accomplishments and achievements of the recipient of the honor in the presence of many of his colleagues. The preparation is much the same as for the eulogy, and somewhat like the speech of presentation.

The Commemorative Speech

The speech of commemoration is an inspirational speech which celebrates an important or a significant day, or an important event. Centennials, bicentennials, the Fourth of July, Labor Day, Armistice Day, Memorial Day, and so on, frequently bring forth commemorative speaking. The laying of a corner stone, the completion of a building, or the erection of a monument may also inspire this type of speech. At both the laying of the corner stone and the dedication of the Bunker Hill Monument Daniel Webster gave commemorative speeches.

The speech of commemoration is similar in method and substance to the other types of inspirational talk.

1. The central theme ordinarily stresses the importance of the day or the event.

2. The speaker works to arouse feelings of loyalty, pride, and patriotism. Webster in his Plymouth Oration expressed the purpose of his speech in these words:

> We have come to this Rock [Plymouth], to record here our homage for our Pilgrim Fathers: our sympathy in their suffering; our gratitude for their labors; our admiration of their virtues; our veneration for their piety; and our attachment to those principles of civil and religious liberty, which they encountered the dangers of the ocean, the storms of the heavens . . . to enjoy and to establish.

Homage, sympathy, gratitude, admiration, veneration, and attachment are the sentiments which most talks of this type attempt to arouse.

3. The supporting materials may be of a variety of types, but the historical example and the analogy or comparison again find frequent use. In the Plymouth oration, Webster, for example, developed the importance of the New England colonies by comparing them with the colonies of Greece, Rome, and the colonies in Asia and the West Indies. Naturally he stressed how the Pilgrims were far superior to other colonists.

SPEECHES OF GOOD WILL

Each year large corporations spend millions of dollars in quest of an intangible something in the public attitude which is called good will. Keeping their names and trademarks before the public in a favorable light, and maintaining happy relations with actual and potential customers are significant phases of this campaign. Great efforts are made to give the public information which casts a favorable light on the company's activities. Complaints are answered promptly. "The customer is always right." High powered public relations experts are employed to devise new ways to build up good will.

By arousing good will the company is building its reputation, that is, the favorable attitude of the friends that it already has; it seeks further to create a similar attitude among as many others as possible. Many advertisements do not even suggest that the reader buy the product described, or even become a customer of the company. The speech of good will, as an aspect of such a campaign, has for its purpose therefore to *win friends*—nothing more, at least in organization and apparent objective.

In the speech of good will the speaker attempts to make friends for a movement, for an organization, for a business firm, or even for a person. Every year thousands of talks are presented in behalf of the Boy Scouts, the Girl Scouts, the Y.M.C.A., the Y.W.C.A., the Red Cross, the Salvation Army, the March of Dimes, the Community Chest, the Cancer Fund, blood banks, and savings bonds. These talks are usually delivered under the form of informative talks, and from one point of view, that is just what they are. The immediate goal of the speaker is to elicit understanding, to add to the knowledge of the listeners; but the ultimate goal, closely connected with persuasion, remains unexpressed. Such speeches are related to persuasion in that, by giving information and establishing attitudes, they are directed ultimately to overt response.

So long as the information presented is true to fact, and so long as the ultimate purpose is neither concealment nor misleading, there is nothing whatever in this type of speech that is inherently unethical.

The formula of the good-will speech is something like this: information concerning worthy activities or worthwhile products makes friends; these friends will make other friends; as a result of acquiring strong friendships contributions of effort and money may be expected in the future; or, all these friends will buy the things they need, when the need arises, from the organization that has created the good will for itself.

The plan of the good will talk is often developed around the following pattern:

1. The introduction relates the organization or cause to the auditors.
2. The background of the organization or campaign is traced.
3. The present needs are presented.
4. The results of the organization's efforts or of the campaign are related to the self-interest of the audience, or to their interest in the well-being of others.
5. An appeal is made for sympathy and understanding.

SPEECHES TO ENTERTAIN

Despite the drawing power of movie thrillers, radio serials, television shows, and sports events, the speech continues to rank as a significant type of diversion, and the speaker who can talk entertainingly is in great demand. In fact, a business, the lecture bureau, thrives on supplying speakers to hundreds of organizations in quest of this type of entertainment. These booking agencies direct the efforts of thousands of lecturers who go forth to address millions of Americans. But the professional speaker by no means dominates the lecture platform or comes near supplying the requests for entertaining speakers. Town Hall groups, Toastmaster Clubs, service groups, women's organizations, and directors of school assemblies, search the community diligently for program material for their weekly meetings, and local citizens are frequently drafted into service. As any program chairman will tell you, there are far too few persons in any given community who can give a really clever, entertaining speech.

Immediately one common misconception concerning the nature of the entertaining talk should be clarified. A speech to be entertaining need not be funny, side-splitting, or laugh provoking. We have all encountered the so-called speech which was composed solely of unrelated jokes. These efforts are frequently not speeches, and they are often not even entertaining. The entertaining speech has one basic requirement: *it must hold attention and interest in itself.* The response sought may be either covert or overt. The well told story, serious and dramatic in detail, although it may not elicit laughter, may provide the listener with pleasant diversion and may make him forget his more serious problems. In summary, there are four characteristics which most entertaining speeches possess:

1. An entertaining speech is well organized and unified. Like other good speeches it is built around a central theme and is developed in planned sequence. It is the product of careful preparation.

2. An entertaining speech is ordinarily brief. As a rule entertainers strive to leave their audiences not quite satisfied; they leave the listeners in the frame of mind of wanting more. It is better to have your hearers want you to continue rather than that they should want you to stop.

3. The entertaining speech strives for an immediate, momentary response either covert or overt. The speaker seldom hopes to control his audiences beyond the limits of his talk, although, it is true, he may give them worthwhile information that they will remember for a long time.

4. In the entertaining talk emphasis is placed on the utilization of the factors of attention and interest. Novelty and suspense are frequently employed. The example and the episode are often included for supporting material. Delivery may be more sensational and animated, but it must always remain within the bounds of good taste.

5. In most of its forms, the entertaining speech is usually delivered extemporaneously. Certainly it must be spontaneous and natural. Giving the "illusion of the first time" is extremely important in maintaining interest.

After-Dinner Speaking

A banquet or dinner of consequence is seldom planned without the inclusion of a formal program of speeches. The toastmaster, as the "master of ceremonies" is called, and the after-dinner speaker are considered no less important than the food, the atmosphere, and the service. Why, you ask. Seemingly when men are in the mood of joviality they feel the urge to express themselves, and they like to hear others speak, so long as the speaking is not overdone. For hundreds of years feasting and speaking have gone together.

The after-dinner speech is difficult, if not impossible, to define. Perhaps the explanation is that it is actually not a type of speech at all, but a class of speeches which possess only two distinguishing characteristics: they are speeches and they follow a dinner, or some other meal. In other elements after-dinner speeches may vary widely. They may be humorous or serious; they may seek to entertain, to inform, to stimulate, to convince, or even to actuate. Dependent upon the nature of the dinner they may be reminiscent, commemorative, or congratulatory, or they may fit into almost every other type. Obviously there are few rules that can be laid down for after-dinner speaking, for it employs the same principles that other effective speaking possesses.

Almost any subject the speaker may choose will be appropriate if it fits the requirements of the occasion and the audience. A study of the three hundred after-dinner speeches included in the collection of *Modern Eloquence*[14] offers convincing proof of this observation. Here is a representative sample of titles chosen at random from this collection:

Faith and Duty	The Drama
The Lessons of Life	My Farm in Jersey
Washington's Birthday	Cape Cod Folks
A Cincinnatus from Indiana	Direct Democracy
Virginia	After-Dinner Speaking
The Republic that Never Retreats	The Ladies
Finding God Among the Tommies	Commerce
America's Mission	Prayer and Politics

[14] *Modern Eloquence*, Edited by Ashley A. Thorndike, Modern Eloquence Corporation, 1923, Vols. I, II, III.

Progress in Medicine	The Southland
The Pilgrim Mothers	The American Ideal
The Babies	Sires and Sons
The Battle of Manila	Across the Flood
Invention	The Salt of the Earth
Woman	The Hollander as an American
Friends Across the Sea	Business and Politics
Truth and Light	Russia
North and South	The Pious Pilgrimage
Music in the United States	The Qualities that Win
Joys of the Trail	Yankee Notions
The New South	The Ideal Woman
Mere Man	My Creed for the Nation
Business Education	Behold the American
My Garden	Alaska, Fish and Indians
Dorothy Q.	The President's Prelude
The Class of '61	The Critic
Our Reunited Country	The Bright Land to Westward

After reading the list above you can readily understand why the editor describes the collection as "ranging from persiflage and nonsense to the most eloquent utterances on greatest themes."[15]

What has been said in earlier chapters concerning speech preparation is equally applicable here and certainly does not need repeating. The preparation of an after-dinner speech is just like the preparation for any other speech, because exactly the same factors are involved.

Perhaps some special consideration should be given to the following elements:

1. The audience will ordinarily be in a friendly and receptive mood, for good food, pleasant surroundings, and boon companions are conducive to geniality.

2. The auditors will probably be an inactive audience. They have come to be entertained or inspired, and they expect to give little except attention. Many will resist any effort on the part of the speaker to be serious.

[15] *Ibid.*, Vol. I, p. v.

3. The speaker must make his speech consistent with the theme and the spirit of the occasion. If the general atmosphere emphasizes the reminiscent or the commemorative, then the after-dinner speech must follow in the same spirit.

4. The after-dinner speech should be clever, but *not laboriously so*. There must be no evidence of striving for cleverness. A tradition has developed that effective after-dinner speakers are masters of wit, language, and delivery. The speaker should strive to show definite marks of originality. Particularly in the introduction sparkling repartee is often desirable in adjusting to the remarks of the toastmaster or of previous speakers. This requirement does not imply that the speech must be humorous; on the contrary, it may be deeply serious. But even the seriousness may now and then be relieved by a sudden, rapier-like thrust of wit or humor.

5. The after-dinner speech usually does not make serious demands on the audience. The banquet is not a fitting place to reform the listeners, to develop a complicated formula, or to teach a profound truth. People who have just eaten a large meal are not as a rule in any mood for anything that demands great concentration.

6. The after-dinner speech is usually regarded as a short speech. James Russell Lowell once said, "There is one virtue, I am sure, in after dinner oratory and that is brevity."[16] There is good reason for this convention. A prolonged speech after an hour or more of eating may indeed be too much for most audiences. The fact is doubly true if several speeches are delivered on the same program. You will win favor with the audience, the toastmaster, and the other speakers if you stay rigidly within the time limit.

After-dinner speakers sometimes fail because of some very minor violations of good speaking practice. The following list

[16] From a speech entitled "After Dinner Speaking," delivered July 4, 1883, in London at a banquet in honor of Sir Henry Irving. *Modern Eloquence*, Vol. II, pp. 359-362.

of "don'ts" suggests some of the pitfalls that effective speakers will avoid:

1. Don't speak impromptu, and don't let the repartee ruin your planned speech. An after-dinner speech should be well organized and carefully rehearsed.
2. Don't speak solely to the honored guests or to the head table; speak to the entire assembly.
3. Don't try to clown.[17] Ordinarily the clown's place is in the circus, not at the banquet table. Pounding glasses or dishes with silverware, hammering the table, climbing on chairs, or hitting nearby guests is usually considered extremely poor taste.[18]
4. Don't insert into your speech jokes or anecdotes that are unrelated to your development. The best humor usually grows out of the speaking situation.
5. Don't preface a humorous story by telling your listeners how funny it is.
6. Don't laugh at your own stories.
7. Never tell stories that you would hesitate to tell in mixed company or in your own home.
8. Don't select any one person—even the toastmaster—as the butt of your wit. The audience may feel that you are taking an unfair advantage of the victim.
9. Don't overdo the use of puns; they may not be understood, and can become very tiresome.
10. Don't allow an irritating or rattling noise, or any other disturbance, in or out of the room, to upset your composure.

The Toastmaster

The duties of the toastmaster are the same as those of any other presiding officer: he presides over the banquet and introduces the speakers on the program; if other types of entertainment are offered, he introduces them as well. Ordinarily he is expected (1) to call the banquet to order, (2) to determine when the

[17] Some of the worst violations of this principle may be observed occasionally in intercollegiate after-dinner speaking contests.
[18] Bad as they seem, these have all actually been seen relatively recently in after-dinner-speaking!

various activities shall commence, (3) to introduce honored guests, (4) to maintain the unity of the program, including what may be described as "setting the tone" of the occasion, (5) to keep the program on schedule, (6) to deal with difficulties such as testing the public address system, and (7) to introduce the speakers or other items on the program. In introducing speakers his talk is the same as in any other introductory talk; that is, he attempts by his remarks to make it easier for the speaker to present his speech. He should not attempt to compete with the speakers or to be the stellar attraction. The idea of the "roastmaster," one who tries to tell good natured but embarrassing jokes about each speaker, is regarded as inappropriate for most occasions and certainly always out of place on an occasion which demands dignity. If you are a toastmaster, be a "builder-upper," not a contestant for attention.

Planning a Toast Program

A banquet and toast program (one making use of a program in which several speakers participate with very short speeches) requires careful planning. You have no doubt witnessed the tragic results of the failure to plan—inadequate table space, failure of persons to arrive on time, poor ventilation, a seemingly endless program, a drowsy audience. When the committee fails to do an adequate campaign of preparation they do both the audience and the speakers a great injustice.

The planning committee for a banquet should make sure that they have solved the following problems:

1. Arrangements should be made for the banquet; that is, the menu should be determined, the caterer should be instructed as to what service you want and when you want it; ventilation and checkroom facilities should be arranged.

2. The seating arrangement should be determined, particularly that for the head table. Speakers should be located in places from which they can speak to all the audience.

3. A banquet theme must be selected. The committee may actually wish to determine the topics on which the speakers are to talk.

4. Speaking facilities must be checked. The availability of a lectern, public address system if needed, and controls over lights should be considered.

5. A committee to help guests find places at the tables and to serve as hosts should be appointed.

6. Invitations must be extended to the speakers. Each speaker must understand the theme, his specific subject, and his time limit. The committee should make clear to the speakers the nature and significance of the occasion.

7. The chairman must be instructed as to what his duties are. He cannot carry out the plan of the committee if he is not given specific instructions.

Other Types of the Entertaining Speech

STORY TELLING. In an earlier chapter the narrative was discussed as a means to inform. Now let us view it from the point of view of entertainment. Stories of personal adventure, travelogues, and stories concerning exciting exploits of others make splendid ways to pass the time. The explorer back from an exciting expedition may be asked to relate some of his experiences. The lover of history may give fascinating talks concerning olden times. A person who has just returned from a trip is frequently called upon to relate his experiences. In each case the speaker usually has no goal beyond entertaining, although here again he may present information; he may add to the general knowledge of the listeners.

The difference between the informative narrative and the entertaining narrative lies primarily in the emphasis given to the materials. In the first case the speaker is guided by the desire for accuracy and objectivity. In the second case the story teller attempts to maintain interest by the development of characterization, plot, and mood. The elements are presented in a way to stimulate suspense. Distortion of detail, omission of a few details of fact here and there, and the choice of loaded words become aids in achieving the speaker's purpose.

Much of what was said in the chapter on the informative speech concerning development also applies here;[19] consequently there is no need to repeat the discussion of partition.

THE BOOK REPORT AND REVIEW. A study of club programs will reveal that the book review is another type of speech which frequently appears in the schedule. Women's clubs have book study groups that devote all their time to this type of activity. The good reviewer is dated up months in advance.

Like the narrative, the book review may have either of two purposes, to inform or to entertain. A passing mention, made in the chapter on the informative speech, refers to the first type as a kind of criticism. In this form the reviewer strives to evaluate the worth of a book. More specifically he may speak with the idea of revealing his own opinion of the work in order that others may make comparisons of their standards of value; he may make an attempt to guide his auditors in their book choices; or he may hope to give information that will aid his listeners in understanding literary trends. The book review may be developed along the following lines:

1. Title and author
2. Sentence summary classifying the book as to type and content
3. Presentation of elements of the book including for the novel, the plot, setting, theme, characters, and purpose
4. Interpretations of the book in the light of literary trends and contemporary developments
5. Final critical evaluation

In the critical review the reviewer may attempt his consideration of the book without revealing the entire content or fully developing the plot. In other words, he does not want to deny the listener the pleasure of reading the book for himself.

The book review having as its purpose to entertain should

[19] See Chapter VIII.

more properly be referred to as a book report, for the speaker's goal is not to give information, but to provide pleasant diversion for his listeners. In this type the speaker or reporter does little more than summarize the contents of the book. In his development he may include representative passages in order to reveal an interesting characterization, a vivid bit of description, or a particular mood. The plan of presentation follows closely that order of development used by the author of the book itself. The outline of this type of report may be summarized as follows:

1. The introduction is devoted to the presentation of necessary background material for understanding. This may include information concerning the author, his other works, and the setting of the book.
2. The development is devoted to retelling the story or summarizing the content, if non-fiction.
3. The conclusion is the final interpretation of the book in the light of current literary trends.

Some book reporters prefer to read what actually amounts to a condensed version of the book. The speaker selects important passages which contain the chief elements of the plot or development, and then he ties these together by short transitional paragraphs in his own words. In his presentation, he actually reads a major portion of his manuscript, suggesting characterization by subtle changes of voice, posture, and restrained gestures. In its extreme form this type of performance falls outside the realm of public speaking, and belongs to the field of interpretative reading.

EXERCISES

1. *Speaking Assignment.* Deliver a speech of introduction in which you present one of the following persons to your speech class or

A SPEECH OF WELCOME FOR MRS. ELEANOR ROOSEVELT

Miss Tellegen, Doctor of Laws, in behalf of her country welcomes Mrs. Roosevelt to the Netherlands. The speech was delivered in the Hall of Knights in the presence of a distinguished audience. (Photo, Black Star.)

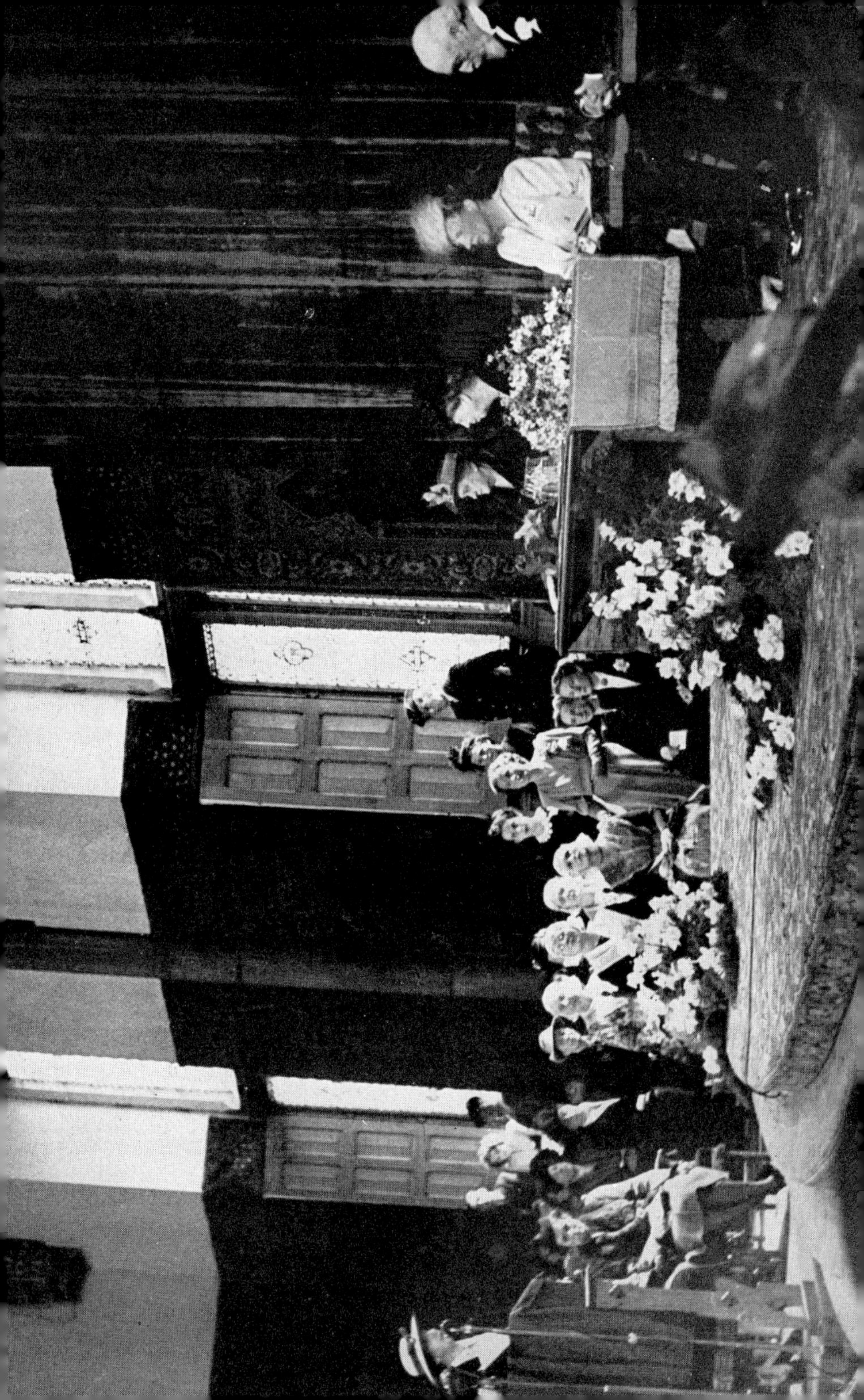

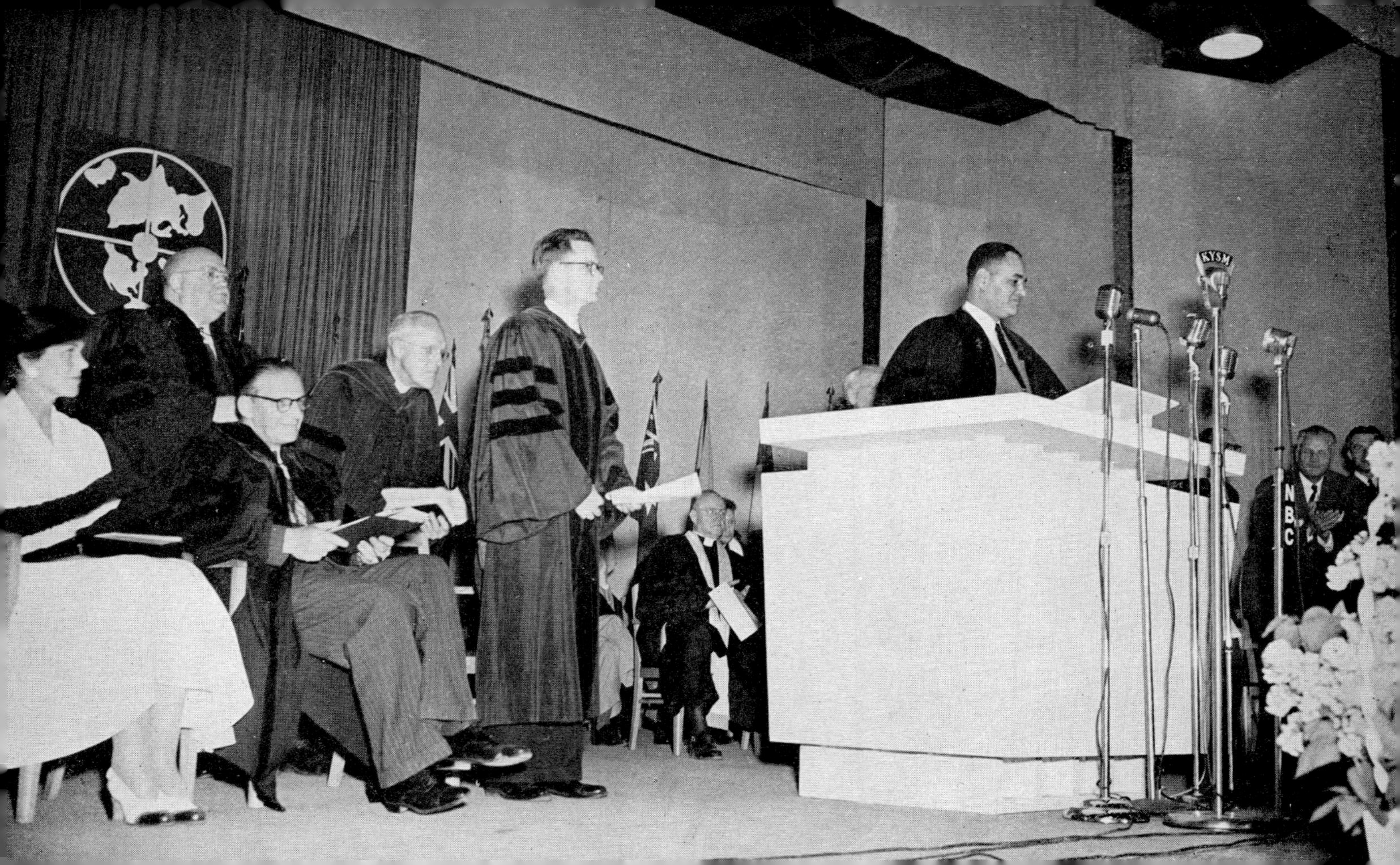
KYSM
NBC

to any other group of college students: the president of a neighboring college or university, a local attorney or doctor, a social worker, a prominent professor, a Jewish rabbi, a Negro educator, a labor leader, or a woman lecturer.
2. *Speaking Assignment.* Deliver a speech of welcome to one of the following:
   a. A new minister in your church
   b. A new resident in the community
   c. The governor of the state
   d. The football, basketball or baseball team of a neighboring school
   e. A Boy Scout troop
   f. A similar group of your own choice.
3. *Speaking Assignment.* Deliver a five- to eight-minute eulogy on some great American. In planning your organization use a topical arrangement. In other words, do not just repeat the events of the man's life in chronological order, but attempt to discuss his great traits of character.
4. *Speaking Assignment.* Deliver a eulogy on some person whom you have known personally.
5. *Speaking Assignment.* Deliver a five- to eight-minute commemorative speech fitting for the celebration of some national holiday or anniversary important in the life of the university or local community.
6. *Speaking Assignment.* Deliver a brief speech of presentation suitable for one of the following occasions:
   a. Awarding letters to the athletic team
   b. Awarding a prize for establishing a record for safe driving
   c. Awarding a $5,000 scholarship for study abroad
   d. Presenting a substantial gift to the college or university
   e. Establishing a foundation for some worthy inquiry in the field of medicine, science, or social welfare

DR. RALPH BUNCHE DELIVERS AN OCCASIONAL SPEECH

Dr. Bunche, Nobel Prize winner, delivers a speech at ceremonies honoring the Count Bernadotte Memorial Library, Gustavus Adolphus College at St. Peter, Minnesota, June 4, 1950. Other persons on the platform are (left to right) Countess Bernadotte; the Swedish Ambassador, Erik Boheman; and Dr. Edgar Carlson, president of the college. (Photo, Wide World.)

274   PUBLIC SPEAKING

    f. A presentation of your own choice (serious in nature)
7. *Assignment for After-Dinner Speaking.* Divide the class into groups of five or six. Each group will be responsible for preparing a "toast" program of not more than forty minutes in length. Each group will elect its own toastmaster, decide upon a theme appropriate for a speech class, and partition the theme. Some classes may actually want to have a dinner at which the five or six best speakers prepare the program.
8. *Speaking Assignment.* Deliver a five-minute oral analysis of an effective or ineffective occasional speech which you have personally heard.
9. *Research Assignment.* Make a comparative study of several eulogies of the same man. Consider structure, content, and language. Your best source will probably be the *Congressional Record.* Check the index of the session under such headings as "Eulogies," "Memorial Services," or under the name of the deceased Congressman (or other person). You will find numerous eulogies of Lincoln in the various collections of speeches.
10. *Speech Analysis.* Bring to class six or eight display advertisements from popular magazines, which are designed solely to create good will. Make a talk showing how the copy writer has adapted the principles of the good-will speech to the writing of the advertisements.
11. *Speech Analysis.* Senator Arthur H. Vandenberg of Michigan gave the following eulogy on William E. Borah, Senator from Idaho from 1907 to 1940, before a Senate memorial service, April 25, 1941.[20] It should be recalled that Mr. Borah was highly respected by his colleagues and greatly admired by millions of Americans. In this eulogy Mr. Vandenberg makes frequent use of superlatives. Study the speech carefully and determine if you think it is a fitting tribute to the Idaho Senator. In your analysis you may need to familiarize yourself with other estimates of the man. You may find it profitable to turn to the *Congressional Record* and read other eulogies on Borah. If you want to compare this eulogy with another, read William E. Borah's eulogy on Robert M. LaFollette, found in the *Congressional Record,* Vol. 67, Part 11, p. 11648.

    Mr. President, no mortal words can add to the stature of a great character in human history. They can but acknowledge the vast and eternal debt of lesser men to the Olympians

[20] *Congressional Record,* Vol. 87, Part 3, pp. 3307-3308.

whom God occasionally gives to the Republic. It is in this humble spirit that I rise to speak a few simple sentences regarding the greatest man I ever knew. That he was the greatest friend I ever had in public life is my own personal legacy. That he was the greatest friend America had in my time and generation is the measure of the Nation's debt to the life and service and the vivid memory of the late United States Senator WILLIAM E. BORAH, of Idaho.

There was something in him of the rugged strength of the mighty mountains of the West whence he came. There was something in him of the lonely pioneer who dares against all odds for the faith of his objectives. There was something in him of the divine genius with which God occasionally touches one among us and bids him lead the sons of men. There was honor—against which no shadow of a syllable was ever lisped. There was power—the like of which this Senate Chamber has not known since the founding fathers made us what we are. There was simplicity—the badge of a great soul. And there was the gentle, kindly friendliness and simplicity which made him as beloved as he was respected and revered.

Others have spoken in detail of his great career. Volumes would fail to do it justice. I but add a postscript, as it were, in behalf of what I know was the aching sorrow of tens of millions of his fellow countrymen when they learned, in veritable consternation, that his great heart had ceased to beat and that his invincible eloquence was no longer available to the defense of truth and justice and the American way of life. He was one of those few statesmen—I can think of but two or three others in our history—who was greater than any President under whom he served, and for whom the Presidency itself could have added nothing to his stature or his laurels. He was an institution within himself. His patriotism is part of the American inheritance. When he died one of the Republic's pillars fell. We shall not soon look upon his like again.

Thirty-three fertile years he served within these walls. Within these walls? Ah, Mr. President, he grew so swiftly that no walls could encompass his influence and his authority. Swiftly he became not merely the Senator from Idaho but the Senator of the United States. Nay, more; his fame leaped the boundaries of his native land and spanned the earth. BORAH! It was an electric name in any capital on earth. BORAH! It was a magnet to draw the throngs of our common citizenship wherever he appeared. BORAH! It was the personification of human aspiration at countless hearthstones beneath the Stars and Stripes. BORAH! If only we could still hear him answer "present" in these cataclysmic times.

Swiftly he grew in the talents which made him the greatest advocate and orator of his time. He became the greatest expounder of the Constitution since Daniel Webster. He seemed to be the living resurrection of all those voices which, for 150 years, have invincibly responded whenever reveille has called the defenders of the faith to their unyielding battle line. He became the greatest apostle of vibrant, self-reliant Americanism since Washington's Farewell Address. He became the Senate's dean, not alone in years of service but in the personal prestige of a unique and mighty character which was worthy of the Senate in its richest tradition since this Government was born.

He loved America—and America loved him. He believed in America and in her independent destiny with a passion that was the touchstone of his life—and America, whether it always agreed with him or not, believed in him. It knew his courage. It knew his shining probity. It knew his soul-deep sympathy with human needs. It knew his deathless devotion to representative democracy. It knew his dedication to the common weal. It knew he was a man—in the maximum that term may imply—the noblest work of God.

Fifteen months have rolled down the tragic avenue of time since we bade good-bye to him one peaceful afternoon amid yon western hills which he knew and loved so well. Yet he is here among us at this hour as vividly as though in the flesh. Such spirits do not die. They live—they live—to become lamps to light the way.

Farewell, great patriot, great friend.

12. *Speech Analysis*. Study the two speeches given below to determine their structure, content, language, and appropriateness for the occasion.

    a. Introduction of James A. Farley at the dawn-patrol breakfast sponsored by the Boy Scouts of America over radio station WJZ, Hotel Waldorf-Astoria, New York, January 8,

1947.²¹ Mr. Harry J. Delaney, chairman of the Businessmen's Committee, introduced Mr. Farley as follows:

Honored guests, ladies and gentlemen, We all know Jim Farley—if I may be permitted to address him publicly in the way that we all affectionately refer to him in our private conversations—as one of the nation's stalwarts who has valiantly fought to keep America in the path that has made her great.

Likewise, we know that he never loses an opportunity to speak up for those causes which join with the church, the school, and the home to•work for the protection and betterment of youth. It is for these reasons that we thought he was the very best person whom we could ask to help us launch this million-dollar drive for the expansion of the Boy Scouts of America in Greater New York.

It is with the greatest of personal pleasure and with keen appreciation of his coming here this morning to address our dawn patrol breakfast, that I present to you the former Postmaster General of the United States—and a friend of youth—the Honorable James A. Farley.

b. Introduction of Winston Churchill to the joint meeting of the Senate and the House of Representatives, May 19, 1949.²²
The Speaker of the House, Sam Rayburn, said:

Members of the Congress, today is a high mark in the history of the Capitol of our country and of the members of the Senate and House and their guests, because today we receive as our guest one of the outstanding figures of all the earth.

It is my great pleasure, my high privilege, and my distinguished honor, to present to you the Right Honorable Winston Churchill, Prime Minister of Great Britain.

13. *Speech Analysis.* The introduction quoted below violates many of the principles discussed in the preceding chapter. Determine what is wrong with this introduction and rewrite it into appropriate form and content.

Ladies and Gentlemen. Our speaker tonight is Mr. Buck Frank, the world's most famous and most daring explorer, who will address you for thirty minutes on the subject, "The Asiatic Menace."

²¹ *Congressional Record,* Vol. 93, Part 10, Appendix, p. A 155.
²² *Congressional Record,* Vol. 89, Part 4, p. 4919.

Indeed his subject is a timely one, for we all know what is going on in Asia. I am sure you all read last week about the new civil war that has broken out over there. It looks as if the Chinese may be in for another unpleasant time. I shall not say more, for I suspect that Mr. Frank will discuss it.

Certainly so famous a man as our speaker needs no introduction to this audience, for you have seen his handsome pictures so frequently in the newspapers and the newsreels. We are indeed fortunate to have him with us. He is not only a daring adventurer but he is also a superior speaker. I know that you will be interested to know that his lecture fee is $500, the largest sum we have paid this season.

Buck will address you at this time. I hope you like him. I give you Buck Frank, that most daring explorer of far-off China. Mr. Frank.

SUPPLEMENTARY READINGS

1. Butler, Jessie Haver, *Time to Speak Up*, Harper & Brothers, 1946, Chapters 5-8.
2. Crocker, Lionel, *Public Speaking for College Students*, American Book Company, 1941, Chapter 22.
3. Drewry, John E., *Book Reviewing*, The Writers, Inc., 1945.
4. Gislason, Haldor B., *The Art of Effective Speaking*, D. C. Heath and Company, 1934, Chapters 16-17.
5. Haverland, Stella, *Oral Book Reviewing*, Meador Publishing Company, 1938.
6. Hayworth, Donald, *Public Speaking*, Revised Edition, The Ronald Press, 1941, Chapters 14, 19-21.
7. Lee, Josh, *How to Hold an Audience Without a Rope*, Ziff-Davis Publishing Company, 1947, Chapters 17-18.
8. Monroe, Alan H., *Principles and Types of Speech*, Third Edition, Scott, Foresman and Company, 1949, Chapters 25-28.
9. Norvelle, Lee, and Smith, Raymond G., *Speaking Effectively*, Longmans, Green and Company, 1948, Chapter 14.
10. O'Neill, James M., and Riley, Floyd K., *Contemporary Speeches*, The Century Co., 1930. See for additional speech models.
11. O'Neill, James M. (ed.), *Modern Short Speeches*, The Century Co., 1925. This volume contains ninety-eight complete speeches, most of which are speeches for special occasions.

12. Sumner, Lynn, *We Have With Us Tonight*, Harper & Brothers, 1941.
13. Thorndike, Ashley H. (ed.), *Modern Eloquence*, Modern Eloquence Corporation, 1923, 12 volumes. This is an excellent source for speech materials.

CHAPTER XI

Forms of Support

EVERYONE at some time has probably followed the construction of a large building. The excavation for the basement, the driving of the piling, the laying of the foundation, and the maneuvering of the structural steel into place are fascinating and exciting to watch. But even when the last girder has been bolted down, there is yet little to suggest what the final structure will be. It may turn out to be a factory, an auto hotel, an office building, or even a fashionable apartment house. Bricks, finishing materials, hardware, interior design, and decoration finally transform the pile of steel into a building.

In many ways the same is true of a speech. The research, the study of the audience and the occasion, and the outline are necessary forerunners; but no matter how thoroughly done, they do not finish the speech. They are as necessary as excavations, foundations, and structural steel, but they need supporting material to constitute a speech.

The supporting materials for a speech may serve any one of three purposes: (1) to clarify, (2) to prove, and (3) to amplify. They may be evidence, inference, explanation, or even stylistic devices. Their extent and kind are suggested by the following outline:

I. Oral materials
   A. To clarify
      1. Explanation
      2. Description
      3. Narration (illustration)
   B. To prove
      1. Facts
         a. Testimony
         b. Examples
         c. Statistics
      2. Inference—inferred facts
         a. Generalization
         b. Causal inference
         c. Analogy
         d. Deduction
   C. To amplify
      1. Restatement, summary
      2. Adage, maxim
      3. Rhetorical question
II. Visual Supports

SUPPORTING MATERIALS TO CLARIFY

Explanation

In another chapter, explanation, description, and narration are considered as types of the informative speech. Much of what is said there applies to the present discussion. In a short form these types also serve as supporting materials for the stimulating, convincing, or actuating speeches. For example, many times you may clarify the subject by explanation. Such is the case in the following excerpt:

In any big city, the dominant movement within the city, be it on foot, by transit, or by automobile, is from home to work and back again. Between the suburban areas and any big city, the dominant movement is the same, except that the most efficient form of movement, in terms of both highway space and cost, namely on foot, is eliminated because of distance. Despite the invention of air conditioning and excellent artificial light, we still insist on copying our caveman ancestors in the use of time. Business must continue to run on conventional hours; work must continue to be done in conventional hours; and as a result everybody, city dwellers or suburbanite, wants to go to business at about the same time and go home about the same time. This bunches the predominant movements into sharp peaks, of two hours or less duration, in the mornings and evenings of business days. With the coming of the five-day week, the Saturday peaks are getting less and less.[1]

In the paragraph above the speaker is explaining the present traffic situation. His explanation enables him later to present convincingly his solution to the problem.

Description

Frequently description also is helpful in clarifying a topic. If you can make the auditor visualize what is being said, attention and perception are enhanced. The clever real-estate salesman sells a lot by vividly describing a ranch-type house for that location. The more vivid he makes the description, the easier it is for him to weaken the client's sales resistance. The travel agency sells you a ticket to a faraway place by describing for you the warm sun, the romantic nights, the sandy beaches, and the friendly natives. You sometimes select your clothes on the basis of an advertiser's description.

William E. Borah, master orator, concluded one of his important addresses with a passage that contains many descriptive details. Notice how each sentence summons up a picture.

A few evenings ago, in calling upon a friend, I passed by that monument to Abraham Lincoln which stands in Lincoln Park, the monu-

---

[1] Alfred J. Lundberg, "Minimizing Congestion—A Parking Problem," *Vital Speeches*, March 1, 1949, pp. 315-320. Quoted by special permission.

ment representing Lincoln with the kneeling slaves and their broken shackles.

I thought again over the life of Abraham Lincoln and tried to comprehend its greatness. I saw the awkward country boy in his cabin home in the forests of Kentucky. I saw him as he covered his mother's new grave with autumn's withered leaves and went back to his humble home to enter the race for fame. I saw him as he walked near the auction block in the slave market of New Orleans and heard him utter his curse upon the institution of slavery. I saw him in after years when, as one of the greatest rulers upon the earth, he walked with patience and compassion the paths of power. I heard men denounce him as a tyrant and a usurper. I listened for the answer, but he quietly submitted to it all. I saw him in storm of civil strife as he steered the ship of state into the Union Harbor. At last the storm began to clear, the light break through the rifted clouds, and I saw Abraham Lincoln walking in the morning of a new day with four million human beings unloosed of their fetters striving to walk by his side.[2]

Narration (Illustration)

The illustration, which ordinarily is a brief narrative, serves also to clarify difficult points. The speaker may give an actual illustration, or he may invent a hypothetical one.

Roe Fulkerson, lecturer and humorist, once demonstrated that he knew how to hold the attention of a Kiwanis International Convention. He illustrated one point with the following paragraph:

Coming down just a little closer, our ancestors worked in the fields, a great many of them, peasants in Europe, and, like some of the peasants in Europe still, they wore smocks. The smock became annoying when they climbed fences and when they rode a horse, so they gathered her up and stuffed her in. A shirt tail isn't a bit more use to a man than a third hand, and yet, there it is, a foot and a half of it. That thing should have been cut off and buttons put on it as a little boy's shirt waist. But we have worn that foot and a half ever since, as a part of our inheritance tax, and it serves no useful purpose except to give us this balloon tire effect in the center. Those are but

[2] From address on "Constitutional Government," delivered September, 1937, in pamphlet published by J. H. Bordeaux Company, West Springfield, Massachusetts.

the surface, trifling indications of things which we have inherited from our ancestors.[3]

The Bible provided Charles Seymour with an excellent illustration of magnanimity, the subject of his talk:

> The contrast is sharp between this spirit of magnanimity and the Mosaic law, of an eye for an eye and a tooth for a tooth. Yet the Old Testament provides outstanding examples of magnanimous heroes. We remember the story of Joseph's brethren throwing him into a pit and then selling him for twenty pieces of silver; and then, after his own rise to power in Egypt, his treatment of them when they came in supplication for food. "Be not grieved nor angry with yourselves that ye sold me hither, for God did send me before you to preserve life." And after their father's death when they feared again that now "he will certainly requite us all the evil which we did him," he gave final assurance: "As for you, ye thought evil against me but God meant it unto good. . . . Now therefore fear ye not. I will nourish you and your little ones, and he comforted them and spake kindly unto them."[4]

Booker T. Washington, famous Negro educator, built an entire speech around the hypothetical illustration given below. Indeed he did an excellent job of telling the narrative.

> A ship lost at sea for many days suddenly sighted a friendly vessel. From the mast of the unfortunate vessel was seen the signal: "Water, water, we die of thirst!" The answer from the friendly vessel at once came back: "Cast down your bucket where you are."
> A second time the signal, "Water, water; send us water!" ran up from the distressed vessel, and was answered: "Cast down your bucket where you are." And a third and a fourth signal for water was answered: "Cast down your bucket where you are." The captain of the distressed vessel, at last heeding the injunction, cast down his bucket, and it came up full of fresh sparkling water from the mouth of the Amazon River.[5]

---

[3] Roe Fulkerson, "Inheritance Tax," *Classified Speech Models*, William Norwood Brigance (ed.), F. S. Crofts & Co., 1928, pp. 407-413. Quoted by permission of the publishers.

[4] Charles Seymour, "Live Magnanimously," *Vital Speeches*, August 1, 1949, pp. 635-637. Quoted by special permission.

[5] Booker T. Washington, "A Plea for the Negro Race," *Classified Speech Models*, pp. 8-12. Quoted by special permission of the publishers.

SUPPORTING MATERIALS TO PROVE: FACTS

When the speaker and auditor disagree on the validity of a line of thought or on the desirability of a course of action, proof is necessary. Proof, as it is used here, is composed of two types of supporting material: *facts* (evidence) and *inference*.

What are facts? Larrabee says,

> What we usually think of as a fact is something known to us directly in experience. It is what is appealed to as the ground for some human assertion or judgment. It is the stuff of evidence; it is the foundation or primary datum upon which a claim to knowledge rests. When we use such expressions as: "To get down to the facts . . . ," "Now the fact of the matter is . . . ," we call attention to some lower or more fundamental stratum upon which our assertions rest. To talk about "true facts," as people often do, is redundant: facts just *are*. They cannot be false. To demand the facts is to signify our intention to find out what it is that we are obliged to take account of—that is, to move away from the sphere of the merely possible: guesses, conjectures, and fancies, toward actuality—"the world as it really is."[6]

Facts for a speech normally come in three forms: testimony, statistics, and examples.

Testimony

Much of what we know necessarily must come from the observations and experience of others. "Seeing is believing," goes the old adage, but our lives are so short and our spheres so limited that we are forced to depend on other persons for information. Facts or judgments coming from people are usually referred to as *testimony*.

Regardless of the type of testimony, it behooves the speaker to check his informants carefully. If possible, you want to draw upon the authority or expert, the one most qualified by training and experience.

---

[6] Harold A. Larrabee, *Reliable Knowledge,* Houghton Mifflin Company, 1945, p. 128. Quoted by special permission.

Who is an authority? In checking on a source, such questions as the following should be considered:

1. *Is he recognized by his colleagues?* His training, his degrees, his professional affiliations and connections, his publications, his reputation, and his experience are indications of recognition. *Who's Who, Current Biography*, and professional directories are valuable sources in this connection.

2. *Are his findings supported by other authorities and other evidence?* Or what kind of company does he keep? Of course, in cases of original discoveries, such criteria cannot be applied; but for most authorities, this test is a valuable one. The fact that many psychologists question some of Dr. Smith's conclusions on extrasensory perception should be a sufficient reason to question his findings.

3. *Is he an unbiased observer?* Or to put this question in popular jargon, "does he have an ax to grind?" Objectivity is essential if facts are to be found. The true scientist or scholar takes great care to ensure impartial observations and reporting. Any indication of prejudice or bias should be enough to cause you to discard testimony. When we read Plato's harsh criticism of the sophists of his day, for example, we must remember that Plato, although a contemporary of the sophists, was also a bitter enemy of this group of teachers. As the utterances of a partisan, therefore, Plato's evaluations must be discounted somewhat. Although Woodrow Wilson is considered an authority on many aspects of politics, much of what he said about the Democratic Party must be discounted because he was a Democrat.

4. *Has the authority had an adequate opportunity for observation?* Under this heading many subquestions should be considered. How long has he studied in the given field? Does he report his own observations or those of others? Under what conditions did he make his observations? How much time elapsed between his observation and his reporting?

The fact that a person is an authority or expert in one area does not make him an authority in another line of endeavor. A flagrant violation of this principle is found today in the endorsements used by advertisers. The fact that Dizzy Smith is the home-run king of the American League does not make him an authority on breakfast food; nor does the consumption of a bowl of this or that cereal qualify him in this regard.

Statistics

Whether they are based upon your own experience or that of someone else, facts usually come in one of two forms: statistics or examples. The first permits the speaker, through the use of a numerical technique, to make a large collection of data meaningful. In a few words vast amounts of information may be drawn together in a usable and understandable form. The common numerical medium makes possible striking comparisons. In the example given below, observe how in about fifty words the speaker has summarized total production, total exports for two significant years, and has pulled together a conclusion about "inflationary demand."

For example, we all have heard the accusation that inflation and the scarcity of materials is largely caused by exports, but the facts fail to substantiate this charge in any respect. In 1938 the United States produced $84 billion worth of goods and exported $3.5 billion, or 4 percent. In 1947 we produced $230 billion worth of goods and exported $14 billion, or about 6 percent. In other words, foreign inflationary demand on our economy in 1947 was not greater than 6 percent. The bulk of the pressure, or 94 percent, was caused right at home by domestic demand.[7]

In using the example, you need to guard against oversimplification or dependence upon too few instances. Still, statistics must be kept in as simple a form as possible. Too many or too complicated statistics only confuse the listener. Some engineers and scientists frequently ignore this principle. As a result, they may present statistical data in table form, forgetting the span of

[7] W. C. Haddon, "Give and Take," *Vital Speeches,* February 1, 1949, pp. 239-242.

attention, with the result that soon their colleagues doze off or lose track of what is said.

The following simple rules may increase the effectiveness of statistics.

1. *Reduce statistics to round numbers.* Instead of telling your listeners that the population of your state is 9,543,676, simply say, "nine and a half million." Mr. Ernst, in an illustration cited a little later in this chapter, says, "1000 daily newspapers," and "2500 weeklies." Many times percentages may be more effective than the raw data. Keep the number simple. The eleven miles per second recently added to the velocity of light will make no appreciable difference to most of us.

2. *Present statistics in a form familiar to your auditors.* To European audiences or groups of scientists, the metric system may be entirely clear, but to the average English-speaking audience you will be ineffective if you speak in terms other than inches, feet, yards, etc. The same is true in discussing temperature; you must choose between Fahrenheit and centigrade. When it is necessary to employ a system not in common usage, you must take special precautions to compare and contrast the unfamiliar with what the audience knows.

3. *Use as many visual aids as possible.* Since statistics are a compact representation of numerous facts, you may discover the desirability of making your listeners see as well as hear these abstractions. As we have suggested in the chapter on visual support, charts, diagrams, and graphs skillfully presented will reduce the likelihood of misunderstanding.

4. *Avoid presenting too many statistics at a given time.* Their abstract nature requires that we give to them greater attention and concentration than to some other types of material. Long lists should be avoided. Thought breaks in the form of illustrations and humor should be included to ensure attention and interest.

5. *Dramatize your statistics.* In other words, make the listeners see what is back of a given number. If you are discussing the

thousands of automobile accidents, describe a wreck or two in order that the listener will realize the full implication of your remarks. Observe how Mr. Ernst employs this technique in the example given below.

Here is the indictment I make in behalf of the readers of the nation: We have lost 1000 daily newspapers in 20 years. We are down to only 1700. More than 2500 weeklies have disappeared. There are only 117 cities left in this vast country where there is any competition left in daily newspapers.

I ask what price freedom and what price free enterprize? One boiler plate company supplies the inside pages for 3000 weeklies and even these pages are sold packaged with advertising.

One man owns about one half of all the independent papers of his state. What if he owns all papers in the state? Do we sit by idly until that happens?

Twenty-five per cent of the total circulation of all our daily papers is owned by a handful of chains. In 10 states, there is not a single city with daily newspaper competition today, and in 22 states there is not a single city with any Sunday competition.

Now I submit to you that it is no answer for you to say, but we have done well in total circulation.

Take Springfield, Massachusetts, for example. It has four papers, but all owned by the same interest. What good does total national circulation do to the people of that area? It is no answer to say that the papers that are left are better than those of 70 years ago. Let's admit it. The question and the answer duck the issue. Even if better, what would keep the few remaining papers on their toes without competition if monopoly continues?[8]

Example or Specific Instance

As suggested earlier, statistics are frequently more effective and more meaningful if examples are interspersed among the statistical data. In the case given above, the speaker humanized his cold figures by inserting the example of Springfield, Massa-

---

[8] Morris Ernst, "Is the American Press Really Free?" a speech delivered on America's Town Meeting of the Air, *Representative American Speeches: 1946-1947*, A. Craig Baird (ed.), The H. W. Wilson Company, pp. 160-176. Quoted by special permission of America's Town Meeting of the Air.

chusetts. From the point of view of interest and attention, the example is one of the most effective forms of proof.

On other occasions the speaker may not have time to review innumerable instances in his presentation; consequently, he may select one or two instances which he considers typical and sufficient to establish his point. This is the situation with the proud farmer who hands his friend an ear of corn, commenting, "That is the kind of corn I grow on my farm." The validity of such a generalization depends upon whether the farmer selected a representative ear of corn. The more ears he displays the more likely that his statement will give the true facts of the case.

Notice how Charles Seymour gives specific instances or examples of "magnanimous men" in history:

It would be illuminating if we should make up a list of the magnanimous men of literature and history. Those would stand out as objects of our admiration who combine the particular traits that we are considering: Such men as Marcus Aurelius, Chaucer's knight, Francis of Assisi, the Black Prince, St. Louis of France, Henry V, Sir Walter Raleigh, Henry of Navarre, Charles Darwin, and above all in modern times—Abraham Lincoln. It would be equally instructive to note the men no matter how courageous and intelligent, who would have to be excluded from the list: Oliver Cromwell, Louis XIV, the Duke of Marlborough, Frederick the Great, Napoleon Bonaparte. If you consider the implications of these lives you see how just is the emphasis that was laid by John Milton on learning how to perform magnanimously.[9]

The two tests that you and the listener should apply in evaluating examples as evidence are the following:

1. *Are examples representative of their class?* If a generalization is to be drawn upon a limited number of cases, those instances must be typical; they must be the rule, not the exception.

2. *Has a sufficient number of examples been presented to constitute a fair sample?* The more cases presented, the more the likelihood that the conclusion will be valid.

The presentation of numerous examples in a speech may be

[9] Seymour, *op. cit.*

difficult on account of limitations of time. The ethical speaker should take great care that the instances presented are representative. When called upon, he should be able to summon up additional evidence of a statistical nature to support his conclusions.

SUPPORTING MATERIALS TO PROVE: INFERENCE

Woodrow Wilson once said, "There are whole worlds of fact waiting to be discovered by inference."

What did he mean? Facts in isolation are meaningless and neutral: but depending upon the industry and resourcefulness of the thinker they may be "diadems or fagots." Through analysis and synthesis, the thinker seeks out their implications, drawing therefrom *inferred facts*. Baird has aptly described this mental process of inference as "an intellectual leap in the dark, a voyage from the known to the unknown. It is mental exploration."[10]

Perhaps you will be able to see the relationship between facts and inference more clearly by comparing the thought process to a manufacturing process. The raw materials of thought should be facts; the manufacturing process of these raw materials is the process of inference by which facts are put together in various combinations. The result of the processing is a conclusion or an inferred fact or facts.

The Reflective Thought Process

Raw Materials	Processing	Finished Products
Facts	⟶ Inference ⟶	Conclusions

The types of inference are four in number:

1. Generalization
2. Deduction
3. Causal reasoning
4. Analogy

---

[10] A. Craig Baird, *Discussion: Principles and Types,* McGraw-Hill Book Company, Inc., 1943, p. 147.

Generalization

Generalization, sometimes called argument from specific instance, which involves drawing conclusions from statistics or specific instances, has already been partially described in the earlier section on example. To reiterate, it involves drawing conclusions from a number of observed instances. It may be represented as follows:

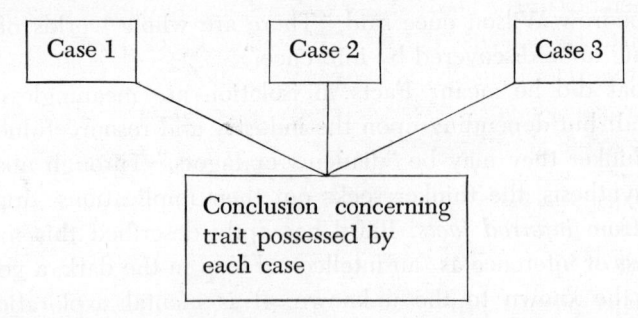

```
  ┌────────┐      ┌────────┐      ┌────────┐
  │ Case 1 │      │ Case 2 │      │ Case 3 │
  └────┬───┘      └────┬───┘      └────┬───┘
       └───────────────┼────────────────┘
                  ┌────┴──────────────────┐
                  │ Conclusion concerning │
                  │ trait possessed by    │
                  │ each case             │
                  └───────────────────────┘
```

When the judge polls the jury for its verdict, he utilizes such an inductive process. After hearing each juror's response, he generalizes concerning their opinions and thus determines the guilt or innocence of the accused.

If each member of the advanced public-speaking class makes a low grade on a snap quiz, the teacher may conclude that the students have not studied. (What other generalizations might explain such a result?)

It becomes obvious that the more cases considered, the more likely that the conclusion is valid. Absolute certainty is possible only in cases of *perfect induction* or when all members of a class are examined. Since this possibility seldom occurs, the conclusions reached are ordinarily probabilities, that is, likely to be true.

In summary, the two essential tests of generalizations are the following:

1. Is a sufficient number of instances considered to draw a generalization?
2. Are instances observed representative of the class?

Deduction

Deductive reasoning consists in applying a general law or accepted principle to a particular case. It is based upon the tenet that what is true of an entire class is likewise true of any member of the class. Such reasoning may be arranged in the form of three propositions: a major premise, expressing a generalization about an entire class; a minor premise, identifying a specific instance as a member of the class; and a conclusion, applying the generalization to the specific instance. Logicians speak of this form of deductive reasoning as the categorical syllogism.

Below are some syllogisms which we frequently hear in our society in one form or another:

> Major premise: All men are created free and equal.
> Minor premise: John is a man.
> Conclusion: Therefore John is created free and equal.

> Major premise: All men twenty-one or over have the right to vote.
> Minor premise: John is a man.
> Conclusion: John has the right to vote.

> Major premise: All men should be educated.
> Minor premise: John is a man.
> Conclusion: John should be educated.

> Major premise: All able-bodied men over eighteen years old come under the provisions of the Selective Service Act.
> Minor premise: John is an able-bodied man over eighteen.
> Conclusion: John comes under the provisions of the Selective Service Act.

In a speech the syllogisms given above would probably not be formally stated, but they might be combined in a form similar to the paragraph below:

Democratic society bestows many privileges and many duties. It recognizes that each one is free and equal, that each should be educated, and that each should have the privilege of voting. Therefore

John Jones has a right to demand these privileges. His race and color should not be made the bases for denial of any of these privileges.

On the other hand, John Jones must also meet his obligations. The able-bodied over eighteen years old come under the provisions of the Selective Service Act. In time of war, they must defend their country.

The validity of the categorical syllogism depends upon the following tests:

1. Is the general principle (major premise) true or accepted as true?
2. Does the major premise generalize concerning an entire class? If it refers to "most" or "some" cases, the conclusion is not a certainty but a probability.
3. Is the specific case (minor term) a member of the class about which the generalization is made?

In addition to the categorical type, there are two types of conditional syllogisms: the hypothetical and the disjunctive. In the former, the major premise is qualified by an "if" clause. Notice the following statements, which may easily be transformed into syllogisms:

If you study, you will pass.
If you take chemistry under Dr. Jones, you will have difficulty making a good grade.
If you join the Y.M.C.A., you will make some fine friends.
If you obtain a college degree, your future is secure.
If you take History 344, you will be sorry.

The average college student will have no difficulty completing these syllogisms. But in case some may ponder unnecessarily, a complete hypothetical syllogism appears as follows:

Major premise: If you fail the final examination, you failed the course.
Minor premise: You failed the final examination.
Conclusion: You failed the course.

Note that the minor premise affirms the "if" clause (antecedent). An absolute rule which applies to this type is that the minor premise *must affirm the "if" clause* (antecedent) *or deny the main clause* (consequent). Obviously, "if you fail the course," it does not necessarily mean that "you failed the final examination," which is only one of many possibilities. You may not have turned in a term paper, or attended class, or completed the daily assignment, or pleased the instructor.

Notice the deductive pattern in the following sentences from Patrick Henry's famous address, "Liberty or Death." "If we wish to be free—if we mean to preserve inviolate those inestimable privileges for which we have been so long contending—if we mean not basely to abandon the noble struggle in which we have been so long engaged, and which we have pledged ourselves never to abandon until the glorious object of our contest shall be obtained—we must fight! I repeat it, sir, we must fight! An appeal to arms and to the God of Hosts is all that is left us!"

From the example above you will observe that Patrick Henry did not put formal syllogisms into his speech. In fact, in the part given here, the syllogisms are only suggested, and some of the premises must be implied. The listener following the speaker automatically supplies what is missing. In this popular form the syllogism is often referred to as an *enthymeme*.[11]

The disjunctive syllogism involves an "either . . . or" major premise: two possibilities are presented.

> Jones will play either guard or tackle.
> You must take either "math" or science.
> The fraternity will either build a house or lose its popularity.

Again the reasoning process is easily discernible.

> Major premise: You may either enter law school or work on a Master's degree.
> Minor premise: You will work on a Master's degree.
> Conclusion: You will not go to law school.

If the minor premise affirms one alternative, the conclusion denies the other, and vice versa. For this type to be valid, the

---

[11] For further explanation, see A. Craig Baird, *Public Discussion and Debate*, Ginn & Company, rev. ed., 1937, pp. 139-141.

possibilities given in the major premise must embrace all the possibilities, and there must be no overlapping.

The explanation above is by no means complete. For those interested in understanding the intricacies of the deductive reasoning, a course in logic is recommended. However, the student speaker should be aware that much of our thought is deductive. Seldom does the formal syllogism appear in a speech, but frequently in a contracted form it is presented as an enthymeme (with one or more premises suppressed). In one paragraph there may be stated or implied an entire series of syllogisms. Oftentimes these are extremely difficult to untangle. The following paragraph illustrates this point: "The Shantung affair is indefensible from any standpoint of moral or international justice or common decency.... It will dishonor and degrade any people who seeks to uphold it. War will inevitably follow as the result of an attempt to perpetuate it. It is founded in immorality and revolting injustice."[12]

Causal Reasoning

Recently a student at Louisiana State University became so irritated by true-false examinations that he wrote a letter to the campus paper. His complaint was that he had failed a certain course because the professor tested solely by this method. Whether he knew it or not, this young man indulged in some causal reasoning. His failure to pass the examination, he thought, was the *effect* of the true-false test, the *cause*.

Cause-to-effect sequence moves toward the future. If two events in the past are considered, the one which occurred first is the *cause* and the second is the *effect*. Historians agree that the murder of Archduke Ferdinand in 1914 was an immediate cause of World War I. Causal reasoning may enable the reasoner to hazard a guess about the future. The small child may be admonished with the statement, "If you get too close to the stove (cause), you may get burned (effect)."

[12] From speech delivered by William E. Borah before the Senate August 26, 1919, *Congressional Record*, Vol. 58, Part 5, p. 4355.

Some time ago the police of a southern city arrested twenty-one hoboes who had drifted into the town. When a reporter asked the oldest one, "What do you think makes men go on the bum?" he received the following causal analysis: "That's easy, it's liquor. Liquor and women. Oh, well, some of them just got the wanderlust. But mostly it's liquor. A man gets to drinking. He loses his job. His wife leaves him. He goes on. Gets arrested. Told to get out of town, and then there he is. He's sunk."

In this example, the speaker gave numerous causes explaining why there are hoboes. Interestingly, each *result* becomes a *cause* for the next event. Usually causality is exceedingly complex, consequently difficult to untangle.

Effect-to-cause sequence moves toward the past. A given event becomes an effect with a cause somewhere in the past to be located. A man's car is ruined by fire during the night. When he investigates, he finds the dashboard melted and the wiring still smoking. He concludes therefore that the cause was defective wiring.

In the following passage both types of causal inference are employed:

That tax-supported education in America has not followed the path which education, and especially higher education, in Germany took prior to World War II has been due almost altogether to the independent college. It has provided the intellectual milieu for our entire educational system in this country. Remove these institutions, and if recent history in Europe and Asia means anything, it means that the entire atmosphere of all education with us will become a different thing. One is compelled to wonder, especially in view of the educational backgrounds of the majority, how much the members of the President's Commission considered the basis of their own freedom in the making of their recommendations. Much of the philosophical background of the report stems from setting almost the reverse of the educational system which they envision, and yet they have really made no provision for that which is so basic in their own recommendations.[13]

[13] Walter Alexander Groves, "The Christian College Today," *Vital Speeches,* January 1, 1949, pp. 166-168. Quoted by special permission.

Effect-to-effect inference attempts to relate two events by locating a common cause. Persons who make high scores on I.Q. tests seem to be able to perform intellectual feats more readily than those who make low scores. The test score, seemingly, is the result of the same factor which accounts for performance in intellectual feats. William Trufant Foster, director of the Pollack Foundation for Economic Research and prominent writer on public speaking, makes significant use of this type of reasoning in his speech "Should Students Study?" Below is a part of that speech:

Is it a fact that good students in high schools are more likely than others to become good students in college? Professor Walter F. Dearborn . . . compared the records of hundreds of students at the University of Wisconsin with their records in various high schools. He found that above 80 per cent of those who were in the first quarter of their high-school classes were in the upper half of their college classes throughout the four years, and that above 80 per cent of those who were in the lowest quarter in their high-school classes failed in college to rise above mediocre scholarship. The parallelism is striking. Except in scattering cases, promise in high school becomes performance in college. Indeed, only one student out of five hundred in this investigation who fell among the lowest quarter in the high school attained the highest rank in the university. . . .[14]

Causal inference is full of hazards. Certainly the speaker who employs this type of thought needs constantly to guard against oversimplification. A given event may and probably does have many causes. For example, let us analyze the case of the young man who thought he failed the course because the instructor gave true-false examinations. Any of the following causes could have accounted for his failure:

1. Too little study
2. Poor eyesight
3. Defective hearing

[14] William Trufant Foster, "Should Students Study?" Lew Sarett and William Trufant Foster (eds.), *Modern Speeches on Basic Issues*, Houghton Mifflin Company, 1939, pp. 64-75. Quoted by special permission of the publishers.

4. Malnutrition
5. Purchase of wrong textbook
6. Mirror reading
7. Limited vocabulary
8. Too little sleep
9. Too much social life
10. Lack of confidence in his own ability

Causal reasoning may be checked by the following tests:

1. *Are the alleged facts true?* Before attempting to ascertain whether a causal relation exists, it is necessary to verify the actual occurrence of the events. In a murder trial, the lawyer must prove first that the murder did take place before he can attempt to establish a motive.

2. *Is there a genuine connection between the events under consideration?* The causal reasoner must distinguish between the coincidental sequence and the causal sequence. In other words, Spanish moss on a dead tree does not necessarily indicate that the moss killed the tree.

Here are some questions that may aid you in determining if a connection is genuine.

   a. Does the alleged cause ever occur without the effect?
   b. Does the effect ever occur without the alleged cause?
   c. Are other alleged causes operating which may explain the effect? And vice versa?

3. *Is the cause of sufficient magnitude to produce the alleged effect, and vice versa?* The likelihood of a single mole moving a mountain is indeed remote. How shall we evaluate the long series of tragic events that supposedly accompanied ownership of the famous Hope Diamond, at present insured for over one million dollars? Does the fact that Marie Antoinette wore this notorious gem explain why she was beheaded? Did possession of it account for the fact that Sultan Abdul Hamid lost the Turkish throne? Or did this forty-four-and-one-half-carat stone cause the deaths in the family of the late Evelyn Walsh McLean, Washington society leader, who recently owned it? In spite of the chain of

events, we have to conclude that the diamond had nothing to do with the tragedies because it is too limited in its power to produce the alleged effects.

4. *Are other causes operating which may explain the effect?* Let us repeat, causality is indeed complex; a single effect seldom has a single cause. Remote as well as immediate causes may have operated. Return for a moment to the example of the Hope Diamond. When jeweler Harry Winston received the famous jewel, he scoffed at the legend of tragedy. He then engaged in some causal analysis, saying: "It is childish to suppose that diamonds themselves exert any influence for good or evil. It's not the diamonds themselves that cause misfortune but the people who handle them." Mr. Winston, an expert in his field, concluded that other causes were operating which resulted in the tragic events.

Analogy or Comparison

Analogy is that form of inference by which it is reasoned that, if two objects or events are alike in certain respects, they resemble in other respects. The reasoner, knowing the characteristics of one, can ascertain the unknown characteristics of the other. Many times we select our reading matter by analogy. If we find John Smith's short story about the Caribbean exciting, we are likely to conclude that other stories by him with a similar locale will be equally good reading. Our reasoning may be diagrammed as follows:

First Case	Second Case
1. By John Smith	1. John Smith
2. A short story	2. A short story
3. About the Caribbean	3. About the Caribbean
4. In *Redbook*	4. In *Redbook*
5. Was exciting	5. Must be exciting, since first one was.

Ordinarily, analogies are divided into two types: *literal* and *figurative*. The literal analogy compares objects or events in the same class. For example, World War I is compared with World War II, or the White Sox baseball team is compared with the New York Yankees. On the other hand, the figurative analogy makes comparisons between objects in widely different fields. For example, we may compare the federal government to a three-legged stool. The literal analogy is usually considered a superior form of proof.

Note the literal analogy in the following paragraph taken from a speech by W. Norwood Brigance:

But because we have been fighting a war against militarism, we ourselves in this backwash of war are tending to become militaristic. It is an old story. Read your Bible, and you will find where the early Hebrews fought mightily against tribes with pagan gods—and then for a time adopted those gods. Read your history, and you will find that in 1789 the people of France arose against tyranny and began a revolution, having as its aim "liberty, . . . fraternity, . . . equality"—and ended by having (1) a Reign of Terror, in which thousands of its people were executed, (2) compulsory military training, and (3) a dictator by the name of Napoleon. Now the United States is following this same time-worn paradoxical human pathway. We, who set up liberty in a new world, who gave shelter to emigrants that fled from tyranny in the old world, we are now debating whether we should fasten compulsory military training upon ourselves.[15]

Contrast the quotation given above with the following figurative analogy used by William E. Borah for exposition and vividness, which ordinarily is the primary function of this type:

"You might just as well say, 'I will stop midway after I start over Niagara Falls' as to say, 'I will advocate a super state, but I will not accept internationalism.' "[16]

The essential tests of analogy are four in number.

[15] William Norwood Brigance, "The Backwash of War," *Representative American Speeches: 1945-1946*, pp. 75-84. Quoted by special permission.

[16] From speech by William E. Borah delivered February 4, 1919, before the Senate, *Congressional Record*, Vol. 57, Part 3, p. 2656.

1. *Do the points of likeness outweigh the points of difference?* If valid conclusions are to be reached, it is evident that the two objects compared must be alike in essential particulars or in those which have a direct bearing on the point under consideration. The first step in checking an analogy is more or less to tabulate the points of similarity and those of dissimilarity.

2. *Are the characteristics considered of major importance?* Once you see the points of likeness listed in tabular form, you need to weigh them carefully to determine whether they are essential in your consideration. If you are comparing the literacy in Denmark with that in the United States, you must show that the two nations are essentially alike. The fact that one has a sparse population and the other has a dense population may be a significant consideration, but the size of the two may not be of any significance.

3. *Are the facts upon which the analogy is based accurate?* Valid conclusions cannot be based upon assertions or what seems to be true. A comparison of public ownership of utilities in Australia with that in the United States must be based upon verified facts.

4. *Is the analogy supported by other forms of reasoning?* Comparisons may give us a hint as to a relationship; they should be checked by argument from specific instances, by causality, and by deduction. What are the opinions of experts on the subject?

SUPPORTING MATERIALS TO AMPLIFY

Jones's paper was so dull that it put his listeners to sleep. They wanted to listen, but it was dull. Why? His presentation reflected careful study and thorough analysis and indicated that he had checked and rechecked his references. Furthermore, he had written his paper with great care, hoping to pack into his five thousand words as much meaning as possible. In fact, he bragged that he had not wasted a single word or a single sentence. Herein Jones forgot one important principle: an oral presentation must be planned to elicit almost immediate comprehension. For this reason some good written paragraphs may be very ineffective when delivered orally.

The successful speaker highlights important ideas, devotes to them sufficient time to ensure immediate understanding. Thoughts may be given emphasis by restatement, a technique sometimes referred to as amplification.

Says Winans, "But often single ideas need to be dwelt upon. It is evident that for clearness and for conviction, information and evidence must be introduced; but there are other reasons for amplification. Some ideas are too difficult for a hearer when put into condensed statement. Moreover, if you succeed in setting your hearer to thinking he needs time to consider and assimilate...."[17]

An idea may "be dwelt upon" in a variety of ways. In fact, any type of supporting material, such as testimony, examples, or statistics, serves to amplify a thought expressed. If you prove an assertion by an extended illustration two or three minutes long, you have "dwelt upon" the thought long enough so that your listener should more readily comprehend.

Some stylistic devices, however, serve little purpose except amplification. You may recast your thought in different words in order to enhance the auditors' appreciation.

You may restate the sentence in your own words. Winston Churchill does so in the following:

In the first half of the twentieth century, fanned by the crimson wings of war, the conquest of the air affected profoundly human affairs. It made the globe seem much bigger to the mind and much smaller to the body. The human biped was able to travel about far more quickly. This greatly reduced the size of his estate, while at the same time creating an even keener sense of its exploitable value. In the nineteenth century Jules Verne wrote "Round the World in Eighty Days." It seemed a prodigy. Now you can get round it in four; but you do not see much of it on your way. The whole prospect and outlook of

[17] James A. Winans, *Speech-Making*, Appleton-Century-Crofts, Inc., 1938, p. 191. Quoted by special permission.

mankind grew immeasurably larger, and the multiplication of ideas also proceeded at an incredible rate. This vast expansion was unhappily not accompanied by any noticeable advance in the stature of man, either in his mental faculties, or his moral character. His brain got no better, but it buzzed more. The scale of events around him assumed gigantic proportions while he remained about the same size. By comparison therefore he actually became much smaller. We no longer had great men directing manageable affairs. Our need was to discipline an array of gigantic and turbulent facts. To this task we have certainly so far proved unequal. Science bestowed immense new powers on man and at the same time created conditions which were largely beyond his comprehension and still more beyond his control. While he nursed the illusion of growing mastery and exulted in his new trappings, he became the sport and presently the victim of tides and currents, of whirlpools and tornadoes amid which he was far more helpless than he had been for a long time.[18]

In this statement, Churchill does little more than reword his second sentence, "It [airplane] made the globe seem much bigger to the mind and much smaller to the body."

At first glance the sentence which reads "This vast expansion was unhappily not accompanied by any noticeable advance in stature of man, either in his mental faculties or moral character" will seem to be another thought, but in reality Churchill is clarifying what he means by "seem much bigger to the mind."

If you wish to be more subtle, you may give a quotation or epigram which rephrases your thought. In addition to amplify-

[18] Winston Churchill, "United We Stand Secure," delivered March 31, 1949, at the Mid-Century Convocation of Massachusetts Institute of Technology, *Representative American Speeches: 1948-1949*, pp. 35-50. Quoted by special permission.

SUPPORTING MATERIALS

Supporting materials must be carefully selected. They must be appropriate for the occasion and must be adapted to the peculiar requirements of the audience. Top, foreman talking to men. (Photo, Esso Standard Oil, Baton Rouge Refinery.) Center, instructor and boys. (Photo, Ethyl Corporation, Baton Rouge Plant.) Bottom, speaker talking to middle-aged group. (Photo, U.S.D.A. Extension Service.)

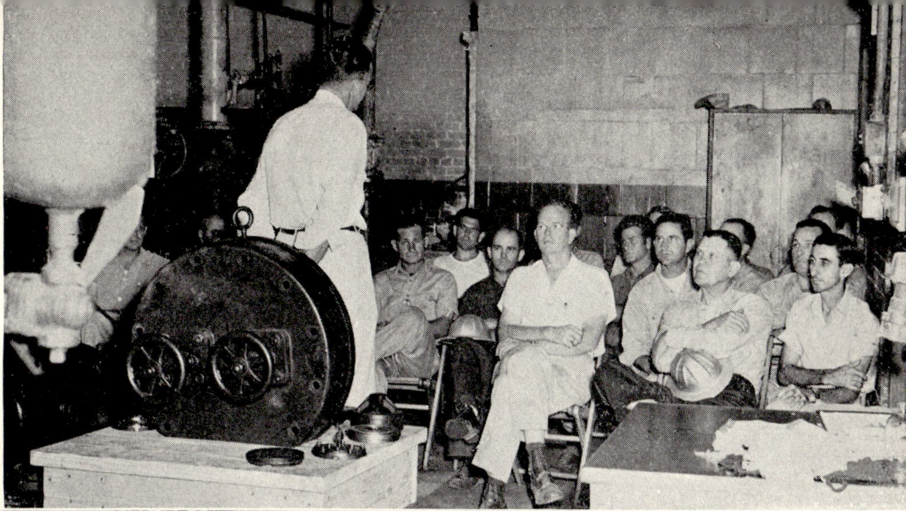
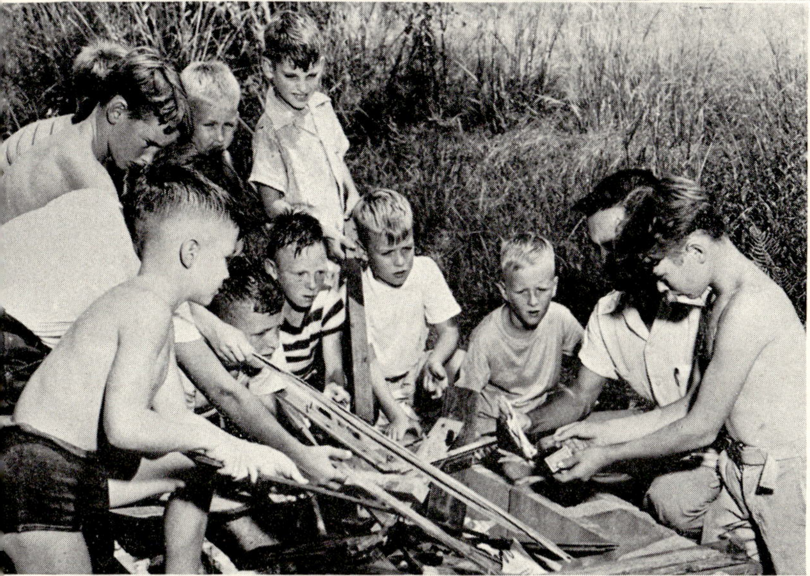
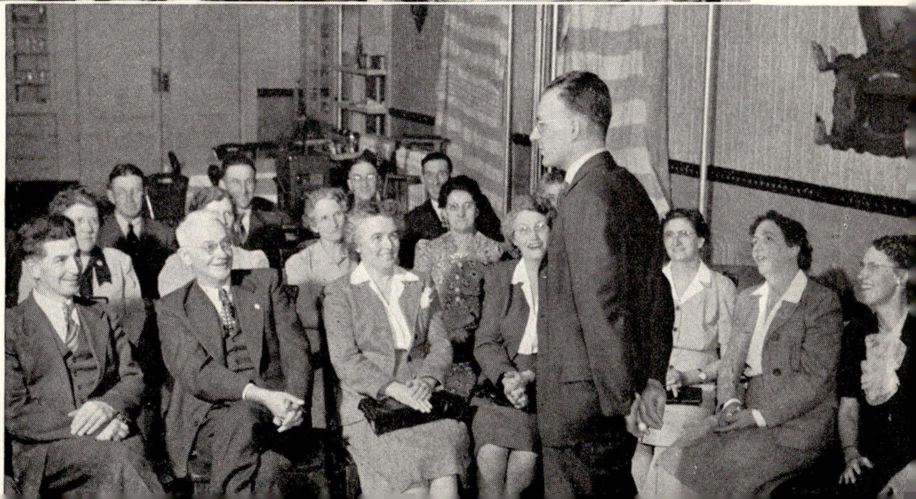

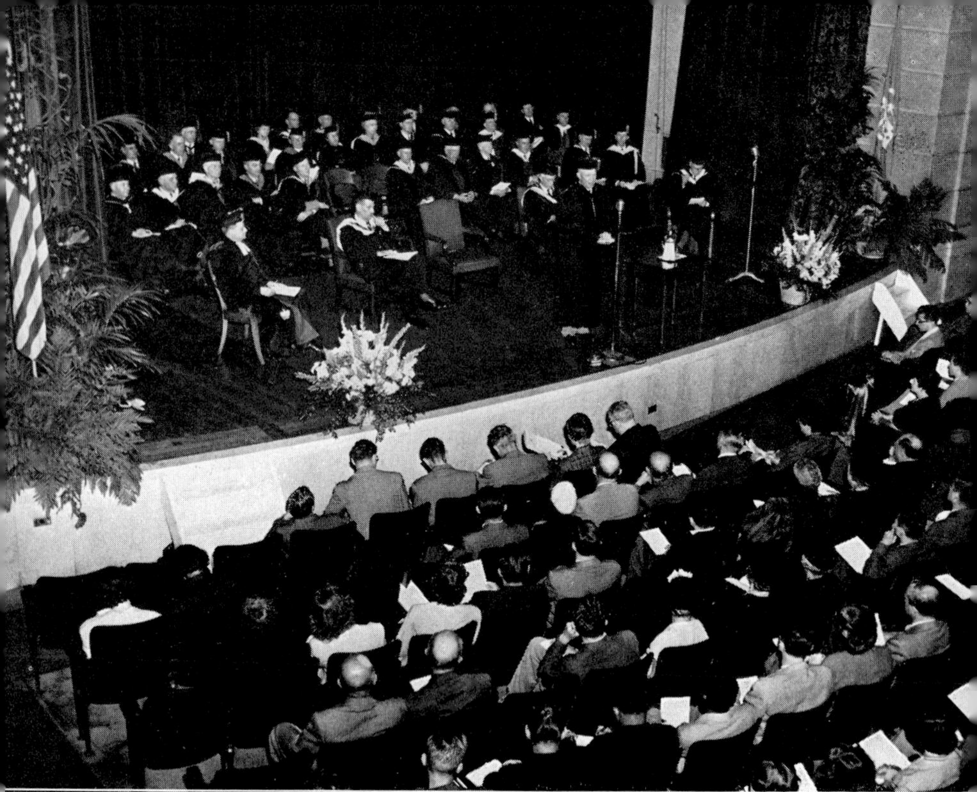

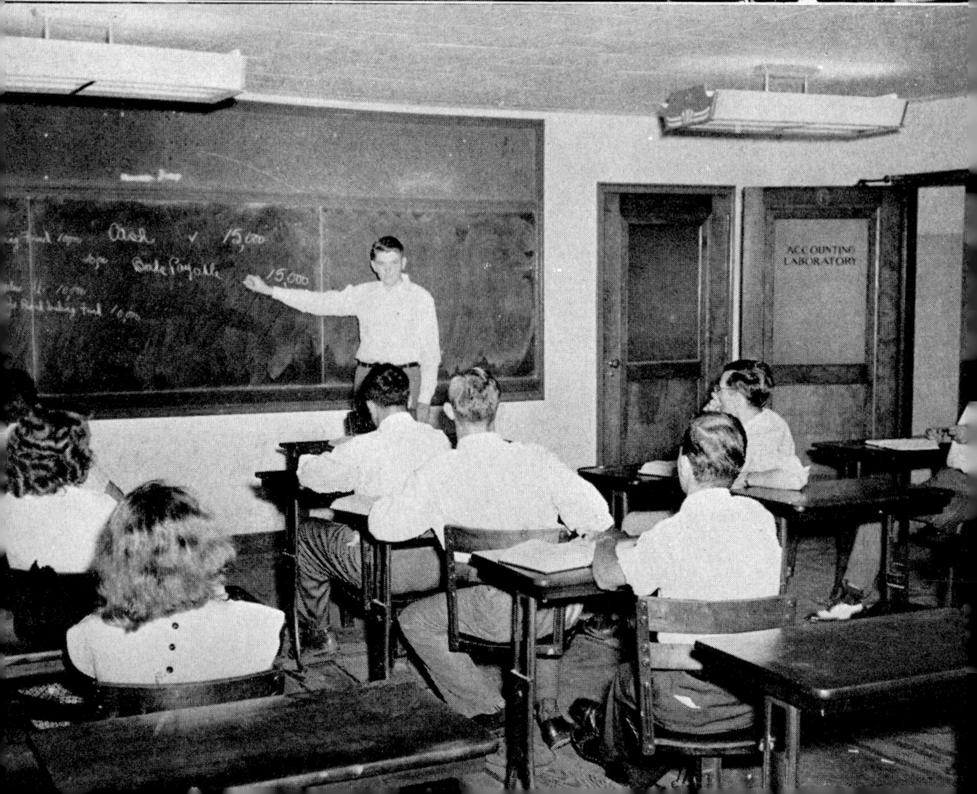
ACCOUNTING
LABORATORY

ing your idea, you may also impress your auditor with your learning. Such is the case in the following quotation: "The time in the life of a child when a mother can exert her influence is terribly brief. 'Give me a child until he is seven years old,' a great philosopher said, 'and I care not who has him afterwards.' Seven years in which to mold character; seven short, fleeting years! What a tragedy that a single moment of these years should be wasted in work which an electric machine can do."[19]

The rhetorical question may be used as a form of amplification. The loaded question demands a rethinking of the thought to be amplified. Bruce Barton effectively puts to use this means in the following sentences: "Some day you gentlemen expect to have every home in the United States electrified. My friends, why should you wait until *some day*? Why don't you do it immediately, next year, within the next twelve months? Does that seem impossible? I tell you that I believe it would be possible, by the right sort of concerted advertising, to arouse such a sentiment in the minds of the women of this country that *every* woman would realize that it is beneath the dignity of human life for her to work for three cents an hour."[20]

In summary, therefore, amplification may be accomplished by three means: (1) recast the thought in different words, (2) give a quotation which restates it, and (3) use rhetorical questions.

[19] Bruce Barton, "How Long Should a Wife Live?" *Contemporary Speeches*, J. M. O'Neill and Floyd K. Riley (eds.), The Century Co., 1930, pp. 255-257. Quoted by special permission of Bruce Barton and the publishers.
[20] *Ibid.*

SUPPORTING MATERIALS

Supporting materials must be suited to the intellectual capacity of the audience. In the first picture Dwight D. Eisenhower is addressing a convocation at Columbia University. (Photo, Columbia University.) In the second picture an instructor is addressing a class. (Photo, L.S.U. Alumni News.)

EXERCISES

1. *Speaking Assignment.* Deliver a five-minute argumentative speech in which you develop your proposition by an extended illustration. (Christ used this method in the parables.)
2. *Speaking Assignment.* Deliver a five-minute talk in which you develop your speech by using only one or two types of supporting material.
3. *Speaking Assignment.* Deliver an oral analysis of the forms of support used in a passage (one hundred fifty to two hundred words) taken from a current speech. Show to the class that the speaker supported or did not support his inference adequately.
4. Make an analysis of the forms of support used by one of your colleagues in a speech. After the speech, check with the speaker to see if you have found the ones he thought he used.
5. Bring to class five examples of inference that you have found in your local newspaper (look on the editorial page). Be able to present an oral analysis of these for your classmates.
6. Make a list of ten situations in which you can have perfect induction.
7. Make a list of ten situations in which you have a valid "either . . . or" situation. Remember that the choice must be mutually exclusive, and there must be only two possibilities.
8. Bring to class several unsupported popular generalizations you have heard recently.
9. Bring to class several generalizations that have been proved by exceptional instances.
10. *Discussion Questions for Class Symposiums.*
    a. What is the strongest type of proof?
    b. Is it possible to prove a proposition conclusively? Is it necessary for a speaker to give conclusive proof of a proposition? What is conclusive proof?
    c. Why should one use with care the following terms: "all," "every," "none," "not one," "never," "always?" What words would you ordinarily substitute for these?
    d. Why should one test carefully an "either . . . or" statement?
11. Each of the following statements reflects an attempt to make a popular application of some test of inference. Determine whether these statements are sensible.
    a. "Figures don't lie, but liars figure."
    b. "You can prove anything by the Bible."

c. "An expert is a man who is away from home."
d. "It's the exception that proves the rule."
e. "An analogy is a weak type of proof."
f. "The Devil can quote Scripture to his own purpose."
g. "A prophet is not without honor save in his own country."
h. "There is honor among thieves."
i. "All I know is what I see in the papers."
j. "A foolish consistency is the hobgoblin of little minds."

12. Identify the type of inference used in the examples given below. If the inference is not valid, explain wherein the error lies.
    a. Mississippi is poor because it has few material resources.
    b. Dr. Earl Jones, professor of speech at Warren University, says, "My book *Argumentation* is a good textbook."
    c. Students who make high grades in high school are likely to make high grades in college.
    d. Bill Smith makes good grades because he studies.
    e. Dr. A. M. Smith, professor of speech at the State University, says, "Jones's *Argumentation* is a good textbook."
    f. If I go to college, I will be assured a position that pays a high salary. I will not go to college. Therefore I will not be assured a position that pays a high salary.
    g. The Y.M.C.A., the Y.W.C.A., the Methodist Youth Center, the Baptist Youth Center, Tau Kappa Alpha, and Kappa Kappa Gamma did not contribute to World Student Service Fund. Therefore, it is probable that the campus organizations did not support the World Student Service Fund.
    h. I shall get either B or C in this course. I shall not receive B. Therefore I shall get C.
    i. John Brown belongs to a fraternity and he is popular.
    j. Since all members of class Speech 99 got high grades last semester, I am enrolling in Speech 99 this semester.
    k. The enemies of Russia include all American businessmen. John Morris is a businessman. Therefore John Morris is an enemy of Russia.
    l. Each year more persons are killed or injured by automobiles than were killed in World War I.
    m. Labor leaders are radicals.
       John B. Lee is a labor leader.
       Therefore John B. Lee is a radical.
    n. From my experience with the Iroquois Indians I have decided that you cannot trust Indians.

o. All slaves are men.
   This machine is a slave.
   Therefore this machine is a man.
p. A man who makes a million dollars is a success. It seems evident, therefore, that John D. Rockefeller was successful.
q. Since several students failed to return last semester, it is evident that M.S.U. is not pleasing its students.
r. Louisiana is a great state because it is located upon the Mississippi River.
s. The richest man in my home town has a fourth-grade education. It seems to me that proves that schooling is not important.

13. Analyze the forms of support used in the following speech. Attempt to differentiate among those materials which clarify, prove, and amplify.

Live Magnanimously[21]
By Charles Seymour

Text: I Samuel 24:12: And David said to Saul, "The Lord judge between me and thee, and the Lord avenge me of thee; but mine hand shall not be upon thee." In a lecture delivered in London some eighteen months ago, Sir Richard Livingstone surveyed with breadth and insight the general quality of university education in Great Britain and America today. "What," he asked, "is the minimum equipment needed by an educated man, if he is to live effectively in the modern world: and how should the university provide the student with that equipment?"

The lecturer accepted as essential and obvious the principle that the educated man must be aware of the chief social and political problems of his time; and that he must have an idea of the nature and power of science. But Livingstone laid chief emphasis upon the greatest of all problems—the problem of living, and the university's obligation to give the student some guidance in meeting it. The educated man must acquire an understanding of "the spiritual forces which alone give meaning and value to human existence, in order that, in the words of John Milton, he may become fit 'to perform justly, skillfully, and magnanimously all the affairs both private and public of peace

[21] Dr. Seymour, president of Yale University, New Haven, Connecticut, delivered this Baccalaureate address at the Yale Commencement Exercises, June 19, 1949. It is quoted by special permission of Dr. Seymour and the editor of *Vital Speeches*.

and war.'" "All the adverbs in this quotation," comments Sir Richard, are important. "The one most easily overlooked is the last."

What are the qualities that enable a man to live and perform "magnanimously," and why does Milton regard the magnanimous life as of such vital importance? What did the eulogist of Queen Elizabeth, Sir John Hayward, have in mind, when he described the Queen as not merely just but magnanimous?

The word, taken etymologically from the Latin, connotes a large spirit. When Aristotle describes the magnanimous man he finds this spirit so large that he includes no less than twelve virtues that go to make up the quality. Three of them deserve especial emphasis. First, intelligence, which inspires all the other virtues. Second, self-reliance based upon courage. "It is characteristic of the great-souled man never to ask help from others or only with reluctance. . . . The great-souled man does not run into danger for trifling reasons; but he will face danger in a great cause and when so doing will be ready to sacrifice his life, since he holds that life is not worth having at every price." And third, generosity. The great-souled man "does not bear a grudge for it is not a mark of greatness of soul to recall things against people, especially the wrongs they have done you, but rather to overlook them."

With this we may compare the emphasis which the philosopher Spinoza, discussing the virtue of the free man who follows the guidance of reason, lays upon strength of mind and upon generosity. "By strength of mind," he avers, "I mean the desire by which . . . each person endeavors alone to preserve his own being." Let us note here, parenthetically, the idea of individual initiative, of enterprise, of Yankee "gumption." "By generosity," Spinoza continues, "I mean the desire by which from the dictates of reason alone, each person endeavors to help other people and to join them to him in friendship."

Compare with these analyses a contemporary appreciation of the qualities that characterize the spiritual leader: "He is a seer and sees clearly; he is a great heart and feels deeply; he is a hero and dares valiantly, with a consuming passion for righteousness."

These are interesting clues to an understanding of what we mean by the magnanimous man. For myself I like that which is offered in John Bunyan's choice term, as the name of the hero of the second part of the "Pilgrim's Progress"—Mr. Great-heart. You will remember that when the pilgrim Christian's wife and family determined to follow in his footsteps, they were given as guide and protector in their arduous and perilous path, this Great-heart. He was a man of sturdy self-reliance, marched with sword in hand at the front of the party when there were lions in the way; guarding its rear when foul fiends threatened from behind.

He was a man not merely of courage but of generosity. Read again the story of that extraordinary duel between Great-heart and the Giant Maul: "The Giant came up and Mr. Great-heart went to meet him, and as he went he drew his sword but the Giant had a club, so without more ado they fell to it and at the first blow the Giant struck Mr. Great-heart down upon one of his knees. With that the women and children cried out, so Mr. Great-heart recovering himself laid about him in full lusty manner and gave the Giant a wound in his arm. Thus he fought for the space of an hour to that height of heat that the breath came out of the Giant's nostrils as the heat doth out of a boiling caldron ... and Mr. Great-heart with a full blow fetched the Giant down to the ground. 'Nay hold and let me recover,' quoth he, so Mr. Great-heart fairly let him get up. So to it they went again and the Giant missed but little of all to breaking Mr. Great-heart's skull with his club." The fight, however, terminated in the hero's piercing his adversary under the fifth rib and this time, without any false mercy, he cut off his head.

For Mr. Great-heart was wise enough to realize that while courage must be imbued with a spirit of generosity, generosity in turn must be guided by intelligence. No matter how generous the fool, until he is cured of his folly he cannot live magnanimously. Mr. Great-heart himself immediately after the slaying of the Giant emphasized this fact. For when they came on the Pilgrim old Mr. Honest, and learned that he came from the town of Stupidity, Great-heart averred, "Your town is worse than the City of Destruction itself."

The place and the limits of generosity must be determined by our intelligence, in the ordinary affairs of life by common-sense. The professional baseball player would presumably lose his job if, when given a base on balls by the umpire, he insisted that the last ball was in reality a strike and that he should have been called out. But in a tennis tournament it is not uncommon for a player who has been awarded by the linesman an ace which he himself knew was out, to serve intentionally a double fault. That is proper generosity. And it is this attitude that lies at the heart of what Milton meant by the magnanimous. It is the breadth of spirit which, as Aristotle indicates, prevents a man from holding a petty grudge and which is capable also of forgiveness in the most deadly enmities.

The Bible does not use the Greek word signifying magnanimous or great-souled. But the spirit of generosity which is essential to our understanding of it is repeated. This was in St. Paul's mind when he wrote to the Corinthians on the quality which we translate "charity," the spirit not merely of mercy but of fortitude and of the quest for truth which is the mark of the intelligent man. . . .

The contrast is sharp between this spirit of magnanimity and the Mosaic law, of an eye for an eye and a tooth for a tooth. Yet the Old Testament provides outstanding examples of magnanimous heroes. We remember the story of Joseph's brethren throwing him into a pit and then selling him for twenty pieces of silver; and then, after his own rise to power in Egypt, his treatment of them when they came in supplication for food. "Be not grieved nor angry with yourselves that ye sold me hither, for God did send me before you to preserve life." And after their father's death when they feared again that now "he will certainly requite us all the evil which we did him," he gave final assurance: "As for you, ye thought evil against me but God meant it unto good. . . . Now therefore fear ye not. I will nourish you and your little ones, and he comforted them and spake kindly unto them."

Take another dramatic example. King Saul in his hatred and fear of David pursued him in the wilderness with a great force of soldiers. But incautiously and without a guard he entered the cave of Engedi where David was hid, and he went to sleep. Here, as David's followers insisted, was the golden opportunity to slay the implacable and frenzied monarch. David refused. He cut off the hem of the King's robe as a token of the opportunity of which he would not take advantage. Then when Saul had wakened and left the cave, David called to him: "See the skirt of thy robe in my hand, for in that I cut off the skirt of thy robe and killed thee not, know then and see that there is neither evil nor transgression in mine hand and I have not sinned against thee; yet thou hatest my soul to take it. The Lord judge between me and thee and the Lord avenge me of thee, but my hand shall not be upon thee."

This conjunction of courageous strength and generosity is characteristic of the great books of wisdom of the Old Testament.

Observe the reference to the qualities of God in Ecclesiasticus, "As His Majesty is so is His mercy"; and in the 31st Psalm, "Blessed be the Lord for he has shown me his marvelous kindness in a strong city." Or take the oft quoted injunction in the book of Proverbs: "If thine enemy be hungry, give him bread to eat; and if he be thirsty, give him water to drink, for thou shalt heap coals of fire upon his head and the Lord shall reward thee. . . ."

In my own youth, being under parental discipline and accordingly compelled to spend more time in reading the Bible than I would otherwise have consumed, my preference was for the Old Testament. This may have been because of the variety of wars and battles, or perhaps of incidents which I did not wholly understand but which I recognized as attractively unedifying. But it was chiefly, I think, because of the extent to which as it then seemed to me, the New Testament emphasized such uninteresting qualities as mercy, love, loving-kindness, forgiveness, and the like. And it is certain that to most youthful minds these terms denote a type of softness, or as we said sissiness, not closely attuned to the ideals of hardy manlihood.

But if, as adults, you will study the New Testament, it is striking how often the examples given of the personal exercise of these qualities are tied up with the sense of power, of courage, or of wisdom. The father of the prodigal son, in the display of his great generosity towards the returned wastrel, was always master of the situation. He was in a position of strength. Except for that, there could have been little virtue in his spirit of forgiveness. What an instance of courage is there in the martyrdom of Stephen, stoned to death, praying for them that did him wrong and dying with pardon on his tongue! Or the sublime example of Christ crucified: "Father forgive them, for they know not what they do." Our Lord's wisdom, the recognition of the ignorance of his enemies, is knitted in with his courage and his generosity.

It would be illuminating if we should make up a list of the magnanimous men of literature and history. Those would stand

BLACKBOARD SKETCHES

1. Keep the blackboard clean and the printing legible.
2. Make the drawings large enough that every auditor can see them with ease.
Notice that the speakers are talking to the audiences and not to the blackboards. (Photos, Black Star.)

12" NOZ.

POST WAR SURVEY
EMPLOYED (1940) — 4,266
" (1943) — 5,455
" (EST.) (1946) — 5,968
1946
No. SEEKING JOBS — 6,561
5,968
POTENTIAL UNEMPLOYED 593

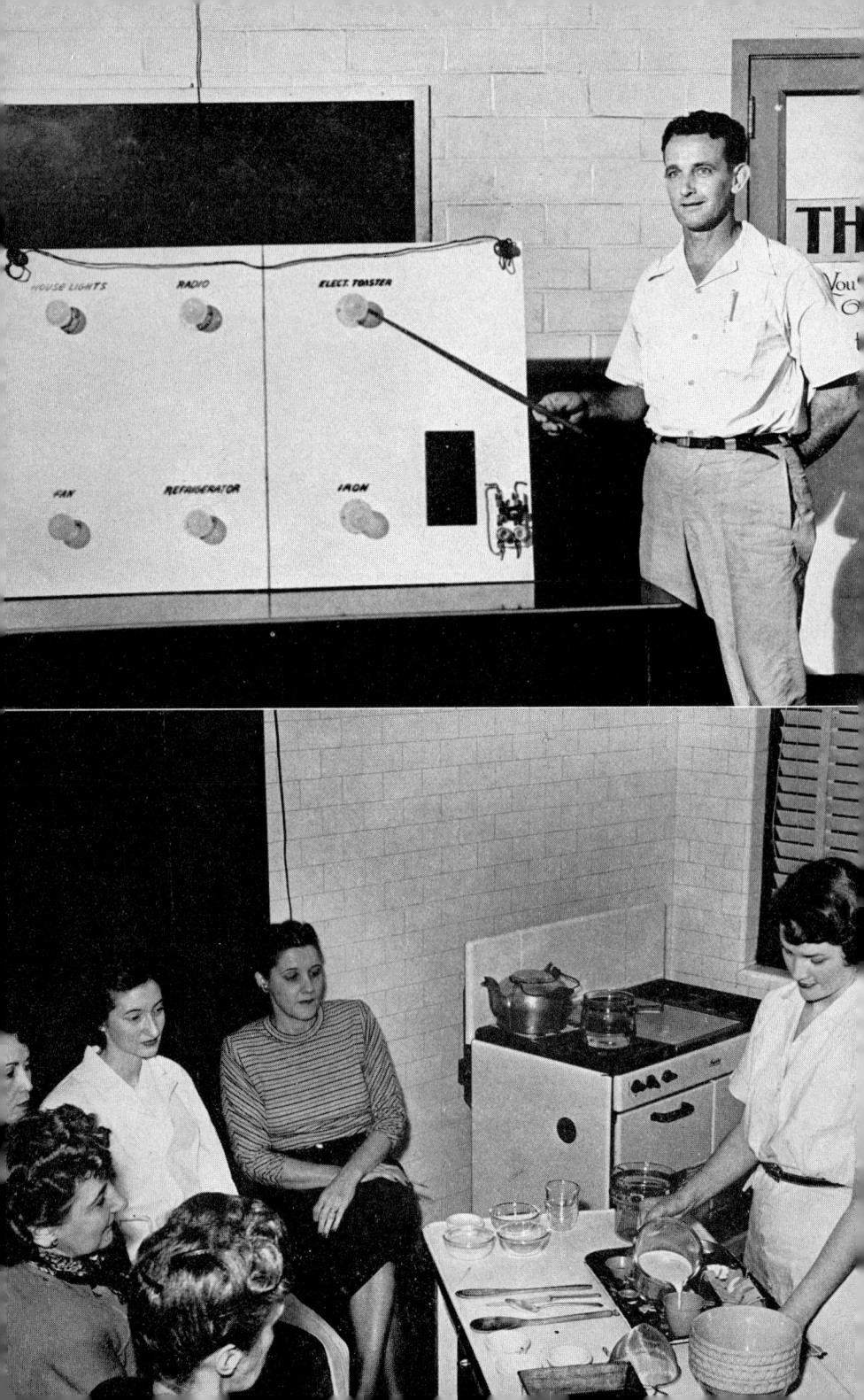
HOUSE LIGHTS
RADIO
ELECT. TOASTER
FAN
REFRIGERATOR
IRON

out as objects of our admiration who combine the particular traits that we are considering: Such men as Marcus Aurelius, Chaucer's knight, Francis of Assisi, the Black Prince, St. Louis of France, Henry V, Sir Walter Raleigh, Henry of Navarre, Charles Darwin, and above all in modern times—Abraham Lincoln. It would be equally instructive to note the men no matter how courageous and intelligent, who would have to be excluded from the list; Oliver Cromwell, Louis XIV, the Duke of Marlborough, Frederick the Great, Napoleon Bonaparte. If you consider the implications of these lives you see how just is the emphasis that was laid by John Milton on learning how to perform magnanimously.

The qualities of courageous self-reliance, generosity, and intelligence are at all times necessary to the conduct of national affairs, but never more so than in the critical years that lie before us. We must be warned by history. Remember the magnificent example of a magnanimous policy that was set by Great Britain at the close of the Boer War. That prolonged and bitter struggle ended in the complete triumph of British arms. The enemy lay helpless. Nothing stood in the way of a Carthaginian peace. Instead, British statesmen, by a series of measures that were at once generous and wise, laid the basis for a reconciliation and a union of peoples and the establishment of an autonomous bulwark of the British Empire. This bulwark could not have been spared in the two world wars that followed. Compare the results of this statesmanship with those of the treaty dictated by the victorious Germans to Russia in 1917 at Brest-Litovsk. That was indeed a Carthaginian peace that took Russia apart and left her with no apparent means of defense for the future; but Germany shortly paid the price and on disastrous terms.

Allied treatment of Germany in the years between the world wars illustrates the failure to adopt a magnanimous policy and the consequent cost to the entire world. During the earlier half of

PRESENTATION

The upper picture demonstrates the importance of labeling parts with simple printing large enough to be read with ease. (Photo, Ethyl Corporation, Baton Rouge Plant.)

The lower picture stresses the importance of careful planning in a presentation. Notice how carefully the demonstrator has arranged her utensils. (Photo, L.S.U. Alumni News.)

that period allied policy was characterized by a stupid relentlessness; in the latter by an equally foolish generosity. In the twenties, by a more prompt and open course designed to set German economic life in order, thus serving the real interests of all concerned, it would have been possible to strengthen the forces of liberalism in central Europe and to have prevented the rise of Hitler. That was the time to be generous. But in the thirties, with the Nazis in control and their aggressive intent clear to the world, the conciliatory gestures of the British and the French could be interpreted only as indications of weakness and timidity and could serve only as an invitation to further aggression. For if generosity is to be effective, it must be based upon strong self-reliance as well as guided by wisdom.

The application of these principles to contemporary conditions seems to me clear. We are living in a time and a world of intense and bitter competition, both in the field of our national economy and in that of international relationships. In the area of domestic political, social and economic problems we are threatened with a type of state socialism which is utterly divorced in spirit from traditional American principles. It is based upon the alleged right of the citizen to receive rather than upon his duty to create. There is real peril in the expanding popular attitude that if the individual cannot make good for himself he will be taken care of by the government. Such an attitude is degenerative in the moral sense, tends to destroy incentive in the economic, and is socialistic in the political. Salvation is not to be found in laying our troubles in the lap of government. On the contrary, as citizens we must strengthen our self-reliance as we meet the difficulties of the day, we must be generous in assistance to those who are less fortunate, and always intelligent in the application of our self-reliance and generosity.

These same qualities are essential to the conduct of foreign affairs. In Russia we face a rival of great strength, the protagonist of a political system basically at odds with American constitutional principles, and in the eyes of most Americans utterly detestable. We cannot be sure of the peaceful intentions of this great power. Certainly we should be foolish to expect an attitude of friendly good-will on the part of those who govern in Moscow.

These are conditions which at the moment are apparently unalterable. We must face them. To meet them in the spirit of appeasement would spell disaster. Courageous self-reliance is the first condition of security. We must not fear to develop and maintain our national strength so as to be able to play our part manfully. All the world, and Russia in particular, should be aware of our determination and our readiness.

But this determination must be tempered with a spirit of generosity. We, on our side, must develop, together with our strength, an attitude of underlying friendliness. We must spare no effort to understand the Russian point of view and to work out methods of somehow getting along with them. Sumner used to talk about "antagonistic cooperation," which involved the frank recognition of hostility but at the same time the necessity of common endeavor. When we speak of generosity in this context, there is no suggestion of a willingness to yield essential principle as a means of staying out of trouble. The generosity I have in mind goes back to St. Paul's ideal quality which "vaunteth not itself, is not easily provoked, rejoiceth in the truth." And the limits to which it will extend must be determined by an instructed intelligence.

Gentlemen of the Graduating Class: The quality of a nation is the sum total of the qualities of the individual citizens. That is why it is so vital that the young men and women now going from the colleges, who will be the leaders of the coming generation, should go out with a sense of moral values. The University can point the way, but it is upon the actual exercise of these qualities by educated men and women that the future will depend. It is for you to show the nation how to live magnanimously. Because of our ancient traditions of service to the community you carry with you a special obligation. Be sure of our confidence that you will worthily fulfill it.

SUPPLEMENTARY READINGS

1. Baird, A. Craig, *Argumentation, Discussion and Debate*, McGraw-Hill Book Company, Inc., 1950, chaps. 8-15.
2. Bryant, Donald, and Wallace, Karl R., *Fundamentals of Public Speaking*, Appleton-Century-Crofts, Inc., 1947, chap. 16.
3. Foster, William Trufant, *Argumentation and Debating*, Houghton Mifflin Company, 2nd rev. ed., 1936, chaps. 4-8.
4. Larrabee, Harold A., *Reliable Knowledge*, Houghton Mifflin Company, 1945.
5. Mander, A. E., *Logic for Millions*, Philosophical Library, Inc., 1947.
6. Overstreet, H. A., *Influencing Human Behavior*, W. W. Norton & Company, 1925, chap. 11.

CHAPTER XII

Visual Supports

IN THE preceding chapter we have discussed at length the various types of verbal supporting materials. Although these are normally the principal substance of a speech, they are not enough many times to accomplish the speaker's goal. Because of the abstract nature of language, oral materials somehow fall short of holding interest, of making the subject clear, or of giving the speech the necessary persuasive quality. Just as it is never wise to "put all of your eggs into one basket," so it is often unsatisfactory to depend upon your voice alone to move your listeners. In this respect you can learn a lesson from authorities on visual education, who emphasize that the number of sensory stimuli and the strength of the stimulation are directly related to learning. They point out that appeals to two senses are more effective than appeals to only one. Two appeals to the same sense or a sustained appeal will also produce greater results than a single momentary effort. A speaker can therefore improve his speech by working for multisensory appeals.

Immediately it is obvious that you can hardly avoid appealing to more than one sense in the face-to-face situation, even if you try. Auditors judge a speech by what they see as well as hear. A listless manner, a blank expression, and awkward gestures will create an unfavorable impression. If you are skillful, you can make your facial expression, gestures, posture, and movement support your ideas. When you explain or describe, you may indicate through the use of gestures size, shape, location, and direction. If you choose, you may reflect horror, disgust, disinterest, or approval through your facial expression. You may suggest a mood or an attitude by your movement or posture. In each of these cases, you reinforce your spoken words by visual imagery.

Of course a speaker can increase his multisensory appeals by including in his speech what are commonly referred to as "visual aids." Among those ordinarily most available are the following:

Graphic and pictorial materials
1. Charts
2. Diagrams
3. Graphs
4. Sketches and drawings
5. Cartoons
6. Posters
7. Maps
8. Globes
9. Pictures
10. Photographs

Practical devices
1. Models
2. Specimens
3. Full-scale objects

Projected pictures
1. Motion pictures (films)
2. Film strips (slide films)
3. Slides

PUBLIC SPEAKING

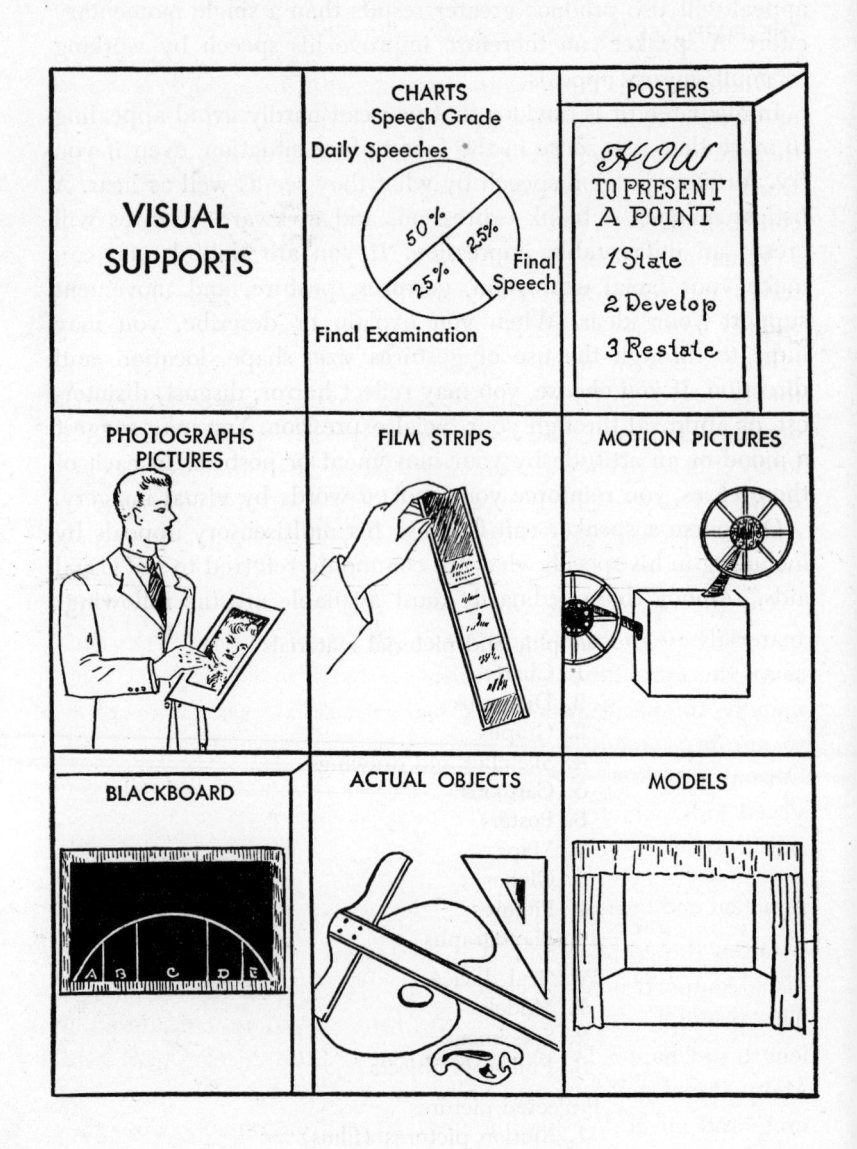

VISUAL SUPPORTS

CHARTS
Speech Grade
Daily Speeches
50%
25%
25%
Final Speech
Final Examination

POSTERS
HOW TO PRESENT A POINT
1 State
2 Develop
3 Restate

PHOTOGRAPHS PICTURES

FILM STRIPS

MOTION PICTURES

BLACKBOARD
A B C D E

ACTUAL OBJECTS

MODELS

THE PURPOSES OF VISUAL AIDS

Under various circumstances visual aids are used in a variety of ways, and hence they accomplish different ends. In some of their functions they are not speech materials in any sense of the word. Let us investigate briefly their relationship to speech composition.

Visual aids such as motion pictures may be complete in themselves and require no additional explanation. The movie maker weaves into his production all the necessary materials to accomplish his predetermined objective. If he wishes to solicit funds for the March of Dimes, he includes powerful persuasive appeals designed to move the audience to deposit dimes in a box in lobby. In this event the visual aid is a complete unit and of course is not a type of speech material. In this form it is a subject for courses in cinematography or visual education, but not for a speech class.

On the other hand, visual aids may be used as supporting materials in the accomplishment of a speech goal. They may serve the same functions that the verbal forms of support serve, namely, to attract attention, to hold interest, to clarify meanings, to amplify, and to prove arguments. The title of this chapter, "Visual Supports," was chosen advisedly to suggest this aspect of visual aids, which does fall within the province of a course in public speaking.

Attention and Interest

Often the speaker may find occasion to include one of these visual supports in a speech to attract attention and direct interest. The principles involved are the same as those considered at length in Chapter IV and therefore need little development here. Many visual aids are especially effective because they are concrete and novel. We like pictures, charts, diagrams because they are definite. They provide the listener with something upon which to focus his attention. Furthermore, because they ordinarily necessitate movement in presentation, they provide a welcome change from a straight oral presentation.

A colorful poster, a vivid picture, an appealing chart, or a carefully selected film strip often adds novelty and keeps interest from lagging. Curiosity can be heightened by a series of drawings or pictures or by a strip chart. In the latter case each point is covered by an easily removable strip of paper. When the point fits with the speech, the speaker dramatically uncovers it.

To Clarify

Visual aids may assist in clarifying what otherwise may seem abstract. They often more nearly approach or suggest "the real thing" which the speaker is attempting to describe or to explain. They illustrate or suggest graphically subjects that are difficult to express orally.

In fact, the clear presentation of some subjects is impossible without visual aids. Things that are too complex, too big, too small, too fast, too slow, too inaudible, too inaccessible, or too untimely for first-hand experience must be presented in a manner to assist normal perception. If first-hand experience is hazardous or unpleasant, such aids become even more desirable. Certainly most auditors prefer to learn about such subjects as malaria, leprosy, poison gas, snakes, atomic explosions, from afar. Diagrams, graphs, flow charts, enlarged photographs, microphotographs, slides, and motion pictures simplify the treatment of these difficult subjects. For example, on the screen the auditor may see pictures of the "real thing": the landing on a distant beachhead, the storming of a pillbox, the eruption of a volcano, or the results of a hurricane. He may become a party to many experiences that otherwise would be denied him.

To Amplify

Amplification makes a subject more vivid and more impressive. Certainly visual aids are excellent ways of dwelling upon a subject in order to make it more real and stimulating. The presentation of a chart, specimen, or film ordinarily provides a means of spending more time in the development of the point. The multisensory appeal requires additional orientation—the listener thinks of the subject in a new light. Hence the shift in medium increases the vividness and impressiveness of the subject. Perhaps this explains the old Chinese proverb that a picture is worth a thousand words.

To Prove

Many auditors who refuse otherwise to believe a speaker may be convinced by a demonstration or exhibit. "Seeing is believing," states the old adage. Frequently a prosecuting attorney moves a jury not by words but by *real* evidence. He startles his listeners by displaying the knife with which the accused supposedly stabbed the murdered man. He points to the blood-stained coat. "Here is where the knife entered," he says. The jurors, shocked and horrified by these gory details, are moved to vote for conviction.

The scientist exhibits a slide, a photograph, or perhaps the real object to support his hypothesis. Upon demand the salesman skillfully pares a potato in order to sell the housewife the peeler. Demonstration and performance make the presentation believable.

SELECTION OF VISUAL SUPPORT

There is no magic in visual aids; their mere inclusion in a speech does not necessarily mean a short cut to success. Since on most occasions they supplement verbal materials, they must be selected with great care; they must be carefully fitted into the speech; and they must be skillfully presented. Like other materials they must be adapted to the speaking situation in a way to keep the speech moving toward the speaker's goal. In selecting a visual aid, you should ask yourself six questions:

Is sufficient equipment available for the presentation? Materials and apparatus available will determine largely what you can use. Anything as simple as a blackboard sketch requires chalk, an eraser, and a board solid enough for sketching and large enough to be seen. Without a projector, a screen, and a darkened room, motion pictures are out of the question. Checking essential equipment becomes a first step in selection of visual supporting materials.

Does the visual aid support the point under consideration? Like any other supporting material, visual support must accomplish its objective—to prove, to amplify, or to clarify. Many of the materials must be adapted or altered to fit into your plan. If they do not support the point or cannot be made to support it, they should be omitted.

Is the visual aid appropriate for the audience? The intellectual capacity and the experience of the auditors will have much to do with the type of visual aid which you decide to include. Elaborate charts or long statistical tables prepared for careful reading may prove highly unsatisfactory for oral presentation because they demand greater concentration than listeners can give. Some types of flow charts, graphs, maps, and diagrams may be too technical for the average audience but very effective for engineers or specialists. These aspects must be considered.

Is the visual aid appropriate for the speaker? Each of these methods requires some special skill for presentation. If you plan to use a blackboard, you must be able to write or print legibly. Projected pictures require a trained projectionist who understands how the slides or pictures are to be presented. You certainly would be foolish to select a visual aid with which you are clumsy and not thoroughly acquainted.

Is it possible to present the visual aid in the time available? By nature these visual means are great time consumers. Their introduction and presentation sometimes may require more time than you can wisely devote to that phase of your talk. A careful timing of a presentation is necessary to determine if you have the time available. Guard against the temptation of becoming so engrossed in the operation of a gadget or projector that you slight or neglect the oral part of your presentation. The visual aids must be kept supplementary to the speaker's development because they are not ends in themselves, but another type of *supporting material.*

Is it possible to make the visual aid an integral part of the speech? Like any other supporting material, the visual supports must be blended into the development in such a way that they do not destroy unity and coherence. A film or slide may be entertaining, but the vital question is, does it stress the point that the speaker wishes to make? The specimen may be novel, but does it support the lecturer's point? These and similar questions should constantly be kept in mind by the speaker who wishes to supplement his oral proofs with visual aids.

DISPLAYING VISUAL AIDS

Visual aids may be adapted to a speech in many ways. One of the first problems in this respect concerns the display of your materials. Two methods are possible: (1) to present the visual aid from the front of the room, or (2) actually to place it in the hands of the auditor.

Display from the front of the room is frequently effective if the visual support is suggestive in nature and if intricate details are not important. Of course the drawing or object must be large enough to be seen and must be placed in a location which the listeners can see with ease. Obviously, most graphic and pictorial materials, practical devices, and projected pictures may be presented from the front of the room. If the visual aid is in the front of the room, the speaker has the advantage of directing attention to those aspects which emphasize his point. Except in the case of projected pictures, he also has the advantages of face-to-face delivery, direct eye contact, and careful observation of audience reaction.

A second method of display is to place the visual aid in the hands of the auditor. Small models or specimens, outlines, summaries, page-size charts and maps, and detailed drawings can be

DISPLAYING VISUAL AIDS

RIGHT

STEPS IN SPEECH PREPARATION
1 Analysis
2 Research
3 Outline
4 Gather Material
5 Rehearse
6 Deliver

WRONG

presented only in this manner. Under these conditions more intricate details may be examined.

When you distribute your visual materials to your listeners, keep in mind four requirements:

First, each auditor should have a copy. The distribution of too few encourages inattentiveness because the listener must examine the visual material while the presentation advances.

Second, the parts should be carefully labeled and numbered. If the listener is to notice details, he must be constantly aware of what part of the visual aid is under discussion. By including numbers and labels frequent reorientation of the listeners is possible.

Third, the speaker must be able to persuade the listener to lay aside the visual aid when it is not under consideration. If the auditor becomes too engrossed in the material that he has in hand, he may fail to follow the development, with the result that he misses the main points. The speaker must be adept at saying to his listeners, "At present, please listen to what I have to say," "Now I should like to have you observe the visual aid which I have given you," and "Will you please lay aside the visual aid while I consider another point." This feat is indeed most difficult.

Fourth, the method of distribution must be carefully planned. The speaker may distribute his material (a) before he starts speaking, (b) during his speech, or (c) at the close of his presentation. The first possibility is usually the most satisfactory, for it avoids prolonged breaks in the actual presentation. The common practice of distribution during the speech can result in confusion, a waste of precious time, and an interest lag. Of course if you have several assistants who have been carefully instructed, you may be able to effect a distribution without serious consequences. Under this latter possibility you can, of course, direct attention more adeptly to the point by withholding materials until they fit into your development.

Distribution following a speech may be used if you expect the auditor to do further study. In your speech you give the highlights and rely on printed material to provide more complete and more detailed information.

FITTING VISUAL AIDS INTO A SPEECH

Visual supporting material may be incorporated into a speech in two ways: it may be interspersed throughout the talk, or it may be presented as a unit before or after some explanation. It is ordinarily desirable to present blackboard sketches, charts, models, and film strips in the first manner, presenting the visual aid as reinforcement in the development of a point.

The speaker should have his material so organized that he can move along without hesitation and long periods of silence. Delays, while you make elaborate drawings or while you set up equipment, are likely to kill interest and to destroy the unity of your talk. If possible you should cut time-consuming operations to a minimum by careful preparation.

The motion picture may be presented in the second way, that is, as a unit. Starting and stopping the projector seriously interferes with the presentation of the thought contained in the picture. Occasionally, after a continuous run, the second showing may be interrupted, but ordinarily such a procedure defeats the entire purpose of *motion* pictures. Introductory and summary remarks must be skillfully planned to point up what you want the auditor to remember.

But regardless of the type of visual aid, there seem to be four steps necessary for the effective use of visual support in a speech. These steps are as follows:

1. *Introduce the visual aid* stressing its importance to the speech. Prepare the listener for what to anticipate and for what to observe.
2. *Present the visual aid.* Make sure that it is clearly visible and that the important points are emphasized.
3. Upon completion of presentation, *review main points* to be remembered.
4. *Relate point stressed* by visual aid to the line of thought it supports.

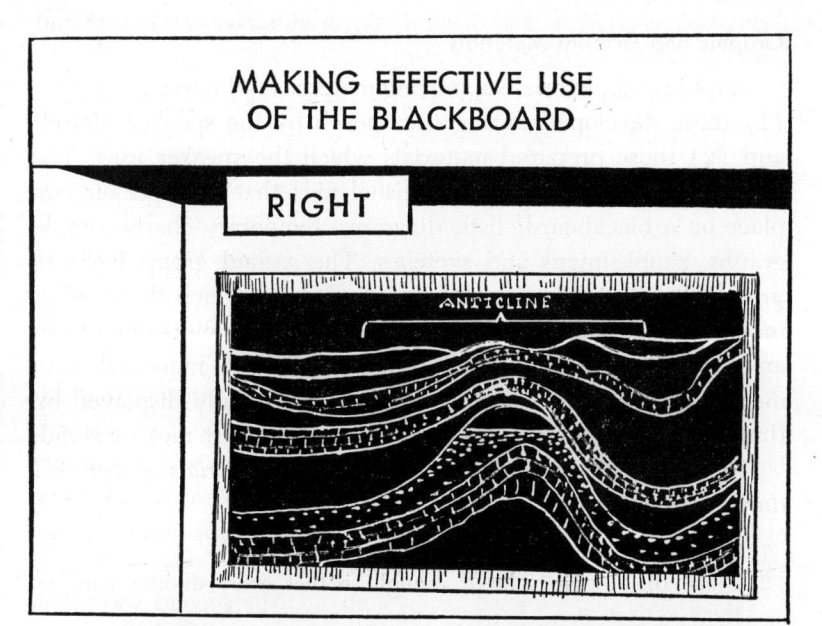

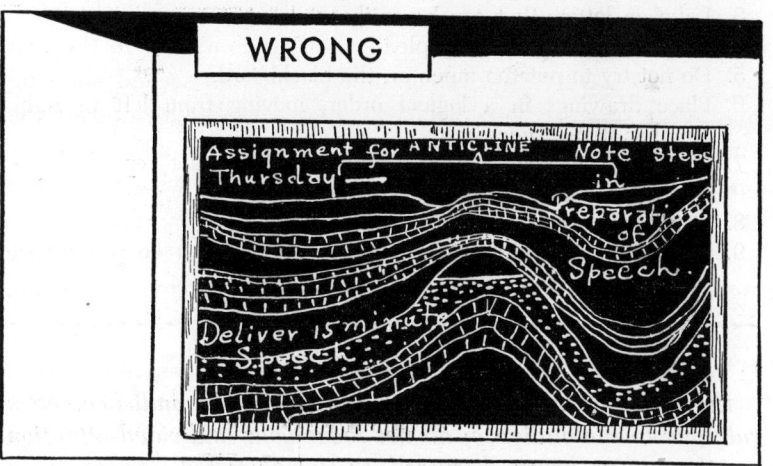

MAKING EFFECTIVE USE OF THE BLACKBOARD

RIGHT

WRONG

PRESENTING VISUAL AIDS

Graphic and Pictorial Materials

Graphic and pictorial supporting materials fall into two classes: (1) those developed during the speech by the speaker himself and (2) those prepared materials which the speaker uses. The first group includes ordinarily visual aids that the speaker can place on a blackboard: lists, diagrams, temporary charts, simple graphs, simple maps and sketches. The second group includes prepared materials, more elaborate in nature, which the speaker may construct himself before the presentation or may obtain from an outside source, that is, charts, cartoons, posters, more elaborate maps, pictures, and photographs. They are usually displayed by thumbtacking them to a wall or board, on a chart rack or stand.

Hints on the presentation of original materials developed during speech:

1. Keep the blackboard clean and legible.
2. Make the drawings large enough so that every auditor can see them with ease.
3. Label in letters that can be easily read.
4. Keep labels short and simple.
5. Do not try to put too much on the blackboard.
6. Place drawings in a logical order, moving from left to right. Number steps if necessary.
7. Suggest main features without attempting exact reproductions. Use schematic drawings.
8. Strive for novelty and variety in drawing.
9. Intersperse drawing and oral presentation. Don't keep audience waiting while you make elaborate drawing.

VISUAL AIDS

In presenting a visual aid do not forget the audience. As a rule talk to the audience; do not focus your undivided attention on the object being discussed or demonstrated. (Photo, Esso Standard Oil, Baton Rouge Refinery.)

Be able to manipulate the gadget or machine with ease and confidence. (Photo, L.S.U. Alumni News.)

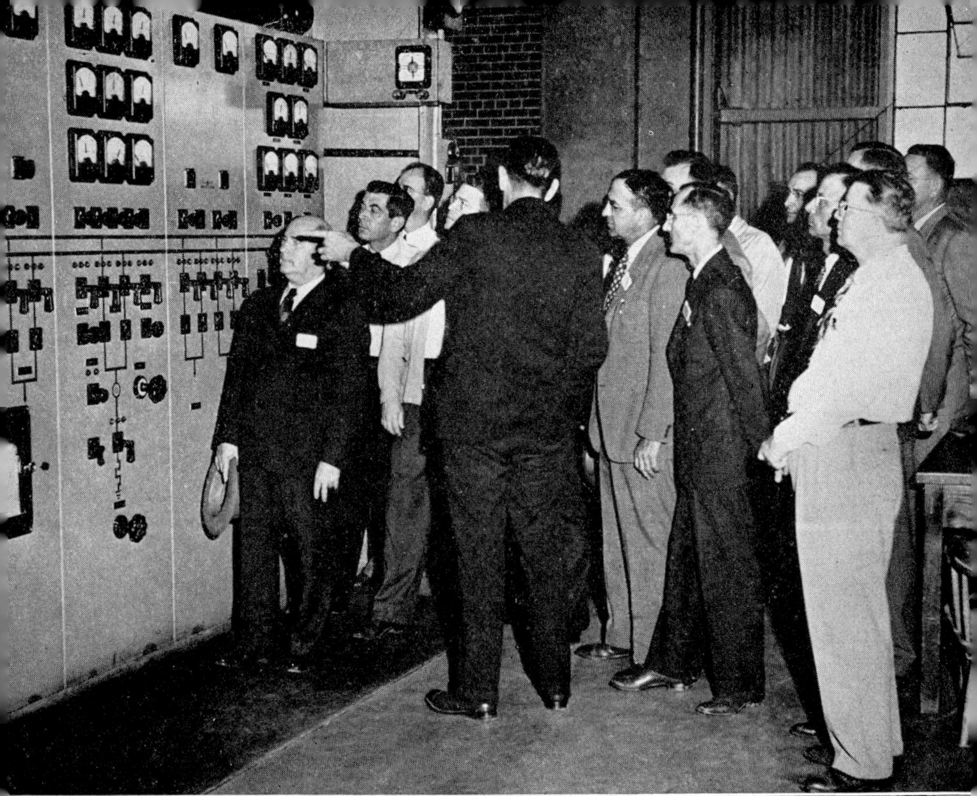

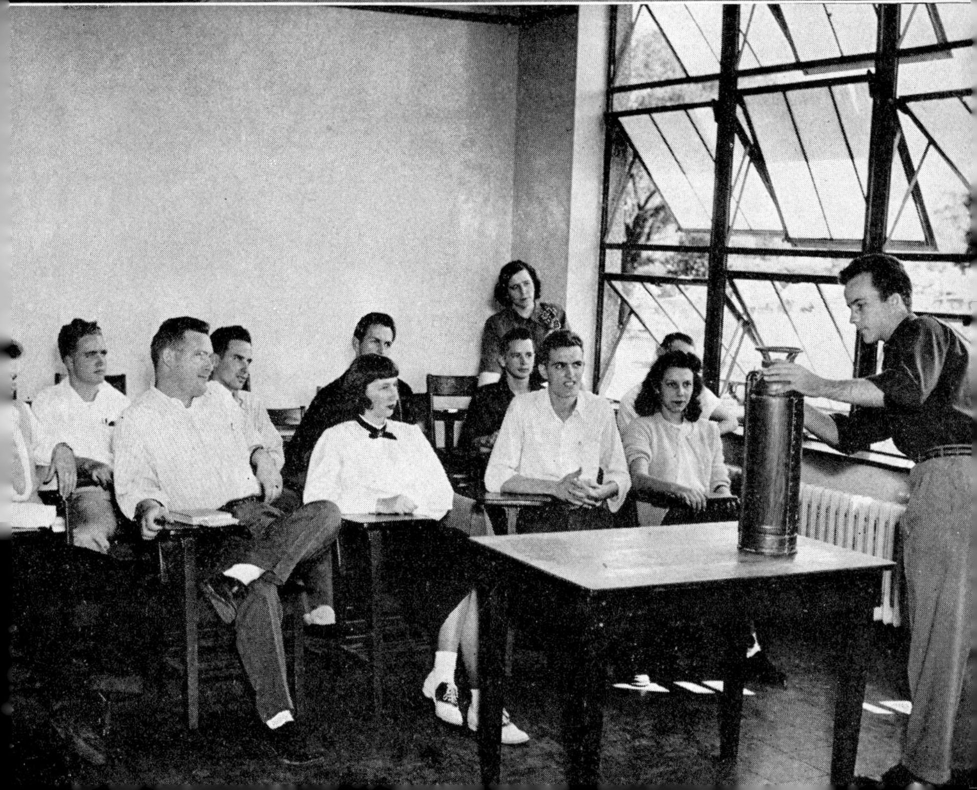

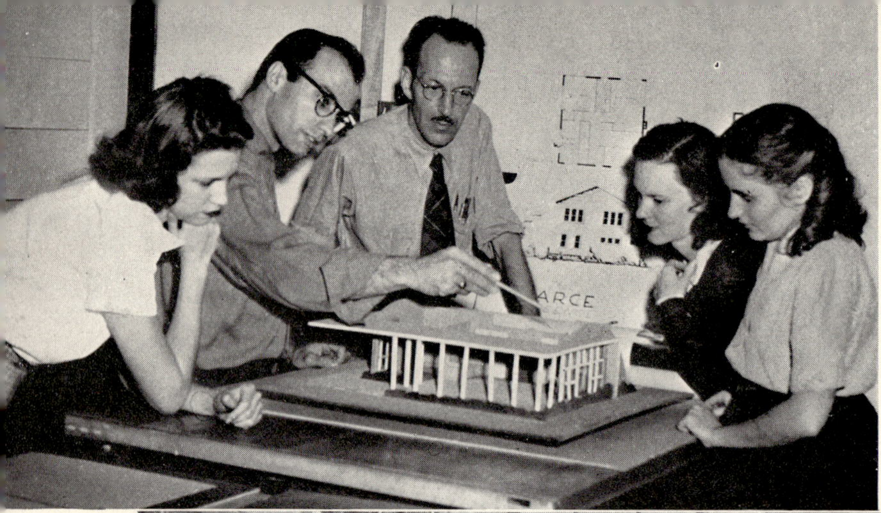

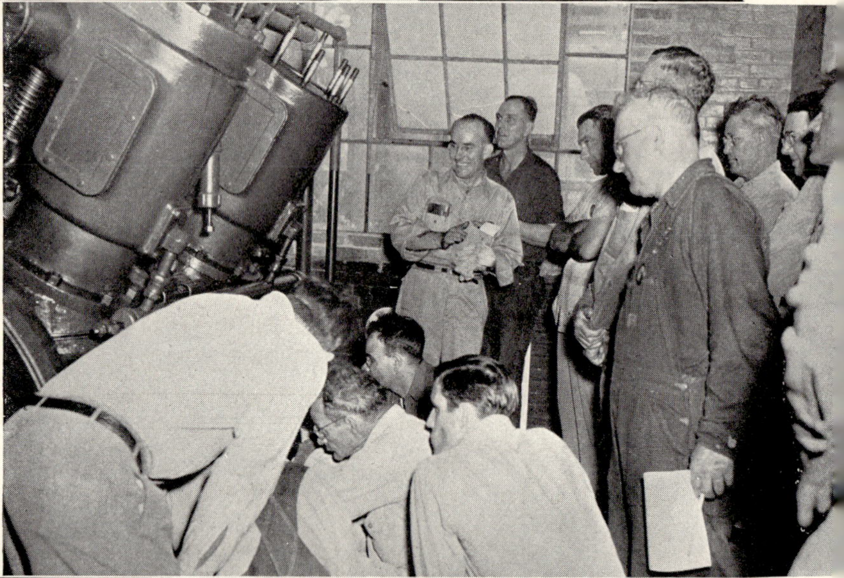

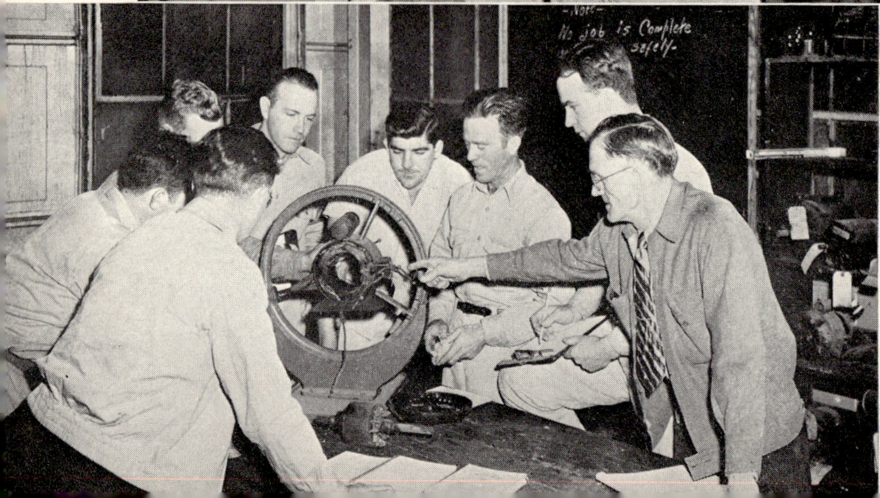
No job is Complete
safely-

VISUAL SUPPORTS

10. Leave the material on board until auditor has had time to see it.
11. Be prepared to draw or sketch with ease and surety; avoid crude drawing, frequent misstarts and slow presentation.
12. Use colored chalk whenever possible for contrast.

Hints on the presentation of prepared materials:

1. Select a visual aid large enough to be seen by all auditors; page-size material can best be presented by using opaque projector.
2. Avoid aids containing unnecessary details not pertaining to subject.
3. Select aids using color.
4. Mount aid in place where all can see it.
5. Mount or display in secure position.
6. Label parts with simple printing large enough to be read with ease.
7. Focus attention on important points by use of pointer.

Practical Devices: Actual Objects, Specimens, and Models

Actual objects are the things themselves; they may be anything about which a speaker might talk: a golf club, potato peeler, even a B-36. A specimen is a small part or sample of the real object. A model is a replica, smaller or larger than the object.

These visual supports come nearer reality than any of the other types discussed: consequently their use is to be encouraged whenever possible. If the speaker wishes to discuss how to hit a golf ball, he will do well to have golf clubs at hand.

General rules concerning effective presentation of such devices are difficult to formulate because each offers unique problems. The following suggestions will probably be helpful, at least in the use of models and specimens.

1. Select only those that are large enough to be seen.
2. If a model is three dimensional, give the auditor an opportunity to view it from different angles.

PRACTICAL DEVICES: MODELS AND ACTUAL OBJECTS

Whenever possible use the real thing in your demonstration talk. These three pictures show an instructor using a model house (photo, L.S.U. Alumni News), a group looking at a large machine, and a group looking at an electrical motor (photos, Esso Standard Oil, Baton Rouge Refinery).

CHARTS YOU MAY WISH TO CONSTRUCT

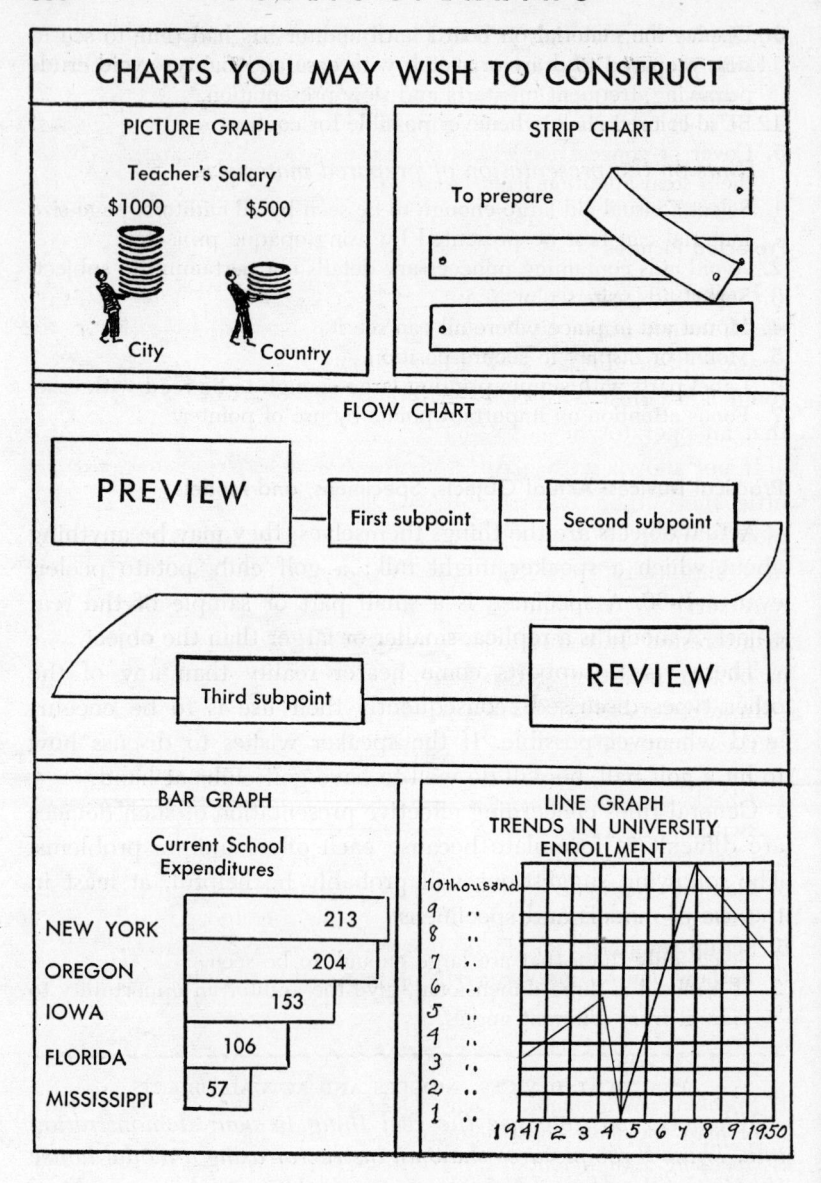

PICTURE GRAPH

Teacher's Salary
$1000 $500

City   Country

STRIP CHART

To prepare

FLOW CHART

PREVIEW — First subpoint — Second subpoint

Third subpoint — REVIEW

BAR GRAPH

Current School Expenditures

NEW YORK   213
OREGON   204
IOWA   153
FLORIDA   106
MISSISSIPPI 57

LINE GRAPH
TRENDS IN UNIVERSITY ENROLLMENT

10 thousand
9 "
8 "
7 "
6 "
5 "
4 "
3 "
2 "
1 "
1941 2 3 4 5 6 7 8 9 1950

3. Display long enough so that all may see; avoid giving the impression that you are attempting to conceal or hurry over difficult points.
4. Be able to manipulate the gadget with ease and with confidence.
5. Cover or conceal models or specimens when not in use; don't let them steal attention from other points.

Projected Pictures

Projected pictures necessitate expensive and technical equipment, namely, a motion-picture projector, strip-film projector, or opaque projector, as well as some kind of screen. A darkened room is a "must." Furthermore, most effective showing requires that an operator be employed.

If not shown with great skill, these materials may amount to little more than entertainment. Ordinarily, the sound motion picture must be completed as a unit. In this time the audience may slip away from the speaker because the darkened room may serve as welcome concealment for the inattentive and the disinterested. Introductions, summaries, and efforts to fit the film or picture into the speech become increasingly important.

In addition, the following hints may increase the speaker's use of these materials:

1. Check carefully physical surroundings, electrical outlets, and switches, lighting, seating, and ventilation.
2. Check time required for presentation of film or picture.
3. Plan presentation so that no note taking is necessary during showing.
4. Rehearse presentation and plan cues with operator.
5. Set up equipment and focus image on screen before speech.
6. Reshow film for emphasis if subject is highly technical or difficult.

EXERCISES

1. *Speaking Assignment.* Deliver a speech in which you use a chart or map you have constructed.
2. *Speaking Assignment.* Deliver a speech in which you make use of colored chalk and blackboard illustrations.
3. *Speaking Assignment.* Deliver a speech in which you make use of a model or specimen.

4. *Speaking Assignment.* Deliver a speech in which you use a filmstrip or motion picture.
5. *Research Assignment.* Check for available film strips or motion pictures on the following subjects:

Telephoning	Soil erosion	Dairy industry
Safety	Citizenship	Gardening
Better health	United Nations	Vocal cords
Conservation	Battle for Britain	City planning

For each subject locate a film title, the place it is available, the rental, and source of your information.
6. *Discussion Questions for Class Symposium.*
   a. How do the following types of persons make use of visual supports in their speaking: (a) clergyman, (b) physics teacher, (c) "gym" teacher, (4) football coach, (e) auctioneer, (f) automobile salesman, (g) Fuller Brush man, (h) home demonstrator.
   b. How do persons fail in the use of visual supports? (Use illustrations from your own observation.)
   c. What visual supports are available to you as speech students?

SUPPLEMENTARY READINGS

1. Dale, Edgar, *Audio-Visual Methods in Teaching*, The Dryden Press, Inc., 1946.
2. *Educational Film Guide*, The H. W. Wilson Company. (See annual volumes and monthly supplements.)
3. Falconer, Vera M., *Filmstrips*, McGraw-Hill Book Company, Inc., 1948. (See sections on "What are Filmstrips," "Using Filmstrips," and "Projection," pp. 1-98.)
4. *Filmstrip Guide*, The H. W. Wilson Company. (See annual volume and monthly supplements.)
5. Haas, Kenneth B., and Packer, Harry, *Preparation and Use of Visual Aids*, Prentice-Hall, Inc., 1946.
6. McKown, Harry C., and Roberts, Alvin B., *Audio-Visual Aids to Instruction*, McGraw-Hill Book Company, Inc., 1940.
7. Miles, John R., and Spain, Charles R., *Audio-Visual Aids in Armed Forces*, American Council on Education, 1947.
8. Oliver, Robert T., Dickey, Dallas C., and Zelko, Harold P., *Essentials of Communicative Speech*, The Dryden Press, Inc., 1949, chap. 10.
9. Strauss, L. Harry, and Kidd, J. R., *Look, Listen and Learn*, Associated Press, 1948.

CHAPTER XIII

The Introduction

UPON meeting someone for the first time, you often, if not usually, make a quick estimate of him. If you know nothing of him, you decide that you like or dislike him entirely on the basis of what you see and hear. If given sufficient time, you may change your opinion, but if your acquaintanceship is brief, that first impulse becomes your permanent impression. Frequently a speaker is judged also on the basis of the first impression he makes in his opening sentences. Winston Churchill has learned this lesson through years of experience. It is reliably reported that England's greatest orator of his time may not be satisfied with an introduction until he has dictated a dozen versions. Churchill knows that those crucial beginning words probably mean success or failure.[1]

[1] Raymond Daniell, "Churchillisms," *The New York Times Magazine,* September 12, 1943, sec. 6, p. 9.

In the opening moments of your speech make sure that you win your way into the good graces of your listeners. Your introduction must be planned to gain for you a *favorable hearing*, in which your listeners are in a state of readiness to give serious consideration to the main part of your speech.

What is a favorable hearing? It involves three aspects:

1. An attentive hearing
2. A friendly hearing
3. An intelligent hearing

An attentive hearing implies sustained attention and directed interest. A friendly hearing means that the listeners respect the character and authority of the speaker and are willing to listen to him discuss the subject. An intelligent hearing implies that the auditors understand the subject and are desirous of further information.

In summary, therefore, it appears that the function of the introduction is (1) to direct the listeners' attention and interest toward the subject; (2) to develop a friendly attitude toward the speaker; and (3) to prepare the listeners for understanding.

SECURING AN ATTENTIVE HEARING

When the door-to-door salesman rings your doorbell, he faces much the same problem that you do at the beginning of a speech. If you answer the doorbell, the salesman momentarily has your attention, but unless he acts immediately you are likely to dismiss him. From the outset his problem is to hold your attention and direct interest toward his product. Somehow he must persuade you to unhook the screen door and to invite him inside to present his canvass. To achieve this objective, the successful canvasser knows how to play upon the factors of attention and interest and how to appeal to your wants. The magazine salesman, to surmount initial obstacles, works on your sympathy by posing as the struggling college student who is attempting to earn his way through college. The Fuller Brush man, if permitted

THE INTRODUCTION

to enter, promises you a free vegetable brush. The encyclopedia salesman flatters you by suggesting that you are one of a select group for a special introductory offer. The insurance man volunteers to advise you without cost or obligation on how to reinvest your money. Each has his way, sometimes not too commendable, of opening the door.

A speaker in his opening sentences must also be adept at *"opening the door."* As we have said earlier, few audiences are inactive, at least when you arise to speak. For a moment they will attend, but the problem is to hold their attention and direct their interest toward your subject. If you are to be successful, you must understand the psychology of attention and motivation.

In securing an attentive hearing you may wish to employ one or more of the following nine methods:

1. Use an animated delivery.
2. Relate the subject to the vital interest of the auditors.
3. Stir curiosity.
4. Make use of humor.
5. Establish a common ground of understanding.
6. Strive to be different.
7. Keep within the framework of the familiar.
8. Hurl a challenge.
9. Be specific.

Use an Animated Delivery

One of the first ways of making an audience want to hear you is to approach your subject with zest and enthusiasm. You need to give your listeners the impression that you sincerely believe what you say and that you believe it to be important for them to listen and accept your ideas.

Animation seems easier to achieve if you possess some or all of the following:

1. An intense belief in your subject
2. Confidence in your ability to present your subject
3. An eagerness to address the particular audience

4. Knowledge of opening sentences (memorize them)
5. A fervent desire to aid the auditors
6. Abundant information on the subject

In addition to your mental attitude, you will give the audience many important cues by your platform behavior: how you sit, how you await your turn to speak, how you respond to the remarks of preceding speakers, and how you approach the platform. In your approach, the following suggestions may help in giving the impression of animation.

1. Listen carefully and intently to what the preceding speakers say.
2. Walk to the platform with restrained vigor.
3. Stand erect and alert.
4. Pause until the listeners are quiet, giving the impression of poise and confidence.
5. Look directly at the auditors.
6. Give the impression that what is to follow will be worthy of attention.

Relate the Subject to the Vital Interests of the Auditors

Ordinarily, when you arise to speak, the listener has foremost in his mind such questions as the following: "Why should I listen to this person?" "What has this speaker to say that is important to me?" "Will he say anything worth while?" It is to your advantage to satisfy these queries as soon as possible by suggesting how your subject is related to your auditor's welfare and self-interest, those vital wants which are powerful incentives. Further it will be to your advantage to make additional application of the principles of motivation discussed in Chapter III. Directly or indirectly, you may weave into your remarks a theme like one of the following:

PROJECTED PICTURES MAY MAKE YOUR TALK MORE EFFECTIVE

Audience viewing projection. (Photo, Esso Standard Oil, Baton Rouge Refinery.) Picture of projection equipment. (Photo, L.S.U. Alumni News.)

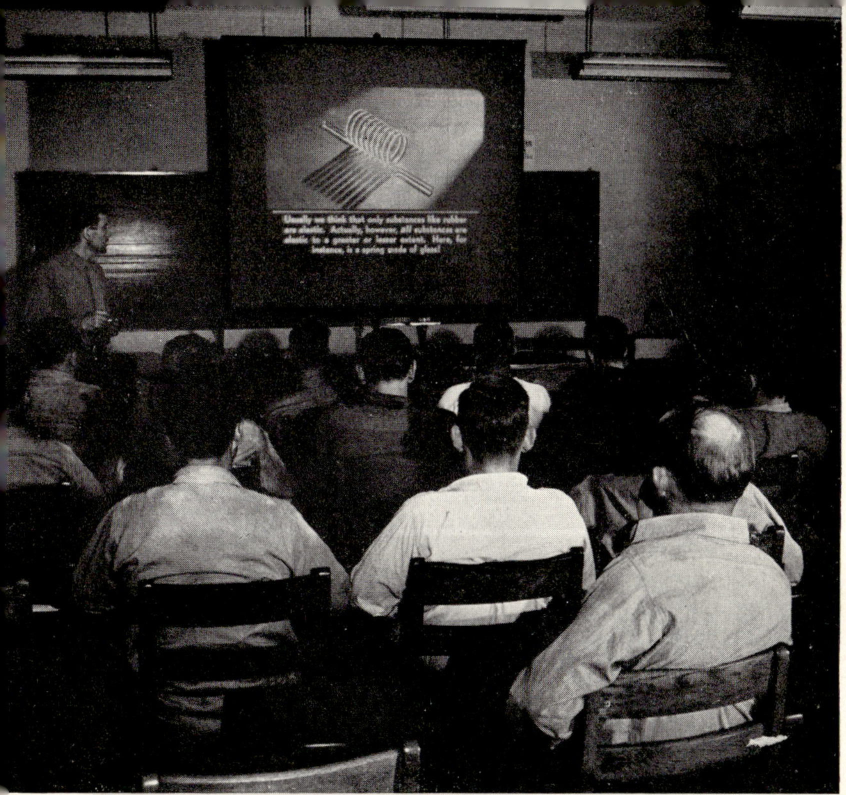

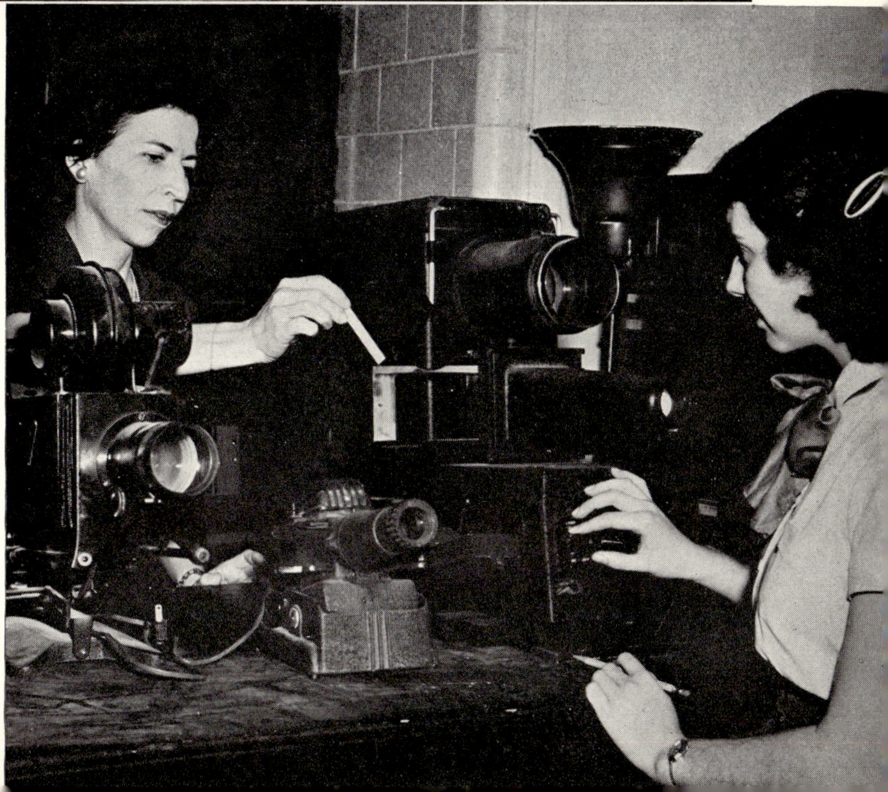

MASSACHUSETTS INSTITUTE OF TECHNOLOG
56
57
58
59
60
61

Have You Seen These?
Louisiana Corn
Louisiana Cotton
COTTON APHID
Louisiana 4H Poultry Manual
Sewing Can Be Fun
Jellies Jams Preserves
MARMALADES
JELLY
PRESERVES
JAMS
4-H DAIRY CALF CLUB MANUAL

THE INTRODUCTION

1. Your life or your property is in danger.
2. The safety of your loved ones may be involved.
3. Your material prosperity is dependent upon my subject.
4. This scheme will save you work and worry.
5. My plan will make you money.
6. Following my advice will make you famous.
7. The God-fearing man believes in this cause.
8. By this means you can be important and respected.
9. Patriotism demands that you listen.

At the opening meeting of the Atomic Energy Commission of the United Nations, June 14, 1946, Bernard Baruch demonstrated how to make use of the vital in an introduction. He said:

My Fellow Members of the United Nations Atomic Energy Commission, and My Fellow Citizens of the World: We are here to make a choice between the quick and the dead. That is our business.

Behind the black portent of the new atomic age lies a hope which, seized upon with faith, can work our salvation. If we fail, then we have damned every man to be the slave of fear. Let us not deceive ourselves: We must elect world peace or world destruction.[2]

No doubt these sober words made Mr. Baruch's listeners attentive. "To make a choice between the quick and the dead" is too

---

[2] Bernard M. Baruch, "International Control of Atomic Energy," *Representative American Speeches: 1945-1946*, A. Craig Baird (ed.), The H. W. Wilson Company, 1946, pp. 120-131. Quoted by special permission.

PICTORIAL AIDS

1. In the first picture Winston Churchill is addressing the Mid-Century convocation of the Massachusetts Institute of Technology. The huge picture in the background aids the speaker in making the occasion more impressive. It sets the mood and focuses attention on the platform. (Photo, Black Star.)

2. Pictorial aids planned for displays may not be suitable for visual supporting material. The chart that the young lady is holding is an excellent one for display; it is a poor poster for a speech because the pictures are too small, the printing is too small, and there is probably too much detail. (Photo, L.S.U. Alumni News.)

serious to be ignored; everyone is interested in any scheme that "can work our salvation"; no one wants to be "the slave of fear."

Stir Curiosity

Earlier we pointed out that persons like the unpredictable, the puzzling, the mysterious. Remembering the exploratory tendencies of the human being, his eagerness to participate in the chase, publishers sell magazines by running continued stories; movie serials, no matter how crudely produced, draw thousands to the theaters; and the soap opera keeps millions of American women close by their radios. This inquisitiveness which always seeks to learn "what happened next" can be put to good use in your introduction. If you can keep your audience "guessing," if you can provoke and encourage them to speculate as to what is going to "happen next," you are assured of continued attention and directed interest.

Methods of arousing the curiosity are so numerous that the following list can be only suggestive:

1. The speech may be given a unique title.
2. The speaker may create doubts as to his real position.
3. An exciting story may be told.
4. A dramatic question or series of questions may be asked.
5. The speaker may give the impression by his manner that he is going to reveal a secret or confidential matter.

Bruce Barton employed curiosity in his speech by saying: "My Friends: My subject today is 'How Long Should a Wife Live?'"[3] The title was unique—it stirred his listeners.

Make Use of Humor

Few persons can resist listening to a witty story or to a clever turn of language. Therefore on many occasions a humorous illustration or anecdote makes an excellent introduction. To be able to tell a witty story puts a speaker in a favorable light, breaks

[3] Bruce Barton, "How Long Should a Wife Live?" *Contemporary Speeches*, J. M. O'Neill and Floyd K. Riley (eds.), The Century Co., 1930, pp. 255-257. Quoted by special permission of Bruce Barton and the publishers.

down resistance, elicits initially a favorable group response, and creates an air of expectancy. Overstreet says about humor:

> Humor should be an attitude—of playfulness, of not too great seriousness; the sudden twist of a word, the flash of a grotesque idea. Humor is invaluable to the speaker because (1) it enlists the audience. It gives them a feeling of good fellowship with the speaker. Hence it breaks down the "wall." (2) It gives to the audience exhilarating bodily reactions. It stimulates the nerves and circulatory system; it raises the emotional tone of the audience. Hence it makes them better listeners. A laugh is the best sleep dispeller. (3) It keeps the sense of proportion, both in speaker and audience.[4]

Among amateurs the impression exists that humor is so important that relevancy or length of the story has little bearing on the situation. Anything for a laugh is their motto. These persons may hold attention momentarily, but they fail to direct interest toward the key idea of the speech. As a result, when the laugh is over, the audience is no nearer the main consideration than before. An irrelevant story may give the listeners a false cue and thus direct their attention elsewhere. The speaker will do well to make his humor grow out of the situation at hand and to point it toward the main idea of the speech.

Henry W. Grady made effective use of humor in his introduction to his famous address "The New South." He said in part:

> I bespeak the utmost stretch of your courtesy to-night. I am not troubled about those from whom I come. You remember the man whose wife sent him to a neighbor with a pitcher of milk, and who, tripping on the top step, fell, with such casual interruptions as the landing afforded, into the basement; and while picking himself up had the pleasure of hearing his wife call out: "John, did you break the pitcher?" "No, I didn't," said John, "but I be dinged if I don't!" [Laughter.]
>
> So, while those who call to me from behind may inspire me with energy if not with courage, I ask an indulgent hearing from you. I beg that you will bring your full faith in American fairness and frankness to judgment upon what I shall say. There was an old preacher once who told some boys of the Bible lesson he was going

---

[4] H. A. Overstreet, *Influencing Human Behavior*, W. W. Norton & Company, 1925, p. 78. Quoted by special permission.

to read in the morning. The boys finding the place, glued together the connecting pages. [Laughter.] The next morning he read on the bottom of one page: "When Noah was one hundred and twenty years old he took unto himself a wife, who was"—then turning the page—"one hundred and forty cubits long [laughter], forty cubits wide, built of gopher-wood [laughter], and covered with pitch inside and out." [Loud and continued laughter.] He was naturally puzzled at this. He read it again, verified it, and then said: "My friends, this is the first time I ever met this in the Bible, but I accept it as evidence of the assertion that we are fearfully and wonderfully made." [Laughter.] If I could get you to hold such faith to-night I could proceed cheerfully to the task I otherwise approach with a sense of consecration.[5]

Establish a Common Ground of Understanding

Finding a common ground of understanding implies the discovery of those areas and activities about which there is no disagreement. Although "Yankees" and "Southerners" may quarrel vigorously over states' rights, they can always find a common ground in their love for the United States. You may disapprove of a man's religion but admire his golf game tremendously. A Democrat will take criticism from a fellow Democrat that he would bitterly resent from a Republican. To remind your listeners of the common grounds that exist between you and them is an excellent way to open a speech.

Elmer E. Ferris, a professor of salesmanship, demonstrated this method when he talked to the New York Advertising Club. Quite frankly he mentioned the common ground he had with his hearers.

Gentlemen of the Advertising Club: It is a pleasure to speak before you tonight because you and I stand on common ground. Sales is the essence of advertising. The gist of salesmanship is getting the other person to take your point of view and act accordingly. That is also the gist of what the advertising man is trying to do. Furthermore, this matter of judging and handling men, which lies at the heart of personal

[5] Henry W. Grady, "The New South," *Classified Speech Models*, William Norwood Brigance (ed.), F. S. Crofts & Co., 1928, pp. 287-297.

contacts, is just as essential a part of advertising skill as of sales ability, and so right at the outset of this talk I can confidently claim your interest because the subject itself ought to hold you.[6]

The means of establishing a common ground of understanding are numerous. Below are given a few suggested sources that you may uilize:

1. Stress the groups, organizations, and institutions in which you and your auditors may both hold membership in common: church, lodge, fraternity, college, service club, business organization. Rotarians like to meet and to hear fellow Rotarians; a Harvard man holds strong ties with other Harvard graduates; a South Carolinian feels a kinship to another South Carolinian.

2. Stress experiences that you have had in common with the audience. Even stronger are those ties that have been formed by common experience, particularly if the events have been dramatic or intense. With an audience of ex-G.I.'s, you can improve your position if you let it be known that you too have served on KP, walked guard, "sweated out" a furlough, and stood in line for "chow." Herein lies a partial explanation for the recent Broadway hit, *Mr. Roberts*. Many who saw the play had recently encountered experiences similar to those of Mr. Roberts; they too had experienced an urge to throw the Captain's palm tree overboard. Student audiences respond more readily if the speaker (especially if he is of an older generation) recalls his own student days and reveals that he too dreaded final exams, disliked class routine, and had an unreasonable professor.

3. Stress attitudes, beliefs, and biases that you hold with the auditors. To learn that the speaker believes as you do ordinarily means that you become more interested in his remarks.

The southern politician knows that in many southern towns adherence to the tenets of white supremacy is a sure way to gather a following. It is equally true that an expression of distrust of Japanese or Mexicans may win an audience in other sections.

[6] Elmer E. Ferris, "The Art of Personal Contact," *Modern Speeches*, compiled by Homer D. Lindgren, F. S. Crofts & Co., 1926, pp. 434-441. Quoted by special permission.

Too often the unscrupulous resort to such sordid biases. However, beliefs of a higher order are equally effective and decidedly more ethical: admiration of cherished heroes, reverence for historical events, love of country, respect for our democratic way of life.

4. Stress common goals and objectives that you and the audience have. In this respect you minimize differences that may arise over method by showing your listeners you are in agreement as to the end desired. Frequently a Republican remembers this method when the majority of his listeners are Democrats. During the war President Roosevelt attempted to play down political differences and sought to emphasize instead the goal of winning the war.

Strive to Be Different

An audience welcomes a change from the usual and commonplace. The speaker who can introduce the same old subject in a novel way is assured of continued attention from the first. David Lilienthal, no doubt, held the attention of an audience of editors when in his opening moments he exhibited a cylinder of pure uranium, saying,

This black object that I hold in my hand is a cylinder of pure uranium. The amount I hold here is small as you can see. It is harmless. Five years ago no man had even seen even this much pure uranium. Not that it was rare, but it was simply of little importance. Tonight this black metal, this inanimate substance is the central figure in the councils of the peoples of the world.

Why this should be so is not difficult to understand. Look at this small cylinder for a moment. It weighs about 2½ pounds. That much coal or oil, burned under the boilers of industry, would provide a trifling amount of useful energy. Compare the technical opportunities of the controlled release of nuclear forces. The energy resulting from the fission of the 3 million billion billion atoms in this small cylinder, converted into electricity, would equal about the total daily use of electricity in the city of Washington, which now requires about 2600 tons of coal.[7]

[7] David E. Lilienthal, "Atomic Energy," *Representative American Speeches: 1946-1947*, pp. 134-143. Quoted by special permission.

Roe Fulkerson employed novelty in the following introduction: "Dearly Beloved: The sermon today will be on the topic of dollar chasing. The text is taken from the first verse of the first chapter of the Gospel of Common Sense, which reads as follows: 'What does it profit a man if he gain the whole world and leave a rich widow?' "[8]

Says Overstreet, "The wise proponent of a new idea will make sure that the new is sufficiently tied to the old to be at least interesting as well as acceptable."[9] As long as the new remains within the framework of what is considered decent and normal, the novelty will not shock or embarrass. But if the auditors draw the conclusion that the speaker is peculiar, that he is ridiculous, or that he exercises poor judgment, then the speaker has stepped outside what is considered the familiar.

Keep Within the Framework of the Familiar

Of equal value in an introduction is the familiar as a means of deriving interest and attention. Many times we enjoy hearing an old story retold; we like to meet old friends; we treasure our memories; we appreciate the speaker who conforms to our ideas of proper behavior. The Fourth of July orator, for example, mentions in opening those revered events held in pleasant memory by those present. Two cautions are in order. First, the familiar must not be confused with the commonplace or the trite. You will do well to avoid stereotyped introductions which open with sentences like the following:

1. "Unaccustomed as I am to public speaking. . . ."
2. "It is a great pleasure to be here."
3. "I have a few remarks which I want to make."
4. "I am sure that someone else is more capable of saying this, but I. . . ."

Second, a nice balance must be maintained between the novel and the familiar. Eisenson explains, "We generally . . . strive for

[8] Roe Fulkerson, "Dollar Chasing," *Modern Speeches*, pp. 359-366.
[9] Overstreet, *op. cit.*, p. 24.

a state of equilibrium, one between the two extremes in which neither too little of the novel, or too much of the familiar is present."[10]

Hurl a Challenge

In planning your opening remarks, remember that almost everyone enjoys a good fight as is evidenced by attendance at football games, horse races, boxing matches, or a common fist fight. If you as the speaker enlist your listeners on your side against a common foe or if you put up a good fight against a real or even an imaginary enemy, you are assured of continued attention.

President Harry Truman used the challenge approach in his radio address of May 24, 1946. In the face of a railroad strike the President opened with these sentences:

> My Fellow Countrymen, I come before the American people tonight at a time of great crisis. The crisis of Pearl Harbor was the result of action by a foreign enemy. The crisis tonight is caused by a group of men within our own country who place their private interests above the welfare of the nation.
>
> As Americans you have the right to look to the President for leadership in this grave emergency. I have accepted the responsibility, as I have accepted it in other emergencies.
>
> Every citizen of this country has the right to know what has brought about this crisis. It is my desire to report to you what has already taken place and the action that I intend to take.[11]

Occasionally inattention may demand a bolder approach, that is, a direct challenge to the audience to listen. Under these circumstances the speaker may question a favorite belief, a sacred custom, or a cherished tradition. Josh Lee relates how an evangelist used this method: "He walked directly to the front of the platform while his eyes searched the audience. He stood for a

---

[10] Jon Eisenson, *The Psychology of Speech*, F. S. Crofts & Co., 1938, pp. 233-240.

[11] Harry Truman, "The Railroad Strike Emergency," *Representative American Speeches: 1945-1946*, pp. 197-201.

moment and then announced his text in a low-pitched voice, vibrant with meaning—'The fool hath said in his heart, there is no God.' "[12]

The more dramatic and sensational the method, the more adroit the speaker must be to avoid stirring up antagonisms which cannot be overcome later. Says Overstreet, "Challenge, therefore, must be fair. It must show good sportsmanship. It must give even the opponent his due. But above all, it is most powerful when it enlists others in the fight. Not 'Come, see me wipe up the earth with this false prophet,' but rather, 'Come, let's join in the fight.' "[13]

Be Specific

In the chapters on language we discuss at length how abstract words, indefinite references, and trite phraseology will kill interest and attention. Trite supporting material has the same effect. Inclusion of names, dates, places, lends reality to an opening. Material taken from the lives of the persons addressed is familiar but also specific. In addition, putting an introduction into the first or second person likewise contributes to directness.

SECURING A FRIENDLY HEARING

Seemingly we listen more attentively to those whom we like or admire than to those whom we distrust or dislike. Early in the speech you need to work your way into the good graces of your hearers, and you need to establish your right to speak on the subject.

Cicero explains that this process involves the speaker's personality, the personalities of the judges, and those of his opponents:

. . . the first steps to secure good will are achieved by extolling our own merits or worth or virtue of some kind, particularly generosity,

---

[12] Josh Lee, *How to Hold an Audience Without a Rope*, Ziff-Davis Publishing Company, 1947, p. 121. Quoted by special permission of Prentice-Hall, Inc.

[13] Overstreet, *op. cit.*, p. 23. Quoted by special permission.

sense of duty, justice and good faith, and by assigning the opposite qualities to our opponents, and by indicating some reason for or expectation of agreement with the persons deciding the case; and by removing or diminishing any odium or the popularity that has been directed against ourselves either by doing away with it or diminishing it or by diluting it or by weakening it, or by selling something against it or by making an apology.[14]

In obtaining a friendly hearing you should consider at least three factors: reputation, appearance, and ethical proof during the speech.

Reputation

Reputation, or "the antecedent impression," embraces what the listeners know about the speaker's past. If at the outset you are held in high regard, you do not need to establish your right to speak on the given subject. The President of the United States receives close attention whenever he makes an official pronouncement because of the dignity and importance of his office; consequently he is assured of a friendly hearing. But when he speaks as a party leader, the same does not hold; his partisanship is challenged, and some may even accuse him of taking unfair advantage of his official position. In this instance he must win a friendly hearing before he can be effective.

In a speech to the Harvard Business School Club of New York, Otto H. Kahn, well-known financier, had the following to say about reputation: "Remember that the most serviceable of all assets is reputation. When you once have it, and as long as you hold it, it works for you automatically, and it works twenty-four hours a day. Unlike money, reputation cannot be bequeathed. It is always personal. It must be acquired. Brains alone, however brilliant, cannot win it. The most indispensable requisite is character."[15]

---

[14] *De Partitione Oratoria*, VIII:28, found in Cicero, *De Oratore*, Harvard University Press, 1948, vol. 2, p. 333. Quoted by special permission.

[15] Otto H. Kahn, "A Talk to Young Business Men," delivered Nov. 13, 1924, *Modern Eloquence*, 1936 ed., vol. 5, pp. 55-61.

The skillful speaker must know when to rely upon reputation and when to pack into the opening sentences some efforts to establish his right to speak on the subject.

Appearance

"Actions speak louder than words," advises the authority on good manners. "Pretty is as pretty does," says the anxious mother to her bobby-sox daughter. "Clothes make the man," insists the clothing salesman. These clichés, overworked and oversimplified as they are, do reflect the importance our society places on appearance. Consciously and unconsciously the speaker's appearance and his platform deportment have a marked influence upon us. If we like what we see, we are more likely to give continued attention, to show greater interest, and to believe what we hear. If we dislike or question what we see, we reserve judgment and become more difficult to persuade.

In the opening moments of the speech, the audience forms many lasting opinions of the speaker, based upon his physique, his clothing, and his manner. A friendly countenance and genuineness in manner arouse enthusiasm; austerity and grimness inspire frigidity. Will Rogers, the humorist, won his way into the hearts of millions of Americans by his simple and unaffected manner. The smile and friendliness of Franklin Roosevelt were significant factors in his great popularity. Abraham Lincoln realized the value of being a humble man. In each case, these men won friendly hearings.

The bodily build of a speaker may even influence the auditors. Large men are often regarded as more commanding in their appearance than men of slight build. Nevertheless, the large man must not attempt to hide his size by slouchiness. It likewise behooves the smaller person to take special precautions to appear dignified and impressive.

Even in the twentieth century, there lingers occasional prejudice against women on the platform. Such attitudes are carry-overs from the past, when some felt that the woman's only place was in the home. Some regard the woman's voice as not forceful enough for public speaking. Of course, such women as Eleanor Roosevelt, Clare Boothe Luce, Helen Gahagan Douglas, and Dorothy Thompson provided proof that such attitudes are unfounded. Nevertheless, a woman speaker needs to take cognizance of such attitudes when she decides to speak.

The speaker's attire must be appropriate for the occasion. To be accused of being overdressed or of being slovenly is damaging to your cause. A dress suit may be a "must" for some banquets, but at other times it is inappropriate. A cigarette holder, pince-nez, or even a loud tie can give a wrong impression. Flashy clothes or overdressing may be a factor in creating an unfriendly hearing. The woman who dares to speak in a startling hat, trimmed with a dangling flower or a waving feather, may direct attention to her hat at the expense of her speech.

A good rule concerning appearance is: *the speaker should strive to be what his auditors expect him to be*; he should mirror what they consider acceptable appearance.

Ethical Proof

The third factor in obtaining a friendly hearing in the introduction has been called ethical proof or *ethos*. It may be defined as the speaker's attempt during his speech to "give the right impression of himself" and by his appearance and manner to give evidence of his own merits, worth, and virtues. Certainly by such efforts the speaker should avoid giving an impression of cockiness or oversureness, but he should establish that he has a right to speak on the subject, that he is interested in the welfare of his listeners, and that he is a person to be trusted. As Aristotle puts it, he must present himself as a man of (1) good character, (2) good will, and (3) intelligence.[16]

Good character. The "good man" is persuasive because his listeners accept what he says without question and because his

---

[16] Lane Cooper, *The Rhetoric of Aristotle*, Appleton-Century-Crofts, Inc., 1932, pp. 90-92.

authority is so impelling that other persuasive devices are unnecessary. Aristotle explains, ". . . we trust men of probity more, and more quickly about things in general, while on points outside the realm of exact knowledge where opinion is divided we trust them absolutely."[17] The speaker who gives the impression of having good character must demonstrate that he possesses some of the virtues: justice, courage, temperance, magnificence, magnanimity, liberality, gentleness, prudence, and wisdom.[18]

Good will and friendly disposition involve the speaker's attitude toward the auditor. Does the speaker have the interests of his auditors at heart? Lincoln once said, "If you would win a man to your cause, first convince him that you are his sincere friend. Therein is a drop of honey that catches his heart, which, say what he will, is the great highroad to his reason, and which when once gained, you will find but little trouble in convincing his judgment of the justice of your cause if indeed that cause really be a just one."[19]

Herein the "high-pressure salesman" or the spellbinder fails, for somehow, in his eagerness to sell his product, he unconsciously gives the impression that he is more interested in making the sale for selfish reasons than for the benefit of the customer. Consequently, the client immediately reacts negatively.

Intelligence. The third aspect of *ethos* is intelligence. Early in the speech, you must establish (1) that you are well informed on the immediate subject, (2) that your experiences qualify you to speak, and (3) that in general you possess sound judgment. A speaker may be sincere and virtuous, but if the audience is in doubt concerning the speaker's information, his cause is lost.

In the opening of a Senate speech in support of the nomination of David Lilienthal, April 3, 1947, Senator Arthur Vandenberg

---

[17] *Ibid.*, p. 8.
[18] *Ibid.*, pp. 46-55.
[19] From address before Springfield Washingtonian Temperance Society, February 22, 1842, found in *Complete Works of Abraham Lincoln*, John G. Nicolay and John Hay (eds.), Lincoln Memorial University, 1894, vol. I, pp. 193-209.

took a direct approach to establish his "intelligence" on his subject. He said: "Mr. President, I have been a member of the Senate Atomic Energy Committee which sat as a jury in the Lilienthal case from January 27 to March 4. I have heard or read every word of the testimony. As a result, I have been driven away from the adverse prejudice with which I started. I have been driven to the belief that logic, fair play, and a just regard to urgent public welfare combine to recommend Mr. Lilienthal's confirmation in the light of today's realities."[20] Vandenberg stresses that he is in possession of the facts about Lilienthal and that these facts had served as the basis of his decision. He wants the audience to know that he is a man of intelligence.

SECURING AN INTELLIGENT HEARING

The third objective of the introduction is to clarify the subject sufficiently to secure an intelligent hearing for the remainder of the speech. The audience must understand what the subject is, what it means, and what the speaker proposes to do with it.

The subject may be clarified by such means as follow:

1. State the nature of the subject to be developed.
2. Reveal the thesis or the proposition.
3. Give the cause for discussion: Why is the topic timely?
4. Define unfamiliar terms.
5. Give the history of the case (narration).
6. Summarize the plan of development (division).

Not all these means are applicable to every speech; the nature of the occasion and the audience will determine whether any or all are necessary.

ADAPTING THE INTRODUCTION TO THE SPEAKING SITUATION

We have stressed constantly in this book that above all else the *audience must remain paramount in your thinking.* At each step

[20] Arthur H. Vandenberg, "For the Appointment of Lilienthal," in *Representative American Speeches: 1946-1947,* pp. 123-133. Quoted by special permission.

in your preparation, you must reevaluate the question: *What means and methods will produce the greatest audience response?* The preparation of the introduction, of course, is no exception. Your opening remarks must grow out of the demands of the speaking situation. In planning your opening strategy, put these questions to yourself:

1. Do I need to strive for interest and attention, or will the audience naturally be curious as to what I shall say?
2. Is it necessary to sell myself to the audience? What do they know about me? Is it favorable or unfavorable?
3. Does the subject need clarification? Is there confusion about the terms?
4. Should the foregoing three elements have equal stress?

Once you have determined where you need to concentrate your fire—on interest and attention, yourself, or your subject, or all three—then you must decide on the kind and amount of ammunition needed. *The best introductions are developed out of the speaking situation:* they involve the speaker or his experience, the audience and its interests, implications of time and place of the speech, the nature of the subject. In other words, the speaker in some way should make reference to the speaker, the audience, the occasion, or the subject.

The following outline is suggestive of some of the possibilities open to the speaker:

1. *Reference to the speaker:*
   a. Relate a personal experience that qualifies you to speak on the subject.
   b. Relate a personal experience that you have had in common with the listeners.
   c. Tell a joke on yourself.
   d. Mention your interest in and an analysis of the subject.
   e. Explain or allude to your desire to help the audience.
   f. Indirectly stress your good character.
   g. Give the impression that the chairman has flattered you.
2. *Reference to the audience:*
   a. Connect the subject with the vital interests of the audience.
   b. Allude to a common experience or goal that you share with the audience.

    c. Praise the accomplishment or aspirations of the group.
    d. Eulogize a hero of the group or a respected member, such as the president.
    e. Hurl a challenge.
    f. Relate the subject to a hero or patriot.
    g. Ask the audience a series of personal or challenging questions.
3. *Reference to the occasion:*
    a. Relate the subject or yourself to a revered day or event (a great battle, a holiday, or historic moment.)
    b. Show why the occasion is important.
    c. Mention in connection with the subject a current event foremost in the minds of the listeners.
    d. Eulogize the history of the group.
    e. Recall other speakers that have spoken in the given meeting place.
    f. Contrast or compare your own views with those of a previous speaker.
    g. Tell a joke on the chairman or a previous speaker.
4. *Reference to the subject:*
    a. Ask a series of questions which lead listeners to think about the subject.
    b. Give a startling statement which focuses attention on the meaning of the subject.
    c. Relate an anecdote or story containing central point of speech.
    d. Plunge into development of significant point.

EXERCISES

1. Study carefully the following introductions. Be prepared to discuss how you would improve each one of these.

Seven with One Blow

"Seven with one blow." Does that phrase seem familiar to you? Think hard. It was the personal motto of the valiant little tailor in Grimm's fairy tale of the same name. Surely you remember having read or heard the story of the little tailor who, after killing seven flies with one blow in his shop one day, becomes convinced that he has a bigger and better destiny than that of a common little tailor. Remember, he makes himself a girdle upon which he stitches the words, "Seven with one blow," and sets out to make his fortune.

Of course he finds that the road to fame and fortune is not an easy one but is filled with pitfalls and obstacles that would discourage an ordinary man. But then he is no ordinary man. He has killed "seven with one blow." Armed with this knowledge and the self-confidence which it gives him, everything blocking his way is only trivial; everything is swept aside with ease as he continues his upward climb toward his goal, until he becomes king of the land.

When you leave Smithfield, will you too be armed with the self-confidence the little tailor had; will you too be able to sweep aside the obstacles blocking the pathway to your goal in life? Will you too have mastered "Seven with one blow?" The chance is being given you; are you taking it?

The instruction here in the speech department is divided into seven phases: drama, interpretation, rhetoric and oratory, speech correction, phonetics, voice science and speech psychology, and radio. With a basic knowledge of each, you can face the world with the self-confidence of the little tailor in your ability in the field of speech. The seven are here; can you make it with one blow?

Crime

We cannot pick up a newspaper or magazine without reading of some crime—whether it be murder or robbery or rape or the kidnapping of some small child. The United States is faced today with a situation which in my opinion is almost as big as any problem that confronts us in the foreign-affairs department, and you are all aware of the problems we have with other countries. That problem is the increasing amount of crime in the United States as a whole, and especially in the larger cities.

In a recent article which appeared in *Collier's* magazine, the criminal situation as it exists in the city of Philadelphia was presented. During the year 1948 the number of serious crimes in the city increased seventeen percent, and during the first half of 1949 there was an increase of sixteen percent over 1948. The cause of these increases in the number of crimes in the city of brotherly love is due, according to the editor of Collier's, to the intermingling of politics and police protection. I agree that where there is an inadequate system of police protection there will be more crime, because hoodlums will flock to those areas in which they will be reasonably safe from the law. However, lack of police protection is not the problem which I wish to discuss, because this is only a method of catching and punishing those criminals who have already completed their work.

The problem that I should like to discuss at this time involves a few of the probable causes of crime. In the short time I have at my disposal, I can hardly hope to cover all the probable causes of crime. Therefore, I should like to discuss those which are most interesting to me.

2. *Written Assignment.* Rewrite one of the foregoing introductions making it into what you would consider an effective introduction.
3. *Research Assignment.* Select a speech which you heard recently, and prepare a report on how the speaker gained (a) an attentive hearing, (b) a friendly hearing, and (c) an intelligent hearing.

SUPPLEMENTARY READINGS

1. Brigance, William Norwood, *Speech Composition*, F. S. Crofts & Co., 1937, pp. 66-85.
2. Bryant, Donald C., and Wallace, Karl R., *Fundamentals of Public Speaking*, Appleton-Century-Crofts, Inc., 1947, chap. 11.
3. Miller, Edd, "Speech Introductions and Conclusions," *The Quarterly Journal of Speech*, April, 1946, pp. 181-183.
4. Monroe, Alan H., *Principles and Types of Speech*, Scott, Foresman & Company, 3rd ed., 1949, pp. 285-295.
5. Sarett, Lew, and Foster, William Trufant, *Basic Principles of Speech*, Houghton Mifflin Company, rev. ed., 1948, chap. 16.

CHAPTER XIV

The Discussion

THE discussion proper is sometimes referred to by such names as the body, the development, the proof, and the argument. In other words, it contains what Aristotle called "indispensable constituents": "the statement of the case" and "the ensuing argument." The putting of these together into an effective whole involves the following:

1. The presentation of the proposition or central thought and the supporting points
2. The ordering of the supporting points
3. The internal organization and development of each point
4. The number and interrelationship of the supporting points to each other
5. The use of oral devices to ensure clearness and coherence

Before starting our consideration of these factors, let us stress again an important observation: *a speech is not an essay.* The well-developed written paragraph may be extremely ineffective when presented orally. Written material may often be subtle, precise, or terse. Sentences may be long, complex, and balanced in structure. The writer may attempt at times to pack into his composition implications evident only to the thoughtful and careful reader.

In direct contrast, the oral paragraph must be so constructed and so presented that the meaning is evident the instant it is heard. Sentences may be loose, and thought breaks must be included frequently. It may be necessary to express a thought in several different ways in order to ensure clearness. Important ideas must be labeled and stressed; frequently summaries must be included, and the overall organization must be made to stand out in order that the listener will know where he is at all times.

Let us contrast for a moment the reader and the listener. The reader has the option of pausing, adjusting his reading rate to the difficulty of the material, looking up troublesome words, and reading a passage until he is satisfied that he has squeezed out the last bit of meaning.

The listener is limited by what he can hear and understand at the moment of utterance. His comprehension rate must be at least equal to the speaking rate, which is usually between one and two hundred words per minute. What are his options when he encounters difficult material? Seldom does he have the opportunity to ask the speaker to talk at a slower rate, to pause, to repeat a word or phrase, or to elucidate. If the listener pauses to reflect, to attempt to figure out what has been said, he stands a real chance of losing the thread of the speaker's thought. Therefore he has only the alternative of skipping over words, phrases, or ideas which are meaningless at the moment, with the hope that information forthcoming will clarify these gaps. Naturally, too many such lapses in understanding doom the speech to certain failure.

In planning a speech, therefore, strive to meet the following requirements:

THE DISCUSSION

1. Attempt to make what you say *immediately intelligible* and *obviously pertinent* and *compelling*.
2. Give the listeners as many clues as possible to the structure of your speech and to what is important.
3. Plan your development in such a way that the confused listener will have frequent opportunities to catch up with the thought development.
4. Adjust your rate of utterance to the listeners' rate of comprehension.

LOCATION OF THE CENTRAL THOUGHT OR PROPOSITION IN THE SPEECH

The overall organization of the discussion proper is largely determined by how and where in the speech the speaker presents the central thought or proposition. Shall he include it near the opening of his speech? Or shall he wait until later for the presentation? The answers to these questions may suggest the basic organization of the speech.

For the informative speech, the location of the central thought is determined on the basis of how much the audience knows about the subject. Since there is little to be gained by concealing the central thought, the speaker is wise to give it early in his development. As a general rule, the real advantage in this procedure is that the listener knows what to look for in the development. As a result, understanding is facilitated. Following these suggestions, the speech is developed as follows:

Introduction
1. Gain attention and arouse interest.
2. State and clarify the central thought.

Discussion
3. Development of central thought
   a. Point 1
   b. Point 2
   c. Point 3

Conclusion
4. Restatement of central thought and summary of points

In stimulating and persuasive speeches, locating the proposition is not so simple. In fact, according to his goal, his subject, and his audience, the speaker may present his thesis in any one of four ways:

Deductive Order

As in the case of the informative speech, the thesis may come early in the speech before any of the main points are presented. In this case, the development follows a deductive order as exemplified below:

Proposition: Baton Rouge offers many advantages to the business man, for
  1. The city is located in the heart of a rich agricultural area.
  2. The river provides cheap transportation.
  3. The state capitol attracts thousands of tourists.
  4. The many industries have large pay rolls.

The deductive arrangement offers both advantages and disadvantages. Its chief asset is that it is possible for the speaker to clarify his topic early, to keep constantly reminding his listeners of his proposition, and to stress the logical relationships that exist between the proposition and the supporting points and between the supporting points themselves.

The principal disadvantage arises if an audience contains many opponents. In this event, the announcement of the proposition may serve to crystallize the opposition before you have had an opportunity to present the speech.

Inductive Order

In the case suggested immediately above, that is, with the hostile audience, it may prove wise to reverse the order—to present the proposition after the main points. An inductive order gives the speaker the opportunity to move from the least controversial points in the direction of the points of greatest disagreement. In other words, you build a sound foundation before risking a direct statement of your proposition. A speech following the inductive order might appear as follows:

1. The Southern states devote a greater percentage of their income to education than do states in other areas.
2. The Southern states have the largest number of children to educate.
3. The Southern states have the least taxable wealth.
Therefore the Southern states should work for federal aid to education.

The inductive development may take a form similar to a special type of refutation called the method of *residues*, in which all possibilities are eliminated but the one which you support. In the 1948 presidential election, a Dixiecrat followed this line of argument:

1. Don't vote for Norman Thomas.
2. Don't vote for Thomas Dewey.
3. Don't vote for Harry Truman.
Vote for Thurmond and the Dixiecrats.

Proposition Between Two Points

At times there may be real advantage in delaying the presentation of the proposition until after one or more points at least have been developed. A strong point may do much to win a friendly hearing, to bolster up the wavering, or perhaps to quiet a militant minority.

This strategy, of course, is the one that guided Patrick Henry the day he thundered out his famous words, "Give me liberty or give me death," before the Virginia Convention. Because of lukewarm patriots and those who opposed direct action, Henry dared not open with his real sentiments on resistance. Therefore, he showed first that the colonists had failed in their peaceful efforts. "Sir, we have done everything that could be done, to avert the storm which is now coming on," he said. At the close of his first point, he dramatically shouted his thesis, "We must fight."

Then followed his second contention that the colonists should resist at once.

Presenting the Proposition by Implication

The speaking situation may demand that you approach the subject by indirection. One excellent method is to make the development so pointed that the audience frames the proposition without being told specifically what it is. This approach demands that the listener be kept active and alert. On the other hand, if he does put the pieces together correctly and does reach the intended conclusion, he may experience such self-satisfaction that he is more easily converted to your way of thinking.

Obviously the presentation of the proposition by implication requires careful planning, great skill, and forceful delivery. For the mature speaker, it may be highly effective, but for the novice it should be used sparingly.

ORDERING THE POINTS

A second phase of speech organization concerns the arranging of the supporting points. Maximum effectiveness demands that your scheme of arrangement meet the following tests:

1. Does it hold attention and interest?
2. Does it fit the peculiar requirements of the subject?
3. Is it designed to facilitate understanding and retention?
4. Does it keep the speech marching toward the speaker's goal?

The chapters on analysis present several patterns of partition which may be adapted to the speech development. Some of these are the following:

1. Chronological or time order.
2. An operational order.
3. A developmental or procedural order
4. Spatial or geographical order
5. Causal order
6. Problem-solution order

In each of these cases, the speech order may be predetermined by the pattern of analysis. If, for example, the analysis has followed a chronological development, then the points of the speech may also be arranged in the order of their occurrence, from past to future or the reverse. The problem-solution approach dictates consideration, first, of the difficulty and, second, of the remedy. So it is with the others; the scheme of analysis offers a plan for arranging the points of the speech.

However, in preparing a speech, it is not always possible or advisable to follow one of these standard patterns. In the first place, some of the schemes mentioned above may require adaptation to a specific speaking situation. Second, other bases of division like those given below may imply no inherent order:

1. According to parties involved
2. According to the fields of endeavor

In these cases, you may wish to let the interests, attitudes, and information of the listeners guide you in planning your speech order. In this event, you wish to consider the factors of

1. Importance
2. Interestingness
3. Complexity
4. Acceptability

Importance

Using the factor of importance the points are arranged in the order of their relative importance in the accomplishment of the speaker's goal; that is, with reference to their potency to satisfy the listeners. Points are arranged in the order from most important to least important or the reverse.

Interestingness

Using interestingness, proceed from the more interesting to the less interesting or vice versa. For this approach, the speaker arranges his presentation in the order which seemingly coincides with the factors of interest. Audience preferences become the determining factor.

Complexity

With complexity as the factor, proceed from the known to the unknown or from the simple to the intricate. For this approach the speaker starts with what the auditors understand or what seems simple and moves in the direction of what they do not know. The experience and knowledge of the listeners are the controlling elements.

Acceptability

When acceptability is the factor, proceed from the less controversial to the more controversial or vice versa. The speaker moves from areas of agreement and acceptance to those which are more controversial.

These approaches are not mutually exclusive; in fact, they overlap in many cases. What is most important may be most interesting and most acceptable. The complex is probably not interesting, but it may be very important. It behooves you to order your points in the scheme which will produce the best effect on your listeners.

FORMULA FOR PRESENTING A SINGLE POINT

The basic unit of the speech is the single point which sometimes is referred to as an argument, subdivision, or a cell. It should be carefully organized and developed. Here is a simple formula for its presentation:

1. State your point in a single sentence.
2. Give your supporting material.
3. Restate the point.

Let us translate this formula into other terms:

1. Tell them what you intend to say.
2. Tell them how, when, why, or where.
3. Tell them what to remember.

In the following example, Professor Edwin W. Kemmerer demonstrates this principle. Read this point with care and note how he follows the formula suggested above.

First, let us consider the college man's chances for success as compared with those of the non-college man. On this subject there have been a number of studies.

In 1893, Dr. Charles F. Thwing published the results of a study of this subject based upon the 15,142 names in Appleton's Encyclopedia of American Biography. Broadly speaking, his conclusion was, that one out of every 40 college graduates succeeded and one out of every 10,000 non-graduates. This gave a ratio of 250 to one in favor of the college man.

Of course this study refers to conditions as they existed some time ago. It may well be that the situation is different today. A larger percentage of the public receives a college education now than did a few generations ago and it is possible that this may be resulting in important changes in the quality of the graduates that the colleges are turning out. In 1880 there were 687 male college graduates for every 100,000 males in the country over twenty years of age. By 1920 this figure had risen to 1,137. Some light on the present situation is given by studies recently made on the basis of the 1928-29 and the 1934-35 editions of *Who's Who in America*. For both these years approximately three-fourths of all names mentioned were for college graduates and approximately 85 per cent for collegians, graduates and non-graduates. Persons whose education was limited to the common and elementary schools represented 6⅔ per cent of these names in the former edition and 7⅙ per cent in the latter. This is true despite the fact that the number of college graduates in the United States is a very small figure compared with the number of adults whose school education ended prior to the college grade. Furthermore, the figures show that from 1900 to 1934-35 the percentage of the names in *Who's Who in America* represented by collegians continually increased. At the present time, therefore, as in the past, the college man seems to have a very much better chance of succeeding than the non-college man.[1]

The example given above contains (1) a statement of the points to be developed, (2) two pieces of evidence to prove the point, and (3) a restatement of the point under consideration.

[1] Edwin W. Kemmerer, "Scholarship in College," *Vital Speeches*, July 15, 1937, pp. 602-604. Quoted by special permission.

NUMBER OF SUPPORTING POINTS

The number of supporting points that you decide to put into the discussion proper must be determined with reference to the complexity of the subject, the time available, and the type of listeners to be present. Opportunities for note taking as well as the possible handicaps inherent in the speaking situation should also be considered.

You may decide to give a single-point speech with a single illustration, similar to the parables in the Bible. Or you may partition your subject into several main points. Under all circumstances, keep the organization as simple as possible. The inclusion of more than four or five points probably will complicate your presentation considerably. Many speakers favor no more than two or three points.

If you find that you have too many points, you ordinarily can combine similar ones, subordinate minor points, and delete others. Or you may solve the problem by using some other basis of division.

PREVIEWS AND SIGNPOSTS

Early we stressed the importance of oral organization, which provides the listeners with many hints concerning the speech structure and the nature of the development. Previews and signposts serve this purpose and therefore improve a speech for oral presentation.

A *preview* is an enumeration of all the points early in the speech. In other words, the speaker says in effect to the listener, "Let me first list my points in order that you may know what to look for during my discussion."

Walter Lippmann gave the following preview of his speech, "Rise of Personal Government in the United States," in the opening two sentences: "My subject this evening is the rise of personal government in the United States. I shall attempt to define the magnitude of this phenomenon, to diagnose its causes, and to indicate the remedies."[2]

The signpost consists of labeling or numbering the points in order that they may be recognized. In other words, you may simply say, My first point is. . . . My second point is. . . . My third point is. . . .

As the name implies, a signpost in a speech, like a road marker, serves as a guide. It tells the listener where the speaker is and how far he has gone. If the listener's attention strays during the first point, at least you give him an opportunity to orient himself upon hearing the announcement of the second point. In his speech, "Which Knew Not Joseph," Bruce Barton introduces his main points in the following manner: "So the first very simple thing I would say . . . is. . . . Now the second very simple thing which I might say to you is. . . . The third very simple thing and last that I suggest is this. . . ."

In a commencement address Reverend Harry Emerson Fosdick found signposts equally valuable. He introduced his four points as follows: "In endeavoring to see the significance of this, consider first that here lies. . . . In the second place, consider that while. . . . In the third place, let us face the imminent impact. . . . Finally, then consider the responsibility which. . . ."[3]

Signposts need to be numerical in nature. The speaker may devise other means of calling attention to his main points. Thomas DeWitt Talmage devised a novel set in his lyceum lecture, *Big Blunders*.

> Blunder the first : Multiplicity of occupations . . .
> Blunder the next : Indulgence in bad temper . . .
> Blunder the next : Excessive amusement . . .

[2] Walter Lippmann, "The Rise of Personal Government in the United States," *Representative American Speeches: 1937-1938*, A. Craig Baird (ed.), The H. W. Wilson Company, 1938, pp. 122-137. Quoted by special permission.

[3] Harry Emerson Fosdick, "Being Civilized to Death," *Representative American Speeches: 1937-1938*, pp. 210-219.

Blunder the next : The formation of unwise domestic relations . . .

Blunder the next : Attempting life without a spirit of enthusiasm and enterprize.[4]

In each of the foregoing cases, the speaker also has relied upon another technique to make his main points obvious: he has worded the key sentences in parallel form.

If the speaker includes a preview, signposts, and a summary, he actually has stated each point four times. First, he previews the points he intends to develop; second, he states; third, he restates each point when it is developed; and fourth, he repeats his points again in the summary.

Addition	Contrast	Result	Alternation	Cause	Repetition or Exemplification
And	But	Therefore	Or	For	Namely
Further	However	Hence	Nor	Because	Indeed
Furthermore	Yet	Consequently	Otherwise	In as much as	In reality
Besides	And yet	Accordingly	Either		In fact
Also	Still	Thereupon	In other ways		In other words
Moreover	Nevertheless	Thus	Either . . or		In truth
Likewise	Notwithstanding	Thereafter	Both . . and		To be sure
Nor	Despite		Not only		That is to say
Too	On the contrary		In a different manner		
Again	On the other hand		On the other hand		
Finally	In spite of		On one hand		
And then			Contrarily		
Over and above			In other respects		
In addition					

TRANSITIONS

W. N. Brigance has aptly referred to connectives and transitional devices as "the glue that holds together all materials of a

[4] Thomas DeWitt Talmage, "Big Blunders." *Classified Models of Speech Composition,* James Milton O'Neill, The Century Co., 1921, pp. 828-844.

speech, large and small."[5] The coherence of your speech depends upon how successful you are in applying "glue" at the right places.

There are many transitional words and phrases that serve as a kind of "glue"; their function is to show the interrelationship between sentences, paragraphs, and parts of a speech. They may indicate addition, contrast, result, alternation, cause, or repetition. The chart on page 366 gives many, but not all, of these connectives.

EMPHASIZING THE IMPORTANT POINTS

Emphasis involves how to make a point or argument more telling in terms of retention and shift of opinion. Aside from verbal techniques, pausing, variations in inflection, and changes in rate, the speaker has three compositional means of emphasis at his disposal: (1) that of significance, (2) of space, and (3) of position.

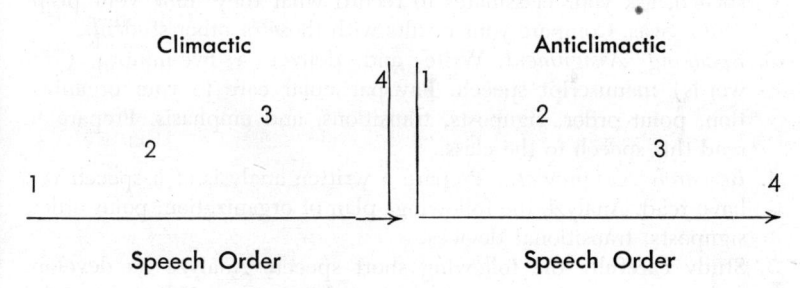

```
        Climactic                    Anticlimactic
                       4 | 1
                   3      |     2
               2          |         3
      1                   |                   4
      ─────────────────►  |  ─────────────────►
         Speech Order              Speech Order
```

Some inference and evidence may touch the auditor more directly. Thus, in his eyes, it assumes greater importance. When such material is incorporated into a point, that point will receive greater attention and produce greater results because of its pertinency.

Space emphasis is a matter of proportions: the more impor-

[5] William Norwood Brigance, *Speech Composition*, F. S. Crofts & Co., 1937, p. 207.

tant point receives more time in the speech. In other words, the two-hundred-word argument is more compelling than a fifty-word argument.

Position emphasis is governed by the order in which the points are arranged. Authorities disagree as to the relative importance of the climactic and anticlimactic order, but they are in agreement that a position at the beginning or near the close is more effective than a medial position.

If you want to make a point more *important*, give it emphasis, pack into it more pertinent supporting material, give it more time than other points, and place it in an initial or final position.

EXERCISES

1. *Speaking Assignment.* Deliver a five- to eight-minute argumentative speech in which you withhold the presentation of the proposition until the last of the speech.
2. *Speaking Assignment.* Deliver a five-minute speech in which you present the proposition by implication. After you have finished your speech, ask your classmates to record what they think your proposition was. Compare your results with those of other students.
3. *Speaking Assignment.* Write and deliver a five-minute (750 words) manuscript speech. Pay particular care to your organization, point order, signposts, transitions, and emphasis. Prepare to read this speech to the class.
4. *Research Assignment.* Prepare a written analysis of a speech you have read. Analyze the following: plan of organization, point order, signposts, transitional devices.
5. Study carefully the following short speech. Analyze its development, its proposition, and its internal structure. What principles

A GREAT GENERAL IS A GREAT SPEAKER

A significant element in the success of Dwight D. Eisenhower, president of Columbia University, is his ability to express himself in public. In World War II his utterances gave confidence to men who had united to overcome tyranny in the world. In the above picture Mr. Eisenhower is addressing the freshmen of Columbia University. In the academic world he has become a foremost speaker. (Photo, Columbia University.)

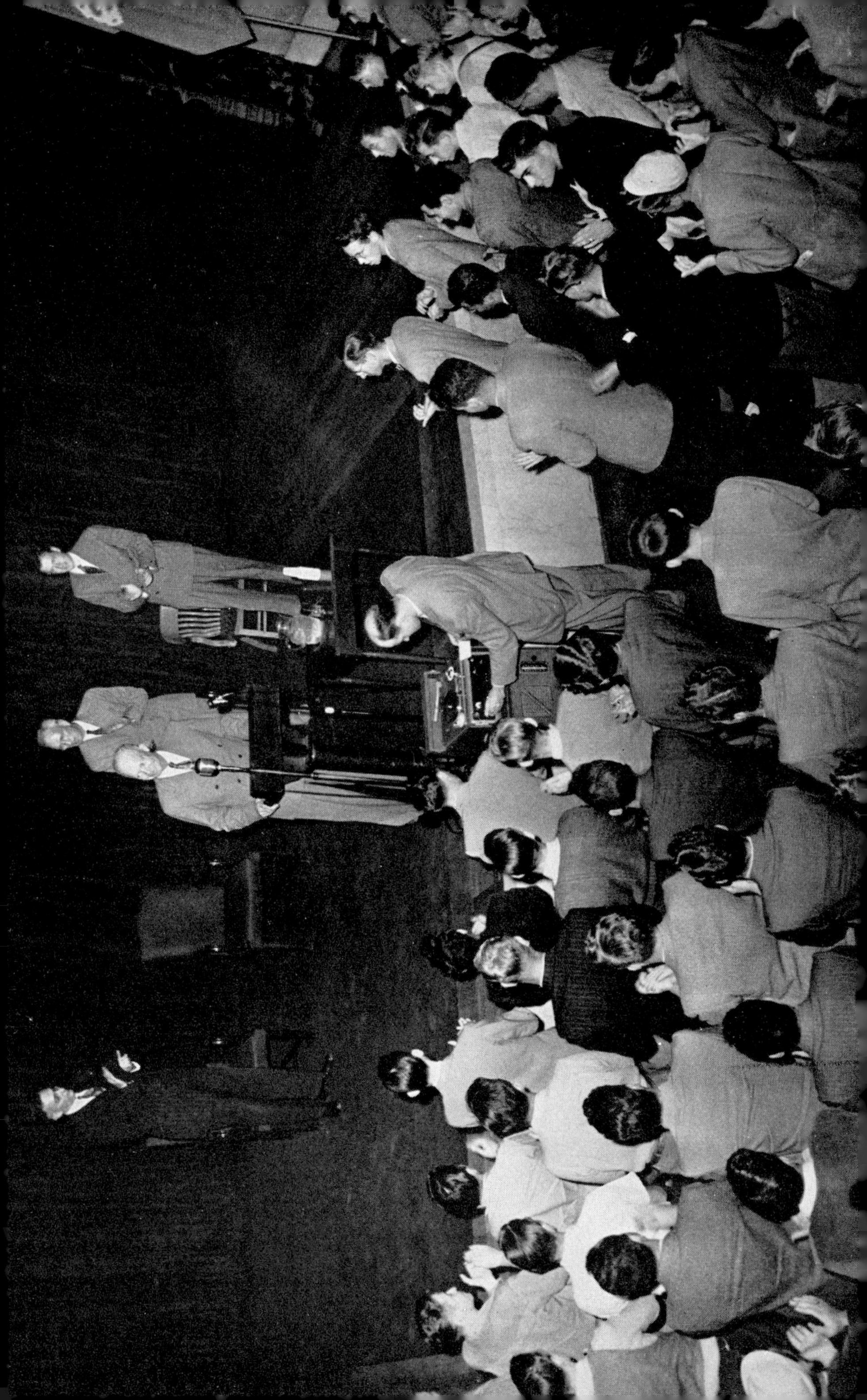

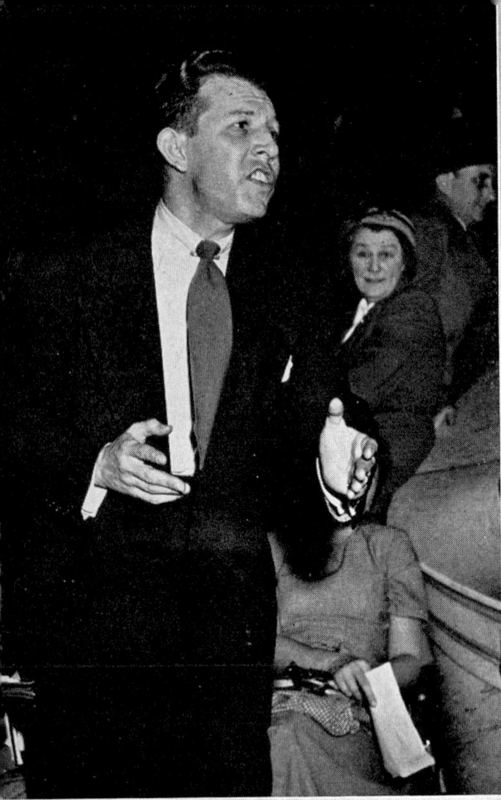
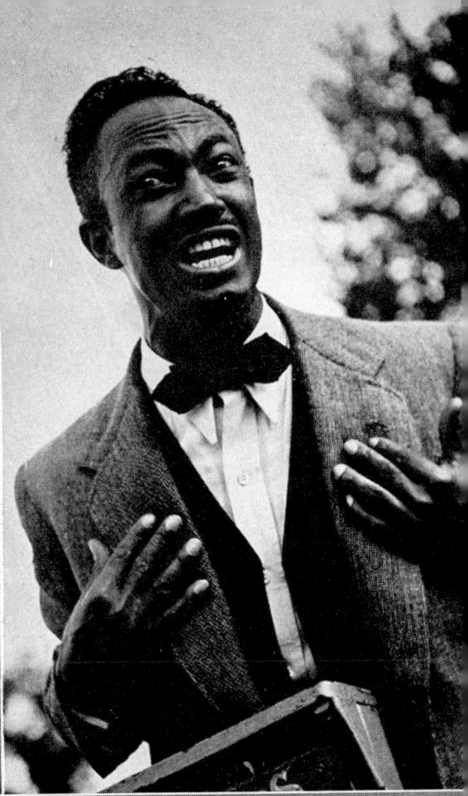
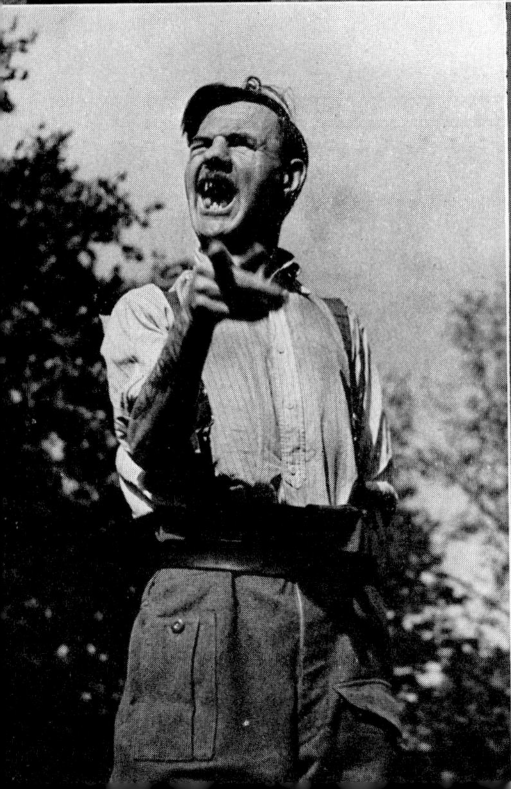
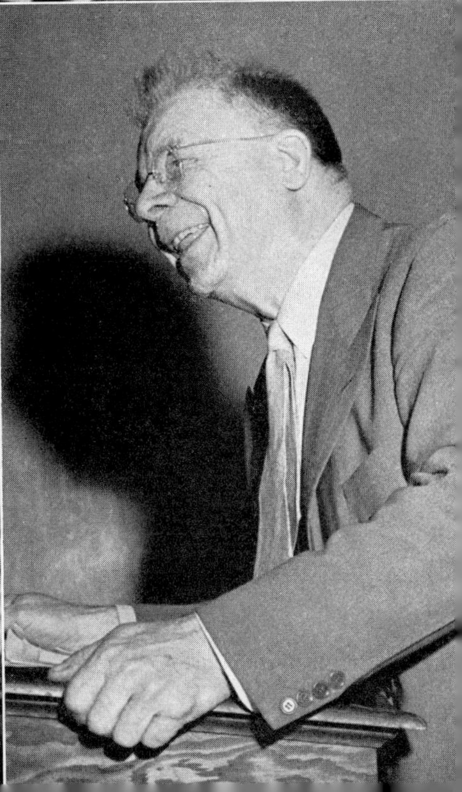

discussed in this chapter does Mr. Barton violate? Is he justified in violating these principles? (If you enjoy Mr. Barton's speech, perhaps you will also enjoy reading his "Which Knew Not Joseph," found in *Classified Speech Models*, William Norwood Brigance (ed.), F. S. Crofts & Co., 1928, pp. 24-29.)

How Long Should a Wife Live?[6]
By Bruce Barton

My Friends: My subject today is, "How Long Should a Wife Live?" My remarks will be brief and informal, and before I reach the end I will refer to the title and answer the question which it raises.

I am emboldened to refer to the ladies because I have been given the privilege of knowing, in advance, something of the wonderful message which Mrs. Sherman, President of the General Federation of Women's Clubs, is to deliver to you tomorrow regarding a nation-wide survey of home conditions. What a vision is spread out before us by the plan which she will outline! If *every* home in the United States were as well equipped with household conveniences as the *best* home, what a difference it would make in the lives of American women! What a difference in their children's lives!

[6] Delivered at the Forty-Eighth Convention of the National Electric Light Association, San Francisco, June 18, 1925. Found in *Contemporary Speeches*, James M. O'Neill and Floyd K. Riley (eds.), The Century Co., 1930, pp. 255-257. Quoted by special permission of Bruce Barton and the publishers.

THE SPEAKER REVEALS MUCH BY THE VISUAL ASPECTS OF HIS DELIVERY

Upper left, the speaker is saying: "St. Louis vital statistics show that the divorce rate in this city has come up to half the marriage rate." *(Photo, Black Star.)*

Upper right, the speaker is saying: "It was not my fault to be born with a black skin." *(Photo, Black Star.)*

Lower left, the speaker is saying: "What are my political views? None, I want to make everybody happy." *(Photo, Black Star.)*

Lower right, the speaker is saying: "Oh, what a panic in the ranks of the economic royalists when labor took political action!" *(Photo, Black Star.)*

Some years ago there was a celebration in Boston in honor of the landing of the Pilgrim Fathers. After several very laudatory speeches had been made by men a bright and vivacious woman was called on. Said she:

"I am tired of hearing so many praises of the Pilgrim Fathers. I want to say a word about the Pilgrim Mothers. They had to endure all that the Pilgrim Fathers endured, and they had to endure the Pilgrim Fathers besides."

Do you know what happened to the Pilgrim Mothers, my friends? I will tell you. They died. They died young. It took two or three of them to bring up one family. The fathers were tough and lived long, but work and hardship made short work of the wives. Listen a minute:

Of the men who graduated from Yale between 1701 and 1745, 418 became husbands. What happened to their wives?

    33 wives died before they were 25 years old
    55 died before they were 35 years old
    59 died before they were 45 years old

Those 418 husbands lost 147 wives before full middle age.

Harvard wives fared no better. Take the Harvard class of 1671 as typical. It had eleven graduates, of whom one died a bachelor at the age of twenty-four. Of the remaining ten

    4 were married twice
    2 were married three times

For ten husbands, therefore, there were eighteen wives.

It has been truly said that you can measure the height of any civilization by the plane upon which its women live. Measured by that standard, we have made great progress in the United States, but we have not made enough. An electric motor which runs a washing machine or a vacuum cleaner works for three or five cents an hour. There are still millions of women doing this work which motors can do; selling their lives at *coolie* wages of three cents an hour, having to neglect the highest work entrusted to human beings, the work of motherhood.

Some day you gentlemen expect to have every home in the United States electrified. My friends, why should you wait until *some day*? Why don't you do it immediately, next year, within the next twelve months? Does that seem impossible? I tell you that I believe it would be possible, by the right sort of concerted advertising, to arouse such a sentiment in the minds of the women of this country that *every* woman would realize that it is beneath the dignity of human life for her to work for three cents an hour.

The time in the life of a child when a mother can exert her influence is terribly brief. "Give me a child until he is seven years old," a great philosopher said, "and I care not who has him afterwards." Seven years in which to mold character; seven short, fleeting years! What a tragedy that a single moment of these years should be wasted in work which an electric machine can do.

It is a thrilling subject. It opens a whole new world of opportunity to us; it gives us a new interest, a new enthusiasm. Every day that we lose in this business of electrifying homes costs the nation in its richest wealth—the training of children, the lives and happiness of mothers. The title of this speech is, "How Long Should a Wife Live?" The answer, in the old days, was "Not very long." The homes of those days had two or three mothers and no motors. The home of the future will lay all of its tiresome, routine burdens on the shoulders of electrical machines, freeing mothers for their real work, which is motherhood. The mothers of the future will live to a good old age and keep their youth and good looks to the end.

SUPPLEMENTARY READINGS

1. Baird, A. Craig, and Knower, Franklin H., *General Speech: An Introduction*, McGraw-Hill Book Company, 1949, chap. 6.
2. Crocker, Lionel, *Public Speaking for College Students*, American Book Company, 1941, chap. 14.
3. Ehrensberger, Ray, "An Experimental Study of the Relative Effectiveness of Certain Forms of Emphasis in Public Speaking," *Speech Monographs*, 1945, pp. 94-111.
4. Sponberg, Harold, "A Study of the Relative Effectiveness of Climax and Anti-Climax Order in An Argumentative Speech," *Speech Monographs*, 1946, pp. 35-44.
5. Winans, James A., *Speech-Making*, Appleton-Century-Crofts, Inc., 1938, chap. 9.

CHAPTER XV

The Conclusion

IN THE conclusion you must pull the speech together into a unified whole. The entire development must be blended into a single, impelling impression designed to accomplish your specific purpose. The audience must feel the impact of the speech in its entirety, must appreciate its significance, and must respond to your suggestions. An effective conclusion demands careful and thoughtful preparation. The inspiration of the moment cannot be trusted. Richard Whately, who wrote a significant book on rhetoric early in the last century, has the following to say about rambling and fumbling: "It may be worthwhile here to remark that it is a common fault of an extemporary speaker to be tempted by finding himself listened to with attention and approbation to go on adding another and another sentence after he had intended, and announced his intention, to bring his discourse to close; till at length the audience becoming manifestly weary and impatient, he is forced to conclude in a feeble and spiritless manner, like a half-extinguished candle going out in smoke."[1]

In order to avoid ending "like a half-extinguished candle," you must prepare your final remarks with great care, and only on rare occasions will you let anything alter your plans. Continue making the speech march toward its goal.

Elements of the Conclusion

Long ago Aristotle suggested that the conclusion or epilogue, as he called it, may involve four elements or parts:

1. You may attempt to render the audience well disposed or favorable toward yourself or your cause.
2. You may amplify what is important and minimize what is unimportant in your speech.
3. You may summarize your speech.
4. You may strive to excite the emotions of your listeners.[2]

Whether you concentrate on one or on all of these elements will depend upon the nature of your subject, your specific objective, and the other aspects of the speaking situation. The informative speech, for example, may require no more than a simple restatement of your central thought or a summary. The conclusion of a persuasive talk sometimes includes all four elements.

PERSONAL ELEMENT IN THE CONCLUSION

In some situations, it may seem desirable to conclude with a reference to yourself or to your own feeling about the subject. During the development of the speech, you may sense that in some way your personal appeal has been weakened and that a defense of your character or your line of attack is necessary. The

[1] Richard Whately, *Elements of Rhetoric,* James Monroe and Company, 1855, pp. 207-208.
[2] Lane Cooper, *The Rhetoric of Aristotle,* Appleton-Century-Crofts, Inc., 1932, pp. 240-241.

criminal lawyer frequently uses a personal reference in his conclusion. A personal reference may be advisable in such situations as the following:

1. You may feel that you need to justify the length of your remarks.
2. You may wish to emphasize that your interests in the subject are not selfish.
3. You may desire to express your appreciation for the attention which the audience has given you.
4. You may want to express your pleasure in receiving the invitation to attend the meeting and to address the group.

Clarence Darrow, famous criminal lawyer, gave a personal justification in the final sentences of his defense of Loeb and Leopold, the youthful murderers of Bobby Franks.

I feel that I should apologize for the length of time I have taken. This case may not be as important as I think it is, and I am sure I do not need to tell this court, or to tell my friends that I would fight just as hard for the poor as for the rich. If I should succeed in saving these boys' lives and do nothing for the progress of the law, I should feel sad, indeed. If I can succeed, my greatest reward and my greatest hope will be that I have done something for the tens of thousands of other boys, for the countless unfortunates who must tread the same road in blind childhood that these poor boys have trod,—that I have done something to help human understanding, to temper justice with mercy, to overcome hate with love.[3]

Darrow, well aware of what the newspapers had written about the trial, apologized for the length of his plea and stressed his high motives in making his defense.

On October 16, 1863, at Liverpool, England, Henry Ward Beecher, fluent American clergyman, addressed a group of British workers out of work because of the blockade of the Confederacy by the North. Naturally, in his attempt to justify the federal action, he faced many who were hostile to his cause. At the close of his hour-and-a-half address he said:

[3] Clarence Darrow, "Defense of Richard Loeb and Nathan Leopold, Jr.," *Classified Speech Models*, William Norwood Brigance (ed.), F. S. Crofts & Co., 1928, pp. 136-205.

Now, gentlemen and ladies—[a voice: "Sam Slick"; and another voice: "Ladies and gentlemen, if you please"]—when I came I was asked whether I would answer questions, and I very readily consented to do so, as I had in other places; but I will tell you it was because I expected to have the opportunity of speaking with some sort of ease and quiet. [A voice: "So you have."] I have for an hour and a half spoken against a storm [hear, hear]—and you yourselves are witnesses that, by the interruption, I have been obliged to strive with my voice, so that I no longer have the power to control it in the face of this assembly. [Applause.] And although I am in spirit perfectly willing to answer any question, and more than glad of the chance, yet I am by this very unnecessary opposition tonight incapacitated physically from doing it.[4]

Your good character and your genuine interest in your hearers, if used effectively, are powerful persuasive forces. Quietly but surely they may exert persistent pressure in behalf of your cause. Therefore, let nothing in the speaking situation weaken your hearers' good opinion of you.

RESTATEMENT

When Aristotle suggested that a speaker may find need to amplify what he has said, he probably had in mind the forceful restatement of the central thought or proposition of the speech or the reemphasizing of an important idea. Restatement in the conclusion may take any of the following forms:

1. In the simplest form you may merely repeat or rephrase your proposition or central thought. For example, you may say, "Let me suggest once more that you urge your Congressman to support the recommendations of the Hoover Commission."

2. A second type of restatement may involve the use of an apt quotation or illustration which embraces the central philosophy of your speech. Naturally, such a quotation adds dignity and authority to what has been said, and the novelty may be a source of renewed interest or awareness.

[4] Henry Ward Beecher, "Liverpool Address," *Classified Speech Models*, pp. 40-65.

Dr. John T. Caldwell closes his address, "The New Birth," thus:

I rather think, finally, that if we strive to do a proper job at Alabama College, and at all our sister and brother institutions, public and private, in bringing about a continual rebirth in the minds of each student of this generation, we shall bring about also a new birth of freedom and prosperity to this whole blessed land. How much will it cost? I did not ask. I only ask my hearers today if there is any task more important, or if there is any need more urgent. I only ask if we are doing all we can. Or whether we think education is just another item on which we can practice "economy."

The words of John in *Revelations* are applicable here: "I know thy works, that thou art neither cold nor hot: I would thou wert cold or hot. So then because thou art lukewarm, and neither cold nor hot, I will spue thee out of my mouth."

This generation cannot afford lukewarmness toward the moral issue of whether or not education is our most important public endeavor. "Through the Looking Glass" contains the final answer to the importance of education in today's battle of ideas. Tweedledee and Tweedledum were preparing themselves for their personal battle with each other. Alice was arranging a neck protector for Tweedledee "to keep his head from being cut off." "You know," he said gravely, "it's one of the most serious things that can possibly happen to one in a battle—to get one's head cut off."[5]

In one of his Fireside Chats, delivered during the darkest days of World War II, President Roosevelt relied on the words of another to restate in his conclusion the theme of his speech. He said,

Never before have we been called upon for such a prodigious effort. Never before have we had so little time in which to do so much.

"These are the times that try men's souls."

Tom Paine wrote those words on a drum-head by the light of a campfire. That was when Washington's little army of ragged, rugged men was retreating across New Jersey, having tasted nothing but defeat.

[5] John Tyler Caldwell, "The New Birth," *Representative American Speeches, 1948-1949*, A. Craig Baird (ed.), The H. W. Wilson Company, 1949, pp. 196-205. Quoted by special permission.

And General Washington ordered that these great words written by Tom Paine, be read to the men of every regiment in the Continental Army, and this was the assurance given to the first American Armed Forces:

"The summer soldier and the sunshine patriot will, in this crisis, shrink from the service of their country; but he that stands it now, deserves the love and thanks of man and woman. Tyranny, like hell, is not easily conquered; yet we have this consolation with us, that the harder the sacrifice, the more glorious the triumph."

So spoke Americans in the year 1776.

So speak Americans today![6]

You will note that President Roosevelt heightened the dramatic appeal of his speech by using the familiar words of Tom Paine.

SUMMARY

Probably the most common type of conclusion is the summary. The oral process demands that the speaker repeat his ideas if he wants them to be remembered; consequently, a terse repeating of your main points in one-two-three order is an excellent way to hammer home your ideas. In some cases, you may find it to your advantage to repeat the same language used when stating your points the first time. You may say, "In this speech I have made three points. First I have pointed out. . . . Second I have said. . . . My final point was. . . ."

Some intercollegiate debaters concluded their argument by saying:

Since there are children in this country that are denied adequate education,
Since the states are unable to provide adequate education for these pupils,
Since these states contain the greatest percentage of our children,
And since education is the responsibility of the entire electorate,
Therefore we urge the adoption of federal aid to education.

[6] Franklin Delano Roosevelt, "Fireside Chat on the Progress of the War," delivered February 23, 1942. In *Nothing to Fear*, B. D. Zevin (ed.), Houghton Mifflin Company, 1946, pp. 312-322.

In a speech before the Third Annual Conference on Public Affairs at Ohio State University, March 5, 1949, Francis B. Sayre used this type of conclusion. In closing he said:

In conclusion, then, may I recapitulate in summary form the four cardinal points in American foreign policy:

First, to build up and fortify in every way possible the youthful and developing United Nations organization;

Second, to continue our full support to ERP and to the movement toward a Western European Union so as to help unify and strengthen the countries of Western Europe;

Third, to assist in establishing an effective North Atlantic Security Pact under the Charter of the United Nations in order to make strong the bastions of human freedom and thus to lessen the likelihood of war;

Fourth, to find ways and means of aggressive action to spread and strengthen the basic principles upon which rests our civilization. America, as a Christian nation, must base its policy unswervingly upon right and justice and humanity. We must believe, in the words of Lincoln, that "right makes might"; and in that faith we "must dare to do our duty as we understand it."

I often think of the verse of Martin Luther, that doughty old fighter, who could not be downed:

> And though this world with devils filled
> Should threaten to undo us,
> We will not fear for God hath willed
> His truth to triumph through us.

With closer political and economic understanding among the free peoples of the world may come a great upsurge of the forces of democracy. The consequences could be electric. Democracy, foundationed upon the deep desires and will of the great masses of mankind, is an unconquerable force.

The time is big with opportunity. Destiny is in the making. The issues call for men of vision and men of courage.[7]

Dr. W. Norwood Brigance used a summary conclusion in his stirring address "The Backwash of War":

[7] Francis B. Sayre, "Major Problems in the United States, Foreign Policies," *Representative American Speeches: 1948-1949*, pp. 51-63. Quoted by special permission.

THE CONCLUSION

These, then, are the especial problems that face us in this backwash of war: First, the problem of the returning soldier adjusting himself to civilian life; second, the danger of transferring our hatred of the Japanese and Germans to other groups; third, the danger that in fighting against militarism, we ourselves shall become militaristic; and finally, the danger of permitting too much of a moral holiday now that we are relieved from the Spartan discipline of war.

We do not face these problems with fear. We do not face them with hesitation. To the timid and faint-hearted who long for security and repose, we quote the answer of Mr. Justice Oliver Wendell Holmes: "Security is an illusion, and repose is not the destiny of man." We shall meet these problems as a people who are conscious of their destiny.[8]

In the example above Dr. Brigance has actually included several elements. Notice his one-two-three summary, his equally effective challenge, and his restatement in the words of Mr. Justice Oliver Wendell Holmes.

APPEAL

The fourth element of the conclusion refers to what Aristotle called putting the audience into the right state of emotion or the appeal for acceptance or action. Facts and inference alone probably will not be enough to achieve your purpose; you will need to appeal to your listeners on the basis of their motives—show how the proposal will bring benefits, pleasures, and satisfactions. Such appeals may be to altruistic motives as well as to selfish ones.

Senator Claude Pepper made a powerful appeal to the Senate to reject a bill giving military assistance to Greece and Turkey:

I proclaim that there is nothing that this Congress could do in its whole life which would so hearten mankind as to rededicate this country to the United Nations and to its high purpose to maintain international peace and security. The world would know that when required to take effective collective measures for the prevention and

[8] William Norwood Brigance, "The Backwash of War," *Representative American Speeches: 1945-1946*, pp. 75-84. Quoted by special permission.

removal of threats to the peace and for the suppression of acts of aggression in the name of this noble charter, we have again pledged our lives, our fortunes and our sacred honor; that America is, and before God and man will continue to be, a democracy dedicated to the people, the servant of their hopes and their dreams, the friend of all the peoples who live in the houses, big and little, beside the roads of the world; that no overweening ambition, no lure of profit or power, no fool's gold of empire shall tempt us to betray our dead or our destiny; that America is not soft, that it is not afraid to fight either for the poor, the oppressed, or the victims of aggression, that we realize that we can neither lift up mankind nor protect their security, strong as we are, alone; and that therefore we shall keep our pledge to achieve international cooperation in solving international problems of economic, social, cultural, or humanitarian character and in promoting and encouraging respect for human rights and for fundamental freedoms for all without distinction as to race, sex, language, or religion; that we turn our faces toward the future with confidence; that we are on God's side because we are on man's side, and as our cause is just we are strong in His strength. If, God forbid, we shall ever have to fight, let us fight to save the Union, as did Lincoln, because the Union is all that can save men. As Washington said, "Let us raise a standard to which the wise and the just may repair." And now, as it was when Washington rose to defend the new Charter of the United States, "The event is in the hands of God."[9]

Arthur Vandenberg gives us another example of a dramatic appeal. In the conclusion of a Memorial Day speech delivered at Gettysburg, Pennsylvania, May 30, 1938, the Michigan senator said:

There is a bivouac of heroes on the shores of the eternal life. They come from Valley Forge and the conflict that wrenched the Republic from the tyrannies of George III. They come from the War of 1812, and then from the Alamo and Monterrey. They come from Gettysburg and the travail of rebellion. They come from Chateau Thierry and the unrequited crusade for world democracy. To the memory of each we bring the rose of our deathless affection. To each we would pay our debt. But we cannot pay, we do not pay, except as, in our easier way,

---

[9] Claude D. Pepper, "Against Aid to Greece and Turkey," *Representative American Speeches: 1946-1947*, pp. 67-88. Quoted by special permission.

we pledge ourselves, with the earnestness of deep conviction, that the traditional spirit of the Republic shall survive and that—no matter what the lure to other paths—here in the United States, now and forever, government of the people, by the people, and for the people shall not perish from the earth.[10]

Much of Vandenberg's emotional appeal in these sentences depends upon associating his present speech with heroic events of the past—Valley Forge, the War of 1812, the Alamo and Monterrey, Gettysburg, Chateau Thierry, and "the unrequited crusade for world democracy." Furthermore, by his word choice, particularly his last sentence, he recalled for his listeners Lincoln's "Gettysburg Address" and thus heightened the emotional inpact.

In its simpler forms, an appeal merely stresses how the listener will benefit from the adoption or acceptance of the speaker's ideas. You may have occasion to want to dress up your final remarks, add a bit of grandeur to the tone of your speech. Perhaps you may wish to employ one of the following special types of appeals:

1. Challenge
2. Declaration of personal intention
3. Visualization of the future

Challenge

It will frequently be to your advantage if you can make the audience feel that they are a part of a struggle against some common foe. Such an approach says in substance, "Let us unite," "Let us put down our enemy," "Let us even this battle." Most persons are flattered to think that they are part of a good cause.

Former President Franklin Roosevelt frequently packed powerful motivation into his closing sentences. The conclusion to his "Victory Dinner Address," delivered March 4, 1937, challenged the Democratic party to follow his lead in dealing with the pressing problems of the nation. He said,

[10] Arthur H. Vandenberg, "Memorial Day Address," *Representative American Speeches, 1937-1938*, pp. 39-44. Quoted by special permission.

It will take courage to let our minds be bold and find the ways to meet the needs of the nation. But for our party, now as always, the counsel of courage is the counsel of wisdom.

If we do not have the courage to lead the American people where they want to go, some one else will.

Here is one-third of a nation ill-nourished, ill-clad, ill-housed—now!

Here are thousands upon thousands of farmers wondering whether next year's prices will meet their mortgage interest—now!

Here are thousands upon thousands of men and women laboring for long hours in factories for inadequate pay—now!

Here are thousands upon thousands of children who should be at school, working in mines and mills—now!

Here are strikes more far-reaching than we have ever known, costing millions of dollars—now!

Here are spring floods threatening to roll again down our river valleys—now!

Here is the dust bowl beginning to blow again—now!

If we would keep faith with those who had faith in us, if we would make democracy succeed, I say we must act—now![11]

Notice that President Roosevelt intensified the effect of his closing words by effective use of repetition and parallel structure.

Woodrow Wilson issued a challenge when he closed the speech in which he submitted the Peace Treaty to the Senate: "The stage is set, the destiny closed. It has come about by no plan of our conceiving, but by the hand of God who led us into this way. We cannot turn back. We can only go forward, with lifted eyes and freshened spirit, to follow the vision. It was of this that we dreamed at our birth. America shall in truth show the way. The light streams upon the path ahead, and nowhere else."[12]

Chaplain Roland B. Gittelsohn delivered a fervent plea to end discrimination, prejudice, and hatred among all religions and between white men and Negroes in his sermon delivered at the dedication of the Fifth Marine Division Cemetery on Iwo Jima, in March, 1945. In concluding, he said to his audience of battle-hardened soldiers:

[11] Franklin Delano Roosevelt, "Victory Dinner Address," *Representative American Speeches, 1937-1938*, pp. 101-110.

[12] Woodrow Wilson, "Submitting the Peace Treaty to the Senate," *Classified Speech Models*, pp. 208-221.

THE CONCLUSION

When the final cross or star has been placed in the last cemetery, once again there will be those to whom profit is more important than peace, who will insist, with the voice of sweet reasonableness and appeasement, that it is better to trade with the enemies of mankind than, by crushing them, to lose their profit. To you who sleep here silently, we give our promise: We will not listen. We will not forget that some of you were burnt with oil that came from American wells, that many of you were killed by shells fashioned from American steel.

We promise that when once again men seek profit at your expense, we shall remember how you looked when we placed you reverently, lovingly, in the ground.

Thus do we consecrate the living to carry on the struggle you began. Too much blood has gone into this soil for us to let it lie barren. Too much pain and heartache have fertilized the earth on which we stand. We here solemnly swear: This shall not be in vain. Out of this, and from the suffering and sorrow of those who mourn this, will come—we promise—the birth of a new freedom for the sons of men everywhere.[13]

The chaplain touched the very heartstrings of his listeners. He made them resolve that the struggle "shall not be in vain."

Declaration of Personal Intention

On some occasions you may find that a forceful statement concerning your own future personal course of action may serve as a powerful appeal. By declaring what you want to do, you hope to stimulate the auditors to take up the cause also. If this type of ending is to be effective, you must enjoy the high regard of your listeners.

Webster used this technique in the peroration of his Reply to Calhoun, February 16, 1833:

If the Constitution cannot be maintained without meeting these scenes of commotion and contest, however unwelcome, they must come. We cannot, we must not, we dare not, omit to do that which in our judgment, the safety of the Union requires. Not regardless of consequences, we must yet meet consequences; seeing the hazards which surround the discharge of public duty, it must yet be dis-

[13] Roland B. Gittelsohn, "That Men Might Be Free," *Representative American Speeches, 1945-1946*, pp. 16-19. Quoted by special permission.

charged. For myself, sir, I shun no responsibility justly devolving on me, here or elsewhere, in attempting to maintain the cause. I am bound to it by indissoluble bands of affection and duty, and I shall cheerfully partake in its fortunes and its fate. I am ready to perform my own appropriate part, whenever and wherever the occasion may call on me, and to take my chance among those upon whom blows may fall first and fall thickest. I shall exert every faculty I possess in aiding to prevent the Constitution from being nullified, destroyed, or impaired; and even should I see it befall, I will still, with a voice feeble, perhaps, but earnest as ever issued from human lips and with fidelity and zeal which nothing shall extinguish, call on the PEOPLE to come to its rescue.[14]

A more famous example of this type is Patrick Henry's ringing final words delivered to the Virginia Convention, March 23, 1775. Said Henry,

It is in vain, sir, to extenuate the matter. Gentlemen may cry, Peace, Peace—but there is no peace. The war is actually begun! The next gale that sweeps from the north will bring to our ears the clash of resounding arms! Our brethren are already in the field! Why stand we here idle? What is it that gentlemen wish? What would they have? Is life so dear, or peace so sweet, as to be purchased at the price of chains and slavery? Forbid it, Almighty God! I know not what course others may take; but as for me, give me liberty or give me death.[15]

Visualization of the Future

Perhaps this type of appeal could appropriately be called "the new-day" appeal, that is, the speaker presents the auditor with a picture of conditions as they will be if his scheme is adopted. Your aim in such a close is to make the listener so eager for the "new times" that he takes the plunge for which you plead.

Chester Bowles used this strategy in the conclusion of a speech that he delivered to the national convention of the Farmers

---

[14] Delivered in the Senate February 16, 1833.

[15] Patrick Henry, "Liberty or Death," *Classified Models of Speech Composition,* James Milton O'Neill (ed.), The Century Co., pp. 328-330.

Union at Topeka, Kansas, on March 6, 1946. He used a series of rhetorical questions to achieve his goal:

> Will we move ahead under a vigorous democracy to greater and greater heights of production? Will we move ahead to higher incomes for all of us, toward the elimination of slums, disease, ignorance, and ill health? Or shall we embark on an inflationary joy ride to disaster, with the spectacle of some strange new American fascism arising out of the bitterness and the disillusionment which will surely result? What will our American answer be to this gravest of all questions which ever faced our nation during peacetime?
>
> Will it be the answer of the NAM which has fought on the wrong side of every public question for the last thirty years? Will it be the answer of the pressure groups, the answer of organized greed?
>
> Or will it be the voice of the everyday people of America, clear, strong, determined, confident—with their heads held high, and their eyes firmly fixed upon a future that for generations to come means the difference between hope and despair not only for 140,000,000 Americans but for all the people everywhere throughout the world?[16]

ADAPTING THE CONCLUSION TO THE SPEAKING SITUATION

There is no formula that the speaker can use in selecting what elements of the conclusion he will use under given conditions. Some speeches may require only one, while others necessitate the inclusion of all four. The speech goal gives some aid in selecting the elements to be used. The informative speech may demand a summary or a restatement or both. The persuasive speech ordinarily requires some type of appeal. Indeed, it would be difficult to generalize about the speech to inform.

Actually, two or three or all the elements are frequently combined into a conclusion. Bruce Barton, in the example given earlier, used both summary and restatement. Brigance utilized three elements: summary, restatement, and appeal.

[16] Chester Bowles, "Price Control and Inflation," *Representative American Speeches: 1945-1946*, pp. 144-153. Quoted by special permission.

EXERCISES

1. *Speaking Assignment.* Deliver a speech in which you include the personal element in your conclusion.
2. *Speaking Assignment.* Deliver a speech in which you conclude with one of the following:
    a. A quotation
    b. A challenge
    c. A declaration of personal intention
    d. A reference to the dawn of a new day
3. *Research Assignment.* Prepare a written analysis of the conclusions of five speeches found in a recent issue of *Vital Speeches* or *Representative American Speeches.* Determine what elements were used and why they were used.
4. Below are the conclusions to three student speeches. Study them carefully and then rewrite them if you believe that they can be improved.

    a. Let me summarize my three points: First, the United States has a strong medical service and the best in the world today. We are much better off than any other country and on a steady and increasing medical achievements.

    Second, socialized medicine would support a certain few who are ill at all times. It would tend to increase and encourage illness among those who might not be.

    Third, the quality of medical care would suffer if a system of free medical service were adopted. Others have tried it, and their medical efficiency is on the decrease.

    For we cannot afford to take one more pillar from our democratic structure. For you know when you keep taking pillars from a structure, the removal of each one weakens that structure until the few that are left are unable to hold it, and it collapses, even breaking its own foundation. Our medical service is strong and good in America today—let us not weaken our country by having socialized medicine.

    b. I have tried to show you why you should be well informed and how you can effectively make the effort. To those who want to know the truth about what goes on in the world, it is a worthwhile effort. To those who want to think for themselves and who want to have a voice in government, it is a necessity. If only for purely selfish reasons, you should keep up with the world. Remember, one of your greatest assets is an intelligent outlook, an outlook distilled from accurate facts and wise opinions.

c. In short, we must see that driving conditions in our State are improved. We must see that our friends realize that carelessness is folly—and we must ourselves BE CAREFUL. We must reduce that 33,000!!
5. Write a detailed evaluation of the following student speech. Consider all the elements that you have studied thus far in the course. Pay particular attention to aspects discussed in the last three chapters.

A Citizens' Marshall Plan[17]
By Charles Fellers

   The French woman and her two children waited patiently for us to empty our scraps into the garbage can. When I scalded my mess kit, I glanced back and saw that she was busily sorting our leftovers. She gave a meaty bone to each child. Then she commenced to put bread crusts, bones, tiny pieces of meat, and bits of fat into her wicker basket. When she had salvaged a basketful she and her children began to walk slowly back to Le Havre.
   Since that day I have thought many times about that French family who felt lucky to have a chance to gather food from a garbage can. What happened to that little trio? I have wished that somehow I could help those two kids. But most of all I have uttered many silent prayers of thanks that my mother and brothers have plenty to eat. I have asked myself, Will my family ever stand by for a turn at a garbage can? I wish I could forget the expression on that Frenchwoman's face and the eagerness with which her children gnawed on those bones!
   As a G.I. I could and did occasionally share my food with the French people, particularly with the children. But what about now? Today the situation in France is desperate. The trouble is not difficult to understand. Many persons there are existing, and I mean existing, not living, on less than 1400 calories per day. I know you've heard that before. Fourteen hundred is just a number to you and it even sounds like a large number. But science has shown that the human body cannot function properly on less than 1700 calories per day. Let me illustrate what I mean. I eat only two meals a day because I'm too lazy to get up for breakfast. In my two meals I receive 2,100 calories. My roommate over a period of two weeks averaged 2,300 calories each day. Compare that with 1400. The French worker today is receiving approxi-

[17] A speech presented by a student in a public-speaking class at Louisiana State University in 1948.

mately 900 calories less each day than a college student who does little physical labor. Skip your heaviest meal tomorrow and you will have a faint idea by nightfall how a French worker feels.

After losing four pounds in nine days a girl of my acquaintance decided to break her diet. On a diet of about 1400 calories a day she lost four pounds in little more than a week. Now imagine, if you can, the effect of such a diet over a prolonged period of time.

I think all of us understand the causes of this deplorable condition that exists in France today: the long occupation by German forces, the complete destruction of industry, and the gradual collapse of the agricultural system. Dairy herds were slaughtered, and seed grain was ground for food or sent to Germany.

None of these conditions that contribute to starvation in France can be solved in one year, or two, and without help from the American people. The French need our help desperately.

Now let us consider why the French people deserve our help. During the Revolutionary War there was a time when our country was in a precarious position. Do we realize that France, who has fought for freedom many times, saw peril, and sent soldiers to fight with us against the Redcoats? France sent generals to train our armies and most of all she sent supplies, arms, and ammunition.

We have been allies in two World Wars, struggles which have been fought on French soil, in French villages, in French homes, wars in which their "little" people were slain the same as soldiers at the front.

Not many years ago, we, the citizens of this country, received a gift from the French people,—from the farmers, the bakers, the school teachers, the children, those persons who admired and respected us. That gift, to the fellow known here as John Q. Public, was called the "beacon light of freedom and friendship." It is the Statue of Liberty.

A student like myself might sum up my plea for help to France in this way, "Give a buddy a hand," or "Help a friend in need."

In Washington our legislators have been debating the Marshall Plan for months and indications are that it will probably not be passed in the near future. The Marshall Plan proposes to give financial aid to most of the depressed countries of Europe, and is primarily a stopgap measure against the spread of Communism. With the Marshall Plan stymied by political debate, the weed of

Communism is spreading in the fertile soil of hunger. Starving people cannot wait for the outcome of congressional debate. They need help now. That brings me to my third point. Let us participate in a Citizens' Marshall Plan. The Citizens' Marshal Plan is not an organization, but a state of mind, a realization of the dire need, a knowledge of the solution combined with the stimulus to act. The French people need food. From that day when I saw the children gnawing bones from the garbage can, to the present, I doubt whether that mother has been able to provide a proper meal for her family.

What can we do? Let me tell you about CARE, C-A-R-E, Cooperative for American Remittances to Europe. CARE will deliver 49 pounds of foods to any designated person in most of the countries of Europe. This parcel contains 40,000 calories. Forty thousand calories, another number, but this time a large one. Food for twenty days of life, twenty days of life with a human diet. To those people, food as luxurious as an American Thanksgiving Dinner. CARE, this forty-nine pounds of food and immeasurable good-will, costs you only $10.

You may designate the individual you wish to receive the food, or the overseas officials of CARE will see that it is received by a worthy person. This person will sign a receipt, acknowledging the food, which is returned to you. In most cases the receipt is accompanied by a grateful letter.

For further information, write CARE, 50 Broad Street, New York 4, New York.

In conclusion, let me summarize briefly. There is little chance that France can successfully recover without outside aid. Shall this aid come from us, or from Communist Russia?

Second, when we consider the past, the bonds of friendship that unite, not just our governments, but more important, the people of our countries, it is clear that we must have a Citizens' Marshall Plan, we must help those who are now at the great crossroads of history. Are the deeds of the French in our American Revolution, and the symbol of the Statue of Liberty to be forgotten?

CARE offers us an easy way to repay our debts, and more, to show what is really in our hearts. Each package is a breath of freedom, and a bit of appreciation, a part of the Statue of Liberty going back across the ocean.

Write CARE, 50 Broad Street, New York 4, New York, for

complete information, or better still go to your church and inquire what arrangements they have made to send relief to Europe and help you join the Citizens' Marshall Plan.

The need is great, the cause worthy, the future imponderable. Let us all act now, let's join in doing our part in a Citizens' Marshall Plan.

SUPPLEMENTARY READINGS

1. Brigance, William Norwood, *Speech Composition*, F. S. Crofts & Co., 1937, pp. 109-119.
2. Monroe, Alan H., *Principles and Types of Speech*, Scott, Foresman & Company, 3rd ed., 1949, pp. 295-305.
3. Sarett, Lew, and Foster, William Trufant, *Basic Principles of Speech*, Houghton Mifflin Company, rev. ed., 1946, chap. 20.

CHAPTER XVI

Using Language for Clarity

ONCE you have made your analysis of the occasion and the audience, determined your purpose, assembled and organized your material, your next problem is to put the speech into words. Much of the success of your speaking will depend on your effective use of language.

When we speak of communicating ideas, of conveying thoughts, to other people, we are speaking figuratively, for thoughts cannot be conveyed from one to another. Ideas cannot actually be communicated to anyone else. Despite occasional reports of mental telepathy, there is no known way by which thoughts can reliably and consistently be transmitted from one person to another. Certainly in the normal speaking situation nothing passes from the speaker to the listener but sound waves and, in the case of visible bodily action, light waves.[1] For the present we are concerned only with the former, and they do not convey thought; they only stir it up in the listener.

BASIS OF WORD MEANING

While you were learning to speak you learned, by repeatedly hearing certain vocal sound sequences in close association with things, actions, events, or qualities, to use these sequences yourselves as substitutes for the nonverbal happenings; these sounds came "to stand for" them, to be symbols for them, to "mean" them. When they were used in your hearing, they called to your mind the things for which they had come to stand; you yourself learned to use them for the same purpose. Other people had also learned in the same way that you had that these sound sequences could be used to symbolize, or "mean," the things with which they had been so often and so closely associated. These sequences, which may now be called words, you and those about you could now use in speaking whenever you wanted to refer to the things for which they stand without bringing up the objects themselves or demonstrating the action. Our entire structure of language is made up of just such words, so arranged and systematized as to have highly complex meanings.

To put it briefly, language has meaning for you and for those with whom you may speak solely on the basis of the associations which have been built up between the sound sequences and the things for which they have come to stand. Meaning for you is thus based entirely on your own individual experiences in associating symbol, that is, word, with object.[2] For your listeners meaning is likewise based on their individual experiences. Hence, since those experiences can never be the same for different per-

[1] In radio and television, electromagnetic waves are transmitted as "carriers" for sound and light waves, but the essential principle holds true, that the speaker emits only sound waves and reflects only light waves. The listener is not sensitive to electromagnetic waves at all.

[2] The word *object* is used here to refer to any nonverbal fact or experience.

sons, no word can have exactly the same meaning for two or more individuals. Communication is possible only because those experiences are sufficiently similar for different persons to permit more or less common meanings to be aroused or stimulated by the symbols.

In Chapter I it was pointed out that the basic purpose of speaking is to bring an audience and an idea together. It would be a little more accurate to say that when you speak you use language not to transmit ideas or thoughts but to arouse in the minds of your listeners ideas or thoughts very similar to those which you yourselves have when you speak; for, as stated earlier, thoughts cannot be passed on to anyone else. Language is used merely as a stimulus to arouse thoughts in the minds of others.

Since the thoughts or ideas which other people get from your speaking are aroused by the words you use, it is evident that they are therefore dependent upon your language. If then you are impelled by what has been called the *urge to communicate*, if you really want to arouse certain definite ideas in the thinking of your listeners, you must choose your language with extreme care. The wrong use of a word, or the use of a wrong word, or a sentence poorly phrased, may utterly destroy the meanings that you want to arouse.[3] You must be sure first of all that the meanings of your language are clear and definite *for you*. Then you must see to it that the words are so chosen and so organized that the associations which your hearers have built up, the meanings, will be as clear and definite and as like your own as possible.

OBJECTIVES IN THE USE OF LANGUAGE

When you plan the wording of your speech, therefore, you should strive to accomplish three specific objectives: *clarity*, *vividness*, and *impressiveness*.

---

[3] We shall see in a later chapter how the manner in which words are spoken has a strong influence on their meaning.

By *clarity* is meant that attribute in your language which arouses definite and specific meanings. It provides for understanding. You have undoubtedly observed that your ideas themselves often lack clarity mainly because you have never gone to the trouble of putting them into language of definite meaning. It was said of Albert J. Beveridge, with whose political theories one might not always agree, but who spoke with such clarity that no one could misunderstand him, that in his youth he never let an idea get away from him without his first casting it into phraseology that expressed exactly what he wanted to say. Like Beveridge, when you have expressed your thoughts in clear, definite language, you have clarified and made definite the thoughts themselves.

Vividness has its primary basis in imagery, which in turn arises from concrete experiences. This imagery may be visual, auditory, motor, thermal, and so on, or any combination of them. The more definitely your language recalls such imagery, the more vivid it will be.

Impressiveness refers to the stimulation of the emotional coloring which is an integral part of the meanings of most of the language you use. "Meaning *for speech*," says Woolbert, "*is always twofold*. . . . It is not enough that a speaker use a type of expression that carries only a logical meaning; he must show the hearer *how he himself feels about the matter*. He must not only let the hearer know what the idea is, but how well or ill he himself thinks of it."[4] In arousing definite logical meanings and securing understanding, you must ensure the attribute of *clarity*; in stimulating rich and varied imagery, you seek to provide vividness; in arousing the emotional aspects of meaning, you attempt to achieve *impressiveness*.

These three objectives are by no means incompatible. It is not only entirely possible, it is usually highly advantageous, for you to choose language that will accomplish all of them at the

---

[4] Charles Henry Woolbert, *The Fundamentals of Speech*, Harper & Brothers, rev. ed., 1927, p. 195.

same time. In a single sentence you can be clear in arousing logical meanings, vivid in your recall of personal experiences, and impressive in your stimulation of emotional attitudes. When you can accomplish all three of these, your chances of success in speaking will be more nearly assured. Let us now consider each of these objectives in somewhat more detail.

ACHIEVING CLARITY

If you would make your own ideas clear to your listeners, you must first of all make them clear to yourself. What we call thinking is largely a matter of the use of language. If your own concepts are vague and hazy, it will not only be impossible for you to make them anything else for your hearers; you yourself will be going about in a perpetual fog. Clarification of concepts, then, is an absolute essential to clear thinking as well as to clear speaking. "A term misunderstood is a term falsified," said a medieval scholar.[5] Four hundred years ago a famous Renaissance scholar, Juan Luis Vives, insisted that "Words behind which there is no meaning are mere bombast."[6] Be sure, then, that you have a clear understanding of your own words. Even though you may have to hunt for the facts of experience to which your language refers, word meanings must be true to the facts.

Finding the Meanings of Words

For many of our words, little or no difficulty is encountered in knowing with sufficient exactness what they mean when we use them. You hear and use such words as *book, horse, automobile* (usually *car*), *credits, football, shoes, walk, write, study, speak, red, cold, hard,* and the like; and with some variations for individual differences in the details of your experiences, they "mean" pretty much the same for most college students all over

[5] Cassiodorus, cited by J. W. H. Atkins, *English Literary Criticism: The Medieval Phase*, The University Press, Cambridge, 1943, p. 46.
[6] Cited by J. W. H. Atkins, *English Literary Criticism: The Renaissance, 1500-1600*, Methuen & Co., Ltd., 1947, p. 43.

the country. Because they refer to fairly definite things or experiences, because their meanings are recognizably representative of facts, you can use them in an intelligent context with little fear of misunderstanding either on the part of yourself as speaker or on the part of your listeners. They are often called *concrete* terms. But even though the meanings of such terms are on the whole fairly definite, confusion often results from their careless use.

On the other hand, there is a large number of words whose meanings are not so easily determined. They come under the classification commonly known as *abstract* terms. It is in the use of these words that the greatest indefiniteness and confusion may arise.[7] And it is with these words that you must be most careful to ensure that your own understanding is clear, if you are to make your meanings clear to your audience.

For instance, you may use the term *big business* in a speech. Precisely what does it mean to you? What are the facts of experience to which this term corresponds? How "big" must a business be to come under this classification? Is mere "bigness" the sole criterion, or does the term imply some particular type of organization, like a corporation, a "trust," a monopoly—any of which terms may themselves require some explanation? You may similarly want to talk sometime about "free enterprise," the "welfare state," "social security," "states' rights," or any of a great number of terms that have come into common use during recent years. Exactly what do these terms mean to you? To what facts of experience do they refer? If they have no clear meanings even to you, how are you going to be able to use them intelligently in talking? How, in fact, are you going to be able even to think intelligently about the things for which the words stand

---

[7] NOTE: All words are in a sense abstract, in that it is impossible to know completely the full meaning of any term, any more than Tennyson could know the full meaning of the "Flower in the crannied wall." For a more extended discussion of this principle, see Giles Wilkeson Gray and Claude Merton Wise, *The Bases of Speech*, Harper & Brothers, rev. ed., 1946, pp. 517-522. The difference between concrete and abstract terms is mainly one of degree.

unless your own ideas about those things are clear? The clarity and honesty of your thinking is largely revealed by the definiteness of meaning of the words in which your ideas are framed.

Some years ago we heard much about the Nazi form of government, and today we hear much about communism. Perhaps sometime you will want to talk about one of these forms of society, particularly the latter. Just what is that form which today goes under the name of communism? For that matter, what are the essential characteristics of what we term the "American way," or democracy?

The relation of meaning to experience is brought out clearly by Professor Schlesinger: "The key to the meaning of democracy ... is to be found in history rather than in philosophy. We must look at the record. What range of possibilities has democracy, in fact, unfolded? What methods has it found legitimate? What have been its values and resources?"[8]

One might enumerate scores of such words which we use daily without actually having a clear notion of just what they do mean. Their meanings are not clear to us because we have never checked them closely as to their correspondence with any facts of experience. The consequence is that not only is our own thinking muddy and indefinite, but because we ourselves do not understand, we find it impossible to make others understand us. There is nothing in our discussions for our listeners *to* understand. We have not gone to the trouble of discovering adequately specific meanings for the terms we use.

Deliberate use of language which is not clear either to ourselves or to our listeners does not meet the demand for honest thinking discussed in Chapter I, for honest thinking requires clear thinking. When such language is used for the purpose of concealing thought or perpetuating confusion on the part of the listeners, then such speaking fails to measure up to the requirements of social ethics.

[8] Arthur M. Schlesinger, Jr., "Democracy: What Does It Mean?" *Vital Speeches,* April 15, 1948, pp. 401-402.

General rather than specific words are sometimes used, according to Adams Sherman Hill, by those "who wish, for good reasons, to disarm opposition or to veil unpleasant facts; but too frequently they are a resource for those who try to hide poverty of thought in pompous language, to give obscurity an air of cleverness or shallowness the dignity of an oracle, to cover the fact of having said nothing with the appearance of having said much."[9]

Methods of Determining Meanings

There are a number of methods by which the meanings of words may be determined either for yourself or for your listeners. All of them are concerned with attempts to point out the specific referent, to trace or, in many instances, to retrace the association of sound sequence to the particular fact of experience to which the word refers, for which it stands.

EXPLANATION. Explanation is the typical definition found in any dictionary. It consists essentially of using one word or set of words to explain the meaning of another word. When the terms used in such definitions are themselves clear in their own meanings, when they lead us directly back to an associational experience, then the definitions themselves and the words being defined are intelligible. Thus, the *American College Dictionary* explains the term *conspire*, in one sense, as "To agree together, esp. secretly, to do something reprehensible or illegal." Such a definition makes use of no terms which are too difficult to understand; hence, we can arrive at a fairly acceptable definition of the term itself.

The definition of democracy given by Stuart Gerry Brown approaches an equal degree of intelligibility. He defines democracy as a system in which ". . . the controls upon social evolution are determined by free discussion of men, events, and things, in the clear light of day, followed by consent to the will of the majority.

---

[9] Adams Sherman Hill, *Beginnings of Rhetoric and Composition Including Practical Exercises in English,* American Book Company, 1902, p. 396.

This, it would seem, is the most useful meaning of democracy."[10] Contrast such a statement with Herbert Spencer's definition of evolution: "Evolution is an integration of matter and concomitant dissipation of motion; during which the matter passes from a (relatively) indefinite, incoherent homogeneity to a (relatively) definite, coherent heterogeneity; and during which the retained motion undergoes a parallel transformation."[11] This is not to say that Spencer's statement is unintelligible; but in order to trace it back to any recognizable facts of experience, the reader would have to study laboriously through two long chapters in which Spencer leads up to his final definition. To the ordinary reader it contributes nothing to an understanding of the process of evolution.

Verbal definitions are often the only kind available. The dictionary is an extremely useful work, and its frequent use is to be encouraged. If you seek your definitions in the dictionaries, however, be sure that you understand all the terms used in those definitions. It should be borne in mind, moreover, that the chief function of the dictionary is not to prescribe definitions but to record the senses in which words are used by large numbers of people.

CLASSIFICATION AND DIFFERENTIATION. In the classification and differentiation type of definition, usually combined with the preceding type, the thing being defined is first indicated as belonging to a large class of similar objects and is then shown to differ in certain respects from other objects in that class. An *automobile* is thus *classed* as a vehicle but *differentiated* from other vehicles by being (1) especially for carrying passengers, (2) carrying its own power-generating and propelling mechanism, and (3) for travel on ordinary roads.[12]

---

[10] Stuart Gerry Brown, *We Hold These Truths,* Harper & Brothers, 2nd ed., 1948, p. 8.

[11] Herbert Spencer, *First Principles,* C. A. Watts & Co., Ltd., 6th and final ed., 1946. The Thinker's Library, No. 62, pp. 358-359. The word *relatively* was inserted by Spencer himself in a note following the definition at the end of chap. XVII, 6th ed., dated Apr. 27, 1900.

[12] Clarence L. Barnhart (ed.), *American College Dictionary,* text ed., Harper & Brothers, 1947.

USE OF CONTEXT. Many words are difficult to explain, classify, or define in specific terms. In such cases it is helpful to put them into context, that is, to use them in phrases or sentences by which the meaning is more easily understood. Moreover, since so many of our words are used in different senses, context aids in determining which of these senses is intended. A familiar example is the word *get*, which may have the sense of acquiring (to *get wealth*), of finishing some task (to *get the job done*), of learning (to *get one's lesson*), of departing or escaping (to *get away*), of donning (to *get one's coat on*), of persuading (to *get someone to do something*), and so on.

SYNONYM. Often a word may be satisfactorily defined by using another single word or phrase whose meaning is so close to the first that a clear understanding is obtained. Thus, to *alter* is to *change*; *illicit* and *unlawful* are near enough in meaning usually to permit the use of one in defining the other. Eberhard P. Deutsch uses synonym in defining "fascism as totalitarian reaction, Nazism as totalitarian socialism, and communism as totalitarian collectivism."[13] In this speech he insists that "any discussion of international relations today ought to begin with accepted terminology" and demands that common terms be clearly defined. "Communism," he goes on to say, "as a term does not have the same significance today that it had a quarter of a century ago. The term is no longer used to express an idea or even a philosophy. It refers to a realistic form of government involving an extremely distasteful totalitarianism as its principal ingredient." Of course, the terms which he himself uses in his explanation may in turn need some clarification.

The careful study of synonyms and antonyms may be valuable further in that delicate shadings of differences in word meanings may be learned. For example, consider such groups of synonyms as *command, order, dictate, regulate, instruct, rule,* and so on.

Two cautions should be observed in the method of definition by synonyms. In the first place, no two words have precisely the

[13] Eberhard P. Deutsch, "Toward Total Peace," *Vital Speeches,* February 15, 1948, pp. 263-265.

same meaning. If great precision is required by the situation or to make the sense unmistakable, synonyms alone are seldom sufficient. They should be supplemented by other methods. Furthermore, since the synonym itself may often be used in various senses, it is easy for you to select the wrong sense, so that you will have an erroneous understanding of the word whose definition you are seeking. Thus, in some dictionaries to *enunciate* may be defined as to *articulate*; but to *articulate* may be defined as to *unite by joints*. It would take considerable interpretation to think of *enunciate* in the sense of *unite by joints*.

In the second place, the use of synonyms, like other methods of definitions, is of no value at all unless the synonyms themselves serve to clarify the meaning. It will not help you to define *turgid* as *tumid* unless you know the meaning of the latter term. If you use synonyms, therefore, be sure that you know their meanings.

ETYMOLOGY. You will sometimes find that knowing the derivation of a word will help you to understand its meaning. Many of our words have interesting histories. Salary, for instance, comes from the Latin *salarium* and originally referred to money paid to Roman soldiers for the purchase of salt. The prefix *sal*, used in chemistry as in *sal ammoniac*, comes from the same origin. There is a suggestion of this original meaning when we say that someone is "not worth his salt." English *starve*, meaning to perish from lack of food, comes from the same origin as German *sterben*, which means simply to die from any cause.

Again, you must use caution in attempting to determine meanings from etymologies. One recognized characteristic of words is that most of them are in a fairly constant process of change in meaning, so that often their original meanings no longer apply. It is quite essential that you be aware of this phenomenon of change, for the meanings of many of our words are today greatly different from those they had originally or even some years ago. *Fond*, for example, which has the general meaning of *affectionate*, once meant *foolish* and is still used occasionally in that sense, as in referring to *fond mammas*.

PURPOSE OR EFFECT. Many words may be defined by indicating the purpose of the thing referred to. A *league* may be defined briefly as a compact or agreement among persons or groups for the purpose of maintaining or promoting mutual interests. A *rhetorical question* is a question intended to create some specific effect not to be answered verbally.

NEGATION. An understanding of the meaning of a word may often be made clearer by telling what the word does not mean. Usually a negative statement is coupled directly or indirectly with a positive definition: "not this, but that." For example, conscience, as Shakespeare used the word in the line, "Thus conscience does make cowards of us all," referred then not to a sense of guilt and a fear of future punishment, as it does today (negative), but to *thoughtful meditation* (positive).[14]

EXAMPLE. There are many words which it is difficult if not impossible to define in other words, or by any of the methods here described. Our own understanding of them has grown up with our direct experience, and we have never been forced to frame into words any adequate brief statement which would reflect their meaning. Most American boys (and many girls) are so familiar with the game of *baseball* that no verbal definition is felt to be necessary. We use the term freely and for the most part intelligently, often qualifying it with some such designation as *sandlot, major* or *minor league,* or sometimes *bush league,* so that there is little likelihood of our own misunderstanding of the term. If you were to attempt to explain this word to someone, say a European, entirely unfamiliar with the game, your best method would probably be to take him out to the ball park and let him watch two teams in action. Of course some verbal explanation might help him to comprehend what was going on, but his own understanding would be immeasurably increased by having made the direct association of word and experience. It would be still better if he could get into the game himself as a

---

[14] Charles Hubbard Judd, *The Psychology of Social Institutions,* The Macmillan Company, 1926, p. 205. Cf. Gray and Wise, *op. cit.,* p. 532n.

participant. You would understand the English game of cricket if you were to see it played or attempt to play it yourself. How many of you know from first-hand experience, or can describe briefly in words, the game called "bowling on the green"?

If we were to obtain more of our meanings, especially of the so-called abstract terms, from the same type of experience as for such words as *baseball,* our thinking and speaking about the things they stand for would be less vague and indefinite. We do not fully grasp the meaning of such abstract terms as democracy, for instance, because, even though living in the midst of what is called democracy, too many of us do not avail ourselves of the opportunity of learning the meaning of the term by close observation of or participating in the processes involved. Such experience through participation is often the only effective means of acquiring meanings. The more directly our understanding of these meanings comes from experiences and with the actual associating of word with thing, the more complete and exact that understanding will be. Obviously, then, when opportunity for such direct experience is wholly lacking, we must derive our meanings by other methods.

Multiple Terms

If the terms used in speech or writing were always composed of single words, the difficulty of understanding language might be considerably lessened. Often, however, our terms are word combinations which cannot be adequately understood merely by combining the meanings of the separate word elements. The term *big business* mentioned before is not to be defined by adding the definition of *big* to the definition of *business*; it has come to mean something more than the sum of these two. Similarly, the term *labor union* cannot be understood by first defining *labor*, then *union,* and putting the two together. Whenever multiple terms are used as single concepts, their definitions must refer to the combinations as wholes, and your understanding must be of the whole.

Further examples of such multiple terms, which you might be interested in attempting to define as wholes, are *laissez faire, hillbilly, cross reference, dollar diplomacy, economic royalists, open door, fellow traveler, forlorn hope, body politic, free coinage, left wing, core curriculum, rugged individualism*, and so on.

Technical Terms

Every specialized field of thought has its own peculiar vocabulary or set of terms which are used in senses restricted to that particular discipline. These same terms are in many instances also used in ordinary everyday discourse. When you say that you have "made up your mind," you are not using the term *mind* as the psychologist uses it but in what has often been called the *language of the street*. If you insist that you have *work* to do, you probably are not using *work* according to its meaning in physics.

Specialists are not as a rule good speakers.[15] One reason is that, being so familiar with the highly specialized vocabulary of their particular profession, they forget that to the uninitiated much of the language they are using has no meaning. The sign of the integral in mathematics is just as unintelligible to people who have not studied the calculus as Greek is to those who have not studied that language. Not all your speaking will be to groups of fellow scientists; you will also have to address people who are quite unfamiliar with your technical language. Aside from any other requirements of good speaking, you will need to learn how to translate your technical terms into language that will be intelligible to the layman. Mysticism in some fields of thought may be deeply impressive, but it contributes nothing to the understanding. Whether or not the words you use technically are also used in the nontechnical sense, you must be sure that you yourself have a clear understanding of the sense in which you are using them at the moment; and *you must see to it that the audience understands them in that same sense.*

[15] James A. Winans, *Speech-Making*, Appleton-Century-Crofts, Inc., 1938, p. 183.

Stereotypes

Our conversation, as well as much of the public speech that we hear, contains many terms the meanings of which have a high emotional, but often a very low logical, component. That is, they have come to have for us meanings which are vague as to understanding but yet which are effective in arousing strong emotional responses. They call up some picture, some image, pleasant or unpleasant according to the connotations in the terms, about which we are not called on to think; all we are expected to do is to feel. In fact, because most of us *think* we know what they mean, without ever having clarified our concepts, they may be used to give the impression of reasoning without actually stimulating the rational processes at all. It is not necessary to specify who or what is indicated by the term *selfish interests*; whatever or whoever they may be, mere mention is often enough to generate vigorous opposition.

The use of these terms may not be wholly reprehensible; sometimes they stimulate entirely praiseworthy attitudes which may in turn be carried over into eminently worth-while undertakings. There is a type of stimulating speech, for instance, that does not demand close logical argument; your listeners are willing to agree with you at the outset. What is demanded is an intensification of attitudes already held.[16] In such cases the occasional use of terms which carry a large proportion of emotional meaning may be entirely permissible. But *such terms should not be used as a substitute for thinking.* They are often employed not to stimulate thought but to furnish ready-made judgments without giving the opportunity to the audience to make their own judgments on an objective basis. Such terms are often designated as stereotypes.

Many of our stereotypes have arisen from beliefs which are the result of oversimplification of solutions of problems, or of answers to questions, which may be a little more difficult than we are willing to undertake. Primitive taboos are illustrative of such

[16] See chap. VI, "Speech Goals."

beliefs; but such unthinking generalizations are not confined to the primitive mind. We generalize often before we have made an adequate examination of a sufficient sampling to make the generalization valid. From what we have heard about a few Scotsmen we conclude that all Scots are miserly. In the thinking of many people, all college professors are "visionary," all corporations are predacious, all labor leaders dictatorial; and, according to those who oppose it, the Taft-Hartley Law is a "slave-labor" law. These and other labels we use to stimulate either approval or disapproval without examining a sufficient body of evidence on which to base a rational judgment.

Test your terms before you adopt them into your own thinking and thence into your speaking vocabulary. Determine whether they represent objectively ascertainable fact or a subjective evaluation only. Does the meaning of the term carry a preponderance of emotional component, or does it have a large proportion of the logical; that is, does it mainly arouse an emotional reaction, or does it refer you and your listeners to direct objective experience?

Slogans, as typical stereotypes, are generally to be avoided when you want to base your argument on sound reasoning. If you attempt to analyze the usual advertising slogan, you will find that often it does not mean a great deal. What does it mean, for example, to announce week after week that a certain brand of cigarettes is the "product of two hundred years of tobacco experience," when ten years of experience (the specific nature?) of each of twenty persons would total "two hundred years of tobacco experience?" Another brand insists that not a single case of throat irritation is reported as resulting from a thirty-day test; but the fact is that hundreds of people who have used that brand as well as others have had to discontinue smoking entirely because of throat irritation. Many radio advertisers seem to believe (with Hitler) that if a statement is repeated often enough and long enough and loudly enough, it will be believed whether it makes sense or not. Whether the name of some product is another word spelled backward has no bearing whatever on the efficacy of the product itself.

Brevity

As a rule, long, involved sentences are to be avoided in speaking in favor of brief, concise statements. Aristotle writes of making speeches "obscure through wordiness."[17] Superficial impressiveness achieved through verbosity is no substitute for clarity; if you can say what needs to be said in five words, do not use fifteen. You will often find that brevity itself has an impressiveness achieved through its very directness.

Occasionally, however, one hears something like the following examples, which are intended to illustrate the point of view apparently held by some, that ". . . brevity is the mark of a Very Unimportant Person." The samples present the "right" and the "wrong" way of making statements.

Politician Available for Office

Wrong: "I'd like to be elected."

Right: "While I am not, and never have been, beset with ambitions to aspire to this high office, I am deeply conscious of the necessity, duty and obligation of acceding to the people's wishes in the event that these wishes may be summarized as a desire that I make clear my availability. I shall not, therefore, raise obstacles to the consummation of this wish."

Company Unable to Fill Orders

Wrong: "We can't make billipers fast enough."

Right: "The current crisis in the billiper industry is a manifestation of the law of supply and demand, in that the public's desire to obtain billipers is thwarted by our present inability to supply the demand within the time at our disposal. When a point is reached where the volume of billipers equals the quantity demanded by potential customers, it is our considered opinion that this situation should terminate."[18]

---

[17] Lane Cooper, *The Rhetoric of Aristotle,* Appleton-Century-Crofts, Inc., 1932, p. 191.

[18] Parke Cummings, "How to Make Statements to the Newspapers," *Saturday Evening Post,* March 25, 1950, p. 44. Used by special permission.

In choosing your language for purposes of clarity, then, you must take every precaution to ensure that you yourself have a clear, definite understanding of the meanings of the terms you use. Otherwise not only will your own thinking be vague, but you will be entirely unable to stimulate in the thinking of your audience the meanings you would like to arouse. Speak in familiar terms; use concrete, specific terms; be simple, direct, and brief.

Community of Reference

It is not enough that you as the speaker have a clear understanding of the meanings of your words; your listeners must also understand them. If there is not sufficient similarity in the associations which you and your hearers have attached to your language to make it mutually intelligible, then no communication at all is possible. Either your words must come within the vocabulary of your audience, or you must give your listeners enough of a definition, using one or more of the methods described above, to make your words understandable. You cannot talk about *parity* and *parity prices* to a group which knows nothing of the principle of parity or its application. You are at liberty to talk freely about a "liberal" education or about the value of the "humanities" in education, provided only that you know definitely what the term *liberal education* means and precisely what are those disciplines to which the term *humanities* is applied, and provided further that your listeners have the same understanding as you have, or as nearly the same as is reasonably to be expected.

It is unlikely that confusion will result from the use of many terms in our language. For your general purposes, such divergencies in meaning as exist are usually immaterial. But there are a great number of words whose associations among different people are so divergent that understanding among individuals, as among peoples, is difficult if not impossible. As this is being written, the Russians are insisting that it is they who are trying to build up a "democratic" order, while the western powers are "fascist" and "reactionary." It is quite evident that there is no common ground for understanding these terms. To one people (or to their rulers) "democratic" has one range of possible meanings; to the other the range of meanings hardly touches the first at any point. Essentially the same might be said with respect to the terms *Fascist* and *reactionary*. Any discussions between these two groups about the desirability of democracy or the dangers of fascism are futile until all the conferees are willing to agree upon the body of principle, method, or procedure for which the terms shall be permitted to stand *for both groups*.

Descriptive of the absence of common reference in this particular connection is the following:

... Many of the Russian people consider their recent election a thoroughly democratic operation and a bona fide expression of the popular will.

This ... is due ... to the fact that they have never taken part in a real election. In all the history of Russia there never has been a democratic election in which two or more candidates debated the matters at issue and the people made known their decision in a secret ballot. ... The Russian people, slaving under a long series of tyrants in the isolated vastness of their mysterious land, never have known freedom or had any contact with democracy.

To try to explain freedom and democracy to such people is like trying to explain electronics to a Hottentot. It is true that the Russians have in their language words which appear to mean the same things that "freedom" and "democracy" mean to us. But actually the meaning is different, because it is impossible for a people to have words for things that they have never known and never have been able to imagine clearly.

Obviously, this raises a certain obstacle to our efforts to reach the Russian people and tell them more about the freedom that we enjoy. A man who lived all his life in a dark cellar would be unable to imagine sunlight. A man who dwelt in a cave could not imagine the vastness of the world above. So it is with Russians who have lived all their lives in slavery and cannot imagine freedom or understand the words that describe freedom. ....[19]

[19] Editorial, *The Morning Advocate,* Baton Rouge, Louisiana, March 30, 1950. Used by special permission.

PUBLIC SPEAKING

Be sure that your listeners know the sense in which you are using a given word, especially if there is likely to be any question about its meaning. The first requisite of language is that it clarify meanings rather than obscure them. You and your hearers must, if meanings are to be made clear, have had an essential community of reference. Any willful neglect of this principle may betoken a lack of honest thinking and purpose. A good criterion to observe in choosing language for clarity is to use terms, as Dewey suggests, which "convey meaning so directly that no effort at translation is needed."[20]

Study the following address from the point of view of clarity. Attempt to determine the degree to which it meets the criteria described in this chapter. Select a short passage from the address, and see if you can restate it with greater clarity, still preserving the additional elements of vividness and impressiveness.

Second Inaugural Address
Abraham Lincoln

At this second appearing to take the oath of the presidential office, there is less occasion for an extended address than at the first. Then a statement somewhat in detail of the course to be pursued seemed very fitting and proper; now at the expiration of four years, during which public declarations have constantly been called forth concerning every point and place of the great contest which still absorbs attention and engrosses the energies of the nation, little that is new could be presented. The progress of our arms, upon which all else chiefly depends, is as well known to the public as to myself. It is, I trust, reasonably satisfactory and encouraging to all. With a high hope for the future, no prediction in that regard is ventured. On the occasion corresponding to this four years ago, all thoughts were anxiously directed to an impending civil war. All dreaded it. All sought to avoid it. While the Inaugural Address was being delivered from this place, devoted altogether to saving the Union without war, the insurgent agents were in the city seeking to destroy it without war,—seeking to dissolve the Union, and divide the effects by negotiating. Both parties deprecated war, but one of them would make war rather than let it perish, and war came. One-eighth of the whole

---

[20] John Dewey, *How We Think*, D. C. Heath and Company, 1910, p. 136.

USING LANGUAGE FOR CLARITY 411

population were colored slaves, not distributed generally over the Union, but located in the southern part. These slaves contributed a peculiar and powerful interest. All knew the interest would somehow cause war. To strengthen, perpetuate, and extend this interest was the object for which the insurgents would rend the Union by war, while the Government claimed no right to do more than restrict the territorial enlargement of it. Neither party expected the magnitude or duration which it has already attained; neither anticipated that the cause of the conflict might cease even before the conflict itself should cease. Each looked for an easier triumph and a result less fundamental and astonishing. Both read the same Bible and pray to the same God. Each invokes His aid against the other. It may seem strange that any man should dare to ask a just God's assistance in wringing bread from the sweat of other men's faces; but let us judge not, that we be not judged. The prayer of both should not be answered; that of neither has been answered fully, for the Almighty has His own purposes. "Woe unto the world because of offenses, for it must needs be that offense come; but woe unto that man by whom the offense cometh." If we shall suppose American slavery one of those offenses which, in the providence of God, must needs come, but which, having continued through His appointed time, He now wills to remove, and that He gives to both North and South this terrible war, as was due to those by whom the offense came, shall we discern that there is any departure from those divine attributes which believers in the living God always ascribe to Him? Fondly do we hope, fervently do we pray, that this mighty scourge of war may speedily pass away; yet if it be God's will that it continue until the wealth piled by bondsmen by two hundred and fifty years' unrequited toil shall be sunk, and until every drop of blood drawn with the lash shall be paid by another drawn with the sword, as was said three thousand years ago, so still it must be said that the judgments of the Lord are true and righteous altogether.

With malice towards none, with charity for all, with firmness in the right, as God gives us to see the right, let us strive on to finish the work we are in, to bind up the nation's wounds, to care for him who shall have borne the battle, and for his widow and orphans; to do all which may achieve and cherish a just and lasting peace among ourselves and with all nations.

EXERCISES

1. Select a passage from some speech (as in *Vital Speeches*), and determine the techniques used in achieving clarity; or point out in

what ways the speaker failed to achieve clarity or might have succeeded.
2. Set down ten of the most nearly concrete terms you can think of. Now study these words, and discover to what degree they are actually abstract or represent abstractions.
3. Put into intelligent context the following words:

arrogant	encomium	opprobrium
arrogate	entrenched	partisan
capacious	intrinsic	random
capricious	meretricious	specious
covert	meritorious	supercilious

Add to this list any others which you may discover, the meanings of which need clarification by use.
4. Make a list of ten words you have recently encountered, the meanings of which were not clear to you. Find the meanings according to the context in which you discovered them.
5. Select one of the words mentioned in this chapter, the meanings of which are often confused, and give to the class in a three- to five-minute speech a clear definition. Use two or more of the techniques of definition described in the chapter. Do not discuss the various ways in which the word may be used; give one extended explanation of one of the senses in which it actually is used.
6. Select a two-word term now in current use, and give a statement of its meaning in from three to five minutes. Several such terms are suggested in this chapter.
7. Select some *technical* term, and explain its meaning to a group of uninitiated listeners. Make them understand the term as nearly as possible as it is used in its technical sense.
8. Select a group of words of similar meanings (synonyms, approximately), and differentiate their meanings and connotations.
9. Give the etymology of some word of interest, showing how its meaning has developed and changed since the original use of the source words.
10. Study some speech, either from *Vital Speeches* or from some other source, and list the stereotypes to be found there.
11. Evaluate the following definition from the point of view of clarity:

By highbrowism I mean the highest degree of unapologetic, unflinching excellence that can be achieved in any field of knowledge—from agriculture to zoology. I mean a devotion to that high truth even though the truth be difficult, unpopular, unprofitable, unconsoling, unflattering, and entirely out of accord with dominant prejudices. Yet I am speaking here not primarily of a moral fact—the moral fact of courageous adherence to a conviction—but rather of a cast of mind, of the intellectual personality, of the unwillingness to be satisfied with anything less than the best, the most highly refined, the most penetrating and inclusive version of truth permitted by the present state of knowledge and by our inherited wisdom.[21]

12. In order to be able to discuss some matters intelligently, agreement is necessary on the accepted meanings of terms. Such agreement may often be arrived at through the processes of discussion. Organize a series of symposiums of five members and a chairman each, which will attempt to frame in specific language a definition of some commonly used terms on which there may be no common agreement. Work toward the smoothing out of differences. Emphasize common understandings at first, rather than divergences, eliminating as many of the latter as possible, and attempting to arrive at a statement on which all can agree. The following are examples of terms that may be used:

democracy	big business
communism	government in business
welfare state	liberal education
socialism	humanities
social security	statism

13. Where the facilities are available, make a recording on wire or tape of one of your speeches of this group of exercises. Listen to it critically, studying it for ideas, organization, language. Revise wherever it seems necessary for greater effectiveness. Record again and listen. When you are satisfied that you can make no more improvement yourself, present it to the class.

SUPPLEMENTARY READINGS

1. Baird, A. Craig, and Knower, Franklin H., *General Speech: An Introduction*, McGraw-Hill Book Company, Inc., 1949, pp. 134-156.
2. Blair, Hugh, *Lectures on Rhetoric and Belles Lettres*, Collins and Hannay, 1819, Lecture IX, "Style—Perspicuity and Precision."

[21] Robert B. Heilman, "An Inquiry into Highbrowism," *Bulletin of the American Association of University Professors*, 1949, pp. 611-627.

3. Bryant, Donald C., and Wallace, Karl R., *Fundamentals of Public Speaking*, Appleton-Century-Crofts, Inc., 1947, pp. 171-190.
4. Campbell, George, *The Philosophy of Rhetoric*, Harper & Brothers, 1846, Book II, chap. VI, "Of Perspicuity."
5. Dolman, John, Jr., *A Handbook of Public Speaking*, Harcourt, Brace and Company, Inc., rev. ed., 1934, chap. 9, pp. 67-70.
6. Quintilian, *Institutes of Oratory*, Book VIII, chap. II, "Concerning Perspicuity."
7. Sarett, Lew, and Foster, William Trufant, *Basic Principles of Speech*, Houghton Mifflin Company, rev. ed., 1946, chap. 22, "The Language of Speech," pp. 545-568.
8. Soper, Paul L., *Basic Public Speaking*, Oxford University Press, 1949, pp. 203-216.
9. Spencer, Herbert, *The Philosophy of Style*, Appleton-Century-Crofts, Inc., 1871, Part I, sec. 1.
10. Williamson, Arleigh B., Fritz, Charles A., and Ross, Harold Raymond, *Speaking in Public*, Prentice-Hall, Inc., rev. ed., 1948, chap. XIII, "Clearness," pp. 203-222.

CHAPTER XVII

Using Language for Vividness

TO SECURE understanding, as explained in the previous chapter, you must give your language clarity; to arouse and maintain interest and attention, you must give it vividness. The primary sources of vividness lie in the sense imagery you are able to arouse in the minds of your listeners. "Vividness," says Brigance, "is the *sine qua non* of style."[1]

This is not to imply that vividness and clarity are necessarily separate and distinct. On the contrary, in order to achieve vividness you must first of all be clear; clarity is the first step to vividness. If you are giving instruction, for instance, you will need to be clear in your verbal explanation; you will also need to make your listeners see at least in imagination the details of the subject

---

[1] William Norwood Brigance, *Speech Composition*, Appleton-Century-Crofts, Inc., 1937, p. 218.

matter. The chief advantage of visual aids in instruction, as well as of the other visual forms of support discussed in an earlier chapter, lies in their potency in providing an experience which forms the basis for arousing clear, vivid imagery. It is this imagery which makes possible both immediate understanding of the points being discussed and the later recall of the experience itself.

But imagery provides more than clarity. We have all experienced the rise of interest and attention when the speaker introduces the phrase, "To illustrate," or "For example," or when he draws some striking word picture to enable us to see mentally what he is talking about. They are almost as effective in recapturing the attention as the expression, "In conclusion." Vividness, created by copious use of imagery, has as one of its main values the holding of attention and interest. This chapter, then, can easily be studied in connection with the chapter in which attention and interest are discussed.

IMAGERY

Imagery as Recall

While the exact nature of images and of imagery may not be fully known, the phenomenon itself is a familiar one. In one sense, imagery is a form of recall. We cannot relive actual experiences; we can bring them back into consciousness only through some form of imagery. It is not important here that we understand fully just what goes on in the physical and mental organization of the individual to produce what is called imagery; it may be of some significance to understand something of its importance in thinking.

Much of our thinking goes on in the form of the recall of past experiences, and the organization of those experiences into new combinations. It is the reliving of these experiences, their recall in terms of the sensory avenues by which the data of experience became known to us in the first place, that constitutes imagery. If, for example, you have attended a symphony concert, you may have relived that experience by recalling how the orchestra appeared on the stage, the graceful movements of the conductor as he drew the players out in their various passages, the unison bowing of the first violin section, the movements of the hands of the harpist as she plucked the strings of her instrument. Your renewal of the visual experience constitutes your visual imagery. At the same time, you may recall also the sounds you heard: the exquisite blending of the tones from the different sections, the development of the motif of the symphony, the crashing of the cymbals or the blare of the brasses, the plaintive nasality of the oboes or the tinkle of the celesta. Your reliving of that auditory experience constitutes your auditory imagery.

Have you ever taken a boat ride when the waves caused the vessel to rock noticeably? For a time after you landed, what were your sensations? Did you not relive for some time that rocking? Did you not have a distinct imagery of shifting of balance, of movement?

Verbal Imagery

Many people have considerable difficulty in arousing a strong sense imagery; they have, however, a strong imagery for *words*. Moreover, there are many abstractions for which no direct experience can be recalled and for which there is no immediate sense imagery. As we hear and use such terms as *justice, truth, beauty, honor, charity*, and scores of other abstract ideas, we find it difficult to visualize such generalizations. There is nothing to see, to hear, to sense directly. The words, however, are of the greatest importance in the thinking process, for we can and do use words in the formulation of ideas; we use them, first, in referring directly and specifically to things of sense, thereby calling up the direct imagery of those things; we use them, second, quite as often for those abstractions for which it is difficult to recall direct experience. We combine words into new combinations, we put them into new relationships, and develop new ideas—always provided that the things for which the words stand, even abstractly, can by themselves be combined into the new relationships indicated by the new word combinations. Word relations which have no correspondence to fact relationship simply do not make sense outside of fairy tales and fantasy. As Roderigo said to Iago, "... your words and performances are no kin together."[2]

FORMS OF VERBAL IMAGERY. Verbal imagery itself may take one or more various forms. These words in which we think may come to us through the auditory sense as though we hear them spoken, through the visual sense, as if they appeared on the page, kinaesthetically as if we pronounced them or even as in imagination we pound them out on a typewriter, or through any other mechanism by which we symbolize. Verbal imagery of the deaf may be through manual symbols.

Verbalization in whatever form it may occur thus provides the imagery in which most of our thinking goes on, mainly for the reason that so much of it involves abstract concepts for which the only method of recall we have is through verbal imagery. These concepts are so general and so removed through the processes of abstraction from direct experience that clear, vivid imagery *of the generalization* itself is impossible. Imagery is specific: we do not recall abstract beauty, we recall things that are beautiful. We have no experience and hence no imagery of abstract harmony: we can recall the blending of tones that produced harmony. There is no experience of truth as such; we know directly only those things which are true. All we have of any of these generalizations is a *concept* of beauty, of harmony, of truth, in the formulation of which concept the *word* is the final step; and the word itself is concrete. The only way in which we can recall the concepts is through the imagery of the words which have come to stand for the generalizations. Of course, the concepts themselves are made up of innumerable specific instances, of a large number of direct

[2] Othello, IV, scene 3.

experiences for any one of which, or for a combination of which, we might easily call up a rich imagery.

Because abstractions are so difficult to interpret in terms of actual experience, your listeners will soon tire of an unbroken succession of such generalized ideas. Their interest and attention will waver unless you can find a way of bringing these abstractions to life. You must make them vivid; you must put them into language that will be more directly related to their experiences. Vividness in language demands imagery, which is aroused by concrete terms. You will not be able to avoid abstract terms entirely, but your listeners' understanding of such terms will be made clearer, the ideas will be more vivid, if you will express the abstractions in terms that will arouse specific imagery. George William Curtis might have spoken in general terms of the patriotism that fired the men of the Revolution; instead, he gives a vivid picture: "The inspiring statue of the Minute Man at Concord . . . commemorates the spirit that left the plow standing in the furrow, that drew Nathanael Green from his anvil and Esek Hopkins from his farm."[3]

Imagery and Imagination

Simple imagery itself is a simple act of recall, an act of memory. When the sense images are combined into new arrangements, often quite logical, often fantastic, the process is known as imagination. James Watt, seeing the force of the steam raise the lid of the teakettle, combined these elements into new relationships with other known elements, "saw" the steam moving a piston in a cylinder—and the steam engine was born. Every new invention is the result of an active imagination. Every new relationship is a product of old images in new combinations. It is these new combinations of old elements that the speaker describes whenever he proposes something different from what is already known.

[3] George Williams Curtis, "The Leadership of Educated Men," *Classified Models of Speech Composition*, James Milton O'Neill (ed.), The Century Co., 1921, pp. 816-828.

Types of Imagery

Many writers recognize seven principal types of imagery, each one corresponding to one of the physical senses. These seven are:[4]

1. *Visual*: the recall of things and events that have come into our awareness through the sense of vision, such as familiar scenes, faces, happenings, localities, pictures, etc.
2. *Auditory*: the recollection of impressions that have entered our experience through the sense of hearing, such as the voices of friends, musical melodies or harmonies, the noise of crowds, the roar of the waves, the gentle drip of rain, and so on.
3. *Gustatory*: the recollection of impressions reaching our consciousness through the sense of taste, such as the tartness of lemon juice, the richness of pecan pie, the bitter of quinine, the salt of sea water, the flavor of a well-cooked steak, and so on.
4. *Olfactory*: the recall of impressions that have come to us through the sense of smell, such as the fragrance of new-mown hay or freshly ploughed land, the heaviness of cape jasmine (gardenia), the aroma of breakfast coffee or of cooking cabbage (if you like it, *stench* if you don't!), the freshness of the air after a summer rain, the pungency of onions, etc.
5. *Kinaesthetic*: the memory of sensations of movement, such as running, or strolling, of driving a golf ball, or of striking a tennis ball, of kicking a football, of paddling a canoe, or deftly tossing a dry fly on the surface of a quiet pool, of driving over the mountains or through heavy traffic.
6. *Tactual*: the remembrance of things felt through the sense of touch, such as the smoothness of silk, the roughness of an unshaven chin, the wind across the forehead, the sleekness of fine fur, etc.
7. *Thermal*: the recall of impressions of temperatures, such as the extreme heat or cold of an August or a January day, the cooling breeze from the Gulf or the freezing winds across the prairie, the hot coffee for breakfast, or the cold "coke" in midafternoon.[5]

---

[4] See also William Phillips Sandford and Willard Hayes Yeager, *Principles of Effective Speaking*, The Ronald Press Company, 4th ed., 1942, p. 194.

[5] It should be observed that each of these items calls up other types of imagery than the particular one being described.

USING LANGUAGE FOR VIVIDNESS 421

These seven are not all the avenues by which impressions may enter our awareness. Several other senses are generally recognized by psychologists, each of which gives rise to an additional kind of imagery. Among these are hunger, thirst, pain, nausea, fatigue, pressure, balance, to all of which there may be a related imagery just as vivid as that based on the seven listed above.

When the listener hears you give a description or use a word or phrase involving one or more of these types of imagery, he bases the imagery thus aroused upon his own past experiences involving sense impressions similar to those represented in the words. Upon the basis of those experiences, he constructs in his own consciousness an imagery pattern through which he tends to relive mentally, if only for a fleeting instant, the original experience. In that process he is *creating for himself* a vivid reconstruction of his own experiences and is himself materially aiding you in achieving vividness in your descriptions. Listening thus becomes in a very real sense a creative process.

Notice the different sense images which are aroused by the following passage from Dr. Kincaid's "The New Portrait of Abraham Lincoln." Referring to a letter written to Lincoln by his step-brother, J. D. Johnston, May 25, 1849, asking Lincoln to come to see his presumably dying father, he says, "The son of Sarah Bush Johnston, Lincoln's step-mother, was speaking plaintively for a lonely father who 'craved to see' his own 'flush & blood.' Picture if we can this old and infirm father, lying ill and wasting away, in the humble log-cabin home on the Goose Neck prairie. Far away in Springfield was his stalwart son, a rising young lawyer, a former Congressman and political leader, beginning to evolve a political philosophy which would lead him to the highest office in the land."[6]

Although any or all of these types may be strong and vivid, it is generally believed that for most people visual imagery is

[6] Robert L. Kincaid, "The New Portrait of Abraham Lincoln," *Vital Speeches*, February 15, 1948, pp. 265-269. Dr. Kincaid is President of Lincoln Memorial University, Harrogate, Tennessee. Quoted by permission.

stronger and more vivid than any other type. Word pictures, then, that recall visual experiences or images would seem to stand the greatest chance of being effective for the greatest number of listeners. Notice how Grady makes use of the visual in his moving description of the Confederate soldier at the close of the Civil War:

> Let me picture to you the footsore Confederate soldier, as, buttoning up in his faded gray jacket the parole which was to bear testimony to his children of his fidelity and faith, he turned his face southward from Appomattox in April, 1865. Think of him as ragged, half-starved, heavy-hearted, enfeebled by want and wounds; having fought to exhaustion, he surrenders his gun, wrings the hands of his comrades in silence, and, lifting his tear-stained and pallid face for the last time to the graves that dot the old Virginia hills, pulls his gray cap over his brow and begins the slow and painful journey.

Visual is not, by any means, of course, the only type of imagery in the passage.

Although visual imagery seems to be strongest for most people, many are especially strong in auditory imagery and have little difficulty in recalling the various sounds that have come into their experience. Patrick Henry uses the appeal to the auditory in this passage from his famous "Liberty or Death" speech delivered in 1775: "The next gale that sweeps from the north will bring to our ears the clash of resounding arms!"

In his repeated use of such terms as "a snare to your feet," "subjugation," "bind and rivet upon us those chains which the British Ministry have been so long forging," "we have been spurned, with contempt, from the foot of the throne," "until our enemies have bound us hand and foot," he arouses a strong kinaesthetic imagery of coercion, of forcible restraint from an outside agency.

Some people are apparently able to call up vivid imagery of all types; others insist that their entire imaginal experience is very weak, that they are able to call up any imagery at all only with extreme difficulty, and even that tends to be faint and indistinct. They do respond to language or verbal imagery, which seems to serve in lieu of imagery based on the senses indicated above. Yet, as pointed out, even verbal imagery depends, it would seem, on other types, such as auditory, visual, kinaesthetic, and so on. It is probable that people devoid of a considerable amount of imagery of one kind or another are extremely rare.

CHOOSING WORDS FOR VIVIDNESS

"No style can be vivid," says Brigance, "which is not clear, yet clearness alone cannot give vividness for there must be the added quality of force."[7] Whatever may have been said with respect to the use of language and the choice of words for clarity, therefore, applies with equal potency with respect to their importance in the development of vividness. Language may have a few attributes, however, which seem to contribute especially to vividness.

Concreteness

In the previous chapter, "Using Language for Clarity," it was pointed out that, whereas abstract words are remote in their reference to experience, concrete terms, on the other hand, lead much more directly back to actual association which gave original meaning to the terms themselves. The result is that the meanings of these terms are much more definite and clear than abstract terms. They are far more likely to arouse specific imagery and hence contribute to vividness to a much greater degree. Thus, *parliamentary procedure*, with which many people have had direct, concrete experience, may have a more specific meaning than *democracy*, although both are based on identical philosophies and are put into practice through the functioning of identical principles. Churchill made the severity of the coming

[7] William Norwood Brigance, *op. cit.*, p. 218.

struggle highly vivid when he proimsed the British people nothing but "blood, toil, sweat, and tears."

In his *Philosophy of Style*[8] Herbert Spencer explains the force of "specific" as compared with "generic" words on the basis of economy of effort:

> This superiority of specific expressions is clearly due to a saving of the effort required to translate words into thoughts. As we do not think in generals but in particulars—as, whenever any class of things is referred to, we represent it to ourselves by calling to mind individual members of it; it follows that when an abstract word is used, the hearer or reader has to choose from his stock of images, one by one, by which he may figure to himself the genus mentioned. In doing this, some delay must arise—some force be expended; and if, by employing a specific term, an appropriate image can be at once suggested, an economy is achieved, and a more vivid impression produced.

One implication at least is that your listeners simply will not go to the trouble and effort to trace the reference in abstract words to original experiences, with the result that meanings for them continue to be hazy, vague, and indefinite. "Eloquence," says Emerson, "is *the power to translate a truth into language perfectly intelligible to the person to whom you speak.*"[9] "Instant intelligibility" is the goal set by Winans.[10]

Instead of using general terms, then, use words and expressions whenever possible that will stimulate definite sense imagery. Remember that your listeners have no imagery of abstract beauty; they will recall with any degree of vividness only the *things* that are beautiful. Rather than saying that a certain scene was beautiful, point out the specific elements of beauty, whether they be the rolling hills, the verdant pastures with grazing cattle, the

[8] Herbert Spencer, *The Philosophy of Style*, Appleton-Century-Crofts, Inc., 1871, pp. 15 ff.

[9] Ralph Waldo Emerson, "Eloquence," *Letters and Social Aims*, vol. VIII of the Centenary Edition of the Complete Works of Ralph Waldo Emerson, Houghton Mifflin Company, 1904, p. 130. Italics are in the original.

[10] James A. Winans, *Speech-Making*, Appleton-Century-Crofts, Inc., 1938, p. 180.

acres of ripening wheat waving in the breeze, the pattern of well-marked fields that lie spread out before you from your vantage point on a high eminence—these are all descriptive details which require, in Spencer's terms, a minimum of translation into "thoughts" in order to establish vividness. "Beautiful" is an abstract term which requires considerable translation into concrete language; alone it cannot arouse definite, concrete imagery.

Mark Twain in his after-dinner speech on "New England Weather" concludes with an effective description of a winter scene, in which the element of vividness is achieved through the use of concrete terms:

> If we had not our own bewitching autumn foliage, we should still have to credit the weather with one feature which compensates for all its bullying vagaries, the ice-storm—when a leafless tree is clothed with ice from the bottom to the top—ice that is as bright and clear as crystal; every bough and twig is strung with ice-beads, frozen dewdrops, and the whole tree sparkles, cold and white, like the Shah of Persia's diamond plume. Then the wind waves the branches, and the sun comes out and turns all those myriads of beads and drops to prisms, that glow and hum and flash with all manner of colored fires, which change and change again, with inconceivable rapidity, from blue to red, from red to green, and green to gold; the tree becomes a sparkling fountain, a very explosion of dazzling jewels; and it stands there the acme, the climax, the supremest possibility in art or nature of bewildering, intoxicating, intolerable magnificence. One cannot make the words too strong.[11]

DESCRIPTIVE WORDS. The above quotation from Mark Twain illustrates the effective use of descriptive words in achieving concreteness and thereby vividness. He states a number of facts of experience, but he also employs such words as both state and characterize those facts. He does not say merely that the ice-

[11] Samuel L. Clemens, "New England Weather," *Modern Eloquence*, Ashley Thorndike (ed.), Modern Eloquence Corporation, 1923, vol. 1, pp. 288-292. (This speech also appears in the writings of Samuel L. Clemens, in the volume, *Tom Sawyer Abroad*, Harper & Brothers, 1896, pp. 364-376, under the less familiar title, "Speech on the Weather.")

storm is beautiful; he chooses his details, and then uses his descriptive words to give a series of vivid images that impress us with its beauty.

Similarly, in the passage from Grady, quoted on page 422, observe that nowhere does the speaker use a term intended to describe in general the returning soldier; instead he chooses his particular details and, by selecting his words for their descriptive value, creates an effect which could not have been achieved with a less skillful use of language. Every one of those details stands out in vivid imagery: *footsore, faded gray jacket, turned his face southward, ragged, half-starved, heavy-hearted, enfeebled, fought to exhaustion,* and so on. Note the effect of the statement, "wrings the hands of his comrades in silence," and of "lifting his tear-stained and pallid face for the last time to the graves that dot the old Virginia hills," "begins the slow and painful journey." The picture is as vivid as if it had been painted, and it is made so by the skillful use of descriptive words, which give concreteness and arouse strong imagery.

Familiarity

A second attribute of words that may contribute to vividness is familiarity. Whenever possible use words that are well within the vocabulary of your listeners. If, as Spencer suggests, you must use new, strange terms, be sure to translate them yourself. Do not make it necessary for your listeners to translate your language for themselves. ". . . the more time and attention it takes to receive and understand each sentence," says Spencer, "the less time and attention can be given to the contained idea; and the less vividly will that idea be conceived."[12]

Shaded Words

Much of the clarity and vividness of your language will depend on your careful use of fine shadings of meaning. It is said that no two words are identical in meaning, that there is between

[12] Spencer, *op. cit.*, p. 11.

USING LANGUAGE FOR VIVIDNESS

every two words, however closely related they may be, some slight distinction that can make the difference between ordinary language and vivid usage.

About twenty-four hundred years ago an old Greek by the name of Prodicus attempted to point out shadings of meaning in such groups of words as *bravery, boldness, rashness, courage, fearlessness; adversary, opponent, antagonist,* and *enemy; argue* and *wrangle; esteem* and *praise; gratify* and *please; will* and *wish,* and so on. Even at that early date he recognized the importance of choosing the right word to give the exact shade of meaning desired and to add vividness as well as clarity to the language.

A careful study of the dictionary will reveal to you a great number of these word groups, that is, groups of words having somewhat similar meanings yet sufficiently different to justify great care in the selection. It might make quite a difference which word you were to choose in the following groups:

detriment	have	gaudy	complete	doubtful
harm	hold	flashy	entire	dubious
damage	own	garish	intact	skeptical
injury	occupy	tawdry	perfect	incredulous
manner	melt	refuse	hint	rectify
air	thaw	decline	insinuate	remedy
bearing	fuse	reject	suggest	correct
mien	dissolve	spurn	intimate (v.)	reform
				amend
compete	map	fate	irony	
contend	chart	destiny	satire	ease
contest	graph	doom	sarcasm	comfort
mutual	ripe	fair	modify	counsel
reciprocal	mellow	impartial	qualify	advise
	mature	disinterested	temper (v.)	recommend
		uninterested		
		unprejudiced		

Do your windows have *curtains, shades, shutters, blinds,* or *drapes*? Is your way of doing things a matter of *custom, habit, wont,* or *practice?* In your social relations are you merely *civil,* or are you *affable, genial, courteous,* or *polite?* Was the murder described in this morning's paper *premeditated, voluntary, intentional, deliberate?*

Textile manufacturers and dyers are continually bringing out new shades of old colors, to each of which a new name is given. Those who deal in fabrics and their colors learn these names and are able to discuss them consistently. Thus there are large numbers of reds, blues, greens, and yellows and of shades, hues, and tints made up of combinations of the primary colors, each with its own designation. In cases where the precise shading is significant, learn these differences and be able to use them.

To the person keenly interested in such things, these differences are important. Hester Prynne wore a *scarlet* letter, not one of carmine or crimson. Fine differences in human relations are just as important as differences in colors, perhaps even more so, and the terms that are used to designate them are likewise important in giving to your language both vividness and clarity. The merchant must know the difference between the *cost*, the *price*, the *worth*, and the *value* of his goods. In your speaking you will be dealing not only in material things but in human relations as well. In these relations are many fine shadings, the perception of and response to which may be said to constitute in part that elusive human quality known as refinement. "To be refined," says Woolbert, "is to be able to make fine distinctions."[13]

SIMPLE WORDS. Short, simple words will ordinarily lend themselves more readily than long ones to translation into imagery and hence to vividness. In Lincoln's "Gettysburg Address" are found only twelve different words of more than two syllables. Of these twelve, one *dedicate(d)*, is used six times, and two others, *consecrate* and *devotion*, twice each. None of these nor

[13] Charles Henry Woolbert, *The Fundamentals of Speech*, Harper & Brothers, rev. ed., 1927, pp. 46.

USING LANGUAGE FOR VIVIDNESS

of the other nine can be thought of as other than plain, simple language.

Often your choice will be not so much between short and long words as between simple, easily understood phraseology and those long, complex conceptions that may be difficult to translate. The words must not only be in good usage; they must be so familiar to the listener that they facilitate rather than retard the translation into concrete imagery. Length is often of less importance than intelligibility. Do not attempt the restricted idiom of a relatively small section of the country unless you are thoroughly familiar with it. During World War II, after the fall of Italy, many Americans took up the slogan from baseball, "One down and two to go." Unfortunately, many Japanese were also familiar with American baseball lingo, for one of them came up with the comment, "Much depends on who's coming to bat!"

Notice how Winston Churchill uses a complex conception and then proceeds to translate it himself: ". . . profound scientific, social and philosophical issues . . . are to be examined . . . not only in their integrity but in their relationship, meaning thereby not only one by one but all together."[14]

It is here that the difference between simplicity and floridity might be pointed out. Generally the latter refers to a type of language, a style, exalted far beyond any fitness to the speaker, the audience, the subject, or the occasion. An experienced speaker, known to be widely read, speaking on some highly important subject on a great, formal occasion, might use language that would be entirely out of place for a younger speaker on a less exalted subject on an informal occasion. An exalted style, a part of which may consist in the use of words that would rarely be used in conversation, may on some occasions be appropriate; but the occasion must call for that style. Even then, it can easily be overdone.

[14] Winston Churchill, "United We Stand Secure," *Representative American Speeches: 1948-1949*, A. Craig Baird (ed.), The H. W. Wilson Company, 1949, pp. 36-50.

FIGURES OF SPEECH

Not all vividness comes from single words, although they are in themselves important. Probably more comes from the ways in which we put words together into expressions that arouse definite, sharp imagery. In addition to direct literal narrative and description there are more indirect methods of giving vividness to language which are often, because they are indirect, even more effective. Our language is filled with words and phrases that originated as "figures of speech" but have become so deeply embedded into our daily usage that we no longer think of them as figurative at all. We have all heard much about the *New Deal* or the *Fair Deal*; we *ruminate* on a subject, *drive a hard bargain*, weigh our *arguments*, *ponder* a situation; a campaign speaker *takes the stump*; *brass hats* is a term familiar to everyone. As this is being written we hear and read much about the *Iron Curtain* separating Eastern from Western Europe. Such expressions are especially effective mainly because they suggest rather than state outright. They arouse imagery but leave the details of the images for the listener to supply out of his own background of experience.

Simile and Metaphor

Probably the two most useful figures which the speaker will have occasion to use are the *simile* and the *metaphor*. They resemble each other in that both are comparisons of things essentially unlike; they differ in that the former *states* that a likeness exists; the latter simply *implies* it.[15]

Churchill makes use of simile when he says that "The blockade of Berlin . . . is like a contest in endurance between two men, one of whom sits quietly grinning in his arm chair while the other stands on his head hour after hour to show how much he

[15] A simple statement of likeness between two similar things is known as a "comparison." When General Eisenhower in his Inaugural Address at Columbia University said, ". . . or your republic will be as fearfully plundered and laid waste by barbarians in the twentieth century as the Roman Empire was in the fifth; . . ." he was stating a simple comparison rather than a simile.

is in earnest."[16] But when he says that he "foresaw . . . that the armies of democracy would melt in the sunlight of victory,"[17] he is using metaphor. Similarly, when Dorothy Thompson gave as the title to her Commencement Address at Russell Sage College, June 8, 1937, "Freedom's Back Is Against the Wall!"[18] she was using a mixture of metaphor and personification, to be described later. Both metaphor and simile are used by Grady when he speaks in "The Homes of the People" of ". . . night falling gently as the wings of the unseen dove," although the concept of night "falling" has been so completely accepted into our language that it is rarely thought of as metaphor.

Herbert Hoover speaks of "The frozen class barriers of Europe" and "the hurricanes of social and economic destruction that have swept the world."[19] Daniel Webster, in his famous Knapp-White murder case speech, refers to "the key which unlocks the whole mystery."[20] According to George William Curtis, Patrick Henry was "That Virginian tongue of flame";[21] and the same orator refers to a sermon preached in 1750 by Jonathan Mayhew as "the morning gun of the Revolution."[22]

Other examples of the use of metaphors and similes are these:

I believe most labor leaders are well aware that when "pork chops" and "wage earners" get into a race, the wage earner always loses. He is slower on his feet than a pork chop.[23]

---

[16] Winston Churchill, "Peace Rests Upon Strength," *Vital Speeches*, November 1, 1948, pp. 44-46. The speech was given October 8, 1948.

[17] *Ibid.*

[18] Dorothy Thompson, "Freedom's Back Is Against the Wall," Lew Sarett and William Trufant Foster (eds.), *Modern Speeches on Basic Issues*, Houghton Mifflin Company, 1939, pp. 185-199.

[19] Herbert Hoover, "The Meaning of America," *Representative American Speeches: 1948-1949*, pp. 89-95.

[20] Daniel Webster, "Prosecution in the Knapp-White Murder Case," *Classified Models of Speech Composition*, pp. 3-47.

[21] George William Curtis, "The Leadership of Educated Men," *Classified Models of Speech Composition*, pp. 816-828.

[22] *Ibid.*

[23] Charles Luckman, "Where Freedom Begins," *Vital Speeches*, July 15, 1948, pp. 583-586.

A monarchy is a man-of-war, stanch, iron-ribbed, resistless when under full sail; yet a single hidden rock sends her to the bottom. Our republic is a raft, hard to steer, and your feet always wet; but nothing can sink her.[24]

Fifteen years ago we hung by our eyelashes over the precipice of the police state.[25]

Paradoxically we are becalmed on a sea of power. . . . power, power everywhere and yet no strength to save us.[26]

If my neighbor allows his garden to grow up with weeds how can I keep those weeds out of my property? I cannot fence against weeds when the seeds are in the air. The only way to keep a garden a garden is to cultivate it. And the only way to keep America a free democratic society is to cultivate our civic, social and spiritual institutions.[27]

If we live in our communities like grains of sand in a pile we loosen the whole structure. Only as we are cemented together by social responsibility do we form the foundations of our freedom.[28]

. . . recharge the batteries of our personal faith.[29]

. . . there arises the question of how and whether Communism should be "taught." Of course it should be. There is a considerable difference between teaching and preaching a doctrine. We do not condone malaria by discussing the anopheles mosquito.[30]

A more extended metaphor used by Henry Watterson in his after-dinner speech on "The Puritan and the Cavalier," gives an unusually clear, vivid pattern of imagery: "Grady told us, and told us truly, of that typical American who . . . in Abraham Lincoln's actuality, had already come. . . . from that rugged trunk, drawing its sustenance from gnarled roots, interlocked with

[24] Fisher Ames, as quoted by Wendell Phillips, in "The Scholar in a Republic," *Classified Models of Speech Composition*, pp. 795-816.

[25] Ruth Alexander, "Which Way America," *Representative American Speeches: 1948-1949*, pp. 145-154.

[26] Dr. Ralph W. Sockman (Minister, Christ Church, New York), "The Worth of One," *Vital Speeches*, August 15, 1949, pp. 654-655.

[27] *Ibid.*

[28] *Ibid.* Dr. Sockman had just said that "A sense of community is the best defense against Communism."

[29] *Ibid.*

[30] Rufus Carrollton Harris (President of Tulane University), *Report of the President*, 1948-1949, p. 4.

Cavalier sprays and Puritan branches deep beneath the soil, shall spring, is springing, a shapely tree—symmetric in all its parts—under whose sheltering boughs this nation shall have the new birth of freedom Lincoln promised it, and mankind the refuge which was sought by the forefathers when they fled from oppression."[31]

Personification

Another type of figure useful in achieving vividness is that known as *personification*, in which things or ideas are treated as living beings; they are by implication endowed with the attributes of people, or sometimes, if inanimate, with the characteristics of animals.

The following are illustrations of personification:

The nation which plays a lone hand for stakes of selfish power is bound to lose in the twentieth century world.[32]

... three powerful dictatorships have bluffed the democracies. . . .[33]

If democracy is to continue in any form, it must assert the power which belongs to it as a great ruler.[34]

The first social responsibility of science is to shout from the housetops whenever it sees science and technology being used in the dangerous ways in which they have been used in the past.[35]

... if a man stand up for the right, though the right be on the scaffold, while the wrong sits in the seat of government; if he stands for the right, though he eat, with the right and truth, a wretched crust; if he walk with obloquy and scorn in the by-lands and streets, while falsehood and wrong ruffle it in silken attire—let him remember that wherever the right and truth are there are always "troops of

---

[31] Henry Watterson, "The Puritan and the Cavalier," *Classified Speech Models*, William Norwood Brigance (ed.), F. S. Crofts & Co., 1928, pp. 297-302.

[32] Francis B. Sayre, "Major Problems in the United States Foreign Policies," *Representative American Speeches: 1948-1949*, pp. 51-63.

[33] Dorothy Thompson, "Freedom's Back Is Against the Wall," *Modern Speeches on Basic Issues*, Lew Sarett and William Trufant Foster (eds.), Houghton Mifflin Company, 1939, pp. 185-199.

[34] *Ibid.*

[35] Harrison S. Brown, "Social Responsibility of Science," *Representative American Speeches: 1948-1949*, pp. 139-144.

beautiful, tall angels" gathering round him, and God Himself stands within the dim future and keeps watch over his own![36]

Using Figures of Speech

A judicious use of figures of speech adds greatly to vividness, as it often does also to clarity. A few precautions must be observed, however, in order that the effect may not be ludicrous or otherwise unfortunate.

1. *Whether you use similes, metaphors, personifications, or other figures, they must not be far-fetched.* The imagery aroused by their use must not be grotesque or ludicrous, unless that is the specifically intended effect. Occasionally a humorous effect is intended and is entirely permissible on occasion; but care should be taken that its use does not destroy a prevailingly serious mood.

2. *The figures must not offend; they must be in good taste.* As in working for clarity, avoid the cheap, the off-color, the risqué, the repulsive, and the disgusting. On the other hand, language does not need to be exalted to be on a high plane.

3. *Your figures must be consistent.* Incongruous figures usually arise from the failure on the part of the speaker himself to visualize the particular things which are being used as a basis for comparison. In his *Beginnings of Rhetoric and Composition*, Hill lists a number of "bad" figures:

> He took the stump, platform in hand.
> We must bring the viper to his knees and force him to apologize.
> The Bible needs no smoothing-iron to make it palatable to delicate ears.
> We see now that old war-horse of the Democracy waving his hand from the deck of the sinking ship.[37]

4. *The figures must be "harmonious with the tone of the context."*[38] If the subject and the treatment are plain and simple,

---

[36] John B. Gough, "What Is Minority," *Selections for Public Speaking*, Leslie C. Procter and Gladys Trueblood Stroop (eds.), Charles Scribner's Sons, 1930, p. 90.

[37] Adams Sherman Hill, *Beginnings of Rhetoric and Composition*, American Book Company, 1902, p. 406.

[38] *Ibid.*, p. 417.

the figures themselves must be plain. Such simplicity was one of the sources of effectiveness in Lincoln's use of the homely anecdote to carry a point.

5. *The use of figures must not be overdone.* There are occasions when direct language is more effective than the indirect language of figures. Your listeners will sometimes want and demand facts and straightforward statements without embellishment. Under such conditions it is best to use figures of speech sparingly or not at all. It is probable that objectionable floridity, which often makes use of inappropriately exalted language, also makes excessive use of figures, employing them chiefly for their ornamental value rather than for their illuminating significance.

Vividness, then, arises from sense imagery, which is a process of reliving experiences and impressions which have entered our awareness through one or more of the senses. The speaker's problem, if he wishes to make his language vivid, is to arouse those images. This can be done by the use of concrete, descriptive, familiar, and simple words and by the judicious use of figures of speech.

EXERCISES

1. Listen to several sports broadcasters announcing different kinds of sports events. Discuss them on the basis of these points:
    a. What makes some sportscasters "better" than others? (a) Is it their fluency, their ability to keep up a constant flow of description and comment? (b) Is it their ability to make you "see" what is going on?
    b. Compare the announcers as to their ability to give you vivid imagery of the event that is taking place.
    c. What other types of imagery do these different speakers stimulate?
    d. To what extent are they able to arouse in you something of the excitement, suspense, response to conflict?
    e. Do you agree with what many people have insisted, that they get more out of hearing a game broadcast than out of actually seeing it played? Is that attitude stimulated by all the sportscasters under consideration?

f. What devices *of speech* have your announcers used in order to give you a more satisfactory experience of the game?
2. Estimate (*not* statistically) the relative vividness of your own types of imagery. Which type, if any, gives you a sharper, more "realistic" image than the others? Have you in any sensory field experienced what are known as eidetic images, so vivid that they seem like actual sensory experiences?
3. Read a short poem (such as "Trees," "Crossing the Bar," "The Wolf Cry," "The Loon," "Cupid Swallowed," "Abou Ben Adhem," or the like), and determine the different kinds of imagery aroused. To what extent did the reading actually arouse vivid imagery? To what extent do such images as were aroused contribute to your understanding or appreciation of the poem?
4. Study some good speech (in *Vital Speeches, Representative American Speeches,* or some other collection), and analyze the imagery aroused. What different types? What is the preponderant type? Would you say that the speaker is mainly of one type or another? In your reading of the speech, how vivid was the imagery in your own mind? Did the imagery contribute to your understanding and appreciation of the speech?
5. Bring to class and be prepared to discuss specific examples of the appeal to various types of imagery which some speaker has used.
6. Give a three-minute talk in which you differentiate among the words of one of the groups on page 427, or any other group of not fewer than three words. Make use of imagery-arousing language in order to make your differentiation vivid.
7. Bring to class and be prepared to discuss the use which some speaker has made of figures of speech in making his ideas vivid. To what extent has the speaker avoided the pitfalls discussed in the chapter? Was his use of figures effective?
8. Find in the speeches of Winston Churchill (or some other acceptable speaker) five examples each of simile, personification, metaphor. What figures not discussed in the text do you find?
9. Give a three- to five-minute speech in which you make specific use of three or more specific techniques for securing vividness. *Be able to identify the techniques you have used.*

SUPPLEMENTARY READINGS

1. Brigance, William Norwood, *Speech Composition,* F. S. Crofts & Co., 1937, pp. 218-268.

2. Quintilian, *Institutes of Oratory*, Book VIII, chap. III, "Concerning the Embellishments of Style;" chap. VI, "Concerning Tropes."
3. Overstreet, H. A., *Influencing Human Behavior*, W. W. Norton & Company, 1925, chap. III, "The Problem of Vividness," pp. 50-70.
4. Sandford, William Phillips, and Yeager, Willard Hayes, *Principles of Effective Speaking*, The Ronald Press Company, 4th ed., 1942, pp. 193-196.

CHAPTER XVIII

Using Language for Impressiveness

YOU must do more than make your ideas intelligible to your audience. It is not enough that your listeners know what you think about your subject; you must let them know also how you feel about it. You must create or intensify attitudes as well as provide understanding. You must, in other words, go beyond the logical development of your subject; you must stimulate the emotional component which is associated with that subject in the minds of your audience.

Your language must therefore have more than clarity, more than vividness. It must have that element which we shall call *impressiveness*. This characteristic has been called variously *vivacity, energy, strength, force*. Whatever term is used, the point is that you must use language that will give enough force, energy, strength, vivacity, to make your ideas impressive.

Impressiveness is important also because of its contribution to retention and recall. Psychologists tell us that learning, and hence the power of recall, depends mainly on three factors, recency of the stimulus (or response), the frequency of occurrence or repetition, and the intensity of the stimulus or of the response. That is, we remember most easily occurrences of the immediate past, those which have taken place repeatedly, and those which involved an intense or allover response, such as a profound emotional reaction. It would seem, then, that whatever adds to the intensity of the stimulus or to its emotional coloring would also add to one's ability to recall that experience.

These emotional responses can be stimulated by the proper use of language which will make your ideas so impressive that they will be more readily recalled, and when recalled they will have a strong emotional coloring. Use language, therefore, that can easily be translated into experience to which a strong emotional component is attached.

Still another reason for the importance of making your language impressive lies in the fact that, in the very nature of the speaking situation, the listener has no time for reflection; he must grasp your idea immediately. A reader can go over an obscure passage as many times as necessary in order to grasp its full significance. He can stop entirely if he feels like it and meditate for as long as he pleases before reading further. The need for making an instant impression is not vital for the writer. As a speaker, on the other hand, you must create your impression at once. There is no time for meditation; your listeners have no opportunity to go back and listen again to a point you have just made. They cannot review the development up to the present moment, or, while they are thinking back over what has been said, you have been going forward, and much of what you have been saying is lost. If you are to make your impression at all, you must do it as you proceed. Impressiveness is a means of getting the point to the audience on the instant and making it "stick."

IMPRESSIVENESS, VIVIDNESS, AND CLARITY

In achieving impressiveness, clarity is not an essential, although clarity may be used to intensify it, as may also vividness. Your speech may be perfectly clear without its being either vivid or impressive. A classroom lecture may be quite intelligible and yet, because it is neither vivid nor impressive, be utterly dull. A speech of instruction, of information, clear though it may be, which lacks the spark of impressiveness is likely to be most uninteresting. Do not take the attitude that, because a group of people has assembled to hear your discussion or because a class of students is under a certain degree of compulsion to listen to you lecture, you are therefore justified in assuming that they will listen attentively to a dull, unimpressive enumeration of unadorned facts.

On the other hand, to the uncritical a speech may be highly impressive without actually meaning a great deal if it consists of a succession of vague, emotional ideas strung together, none of which, when analyzed, has a close reference to any reality. A highly dramatic description of the deplorable conditions in some far-away area may sound impressive, but it may not correspond in any detail with conditions as they actually exist. The descriptions of American life as published in *Izvestia* and read by the Russian people have little in them that bears any resemblance to reality. Much of the gobbledygook of official and diplomatic language sounds very impressive; but translated as Spencer suggests[1] into intelligible language, when and if it can be, it adds up to little more than nonsense. Someone has described much of what goes by the name of oratory as "The art of making deep rumblings from the chest sound like deep thoughts from the

[1] Herbert Spencer, *The Philosophy of Style*, Appleton-Century-Crofts, Inc., 1871, pp. 11-12.

brain." The ideal use of language achieves clarity or clear ideas, vividness or strong imagery, *and* impressiveness through emotional coloring—all three.

METHODS OF ACHIEVING IMPRESSIVENESS

Some of the methods by which clarity and vividness are achieved are also helpful in achieving impressiveness. The use of many of the figures of speech, for instance, contributes to all three characteristics of language. Hill points out that ". . . many of the principles of selection which render language clear also render it forcible. The univocal, brief, specific, and familiar word will, in the great majority of cases, be the forcible word; for though men may admire language they do not understand, they will not be influenced by it."[2]

Ideas are made impressive [says Woolbert] by being made to live again. Old truths lie dormant and then blaze into liveliness when brought out into the light. In many ways "Old things are best." This reviving of the long beloved can be done in the following ways:
> Recall vivid and concrete pictures of old experiences, old descriptions, old impressions of all kinds; stir up concrete mental imagery.
> Relate old and lively adventures, escapades, dramatic moments, crises, incidents charged with emotion.
> Quote old and reliable authorities, opinions of authors, leaders, heroes, divinities, anyone especially beloved; especially poetry and "holy writ."[3]

George Campbell, in his *Philosophy of Rhetoric,*[4] first published in 1775, uses the following passages to show the effectiveness of the specific word as compared with the general:

| Consider the lilies how they grow; they toil not, they spin | Consider the flowers how they gradually increase in their size; |

[2] Adams Sherman Hill, *The Principles of Rhetoric,* Harper & Brothers, 1885, pp. 85-86.

[3] Charles Henry Woolbert, *The Fundamentals of Speech,* Harper & Brothers, rev. ed., 1927, p. 358.

[4] George Campbell, *The Philosophy of Rhetoric,* Harper & Brothers, new ed., 1846, pp. 307-308.

not; and yet I say unto you, that Solomon in all his glory was not arrayed like one of these. If, then, God so clothe the grass which to-day is in the field and to-morrow is cast into the oven, how much more will he clothe you? (Luke xii: 27, 28.) they do no manner of work, and yet I declare to you that no king whatever, in his most splendid habit, is dressed up like them. If, then, God in his providence doth so adorn the vegetable productions which continue but a little time on the land, and are afterward put into the fire, how much more will he provide clothing for you?

The two passages are equally clear, but the reference to a specific flower and a specific king, rather than to flowers in general and rulers as a class, impresses us with the belief that whatever is true for this particular individual is true as well for all, whether it be flowers, kings, or people in general. Campbell himself has already stated the broad principle: "The more general the terms are, the picture is the fainter; the more special they are, it is the brighter. The same sentiments may be expressed with equal justness, and even perspicuity [clarity], in the former way as in the latter; but as the colouring will in that case be more languid, it cannot give equal pleasure to the fancy, and, by consequence, will not contribute so much either to fix the attention or to impress the memory."

An unimaginative writer might have told us simply, but without the "colouring" which Campbell mentions, that "It is evening; the cows are coming in from the pasture, and the tired farmer is going home from his fields." It took a poet, with his rich appreciation of imaginary detail, to phrase the picture differently:

> The curfew tolls the knell of parting day,
> The lowing herd winds slowly o'er the lea,
> The plowman homeward plods his weary way,
> And leaves the world to darkness and to me.

Instead of flatly stating that Karl Marx was wrong in his economic and social theories and actually had contributed little or nothing to human welfare, Samuel B. Pettengill makes telling use of specific language in achieving impressiveness:

Was the conquest of starvation a humanitarian thing? What conquered it? Who conquered it? Karl Marx? *No*.

The time in the field required to raise a bushel of wheat in America has gone down from 60 hours of human labor to 2 hours or less today. What did it? The steel plow, the tractor, the harvester, better fertilizer and seed, the conquest of insects and plant diseases, and cheap transportation. American wheat now feeds millions today in the Europe that is adopting the philosophy of Karl Marx.

Aluminum was so expensive in 1870 that Napoleon III of France had an aluminum table set for state dinners, more valuable then than gold. Today aluminum is found in the American kitchen.

. . . The answer [to the problem of improving conditions] is to substitute slaves of iron and steel for the sweat and toil of human backs.[5]

Using Characteristic Traits (Metonymy)

General ideas can often be made more impressive by using some characteristic or some part of the broad class of objects to represent the whole. Use *the bench*, for example, rather than the judiciary department of the government; *the bar* and *the pulpit* (sometimes *the cloth*) instead of the legal profession and the ministry. *Red tape* is too familiar a term to require explanation. In parliamentary law we address *the chair*; the presiding officer refers to himself as *the chair*, members of the organization *obtain the floor*, rather than the right to speak, and motions are put before *the house*.

Our language is full of such expressions. "The pen is mightier than the sword"; "a Daniel come to judgment." We say, "Use your head," or that someone is "all eyes." We attribute certain emotions to the *heart*; even though that organ is no more the seat of emotion than is the stomach, the meaning is not ambiguous, so long as we are not attempting to speak in scientific terms. We say we are reading Shakespeare, or Milton, or Homer; of course we are doing no such thing. But the occasional use of such expressions gives concreteness to speech, just as Byron, instead of saying that there were a great many ships sailing the

[5] Samuel B. Pettengill, "Where Karl Marx Went Wrong," *Vital Speeches*, May 1, 1949, pp. 442-444.

oceans, wrote instead, "Ten thousand fleets sweep over thee in vain." Lloyd's of London would not be satisfied with such an enumeration as a basis for determining insurance rates, but for Byron's purpose the figure was more impressive than a precise count.

Use of Allusions

Often an idea which might require several words or sentences to present, and even then might be flat and uninteresting, may be made more impressive by the use of an appropriate allusion to something already known, toward which certain attitudes have been built up. Such allusions may be direct or indirect, literal or figurative, historical, literary, Biblical, or legendary.

Typical as an instance in the use of historical allusion is "The march of civilization is as romantic as the Crusades."[6] In various passages cited earlier various speakers have referred to the Puritan and the Cavalier stock who formed the first wave of immigration into this country.

David E. Lilienthal, speaking on "The Spirit of Democracy,"[7] refers repeatedly to Walt Whitman and bases much of his speech on the poet's expression of faith in America. Incidentally, he makes effective use of a quotation from Whitman as a conclusion to his speech. Somewhat similarly, President John Tyler Caldwell, in his Inaugural Address at Alabama College, bases much of his speech on the adventures of *Alice in Wonderland*:[8] James Bryant Conant, President of Harvard University, speaks of "those *Cassandras* who would have us believe that there is no spiritual

---

[6] Edwin P. Morrow, "The Cost of Heritage," in *Classified Speech Models*, William Norwood Brigance (ed.), F. S. Crofts & Co., 1928, pp. 279-287.

[7] David E. Lilienthal, "The Spirit of Democracy," *Representative American Speeches, 1948-1949*, A. Craig Baird (ed.), The H. W. Wilson Company, 1949, pp. 65-73.

[8] John Tyler Caldwell, "The New Birth," *Representative American Speeches, 1948-1949*, pp. 196-205.

unity in the United States."⁹ Cassandra, daughter of Priam of Troy and one of the survivors of the siege, was granted by Apollo the gift of prophecy; but afterward he "rendered the gift unavailing by ordaining that her predictions should never be believed."¹⁰ In the same speech President Conant mentions the *"doubting Thomases* who are skeptical of our capacity as a nation to remain unshaken in troubled times." To what Biblical incident does the expression "doubting Thomas" refer?

Herbert Elliston, speaking on "Balance of Power for Peace,"¹¹ does not want to say in so many words that the achieving of a complete and permanent balance of power is impossible; he says, instead, that "The job of achieving a balance of power, of winning the Cold War, is the job of Sisyphus." Sisyphus, it will be remembered, was the mythical king in ancient Greece who was condemned in Hades forever to roll a heavy stone to the top of a mountain, only to have it slip each time he had almost reached the top and roll back down to the foot again.¹² A somewhat similar use of a mythological allusion is that of Chauncey M. Depew, who at the laying of the cornerstone of the *New York World* building, speaks of the "argus-eyed watchfulness of the press."¹³ A historical allusion is used by Edwin P. Morrow in referring to "Lewis and Clark . . . starting from the Missouri, guided by the pointing finger of an Indian girl,"¹⁴ reminding us of the Shoshone Indian girl, Sacajawea, who, with her French husband, led the explorers through the wilderness.

When Theodore Roosevelt announced, "We stand at Armaged-

⁹ James Bryant Conant, "Challenge of the Times," *Vital Speeches*, August 15, 1948, pp. 642-645.
¹⁰ See Charles Mills Gayley, *The Classic Myths in English Literature and in Art*, Ginn & Company, 1911, p. 313. This book might well be studied as a source of many allusions to classical mythology.
¹¹ Herbert Elliston, "Balance of Power for Peace," *Vital Speeches*, February 1, 1949, pp. 228-232.
¹² Gayley, *op. cit.*, p. 358.
¹³ Chauncey M. Depew, "At Laying of Cornerstone of the New York 'World' Building," *Classified Speech Models*, pp. 354-359.
¹⁴ Edwin P. Morrow, "The Cost of Heritage," in *Classified Speech Models*, pp. 279-287.

don and we battle for the Lord," he was referring to the passage in *Revelation*[15] in which Armageddon is mentioned as the place where the final battle is to be fought between the forces of good and evil. Theodore Roosevelt also coined an expression which has since been used many times. Charles Luckman paid tribute to the former President when he said, ". . . the only way for peace to endure is for us to *talk* fairly *softly* and *carry* a *bigger* production *stick* than any other nation."[16] Such allusions to some well known phrase which has been coined by a favorite writer or speaker may be used with striking effect.

A contemporary allusion to the perspective of the astronomer is made by Raymond B. Fosdick in dedicating the two-hundred-inch telescope on Mount Palomar, and with it is coupled a striking turn of phase: "In the last analysis, the mind which encompasses the universe is more marvelous than the universe which encompasses the mind. 'Astronomically speaking,' said the philosopher, 'man is completely negligible.' To which the psychologist answered, 'Astronomically speaking, man is the astronomer.' "[17]

Allusions, which are figures of speech, can often be coupled with other figures for an especially impressive effect. In a recent classroom speech a Latin-American student referred to the famous General Bolivar as a Casanova, thereby drawing a one-word character sketch of the great Liberator. Excessive love of wealth is often designated as the *worship of mammon*,[18] an allusion taken directly from the Bible.

Be sure that in your use of allusions your audience will understand the reference; otherwise the allusion will add little to

---

[15] Rev. xvi:16. See also Whittier's "Rantoul":
    We seemed to see our flag unfurled,
    Our champion waiting in his place
    For the last battle of the world,—
    The Armageddon of the race.

[16] Charles Luckman, "Where Freedom Begins," *Vital Speeches*, July 15, 1948, pp. 583-586. (Italics not in the original.)

[17] Raymond B. Fosdick, "The Challenge of Knowledge," *ibid.*, pp. 586-587.

[18] Matthew vi:24; Luke xvi:9, 11, 13.

impressiveness. Probably the only aspect of speaking unfamiliar references will enhance in such a case is the audience's impression of your own learning; but they will be of very little help to you in getting the idea and the audience together. Instead of making the idea impressive, such a usage serves only to make you yourself impressive. Use allusions, then, that are within the understanding of your listeners and that will probably arouse or deepen the attitude you want to establish. When so used they can add greatly to the impressiveness of the speech. It should be unnecessary to add that you should of course be thoroughly familiar with the significance of your reference in relation to the point you are trying to make. Otherwise there is a strong chance that you may make yourself ridiculous.

Quotation

Quotations may in one sense be thought of as extended allusions. Frequently you can use a familiar passage from some well-known writing to increase impressiveness and hold interest. These quotations may be from any recognized source; they will be especially effective if the source itself is highly regarded. Henry W. Grady opened his address before the New England Society of New York on "The New South" with a quotation from Benjamin H. Hill and closed it with one from Daniel Webster, both highly regarded in New England.

Winston Churchill expressed his faith in the future of the human race in the following passage from Tennyson's "Locksley Hall":

Men, my brothers, Men, the workers, ever reaping something new;
That which they have done but earnest of the things that they
    shall do.[19]

Biblical passages are often used as the basis for speeches by laymen as well as by ministers of the church. Dr. Karl T. Compton chose for the thesis of his Baccalaureate Address to the class

---

[19] Winston Churchill, "United We Stand Secure," *Representative American Speeches, 1948-1949,* pp. 35-50.

of 1937 at the Massachusetts Institute of Technology the Parable of the Talents, putting especial stress on the verse, "Well done, thou good and faithful servant; thou hast been faithful over a few things, I will make thee ruler over many things; enter thou into the joy of thy Lord."[20] It is no sacrilege to say that Biblical quotations are almost always effective, provided they are appropriate to the subject and the occasion.

Even in a lawyer's address to a jury in the courtroom, quotations are occasionally used to secure impressiveness. Jeremiah S. Black, in his famous "Right to Trial by Jury," delivered before the Supreme Court of the United States, made frequent use of quotations throughout the speech, some of these being from the Constitution, some from the Bible, some from secular literary sources. Each one was introduced to make the argument more impressive.[21]

Repetition

Some of the techniques of speech which are useful in creating certain effects are also valuable in achieving at the same time additional results. Repetition was discussed in connection with attention and interest; it was pointed out how it could be used for such objectives. With some adaptation, it can also be used to make ideas impressive. Sometimes a single word will be repeated, sometimes a phrase, sometimes an entire clause. Shortly after the Spanish-American War, in which the United States had suddenly acquired more territory than it knew what to do with, Senator Albert J. Beveridge, spokesman of the "imperialists," raised in his "March of the Flag" speech the stirring question and challenge, "Who will haul down that flag?" He was answered by John Sharp Williams, who repeated the question several

---

[20] Karl T. Compton, "The Stuff of Life: Our Talents and Their Care," *Modern Speeches on Basic Issues*, Lew Sarett and William Trufant Foster (eds.), Houghton Mifflin Company, 1939, pp. 13-21.

[21] Jeremiah S. Black, "In Defense of the Right of Trial by Jury," *Classified Speech Models*, pp. 101-136.

times, each time answering it himself by insisting that the American people themselves would "haul down that flag" because it was the sensible thing to do.[22]

Observe also how in his radio speech to the American people on December 9, two days after the bombing of Pearl Harbor, former President Roosevelt makes use of the technique of repetition both to maintain high interest and to achieve the maximum of impressiveness:

> The course that Japan has followed for the past ten years in Asia has paralleled the course of Hitler and Mussolini in Europe and in Africa. Today it has become far more than a parallel. It is collaboration —actual collaboration—so well calculated that all the continents of the world, and all the oceans, are now considered by the Axis strategists as one gigantic battlefield.
> In 1931, ten years ago, Japan invaded Manchukuo—without warning.
> In 1935, Italy invaded Ethiopia—without warning.
> In 1938, Hitler occupied Austria—without warning.
> In 1939, Hitler invaded Czechoslovakia—without warning.
> Later in 1939, Hitler invaded Poland—without warning.
> In 1940, Hitler invaded Norway, Denmark, The Netherlands, Belgium and Luxembourg—without warning.
> In 1940, Italy attacked France and later Greece—without warning.
> And this year, in 1941, the Axis powers attacked Yugoslavia and Greece and they dominated the Balkans—without warning.
> In 1941 also, Hitler invaded Russia—without warning.
> And now Japan has attacked Malaya and Thailand—and the United States—without warning.
> It is all of one pattern.[23]

Repetition is used with strong effect also in Dr. George Hedley's refutation of the well-known statement of Karl Marx, that religion is the "opium of the people." After quoting directly from

[22] John Sharp Williams, "Who Will Haul Down That Flag?" *Classified Speech Models*, pp. 206-208.

[23] Franklin Delano Roosevelt, "America Accepts the Challenge," radio address December 9, 1941, *Representative American Speeches, 1941-1942*, pp. 30-39.

the writings of Marx himself, Dr. Hedley insists that "from the very beginning religion had been, and has continued to be, a vital force of social criticism, social protest, and social change; that the great leaders of religion, so far from being defenders of the *status quo*, were one after another revolutionaries. . . ." He then goes on to name many of the great leaders, introducing each one with the challenging question,

> Will you grant that Moses was a religious leader?
> Were the prophets Amos and Micah religious leaders?
> Was the prophet Jesus, of Nazareth in Galilee, a religious leader?
> Was St. Paul a religious leader?
> Was St. Francis of Assisi a religious leader?
> Was John Bunyan a religious leader?
> Was John Wesley a religious leader?
> Was John Woolman a religious leader?[24]

In arguing that the term "slave-labor law," as applied to the Taft-Hartley Act was grossly inaccurate, a "flagrant lie," Maurice R. Franks, Director of the National Labor-Management Foundation, discusses a number of benefits which he insists were brought about through the functioning of the law. In connection with each one of these benefits, he raises the question, variously framed, "Is it a slave-labor law?" The constant repetition of the term "slave-labor law," together with the repeated rhetorical question, produces an impressiveness which would have been difficult to achieve otherwise. With but one break, he propounds a series of forty-three consecutive questions, most of them so framed as actually to state a proposition intended to refute the charge of "slave-labor law."

> Is it a slave-labor law . . . ?
> And what of the law which . . . ?
> What do we say when we find . . . ?
> Do we right away think of enslavement . . . ?
> Do we immediately visualize a long line of regimented slaves . . . ?
> What is our definition of a slave-labor law?

[24] George Hedley, "Religion: What It Isn't, and Is," *Vital Speeches*, December 15, 1947, pp. 148-152.

IMPRESSIVENESS

Is it in our mind to describe a slave-labor law as one which . . . ?
Is a single one of these provisions . . . ?
. . . wouldn't it be more reasonable for us to assume . . . ?[25]

In his Madison Square Garden Address during the 1948 presidential campaign, President Truman used the technique of repetition with great effectiveness in playing repeatedly on the proposition that, although his opponent had followed him in his itinerary, he would not follow him into the White House. Over and over again he repeated that his opponent could follow him into Framingham, Massachusetts, into Cleveland, into Chicago, Boston, and elsewhere, but he would not follow in raising minimum wages, in broadening the base of social security, in providing for health insurance, for federal aid to education, or in any of the other issues which the President was placing before the American voters.[26]

Similarly, in his speech accepting the nomination of the Progressive Party, as candidate for the Presidency, Henry A. Wallace introduces each "plank" of his platform with an introductory phrase, "I am committed. . . ." Twice this formula is broken by "I am pledged. . . ."[27]

These examples should be enough to indicate some of the ways in which you may be able to use the technique of repetition in order to make your ideas impressive. It is not always necessary that the repeated idea be in identical language, although a short phrase can be repeated verbatim. Be sure not to overdo the practice; once you have made your point, go on to the next idea.

Use of Facts

It often happens that you will not need to resort to any of the techniques described above in order to make your ideas

[25] Maurice R. Franks, "Lift the Iron Curtain on the Taft-Hartley Law," *Vital Speeches,* January 15, 1949, pp. 204-207.
[26] Harry S. Truman, "Madison Square Garden Address," *Representative American Speeches, 1948-1949,* pp. 112-121.
[27] Henry A. Wallace, "Progressive Party Commitments," *Representative American Speeches, 1948-1949,* pp. 123-133.

impressive if your facts themselves are sufficiently significant. There is some validity to the old saying that "Truth is stranger than fiction." Plain, unvarnished facts are often so striking that they need no embellishment or figures of speech to dress them up. The "startling statement," the "believe-it-or-not" technique can make a statement of fact impressive." An excellent illustration of such a method is the opening of Gordon L. Hostetter's speech on "Human Liberty." "Of all the people who have ever lived on the earth's surface only about 3 percent have ever known freedom, and only as they have been free politically have they been relatively free from the most elemental pang of human nature—hunger."[28]

It is an impressive fact that more people have been killed in America in automobile accidents than in all the wars we have ever fought, beginning with the Revolution. Some years ago the *Reader's Digest* carried an article which had to do with the immediate results of many fatal traffic accidents. Many of these effects were described quite without emotional coloring but were presented as simple, straightforward facts, without elaboration. The descriptions were so detailed and so realistic that hundreds of drivers felt the full impact of the pictures. Shortly after that particular issue appeared on the stands, one student gave as her speech a résumé of the article, "And Sudden Death."[29] Although such résumés are not encouraged, are even definitely discouraged and sometimes prohibited, the speaker was permitted to continue. Her presentation of this particular subject was so impressive that when she sat down her listeners drew a sigh of relief, and one young man was heard to say, as if to himself, "I've had enough of that!" Incidentally, the title of the article itself is an effective quotation probably not recognized as such by all who use it or hear it.

[28] Gordon Hostetter, "Human Liberty," *Vital Speeches*, November 15, 1948, pp. 83-87.

[29] Joseph Chamberlain Furnass, "And Sudden Death," *Reader's Digest Reader*, Theodore Roosevelt and Staff (ed.), Doubleday, Doran & Company, Inc., 1941, pp. 295-300.

It may be regarded as an impressive fact, also, that the *Reader's Digest* has the largest circulation of any magazine in the United States—over eight million.

It is another impressive fact that the teaching of speech goes back almost to the time of the building of the Great Pyramid of Khufu. It is an impressive fact that the theater in the South flourished all through the existence of the Confederacy. It is likewise an impressive fact that the radio program, "The Voice of America," according to the evidence, is penetrating the Iron Curtain and that this penetration is having highly desirable results, so far as can be ascertained.

Facts in themselves, then, may be highly impressive. Ripley's "Believe-It-Or-Not" series, which has been running for years, together with several similar series such as "This Curious World," and "Strange As It Seems," is sufficient evidence that the unusual has both attention value and the quality of impressiveness and can be used with strong effect.

Statistics

You may be surprised at what can be done with statistics to make your ideas impressive. Quantitative comparisons need not be dull and uninteresting; they will not be if they are chosen because they represent wide departures from the usual or the expected and if they can be related to human interests.[30]

It is an impressive statistical fact, for example, that the Federal government spent more in the year 1945 than it had spent in the one hundred forty years from the beginning of Washington's first term to the inauguration of President Hoover, and that the average annual expenditures of the government for the first four postwar years were eighty times what they were for the first decade of the twentieth century. Lane D. Webber, showing how government income and expenditures have increased during fifty years of the present century, uses these data:

[30] For an illustration of the interpretative use of statistics in written discourse, see the editorial, "Statistics and the National Association," *The Quarterly Journal of Speech*, October, 1939, pp. 462-464.

For the first ten years federal expenditures averaged $575 million—half a billion. In the teen age decade—which witnessed World War I—that average was $3.8 billion. During the 1920's—notwithstanding some $10 billion of debt reduction—the average was $3.7 billion. Throughout the 30's—with its depression—$6.2 billion. The 40's—cursed with World War II—hit the jackpot with $51.7 billion. For the four postwar years—'46 through '49, and using the current budget for the latter year ending June 30 next—the average will be $48 billion—80 times that of the first decade, 12 times that of the second, and 7 times that of the 30's.[31]

These figures are in themselves impressive. They are accompanied in the same speech with many more of the same nature.

You can make these comparisons much more impressive if you relate them to things your audience already understands. Charles Luckman illustrates this principle in pointing out what a ten-percent annual increase in productivity would mean. It would represent over five billion dollars a year: "If put to work it would run the whole Federal Government for almost two months. It would carry the Marshall Plan for a year. It would build over a half million houses. It would provide the money we need to run all the public and private schools and colleges in the entire United States for the next two years. . . ."[32]

The following statistical data are impressive as fact:

When Colonel Drake struck oil in Pennsylvania in 1859, Russia and the United States probably had about the same amount of oil in the ground, perhaps 110 billion barrels each. Russia had little liberty under the Czars; we have always had much. By 1923 we had found about 12 billion barrels; Russia had found about 3 billion. In 1923, then, Russia had some 9 billion barrels more undiscovered oil than the United States.

Since 1923, to the end of 1947, we have found nearly 44½ billion barrels; Russia has found 5 billion at most. In that time we have produced 28 billion barrels; Russia has produced about 3 billion. Under

[31] Lane D. Webber, "Bubonic Budgets," *Vital Speeches*, December 15, 1948, pp. 150-153.

[32] Charles Luckman, "Where Freedom Begins," *Vital Speeches*, July 15, 1948, pp. 583-586.

American liberty, we have found nine times as much oil, and produced nine times as much, as Russia under Communist authority. "Freedom is necessary to industry."[33]

To show the economic progress of Canada, these impressive facts are cited: "Retail sales in Canada compared with 1938 have advanced from 2,400 Million Dollars to over 5,000 Million. Bank deposits from 31,000 Million to over 75,000 Million. Newsprint exports from 2½ million tons worth $64,000,000 to 4½ million tons worth $356,000,000. The output of electricity has climbed from 26 million to 40 million Kilowatt hours. Flour from 14 million barrels to 30 million barrels. Pig Iron from 705 thousand tons to 1 million 840 thousand tons. Mineral production has gone to 620 Million Dollars, and our production of Newsprint has gone beyond all previous expectations."[34]

Such data as these are impressive in themselves; they need no elaboration. In the development of many of the subjects you will want to talk about you will find that there are startling facts, items of simple numerical information that are so divergent from the expected or the usual that they arouse instant attention and keen interest. A single statistical item may be so striking as to draw attention itself; but its impressiveness may be greatly enhanced if it is supplemented by further data of much the same general type, so that the factor of cumulation becomes operative. The isolated facts may be impressive; a great mass of fact may give additional weight to the point you are trying to make.

Detailed Description

It often happens that the best way to make your ideas impressive is to use detailed description, adding one descriptive item after another, so that a complete picture is created in all its fine detail. In recasting the actual crime for which Knapp was

[33] Max W. Ball, "Government for the People," *Vital Speeches*, February 1, 1949, pp. 236-239. Mr. Ball is Director, Oil and Gas Division, United States Department of the Interior.

[34] Ernest C. Bogart, K.C., LL.D., "Canada's Relation with Great Britain and the United States," *Vital Speeches*, July 15, 1948, pp. 598-600.

being tried, Webster went into such a minute description of every movement that the incident was both exceedingly vivid and deeply impressive:

Deep sleep had fallen on the destined victim, and on all beneath his roof. A healthful old man, to whom sleep was sweet, the first sound slumbers of the night held him in their soft but strong embrace. The assassin enters, through the window already prepared, into an unoccupied apartment. With noiseless foot he paces the lonely hall, half lighted by the moon. He winds up the ascent of the stairs, and reaches the door of the chamber. Of this he moves the lock, by soft and continued pressure, till it turns on its hinges without noise, and he enters, and beholds his victim before him. The room is uncommonly open to the admission of light. The face of the innocent sleeper is turned from the murderer, and the beams of the moon, resting on the gray locks of his aged temple, show him where to strike. The fatal blow is given, and the victim passes, without a struggle or a motion, from the repose of sleep to the repose of death! It is the assassin's purpose to make sure work; and he plies the dagger, though it is obvious that life has been destroyed by the blow of the bludgeon. He even raises the aged arm, that he may not fail in his aim at the heart, and replaces it again over the wounds of the poniard! To finish the picture, he explores the wrist for the pulse! He feels for it, and ascertains that it beats no longer! It is accomplished. The deed is done. He retreats, retraces his steps to the window, passes out through it as he came in, and escapes.[35]

Not all descriptions, needless to say, are of the "horror" type. Grady, in his "Homes of the People," gives an impressive and detailed description of his friend's home, to support his thesis that ". . . here in the homes of the people lodge at last the strength and the responsibility of this government, the hope and the promise of the republic:" "It was just a simple, unpretentious house, set about with great trees and encircled in meadow and field rich with the promise of harvest; the fragrance of pink and hollyhock in the front yard was mingled with the aroma of the orchard and the garden, and the resonant clucking of poultry

---

[35] Daniel Webster, "Prosecution in the Knapp-White Case," *Classified Models of Speech Composition*, James Milton O'Neill (ed.), The Century Co., 1921, pp. 3-47.

and the hum of bees. Inside was quiet, cleanliness, thrift, and comfort...."[36]

Loaded Words

Another technique by which you can often make your ideas impressive is by the use of words or phrases which are so rich in connotation that they immediately arouse an emotional response: the affective, or emotional, component in the meaning is so strong that for the moment it outweighs whatever there may be of logical meaning. Webster, in the Knapp-White case previously referred to, speaks of "extraordinary guilt, exquisite wickedness, the high flights and poetry of crime," and "murder; deliberate, concerted, malicious murder"; and again in the same speech, "What is innocence? How deep stained with blood, how reckless in crime, how deep in depravity may it be, and yet retain innocence?"

Henry B. DuPont, in referring to criticism of "Big Business" merely on the ground of size, points out that "These criticisms have, in the main, come from the lips of many people in politics, bureaucrats, irresponsible labor elements and, unfortunately, also from many well-meaning but uninformed people, and they have been fanned by the radical section of the press and radio. The little businessman has been depicted as a poor little fellow living and working in a continual state of oppression at the hands of Big Business."[37]

It is not at all difficult to pick out of this passage a number of words which carry logical meaning but which have been chosen also because they have strong emotional connotations. The intent is obviously to create an attitude unfavorable to the criticism of "Big Business" which comes from prejudiced sources.

Somewhat similarly, Helen Gahagan Douglas, speaking against

[36] Henry W. Grady, "Plymouth Rock and Democracy," *The Complete Orations and Speeches of Henry W. Grady*, Edwin Dubois Shurter (ed.), Hinds, Noble & Eldredge, 1910, pp. 221-233. A similar passage appears in Grady's speech, "The Farmer and the Cities," delivered at Elberton, Georgia, in June, 1889. See pp. 158-191, and especially p. 186.

[37] Henry B. DuPont, "That No Man Shall Be Poor," *Vital Speeches*, July 15, 1948, pp. 587-590.

the Taft-Hartley Law, chooses words with the intent of building up an attitude of opposition to the act: "Is it fair or just for the Congress of the United States to impose, by statute, restrictions which make it almost impossible for labor organizations to grow, or even to survive while at the same time granting to big business full permission to expand until it has achieved a virtual monopoly of practically all lines of industry?"[38]

For their maximum effect most speeches will require a certain amount of impressiveness, the degree being determined by the occasion and the purpose of the speaker. It is only such colorless reports as the minutes of meetings, intended to present nothing more than the bare record of proceedings, that can be devoid of this particular characteristic. In most of your speaking you will want to do more than present cold, barren, colorless fact. Even the report of an especially interesting and significant bit of research may be made impressive by pointing up its significance, its departure from commonly held theories, its distinctive contribution to the field of knowledge. When Professor Shapley discusses a number of astonishing astronomical facts in his lecture, "The Expanding Universe," his listeners are deeply impressed by the information he presents.

Through the study and application of the techniques discussed in this chapter, you should be able to add to your elements of clarity and vividness in your speaking that of impressiveness.

EXERCISES

1. Bring to class one example of each of the specific techniques of impressiveness discussed in the chapter, taken from some speech or speeches.
2. Select some general term the meanings of which are very broad and indefinite, and then not fewer than ten words having specific, concrete meanings related to that of the general term.
3. Find five to ten illustrations of allusion in a speech, and give a

[38] "Repeal of the Taft-Hartley Law," from a Debate in the House of Representatives, Apr. 26th-May 4, 1949. The participants were Helen Gahagan Douglas, Joseph Martin, Samuel Rayburn, and Harold Donohue. The debate is printed in *Representative American Speeches, 1948-1949*, pp. 155-164.

IMPRESSIVENESS

talk discussing the references in each one. What, for example, is alluded to by Depew's expression, "argus-eyed watchfulness," mentioned on page 445.
4. Summarize in a single word a particular trait of some individual, somewhat like the example of General Bolivar as a "Casanova."
5. Give a two- or three-minute talk in which you make use, for the purpose of impressiveness, of at least three quotations.
6. Prepare a talk based on a passage from a well-known source, which in itself is highly regarded by your audience.
7. Give a three- to five-minute speech in which you make use of (a) "impressive facts," (b) "impressive statistics," or (c) a combination of the two.
8. Select from a recent speech in *Vital Speeches* not fewer than ten examples of "loaded words." Analyze the effect of these terms with reference to impressiveness.
9. Write a speech which will take you approximately ten minutes to deliver in which you make use of at least five specific techniques of impressiveness. Do not neglect in your writing the principles of clarity and vividness. Keep constantly in mind how the speech will sound when read aloud to an audience, rather than how it will appeal to one reading it to himself. Record the speech, and make corrections before presenting it to the class.
10. Organize a symposium of from five to seven members of the class as participants. Select one of your members who is to serve as spokesman for the group in presenting a point of view, an argument, or in submitting a set of important facts. The task of the symposium is to consider how those facts can be made more impressive through the application of specific techniques. The spokesman will then give the finished speech on behalf of the group. Each participant should bring to the discussion material emphasizing the use of one of the specific techniques.

SUPPLEMENTARY READINGS

1. Quintilian, *Institutes of Oratory*, Book VIII, chap. IX, "Concerning the Embellishments of Style"; Book XI, chap. I, "Of Figures. . . ."
2. Overstreet, H. A., *Influencing Human Behavior*, W. W. Norton & Company, 1925, chap. VII, "Making Ideas Stick," pp. 125-139.
3. Thonssen, Lester, and Baird, A. Craig, *Speech Criticism*, The Ronald Press Company, pp. 431-432.
4. Whately, Richard, *Elements of Rhetoric*, James Monroe and Co., 1858, Part III, chap. II, "Of Energy."

CHAPTER XIX

Memory

THE classical rhetorician considered memory important enough to give it a distinguished place among the other speech canons, namely, invention, arrangements, style, and delivery. Quintilian declared it "the treasury of eloquence," and Cicero referred to it as "the treasury and guardian of all things." Indeed there can be little doubt that the other canons are dependent upon the speaker's ability to remember his materials. It is not an infrequent occurrence to hear a speaker lament, "I didn't say half of what I wanted to," or "I forgot my most important point," or "My speech was nothing like what I had intended." These comments all reflect problems of memory.

It is not the function of a public-speaking course to assume the responsibility of improving the memory in all lines of thought, but neither is it advisable to fail completely to give the student as much help as possible in devising ways by which he can more effectively master and remember his materials when he needs them.

NATURE OF MEMORY

Memory is the capacity to remember or to make "direct use of what has been learned."[1] Actually, within this process are three closely associated phases: first, memorizing or learning the material; second, retention for a period of time; and third, remembering or reproducing at the moment of need. This last phase may be further subdivided into recall and recognition. The first refers to reviving or reproducing previously acquired knowledge. When in the middle of a speech you feel it appropriate to quote Shakespeare, you "cudgel your memory" for a suitable quotation; hence in remembering the passage, you have used recall.

Recognition is the capacity to identify something with which you have had previous experience. No doubt you have all had the experience of recognizing an acquaintance without being able to recall his name. Our vocabulary usage aptly illustrates the distinction between these two aspects of memory; we recall our spoken vocabularies, but we recognize our reading vocabularies.

Memorizing, retention, and remembering play an important part in a speech. Quintilian put the case this way: "It is the power of memory that brings before us those multitudes of precedents, laws, judgments, sayings, and facts, of which an orator should have an abundance, and which he should always be ready to produce. The memory is accordingly not without reason called the treasury of eloquence."[2] Interestingly enough, Quintilian put stress on the speaker's ability to be "ready to produce" facts. It is certainly true also that the speaker relies more on recall than

[1] Robert S. Woodworth, *Psychology*, Henry Holt and Company, Inc., 4th ed., 1940, pp. 328-329.
[2] Quintilian, *Institutes of Oratory*, John Selby Watson, translator, Henry G. Bohn, 1856, vol. II, p. 333.

on recognition. However, in speechmaking, memory involves, in addition to the reproducing of facts, the recall of the other previously prepared materials, namely, the plan of development, the order of the points, the language, and the planned mode of physical and vocal behavior.

Different degrees of preparation place varying demands upon this triple process of memory. The carefully prepared speech will naturally contain more elements to be recalled than the ones which have been thrown together hastily. An extempore effort requires the speaker to remember his previously prepared plan, his forms of support, his planned mode of behavior. In addition to these elements, the memorized speech demands recall of the verbatim wording of the manuscript. This entire problem is closely associated with methods of preparation. Let us, therefore, consider more in detail the relations of memory to the impromptu, the extemporaneous, the manuscript, and the memorized speech.

MEMORY IN THE IMPROMPTU SPEECH

Many persons may say that memory is not a factor in the unprepared, spur-of-the-moment speech in which you must collect, organize, and present your thoughts almost simultaneously. It is true that the speaker has no previous opportunity to memorize, but he does have a serious problem of recall in pulling together materials that he can present.

At such a time there can be no doubt that a large storehouse of information, a broad background of reading and experience, are invaluable in meeting the impromptu situation. But background is not enough. If you are going to collect your thoughts and supporting material, you must be able first to free yourself of the bewilderment that may come when you are singled out to speak. The beginning speaker is ordinarily so busy thinking about himself that he has little time to concentrate upon his subject; consequently, he experiences what the psychologist refers to as interference. Explains Woodworth, "One type of interference is emotional. Fear may paralyze recall. Anxious self-consciousness or stage fright has prevented the recall of many a well learned speech, and disturbed many a well practiced act."[3] If this is true in the "well-learned speech," it is evident that emotions interfere when you must think on your feet. Of course, the emotional reaction to the impromptu speech may be of a slightly different type, for the speaker does avoid the cumulative effect of devastating anticipation. But the surprise of being asked to speak may make him almost as uncomfortable.

A second type of interference occurs when the speaker has difficulty in deciding what thoughts to present. Two or more ways of expressing an idea may flash into his mind at the same time, with the result that one serves to block the others. As a consequence, the speaker is faced with indecision, becomes hesitant, and utters meaningless vocalizations such as "and-a" and "uh."

What can the speaker do to relieve himself of these tensions? Our first suggestion may seem only remotely related to memory, but we advisedly include it, because it does provide a way to master the fears that tongue-tie the speaker. The best general preparation for impromptu speaking is frequent practice in extempore speaking. In this manner you develop confidence and the ability to phrase your ideas meaningfully in spite of your fears. The intercollegiate debater, for example, develops this skill to summon his thoughts rapidly because, being constantly under pressure to extemporize upon the unexpected, he soon learns how to collect and organize his thoughts while he speaks. He discovers ways to "tie" his thoughts into what has been said and to marshal arguments and evidence.

The following additional suggestions may further help you to overcome fears and to concentrate upon what to say.

1. When you are called upon to speak, immediately start searching in what has already been said for an opening remark.

---

[3] Woodworth, *op. cit.*, p. 350.

Do you agree or disagree with the previous speakers? Has the chairman said something that you can use? Why have you been called upon to speak? What has the previous speaker said that you can further develop?

2. In order to avoid indecision about what to say, attempt immediately to formulate a brief and concise answer to the problem. Put your answer into a single short sentence, and then develop it. You may start your impromptu remarks in the following manner: "Our chairman has asked me how I think we can increase production on the night shift. It is my opinion that we need a complete reorganization of our personnel." Notice that the first sentence relates the speech to what the chairman has said and that the second is a concise statement of what the speaker intends to discuss. On another occasion, you might open by saying, "For the last thirty minutes we have been discussing the advisability of constructing a new school building. From what has been said it is evident to me that we must have a new school. The only problem now is how much shall we invest in this project."

The formula for opening an impromptu speech may be summarized as follows:

a. Relate speech to what has been said,
   (1) By a previous speaker
   (2) By an authority
   (3) By the chairman
b. State concisely your point of view.
c. Develop by illustrations, examples, etc.

3. What we have advised on stage fright earlier is equally applicable here. Woodworth says, "One good general principle, applicable to ... the making of a speech, is to avoid the interference of self-consciousness and worry, by forgetting about yourself and becoming thoroughly immersed in the matter in hand."[4] Furthermore, physical activity, such as drawing a sketch, and the use of gestures and vigorous bodily movement release your tensions and let you think about your subject.

[4] *Ibid.*, p. 356.

4. In opening your speech, attempt to create a favorable impression. Many speakers advertise their nervousness unnecessarily by their first remarks because they insist on starting with an apology such as "I just don't know what I can say on the subject," "I am sure someone else knows more about this question than I do," or "I don't feel qualified to discuss the topic, but. . . ." When they conclude, they make an equally unfavorable impression with another apologetic statement like one of the following: "Now let me see if there is anything else that I should say," "That is about all I can think of," or "I hope that is what you wanted from me." Such apologies accomplish nothing but an unfavorable reflection on the speaker.

MEMORY IN THE EXTEMPORANEOUS SPEECH

Quintilian observed that "the ability of speaking extempore" depends on "no other faculty of mind" than memory.[5] The extemporaneous speech should embrace careful planning and thorough rehearsal, but it does not require an attempt to set the language for delivery. Therefore, at the moment of presentation, the speaker must recall only his organization, his supporting materials, and his planned mode of delivery, but not the verbatim language which he uttered in rehearsal.

Systematic speech preparation at spaced intervals and thoughtful speech composition assure thorough learning and hence assure longer retention and easier recall. It becomes apparent that much of what has been said in earlier chapters might be repeated in this section. For the sake of review, let us summarize some of these memory aids.

We advised earlier that in preparation the speaker should try to memorize the main points expressed in the form he intends to use in his speech. These key sentences more firmly establish a chain of association which binds the speech together and hence aids recall.

[5] Quintilian, *op. cit.*, p. 333.

The parallel wording of main points, the use of signposts, and the employment of other transitional devices also strengthen the chain of association. In the same sense, the preview and pattern of development serve as much for memory aids for the speaker as they do for clarity.

The oral method of preparation, in which the speaker rehearses his speech aloud simulating delivery before an audience, is based upon equally sound learning principles. The speaker develops characteristic ways of expressing his thoughts without attempting definitely to crystallize his language. After several debates, the school debater usually develops ease and confidence in speaking because he becomes familiar with his line of argument and that of the opposition; his subject is so much a part of his thinking that he develops fluency. Many persons marveled at Daniel Webster's ability to answer Hayne after only one night of preparation,[6] but the truth of the matter was that Webster had been thinking about and discussing the subject for years. Furthermore, he had heard many speeches on the subject of the Union. He was so full of his subject that memory presented no problem for him.

The more you talk about a subject in conversation, in round-table discussions, before clubs, or in the classroom, the less recall will trouble you.

Oral rehearsal of a speech at regularly spaced intervals makes learning easier and further assures retention. Five half-hour workouts are probably superior to two and a half hours of continuous work. Actors discover that "walking through" their lines, associating them with stage business and movement and with the lines of other actors, makes memory easier. Actually, the same is true in preparing a speech. The rehearsal of the presentation of charts, blackboard drawings, and manipulation of models at the same time you rehearse your speech facilitates recall at a later time.

[6] Before the United States Senate, Jan. 26, 1830.

In addition to what we have already said about your mental attitudes, let us recommend that in the process of developing a speech you avoid *constant* evaluation of your progress, for in many cases it fosters dissatisfaction and discouragement. In support of this suggestion, Knight Dunlap says, "Ideals, purposes, and plans are the indispensable conditions of effective learning. These, however, do their work best when let alone. Constant purposing, constant planning, constant determining of ideals are damaging. These important operations should be undertaken at specific times, with reference to definite succeeding periods, and then dropped from thought."[7]

First attempts at rehearsal of a speech are ordinarily hesitant and awkward, with words difficult to find and thoughts confused. Repeated attempts bring greater fluency. It is only after considerable experience before audiences that many persons develop the ability to express themselves with ease.

MEMORY IN THE MANUSCRIPT SPEECH

Many speakers will not risk speaking "off the cuff" before live audiences. In order to avoid making statements for which they will be sorry later, they insist upon reading their speeches from manuscript. Furthermore, radio has increased the demand for the manuscript speech because broadcasters cannot risk the putting on the air material that has not been carefully checked and timed. Is memory a problem in this situation? In truth, the memory problems are greatly reduced, for the speaker does not have to recall his materials; they are immediately before him, and if he wishes, he may read them word for word without lifting his eyes from his prepared copy; but as a result, he sacrifices directness. On the other hand, if the speaker is to look at his auditors occasionally, he must be able to continue speaking while look-

[7] From *Habits—Their Making and Unmaking* by Knight Dunlap, Copyright 1932, Liveright Publishing Corp.

ing away from his manuscript. Herein is a memory problem. It necessitates increasing the speaker's powers of recognition and preparing the manuscript with as many reading cues as possible. Below are some suggestions which should help you in preparing your manuscript for effective delivery.

1. Type your manuscript with double or triple spaces without too many words to the line and with ample margins on all sides.
2. Underline or type in red sign posts or other parts of the speech which will enable you to note your progress and to find your place in case of confusion.
3. Read and reread your speech until you are thoroughly familiar with it, having many passages partially memorized. In your preparation, actually plan when you intend to look at your auditors and then practice looking at your simulated auditors. You may wish to memorize completely occasional passages so that during delivery you can give the impression of extemporizing upon your subject.

MEMORY IN THE MEMORIZED SPEECH OR THE MEMORIZED PASSAGE

At times you may find advantage in memorizing a short speech, such as an introduction, a speech of presentation, a speech of welcome or farewell. Or at other times, you may wish to commit to memory a portion of a speech—the introduction, the conclusion, or an apt quotation. In these particular situations, your memory is put to a severe test because you must have perfect recall.

When should you attempt to memorize? To put the answer briefly, when you are alert, at ease, and rested. If you are tired or harassed about other matters, you will have difficulty concentrating on the matter at hand. Your mind will wander away from the passage under consideration. In order to conserve energy, therefore, select carefully your study period.

For short units, the *whole* method of memorizing is generally considered superior to the *part* method. By this method, you commit to memory a whole passage instead of attempting to master lines or sentences and then assembling these into a whole. The chief advantage of the whole method seems to be that a strong train of association is more firmly established in your mind, and transitions are made with greater ease and with less risk of forgetting. The passage as a whole makes sense, and it is easier to memorize sense passages than nonsense.

In using the whole method, follow these steps:

1. First read the whole selection for understanding, noting how the passage is put together, the pattern of partition, and how the points are arranged. If you are memorizing the writing of another person, you may discover real advantage in attempting to place the selection in its proper context; that is, you may be acquainting yourself with the author, with the sources of his ideas, and with the source from which the specific quotation is taken.

2. When you are confident that you understand the selection, put the manuscript aside and attempt to think of the selection as a whole. You may find it helpful to summarize the selection orally.

3. Reread the manuscript several times, simulating how you intend to deliver it to an audience and of course using a conversational approach. Stay on your feet while working, and associate gestures and bodily movement with the various parts.

4. Use several short periods of work in preference to longer periods.

5. As soon as possible, lay aside the manuscript and force yourself to recall, no matter how hesitant you may seem or how difficult it may be.

6. To ensure accuracy, have someone check your recitation against the manuscript. Make yourself strain, however, to remember, and do not consent to prompting until it is absolutely necessary. During your first attempts without the manuscript, you may have to ask for prompting several times.

7. Shortly before delivery, perhaps an hour or more, reread your manuscript straight through aloud and concentrate upon the thoughts instead of on how you sound.

The best insurance against forgetting is "overlearning," or "learning beyond the point when it can barely be reproduced."[8] The best way to forget is not to review. Cramming for an examination should have taught you what happens when learning is hurried and concentrated. Once you have written the test, the information that you have just barely learned slips away rapidly. In contrast, with the necessary review at spaced intervals, you retain what you have learned much longer.

Overlearning of speech materials is particularly important for effective delivery. If the speaker is to give the impression that he is spontaneously conversing with his listeners, he must not have to struggle to recall words, phrases, and sentences. When the memorizing is imperfectly done, the speaker ordinarily loses his "urge to communicate," with the result that he concentrates upon recall instead of upon "putting over" his thoughts to his listeners. In addition, the threat of forgetting increases his nervous tensions and thereby reduces his effectiveness.

Therefore, one of the most difficult problems in repeating memorized or partially memorized material is to maintain what is commonly referred to as "the illusion of the first time," giving the impression of spontaneous and thoughtful presentation. Often there is the tendency to forget meanings and to concentrate on remembering words. Says Woolbert, "In fact, it rather seems as if the great majority of speeches which are committed word for word are remote from the audience, strained, unnatural, even affected. It takes an artist to deliver a memorized speech well; the tendency always is to quit thinking while thus reciting and so to break up the fine adjustment between thinking, voice, and body necessary for vital speaking."[9]

[8] Woodworth, *op. cit.*, p. 348.
[9] Charles Henry Woolbert, *The Fundamentals of Speech,* Harper & Brothers, rev. ed., 1927, p. 372.

If naturalness and directness are to be achieved, you must memorize your vocal and bodily patterns as well as your thoughts and words. The importance, therefore, of memorizing aloud and of attempting during practice to simulate a speaking situation cannot be overstressed. Failure to memorize properly may result in the following difficulties:

1. Speaking too rapidly
2. Emphasizing words of little importance
3. Repeating words and phrases without communicating
4. Falling into monotonous vocal patterns
5. Speaking with little facial expression
6. Failing to synchronize gestures with the presentation of thoughts
7. Neglecting to adjust the loudness of the voice to the room

BREAKING MEMORY BLOCKS

In the midst of a memorized selection, a speaker sometimes experiences memory failure. What can he do to break a memory block? Frequently this question is posed by students who participate in speech contests, by persons who have difficulty recalling names, by those who are absent-minded, and by many others. As we have just pointed out, "overlearning" is the best insurance against forgetting, but in spite of such efforts, you may suffer occasional lapses of memory.

Seemingly no magic formula exists to ensure the speaker against such difficulties. As a rule, however, if you permit memory failure to stir you up emotionally, the problems of recovery are intensified. In case of memory lapse, you will be wise not to attempt to force yourself to remember. Shifting your attention momentarily away from the matter sometimes results in spontaneous return of the desired item. All of us have frequently found this to be true in remembering names and faces. Try as we will, the name won't come, but five minutes later, when we turn to other things, it flashes into the mind. Mental straining too often just intensifies your emotional reaction. Speech contestants who forget often find it valuable to walk around a moment and then start again on a paragraph preceding the place where the forgetting occurred. If they think about the thoughts as they occur without trying to think ahead to the troublesome spot, by the time they arrive at the difficult place, they are able to bridge the gap without difficulty.

SUMMARY

Let us summarize briefly some of the principles that will aid a speaker in memorizing, retaining, and remembering his speech materials:

1. In memorizing, attempt to keep the learning process active by thinking the thoughts as you go over them. Repetition alone is not enough.
2. Oral rehearsal of a speech is superior to silent study.
3. Spaced repetitions are probably superior to longer periods of study.
4. Generally the "whole" method is superior to the "part" method.
5. Eagerness to learn, or "the will to learn," facilitates learning.
6. "Overlearning" is necessary for retention. One of the best ways to overlearn is to review the material frequently.
7. A brief review an hour or so before presentation will ensure more effective recall.
8. Association of the idea or thought with physical activity such as bodily movements, gestures, or manipulation of a visual aid facilitates remembering.
9. As a rule do not attempt to force yourself to remember. If a name or word will not come, shift your attention elsewhere momentarily.
10. Unnecessary interference resulting from extreme anxiety over the occasion should be avoided. Crowding your mind with too many details should be avoided.
11. A sure way to forget is not to review.

EXERCISES

1. *Impromptu Speaking Assignment.* Your instructor will prepare a list of speaking topics from recent issues of a local newspaper or news magazine that you as a class have selected. He will prepare as

many topics as there are students in the class. Each topic, typed on a separate slip of paper, will be placed face down on a table. When your turn to speak comes, you are to go to the table, pick up three topics, select one, and return the other two face down. You then are to discuss the topic you have drawn.
2. *Extemporaneous Impromptu Speaking Assignment.*
   a. *Selecting a subject for the unit.* As a class you are to select a general proposition similar to the intercollegiate debate question or some other broad subject such as capital punishment, socialized medicine, or relations with China. The topic should be worded in the form of a proposition and partitioned carefully.
   b. *Extemporaneous speaking phase.* The class will be divided into groups of five or six; each group will be assigned a phase of the proposition and on an assigned day will conduct a symposium with each member delivering a five-minute speech on some limited aspect. Following the formal speeches, the discussion will be opened to questions from the floor.
   c. *Impromptu speaking phase.* After each group has presented its phase, the instructor (or a class committee) will prepare a list of topics for impromptu speaking. When your turn comes, your instructor will give you a topic to discuss. At the close of your speech you will be expected to answer questions from the floor.
   d. *Group evaluation.* After each member of the class has delivered an impromptu speech, each member will be asked to rank his classmates in a rank order, listing them from the student who has been the most effective to the least effective in the two assignments. Ranks can be averaged by a class committee to determine final rating.

SUPPLEMENTARY READINGS

1. Crocker, Lionel, *Public Speaking For College Students*, American Book Company, 1941, chap. 7.
2. Dunlap, Knight, *Habits—Their Making and Unmaking*, Liveright Publishing Corp., 1932, chaps. 7, 8.
3. Hayworth, Donald, *An Introduction to Public Speaking*, The Ronald Press Company, rev. ed., 1941, chap. 11.
4. Hoffman, William G., *Public Speaking for Business Men*, McGraw-Hill Book Company, Inc., 3rd ed., 1949, chap. VI.

5. Scott, Walter Dill, *The Psychology of Public Speaking*, Walter Dill Scott, 1907, chaps. 13, 14.
6. Wells, Earl, "Methods of Memorization For the Speaker and Reader," *The Quarterly Journal of Speech*, February, 1928, pp. 39-64.
7. Woodworth, Robert S., *Psychology*, Henry Holt and Company, Inc., 4th ed., 1940, chap. 10.

CHAPTER XX

General Principles of Delivery

NOW that you have studied the planning of a speech in detail, the organization of material, and have given some thought to the wording and the style in which your ideas are to be clothed, you are ready to study the final step, the delivery of the completed speech; for your speech is not a speech at all until it is presented to and heard by an audience. The manner in which you present your ideas is of much greater importance than is often realized by students of public speaking.

IMPORTANCE OF DELIVERY

The idea is held by many people that the delivery of a speech is unimportant, that so long as the material is well organized and well worded, it makes little or no difference how it is presented to the audience. It is partially because of this belief that we hear so much ineffective speaking. Lecturers in college and university classes are especially faulty in this respect, apparently holding that their subject matter is of such importance that the students ought to listen whether or not their presentation is interesting.

Such ideas arise from the point of view that a speech and its delivery are somehow two different things, that in the matter of relative importance there is a choice to be made between the content of a speech and its presentation. Actually, no such division can be made. *A speech to be a speech must be delivered to an audience.* It is obvious that the heart of any discourse is the idea, the content, and that the purpose in speaking is to gain acceptability with an audience for that content. Because this is true, the belief has become prevalent that the content is therefore of greater importance than the delivery. But the content of the speech depends, as will be shown, quite as much on the manner of its delivery as on the wording. Delivery helps to make the content clear, vivid, and impressive. Any belief to the contrary implies a duality that does not exist.

Whatever differences there are between speaking and writing exist wholly because of the one factor of delivery. Without these differences there would be no point at all in the trouble and expenditure involved in bringing people together for personal and group conferences; they could simply write notes. Differences in vocabulary, in sentence structure, in style arise out of the fact that in one case the discourse is to be read, whereas in the other it is to be heard. The speaker needs to make his language instantly comprehensible. This imposes upon him certain limitations of verbal language but in return gives him the added facilities of vocal variety and visible action.

The significance of these differences arising out of the factor of delivery may be noted in the intensive efforts to provide for the inclusion of both voice and action in our electrical and mechanical systems of mass communication. The telegraph was a highly significant invention because it brought all parts of the country immeasurably closer together and contributed greatly to the speed of transmission and to the diffusion of information to all sections.[1] But the telephone, which carries the living voice, reaches into almost every home. The "wireless" of Marconi was in a sense an adaptation of the Morse telegraph; but radio carries the voice over the air, bringing speech and music to millions of listeners. Added to that now is television, which makes possible the full delivery of both voice and action directly into your own home *at the instant of their occurrence* miles away.

The old silent motion pictures provided entertainment for almost three decades, but they were incomplete. The addition of voice and other sound effects has brought to the audience the full presentation of the drama instead of only a part of it. Current experiments with tridimensional projection, providing for perspective, are directed toward making talking pictures even more lifelike.

The telephone, the radio, television, and the talking pictures have cost immense sums of money, many years of labor, and have required for their development some of the best scientific brains of the country. Why? For the simple reason that delivery, how the message is presented, is of great importance in the process of communication, of bringing audience and idea together. In fact, it is of such importance that no living language can be adequately or completely written. The word *language* itself is derived from the Latin *lingua*, tongue, implying that originally language and speech were identical.

DELIVERY AND MEANING

The delivery of a speech is important specifically because the meanings, the ideas you want to present to your listeners, are determined as much by the way you use your voice, your body, your hands, fingers, your facial expression, as they are by your

[1] See Charles Horton Cooley, *Social Organization*, Charles Scribner's Sons, 1912, Part II, "Communication."

choice of words and the way you put them together. By changing your manner of speaking, you can completely alter the sense of almost anything you want to say. You can call your best friends by the most scurrilous names if, as Owen Wister's Virginian insisted, you "smile when you say that!"

In the argument between Macbeth and Lady Macbeth as to whether they shall proceed with the murder of Duncan, Macbeth raises the question, "If we should fail?" To which Lady Macbeth replies, "We fail! But screw your courage to the sticking place, And we'll not fail." Now there has been considerable discussion of the specific manner in which Lady Macbeth would say "We fail!" If spoken one way it means one thing, and the succeeding line will be given one pattern; if spoken another way, it means something else, and the pattern of the next sentence will also be different. The whole sense will be altered. For example, read these two words first with a very slight rising inflection, or none at all, on *we* and a strong downward inflection on *fail*, and note the finality of the meaning expressed. Now simply reverse the inflection on *fail*, giving both words a wide rising movement, and observe the complete change in meaning.

In a little German playlet, *Come Here*,[2] an actress is applying for a part in a play. In the tryout the director gives her only two words to speak, "Come here!" and then suggests a number of situations in which those words would be appropriate. The actress speaks them in no less than twenty different ways, each suitable for one situational context and no other and each "meaning" one thing, different from all the rest.

Delivery and Your Meaning

When you speak to an audience, whether it be large or small, you have in mind certain ideas which you want to impart to your listeners. If you were to write those ideas down on paper, you would be limited in your expression to words alone. It is quite

---

[2] In Alice Evelyn Craig, *The Speech Arts*, The Macmillan Company, rev. ed., 1937, pp. 431-434.

true that a great deal can be expressed solely through words, as is evidenced by the great mass of literature that has accumulated through the centuries. But when you write, no reader can possibly know the particular inflections of voice, the stresses you put on the words, the exact phrasing of the sentences, as you write them down; for if you write meaningfully, you probably do write with a great deal of subvocal expression and perhaps with certain facial expressions as well. If the ideas contain a strong emotional component, you may lean a little more heavily on your pen or strike the keys of your typewriter a little more vigorously. All these are lost to the reader, especially if what you wrote is put into type and printed, for then even the possible effect of your handwriting is gone.

Your delivery, then, is not a matter of adding something to your language just for the sake of making a good appearance. Delivery is an integral part of effective communication. It helps to make your language clearer by making your meanings more complete and more specific. It contributes to vividness in helping to arouse more vivid imagery, and it helps to make your speech more impressive in part by revealing in your very manner your attitudes and feelings toward the matter under discussion.[3]

TWO ASPECTS OF DELIVERY

Speech in its completeness consists of a dual system of symbols, those which we hear and those which we see. The audible system or code includes both the words we use and their manner of utterance, the latter being the first of the two aspects of delivery. Since the use of words (verbal language) has already been discussed, our further study of language will be directed, so far as the audible code is concerned, to the manner of utterance of that verbal language and will be the subject matter of Chapter XXI.

[3] See also Giles Wilkeson Gray, "Problems in the Teaching of Gesture," *The Quarterly Journal of Speech,* October, 1924, pp. 238-252.

The visible system or code of symbols consists of all that we see the speaker doing that contributes in any way to, or detracts in any degree from, the communication of the ideas which he is trying to convey to us. This visible code is important, too, and we shall give it much attention. Since this visible behavior is the second of the two aspects of delivery, we shall devote to the discussion the entire final chapter of this text.

DELIVERY IN SPEECH IS INESCAPABLE

In speech, meanings are conveyed (so long as we understand what we mean by that expression) not by language *and* delivery but by *delivered language*. In reinforcing meanings and making them more specific, delivery is as much a part of the total language pattern as are the words themselves. Do not permit yourself to be misled into thinking that if you do nothing by way of visible action you thereby eliminate the factor of delivery entirely, for even making no observable movements at all is in itself a mode of delivery; furthermore, you cannot avoid the effects produced by your voice, for although you speak in a monotone, you are using a definite manner of utterance—in this case, one that is particularly ineffective.

If you speak at all, then, you cannot avoid the element of delivery. The question remains one of the degree to which your manner of presentation contributes to or detracts from your intended meanings, to which it reinforces or negates the ideas which you intend your words to convey.

BASIC PRINCIPLES OF DELIVERY

In speaking your general delivery should be governed by a few basic principles. Among these the following may be mentioned:

1. *To be fully effective you must establish with your audience what has been called* rapport. Oliver explains the concept as follows:

There must be a bond of sympathy uniting a great speaker and his audience. There ought to be a current of warm and cordial understanding which flows both ways. For genuine communication, the speaker and his auditors should become almost one unit. They may not always agree with him, but they should be stirred by his feelings, and he should respond quickly and accurately to theirs. This, I take it, is the general meaning of the term *rapport*. A speaker without *rapport* may be clear, fluent, intellectual—even convincing—but he cannot be great. To arouse his auditors, a bond of strong feeling must unite the speaker with them.[4]

This *rapport* with the audience, this "bond of sympathy," this "current of warm and cordial understanding," is largely the result of a good delivery, which is based, first, on the speaker's own (initial) attitude toward the audience, and second, on the "urge to communicate" with them. One may feel justified in going a bit further than Oliver and insisting that a speaker will not even be fully effective unless through his manner of speaking he is able to establish and maintain *rapport* with his listeners. This is indeed one of the primary factors in the difference between speaking and writing as modes of communication, namely, that because spoken language is delivered in a face-to-face situation, it is possible to create a strong bond of sympathy between speaker and audience. It is the factor of delivery that makes the difference.

2. *Good delivery should not attract attention to itself.* As we have said, the primary objective in a speaking situation is to bring an idea and an audience together. Whatever in the process distracts the listeners' attention away from the idea makes the basic process of speaking that much less effective. Only in rare instances is speech exhibitory; it is very seldom that one should want to impress his hearers with the excellence of his speaking technique. The good speaker who has an idea to communicate and the urge to impart that idea has no desire to place himself on exhibition. Exhibitionism and communicativeness are mu-

---

[4] Robert T. Oliver, "Wilson's *Rapport* with His Audience," *The Quarterly Journal of Speech*, February, 1941, pp. 79-90.

tually antagonistic. If you want to put on a show, your effort may be entirely legitimate; but don't try at the same time to say anything worthwhile. If you want to communicate an idea, don't do anything to direct attention to any phase of your delivery and thus to create a barrier which will interfere with the process.

3. *Good delivery must be consistent with the total speaking situation.* This situation includes the occasion, the audience, the physical surroundings, the subject, and the speaker himself. Some situations permit a strong, vigorous, even vehement, delivery; others demand a restrained, quiet, reserved manner. Small audiences as a rule call for a more restricted type of delivery than a large audience in a large auditorium or outdoors. Some subjects do not lend themselves to vigorous tones and strong gestures. People accustomed to making fine distinctions, to sedentary occupations and intellectual pursuits, do not as a rule like to be stirred too deeply by the overdynamic type of speaking. Learn to gauge your situation; determine as many aspects as you can, and let your delivery be governed by those factors.

4. *Good delivery should make full use of the principle of variety in both voice and action.* No one likes to hear the speaker who within a few sentences is shouting at the top of his voice and maintains that loudness throughout his speech. He soon loses his effectiveness. For the same listeners do not like to see a speaker use the same gesture over and over, trace and retrace the same path in his movements about the platform, or follow any other persistent pattern in his manner of presentation.

In your practicing on delivery, then, work for variety for two reasons: first, it makes you much less tiresome to listen to and to look at; second, just as the ideas themselves and the words in which you express those ideas are changing from moment to moment, so also should the delivery vary in keeping with the shifting thought.

5. *Good delivery is animated, alert.* Good speaking is characterized by an alertness, an animation, that grows out of the speaker's attitude toward the total situation. It reveals itself in

the general tonus of the body, by alert bearing, flexible voice, expressive face and eyes, by clear, distinct utterance. The speaker's attitude, out of which animation develops, is one of liveliness, of keen interest in both the subject matter of his speech and in the talking about it. Closely related to this attitude is what has been referred to repeatedly as the "urge to communicate," which is in itself an emotional attitude.

One of the essential characteristics of emotional states is that they are "allover" conditions. One cannot localize an emotion; when we are angry we are angry all over; when we are happy we are happy all over. Our moods and attitudes, then, are expressed by such allover activity. Hence it is that the urge to communicate, with other associated attitudes, is revealed by animation, by this allover behavior. The whole bodily mechanism is involved.

To the audience animation denotes sincerity and honesty of purpose, as a rule, although many a speaker has attempted to compensate by an excess of animation for what was actually shallow content or questionable ethics. It is easily possible to overdo the matter of liveliness, but the beginning speaker is much more likely to underdo, to use far too little activity, than to overdo. Whether you use much or little, your delivery must be purposeful, not random, communicative, not exhibitory.

6. *Good delivery is simple, unaffected, "natural."* A belief held by many people is that in speaking all one has to do to ensure a good delivery is to be "natural"; that delivery will somehow take care of itself. This is the same as the idea that if one has the thought well in mind an effective presentation is assured. As a measure of delivery, however, *naturalness* is misleading. What is often called *natural* is likely to be nothing more than the "habitual." You are so accustomed to doing certain things in certain ways—like tying your shoe, for example—that that way feels perfectly natural, and any other way is awkward. Any other habit that we may have learned feels just as natural because it is performed almost automatically. It is removed from the focus of

consciousness. But any *new* habit which is built up to replace the old one comes to feel just as natural as the old, when it too can be performed without conscious thought.

Whenever you want to relearn to perform more skillfully, more effectively, any activity which you have been performing for some time, you must unlearn a number of old, ineffective habits and learn a number of new ones. Anyone who has ever attempted to learn to play golf under a good instructor, after having played for a number of years, will attest to the validity of that statement.

To say, then, "Be natural," is usually to say no more than "Do the thing as you habitually do it." The "natural" in speech may or may not be good, depending on whether your early habits of speech are effective or ineffective. You acquired those habits from many sources; most of them you learned years ago by imitating models which in many instances were none too good. This is one case in which practice has not made perfect; all it has done is to fix habits, many of them bad. As a result, your "natural" mode of speaking is in all probability characterized by many ineffective habits.

The procedure obviously is to replace as many of these as possible with more effective modes of speaking behavior, to practice on the new ones until they in turn become habits and hence seem just as "natural" as the ones they replaced.

There is a sense, however, in which "naturalness" may be recommended. This more usable interpretation of the term is analyzed by Woolbert as follows:

1. Be unaffected; use a minimum of display; show off only enough to reveal power; make the exhibitory factors of speaking thoroughly secondary to the communicative factor.
2. Be normally vigorous; speak as you do when you are in earnest anywhere, earnest enough to convince people that you mean what you say.
3. Seem to be at home; speak as you speak freely among those you know and trust. Be unconstrained and as free from nervousness as among your own people.

4. Be at your best; eliminate awkwardness, dullness, and inefficiency. Be what you believe your most interesting self to be.
5. Be free from stiffness, equally tight or loose all over; not stiff in the neck and limp in the knees or stiff in the knees and limp in the neck.
6. Be simple; beware of undue exaggeration. Don't be highflown, pompous, puffed up.
7. Be forthright; connect straightaway with your hearers; count yourself one of them.
8. Be communicative; cultivate what has been called "a lively sense of communication."[5]

7. Good delivery should be free from excessive tensions. If you are like most speakers, especially the better ones, when you contemplate appearing before an audience you may be seized with a sort of nervous apprehension, which will attack you in various forms and degrees. Usually it manifests itself beforehand in such bodily changes as an increase of the pulse rate, clammy palms, an "all-gone" feeling in the pit of the stomach, thick, uncontrollable tongue, dry throat, trembling fingers, knees, and generally excessive tensions of the entire musculature. Every speaker has felt the symptoms, and many of even the most eminent have never arrived at the point where they are no longer affected. The phenomenon is commonly known as stage fright and is identical with the feeling a football player has while waiting for the opening kick-off in a game or a runner awaiting the "On your marks!" of the starter in a race.

To most beginners in public speaking this nervousness is a matter of deepest concern. One of the first questions raised in speech classes is often, "Why do I get so nervous when I try to speak?" or, "How can I get rid of my nervousness?" Many apparently feel that such feelings are evidence of some pathological condition, that if they were perfectly normal they would be completely at ease before an audience.

The truth is probably that nervousness before an audience, and

---

[5] Charles Henry Woolbert, *The Fundamentals of Speech*, Harper & Brothers, rev. ed., 1927, p. 23.

especially when looking forward to facing an audience, is a very common experience. It is likely that practically every speaker since the time of Demosthenes has experienced the same symptoms. So common is it, in fact, that one might almost say that its presence, rather than its absence, is an indication of normality.

Stage fright rises in part from a type of fear, not of physical danger or harm, but rather of loss of status with the audience. The good opinion of others, psychologists recognize, is a powerful incentive to behavior; and the prospect of losing that good opinion fills us with dismay. When you appear before a group of listeners as a speaker, you stand to lose that regard unless you are effective in your presentation. The apprehension felt because of some doubt of your ability to measure up to the demands of the occasion may give rise to nervousness. For the beginner, then, it comes in large part from a lack of self-confidence.

Many people, even with extensive speaking experience, as soon as they are aware of the fact that they are being observed, immediately become self-conscious. They begin to get nervous and to worry about making mistakes. They too develop all the symptoms of stage fright and make the very errors they are afraid of making. The feeling is not limited to beginners by any means.

The underlying causes of stage fright are not entirely understood; it is highly probable that there are factors in the social situation, in the consciousness of being the focus of attention, in the feeling of responsibility, which contribute to nervousness. The whole phenomenon appears to be highly complicated.

You are of course interested in knowing what all this has to do with delivery and what if anything you can do about it. It should be quite obvious, as many of you will testify, that nervousness has a definitely inhibiting effect on your presentation of a speech. It is only when you are at ease that you are able to speak with the maximum effectiveness. Remedial measures should follow two definite lines, both of which are essential, and about both of which you yourself can do everything that can be done at all.

The first of these two measures involves the development of *a different attitude toward the phenomenon of nervousness*. Attempt to change your habitual way of looking at stage fright. You will find it possible to make such a change if you consider these three aspects of the problem of attitudes:

a. Nervousness in itself may or may not be of importance. What is important is the *degree to which you permit it to prevent your doing what you set out to do*. The story is told of General Grant (and probably has been told of many others) that when he was a young lieutenant in the Mexican War he observed just before one of the battles that his knees were knocking together. Looking down at them he said grimly, "Go on and shake! You'd shake worse than that if you knew where I am going to take you!" Most men who have seen active service in the armed forces will readily admit to experiencing the same feelings just before going into combat. Once they become engrossed in what they are doing, the nervousness tends to disappear. Don't give way to it.

b. Realize that *nervousness when you face the prospect of making a classroom speech or any other public appearance is no evidence of a pathological personality*. On the contrary, it is a perfectly normal reaction. The world's greatest speakers, almost without exception, have felt exactly as you and your fellow students do, and most of them, for all their experience, were never able completely to dispel their trepidation as they looked forward to facing an audience. They simply refused to allow themselves to be overcome. In your experience, you are in the company of the oratorical immortals!

If it had been possible for all of you to have come up from the first grade accustomed to making public appearances, so that they were all a part of the day's work and to be taken largely for granted, you probably would not be troubled today. Unfortunately, except for a few of the especially "talented," public appearances are the exception throughout the school system, with the result that for most of you it is a relatively new experience, one which you have seldom had to face. The very newness in itself leads to uncertainty and nervousness. You will find, however, that each speaking experience will reduce your perturbation, so that by the time you have finished your course you should be able to stand before most audiences with considerable poise and equanimity.

c. Develop the urge to communicate. The development of such an attitude toward the function and the process of speaking will serve to direct your attention away from yourself and to the thing you set out to do. The football player, when he gets into the play, has little time to think about himself; there is no place for "grandstanding"; his interest is in fulfilling the particular assignment the play calls for. Your assignment when you are making a speech is to bring an idea to a group of listeners. The attitude that you *have a message* will enable you to concentrate on what you are actually trying to do so that you will not have a great deal of time to devote to yourself. As Woolbert says, "A speaker ought to be reaching out to meet his hearers, eager to get in touch with them, even to mingle with them; but the shaking, stammering novitiate on the platform giving one of his earliest public addresses has little inclination to get in touch with anybody; what he wants is to get away from people; he would much rather run. In fact, that is just what half of him is trying to do when he shakes and quakes."[6]

The second remedial measure necessitates *the adoption of a few simple procedures* which, although they may not entirely rid you of your nervousness, should help you to overcome its effects.

a. Be sure that you have made adequate preparation. Stage fright arises, as has been indicated, partly from a lack of self-confidence, a feeling of inadequacy. Probably nothing else you can do will increase your confidence in yourself, your sense of

[6] Woolbert, *op. cit.*, p. 75.

adequacy, quite so much as knowing that you are fully prepared for the thing you have to do.

Know your subject thoroughly, know the sequence of ideas, your supporting materials; have your facts and their interpretations well in mind, and take whatever steps may be necessary to recall them when you need them. A few notes may be a great help in your early speeches. You should even do some thinking about the language you are going to use.

The most thorough preparation involves also some consideration of the manner in which you are going to present your material; *it involves practicing* your speech aloud. No skill or art was ever learned to any degree of proficiency without much practice and then more practice.

Complete preparation, including practice, will give you, as nothing else can, increased self-confidence, which in turn is conducive to ease in speaking. With a reduction of your feelings of inadequacy, your nervousness and stage fright themselves will tend largely to fade out and finally to disappear altogether.

b. Do not try to conceal your nervousness;[7] you will succeed only in tightening up your muscles all the more. Trying to hold your hands still or to keep your knees from quaking is mainly an effort to hide their trembling. Such an effort results in bringing still other muscles into play and merely adds to the total effect of nervous tension. Relaxation, rather than more tension, is the key to relief.

c. Move about before the audience. A muscle in smooth action is not nearly so likely to stiffen up as one which you are trying to hold rigid. In any fear reaction, an excess of adrenalin is poured into the blood stream which, if not used up, creates a hypertension. Vigorous movement serves to increase that excess; but a moderate amount of movement helps to use up the surplus energy, and the tendency to tighten up is decreased.

[7] See also William Phillips Sandford and Willard Hayes Yeager, *Principles of Effective Speaking*, The Ronald Press Company, 4th ed., 1942, p. 242.

Avoid pacing to and fro; avoid playing with a pencil, a button on your coat, a piece of chalk, or any other article. You can walk to the blackboard and draw a chart; you can exhibit some visual aid and point out significant features on the chart, drawing, or diagram; you can use a pencil somewhat as a pointer or wand, so to speak; you can move freely from one side of the lectern or table or pedestal to the other, so long as you do not move in a rhythmical pattern. You can turn from one side of the audience to the other, making sure that all parts are given equal attention during the speaking. You can use your hands, arms, whole body, facial expression, to give added meaning to what you are saying, as well as to give you relief from the excessive tensions that interfere with your speaking.

With such an attitude toward the phenomenon of stage fright as has been suggested and by following the procedures outlined, you should be able to overcome the effects of any excessive nervousness you may feel at the outset of your speaking experiences. Other procedures may help—whatever will enable you to put your muscles into moderate action and at the same time contribute to the total impression you are trying to make and to your main purpose as a speaker should be of some value. Nervousness at its worst is seldom fatal; speakers are in no greater danger than expectant fathers.

SUMMARY

Delivery, then, is highly important in speaking because of the contribution it makes to the arousing of meanings in the minds of the listeners. Good delivery is governed by a few basic principles:

1. To be fully effective you must establish *rapport* with your audience.
2. Good delivery should not attract attention to itself.
3. Good delivery must be consistent with the total speaking situation.
4. Good delivery should make full use of the principle of variety.
5. Good delivery is animated, alert.
6. Good delivery is simple, unaffected, "natural."
7. Good delivery should be free from excessive tensions.

EXERCISES

1. Demonstrate how, by changing your manner of presentation, the same passage or sentence can be given quite different meanings.
2. Give the statement, "I'll get you for that," in the following ways:
   a. Playfully, as to someone who has played a light joke on you
   b. Mildly reprimanding, as if to a teasing child
   c. Threateningly, as if to someone who has done you irreparable injury

   Work out similar variations for other statements.
3. Give a talk on some subject which touches the everyday affairs of your listeners. Get as close to the front row as you conveniently can, and try to get a direct response from the audience. You may address specific questions to individual members, asking for additional information, for verification, for opinion, etc. Establish as high a degree of *rapport* as possible.
4. Discuss frankly your own experiences with stage fright. Relate specific instances when you were affected, how it felt, and whether you were able to overcome the effects. You need not limit your discussion to speaking situations.
5. Before giving your next speech in class, give it some place—in your room, out in the field, in some vacant classroom—where there is no audience to hear you. Then give the same speech in class. Describe in a written report or orally the difference due to the presence or absence of an audience. What do you receive from an audience that is lacking without one?
6. In the recording laboratory, not in the classroom, record your next speech on either tape, wire, or disk. Do not listen to it. Later on, give the same speech to the class, and at the same time record it again. Now listen to both presentations. What differences do you observe? To what may these differences be attributed?

SUPPLEMENTARY READINGS

1. Bryant, Donald C., and Wallace, Karl R., *Fundamentals of Public Speaking*, Appleton-Century-Crofts, Inc., 1947, chap. 3, "Essential Aspects of Delivery," pp. 45-59.
2. Quintilian, *Institutes of Oratory*, Book XI, chap. III, "Concerning the Best Manner of Delivering a Pleading or Discourse."
3. Sandford, William Phillips, and Yeager, Willard Hayes, *Principles of Effective Speaking*, The Ronald Press Company, 4th ed., 1942, chap. 16, "Fundamental Qualities of Delivery," pp. 223-235.

4. Thonssen, Lester, and Baird, A. Craig, *Speech Criticism*, The Ronald Press Company, 1948, chap. 16, "The Delivery of a Speech," pp. 434-447.
5. Whately, Richard, *Elements of Rhetoric*, James Monroe and Co., 1855, Part IV, "Of Elocution."
6. Winans, James A., *Speech-Making*, Appleton-Century-Crofts, Inc., 1938, chap. II, "Conversing with an Audience," pp. 11-45; chap. XX, "Further Study of Delivery," pp. 404-427.
7. Yeager, Willard Hayes, *Effective Speaking for Every Occasion*, Prentice-Hall, Inc., 1940, chap. 3, "Audience Interest and Effective Speech Delivery," pp. 78-99.

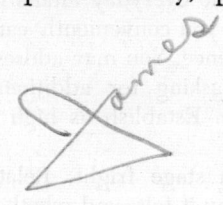

CHAPTER XXI

Vocal Aspects of Delivery

ALTHOUGH speech is an allover activity, as has been pointed out, and although your delivery involves your whole bodily mechanism, it may still be possible for the sake of convenience to discuss separately the two principal aspects of delivery—voice and action. In this chapter, therefore, we shall consider the voice and its various phases in relation to the delivery of your speech and to the meanings you want to arouse.

Keep constantly in mind that the way in which you use your voice is an integral part of your speech, as important as the words themselves. The *spoken* word is a different phenomenon from the *written* word. Both have to do with the communication of ideas, as we have come to understand that process; actually, the voice and the word can no more be separated in speech than can the notes and the melody of music.

The vocal or audible aspects of speech may be considered

somewhat as one considers the production and modification of any sound. We must have some source of energy which initiates a vibration in some elastic body. This vibration produces sound which is modified and amplified so that it creates all the effects of which the voice is capable. The intensive study of these many phases of voice is a study in itself, worthy of many years of inquiry. It is doubtful if the meagre information on the anatomy, physiology, and physics of voice that could be given here would be of much assistance in helping you to improve your own speech. Perhaps a few principles, however, may be helpful.

BREATHING

It has long been held that, for the greatest effectiveness of voice, for the greatest volume (loudness), and for the best tone quality, it was necessary to breathe in a certain definite way, with the maximum expansion of the torso around the region just above the belt line. This method of breathing is ordinarily called the "diaphragmatic" or "abdominal," on the theory that it is produced by a downward movement of the diaphragm in inhalation and by the action of the abdominal muscles in exhalation. It has even been suggested that the diaphragm gives an upward thrust to help force the air out of the lungs in exhalation. Unfortunately for the theory, the general respiratory apparatus is so closely tied up neurologically that it functions pretty much as a unit and is not easy to control in its separate parts. Furthermore, you cannot inhale *without* using your diaphragm, and you cannot exhale actively *without* using your abdominal muscles, since there are no others to use. It seems certain that of the different types of breathing the so-called *abdominal* or *diaphragmatic* is the least susceptible of conscious control; and even if one could control it, there would be no advantage whatever so far as more effective voice production is concerned.[1]

[1] Wesley A. Wiksell, "An Experimental Study of Controlled and Uncontrolled Types of Breathing," *Studies in Experimental Phonetics,* Giles Wilkeson Gray (ed.), Baton Rouge, Louisiana, University Studies No. 27, Louisiana State University Press, 1936, pp. 99-164.

Does this mean that one should pay no attention whatever to breathing? Probably not. The purpose of breathing, so far as speech is concerned, is (1) to set and keep the vocal bands vibrating, (2) to produce through modification the "voiced" sounds,[2] (3) and to direct a stream of air through the throat and oral passages where it can produce the "voiceless" sounds.[3] For good breathing three requirements seem to be necessary:

1. *The breath stream must have adequate pressure back of it* so that the sounds will be plainly audible as far as your voice is intended to carry. It is possible for you to be heard in a whisper for a surprising distance if your sounds have sufficient pressure and distinctness back of them. Adequate pressure will give to your consonants more clearness, greater distinctness, and to your vowels more carrying power so that your voice may be heard more easily over greater distances. Unfortunately, the prevalent use of microphones and public-address systems seems to have minimized the importance of developing voices with strong carrying power. With an adequate voice there should be no need of mechanical and electrical aids to speech for an audience of fewer than several hundred in an auditorium with fair acoustic characteristics.

2. *Maintain at all times an adequate reserve of breath* so that your speech will not trail off into inaudibility. Do not speak with your lungs either entirely full or almost empty. In ordinary speaking you do not need a great amount of breath at any one time; the average amount expelled between inhalations is only about thirty cubic inches, approximately one pint. Your natural tendency will be to take a short breath at each short pause and a full breath at the long pauses. With these short "catches" of breath you will ordinarily be able to speak or read a sentence of any length without running out of breath. Whenever you come to

---

[2] "Voiced" sounds are those in the production of which the vocal bands are vibrating. They include all the vowels and such consonants as *b, d, g, l, m, n, ng, r, v, w, z,* and others.

[3] "Voiceless" sounds are those which do not require for their formation the vibration of the vocal bands. Among these are *p, t, k, s, sh, f, wh,* and *h.*

a full stop in your speaking or reading, as at the ends of sentences, take a full breath (*not* your maximum capacity), whether that full stop comes at the end of a sentence or not. If your sentence divisions (phrases) are well worked out and you replenish your breath with every short pause, you should have no difficulty in maintaining an adequate reserve of breath in your lungs at all times.

3. *Control your breath so as to produce a steady pressure of air against the vocal bands, tongue, teeth, and lips.* These are the modifiers of voice which enable you to produce all the various sounds and tonal effects of speech. Steadiness does not mean constant uniformity of pressure, for you will want to vary it to produce changes in loudness and for accent and emphasis. But your voice should not be wavering or jerky, now booming and now fading into a whisper. Changes in loudness should be because the meaning demands them rather than because you are unable to maintain a smooth, steady tone.

If your breathing enables you to have adequate pressure of breath, an adequate reserve of breath, and a steadiness and smoothness of breath pressure, it is unlikely that you will experience great difficulty with your voice production in speaking, so far as respiration is concerned.

PRESIDENT FRANKLIN D. ROOSEVELT SPEAKS TO 30,000

Radio and the modern public address system have greatly increased the power of a man's voice. In a normal conversational style a speaker can address thousands.

In the above picture President Roosevelt addressed an audience of 30,000 from the Peace Tower of the Parliament Buildings, Ottawa, Canada. On another occasion the President is reputed to have talked to an immediate audience of 100,000. Often his greater audience exceeded 25,000,000. (Photo, Black Star.)

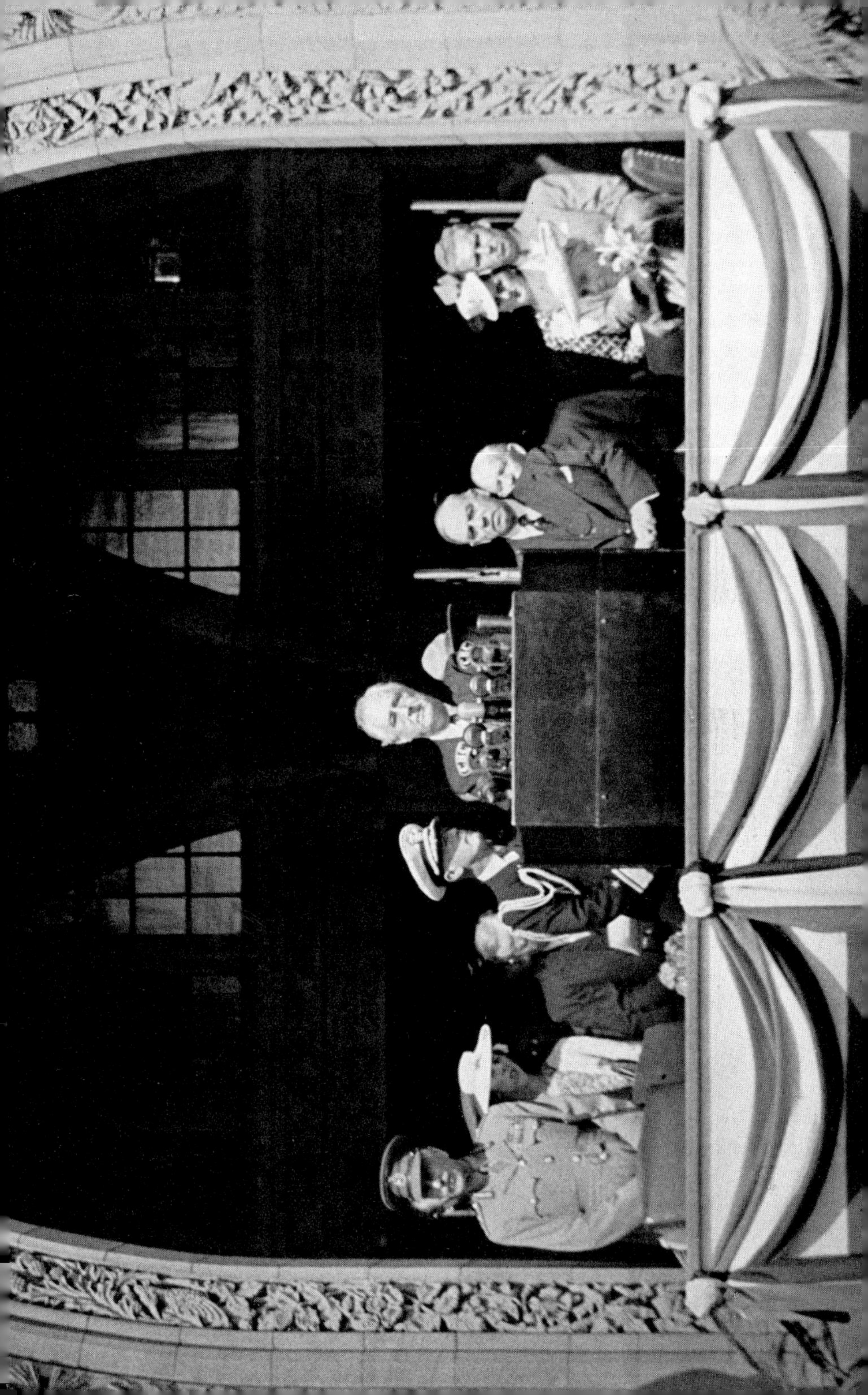

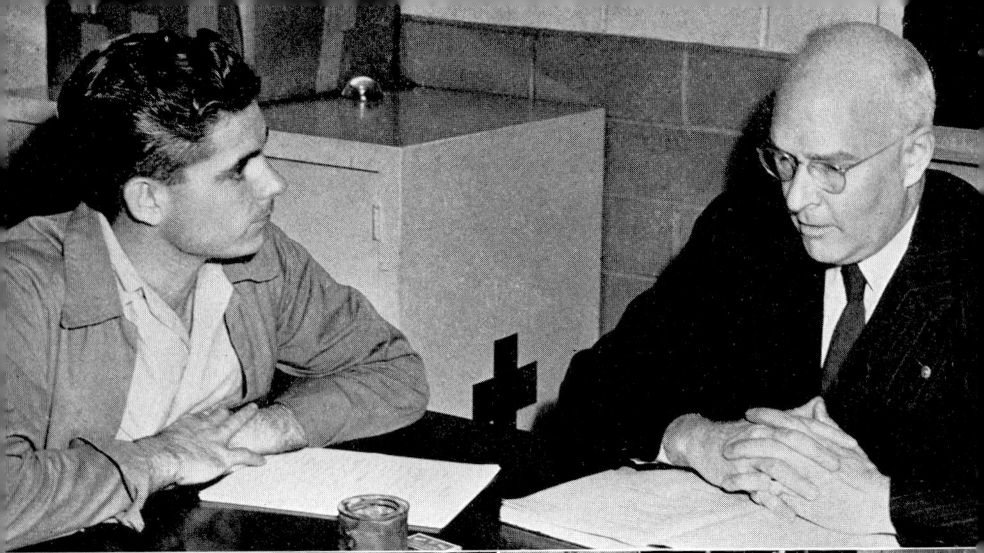

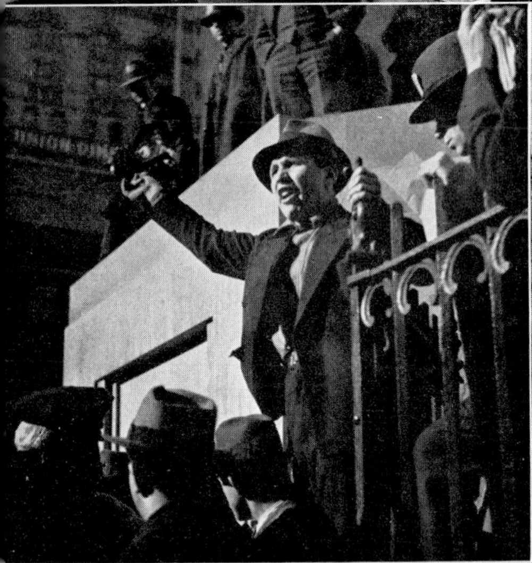

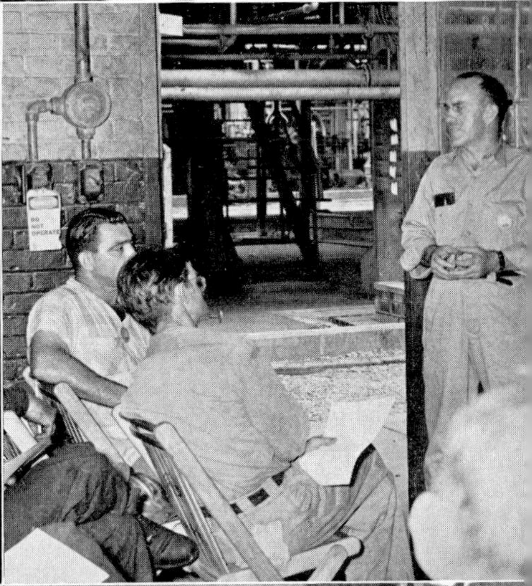
DO NOT OPERATE

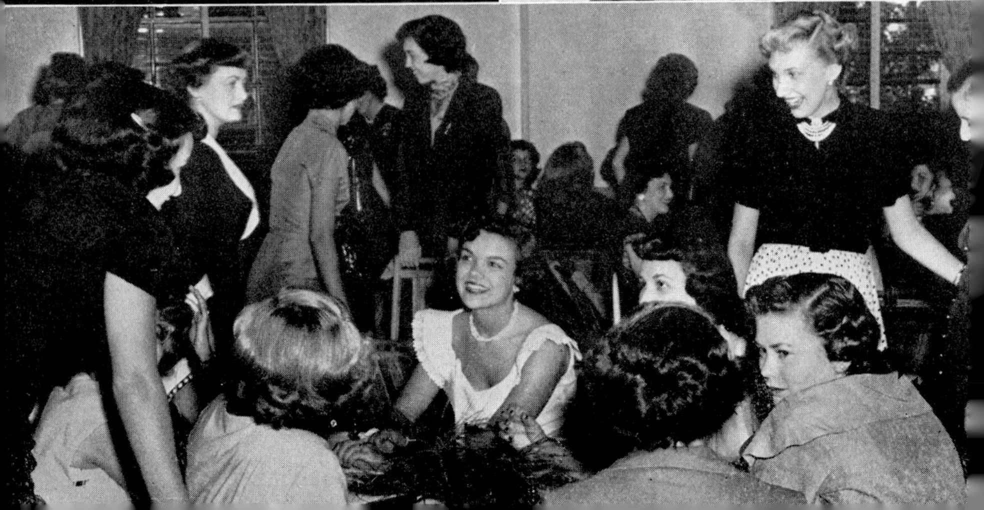

VOICE PRODUCTION

If you will gently stroke down the front of your neck with your fingers you will come to a somewhat rounded projection about halfway down which is commonly called the *Adam's apple*. This little projection, which ordinarily is somewhat more prominent in men than in women, is the foremost point of the *larynx*, which is a most important organ in the production of voice. It contains the two narrow tendinous edges which are called the *vocal bands* or *voice lips*. Through the operation of a number of pairs of muscles of the larynx these vocal bands can be brought together (approximated) or spread apart at one end so as to form a sort of "V" with the apex at the point of the Adam's apple. They can also be tensed and relaxed. They can even be made to vibrate in only a portion of their length. Of course we cannot do all these things consciously, but we can indirectly by producing the effect resulting from these various movements.

When the two vocal bands are brought together just enough to form the proper resistance to the outward passage of breath from the lungs, but not tightly enough to close off the breath entirely, and the breath stream is forced over them, they can be made to vibrate in somewhat the same way a trumpet player makes his lips vibrate in the mouthpiece of his instrument.[4] This

---

[4] Engineers will understand the analogy when such a vibration is compared to a relaxation oscillation.

THE SPEAKER MUST ADJUST HIS VOICE TO THE SPEAKING SITUATION

The four pictures above illustrate a wide variety of situations. The street-corner orator must use an amplified conversational style if he is to be heard. On the other hand, the conference or the drawing room requires a natural conversational style. (Photos, Ethyl Corporation, Baton Rouge Plant; L.S.U. Bureau of Public Relations; Esso Standard Oil, Baton Rouge Refinery; Black Star.)

oscillation of the vocal bands sets up in turn a vibration in the air cavities between the bands themselves and the lips and nostrils of the speaker; between the two, in some way that is not as yet fully understood, a sound is produced.

Through the tensing and relaxing of the vocal bands, the varying of the pressure of the breath stream, the movements of the several organs in the mouth and throat (tongue, lips, soft palate, lower jaw, teeth), this sound may be modified, changed, raised and lowered in pitch, made louder or weaker, and formed into any of the more than two score different sounds that enter into our daily speech. In the formation of words these sounds are combined into well-nigh countless ways to give us an English vocabulary that runs into the hundreds of thousands of words without beginning to use up all the possible combinations. Furthermore, these words in turn can be uttered in an almost infinite number of ways by changes in the tone of the voice, producing a great variety of effects highly important in the meanings that we want to express.

The tones thus produced (quite apart from the words) can be described in terms of four basic attributes, which have been given various names but which ordinarily are called *quality, force, time,* and *pitch.* Let us consider each of these in turn.

QUALITY

Quality is the term usually given to that characteristic of sound (tone) which enables one to identify it as coming from a certain type of source. Another term often used in the same sense is *timbre,* given either the French or the Anglicized pronunciation. Thus you recognize your friend's voice even over the telephone by its individual quality or timbre. Similarly, you are able to hear the tone from a given instrument in the orchestra, the oboe, for instance, by the peculiar "nasal" timbre of its tone. One piano may have a soft, smooth, "velvety" tone, while another may have a bright, brilliant, "hard" tone.

The term *quality* is often used to refer also to the subjective evaluation of a sound, whether it is pleasant or unpleasant, good or poor. We say that the tone from a cheap "fiddle" would have a poor quality, whereas that from a Stradivarius would have a beautiful quality. But both would be recognized as violin tones by their characteristic timbre. Your own voice has an individual timbre which distinguishes it from other voices; but that does not mean that its quality is necessarily either pleasant or unpleasant.

A good quality, if you do not already possess it in your voice, is not to be acquired overnight or in a few easy lessons. If your voice is definitely unpleasant, it is recommended that you enroll in a course in which more emphasis is placed on voice training than can be given in this one. However, there are some things that you can do, under the guidance of your instructor, to eliminate some of the most noticeable faults of voice quality.

1. Nasality

Nasality is generally caused by allowing too much of the tone to go out through the nasal passages.[5] Theoretically, only three sounds of English or American speech are properly nasal, the *m*, the *n*, and the *ng*. As you utter the sound, you will notice that in each instance the breath and the tone are closed off in the mouth and permitted, by dropping the soft palate away from the back wall of the pharynx, to go up and through the nasal cavities. Actually, vowels preceding any of these three in the same syllable are also nasalized in anticipation of the following consonant. The fault of nasality lies in allowing sounds which are not so connected with a nasal consonant also to go up through the nose.

Pronounce the following pairs of words. The two words in each pair should and probably will sound different; but while the

[5] There are a number of theories as to what causes nasality. The one given here will probably explain the great majority of cases.

first of the two will have a definite nasal component because of the nasal consonant, the second should have no trace of nasality.

ban	bad	candy	caddy	pain	paid	sank	sack
bin	bid	come	cup	pawn	pawl	some	sup
Ben	bed	crank	crack	plunk	pluck	think	thick
blank	black	dandy	daddy	ring	rig	trunk	truck
boon	boot	fan	fat	rink	rick	window	widow
brink	brick	flank	flack	rung	rug	wind	wide
bunk	buck	home	hope	Sam	sap	whine	white
came	cape	moon	mood	sang	sag	whimper	whipper

As a partial test of your own nasality, pronounce the first word of each pair a number of times in succession, alternately closing the nostrils by gently pressing in with the forefingers from both sides and then releasing them. The word should sound markedly different when the nostrils are closed and when they are open. Now pronounce the second of each pair similarly, alternately closing and releasing the nostrils. Since these sounds are not normally nasal, it should make no difference whether the nose is closed or not.[6] If there is a difference resulting from opening and closing the nostrils, then your voice is nasal, the degree of nasality probably bearing a direct relation to the amount of difference. Practice on these and other words having no nasal consonants until they sound approximately the same with the nostrils closed and open. When they do, it will mean that only a negligible amount of tone is passing through the nasal cavities.

Make up short sentences without any nasal consonants, and practice on them until they also sound the same with the nostrils closed and open. The following are illustrative:

a. Sister threw out the dish water.
b. A little boy ate a piece of buttered bread with sugar.
c. Set the hook hard to catch your big fish.
d. Prices today are far above average levels for the past decade.

[6] A slight degree of nasal resonance is probably not serious. Some investigators believe that it is neither possible nor desirable to get rid of it entirely.

e. Books will add greatly to your culture if read assiduously.
f. Electric power is a chief requisite to true prosperity.
g. Life without drudgery would be delightful.
h. "Swift as the boreal light which flies. . . ."
i. "The bride kissed the goblet."
j. Puppies are able to sleep at the stable.
k. "Bless the Lord, all ye his works."

2. Huskiness

Huskiness may be caused by various factors. It may be the result of foreign substances or growths on the vocal bands. These may be the effect of overuse or of a pathological development. The best procedure is to visit a doctor and have the growth removed if in his judgment it should be. Often such growths can be reduced or removed entirely by judicious and well-directed exercises under the guidance of a competent instructor. If the huskiness is the result of a cold, the obvious procedure is to have the cold cleared up as soon as possible. While the throat is inflamed, it is best not to put great strain on the vocal bands. When blood vessels are distended, their walls are stretched very thin. Under such conditions the additional stress put on them by excessive use can easily rupture those thin walls, resulting in a huskiness that does not subside as soon as the cold disappears but holds on until the tissues are repaired.

Huskiness, which is often described as hoarseness, may be caused by too great relaxation of the vocal bands, to such a degree that they lack the proper tonus for clear tones. Such relaxation is probably not localized but is more likely to be simply one aspect of an allover relaxation or general lassitude. The remedy in such a case is to build up the general bodily tonus. Since such overrelaxation is often the result of some acquired attitude, as of ennui or boredom, another and probably more effective remedy is to change the attitude.

A fourth possible cause of huskiness, or hoarseness, is the attempt to lower the pitch of the voice far below the normal range. In fact, in one study[7] the conclusion was reached that this is by far the most common cause. When the voice is brought up to the normal range, the hoarseness tends to disappear of its own accord.

3. Muffled Tones

Muffled tones are usually associated with a low pitch, a nearly closed mouth, and loose or flabby lips and tongue. The voice seems not to be permitted to emerge clearly and cleanly. It seems dull, and the whole speech is lifeless. Ordinarily the difficulty can be remedied by opening the mouth wider to let the tone out, raising the pitch to its normal level, and putting greater liveliness into the movements of the tongue, jaw, and lips. Both in your practice and in your speaking emphasize the consonants, particularly those formed near the front of the mouth, that is, with the lips and the front part of the tongue: *p, b, t, d, f, v, l, sh, zh, s,* and *z*. In a later section in this chapter the formation of these sounds will be described in somewhat more detail.

4. Thinness

Thinness is a weakness, a feebleness of tone, resulting in a seeming lack of "body." The tone has neither carrying power nor fullness. It gives the impression of being too high pitched, although it may not actually be pitched any higher than normal. It is often associated with illness or weakness and, if heard in a man's voice, with effeminacy.

5. Stridency

In a sense stridency is hardly a fault of quality; it is often little more than a booming loudness, which is often associated, however, with harshness; it may be almost raucous. It has the effect

---

[7] Arleigh B. Williamson, "Diagnosis and Treatment of Seventy-Two Cases of Hoarse Voice," *The Quarterly Journal of Speech,* April, 1945, pp. 189-202.

of almost overpowering the listener. The possessors of such voices bellow their way through life with no regard for a sense of fitness; their voices are as loud and intrusive in private conversation (they never, in fact, hold any conversation privately) as in the largest gathering. They are often known as "leather lunged"; they are heard frequently as outdoor announcers at sporting events, but one hears them everywhere.

The usual cause of such a quality is hypertension, which again is an allover condition and not merely a matter of the vocal mechanism. The remedy is relaxation, working toward a smoother and easier social adaptation, together, perhaps, with some readjustment of social attitudes. It is possible, too, that some personality readjustment may be necessary. Such stridency may sometimes be the effect of an attempt to overcompensate for an unrecognized feeling of inadequacy or inferiority. On the other hand, it may arise from an exaggerated sense of superiority, although such a cause is probably less often encountered than the former.

6. Breathiness

Some voices have a sort of "featheredge" quality rather than "knife edge." There is a sort of fuzziness about them; one seems to hear about as much breath as voice. This breathiness is probably caused by the failure on the part of the speaker to bring the vocal bands together closely enough to set all the breath stream into vibration; some of the breath thus escapes without being vocalized. It may be that the defect develops sometimes from the frequent and persistent efforts of parents to soften the childish clarion of their children's voices, with a resultant semi-whisper. It is not as a rule heard among people who are alert, animated, and vivacious mentally and physically.

Quality and Personality

An agreeable voice quality is an asset in whatever form of speaking you may have occasion to engage, whether it be public speaking, reading from the printed page, dramatics, or conference and private conversation. Much of the impression which people get of you is due to the quality of your voice; certainly your voice creates one of the earliest impressions, one which may be difficult to change later. In fact, much of what is often called your personality may be found to arise from the impressions you create by the quality and the other attributes of your voice.

Your personality is basically the way you affect other people, whether they react favorably or unfavorably to you. There is no mysterious essence emanating from your organism to which the label *personality* can be attached. The only way you can make an impression of any kind upon anyone else is through what you let others see and hear you doing. If you want to create a favorable impression, that is, if you want to exhibit a pleasing personality, then you must do those things to which others react favorably. Certainly a voice which is extremely nasal, is shrill, muffled, hoarse, strident, or which possesses any of the other unpleasant qualities, does not contribute to the creating of a favorable impression. One of the ways in which social friction can be lessened is through the cultivation of a voice that others enjoy hearing, just for the sound of it if for no other reason.

FORCE

The term *force* is not too well chosen because of its many interpretations. With respect to the voice and its production it refers to the element of loudness, correlated with what is called intensity in the physics of sound. For our present purposes we can think of force as manifesting itself in three ways, all of which may need some study by the aspiring public speaker.

1. Accent

Accent refers to the slight stress or increased loudness you give to certain syllables in a word. It will be discussed further under pronunciation.

2. Emphasis

Just as you stress one syllable of a word a little harder to make that syllable stand out and give the word its correct rhythmic pattern and hence its correct pronunciation, so can you stress one or more words in the sentence a little more to make them stand out and give the sentence meaning. Such stress laid on words in the sentence is known as *emphasis*. The early elocutionists, in distinguishing between accent and emphasis, pointed out that, whereas the former had to do with correctness in the word, the latter had to do with the sense of the passage. "Emphasis," said William Scott more than one hundred and forty years ago, "points out the precise meaning of a sentence, shows in what manner one idea is connected with and rises out of another, marks the several clauses of a sentence, gives to every part its proper sound, and thus conveys to the mind of the reader the full import of the whole."[8]

This differentiation has some foundation; but it should be pointed out here that emphasis (as well as accent) is not entirely a matter of increased force; it involves usually a change in pitch as well. An increase in force for either accent or emphasis is characteristically accompanied by a rise in pitch, although there are occasional deviations from the general pattern.[9]

Observe in the following sentence,

This is the house that Jack built.

the differences in meaning achieved by stressing successively the separate words:

This (not another) is the house that Jack built.
This *is* (believe it or not) the house that Jack built.
This is *the* (It's the only one) house that Jack built.

[8] William Scott, *Essay on Elocution*, Lincoln and Gleason, 1809, p. 37. This is not the first edition of Scott's *Essay* by any means.

[9] See Dwight L. Bollinger, "Inhibited and Uninhibited Stress," *The Quarterly Journal of Speech*, April, 1945, pp. 202-207.

This is the *house* (not a garage or a barn) that Jack built.
This is the house *that* (not some other Jack) Jack built.
This is the house that *Jack* (not Tom or Henry) built.
This is the house that Jack *built* (He didn't buy it; he *built* it).

It will be noted that as these successive words are emphasized they are given not only added force but a different inflectional pattern from that given when they are unstressed. Furthermore, emphasizing the different words involves changes in stress and inflectional pattern throughout the whole sentence. When these and other changes are made in the manner of utterance, the entire meaning of the sentence is also changed.

3. General Loudness

Different occasions call for different degrees of loudness. In a small room it will be unnecessary, it would even be out of place, for you to speak with as great general force as in a large auditorium. The degree of force you will have to use is determined mainly by the distance you will need to project your voice, modified by the interferences (conflicting noises, acoustic peculiarities, and the like) we are likely to encounter in the process. It is a mistake to feel that you must always speak above the audience noise. Often by using a somewhat softer voice, yet one which *could* be heard if the listeners were quiet, you will be able to draw their attention and induce them to be quiet in order to hear at all.

Generally, animated speakers, those who are keenly interested in their subjects and who have the urge to communicate, are more inclined to speak forcefully than are the less enthusiastic. A degree of spontaneous force in the voice is a fairly accurate indication of the speaker's interest and sincerity. However, avoid the type of shouting which superficial speakers often use, as has been pointed out, as a substitute for sound material and honest thinking. With force as with the other attributes of delivery, it is variety which gives to the voice its effectiveness.

TIME

The factor of time as an attribute of vocal tone, having its effect on meaning, is manifested in three principal ways: quantity, length of phrase, and length of pause between phrases. These three together make up the general *rate* of speech.

1. Quantity

The term quantity refers to the length of time a given sound or word is held. It makes a difference, for example, whether you say simply, "all night long" or "A-a-a-all ni-i-i-ght lo-o-o-ng." Lengthening out a sound or a whole word often makes it more impressive; it intensifies meaning which otherwise might be quite casual. On the other hand, by clipping a word short you can give it an incisiveness, a definiteness, a finality it would not otherwise have.

2. Length of Phrase

If you will observe closely, you will notice that you speak not in isolated words but in phrases, which normally are comprised of the words making up a "sense unit." Thus, the opening words of the Gettysburg Address form sense units in this manner: Not "Four / score / and / seven / years / ago," with the words separated just as many of us learned to read "I / see / a / cat," but "Fourscoreandsevenyearsago / ourfathersbroughtforth / uponthiscontinent / anewnation / conceivedinliberty / anddedicatedtotheproposition / thatallmen / arecreatedequal."

It would be possible to vary the length of the phrases here, for example, by combining the second and third (ourfathersbroughtforthuponthiscontinent) and the last two (thatallmenarecreatedequal), which would tend to speed up the total time a little.

When the phrases are too short, the speech sounds choppy, especially if the pauses between the phrases are also too short. Phrasing the above passage thus, "Fourscore / andsevenyearsago

/ ourfathers / broughtforth / uponthiscontinent / anewnation / conceived / inliberty / anddedicated / totheproposition / thatallmen / arecreated / equal," while it might make some sense, would make the whole utterance jerky and choppy. If you want to make this passage very impressive, you will read it in short phrases, and also within each phrase you will lengthen the words somewhat so that the whole will be much slower. On the other hand, if you want to make it sound casual and of little significance, you can produce the effect in part by lengthening the phrases and clipping the words to give the passage a generally faster rate.

Sense units are not fixed and rigid; in any extended passage they can be shortened or expanded. Two or more can sometimes be combined to form a larger unit, or a long one can be broken up into two or three. Much will depend on the effect you want to create. But be sure that your phrases, whether long or short, consist of one sense unit and do not break over from one into the next, for it often happens that the specific phrasing determines the exact meaning. It makes a difference whether one says "The professor insists the student is lazy," or "The professor / insists the student / is lazy."

In determining the sense units in written material, either your own or another's, do not depend on the punctuation, which is primarily a matter of grammar. Phrasing is entirely a matter of meaning, except for the occasional necessity for catching one's breath. The first sentence of the Gettysburg Address is punctuated differently in different texts, usually with commas only after *nation* and *liberty*; thus, "Fourscore and seven years ago our fathers brought forth upon this continent a new nation, conceived in liberty, and dedicated to the proposition that all men are created equal." These commas, however, do not necessarily set off sense units; certainly they do not set off all of them. These are more adequately indicated by such phrasing as is set off in the illustrations given a little earlier. Styles in punctuation change; the same statement cannot be made of the phrasal unit.

As a rule, the more important and weighty the subject matter, the shorter the phrases and the slower the general rate. Speakers often start out very slowly, gathering momentum and speed as they proceed, thus giving the impression of a great mass which accelerates slowly.

3. Length of Pause

In varying the length of phrase, the number of pauses, or periods of silence between phrases, is obviously also varied. But the third way in which the general rate may be affected is through varying the length of the pauses. As a rule, in smooth even speech short phrases are accompanied by relatively long pauses, the whole impression being one of weight, importance, dignity. By lengthening the pauses and using more of them, you can obviously slow down the rate; by shortening them and using fewer, you will speed up your utterance.

Time values are very subtle, for the reason that it takes only slight variations to be significant. These variations may be measured in units of only a few hundredths of a second or, in some instances, in even a few thousandths.

4. Dramatic Pause

Occasionally, when you have just finished some particularly impressive passage and have risen to a climax of thought and utterance, you can add significantly to the impressiveness by suddenly stopping completely and remaining silent for a few seconds while the full import of what you have just said sinks in. One can imagine the effect if William Pitt had made use of such a dramatic pause immediately after his powerful climax, "If I were an American, as I am an Englishman, while a foreign troop were landed in my country, I would never lay down my arms—never—*never*—NEVER!"

Another situation in which this dramatic pause can be used with telling effect arises when, after giving your hearers a strong build-up, you suddenly stop for a moment of dead silence before uttering your final words, to which you have actually been building all the time. Henry W. Grady may have used such a technique in the following passage from "The New South:" "But from the union of these colonist Puritans and Cavaliers, from the straightening of their purposes and the crossing of their blood, slow perfecting through a century, came he who stands as the first typical American, the first who comprehended within himself all the strength and gentleness, all the majesty and grace of this Republic—Abraham Lincoln."

Rate

The elements of quantity, phrase, and pause together make up the general rate at which you speak. There is no optimum rate or average number of words per minute for speech; it may vary from somewhere near ninety words for very slow speech to two hundred or more for rapid speech. Instances have been reported of rates of utterance of more than six hundred words per minute, but the reports say nothing of the intelligibility of the resulting speech.

The general rate will vary somewhat with the type of material and the total situation. Ponderous themes, weighty matters, deep impressiveness, seem to call for slower rates; lighter moods will permit more rapid rates. Larger auditoriums, especially if they have a long reverberation time, require slow utterance; small rooms, with negligible reverberation, place no limit on the rate of speech. On most occasions your best rate will probably be from one hundred thirty to one hundred fifty words per minute.

Such a statement does not mean that every minute you are uttering so many words, no more and no less, say one hundred forty, nor that every thirty seconds you will have spoken seventy words. Rate of utterance is an overall average. You can estimate that, if your tendency is to speak rapidly, in ten minutes you should be able to utter approximately fifteen hundred words; if you are a slow speaker, you will not be able to utter more than one thousand or twelve hundred.

PITCH

The fourth attribute of voice which influences the meanings of our words as we utter them is that of pitch and its variations. Pitch may be defined as the "highness" or "lowness" of a tone as compared with the notes of a musical scale. It is exhibited in the voice in three particular ways in what have been called *key*, *step*, and *slide* or *inflection*.

1. Key

Key refers to the general pitch level at which we speak, whether it be high, low, or medium. The term is not used with anything like the specificity that it is in music, the three ranges being very broad and general. Furthermore, what would be a high pitch for one might be only a normal pitch for another.

OPTIMUM PITCH. For each voice there is a general pitch level which seems to be the norm above and below which that voice moves. Voices are somewhat like musical instruments in that each one is constructed to play within a certain range, some high, some low, some medium, and is most effective when being played within that range. This level is not fixed by any means; the principle simply means that, when a speaker finds the general level at which his voice is easiest and most effective, he has probably found his optimum pitch. This pitch, according to Fairbanks, is about one-fourth the way up from your lowest to your highest singing note, including your falsetto.[10]

The general principle of optimum pitch does not mean that you are limited in your pitch range to that particular level. Some moods call for a low pitch, others for normal, or medium, and still others for fairly high pitches. Deep solemnity, awe, reverence, grief—those moods which seem to inhibit vigorous bodily action—require as a rule low pitches; one can hardly imagine Byron's well-known "Apostrophe to the Ocean" being read in

---

[10] Grant Fairbanks, *Voice and Articulation Drillbook*, Harper & Brothers, 1940, p. 169.

other than a low pitch: "Roll on, thou deep and dark blue ocean, roll. . . ."

At the other extreme, moods of gaiety, excitement, keen pleasure—those that tend to incite bodily activity—call in general for higher pitches and wider ranges, sometimes rising to the upper limit of one's vocal range.

Probably most of your speaking will be in a medium key, that is to say, rising above and falling below your normal or optimum pitch level as a median. It is important for the sake of your own vocal expression, and for the relief of strain on your vocal organs, that you find your most favorable level. At the same time it is also important that you be able to adapt your pitch level to the mood you want to establish. You would not tell ghost stories in the same tone you would use in telling a humorous anecdote.

2. Step

Although the step is one manifestation of the attribute of pitch, it is not likely that you will need to pay much attention to its variations. The term refers to those changes which occur *between* words or syllables when the voice skips, so to speak, from one pitch to another, either up or down. It is comparable to singing the notes D and G (or G and D) successively without sliding from one to the other. If the general pitch level of the voice is used effectively and the inflectional patterns are meaningful, the steps will probably pretty much take care of themselves.

On the other hand, proper use of the step is a requisite to the best use of the inflectional pattern. In the example from *Macbeth* in the preceding chapter, in which both words of the phrase "We fail!" are given the rising inflection, it may be necessary after the rise on *we* to drop down in order to begin *fail* for a rising inflection. Other illustrations will be found in the exercises in connection with inflections.

3. Slide, or Inflection

By far the greater part of the meaningful use of pitch in the voice is to be found in the inflections and the manifold patterns that are made possible by the slides of the voice. The term *inflection* refers to those pitch changes which are accomplished by means of continuous slides or glides from one pitch through a wide or narrow range to another. These patterns may be rising inflections, falling, or various combinations of rising-falling or falling-rising and may cover ranges from as narrow as one semitone or even less to more than a full octave. It is in these variations that the most noticeable aspects of vocal flexibility are to be observed; yet they do not follow the specific intervals of the musical scale. They are indefinite as to range, except that they may be narrow or wide or any degree between.

Although extremely narrow pitch ranges may be employed occasionally to express strong emotional attitudes, a habitually narrow range, when not expressive of specific moods calling for a low pitch level, may denote generally an allover lassitude, a lack of animation, an indifference, or even a dullness of mental activity. It is often accompanied by an inactive articulatory apparatus, by muffled tones, and indistinct utterance, which are further evidences of the same emotional attitude. Extremely wide habitual patterns, on the other hand, may suggest excitability, hypersensitivity to both external and internal stimuli, and in extreme cases, especially when coupled with other phenomena, certain types of manic neuroticism. For the speaker these extremes are useful in the expression of strong emotional attitudes and in stimulating such attitudes in the listeners. Especial care should be taken, however, not to overdo these patterns to the point where your listeners get so used to them that they no longer have any effect.

In your voice development, work toward the cultivation of the ability to use the particular inflectional patterns that will express the specific meaning you intend. Learn to listen to what your own voice is doing, both directly as you speak and as it is recorded for playback. The following exercises may be of some aid in giving you something of an idea of inflections and in giving you practice in flexibility. If you have the opportunity, record them, study them, listen for errors, and try to determine the

514 PUBLIC SPEAKING

degree to which you are able to make your voice do what you want it to do or what you think it is doing. Practice on these expressions, giving them the pitch movements as indicated. A curve slanting upward (/) indicates a rising inflection; a curve slanting downward (\) indicates a falling inflection.

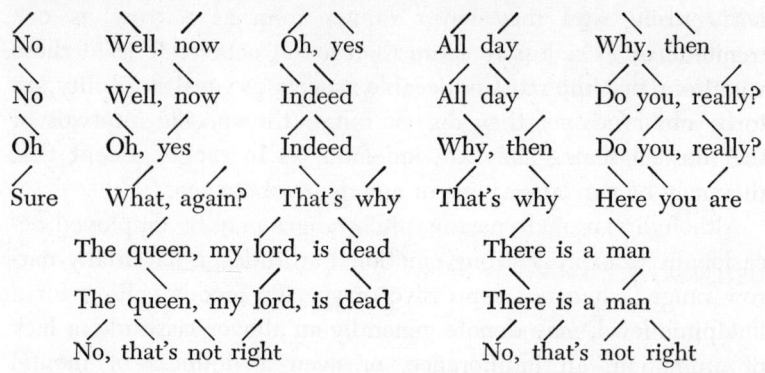

No	Well, now	Oh, yes	All day	Why, then
No	Well, now	Indeed	All day	Do you, really?
Oh	Oh, yes	Indeed	Why, then	Do you, really?
Sure	What, again?	That's why	That's why	Here you are
	The queen, my lord, is dead		There is a man	
	The queen, my lord, is dead		There is a man	
	No, that's not right		No, that's not right	

These four elements, then, quality, force, time, and pitch, are important because their proper use adds variety to the voice and contributes significantly to the meanings which are suggested by the words. Meanings, it will be remembered, are twofold: they have a logical, or intellectual content and a personal, or emotional, content. No effective utterance is wholly one or the other, that is, no good speech is either entirely intellectual or entirely emotional. The latter is necessary to give to speech life, feeling, and to establish or strengthen attitudes; the former is needed to give direction, control, and to add the rational element which distinguishes man from the lower animals. There must be something of both. You must not only express ideas; you must let your listeners know how you feel about those ideas.

Your ability to communicate these two aspects of meaning are, so far as vocal effects are concerned, dependent upon your effective use of changes or variety in the four attributes of vocal tone described above. Your language, of course, and your bodily activity also make heavy contributions to that communication. In general, changes in voice quality seem to have more to do with the stimulation of the emotional aspects of meaning than of the logical.[11] In your speaking you probably will not have a great deal to do with changes of quality, although they may be useful in some situations calling for short characterizations. Changes in the middle ranges of pitch apparently have most to do, though not entirely, with the intellectual component of meaning. Extreme changes in any of the four are essentially emotional, whether these be extremely narrow or extremely wide. Variety in force and in time has to do about equally with the intellectual and the emotional, again with the extremes being expressive primarily of the latter.

LISTENING TO YOUR VOICE

Mention has been made of listening to what your voice is doing. The time for that is in your practice periods and not when you are before an audience. When you are in an actual speaking situation, when the most important thing is getting your idea and audience together, forget your voice. "Consciously selective conduct," says Palmer, "is elementary and inferior. People distrust it, or rather they distrust him who exhibits it."[12] If you have been working on flexibility as you should in your practice, the voice should at other times take care of itself. Practice, therefore, on the various kinds of changes so that you can make your voice do what you want it to do. Learn, if you do not already know, how to place the proper accent in words of more than one syllable, as indicated in the dictionary you use. Learn to make your voice take a rising or a falling inflection whenever you want it to do so or a combination of the rising-falling or falling-rising. Study your phrasing—the sense units of your speaking—and make your pauses correspond to those units. Only by conscious attention to what your voice is doing and by practicing on making it do the

[11] Charles Henry Woolbert, *The Fundamentals of Speech*, Harper & Brothers, rev. ed., 1927, chap. X, "Voice and Meaning."
[12] George Herbert Palmer, *Self-Cultivation in English*, Houghton Mifflin Company, 1908, p. 15.

various things you want it to do during your practice periods will you develop a voice of maximum flexibility and expressiveness as a medium by which you will be able to stimulate in the minds of your audience the meanings you intend.

With a voice of adequate power you should not need microphones and public-address systems for audiences of normal size. Before the advent of such electromechanical boosters to the voice, speakers like Chauncey M. Depew, William Jennings Bryan, Albert J. Beveridge, and scores of others, could address audiences of several thousand listeners and make themselves heard. The public-address systems commonly in use distort the voice and take from it much of the natural quality, making it sound mechanical. Work to make your voice audible to as large audiences as you reasonably can without having to strain or shout.

With a voice of adequate flexibility, you should be able to avoid such vocal atrocities as "quote-unquote" in introducing and ending quoted material. You should be able to indicate either by your voice or by the wording, or both, just when you begin your quotation and just when you resume your own wording. One does not read semicolons, commas, periods, or question marks; they are intended for the eye. No more should one read quotation marks which are also intended only for the eye.

ARTICULATION

Carefully conducted experiments show that the greater part of the carrying power of voice is in the vowel sounds; the intelligibility of speech is mainly a matter of the distinctness of consonants. For speech that can easily be understood for any distance, therefore, you must attend to both your vowels and your consonants—in other words, to your entire utterance. If the quality of your voice is developed so that the faults described earlier in this chapter have been eliminated and if you have developed adequate breath supply, ample reserve, and steady

VOCAL ASPECTS OF DELIVERY

pressure, the vowels and, hence, the carrying power should largely take care of themselves. It will be worth while to examine the consonants in order to understand their importance in distinctness and to form a basis for improvement in articulation.

Consonant Formation

Each speech sound is formed by the modification of the vocal tone or of the breath stream as it passes through the mouth or nasal cavities or both. Many of these sounds include both vocal tones and breath, and in a few cases both the mouth and the nasal cavities are involved. Sometimes this modification is achieved by shaping the oral cavities mainly by movements of the tongue and lips and to some extent by movements of other organs with which we are somewhat less familiar. These modifications by which the *timbre* of the vocal tone is altered produce all the different vowels and some of the so-called consonants. Sometimes the modification consists of putting partial or complete blockages or bars in the way of the emission of voice or breath or both, producing most of what are commonly called consonants. It is with the latter that we are primarily concerned here, although it must be pointed out that there is no generally accepted basis upon which a consistent division of vowels and consonants can be made.

For example, if you close your lips tightly, raise the soft palate at the back of the throat, build up a breath pressure back of the closed lips, and then suddenly release the lips, you produce a sound which is easily recognizable as *p*. Now if while building up the breath pressure behind the closed lips you start your vocal bands to vibrating, you find on releasing your lips that you have produced a clear *b*.

If now you slide the tip of your tongue back along the roof of the mouth, you will notice perhaps a half inch or so behind the base of the upper teeth a sort of rounded ridge. Bring the front part of the tongue (not the extreme tip, but just back of it) up against this ridge, again closing off the passage so the breath cannot get through, again build up the pressure and suddenly pull the tongue away, you will discover that you have made a very respectable *t*. Addition of the vocal-band vibration to this sound will give you a good *d*.

The *k* and *g* (as in *go*) are similarly produced by raising the back of the tongue to the palate just about where the hard and soft palates are joined, building up pressure, and again releasing. The *g* differs from the *k* primarily in that it contains the addition of voice, in the same way that *b* differs from *p* and *d* from *t*.

Did you notice the exact places where the dam was made to prevent the escape of breath? Now if you form the dam again with your lips and hum, allowing the sound to go out through the nasal passages, what sound is produced? It should be *m*. Forming the dam in the same place as for the *t* and the *d* and humming should give you an *n*. The consonant similarly corresponding to the *k* and the *g* should be that ordinarily spelled with *ng* as in *sing*. It should be observed that this *ng* sound actually has no more of a *g* in it than *m* has a *b* in it or the *n* a *d*.

Let us try some different kinds of sounds. If you simply stick the tip (no more) of your tongue between your teeth and blow, the resulting sound should be the initial consonant in *thin* or *thick*. In fact, you don't have to protrude your tongue through; just partially close the opening between the upper and lower teeth and blow. Add the vocal-band vibration to it, and you get the initial sound in *this* and *that* (unless you say *dis* and *dat*!)

It is not intended here to give a detailed description of the formation of all the consonant sounds. These examples illustrate certain important points with respect to distinct utterance, particularly with reference to the production of the consonants.

1. *Every consonant is best produced and is most distinct when the complete or partial closure for the breath or tone is formed in the right place.* In the English language, the *t* and the *d* are correctly formed *only* when the front of the tongue closes off the breath at the "teeth ridge," or as it is more commonly called, the *alveolar ridge*. For every consonant there is a correct place of articulation, and if the sound is formed at that place and other

factors are present, only the one sound can result. After one has learned correct formation habits, some latitude may develop in their production in various phonetic contexts, that is, as the sounds are connected with different sounds in word production.

2. *For a good, distinct consonant the position or movement must be adequately formed.* That is, there must be a strong, firm muscular action of tongue or lips. For such sounds as *p*, *d*, and the like, for instance, the closure must be firm, positive, and complete. All the organs of articulation should have good tonus.

3. *The breath pressure back of the partial or complete closure must be strong,* the degree of pressure being determined by the necessity for more or less incisive speech. For your speech to be understood approximately as far as your voice can be heard, as in a large auditorium, the pressure must be stronger than in a small room, for the same reason that the whole utterance must be louder.

4. *The release, when it is called for by the formation of the sound and its context, must be clean and sharp.* The *t*, for example, is not complete in most instances without such a release. When it precedes another consonant, as in *utmost,* no "explosion" is heard for the first *t*; there should be one for the final sound, and it should be distinctly heard.

Consonants may occupy one of four kinds of positions: *initial, medial, final,* or in a *consonant combination,* in which case the last sound of the group may be in a final position. These positions cannot always be determined by the place of the sound in the isolated word; the place *in the phrase* governs whether it is initial, medial, or final. In the phrase, "Fourscore and seven years ago," *when spoken as a sense unit,* there is only one initial consonant and no final one; all the rest are medial or in combination.

The criteria for well-formed consonants are equally valid for all these positions: the sound must be correctly (*accurately*) formed, it must be *adequately* formed, it must have *sufficient breath pressure* back of it, and the *release,* when demanded, *must be clean and sharp.*

Consonant Combinations

Not all consonants occur singly; they are found frequently in combinations of many kinds. Some of these are relatively easy to produce, but some of them, mainly through force of habit, may be badly slurred. Often the way in which you handle your consonant combinations will set you off as a careful, distinct speaker, one whom it is easy to understand.

The following words illustrate some of the more common types of consonant combination with which you may have some difficulty. Some of them are actually quite simple, others more complicated.

Two-Consonant Combinations

help	least	frost	flask	wrapped	lacked
clasp	first	priest	task	around	correct
crisp	lest	field	risk	fact	exact
east	cast	yield	wept	respect	lived
fast	toast	pulled	apt	waked	arrived
wrist	waste	cold	swept	looked	bribed

In the foregoing words the tendency will be to slur or to omit entirely the second consonant, except in the case of *help*, in which the *l* is often omitted (*he'p*). Be sure to pronounce the *st, lp, sp, kt, pt, nd, vd,* and other combinations, giving each sound its proper value.[13]

Three- and Four-Consonant Combinations

casks	wisps	yields	accepts	fixed
asks	basked	folds	adopts	boxed
hasps	posts	molds	thanked	addled
rasps	costs	pumped	yanked	muddled
tasks	wrists	corrects	bunked	jingled
tusks	pests	Picts	pinked	mingled
whisks	waists	crypts	conked	mangled
asked	fields	battled	mixed	befuddled

[13] *Lacked, correct, looked,* and *exact* do not *look* as if the final sounds were *kt*, nor does *wrapped* look as if the final sound were *t* (*pt*); but those are actually the sounds.

VOCAL ASPECTS OF DELIVERY

The tendency in these combinations may be to omit either the middle element (as in *cas's, wris's, Pic's, cryp's, as't, correc's, fiel's*) or, in some cases, the final one (as in *cask', pest', ask'*, etc.).

Nineteenth-century elocutionists took great pleasure in practicing the following and other archaic consonant combinations, taken from old forms of the verb in the second person singular:

exist'st	(stst)	mixedst	(kstst)	yankedst	(nktst)
yield'st	(ldst)	ask'st	(skst)	heardst	(rdst)
correct'st	(ktst)	askedst	(sktst)	fearedst	(rdst)
accept'st	(ptst)	battledst	(tldst)	governedst	(rndst)
claspedst	(sptst)	jingledst	(ngldst)	earnedst	(rndst)

Whatever may have been said as to the exaggerations of which those speakers and readers were guilty, it can be said on the other hand that there was never any question as to the distinctness of their utterance; they could be understood.

There are many other such combinations, all of which need to be perfectly pronounced. Not every sound in every such letter combination will be heard; but if you want your speech to be clear and distinct, you will have to learn just what sounds are to be included. Be sure that in all such combinations every consonant which is to be pronounced at all receives its proportionate value. Clarity of utterance is as vital as clarity of language; it is to speech as legibility is to writing.

PRONUNCIATION

Correct pronunciation is on a somewhat different basis from distinct articulation; the two aspects of utterance are cultivated for different reasons. Whereas articulation is basic to intelligibility and comprehension, pronunciation is primarily a matter of convention, something that people have come to agree upon.

By way of analogy, if you cannot read someone's writing, you get no idea of what he is trying to say. He may spell atrociously, and while you merely say that he is illiterate, you may still be able to understand clearly; he simply has not learned how good writers spell. Similarly, if you cannot follow someone's speech because of its unintelligibility, the communicative effort is a total loss; if his pronunciation deviates widely from accepted standards, you may again say that he is ignorant, but you can still understand him.

Pronunciation may be defined as giving to the sounds of a word their proper sequence and values and to the syllables their proper accent. "Proper" here is no more than a matter of general agreement; there is no inherently right or wrong way to pronounce any word in the language. We pronounce as we do for no other reason than that that is the way most if not all careful speakers pronounce their words. There is some historical basis for our pronunciations, but even that goes back finally to a matter of general agreement. The processes by which these accepted ways are determined are too involved to be described here; but they have been evolved by dictionary makers and others over a period of more than three hundred years and can be discovered by reading the fine-print introduction to a good dictionary. However determined, though, it is recognized that wherever the language is spoken a pronunciation that follows some accepted convention, some admitted standard, is one of the criteria of an educated person.

Standards of Pronunciation

What constitutes a "standard of pronunciation"? Or what constitutes a "standard pronunciation"? How can one determine what mode of pronunciation to follow with any degree of assurance that his speech will be acceptable? These are some of the questions that inevitably arise to plague the student who is seriously attempting to improve his speech. The answers are not always easy to find, but perhaps a few suggestions will be helpful.

First of all, a "standard of pronunciation" consists broadly of a set of criteria by which it may be determined approximately whether a given pronunciation is "acceptable" or not. Essentially these criteria are determined by the dictates of usage and by the prestige of speakers whose usage is conceded to have some weight and whose pronunciation is therefore taken as a basis for comparison. It is not difficult to understand how authorities, in trying to evaluate these criteria and in weighing the prestige of different speakers, all equally eminent, should occasionally disagree as to the predominant usage with respect to the pronunciation of a given word. The simple fact is that for a large number of our words there is no single accepted pronunciation, although in recording those words, our dictionaries follow these "standards of pronunciation" as rigorously as possible.

Where does all this divergence of opinion, this seeming confusion, leave you who are interested in learning how to use words and to use them correctly? It can safely be said that even though there may be no inherently "correct" pronunciation of any word in our language, the dictionary makers have accomplished a remarkably scholarly task in discovering those pronunciations which are widely accepted as correct.[14] Therefore, any pronunciation which you may find in any up-to-date reputable dictionary is placed there because the makers of that dictionary found ample evidence that it was being widely used by careful, educated speakers, and you may feel quite justified in using such a pronunciation yourself.

It is a lamentable but unavoidable fact that dictionaries, even the latest editions, are usually from five to ten years behind the times in the matter of indicating word usage. The real language of any people is not to be found in their writings but in their speech. This speech is constantly changing, as it has been changing since man first began to speak. If Benjamin Franklin were to be "time-machined" forward to the middle of the twentieth century, we should have difficulty in understanding him, and our

[14] See Thomas A. Knott, "How the Dictionary Determines What Pronunciations to Use," *The Quarterly Journal of Speech*, December, 1935, pp. 1-10.

speech would be jargon to him. Speech is constantly changing; pronunciations are constantly changing. By the time the makers of an unabridged dictionary get around to compiling a new edition, with the new pronunciations indicated, those pronunciations may already have been in extensive use for several years. It takes time to compile a new edition of a dictionary; it takes time to assemble all the necessary information that goes into one.

Despite the time lag between actual usage and the dictionary's recognition of it, your safest course is to follow recommended pronunciations. In using a pronunciation that may be in fairly wide use but which you cannot find indicated in any standard dictionary, it is possible that you may be right; but if you adhere to those recorded by authorities, you are sure to be right.

Regional Variants

It is a matter of common observation, and occasionally some amusement, that different modes of speech may be heard in the various sections of the country. What is known as eastern speech is heard mainly in a narrow strip of country along the Atlantic Coast north of Long Island Sound. What is often called southern speech is commonly heard south of the Mason and Dixon Line, up the Potomac and down the Ohio Rivers, and cutting across southeast Texas, including roughly the area making up the old Confederacy. All the rest of the country, with a few local variations, uses a form of speech fairly uniform—at least with so few variations that it may be thought of as one "dialect." It is commonly known as general American speech.

Even within these large divisions pronunciation is by no means consistent; the three major forms are now so widely distributed, because of increased facilities for travel and more or less permanent migrations, that regional characteristics are rapidly breaking down. About all one can say is that in some sections of the country certain forms of speech are heard somewhat more frequently than they are in others.

Comparative Merits of Regional Variants

The question is often raised, "Which of these modes of pronunciation is correct?" Or, "Which is the *best* of these forms?" Some years ago a fond mama was personally entering her daughter in the university, with the intention of having the girl "major" in speech. During the interview with a member of the faculty the mother asked, "And what do you do about southern speech?" "What do you mean, what do we do about it?" "Don't you try to correct it?" "No, madam, not if it is good southern speech."

There is, of course, no possible answer to the question as to which pronunciation is "correct," or which is the "best" of the three, or even of possible others. No one pronunciation can be considered as *the* correct one when good speakers freely and without embarrassment use other pronunciations. Nor can any one of the three be considered as better than either of the other two. There are equally cultured people, equally careful speakers, people whose usage carries equal prestige, in all sections of the country, so that the speech of no one can be set up as *the* standard for the rest of the country to follow. Any effort to establish a uniform mode of pronunciation in this country is futile nonsense.[15]

If, therefore, you use a good speech modeled on that of the northeast section of the country, centering perhaps in Boston and its environs, you may continue to use it with the full assurance that there is no better speech to be heard anywhere. If your speech is that of the South Atlantic section or of the Gulf States, you have no cause to develop an inferiority complex. Similarly, if you have learned your pronunciation somewhere in the Middle West, or along the Pacific Coast—or at points between—you may rest assured that your speech will be accepted anywhere you

[15] See Giles Wilkeson Gray, "American Modes of Speech," *Opinions and Attitudes*, compiled and edited by Stewart Morgan, Thomas Nelson & Sons, rev. ed., 1938, pp. 220-232. Also "Sidelights on the Pronunciation of English," *The Quarterly Journal of Speech*, November, 1932, pp. 546-560.

go. Any mode of speech, if it is good in one of the broad, general sections, is "legal tender" wherever the English language is spoken.

"Acceptable" Pronunciation

What has been said is not to be interpreted as meaning that you are free to use any pronunciation you may want to use. There are, even with all the possible variations, pronunciations that are acceptable and those which are not. Within each general section of the country are typical errors that are often heard. No general type of error is local. They are all heard everywhere. Make every effort to check on your own pronunciation, look up words about which there is the slightest doubt, and learn how to interpret systems of indicating pronunciations that are widely used. Familiarize yourself with the dictionary; it will tell you many interesting things about words, not the least important of which is pronunciation.

Types of Mispronunciation

Judging from the many words we hear being mispronounced, it would be easy to get the impression that there are countless types of error that can be committed. Actually, there are very few, perhaps a half dozen or so. Let us see what those are. It should be observed that one type of error often leads to another. It should be further noted that some pronunciations which were considered unacceptable not many years ago are recognized now by most authorities.

1. MISPLACED ACCENT. Misplaced accent consists in placing the accent on a syllable other than the one usually recommended. Often the shifting of the accent results in changing some of the sounds in the word. Illustrative of this type of error are the following:

mis chiev ous Often with the accent on the second syllable, resulting in a different vowel in that syllable, and the introduction of an additional syllable before the *ous*, as mis *chiev* i ous.

i *de* a   Often accented on the first syllable, with the third syllable omitted entirely.

mu *nic* i pal   Sometimes with a complete change in syllabication, as mu ni *cip* al.

lam en ta ble   Often with the second syllable accented. This word appeared on page 523. How did you pronounce it when you read it?

gri *mace*   Not *grim* ace, as sometimes heard.

se *cret* ive   Not *sec* re tive.

In some sections of the South, notably in Louisiana, the tendency has been to shift the accent in many words forward, so that Monroe (the city) becomes *mun* roe, police becomes *po* lice, Vermont *Ver* mont, and so on.

Many words are accented differently according to the part of speech, that is, the same word may be accented one way as one part of speech and another way as another. (Incidentally, where did you place the accent on the word *accented* just above and on the word *accent* in this sentence?) For example, *ref* use (noun), re *fuse* (verb); *fre* quent (adj.), fre *quent* (verb); *gal* lant (adj.), gal *lant* (noun); *ac* cent (noun), ac *cent* (verb); *min* ute (noun), mi *nute* (adj.).

As we have said, in the case of many words certain pronunciations not acceptable a few years ago are recognized today as quite good: ad *dress,* *ad* dress; al *ly,* *al* ly; a *dult,* *ad* ult; al *loy,* *al* loy; ab *do* men, *ab* do men, and so on.

In case of doubt, check with the dictionary. If your preferred accentuation is recognized, you are free to use it.

2. OMISSION OF SOUNDS. The type of mispronunciation known as omission of sounds has been partially described under Articulation, which should be reviewed here; but not all errors of this type fall under the discussion of that section. When the accent in *idea* is shifted to the first syllable, for example, the third sound, that represented by the *a*, is usually omitted. Omissions may be of either vowels or consonants. Some examples are these:

help	is often he'p	least	is often leas'
film	is often fi'm	tolerable	is often tol'a'ble
family	is often fam'ly	Saturday	is often Sad'dy
company	is often comp'ny	student	is often stu'ent
asked	is often as't	Louisiana	is often Lou'z'ana

In many words some of the letters are matters of spelling only and actually represent no sound. The *a* in the names of the days of the week (Mond*a*y, Tuesd*a*y, etc.) does not mean that the final syllable in those words is pronounced like *day*; the final sound is like the *y* in *busy*. But you should include all the sounds that properly belong in the pronunciation of the word.

3. ADDITION OF EXTRA SOUNDS. Often sounds are put into words that do not belong there at all. Sometimes this error arises from what is known as *spelling pronunciation*, in which the idea, apparently prevalent, is that because a letter appears in the spelling of a word it must be pronounced; in other cases extra sounds are inserted or added. The following are illustrative:

a'mond	not a*l*mond	drown	not drown*d*
pa'm	not pa*l*m	column	not col*y*um
of'en	not of*t*en	drowned	not drown*d*ed
athlete	not ath*a*lete	World's Series	not World's Ser*i*ous
elm	not elem	mischievous	not mischie*v*ious
film	not fi*l*em	twice	not twice*t*
across	not acros*s*t	close	not close*t*
idea	not idea*r*	once	not once*t*

In speech think what the word should *sound* like, not what it *looks* like on the page. Do not include sounds not indicated by the spelling, but remember that not every letter in the spelling is necessarily pronounced.

4. INVERSION OF SOUNDS. In inversion of sounds the sounds may all be included or approximately all of them, but some of

---

GOOD DELIVERY IS ANIMATED

General Charles de Gaulle shows his enthusiasm by his facial expression, gestures, and posture. (Photos, Black Star.)

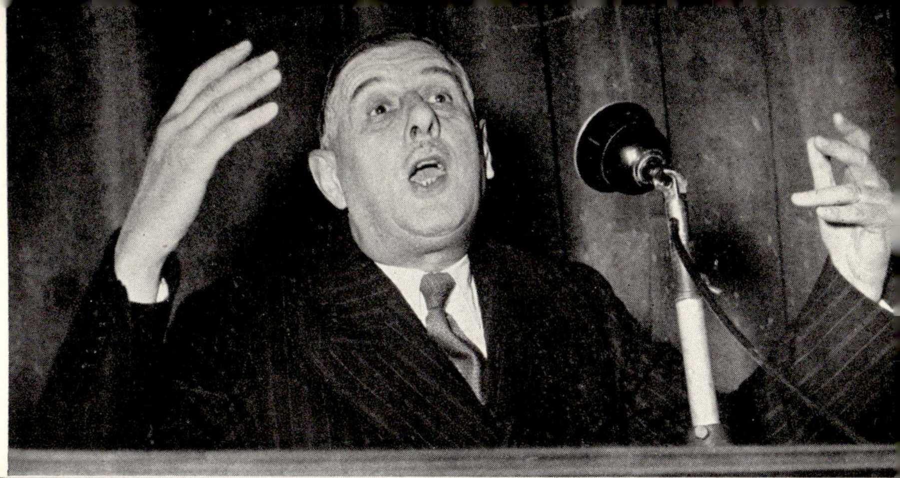

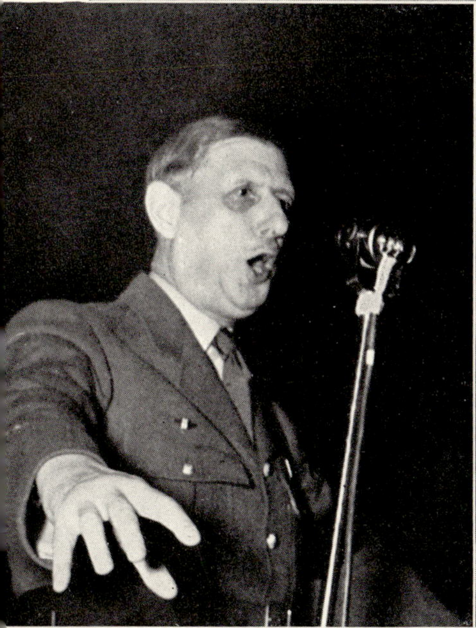

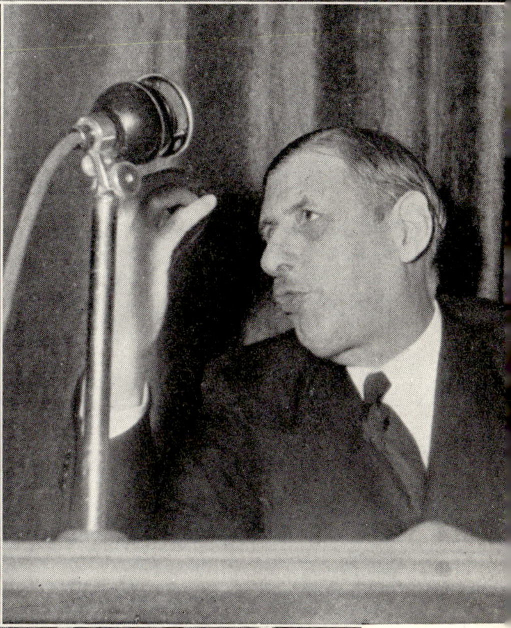

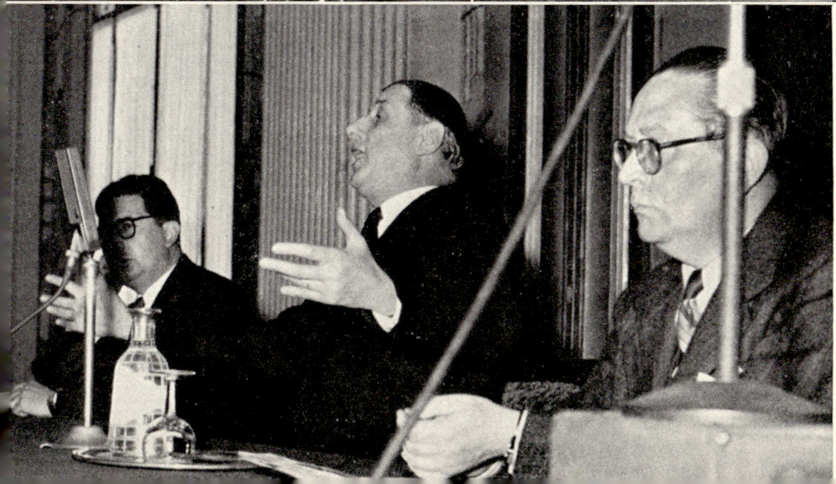

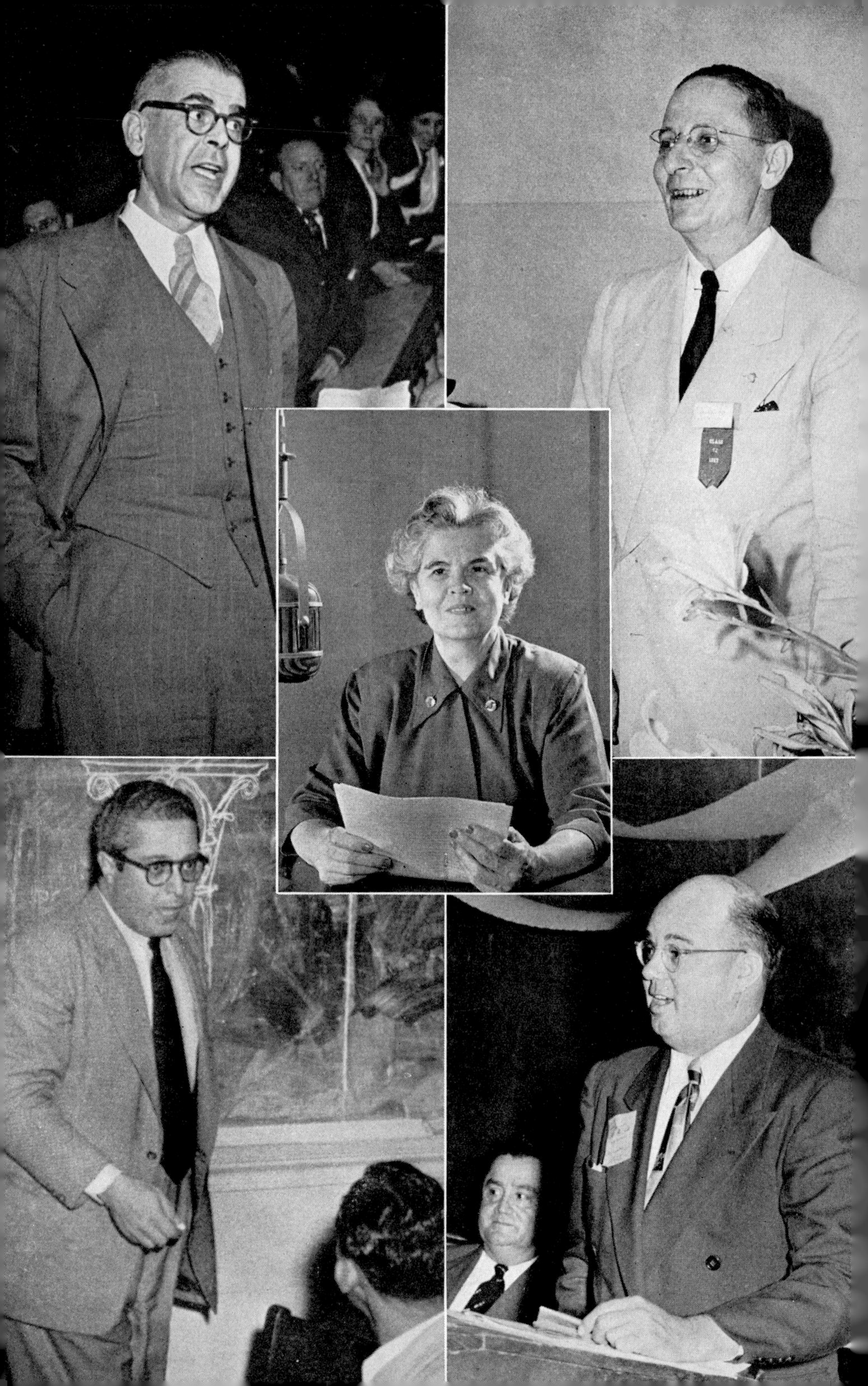

VOCAL ASPECTS OF DELIVERY

them are in the wrong order. Many people do not distinguish between the following pronunciations:

Right	Wrong	Right	Wrong
cavalry	Calvary	prefer	perfer
larynx	larnyx	asked	axed
children	childern	pretty	purty
perspiration	prespiration	hundred	hunderd
perforation	preforation	modern	modren

A student from Puerto Rico some years ago always spoke of the "Thous" instead of the "South." "Casual" and "causal" are often confused because of a letter inversion which results in a combination of sound addition and substitution.

5. SOUND SUBSTITUTION. Sometimes the persistent substitution of one sound for another is classified as a speech defect. Most substitutions, however, are like most mispronunciations, the result of early habits, and can be corrected by the building up of new habits. There are a great many specific types of substitution, both of vowels and of consonants, of which the following are among the most common:

yit for *yet*; *git* for *get*; *tin* for *ten*; *fince* for *fence*, and so on
form for *farm* (where *farm* is intended)
len'th for *length*; *stren'th* for *strength*
champeen for *champion*
talkin' for *talking*; *goin'* for *going*; *writin'* for *writing*, and so on
lugzury for *luxury*
stomp for *stamp*
wether for *whether* (acceptable in some localities)
simular for *similar*
substantuate for *substantiate* (heard among debaters)
interputation for *interpretation* (this misspelling from a debate director)
particalar for *particular*

6. GENERAL ELISIONS. Words are often mispronounced by the

FACIAL EXPRESSION GIVES MANY CLUES TO A SPEAKER'S PERSONALITY process of a general slurring over the sounds. This is so closely related to faulty articulation that little further needs to be said in this connection than was said under the general heading of Articulation.

Reasons for Mispronunciation

It can be said with reasonable certainty that there are four general reasons for mispronunciation, no one of which is irremediable:

1. Not knowing what the correct pronunciation is
2. Too indifferent to look up the correct pronunciation
3. Not knowing how to find the correct pronunciation or how to interpret the symbols
4. Too indifferent to apply what knowledge one has or can obtain

If one wanted to be blunt, even harsh, in attributing reasons even more basic than these, one can say only that they are the result of either ignorance or carelessness, neither of which is an admirable trait of personality.[16]

Learning Good Pronunciation

You have been told of the various types of mispronunciation; your logical inquiry will be, How and where can I learn how to pronounce my words correctly? In general there are three basic sources for learning good pronunciation:

1. *Listen to good speakers.* It was remarked earlier that the use of language, including the ability to pronounce it with fluent correctness without exaggeration or affectation, is one of the marks of the educated person. It must be admitted that many otherwise admirable people, considered to be highly educated and cultured, do make gross errors in their use of language. Sometimes these errors are localized; different small areas have their own peculiarities of pronunciation which stamp the native of those sections as having originated there. The antidote to being

---

[16] For a more complete description of specific errors of pronunciation, see Giles Wilkeson Gray and Claude Merton Wise, *The Bases of Speech*, Harper & Brothers, rev. ed., 1946, pp. 245-258, 265-272, 287-295.

misled by such relatively isolated instances is to listen to speakers from many different localities and try to discover how they pronounce. You will probably settle for the general mode of speech that you have grown up with or in which you will spend most of your lives, eliminating such errors as have crept into your own version of it. If you change your habitat, you will probably find your habitual speech changing slightly in the direction of the speech of your new location. Such changes are neither to be deplored nor hailed with joy; they are one of the factors of linguistic change. *So long as your speech meets the best standards of your linguistic area,* you have nothing for which to apologize.

2. *Study under some competent instructor* who can point out your errors or deviations from the acceptable and help you to correct them. You should not need constant supervision if you learn, first, to recognize your own mistakes and, second, to know when you are successfully making the correction. Practice and then practice more. You may seem to yourself stilted in your conversation if you attempt to maintain what you know to be good pronunciation, but if you will get the habit of correcting yourself each time you recognize an error, it will not be long before you will have eliminated most errors. But do not extend this critical tendency and your habit of correcting, to the speech of your friends and acquaintances! It is an excellent way to "lose friends and alienate people." Besides, since many words have different pronunciations, they too may be right.

3. *Get the habit of consulting a good dictionary,* one that indicates the pronunciations as well as the meanings and other items of interest and significance. Different dictionaries use different methods of indicating pronunciation; you will have to learn the system of whichever one you use. Any of them, if you understand its symbols, will give you all the essential information to help you find the correct pronunciations of words.

The two most widely used systems are first, the diacritical markings of Webster and most other dictionaries and, second, the International Phonetic Alphabet, used in two or three of the most modern pronouncing dictionaries such as Daniel Jones', which gives the pronunciations of southern British,[17] and the Kenyon-Knott Dictionary,[18] which records American pronunciations. Each has its faults and each its merits. For the past four generations every child at home or in school who has studied the dictionary at all has been made familiar with the Webster system of diacritical marks indicating pronunciations. They seem to be a part of the educational heritage of the American school child. Most other general dictionaries use systems similar to those of the Webster series, with a few deviations. The *American College Dictionary*, although it uses diacritical marks, has correlated these with the more specific International Phonetic Alphabet for the purpose of indicating precise pronunciations. It also indicates regional variants more generously than most dictionaries.[19]

The International Phonetic Alphabet also has its advantages. It permits, it even requires, a more specific interpretation of its symbols, since each symbol represents one and only one sound. It makes definite the regional variants, as most diacritical systems do not; and finally, it makes possible the learning of the pronunciation of any language or dialect by one familiar with the symbols.

If you want pronunciations alone, the dictionary with the more specific system of symbolization, like the International Phonetic Alphabet or a set of diacritical marks well correlated with it, is probably preferable. If you want pronunciations together with all the other information usually given by dictionaries, you will need something more than a pronouncing dictionary alone. For most of your purposes the "college" or "desk" editions will be entirely satisfactory. In many circles, however, the "unabridged" editions are still the ultimate authority. The prevalence of mispronunciation and of lack of familiarity with words today is probably less the result of the inadequacy of the usual systems of indicating

[17] Daniel Jones, *An English Pronouncing Dictionary*, E. P. Dutton & Co., 5th ed., 1943.

[18] John S. Kenyon and Thomas A. Knott, *A Pronouncing Dictionary of American English*, G. & C. Merriam Company, 1944.

[19] Clarence L. Barnhart (ed.), *The American College Dictionary*, text ed., Harper & Brothers, 1948.

correct usage and acceptable pronunciations than of the decreased emphasis at the lower school levels on the use of the ones we have.

Fluency

One further aspect of the use of voice in speaking should be considered, and that is fluency. The term comes from a Latin word meaning *to flow*. Fluent speech does just that: it flows. It moves along without hesitation, without groping for words, exhibiting no uncertainty as to either ideas or language.

Fluency is not to be mistaken for rapidity of utterance. You can be just as fluent using only a hundred thirty words per minute as you can using two hundred. Fluency is not speed. Although speech should move without hesitation, that does not mean that it should move continuously without breaks or pauses. You can and should break your speech up into phrases, separating those phrases by pauses of appropriate length. You can and should make the fullest use of variations in quantity. You can make use of all the variations in rate of utterance and still be fluent.

The essential requirements for the achievement of fluency are (1) a thorough knowledge of the points you intend to present and the order in which you intend to present them; (2) an equally thorough knowledge of your supporting materials, the details with which you are going to develop those ideas; (3) sufficient command of vocabulary that you do not have to grope for words in which to clothe those ideas and the supporting details; (4) avoidance of such expressions as *uh, ah, and-a,* and other superfluous vocalizations that are often injected into the utterance when you are groping for the next idea or word; (5) enough self-confidence in your knowledge and skill that you are not overcome by the occasion.

EXERCISES

1. Read a passage in as nearly a normal conversational manner as possible. Count the number of words in the passage, and then

time your reading. Calculate the speed of your reading. Repeat for two or three more passages of different lengths, and find your average rate.
2. Select an interesting passage that will take approximately two minutes to read. Estimate from your findings in Exercise 1 how many words you will need. Divide this entire passage into sense units, and mark these off by short vertical and slanting lines. Now read the passage, making pauses only where you have marked. Does this exercise give you a better idea of phrasing? Be sure to take a short inhalation at short pauses, with a full inhalation at complete stops.
3. Write out an original paragraph, marking off the phrases as in the above exercise. Read the passage with no effort to phrase it, and a second time pausing at the end of each phrase. What is the effect on the meaning of the paragraph?
4. Record the words and phrases on page 514, with the inflectional patterns as indicated. Listen to them as they are played back, and try to discover your errors. To what extent were you able to make your voice move up or down as indicated?
5. Read aloud a short sentence of perhaps a dozen words, and try to plot with slanting lines the inflectional patterns you used. Now arbitrarily reverse some of these patterns and read again. Report on the differences in meaning that you observed.
6. Pronounce very slowly the following words: *pat, bad, plod, blot, flat, bleed, nob, knot, nod, gold, cold, shove, azure, path, bathe, very, ferry, valid, yes, yet, wait, wade*. Describe as accurately as you can the positions of the tongue, lips, and other organs of articulation in pronouncing each word.
7. Find the pronunciations of these words, and practice until you can pronounce them fluently and correctly:

alias	combatant	exigency	gratis
amenable	commandant	extant	grievous
antarctic	comptroller	extrapolate	height
apparatus	culinary	falcon	heinous
arctic	cynosure	flaccid	hypocrisy
beneficence	data	gape	infantilism
biography	diphtheria	genealogy	ingenious
cello	discharge	gesture	ingenuous
clematis	exemplary	gigantism	interstices

intrepid	numismatics	Quincy, Illinois	statistician
intricacies	obligatory	Quincy, Mass.	tarpaulin
irrelevant	onerous	Quincy, Josiah	tremendous
irreverent	orthoepy	quinsy	trephine
leisure	patronymic	research	triglyph
lenient	peremptory	romance	trioecious
lineament	pharynx	salubrious	turmeric
liniment	philately	satiety	umbrageous
livelong	piquant	sinecure	usurious
longevity	precocity	spectator	uxorious
lugubrious	prestige	squalid	vagary
mineralogy	protestation	squalor	verisimilitude
nomenclature	program	statistical	zoology

claustrophobia	dichromaticism	prognathous	supererogate
coelenterate	electroencephal-	prothonotary	tetrabranchiate
cupriferous	ogram	quadruplets	theanthropism
cyclostomatous	hallucinatory	sphygmograph	thoracoplasty
diamantiferous	hamamelida-	sphygmomanom-	
	ceous	eter	

8. The following words may be pronounced differently in the three major dialect areas of the United States and Canada. Indicate by some intelligible and consistent method the pronunciation of your own region:

behalf	demand	insure
telegraph	answer	yourself
after	common	Turner
laughter	fond	fourth
castle	coffee	forty-four
master	pocket	journey
example	possible	tomato
repast	Robert	either
pastor	absurd	neither
command	curdle	purser
reprimand	murder	purpose
advance	murmur	rather
dance	further	raspberry

9. Select a passage from a speech which includes a short quotation of not more than four or five lines. Notice how the speaker introduces

the quotation and makes it clear that he is quoting the words of another without actually using the words "quote" and "unquote." Now write a short passage in which you include a quotation introduced in a similar manner.
10. Give a talk in which you introduce as a quotation what someone else has said. Use in your introduction of the quotation a technique similar to that used in Exercise 9. In your presentation, in addition to your use of language to introduce the quotation, make your voice, through the use of vocal techniques, set off the quotation so that its beginning and end are unmistakable. At the end of the quotation do not announce verbally that you have completed it; show that you are resuming your own words through the use of vocal changes.
11. Suggest by your voice and by appropriate language (a) a small boy begging for a piece of candy; (b) a small boy trying to act grown up; (c) a very old man (Shakespeare's "childish treble"), (d) a whiny old man, or woman; (e) old-fashioned Fourth-of-July oratory; (f) the backwoods preacher; (g) the garrulous gossip; (h) Digger the Undertaker; (i) the teller of ghost stories; (j) the teller of children's stories; (k) the confidential (stage) whisper.
12. By using only simple rising and falling inflections on the three accented words in Shakespeare's line, "*All* the *world's* a *stage*," there are eight ways in which to read the line.

All the World's a Stage.

Read the line in various ways, trying to use all eight of the possible combinations. Record your eight readings and check for both ear and voice. How many of them can you read correctly? (There are undoubtedly many who can give all eight patterns

---

A GESTURE MAY BE WORTH A DOZEN WORDS

Wayne Morse, Senator from Oregon, makes a point with a gesture. (Photo, Wide World.)

Eleanor Roosevelt clarifies an explanation by a gesture. (Photo, Black Star.)

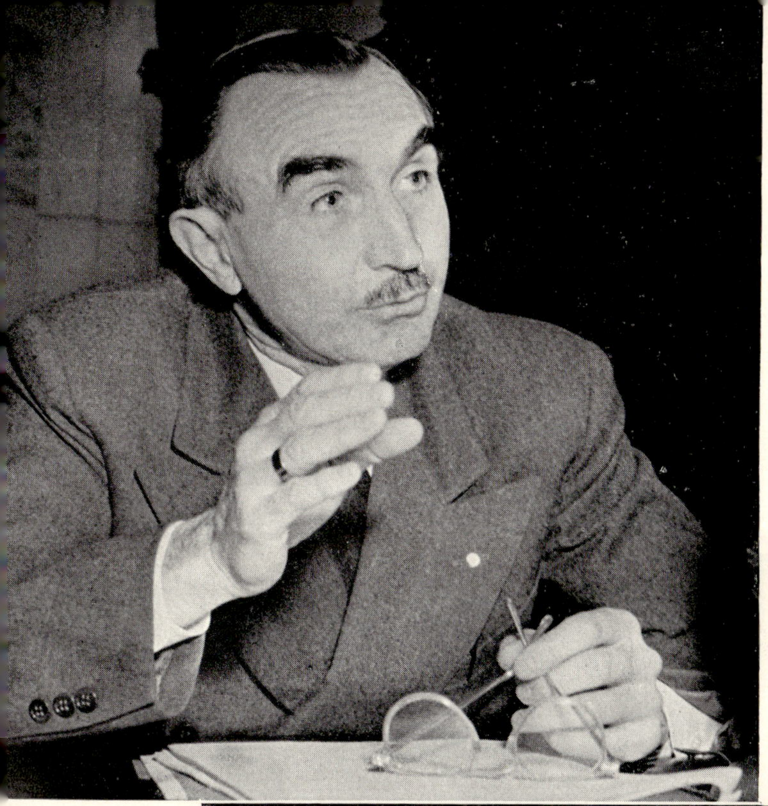

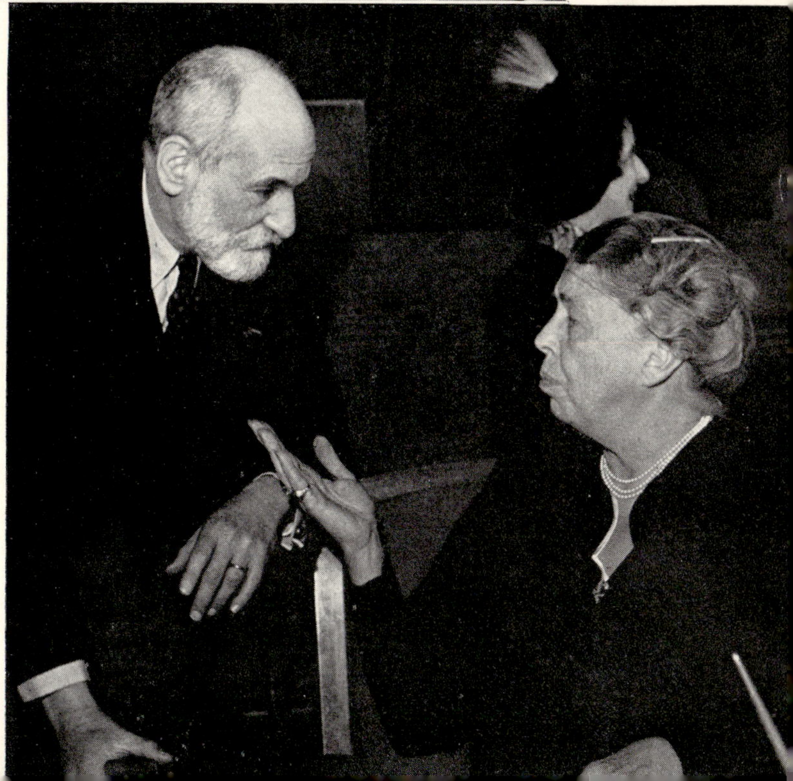

DEMOCRATIC PRESIDENTS

VOCAL ASPECTS OF DELIVERY

correctly on the first trial; but in fifteen years of using this example, the authors have never heard one! (See Gray and Wise, *The Bases of Speech, op. cit.,* p. 33.)

13. Go to a piano, and run the scale from the lowest note you can produce vocally to the highest, including your falsetto. Now count the total number of semitones (both white and black keys) in this range. Go up one fourth of the way from the "bottom" to the "top," and see what the note is. This should be the approximate median for your optimum pitch, according to Fairbanks' *Voice and Articulation Drill Book.*

14. Select three passages, either prose or verse, one of which calls for your normal pitch range, one for a range somewhat higher than your normal, and one lower. Read these selections in the appropriate pitch range to cultivate the ability to speak not only in your normal level but both above and below it.

15. For clearness in consonant combinations practice the following:

> Amidst the mists and fiercest frosts,
> With barest wrists and stoutest boasts,
> He thrusts his fists against the posts,
> And still insists he sees the ghosts.

He first asked the postmistress exactly how the clasps should be wrapped around the casks before the tasks were completed.

The Picts waked in their crypts, looked across the fields, and wept because from the first they had lacked the correct respect.

The crisp clasp on the wrist fixed the pesky pest.

The molds were in fact at last boxed with the casts, but the costs swept skyward.

16. Give a talk in which you describe, in terms of the material of this chapter, the voice of some speaker you have recently heard. Give some illustrations of a few of his mannerisms, if any.

GESTURES MUST BE ADAPTED TO THE SPEAKING SITUATION

Helen Douglas in speaking to the National Convention used broad gestures to reach her thousands of listeners. Hubert Humphrey, Senator from Minnesota, projected his ideas to the audience by his energy and vigor. (Photos, Wide World.)

SUPPLEMENTARY READINGS

1. Baird, A. Craig, and Knower, Franklin H., *General Speech: An Introduction*, McGraw-Hill Book Company, Inc., 1949, chap. 13, "The Speaking Voice," pp. 208-237; chap. 14, "Articulation and Pronunciation," pp. 238-258.
2. Bryant, Donald C., and Wallace, Karl R., *Fundamentals of Public Speaking*, Appleton-Century-Crofts, Inc., 1947, chap. 15, "Voice, Pronunciation and Gesture," pp. 328-345.
3. Gray, Giles Wilkeson, and Wise, Claude Merton, *The Bases of Speech*, Harper & Brothers, rev. ed., 1946, pp. 10-44; chap. III, "The Physiological Basis of Speech," pp. 139-216; chap. IV, "The Phonetic Basis of Speech," pp. 217-302.
4. Monroe, Alan H., *Principles and Types of Speech*, Scott, Foresman & Company, 3rd ed., 1949, chap. 4, "Improving Voice Quality," pp. 76-98; chap. 4, "Developing Vocal Variety," pp. 99-127.
5. Oliver, Robert T., Cortright, Rupert L., and Hager, Cyril L., *The New Training for Effective Speech*, The Dryden Press, Inc., 1947, chap. 10, "The Speaker's Voice," pp. 217-231; chap. 11, "Articulation and Pronunciation," pp. 233-256.
6. Sarett, Lew, and Foster, William Trufant, *Basic Principles of Speech*, Houghton Mifflin Company, rev. ed., 1946, chap. 8, "The Voice," pp. 200-233; chap. 9, "Melody," pp. 234-259; chap. 10, "Time," pp. 260-294; chap. 11, "Force," pp. 295-313.
7. Winans, James A., *Speech-Making*, Appleton-Century-Crofts, Inc., 1938, chap. XXII, "Voice and Speech," pp. 452-478.
8. Woolbert, Charles Henry, and Smith, Joseph F., *The Fundamentals of Speech*, Harper & Brothers, 3rd ed., 1934, Part Three, "Voice," pp. 147-308.

CHAPTER XXII

Bodily Aspects of Delivery

AN INCREASING amount of speaking today is being done over the radio, by which only the voice can be carried. Yet it is highly significant that vast amounts of time, money, and effort are being spent in developing the means of carrying to the radio listener the final element in the complete process of speech, namely, the visible aspects of delivery. The language one uses is undoubtedly of great importance in communication; you have seen how the manner in which that language is uttered also has a bearing on the meaning stimulated. The whole process is made even more complete when the speaker can also be seen.

CONFRONTATION

Almost five thousand years ago a wise old sage of the Fifth Egyptian Dynasty told his children, "If you would judge a friend's character, do not depend on the evaluations of others; seek him out at a mutually agreeable time, and hold discussions with him; 'test his heart in an occasion of speech.' Hear him to the end without interruption, if he wants to open his heart to you, and avoid seeming to be scornful, or withdrawing from him. He will thus give you the opportunity of passing a fair judgment."[1]

Even at that very early period, not long after the building of the Great Pyramid of Khufu, it was recognized that there was "in an occasion of speech" some factor which gives it a peculiar advantage in the formulation of "fair judgments" of other people, which enables us to evaluate the behavior, even the character, of others, with a greater assurance that our evaluation will have a solid basis. Today we still feel that if we can just *see* a friend, talk with him face to face, observe his facial expression, look into his eyes, we can communicate with him with satisfaction to both. Everyone will attest to the fact that during absence letters are more satisfactory than nothing at all. A telephone call is still better because of the added element of voice; but there is nothing that will quite come up to a good visit. None of us likes to listen to a speaker from behind a wall or a post in a lecture hall, even though we are willing if necessary to listen to his voice over the loud-speaker of our radios.

What makes speech preeminent as a means of communication is the factor known as *confrontation*,[2] the face-to-face directness which permits the simultaneous giving and receiving of stimuli: the speaker is receiving stimuli from his listeners at the same time that he is giving visible and audible stimuli to them. Our everyday conversations are our most familiar example of the operation of the principle of confrontation. It is this factor which impels business firms to hold frequent conferences, professional organizations to meet in periodic conventions, and nations to assign diplomatic missions to other nations.

[1] See Giles Wilkeson Gray, "The 'Precepts of Kagemni and Ptah-Hotep,'" *The Quarterly Journal of Speech*, December, 1946, pp. 446-454.
[2] See Giles Wilkeson Gray and Claude Merton Wise, *The Bases of Speech*, Harper & Brothers, rev. ed., 1946, pp. 405-409.

Because of the absence of confrontation in any form of communication other than direct speech, no other form can quite take its place. Radio, television, the motion pictures, excellent as they all may be technically, do not and cannot have the simultaneous giving and receiving of stimuli which is the essential ingredient of direct speech. When a candidate for public office wants to make an effective campaign, he does not satisfy himself or the voters merely by letting them listen to him over the radio or see him on a television screen; he goes out before them, where he can see them as well as be seen by them, where he can get their reactions *even while he is speaking*—an impossibility in any other type of speaking situation.

The speaker is something more than a person to be heard; he is more than a user of words. In the normal and most effective speaking situation he is also a person to be seen. Despite an increasing amount of speaking into the microphone, there is still a vast amount of face-to-face speaking, in which the visible aspect of delivery makes its contribution to the effectiveness of the communication. It is important, therefore, that we examine the question of visible bodily action to determine what principles may be followed to enable us to make that contribution even more significant.

No Actionless Speaking

In the ordinary situation, in which you are facing your audience directly, there is no such thing as actionless speaking. It is doubtful, so far as the speaker is concerned, whether there is any actionless speaking before the microphone; but visible actions contribute nothing directly over the radio, although they may have an influence on the speaker's voice. So long as you are within sight of your hearers as a speaker, what they see you doing is of interest and significance to them. "Every little movement has a meaning all its own," ran a popular song many years ago. That is particularly true in a speaking situation in which confrontation is a factor.

It is therefore no solution to the problem of what to do with your hands, your arms, your feet, to do nothing at all, since even doing nothing, as was pointed out in Chapter XX, is in itself significant. And if you do nothing so vigorously that your muscles become all tense and knotted, it is likely to mean to your listeners most of all that you are a scared and nervous speaker! You cannot hide from your audience so long as you stand before them. The more you try to conceal your movements from them, the more noticeable they become.

It has also been pointed out (Chapter XX) that one of the significant characteristics of emotional behavior is its allover nature. When you are speaking, the emotional component of your meanings reveals itself in allover activity. That does not mean, of course, that you must be perpetually boiling over or even that you bubble up every time you feel the least bit of pleasure. But it does mean that the particular type of emotional response that is strongest at the time is going to show itself in your general behavior. If you are at the moment most strongly moved by the urge to communicate even so "unemotional" a subject as a geometric proposition, that attitude will be revealed in your manner. If at the moment you are most strongly influenced by what is known as stage fright, then certainly you are going to have a difficult time concealing it from your audience. If your speaking has, as it should have, a strong emotional component, your behavior will reveal it.

Subliminal and Supraliminal Stimuli

People are often affected by impressions of which they are totally unaware. They respond, peculiarly enough, to stimuli too faint to be sensed. You have often become suddenly aware of having been hearing for some time a faint sound that has only at the moment entered your consciousness. Sometimes you can tell whether a certain element is present in a given stimulus pattern or not, even though that element would be too weak to be sensed at all if it stood alone.

BODILY ASPECTS OF DELIVERY

You are influenced similarly by little things you see and hear your friends do, even though you are not actually conscious of just what it is that makes the impression on you. It may be an imperceptible tension of a facial muscle, a slight inflectional turn in the voice, a twitch of a finger. Football scouts are trained to detect telltale actions of opposing players and are often able to spot some slight movement, a shift of weight by a player, for example, that gives a play away completely. A boxer may not even see consciously the punch that he "instinctively" blocks.

You all get impressions leading to liking or disliking and are quite unable to isolate in the total pattern the exact elements that have given you those impressions. But even though you are not aware of the significant elements, the impression itself is often so strong that it may outweigh that part of the effect gained from those stimuli which you readily perceive.

Those aspects of the stimulus of which you are quite unaware, because they are below the threshold or *limen* of perception, yet to which you nevertheless respond are known as *subliminal* stimuli. Those of which you are aware, because they are strong enough to be above the lower limit of perception, are called *supraliminal*.

The converse to the principle stated above is that the individual himself is also quite unaware that he is giving out such imperceptible stimuli. He is totally unconscious of the faint movements of his own facial muscles, the inflectional turn of his own voice, the twitch of his own finger. That is, you yourselves are constantly presenting stimulus patterns containing elements well above the threshold of perception for both you and those about you; you are also presenting patterns which contain elements below your own limit of perception and yet which are strongly influential in the impressions that others form of you.

There is a further basis of differentiating between the supraliminal and the subliminal. The former, being within the consciousness, is subject to conscious control and to habit formation. It is possible, for example, to control the gross changes in the vocal attributes, such as inflections, phrasing, pauses, loudness; it is possible to control the larger movements of the body, as of arms, legs, feet, hands; you gain a measure of consistent control over your facial expression. It is possible, though not advisable, for you to develop such habits of observable behavior as are quite incompatible with your actual nature. Contrary to the opinion held by many, most criminals neither look nor behave like desperadoes. Your habitual, overt behavior, as it affects those about you, provides only a part of the basis for others' judgments of what is called your *personality*.

Since you are unaware of the subliminal stimuli you are presenting to others, however, such forms of behavior are not subject to conscious control, nor can they be intentionally incorporated into habit patterns. There is not a great deal that can be done about them on the conscious level.

The sources of these subliminal aspects of behavior lie deep within the individual's nature. They are based on underlying attitudes, emotions, impulses, motives, which themselves provide the unconscious drives for fundamental behavior patterns. Whereas the conscious actions are in a sense superficial and, like other habits, may be and often are changed, unconscious behavior is deeply embedded; it is probably with reference to these underlying forces that it is often said, "You cannot change human nature." These imperceptible factors in the total behavior complete for those about you the bases of their judgments of your "personality."

In a well-motivated person, whose external activities correspond to his underlying impulses and attitudes, there is no conflict between the supra- and the subliminal stimuli which he presents to his listeners. But when one has cultivated habits that are contrary to one's basic nature, then conflicts arise, and the listeners are faced with the necessity of determining which set of patterns is the more authentic, that is, which represents more accurately the man himself. It is significant that, however polished the external form may be, the strongest and most lasting impressions come from the more deeply lying patterns of activity. What you do when you are "off guard" is often of highest significance in the estimates others make of your character; as for the subliminal stimuli, you are *always* "off guard."

If, therefore, you would provide for your hearers what Aristotle called the *ethical proof* for what you say, be sure that those minute, imperceptible movements of which both you and they are quite unaware and against which you can never raise an adequate guard of habit do not betray you.[3] The old principle handed down from ancient times that an orator is a good man skilled in speaking is sound from both the ethical and the psychological points of view.

None of what has been said should detract from the importance of a good delivery, consciously and intentionally developed and consisting of physical attitudes and movements which are entirely obvious to both the speaker and the audience. The important thing to consider, with reference to the subliminal aspects of your behavior, is that, if your speaking is to have its maximum effectiveness, there must be no conflict between these unconscious, unintentional aspects and the conscious, controllable phases of delivery. ". . . unless our public utterances and our moral character are in accord," said Philostratus, "we shall seem, like flutes, to speak with a tongue that is not our own."[4] It will be worth while to consider those aspects of delivery over which we have some measure of control.

Visible bodily activity is usually considered in four divisions or aspects, posture, movement, gesture, and facial expression.

POSTURE

The first thing that an audience will observe when you appear before it, after noting your general appearance, size, and general proportions, is the way you carry yourself—your carriage, bearing,

---

[3] See Lew Sarett and William Trufant Foster, *Basic Principles of Speech*, Houghton Mifflin Company, rev. ed., 1946, pp. 30-37.

[4] *Lives of the Sophists*, Wright Edition, p. 49.

the way you hold your shoulders, your arms, how you carry your head, in other words, your general posture. This is what gives to your audience its first impression, and since first impressions are often difficult to change, you should take pains to ensure that this one is favorable.

Posture, like other aspects of bodily behavior, is an allover matter creating a total impression. It involves the position of the feet, the distribution of weight, the set of the shoulders, the position of the head, the "hang" of the arms when not in use. All parts of the body must work as a unit. Your audience does not see these separate parts or the contribution they make to the total impression; it sees *you* "all in one piece." However, for purposes of analysis and study, it is convenient to consider separately the different parts of the body and their effect on the total pattern.

Position of the Feet

Let it be said at the outset that there is no "orator's position." Many good speakers are so active before their audiences that they do not take any position for more than a few seconds at a time. There is, then, no specific position which the feet should take simply because it is the thing to do. Efforts have been made in the past to fix such positions, to describe them, and to prescribe them for certain attitudes of the speaker, but the rules were too rigid; they became so entirely mechanical that they were finally discarded altogether.

That does not mean that anything that you do with your feet, any position in which you may want to put them, will be acceptable. One can be quite awkward primarily on account of ungraceful positions of the feet. A few elementary principles will govern these positions in general:

1. You will find that the *most flexible* position which your feet can take is for one foot to be a little in advance of the other, with the heel of the advanced foot turned in toward the other, without, however, trying to assume any specific angle. From this basic position you can advance, withdraw, step forward as if to

approach your audience, shift your weight from one foot to the other as you turn from one side of the audience to address the other side or as the idea itself calls for a shift.

The recommendation of such a position does not mean that as you advance to your place before the audience you should place your feet just so, deliberately and mechanically; that would be worse than anything else you might do with your feet. Practicing the position in your room, whenever you stop for a moment, will reveal to you how flexible it really is. It can be used as the basic position from which all others are departures. Moreover, it is not intended to suggest that, once having assumed such a position, you should maintain it throughout the speech. On the contrary, you should move about. But you will find that, with all your movement, the suggested position is the easiest and the most comfortable for you to come back to.

Such advice is not a reversion to the practices of nineteenth-century elocutionists, many of whom made of speech an exhibition rather than an act of communication. The point being made here is that as a basic position, the one just described is at once the easiest to assume and the most flexible.

2. Do not hesitate to shift your foot positions, but vary the type of shift as well as the specific position. Some attitudes call for placing the feet close together, others for a broader "stance," either of which can be achieved without getting too far away from the basic position.

3. Turning from one side of the audience to the other, as you will do from time to time, may be accomplished (a) by simply turning the upper part of the body, (b) by total movement, that is, by walking from one side of the platform to the other, or (c) by turning on the balls of your feet, swinging the heels around. Turning on the heels, swinging the toes around, is not so good.

Distribution of Weight

If you are at all animated in your speaking and if you move about the platform, the problem of weight distribution will for the most part take care of itself, just as foot positions do. You will often, however, stand for some time without changing your position at all. At such times as these the question of weight distribution becomes of some importance. Some of the principles of foot position have just been discussed; but those principles alone will not enable you to achieve poise or to avoid appearing awkward and ill at ease. You will never acquire a good posture or position if you limit your attention to the positions of the feet. What you do with the rest of your body also contributes to the total impression as well as to your own comfort. Woolbert even says, "Get the weight of the whole in the right place, and the feet, if they have any sense at all, have to take care of themselves."[5] The argument here is that the positions of the feet just described, when combined with proper weight distribution, will contribute most to an effective, graceful, flexible posture.

Actually, the possibilities for placing the weight of the body are quite limited; there are only a few:

The ball of either foot
The heel of either foot
The ball *and* heel of either foot
The balls of both feet
The heels of both feet
The balls and heels of both feet

With the general basic position of the feet described above, any of these six distributions is possible. Which one is actually used will depend on the idea to be expressed, the intensity of the attitude to be established, and the strength of the speaker's attitude toward the audience and toward the very act of communication.

A further analysis of the relation of the positions of the feet and the distribution of weight reveals the fact that, of the first three possibilities listed above, the weight can easily and appropriately be placed on either the ball or the heel, or both ball and

[5] Charles Henry Woolbert and Joseph F. Smith, *The Fundamentals of Speech*, Harper & Brothers, 3rd ed., 1934, p. 114.

heel, of either the advanced or rear foot. It is further obvious that none of the last three cases requires that the feet be placed close together, with the heels on the same line; either type of weight distribution can be achieved with one foot advanced. It is quite obvious, then, that there is great latitude in the matter of both foot position and weight distribution.

For attitudes of aggressiveness, of advancing, of reaching out to the audience, throw the weight forward. It makes little difference on which foot it rests; you will soon change anyway. For attitudes of retirement, submission, of casualness, indifference, or for the stronger attitude of defiance, put the weight backward on the heels.

THINGS TO AVOID. In the matter of weight distribution, the latitude is so wide that it is probably easier to suggest a few things not to do than to recommend what can or should be done.

1. Avoid a position of rigid military "attention." As a matter of fact, an experienced Army man can stand at attention and yet be quite relaxed. It is usually the "rookie" who draws himself up with every muscle tense.
2. Avoid placing the feet at an exact angle—any precise angle—intentionally or with the heels pressed tightly together.
3. Do not allow the positions of your feet and the distribution of weight to come into conflict.
4. Avoid placing all your weight on one leg which is held firmly under you, while the other is thrust forward much like the brace on a telephone pole. Keep your feet fairly close together for the most part; it looks better and gives you more flexibility.
5. Avoid constantly shifting your weight back and forth, forward and back on toe and heel or to and fro sidewise from one foot to the other. Hold your position steadily until you have reason to change.
6. On the other hand, avoid holding one position constantly from the beginning of your speech to the end; it will be equally tiresome to you and to your audience.

The Set of Your Body and Shoulders

Your carriage, which is revealed largely by the way you hold your shoulders, indicates to your audience much of your attitude toward yourself, toward them, and toward your relations with the audience. Without overdoing the backward thrust of the shoulders, maintain an erect posture with stomach drawn in and shoulders back, which will exhibit to your audience a decent self-respect. You can as a rule look for much the same degree of respect from your listeners as you reveal that you have for yourself, and little more. Therefore, your general bearing before them should grow out of a reasonable self-confidence in your own knowledge and skill and in your own integrity—your *ethical proof.*

Avoid overdoing such a carriage, however, for exaggeration will create an impression of overconfidence, of conceit, even of arrogance and condescension, attitudes which are certain to arouse unfavorable or antagonistic reactions. At the other extreme, it is equally important that you avoid seeming to be apologetic when you have nothing for which to apologize. There are few occasions when you need to apologize to your audience; on those occasions do it openly, frankly, just as you would under ordinary circumstances. It is the apologetic attitude which you should avoid.

Hold yourself erect, but do not draw yourself up rigidly, with every muscle tense and the shoulder blades pulled back so far they almost touch and all movement of the arms prevented. Let yourself relax, but don't sag; don't let your shoulders droop forward and your whole body slump. Don't allow yourself to assume the "question mark in parentheses" posture. The ideal is a mixture of *strength* and *ease,* the basis of gracefulness. It involves a balance of relaxation and tension—enough tension to give you alertness and enough relaxation to permit easy control of your whole expressive mechanism.

The Hands and Arms

What to do with the hands and arms is always a problem. It is little help to suggest that you do nothing, for doing nothing is in reality one of the most difficult and least effective things you can do on the platform. You will want to do something with them.

Probably the best thing you can do with your arms when you are not using them is simply to let them hang from the shoulders. In your practice you can determine where they should hang by letting them swing like pendulums, and if they are quite relaxed, they will come to rest at about the right place. But don't let them swing like that while you are speaking. There are very few things you cannot do; the occasion will determine some of the limits. On an informal occasion, you may now and then put your hand in your pocket—but don't keep it there. You may for a short while put your arms behind you, but don't allow them to get locked there; get them out where you can use them. If you have a reading stand, you may rest your hands lightly on its edges for a time; you may even lean your weight on the stand momentarily. But unless you are using a manuscript, get out now and then from behind the stand. There are many things you can do with your hands and arms; probably the best thing after all is to use them, as will be explained in more detail a little later in this chapter.

The Head and Neck

What has been said of the body and shoulders is equally applicable to the head and neck. The important thing is that you hold your head up so that you can establish and maintain eye contact with the audience and let your voice get out to them. Even when you are speaking from manuscript, have the paper so placed that you can hold your head up and not have to be bobbing up and down constantly as you shift attention from manuscript to listeners. What will usually happen when the manuscript is not properly placed is that you will finally give up and devote your attention to the paper. Thus the listeners are relegated to a secondary position—a status which they will not relish very long.

On the other hand, audiences are inclined to be long-suffering, at least in America. If they have come to hear a speaker because of his reputation or to hear him discuss something they are really interested in, they will put up with an amazing amount of poor speaking. It hardly seems fair to abuse their patience.

Hold your head up so that your eyes can look straight out; but don't let the whole musculature about the neck go tense. Move your head about, turning from one part of the audience to another, without, however, setting up anything like a rhythmic pattern.

MOVEMENT

However good your posture may be, you will want to vary your position; you will want to move about to give yourself some change and to afford some variety to your listeners. Furthermore, movement often helps you to make a point clearer or more emphatic. Finally, movement is one of the most effective remedies that can be prescribed for the ills resulting from nervousness.

That movement provides variety to yourself and to the audience needs no elaboration or explanation. You can easily become tired of just standing in one spot and will want to move about as a matter of relief. The audience will get tired of having to look constantly in one direction and will welcome the opportunity to move their eyes a little.

Movement may also be instrumental in indicating shifts in thought, in which case it serves somewhat as paragraph indentation does in writing. It furthermore serves to emphasize or to symbolize for the eye the verbal concepts of *but, on the other hand, still, however, therefore,* and so on.

Amount of Movement

You will probably be concerned with the problem of how much movement to use and what should be its nature. Again, the answer to these questions depends on the nature of the occasion

---

TYPES OF GESTURES

Top, the gesture of location. (Photo, L.S.U. Alumni News.) Bottom, the gesture of description. (Photo, Black Star.)

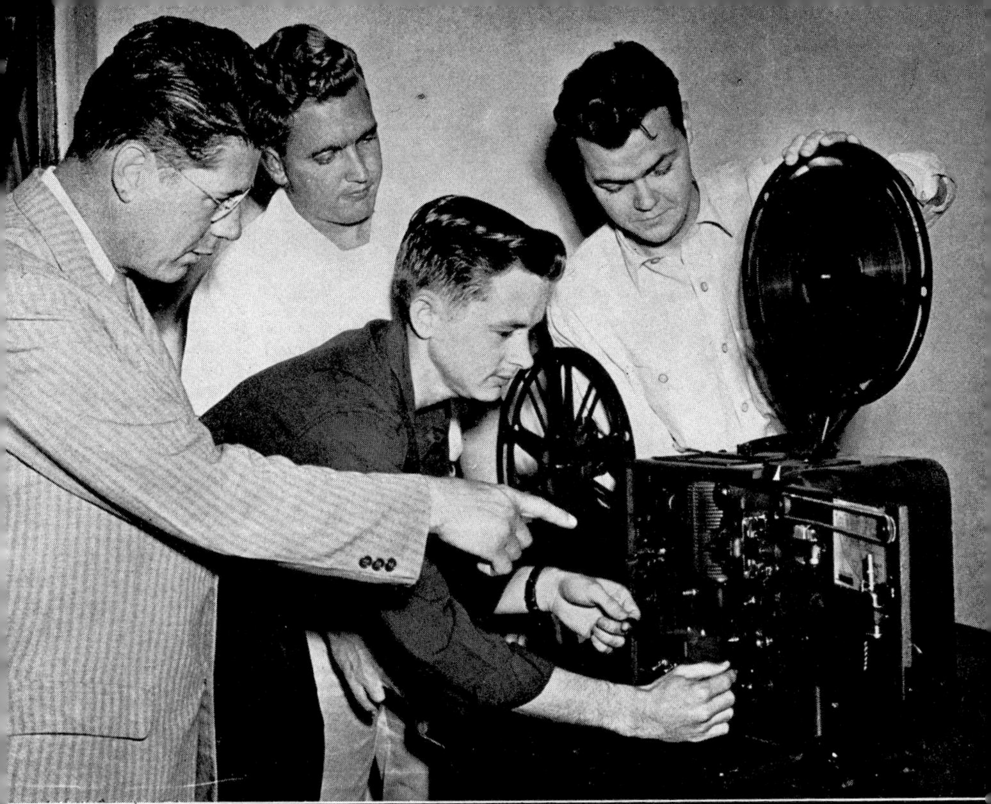
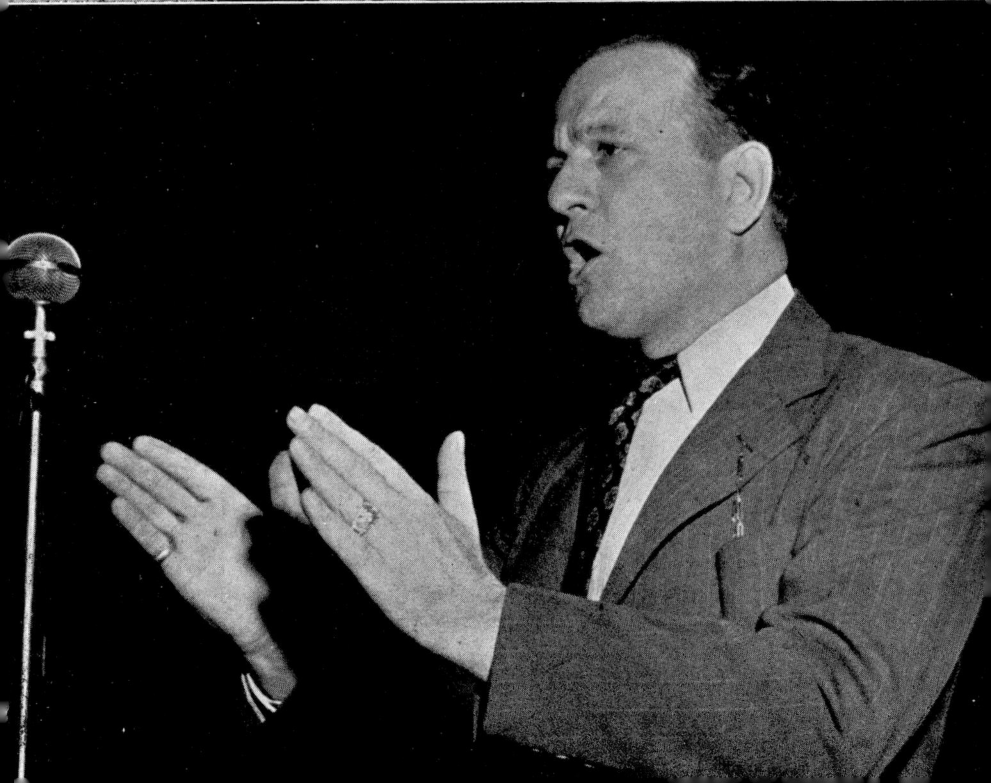

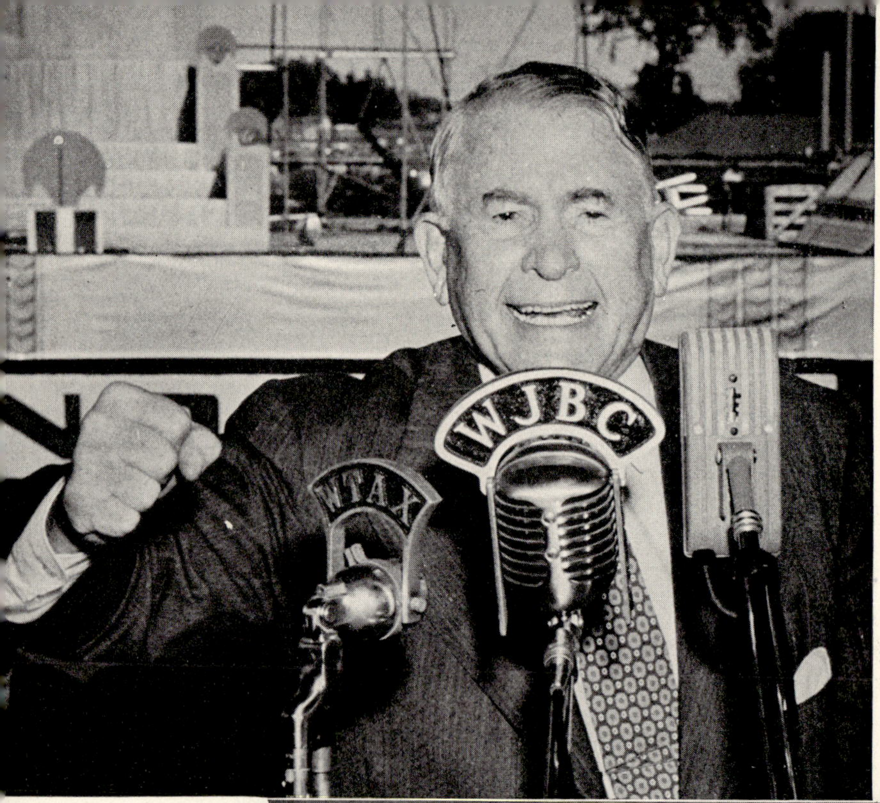
WTAX
WJBC

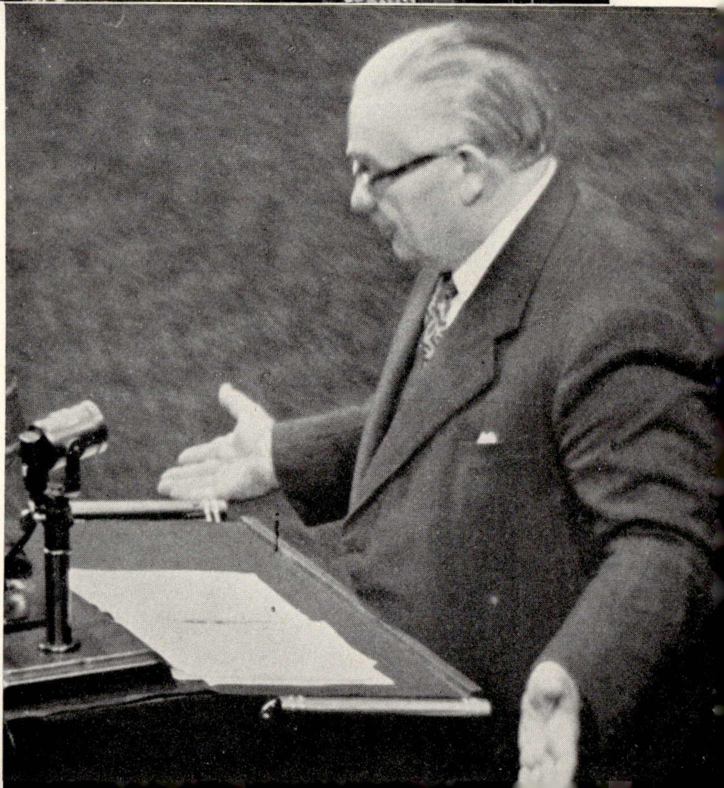

and the audience and on the type of response you are seeking from your listeners.

Sedentary audiences, that is, those whose occupations have accustomed them to relatively inactive existences, are likely to prefer the speaker who uses little movement, whereas those who habitually engage in active pursuits will respond more easily to more extensive and vigorous movement. Those whose interests call for fine distinctions, delicate discriminations, are likely to appreciate the smaller more discriminating actions on the part of the speaker. Occasions calling for highly emotional speaking, particularly when the excitatory emotional attitudes are involved, will likewise call for a large amount of movement; inhibitory emotional attitudes will demand the greatest reserve in the matter of movement.

Develop a keen sensitivity to the nature of the situation, and then learn to control the amount and type of movement to fit the occasion. Some of you will undoubtedly continue to use more than will others; but there are no absolutes; any prescriptions must of necessity be relative. But all of you, whether your tendency is to use much or little, can and should learn to govern your movements according to the demands of the situation.

GESTURE

The term gesture commonly refers to those movements of the hands and arms which often accompany the verbal aspects of speech. However, since in speaking as in other activities of the human mechanism the body tends to act as a whole and is most

---

TYPES OF GESTURES

The gesture of emphasis. Alben Barkley, Vice President of the United States, adds force to his point by using the clenched fist. (Photo, Black Star.)

The gesture of symbolism. Mr. Ernest Bevin, British statesman, uses the open palms to emphasize an attitude. (Photo, Black Star.)

efficient when acting as a whole, gesture properly involves the hands and arms, the head and eyes, the shoulders, body, legs, and feet, all parts of a coordinated whole. Although it is possible to describe a gesture as a matter primarily of the arms from the shoulders down to the fingers, actually with each such movement the head and eyes also move, the shoulders turn, the balance of weight shifts with the body, and the legs and feet change to allow for the shifted weight. One can almost say that in a well-coordinated gesture the whole body follows hands and arms; what the arm and hand do is only a part of the whole. The actual movement begins with the shoulders and as a rule is in a curved line from the center outward.

Functions of Gesture

Gesture serves both the speaker and the listener in the clarification of imagery. Distances, locations, dimensions, even abstractions, can often be clarified through imagery set up by gesture. Such clarification is of value to the speaker in that it is an aid in the development of his own thought; it is also an aid to the listener who is trying to grasp the meaning of the speaker.

But gestures do more than to clarify thought; they also help to intensify and make more impressive the attitudes the speaker is trying to build up. It is generally recognized that the more sensory avenues that can be utilized in entering consciousness, the more impressive the effect will be. Visible action in the form of communicative gestures provides one more sensory appeal.

Empathic Responses

Gestures help to build up what is known as empathic responses on the part of the hearers. You have all noticed when watching a football game how you tend to push in the direction your team is driving; or how, when you are watching a high jumper, you try to raise yourself off the ground as if to clear the bar yourself or at least to assist the jumper. Many of you are familiar with the "body english" often used by billiard players. These responses to observed actions, in which we tend to imitate the movement under observation, are what are called *empathic responses*.

Many such responses are conscious; at least, as in the instances just cited, they are easily observable, even though they are not intentionally made. But much as in the case of the subliminal stimuli, we also respond unconsciously to many types of movement, of lines, of masses, of balance, and the feeling we derive from our own responses determines whether the observed movement is pleasant or unpleasant. If you see someone perched precariously atop an unstable, swaying ladder, you yourself are uncomfortable because you feel the imbalance, the lack of stability, the possibility of falling. Similarly, a massive superstructure supported by thin, reedlike columns, is as unpleasant as a light, lacy structure supported by thick, heavy pillars. Compare the effect produced by pictures of the massive columns of the ancient Egyptian Temple of Karnak with those of the Parthenon. The perfectly proportioned columns of the ancient Greek architecture were so designed as to give a balance of height and thickness in relation to the mass they were supporting. The towering spires which surmounted the medieval cathedral as well as many modern churches achieve their effect through empathic response.

What has all this to do with gesture? Listeners tend, however unconsciously, to follow the actions and movements of the speaker. They enter into what he is doing and in following his behavior experience with him his emotions and feelings. Once you have aroused these attitudes, you have succeeded in large part in getting the response you set out to get in the first place.

Types of Gesture

Gestures may generally be divided or classified into four main types: gestures of location, gestures of description, gestures of emphasis, and gestures of symbolism.

1. GESTURES OF LOCATION. In gestures of location you point out the exact or approximate locations of the things you are talk-

ing about, which you want placed in space for your listeners. You place various objects in spatial relations one with another. You indicate directions, expansiveness, and areas. You visualize these spatial relations for your audience.

In gestures of location you will need to distinguish between the literal and the figurative. You will no doubt describe scenes and actions that are not within the vision of your audience or within the physical limits of your immediate locality. Place them imaginatively somewhere out in front of you, and let the imagination of the listeners fill in the details. As Winans suggests,[6] you do not need to be exact literally in referring to points of the compass, but you do need to be consistent.

If your object is at a distance, indicate that distance by elevating the arm above the horizon and by letting the eyes look off beyond the confines of the auditorium in which you are speaking. Lowering the level of the arm and letting the eyes focus on a point about where you are placing the object will give the idea of nearness. Do not look at your hands—look at the place where the object is supposed to be.

If you want to suggest great distances as covered in some extensive movement, such as from the Atlantic Coast to the Pacific, do not place the two terminals directly opposite with yourself in the middle; let the extent of your own movement be sufficiently broad and sweeping from one side to the other to create the suggestion of the vast distance covered. Great distances can be indicated by an extended sweep of the arm or arms; small distances can be suggested by delicate, fine movements of the hands and fingers.

Develop the ability to suggest locations, movements, positions. Once you have located an object in one position, keep it there, unless in your discussion a change is indicated. In describing a scene, keep yourself out of it; do not build the scene with your-

[6] James A. Winans, *Speech-Making*, Appleton-Century-Crofts, Inc., 1938, pp. 444-445.

self as center. Place it outside of you—out in front—and build it up through suggestion and imagination. Your audience will complete the picture from their own imaginations and probably get a better one than you can draw for them.

2. GESTURES OF DESCRIPTION. You will often be faced with the necessity of giving descriptive details of some object which you do not have with you. You can frequently give enough detail so that your listeners will get a satisfactorily accurate picture for the immediate purpose. You can indicate sizes and shapes; you can suggest the type of movement involved, if any, and the relative location of significant parts. In this respect, gestures of description are somewhat similar to those of location.

In this type of gesture, as in that of location, both literal and figurative (imaginative or suggestive) gestures can be used. In describing sizes and shapes, the literal will probably be most useful; that is, you will attempt actually to indicate the size and shape unless, of course, the size is beyond your reach, in which case you will resort to suggestion.

In representing type of action, you will probably find figurative or suggestive gestures more appropriate. As a rule, attempts to imitate the action or type of action you are describing should be made with extreme caution. Suppose you are telling about an old man tottering down the street, as in the first stanza of "The Last Leaf,"

> I saw him once before,
> As he passed by the door
> And again
> The pavement stones resound
> As he totters o'er the ground
> With his cane.

If you demonstrated the tottering, you would be describing that action in your own individuality and not that of the old man. You cannot, even in imagination, *be* the old man and yourself at the same time. If you were telling about Stephen Leacock's knight and trying at the same time to imitate him, you would certainly encounter difficulties, for you will remember that he mounted his horse and rode off in all directions!

On the other hand, if you are clearly demonstrating some action or movement, such as a dance step or a golf or tennis stroke, you would certainly give an illustration of the movements involved. Then, too, imitation may often be used for humorous effects, although in such instances the imitation may be essentially exaggerated suggestion. As in so many of the techniques of speech, much depends on your purpose and on the effect you want to create.

3. GESTURES OF EMPHASIS. If you speak with due regard to giving proper emphasis to your language, you will find yourself placing more stress on some words than on others. The degree of stress will usually depend on the strength of the attitude you yourself feel and which you want to stimulate in your hearers. If you are permitting the rest of your communicative mechanism to make its contribution to the speaking act, not all this emphasis will be vocal. Part of it will be visible; it will consist of certain definite strokes of the hand and arm which accompany the emphatic word or phrase. These strokes are helpful in giving visible emphasis and thus reinforcing the vocal; they help also in creating vocal emphasis, for it is well-nigh impossible to give a strong, vigorous movement of the clenched hand, for instance, without increasing the force with which the accompanying word is uttered.

Most gestures of simple emphasis consist of such downward strokes, sometimes of the open hand, sometimes of the index finger, sometimes of the clenched fist. Pounding the lectern or stamping the foot for emphasis were once considered good form; nowadays they are indulged in only in extreme cases and then when the speaker is almost beside himself in the intensity of his emotion. Generally they are not to be recommended.

Gestures of emphasis consist of three separate parts, all blended together to make one unified whole: the *approach*, the *stroke* or *ictus*, and the *return*, or *recovery*. In the approach you move into the position for the essential part of the gesture, the stroke. Often this is done unobtrusively, though not secretively; it can be made a significant part of the whole. The stroke or ictus is, as the term indicates, a short, sudden movement of the hand or finger coming exactly on the word or phrase to be emphasized; it embodies the significance of the gesture. On the return the hand and arm are permitted to go back unnoticed to some neutral position, or they may make the approach to the next gesture.

All this sounds as if it might be thoroughly mechanical. In practicing these gestures and parts of gestures, it *will* be mechanical, and it should. Just as in the learning of any skill, you must pass through a stage in which every movement and every aspect of each movement are consciously and rigidly controlled. That is the only way in which you can ever learn effective form for doing anything involving skill. You must pass through a mechanical period; there is no short cut.

But it is only in your practice that you should be conscious of your every movement. In your actual speaking, in which you are attempting to influence your audiences, let the situation take care of itself. Do your practicing before you appear before your listeners and not while you are standing before them.

4. GESTURES OF SYMBOLISM. Gestures of location and of description are for the most part representative of concrete ideas. Gestures of emphasis are somewhat more abstract; they add the increased visible force to an increased audible force to produce a unified effect of emphasis. Gestures of symbolism are for the most part abstract, although they are based on quite understandable physical reactions to various stimuli.

In presenting an idea, for example, you may use a gesture very much like presenting a book or some other object. If you ask a question, you may hold out your hand as if, having asked for a gift, you reach out to receive it. A balance of ideas may be suggested by extending both hands, as if you were either presenting one idea with each hand or comparing the weights of two objects. Aversion may be indicated by turning away or by an outward thrust of the hands with the palms turned outward; benediction by extending the hands up and in front of you with the palms down. The same position with the palms up may suggest supplication.

It is impossible to suggest all the possible movements and positions of the hands and arms that can be used to symbolize attitudes and even simple ideas having a minimum of emotional content. As a rule, the stronger the emotional component of meaning, the more vigorous and intense the gesture; the stronger the logical component, the more restricted, discriminating, and controlled the gesture. As Woolbert says, "There is no limit to which an intelligent person can go in adding expressiveness to his ideas and facts by means of intellectual gestures. He can count and enumerate, point out, indicate place and relations, measure, compare, wipe out, appeal, push, pull, strike, invite, call. He can do many more, in almost infinite permutations and combinations, limited only by his ingenuity and his willingness to help his audience. The more he gains mastery over the intellectual gesture, the more fully and satisfactorily can he carry meaning and convince his audience that he means what he says."[7]

FACIAL EXPRESSION

You may have formed the impression from what has been said as to the importance of posture, movement, and gesture that your listeners are going to be watching closely every movement, every gesture that you make; that they will be conscious of each step you take, each raising of the hand, each change of position. In short, you may by now feel that everything you do will be reviewed in detail and that the success or failure of your speech will depend on what your audience thinks of your physical behavior on the platform.

The sober truth is that, if these actions are what they should be, namely, a part of the total communicative process, your

[7] Woolbert and Smith, *op. cit.*, p. 137.

audience will not notice specifically and consciously just what you are doing. Your listeners are far more likely to notice what you are doing if your physical actions are *not* what they ought to be. Your behavior on the platform will partake somewhat of the nature of the subliminal stimuli discussed earlier in this chapter. Your audience will not be watching your hands, your arms, your feet; these parts of your expressive mechanism, if they are functioning effectively, will be relegated to the fringes of consciousness. They will have their effect; make no mistake about that. But they will make their impression as a part of the *total communicative process.*

What does an audience look at? They will look at your face, your eyes, your hands, your arms, unless you use them all to direct the attention elsewhere. What they see will go far toward determining their judgment of your attitude toward them, toward the subject, toward the speaking situation, more than anything else that your face and eyes reveal.

Audience Contact

It is through the eyes perhaps more than through any other agency that contact with the audience is established and maintained. It is absurd to insist that you must keep your eyes constantly on the audience and to estimate the degree of rapport with your hearers by counting the number of times you look away. Looking off over the heads of your listeners, up at the ceiling, out the window, down at the floor, can all be done without breaking audience contact, provided that you do them only occasionally, that you do them for a definite purpose or effect, and that you constantly return to the audience. Looking now and then at individual members of the audience often gives them the feeling that you are interested in them and in imparting to them what you have to say. It is especially appropriate when there is a measure of audience participation involved. Do not overdo such selection, however; it may be embarrassing to the person so singled out, and it may make others feel that some discrimination is being practiced.

Eye Movement

Shift your glance from one part of the audience to another, so that you will within a short time have recognized the presence of every section. Let them feel that you have seen them and are addressing your speech to them as much as to anyone else. At the same time, avoid giving the impression of "shifty" eyes. Do not let your eyes be constantly moving, apparently never meeting other eyes and never remaining even momentarily fixed on some portion of the audience. In giving the impression of thinking through some solution, you may even fix your eyes on some indefinite spot in space. Generally, however, let your eyes rest occasionally now on one, now on another general area, the movement from one to the other being definite and purposeful. Shifty eyes in a speaker create at least two impressions: first, they give the impression of doubtful personal integrity, and second, of vagueness of thought and purpose. They suggest an unwillingness to meet a possible opposition on comparable terms.

Reflection of Mood

The entire face should mirror the general mood or attitude. It has been said that "the face should wear a genial expression." If the mood is one of geniality, well and good; but sometimes the mood you want has little of the genial in it. You may be deadly serious. You may even be solemn. The face then has no business with a genial expression. If the situation calls for seriousness, you should *look* serious. If it calls for merriment, don't be a "sourpuss."

Do not try, as a rule, to assume the expression of a mood that you cannot feel. Essentially, this means that your expression should be a sincere reflection of your mood. There will be occasions when you are under obligation to speak even though you do not feel like it at the moment. If it is an occasion worthy of your time and effort, though, make every effort to meet the general temper of the situation.

Avoid, too, allowing your face to assume a "dead-pan" expression, without life or animation. A masklike, expressionless face is about as uninspiring and uninteresting as a lump of putty; it has no character, no communicativeness, nothing that will stimulate or sustain the interest of the audience. It indicates a dull, sluggish, uninterested and uninteresting person back of it. Let your entire facial expression be alive, alert, responsive to the constantly shifting moods of the speech. Avoid anything resembling a set expression—one which is assumed at the outset and maintained throughout so that it becomes nothing more than a mask. Keep in mind that what serves as a stimulus is change, variety, deviation from a more or less constant background; the principle is just as valid for facial expression as it is for any other type of stimulus.

Facial Exercise

The essential requirements for effective facial expression are, first, responsiveness to the changing emotional aspects of the total stimulus pattern, and second, mobility of facial muscles. The first of these has already been discussed. For mobility of facial muscles it is necessary to give them plenty of exercise, especially those about the eyes and mouth.

Practice moving the eyes themselves up and down, sidewise, in a rotary motion clockwise and counterclockwise, in order to strengthen the muscles. Practice also focusing them at different distances; far away, close at hand, and at intermediate points. Your audience will be able to tell whether you are looking "a mile or so away" or here, close at hand, by the focus of your eyes. Therefore it is necessary that you be able to adjust the focus just as you do in viewing near and distant objects.

Exercise also the muscles of the eyebrows, the eyelids, and forehead in order to tone them up, for that is one of the regions that make the face particularly expressive. The muscles about the mouth also, which should be very active in the process of articulation, are important in contributing to the expressiveness of the lower part of the face. Strengthening them, therefore, will add to facility of expression and to sharpness of articulation and distinctness of utterance at the same time. Do not be afraid to use the musculature of the lips and tongue vigorously; in practice exaggerate their movements, so that in actual speaking they will tone down somewhat and be just about right.

You may find it helpful as well as interesting simply to stand before a mirror and make all manner of faces at yourself. Do not be afraid of wrinkles. The face which arrives at an advanced degree of maturity without having acquired a few is likely to be an utterly vapid, expressionless, characterless visage, evidence of an individual who has never felt deeply. Wrinkles acquired as a result of honest thinking, the satisfaction of worthy motives, the experiencing of wholesome emotions, and the labor engaged in to advance the welfare of human society are an indication of a life well spent. ". . . whereas Demosthenes himself (we are told) did not succeed in his first attempts, through his having neglected to study action, he arrived afterwards at such a pitch in that faculty, that when the people of Rhodes expressed in high terms their admiration of his famous oration for Ctesiphon, upon hearing it read with a very sweet and strong voice by Aeschines, whose banishment it had procured, that great and candid judge said to them, How would you have been affected, had you seen him speak it! For he that *only hears* Demosthenes loses much the better part of the oration."[8]

EXERCISES

1. Examine your own posture with a view to its improvement. Practice on the correction of faults in general bearing, such as slumping, draping yourself over the reading stand, drawing yourself up too rigidly, locking your arms behind you, or any other things you may do to make your posture ineffective.
2. Practice on the positions of the feet and the various distributions of weight until they seem quite "natural," that is, until they become

[8] Fordyce, *Theocorus: A Dialogue Concerning the Art of Preaching, and Sermon on The Eloquence of the Pulpit*, 1752. Quoted in Increase Cooke, *The American Orator*, John Babcock & Son, 1819, pp. 137-139.

BODILY ASPECTS OF DELIVERY

habitual. Observe whether any of these general postures seem to be associated with any particular emotional attitudes.
3. Practice, while imagining that you are standing before an audience, moving about, changing foot positions, weight distributions, even complete changes of position, seldom turning much more than one quarter away from any major portion of your audience.
4. Study various possible positions of the arms and hands, extending them vertically from straight downward up through various angles to directly overhead. Note whether the different angles seem to suggest different attitudes.
5. Add to the various arm positions described in Exercise 4 various hand positions, with palm down, palm up, palm vertical, palm turned away from the body. Observe and report on any differences you can sense in these different positions. Be sure to achieve, in connection with these positions, a balance with the entire body.
6. Bring to class some object which you will use to demonstrate the construction, the operation, or the product of an operation. Be sure that (a) the article is large enough for everyone to see; (b) that it is simple enough for everyone to see all the significant parts; and (c) that the demonstration itself is communicative.
7. Make use of a drawing or a chart to explain a process, construction, or statistical analysis. As in the exercise above, be sure (a) that your drawing is large enough and that the lines are heavy enough for everyone to see easily; (b) that your drawing is not too complicated to be easily grasped; (c) that the presentation of the diagram is itself an act of communication; and (d) that you give your audience the major part of your attention.
8. Give a descriptive speech in which you make use of your hands to present the descriptive details.
9. Describe a scene, placing it imaginatively out in front of you and placing by gestures of location the various important details of the scene.
10. Tell a story or describe a situation by means of pantomime only. Use no words even as an introduction. Try to make your pantomime so clear that the class will have no difficulty in identifying what you are trying to do.

SUPPLEMENTARY READINGS

1. Baird, A. Craig, and Knower, Franklin H., *General Speech, An Introduction*, McGraw-Hill Book Company, Inc., 1949, chap. 15, "Bodily Action and Visual Aids for Speech," pp. 259-279.

2. Bryant, Donald C., and Wallace, Karl R., *Fundamentals of Public Speaking*, Appleton-Century-Crofts, Inc., 1947, pp. 346-351.
3. Oliver, Robert T., Cortright, Rupert L., and Hager, Cyril F., *The New Training for Effective Speech*, The Dryden Press, Inc., 1947, chap. 9, "The Speaker's Action," pp. 189-215.
4. Sandford, William Phillips, and Yeager, Willard Hayes, *Principles of Effective Speaking*, The Ronald Press Company, 4th ed., 1942, chap. 17, "The Body in Delivery," pp. 236-253.
5. Sarett, Lew, and Foster, William Trufant, *Basic Principles of Speech*, Houghton Mifflin Company, rev. ed., 1946, chap. 5, "Bodily Action," pp. 127-150; chap. 6, "A Method of Self-Motivated Action," pp. 151-164; chap. 7, "Principles of Bodily Action," pp. 165-199.
6. Winans, James A., *Speech-Making*, Appleton-Century-Crofts, Inc., 1938, chap. XXI, "Gesture," pp. 428-451.
7. Woolbert, Charles Henry, and Smith, Joseph F., *The Fundamentals of Speech*, Harper & Brothers, 3rd ed., 1934, chap. VI, "Total Bodily Action and the Speaker," pp. 81-105; chap. VII, "Gesture and the Audience," pp. 106-143.

INDEX OF AUTHORS AND SPEAKERS CITED

Abbott, Lyman, 130
Adler, Mortimer J., 158
Ainslie, George, 251-252
Alexander, Ruth, 432
Ames, Fisher, 432
Aristotle, 355, 375, 407
Atkins, J. Witt, 395
Auer, J. Jeffery, 103

Bacher, Robert F., 103
Baird, A. Craig, 228, 291, 295
Baker, George Pierce, and Huntington, Henry Barrett, 74
Ball, Max W., 455
Barton, Bruce, 93, 96, 305, 338, 369-370
Baruch, Bernard M., 337
Beecher, Henry Ward, 16, 130, 374-375
Behl, William A., 161
Beveridge, Albert J., 38, 164
Bible, 84, 446
Black, Jeremiah S., 448
Bogart, Ernest C., 455
Bollinger, Dwight L., 505
Borah, William E., 282, 296, 301
Borden, Richard C., 38
Bowles, Chester, 385
Boyer, Lee Emerson, 14
Braden, Waldo W., 159
Brigance, William Norwood, 301, 366, 378, 415, 423

Brown, Alice, 62
Brown, Harrison S., 434
Brown, Stuart Gerry, 399
Bryan, William Jennings, 14, 128

Caldwell, John Tyler, 376, 444
Campbell, George, 441-442
Carleton, William G., 46-47
Carter, Boake, 193
Cassiodorus, 395
Churchill, Winston, 120, 303-304, 429, 447
Cicero, 11, 345-346
Clemens, Samuel L., 101, 425
Compton, Karl T., 448
Conant, James Bryant, 444
Conwell, Russell, 116-117, 128
Cooley, Charles Horton, 477
Cooper, Lane, 258, 348, 373
Corwin, Tom, 104
Craig, Alice Evelyn, 478
Cummings, Parke, 407
Curtis, George William, 419, 431

Daniell, Raymond, 333
Darrow, Clarence, 374
Dashiell, John Frederick, 85
Delaney, Harry J., 277-278
Denny, George, 91
Depew, Chauncey M., 445
Deutsch, Eberhard P., 400
Dewey, John, 55, 209, 410

INDEX

Douglas, Helen Gahagan, 457-458
Dunlap, Knight, 467
DuPont, Henry B., 457

Eisenson, Jon, 344
Elliston, Herbert, 445
Emerson, Ralph Waldo, 19, 158, 424
Ernst, Morris, 289

Fairbanks, Grant, 511
Fellers, Charles, 387-389
Ferris, Elmer E., 340
Fordyce, 564
Forrestal, James V., 254
Fosdick, Raymond B., 365, 446
Foster, William Trufant, 298
Franks, Maurice R., 450
Fulkerson, Roe, 283, 343
Furnass, Joseph Chamberlain, 452

Gallup, George, 124
Gayley, Charles Mills, 445
Gehring, Mary Louise, 165
Generazzo, Walter, 10
Genung, John F., 189-190, 195
Gittelsohn, Roland B., 382
Gough, John B., 434
Grady, Henry W., 93, 339, 340, 422, 426, 431, 447, 457, 510
Gray, Giles Wilkeson, 479, 525, 540
Gray, Giles Wilkeson, and Wise, Claude Merton, 72, 396, 530, 540
Groves, Walter Alexander, 297

Haddon, W. C., 287
Harris, Rufus Carrolton, 432
Hedley, George, 449-450
Henry, Patrick, 295, 384, 422
Hill, Adams Sherman, 398, 434, 441
Hitler, Adolph, 20
Hollingworth, H. L., 119, 124
Holmes, Oliver Wendell, 557
Hoover, Herbert, 431
Hostetter, Gordon L., 452
Howell, Wilbur Samuel, and Hudson, Hoyt Hopewell, 257
Humphrey, Laurence, 10

James, William, 92

Jones, Daniel, 532
Judd, Charles Hubbard, 402

Kahn, Otto H., 346
Kemmerer, Edwin W., 363
Kenyon, John S., and Knott, Thomas A., 532
Kincaid, Robert L., 421
Knott, Thomas A., 523

Larrabee, Harold A., 285
Lee, Josh, 344
Lilienthal, David E., 342, 444
Lincoln, Abraham, 15, 84, 255, 349, 410-412, 428, 507
Lippmann, Walter, 120, 365
Lodge, Henry Cabot, 253
Longfellow, Henry Wadsworth, 38
Lowell, James Russell, 267
Luckman, Charles, 431, 446, 454
Lundberg, Alfred J., 282

Manders, H. E., 196
Mann, Thomas, 4
Martin, Dr. M. P., 2
Mathews, Dean Shailer, 247
Mayhew, Jonathan, 431
Mills, Glen, 161
Morrow, Edwin P., 445
Musmanno, M. A., 193-194

Oliver, Robert T., 7, 481
Overstreet, H. A., 116, 339, 343, 345

Palmer, George Herbert, 515
Pepper, Claude, 379-380
Pettengill, Samuel B., 442-443
Phillips, Wendell, 128, 258-259
Plato, 10

Quintilian, 21, 461, 465

Randall, James G., 160
Rayburn, Sam, 247, 277
Reid, Loren D., 101
Robinson, Zon, 120
Roosevelt, Franklin D., 119, 376-377, 381, 449

INDEX

Roosevelt, Theodore, 446
Ruch, Floyd L., 54

St. Paul, 22
Sandford, William Phillips, and Yeager, Willard Hayes, 420, 489
Sarett, Lew, and Foster, William Trufant, 545
Sayre, Francis B., 378, 433
Schlesinger, Arthur M., Jr., 397
Scott, William, 505
Seymour, Charles, 284, 290, 308-315
Shakespeare, William, 132-137, 418
Simpson, Lee F., 17
Smith, Elizabeth, 248
Smith, Joseph F., 21
Sockman, Ralph W., 432
Spencer, Herbert, 399, 424, 426, 440
Stoddard, George D., 11, 103
Sumner, G. Lynn, 246, 249

Taeusch, Carl F., 19
Talmage, Thomas DeWitt, 128, 365
Thompson, Dorothy, 431, 434
Thonssen, Lester, and Baird, A. Craig, 15, 20

Thruelson, Richard, 3
Truman, Harry, 344, 451

Vandenburg, Arthur H., 68, 276, 349-350, 380
Vives, Juan Luis, 395

Wallace, Henry A., 451
Washington, Booker T., 126, 284
Watterson, Henry, 433
Webber, Lane D., 454
Webster, Daniel, 261, 383-384, 431, 456
Whately, Richard, 372
Wiksell, Wesley A., 494
Williams, John Sharp, 449
Williamson, Arleigh B., 502
Wilson, Woodrow, 382
Winans, James A., 72, 89, 303, 404, 424, 556
Woodland, James, 230-235
Woodworth, Robert S., 86, 461, 462, 463, 470
Woolbert, Charles Henry, 394, 428, 441, 471, 484-485, 488, 515, 560
Woolbert, Charles Henry, and Smith, Joseph F., 548

INDEX OF SUBJECTS

Abdominal breathing, 494
Ability to speak important, 2, 3
Abstract terms, 396; abstract words, 424; abstractions, 419
Accent, 504; misplaced, 526-527 *See also* Pronunciation
Acceptability, as basis for order of points, 362
Acceptance, speech of, 254-255; Purposes, 255; Acceptance and Presentation, Speeches of, 252-255
"Acres of Diamonds," 165; theme of, 155
Actionless speaking, non-existent, 541
Activity and Delivery, applied to Attention and Interest, 96-97
Actuating, as form of response, 144-145
Adam's apple, 497
Adaptation, 80
Aeschines, 564
After-dinner speaking, 264-270; difficulty of definition, 265; distinguishing characteristics, 266; elements of preparation, 266-267; planning a toast program, 269-270; subjects for, 265-266; the toastmaster, 268-269; violations of good practice, 268-270
Air cavities, in voice production, 498

Allusions, and Impressiveness, 444-447; literary and Biblical, 9
American College Dictionary, 532
American Medical Association, 17
Amplification, Summary of means of, 305
Analogy or comparison, 300-302; tests of, 301-302
Analysis and Synthesis, Summary of steps, 238
Animation, delivery and, 482-483
Anticlimactic order, 367-368
Antioch, 6
Appeal, as type of Conclusion, 379-381
Appeals to attention and interest, 90-104; activity, 96-97; activity and delivery, 97; concrete, 95; humor, 99-104; new and old, 92-94; struggle, 99; suspense, 98-99; vital, 90-91
Appraisal and criticism, 198-199; analysis of, 199
Approach, in gestures of emphasis, 558-559
Argumentative talk, Biography of, 221-223; evaluation sheet for, 242; framing the proposition, 213-214; kinds of proposition, 210-213; outlining for, 209; 220-227; specimen outlines of, 223-227; summary of steps in analysis and synthesis,

INDEX

238; the proposition, 210-220; wording the proposition, 214-217
Argumentative and Stimulating talks compared, 209-210
Aristotle, 2, 355, 373, 375
Arnold, Matthew, 7
Articulation, 516-521; and breath pressure, 517-519; and consonant position, 519; and distinctness, 516; and timbre, 517; consonant formation, 517-519; criteria for well-formed consonants, 518-519
Ashurst, Senator, 12
Assembling, Basis for, 121-124; and approach, 123-124
Atomic energies, potentialities of, 19
Attention and Interest: appeals to, 90-104; as strain, 87-88; defined, 78-79; derived primary, 87-88; differentiated, 81; factors of, 81-85 (interest, effect of, 85; magnitude, 83; reference to experience, 84-85; repetition, 84); involuntary, 86-87; primary, 86-87; types of, 86-88; voluntary, 87
Attitude, of audience toward speaker, 127-128; of listener, 43-44; of student toward public speaking, 2; toward criticism, 40-42; toward subject, 148
Attitudes, fixed, toward subject, 126
Audible method of delivery, 479
Audience, 116-131; and movement, 552; analysis of, 118-131; analysis based on human relations, 118-119; analysis and motivation, 118-119; analysis, sources of information for, 117-119; attitude toward speaker, 127-128; attitude toward subject, 148; contact with, 561; control and "balance of power," 130-131; homogeneity of, 124-125; immediate and remote, 120-121; knowledge of speaker, 127-128; knowledge of subject, 128-129; nature of, 118-121; neutral, 149; opposed, 149-150; partisan, 149; posterity as, 120-121; radio, 120; response, 139-141; types of: casual or spontaneous, 121-122; concerted, 123; discussional or conversational, 122; inactive, 122-123; selected, 123
Audiences not passive, 89-90
Authority, tests of, 286

Background, general, for speaking, 156-158
"Balance of power" in audience control, 130-131
Barton, Bruce, 385
Basil, St., 6
Beecher, Henry Ward, 7, 130
Beginning speaker, advice to, 28
Behavior, bases of, 52-53; motives and, 54
Beveridge, Albert J., 448, 516
Bibliography, 168-169
"Blood, sweat, and tears," 21
Body and shoulders, set of, 549, 550
Bodily patterns, memorizing of, 471
Book report, 271-272; development of, 271; summary of, 272
Books as reference, 169
Borah, William E., 157, 159, 282
Breath pressure and articulation, 517-518, 519
Breathiness, 503
Breathing, 494-496; abdominal, 494; adequate pressure in, 495; adequate reserve in, 495-496; conscious control of, 494-496; diaphragmatic, 494, purposes of, 495; requirements of, 495-496; steadiness of pressure in, 496
Brevity, 407-408
Brief, The, 227-236; Brief proper, the, 229-235; Conclusion, 236; Introduction, 228-229; Logical structure, 236-238; Parts of, 228-236; Summary chart of, 237; Résumé of rules for, 236
Brigance, W. N., 355
Broad knowledge needed, 8-11
Bryan, William Jennings, 4, 7, 14, 128, 516
Bunyan, John, 96
Burke, Edmund, 156
Byron, Lord, 83

Caldwell, President John Tyler, 444
Calhoun, John C., 156
Carriage, 545, 549, 550; exaggeration of, 550
Carter, Boake, 193
Casual or spontaneous group, 121-122
Causal inference, hazards in, 298
Causal reasoning, 296-300; tests of, 299-300; cause-to-effect inference, 296-297
Census reports, and audience analysis, 117
Central thought, framing a, 30; in discussion, 357-358; in informative speech, 357-358
Chairman, duties of, 249-250
Challenge, as type of conclusion, 381-383
Change, Attention value of, 82-83
Characteristic traits, *see* Metonymy
Chicago Round Table, 163
Chrysostom, St. John, 6
Church Fathers, 6
Churchill, Rev. J. W., 7
Churchill, Winston, 4, 21, 120, 304, 333, 423-424
Cicero, 2, 4, 6, 156; Orations, 6
Clarification, as aim in speaking, 14
Clarity, achieving, 395-410; definition of, 394; Impressiveness, Vividness, and, 440-441
Classification and differentiation, as method of definition, 399
Clearness of thinking, 16
Climactic order of points, 367-368
Commemorative speech, 260-261; compared to speech of inspiration, 261; method and substance, 261
Commendation, The, 260
Communicate, Urge to, 11-13
Communicating ideas, 391-392
Communicative process, the total, 560-561
Communicative situation, 12
Community of reference, 408-410
Complexity, as basis of order of points, 362
Conant, President James Bryant, 444-445

Conclusion, Adapting to speaking situation, 385; elements of, 373-385; personal elements in, 373-375; planning a short, 33; type of, appeal, 379-381; type of, challenge, 381-383; type of, declaration of personal intention, 383-384; type of, restatement, 375-377; types of, summary of, 377-379; type of, visualization of future, 384-385
Concerted audience, 123
Concrete, as appeal to attention and interest, 95
Concrete terms, 395-396
Concreteness and vividness, 423-426
Confrontation, 539-541
Consonant combinations, 520-521; archaic, 521
Consonant formation, 517-519; and articulation, 516-519; criteria for well-formed, 519
Consonants, positions of, 519
Context, as method of definition, 400
Contiguity, as basis for arranging details, 191-192
Conviction, as form of response, 143-144
Conwell, Russell H., 116, 128, 155, 165
Corax, 2
Courtesy, Speeches of, 245-256; characteristics of, 245-246
Criticism, Appraisal and, 198-199
Criticism, Attitude toward, 402; by listeners, 44
"Cross of Gold" speech, 7
Curiosity, methods of arousing, 337-338

Declaration of Personal Intention, as type of conclusion, 383-384
Deduction, as form of reasoning, 293-296
Deductive order in Discussion, 358
Definition, methods of: classification and differentiation, 399; etymology, 401; example, 398-403; negation, 402; purpose or effect, 402;

INDEX

synonym, 400-401; use of context, 400; verbal, 399
Delivery, and animation, 482-483; and excessive tensions, 485-490; and meaning, 477-479; and "naturalness," 483-485; and variety, 482; in the Introduction, 335-336; basic principles of, 480-490; importance of, 475-477; inescapable in speech, 480; of the speech, 37; summary of principles, 490; two aspects of, 479-480; visible aspects of, 539
Democracy, purpose of, 18-20; techniques of, 20
Democratic order, effectiveness of, 3
Democratic way of life, form of society, defined, 18
Demosthenes, 6; and stage-fright, 486
Depew, Chauncey M., 7, 516
Derived primary attention, 87-88
Description, as supporting material, 282-283 details and impressiveness, 455-458, gestures of, 557-558
Descriptive words, vividness and, 425-426
Deutsch, Eberhard P., 400
Dewey, John, formula for reflective thought, 209-210
Diacritical marks, 532
Diaphragmatic breathing, 494
Dictionaries, and pronunciation, 523-524; "unabridged," 532-533
Dictionary, American College, 398, 532; Daniel Jones', 531; Kenyon-Knott, 532; Use of, 531-533; Webster, 531
Discussion, Central thought in, 357-358; deductive order in, 358; plan of, 355; inductive order in, 358-359; patterns of partition, 360-363; requirements of, 356-357
Discussional or conversational groups, 122
Distinctness, important points in, 518-519
Distribution of weight, 547-549; and attitudes, 549; and positions of feet, 548-549; things to avoid, 549

Dixiecrats, 150
Douglas, Helen Gahagan, 348
Douglas, Stephen A., 116, 127
Dramatic pause, 509-510
Dunbar, Paul Lawrence, 7

Early speeches, Approach to, 26
Eastern speech, 524
Effect-to-cause inference, 297; effect-to-effect inference, 298
Egyptians, 1
Einstein, 4
Elisions, general, 529-530
Emerson, 158-159
Empathic responses, 554-555
Emphasis, 505-506; and accent, differentiated, 505; gestures of, 558-559
Emphasizing important points, 367-368
Emotional behavior, significant characteristics of, 542
Emotional biases, 13; affecting thinking, 13-14
Entertain, speeches to, 263-264
Entertaining, as type of response, 142
Entertaining speeches, basic requirements of, 264; book report and review, 271-272; characteristics of, 264-265; story telling, 270-271
Ethical proof, 545
Ethical standards of speaker, 21
Ethical values, 19
Ethics needed, 16-17
Etymology, as method of definition, 401
Eulogy, the, 257-260; sources of evidence used, 258; subpoints for, 259-260; suggestions for preparing, 258-259
Evaluation chart for argumentative talks, 242
Everett, Edward, 112, 167
Evidence, collecting, 174-175
Example, as method of definition, 402-403; as supporting material, 289-291; factual, 96; fictitious, 96, hypothetical, 96-97
Exercises in inflection, 513-514
Experiences, in speaking, 26-27

INDEX

Explanation, as method of definition, 398-399; as supporting material, 281-282
Exploration as motive, 63-65
Exposition, definition in, 195-196; partitioning in, 196-198
Extemporaneous speech, memory in the, 465-467; oral rehearsal of, 466; preparation of, 465-467
Extra sounds, addition of, 528
Eye movement, 562; as agency of audience contact, 561; effect of shiftiness in, 562

Face-to-face speaking 540-541
Facial exercise, 563-564; expression, 560-561
Fact or value, propositions of, 218-220; analysis of, 219-220
Fact, propositions of, 211-212
Facts, and impressiveness, 451-453; as supporting material, 285-291
Familiarity and vividness, 426
Farewell Address, Lincoln's, 255-256
Farewell, Speeches of, 255-256
Fears, overcoming, 463-465
Figures of speech, and vividness, 430-435; precautions, 434-435; Using, 434-435
First principles, 25-50
Fluency, defined, 533; requirements for achieving, 533
Force, 504-506
Form, need for, 8
Fosdick, Raymond, B., 446
Franklin, Benjamin, 523
Freedom from restraint, as motive, 65-68
Freedom of speech, 3, 10
French Academy, 13
Friendship trains, 59
Furnass, Joseph Chamberlain, 452

General American speech, 524
General ends of speech, 11
Generalization, 292
"Generic" words, 424
Gesture, 553-560; empathic reponses and, 554-555; functions of, 554; of description, 557-558; imitation in, 557-558; figurative and literal (description), 557; of emphasis, three parts of, 558-559; of location, 555-557; figurative and literal (of location), 556; of symbolism, 559-560; types of, 555-560
Gettysburg, 111, 160, 507-508
Gladstone, 89
Goals, announced and concealed, 146-147; immediate and remote, 146; methods of obtaining, 141-145; selection of, 147-148; kinds of, 146-147
Golden Rule, for listener, 43
Good will, Speeches of, 261-263; formula for pattern of, 262; objectives, 262; occasions for, 262; plan of, 263
Government publications as reference material, 170
Gracefulness, basis for, 550
Grady, Henry W., 7, 447
Grant, General, 487
Gregory, 6

Hands and arms, and posture, 550-551
Harvard Classics, 158
Head and Neck, and posture, 551-552; in manuscript speaking, 551
Heifetz, Jascha, 4
Hemingway, Ernest, 4
Henry, O., 101-102
Henry, Patrick, 295
Hepburn, Katherine, 4
Hiroshima, 19
Historical trends, effect on speech, 110-111
Hitler, 14, 20, 21, 407; motives, 21
Hoarseness, *see* Huskiness
Homogeneity of audiences, 124-125
Honest thinking needed, 13, 16
Hoover, Herbert, 150
Humor, as appeal to attention and interest, 99-104
Humphrey, Senator, 7
Huskiness, 501-502; causes, 501-502; over-relaxation and, 501; pitch and, 501-502
Hypertension, and stridency, 503

INDEX

Ideas, expression of and capacity for, 8
"Illusion of the first time," 470
Imagery, 416-423; as recall, 416-417; and imagination, 419; Types of, 420-421; verbal, 417-419; forms of verbal, 418-419
Importance, as factor in order of arrangement, 361
Impressiveness, and allusions, 444-447; definition of, 394, detailed description and, 455-458; facts and, 451-453; figures of speech and, 441-443; immediacy of, 439-440; importance of, 438-440; loaded words and, 457-458; methods of achieving, 441-458; metonymy and, 443-444; Quotation and, 447-448; statistics and, 453-455; various terms for, 438; vividness, clarity, and, 440-441
Impromptu speech, memory and the, 462-465; opening the, 464
Improvement in speaking possible, 5
Inactive audience, 122-123
Inductive order in the Discussion, 358-359
Inference, types of, 291-302; analogy or comparison, 300-302; causal reasoning, 296-300; deduction, 293-296; generalization, 292
Inflections, 512-515; and meaning, 513; exercises in, 513-514, patterns of, 513
Informative description, analysis of, 190-192; selection of details, 191
Informative narrative, 192-195; developmental pattern, 193; historical account, 194-195; operational pattern, 193; travelogue, 194
Informative talk, aims of, 184; analysis and organization, 185; appraisal and criticism, 198-199; arrangement of detail, 191-192; Biography of, 199-200; description, 189-192; exposition, 195-198; forms of central thought for, 186-188; forms of, 183-184; gathering and selecting materials, 185-186; informative narrative, 192-195; materials for, 185-186, nature of, 184-185; outlining, 200-205; simple instructions, 188-189; location of central thought, 357-358; as method of obtaining goals, 142-143
Inspiration, speeches of, analysis, 257; goals of, 257; propositions for, 256
Intellectual honesty, 13
Interest, as factor in attention, 85
    See also Attention and Interest
Interestingness, as basis for order of points, 361-362
Interferences in memory, 462-463
International Phonetic Alphabet, 531, 532
Introduction, adapting to speaking situation, 350-351; animation in, 335-336; appearance of speaker, 347-348; attentive hearing, methods of securing, 335; auditors, relation of subject to, 336-337; challenge in, 344-345; common ground of understanding, 340-342 (sources of, 341-342); curiosity, arousing, 337-338; delivery in, 335-336; ethical proof in, 348-350; familiar in, 343-344; friendly hearing, securing a, 345-350; humor, use of, 338-340; intelligent hearing, securing a, 350; interests of auditors, 336-337; novelty in, 342-343; planning for interest-getting, 32; purpose of, 334-335; reputation of speaker and, 346-347; Roosevelt, President, 342; summary of functions, 334
Introduction, speech of, 246-251; brevity, 247; humor in, 249; preparation of, 246-247; rules for, 246-247; summary of points for, 250-251
Inversion of sounds, 528-529
Involuntary attention, 86-87
Isaeus, teacher of Demosthenes, 6

Jefferson, Thomas, 15
Jones, Daniel, Dictionary, 531

Kenyon-Knott, Dictionary, 532
Key, 511-512

Labels, 15
Language, objectives in use of, 393-395
Larynx, 497
Lee, Senator Josh, 7
Libanius, 6
Lilienthal, David E., 349-350, 444
Lincoln, 9, 15, 31, 84, 110, 111, 112, 116, 157, 160, 167
Lincoln-Douglas debates, 116
Listener, attitude as, 43-44
Listening, as creative process, 421-422; to your voice, 515-516
Loaded question, as amplification, 305
Loaded words, and impressiveness, 457-458
Location, gestures of, 555-557
Logical relations, principles of checking, 223
Long, Senator Russell, 7
Loudness, 506
Louisiana, differences between north and south, 116
Luce, Clare Booth, 348

Macaulay, 7
Macbeth, 512
Magazines, general, as reference, 172; special, 173
Magellan, 13
Magnitude as factor of attention, 83
Main points, drafting the, 31
Manner, influenced by attitude, 542
Mannerisms, 40
Manuscript speaking, head and neck in, 551; memory in, 467-468; preparation of, 468
Marshall, Thomas R. 253
Material, special sources of, 171-173
Maw, Governor, 7
Meaning, and community of reference, 408-410; and delivery, 477-479; and experience, 396-397; and inflections, 513; basis of, 392-393, methods of determining, 398-403
Meanings of words, finding the, 395-403
Memorization, 35; failure in, 471
Memorized speech, memory in the, 468-471

Memorizing, of vocal and bodily patterns, 471; steps in, 496-470; summary of principles of, 472; whole method of, 468-469
Memory, a triple process, 461-462; and retention, 461; in the extemporaneous speech, 465-467; in the impromptu speech, 462-465; in the manuscript speech, 467-468; in the memorized speech, 468-471; blocks in, breaking, 471-472; defined, 461; interference in, 462-463; nature of, 461-462; relief of tensions in, 463-465
Metaphor, 430-433
Metonymy, and impressiveness, 443-444
Mispronunciations, reasons for, 530; types of, 526
Mood, and inflections, 513; and pitch, 511-512; reflection of, 562-563
Moral values, 19
Morse, Senator Wayne, 7
Motivation and audience analysis, 118-119
Motives, in speaking, 19; basic to behavior, 54; classification of, 54-55; appeal to, 14, 57-71
Motive appeals, choosing the, 57; types of, 57-71 (exploration, 63-65; freedom from restraint, 65-68; ownership or possession, 62-63; relief of distress, 68-71; security, 58-60; social approval, 60-61); general principles governing, 72-75
Motives, in speaking, 19; basic to behavior, 54; classification of, 54-55; appeals to, 14, 57-71; "higher" and "lower," 55-56; rarely single, 55-56; "selfish" or "altruistic," 55-56; understanding necessary, 52-53
Movement, 552-553; and nervousness, 552; and stage-fright, 489-490
Muffled tones, 502
Multiple terms, 403-404
Mundt, Senator Karl, 7
Mussolini, 20, 21

INDEX

Name calling, 15
Narration, as supporting material, 283-284
Nasality, 499-501; correction of, 500-501; tests of, 500
"Naturalness," delivery and, 483-485
Negation, as method of definition, 402
Nervousness, attitudes toward, 487-488; movement and, 552; not pathological, 487-488
New and old, as appeal to attention and interest, 92-94
Newspapers, and public opinion, 117-118; as reference, 170
Notes, recording, 175-176; use of, 36

Oath of Hippocrates, 17
Objectives in use of language, 393-395
Occasion, the, 110-116; and speeches of welcome and response, 251; understanding necessary, 109
Occasional speech, types of situation, 244
Omission of sounds, 527-528
Opinion, Audience's, of subject, 129-130; division of, 129
Opposition, facing, 150
Optimum pitch, 511-512
Oral method preparation, 466-467
Oral paragraph, 356
Oral rehearsal, 466-467
Orator fit, non nascitur, 4
Oratory, 4
Ordering the points, 360-362: on basis of acceptability, 362; complexity, 362; importance, 361; interestingness, 361
Outline, complete speech, 33-34; model skeleton, 202-203; operational pattern, 203-204; kinds of, in informative talks, 201-205; specimen, 223-227
Outlining the argumentative talk, 220-227
Overlearning, 470
Owen, Ruth Bryan, 7

Ownership or Possession, as motive, 62-63

Parables, as reference to experience, 84-85
Parker, Theodore, 156
Participation, in democratic processes, 3
Partition, of propositions of fact or value, 218-220; of propositions of policy, 217-218; patterns of, 219-220, 360-362
Pasteur, 13
Pause, dramatic, 509-510; length of, 509
Periodicals, as references, 170
Personal elements in the Conclusion, 373-375
Personality, and subliminal and supraliminal stimuli, 542-545; quality and, 503-504
Personification, 433-434
Phillips, Wendell, 7
Phrase, Length of, 507-509
Phrasing, and meaning, 508-509
Physical surroundings, 111
Pilgrims, 110, 111, 112
Pilgrim's Progress, 96
Pitch, 511-515
Place of speaking, 111-112
Planning the speech, 30
Plato, 10, 286
Policy, Propositions of, 212-213, partition of, 217-218
Positions of the feet, 546-547
Posterity as audience, 120-121
Posture, 545-552; and bodily activity, 37-38; and total impression, 546; body and shoulder set, 549-550, distribution of weight, 547-549; hands and arms, 550-551; head and neck, 551-552; positions of the feet, 546-547
Practice, and improvement, 5; "practice makes perfect," 5; oral, 34-35
Practicing the speech, 34, 489
Praise, Speech of, *see* Eulogy
Prejudiced opponents, 150
Prejudices, 14

Preparation, and stage-fright, 488-489; for speaking, 9-11; general, 9-10; immediate, 160-161; mental, 36; of extemporaneous speech, 465-467; oral method of, 466-467; special, 11; specific, 155
Presentation and acceptance, speeches of, 252-255; characteristics of, 253-254; objectives, 253
Previews and signposts, 364-366
Primary attention, 86-87
Prodicus, 427
Pronunciation, 521-533; "acceptable," 526; addition of extra sounds, 528; "correct," 523; dictionaries and, 523-524; general elisions, 529-530; inversions of sounds, 528-529; learning good—, 530-533; misplaced accent, 526-527; omission of sounds, 527-528; regional variants of, 524-526; sound substitutions, 529; sources for learning, 530-553; standard, 522-526; standards of, 522-523
Propaganda, 14-16
Proposition, argumentative, framing the, 213-214; definition, 210; kinds of, 210-213, placing between two points, 359-360
Proposition, by implication, 360; of fact, 211-212: analysis of, 219-220; partition of, 218-220; of policy, 212-213: partition of, 217-218
Ptah-Hotep, 1
Public Address systems, 516
Public opinion polls, and audience analysis, 117
Purpose, of meeting, 115; of speech, 138-152
Purpose or effect, as methods of definition, 402
Putting a speech together, 32

Quality, 498-504; and personality, 503-504
Quantity, 507
Quintilian, 2, 21, 460, 461
Quotation, and impressiveness, 447-448
"Quote-Unquote," 516

Radio audience, 120
Rapport, 480-481
Rate, 510
Rationalization, 14
Reactions to speaking situation, negative, 27; positive, 27
Reader and listener compared, 356
Reasons for speaking, 12
Recall, factors of, 439
Recognition, defined, 461-462
Recovery, the, in gestures of emphasis, 558-559
Red-herring technique of propaganda, 15-16
Reference to experience, as factor in attention, 84-85
Reference works, 168
Reflection of mood, 562-563
Reflective thought, Dewey's formula for, 209-210; reflective thought process, 291
Regional variants of pronunciation, 524-526
Rehearsal, oral, 466
Relief of distress as motive, 68-71
Remedial measures, for stage-fright, 486-490
Repetition, as factor of attention, 84
Research for a speech, 161
Residues, method of, 359
Response, actuating as form of, 144-145; audience, 139-141, convincing as form of, 143-144; duration of, 140-141; entertaining as form of, 142; immediate or delayed, 140; individual or group, 141; information as type of, 142-143; kind wanted, 139-140; stimulating as form of, 143; the aim of speaking, 52; the general goal of all speaking, 138-139
Response and Welcome, speeches of, 251-252
Restatement, type of, in conclusion, 375-377
Retention, as aim of the informative talk, 184; memory and, 461
Reuther, Walter, 6
Rhetorical question, as amplification, 305

INDEX

Roosevelt, Eleanor, 7, 348
Roosevelt, Franklin D., 4, 15, 21, 102, 119, 342
Roosevelt, Theodore, 157, 161

Scholarly journals, as reference, 173
Security, as motive appeal, 58; and altruistic motives, 59
Selected audience, 123
Self-confidence, preparation and, 489
Self-interest, enlightened, 56
Shaded words, 426-428
Shapley, Professor, 458
Signposts, previews and, 364-366
Simile, 430-433
Simple words, and vividness, 428-429
Sincerity, enlightened, needed, 10
Single point, presenting a, 362-364
Situation, listener as part of, 43; need for studying, 71-72
Slide, *see* Inflection
Slogans, 406-407
Smith, Alfred E., 150
Social approval, as motive appeal, 60-61
Social interaction, role of speech in, 19
Social responsibility of speaker, 16-22
Sound substitutions, 529
Sources of material: general magazines, 172; scholarly journals, 173; special magazines, 173; speech magazines, 173
Southern speech, 524
Speaker, audience attitudes toward 127-128; audience's knowledge of, 127-128; notebook of, 159-160
Speaking and writing, importance of delivery in, 476-477
Speaking, can be learned, 4
Speaking situation, adapting conclusion to, 385; adapting introduction to, 350-351; confrontation and, 541-542; delivery and the, 481; movement and the, 552
Specific instance, *see* Example as supporting material
Specific preparation, 155

Specific purpose, wording the, 151-152
"Specific" words, 424
Speaking situation, two factors in, 11
Speech and confrontation, 541
Speech magazines, as references, 173
Speech materials, sources of, 159
Speeches of farewell, points of, 255
Spellman, Francis Cardinal, 6
St. Augustine, 6
Stage-fright, 485-490; and movement, 489-490; and preparation, 488-489; and urge to communicate, 488; attempts to conceal, 489; causes of, 486; Demosthenes and, 486; remedial measures, 488-490
Standard pronunciation, defined, 522-523
Standards of pronunciation, 522-526
Statistics, and impressiveness, 453-455; as supporting material, 278-289; rules for, 288-289
Step, as element of pitch, 512
Stereotypes, 405-408
Stimulating, as form of response, 143
Story-telling, 270-271
Stridency, 502-503
Stimuli, subliminal and supraliminal, 542-545
Stroke, the, in gesture of emphasis, 558-559
Struggle, as appeal to attention and interest, 99
Study an essential in speech improvement, 6-8
Subject, abstract, 29; audience interest in, 29; audience's knowledge of, 128-129; division of opinion on, 129; finding a, 161-163; fixed attitudes toward, 126; narrowing the, 29; selecting a, 28; specific, 29; surveying the, 167-168; testing the, 163-167
Subjects, choosing informative, 30; requiring physical activity, 30; sources of, 162
Subliminal and supraliminal stimuli, 542-545; and control, 543; and habit formation, 543-544; and personality, 544

INDEX

Subversive elements, 3; ideologies, techniques of, 20
Summary type of conclusion, 377-379
Supporting materials: description, 282-283; example, 288-291; explanation, 281-282; gathering the, 31; to prove: inference, 291-302; narrative (illustration), 283-284; purpose of, 281; statistics, 287-289; testimony, 285-287; to amplify, 302-305; to clarify, 281-284; to prove, 285-291
Supporting points, arranging the, 360-362; tests for arrangement, 360-362
Surroundings, difficulties occasioned by, 112
Suspense, as appeal to attention and interest, 98-99
Syllogism, categorical, 293-294; disjunctive, 295-296; hypothetical, 294-295
Symbolism, gestures of, 559-560
Synonym, as method of definition, 400-401

Taboos, 405-406
Taft, President, 101
Taft-Hartley Law, 406, 450
Talmage, Thomas DeWitt, 128
Tarbell, Ida M., 7
Technical terms, 404
Tensions, excessive, delivery and, 485-490; relief of in memory, 463
Testimony, as supporting material, 285-287
Tests of effectiveness, 360-362
Theseus, School of speech, 1
Thinness, in voice, 502
Thinking, clearness in, 16; honesty in, 16
Thompson, Dorothy, 7, 348
Thought process, role of speech in, 19
Timbre, 498, 517
Time, 507-510
Toast program, planning a, 269-270
Toastmaster, duties of, 268-269
Town Meeting of the Air, 91, 163

Transitions, 366-367
Truman, President, 451
Twain, Mark, 101

"Unabridged" dictionaries, 532-533
Understanding, an aim of the informative talk, 184
United Nations, 167
Urge to Communicate, 11-13, 393; and loudness, 506; and stage-fright, 488

Values, ethical and moral, 19
Variety, delivery and, 482
Ventilation, effect on audience, 111
Vergil, 156
Visible system of delivery, 480
Visual aids: actual objects, 329; attention and interest and, 319-320; fitting into a speech; 326; graphic and pictorial materials, 328; hints in presenting, 328-329; methods of displaying, 323-326; models, 329; practical devices, 329-331; presenting, 328-330; projected pictures, 331; purposes of, 319; to amplify, 320-321; to clarify, 320; to prove, 321; types of, 317; selection of, 321-323; specimens, 329; steps for effective use, 326
Visualization of future, as type of conclusion, 384-385
Victorian novel, 96
Vital, as appeal to attention and interest, 90-91
Vividness, and interest and attention, 415-416; and simple words, 428-429; choosing words for, 423-429; concreteness and, 423-426; definition of, 394; descriptive words and, 425-426; familiarity and, 426; figures of speech and, 430-435; impressiveness, clarity, and, 440-441; shaded words and, 426-428
Vocal aspects of speech, 494-495
Vocal bands, 497
Vocal elements, importance of, 514-515
Vocal patterns, memorizing of, 471
Vocal tones, basic attributes of, 498

Vocal sound, variations in, 498
Voice, 38-39
Voice production, air cavities in, 498; mechanism of, 497-498
Voluntary attention, 87

"Walking through" lines, 466
Washington, Booker T., 126
Watt, James, 419
Webster, Daniel, 4, 9, 110, 127, 156, 160, 257, 261, 466
Webster diacritics, 532

Welcome and response, speeches of, 251-252
Welcome, speech of, elements of, 252
Williams, John Sharp, 448-449
Williamson, Arleigh B., 502 n.
Wilson, Woodrow, 7, 89, 157, 286, 382
World War II, 20, 57
Writing the speech, 35

Yancey, William L., 127

Charlie Mudge '53
Jerry Kobe
Jerry Needleman '54
Jim Hoag '54
Jim White '56
"Izzy" Zalkin
3 musketeers { Pete Greenman '56
Toni Giuliano '56
Gil Dedrick '56

Paul Wesser '56
John Myers '54
Bob Schneider

Cindy Hammond '53
Nancy Hoyt '53
Joyce Marchaud '56
Loele Kranish '56
"Marv" Gordon, '54 & last,
but <u>not</u> least:
Ann MacGregor '56
..1/20/53..